Africa's Infrastructure

Africa's Infrastructure

A Time for Transformation

Vivien Foster and Cecilia Briceño-Garmendia

Editors

A copublication of the Agence Française de Développement and the World Bank

ISBN: 978-0-8213-8041-3
eISBN: 978-0-8213-8083-3
DOI: 10.1596/978-0-8213-8041-3

Cover and interior design: Naylor Design

Cover photo: Arne Hoel/World Bank; technician in a chlorination facility at a water treatment plant in Senegal.

Library of Congress Cataloging-in-Publication Data
Africa's infrastructure : a time for transformation.
    p. cm.
  ISBN 978-0-8213-8041-3 — ISBN 978-0-8213-8083-3 (electronic)
  1. Infrastructure (Economics)—Africa. I. World Bank. II. Africa Infrastructure Country Diagnostic.
  HC800.Z9C324 2009
  363.6096—dc22

                   2009025406

Africa Development Forum Series

The **Africa Development Forum** series was created in 2009 to focus on issues of significant relevance to Sub-Saharan Africa's social and economic development. Its aim is both to record the state of the art on a specific topic and to contribute to ongoing local, regional, and global policy debates. It is designed specifically to provide practitioners, scholars, and students with the most up-to-date research results while highlighting the promise, challenges, and opportunities that exist on the continent.

The series is sponsored by the Agence Française de Développement and the World Bank. The manuscripts chosen for publication represent the highest quality in each institution's research and activity output and have been selected for their relevance to the development agenda. Working together with a shared sense of mission and interdisciplinary purpose, the two institutions are committed to a common search for new insights and new ways of analyzing the development realities of the Sub-Saharan Africa Region.

Advisory Committee Members

Agence Française de Développement
Pierre Jacquet, Directeur de la Stratégie et Chef Économiste
Robert Peccoud, Directeur de la Recherche

World Bank
Shantayanan Devarajan, Chief Economist, Africa Region
Jorge Arbache, Senior Economist

Contents

PART 2   Sectoral Snapshots   163

Boxes

Figures

Tables

Preface

This study is part of the Africa Infrastructure Country Diagnostic (AICD), a project designed to expand the world's knowledge of physical infrastructure in Africa. The AICD will provide a baseline against which future improvements in infrastructure services can be measured, making it possible to monitor the results achieved from donor support. It should also provide a more solid empirical foundation for prioritizing investments and designing policy reforms in the infrastructure sectors in Africa.

The AICD is based on an unprecedented effort to collect detailed economic and technical data on the infrastructure sectors in Africa. The project has produced a series of original reports on public expenditure, spending needs, and sector performance in each of the main infrastructure sectors, including energy, information and communication technologies, irrigation, transport, and water and sanitation. This volume synthesizes the most significant findings of those reports.

The first phase of the AICD focused on 24 countries that together account for 85 percent of the gross domestic product, population, and infrastructure aid flows of Sub-Saharan Africa. The countries are Benin, Burkina Faso, Cameroon, Cape Verde, Chad, Côte d'Ivoire,

the Democratic Republic of Congo, Ethiopia, Ghana, Kenya, Lesotho, Madagascar, Malawi, Mozambique, Namibia, Niger, Nigeria, Rwanda, Senegal, South Africa, Sudan, Tanzania, Uganda, and Zambia. Under a second phase of the project, coverage is expanding to include as many of the additional African countries as possible.

The AICD was commissioned by the Infrastructure Consortium for Africa (ICA) following the 2005 G8 (Group of Eight) summit at Gleneagles, Scotland, which flagged the importance of scaling up donor finance for infrastructure in support of Africa's development. The World Bank is implementing the AICD under the guidance of a steering committee that represents the African Union, the New Partnership for Africa's Development (NEPAD), Africa's regional economic communities, the African Development Bank (AfDB), the Development Bank of South Africa (DBSA), and major infrastructure donors. Financing for the AICD is provided by a multidonor trust fund to which the main contributors are the United Kingdom's Department for International Development (DFID), the Public-Private Infrastructure Advisory Facility (PPIAF), Agence Française de Développement (AFD), the European Commission, and Germany's Entwicklungsbank (KfW).

A group of distinguished peer reviewers from policy-making and academic circles in Africa and beyond reviewed all major outputs of the study to ensure the technical quality of the work.

The Sub-Saharan Africa Transport Policy Program (SSATP) and the Water and Sanitation Program (WSP) provided technical support on data collection and analysis pertaining to their respective sectors.

This and other volumes analyzing key infrastructure topics, as well as the underlying data sources described above, will be available for download from http://www.infrastructure africa.org. Stand-alone summaries are available in English and French.

Inquiries concerning the availability of data sets should be directed to the volume editors at the World Bank in Washington, DC.

Acknowledgments

This report was undertaken by the director's office of the Department for Sustainable Development in the Africa Region of the World Bank. A number of directors oversaw the implementation of the project throughout its life, including (in chronological order) Michel Wormser, John Henry Stein (acting), and Inger Andersen.

The task team leaders for the report were Vivien Foster and Cecilia Briceño-Garmendia, and the core team for the project comprised Aijaz Ahmad, Dominique Akele, Sudeshna Ghosh Banerjee, Carolina Dominguez Torres, Sophie Hans-Moevi, Elvira Morella, Nataliya Pushak, Rupa Ranganathan, Maria Shkaratan, and Karlis Smits.

The project team is grateful to a number of World Bank colleagues who acted as advisers on key cross-cutting aspects of the report. These include Antonio Estache, Jose Luis Irigoyen, and Jyoti Shukla, who provided advice on general infrastructure issues; Sarah Keener, who provided advice on social issues; Paul Martin, who provided advice on environmental issues; and Stephen Mink, who provided advice on rural and agricultural issues.

A technical advisory panel provided independent, external peer review on the quality of the background papers on which this report is based. The panel was cochaired by Shanta Devarajan (chief economist, Africa Region, World Bank) and Louis Kasekende (chief economist, African Development Bank), and comprised Adeola Adenikinju (professor, University of Ibadan, Nigeria), Emmanuelle Auriol (professor, University of Toulouse, France), Tony Gomez-Ibanez (professor, John F. Kennedy School of Government, Harvard University), Cheikh Kane (independent expert on infrastructure finance), and Xinzhu Zhang (professor, Chinese Academy of Social Sciences, Beijing).

In order to ensure broad-based participation and consultation of World Bank technical practices, a number of internal peer review groups were formed to provide guidance and feedback on earlier drafts of the document. The individual groups and their members are as follows: *ICT sector*—Mavis Ampah, Philippe Dongier, Clemencia Torres, and Mark Williams; *irrigation sector*—Barbara Miller, Stephen Mink, and Ashok Subramanian; *power sector*—Philippe Benoit, David Donaldson, Vijay Iyer, Luiz Maurer, Rob Mills, Lucio Monari, Kyran O'Sullivan, Prasad Tallapragada, Clemencia Torres, and Tjaarda Storm Van Leeuwen; *transport sector*—Pierre Pozzo di Borgo, Michel Luc Donner, Michel Iches, Marc Juhel, Cornelis Kruk, Alain Labeau, Charles Schlumberger, and Kavita Sethi; *water supply and sanitation sector*—Ventura Bengoechea, Jaime Biderman, Matar Fall, Sarah Keener, Peter Kolsky, Alex McPhail, Eustache Ouayoro, Christophe Prevost, Caroline van den Berg, and Meike van Ginneken; *finance theme*—Gerardo Corrochano, Michael Fuchs, James Leigland, Anand Rajaram, Sudhir Shetty, Jyoti Shukla, Clemencia Torres, Marilou Uy, and Marinus Verhoeven; *poverty and inequality theme*—Judy Baker, Douglas Barnes, Ellen Hamilton, Julian Lampietti, and Kenneth Simler; *institutional theme*—James Leigland and Jyoti Shukla; *urban theme*—Jaime Biderman, Catherine Farvacque-Vitkovic, Matthew Glasser, Sumila Gulyani, and Uri Raich; and *regional integration theme*—Uwe Deichmann, Jakob Kolster, and Mark Tomlinson.

An editorial team comprising Bruce Ross-Larson, Steven Kennedy, and Joseph Caponio contributed significantly to improving the quality of the final manuscript submitted to the World Bank Office of the Publisher for publication.

Abbreviations

$	All dollar amounts are in U.S. dollars unless otherwise indicated.
ADF	African Development Fund
AFRICATIP	Association Africaine des Agences d'Exécution des Travaux d'Intérêt Public
AGETIP	*agence d'exécution des travaux d'intérêt public*
AICD	Africa Infrastructure Country Diagnostic
AMADER	Agence Malienne pour le Développement de l'Energie Domestique et l'Electrification Rurale (Malian Agency for the Development of Domestic Energy and Rural Electrification)
BPC	Botswana Power Corporation
CEAR	Central East African Railways
CREST	Commercial Reorientation of the Electricity Sector Toolkit
DHS	demographic and health survey
EASSy	Eastern African Submarine Cable System
GIS	geographic information systems
GNI	gross national income
GSM	global systems mobile
IBNET	International Benchmarking Network
IBT	increasing block tariff
ICT	information and communication technology
IDA	International Development Association
IPP	independent power producer
JMP	Joint Monitoring Programme
KenGen	Kenya Electricity Generating Company
KPLC	Kenya Power and Lighting Company
MDG	Millennium Development Goal
NEPAD	New Partnership for Africa's Development
NWSC	National Water and Sewerage Corporation
O&M	operation and maintenance
ODA	official development assistance
OECD	Organisation for Economic Co-operation and Development
PPI	private participation in infrastructure
PSP	private sector participation
SAT-3	South Atlantic 3/West Africa Submarine Cable
SEACOM	South Africa–East Africa–South Asia–Fiber Optic Cable
SODECI	Société de Distribution d'Eau de la Côte d'Ivoire
SOE	state-owned enterprise
SSATP	Sub-Saharan Africa Transport Policy Program
TEAMS	The East Africa Marine System
TEU	20-foot equivalent unit
TIR	Transports Internationaux Routiers
VoIP	Voice over Internet Protocol
WiMAX	Worldwide Interoperability for Microwave Access
WSS	water supply and sanitation

Africa's Infrastructure: A Time for Transformation

The Africa Infrastructure Country Diagnostic is an unprecedented attempt to collect comprehensive data on the infrastructure sectors in Africa—covering power, transport, irrigation, water and sanitation, and information and communication technology (ICT)—and to provide an integrated analysis of the challenges they face. Based on extensive fieldwork across Africa, the following main findings have emerged:

- Infrastructure has been responsible for more than half of Africa's recent improved growth performance and has the potential to contribute even more in the future.

- Africa's infrastructure networks increasingly lag behind those of other developing countries and are characterized by missing regional links and stagnant household access.

- Africa's difficult economic geography presents a particular challenge for the region's infrastructure development.

- Africa's infrastructure services are twice as expensive as elsewhere, reflecting both diseconomies of scale in production and high profit margins caused by lack of competition.

- Power is by far Africa's largest infrastructure challenge, with 30 countries facing regular power shortages and many paying high premiums for emergency power.

- The cost of addressing Africa's infrastructure needs is around $93 billion a year, about one-third of which is for maintenance—more than twice the Commission for Africa's (2005) estimate.

- The infrastructure challenge varies greatly by country type—fragile states face an impossible burden and resource-rich countries lag despite their wealth.

- A large share of Africa's infrastructure is domestically financed, with the central government budget being the main driver of infrastructure investment.

- Even if major potential efficiency gains are captured, Africa would still face an infrastructure funding gap of $31 billion a year, mainly in power.

- Africa's institutional, regulatory, and administrative reforms are only halfway along, but they are already proving their effect on operational efficiency.

Finding 1: Infrastructure Contributed over Half of Africa's Improved Growth Performance

Africa's growth improved markedly in the last decade. African countries saw their economies grow at a solid 4 percent a year from 2001 to 2005. Resource-rich countries, which have benefited from rising commodity prices, demonstrate the highest growth rates. Growth overall still falls short of the 7 percent needed to achieve substantial poverty reduction and attain the Millennium Development Goals (MDGs), however. Infrastructure, significant in Africa's economic turnaround, will need to play an even greater role for the continent to reach its development targets.

Across Africa, infrastructure contributed 99 basis points to per capita economic growth from 1990 to 2005, compared with 68 basis points for other structural policies (Calderón 2008). That contribution is almost entirely attributable to advances in the penetration of telecommunication services. The deterioration in the quantity and quality of power infrastructure over the same period retarded growth, shaving 11 basis points from per capita growth for Africa as a whole and as much as 20 basis points for southern Africa.

The growth effects of further improving Africa's infrastructure would be even greater. Simulations suggest that if all African countries were to catch up with Mauritius (the regional leader in infrastructure) per capita growth in the region could increase by 2.2 percentage points. Catching up with the Republic of Korea would increase per capita growth by 2.6 percentage points a year. In Côte d'Ivoire, the Democratic Republic of Congo, and Senegal, the effect would be even larger.

In most African countries, particularly the lower-income countries, infrastructure emerges as a major constraint on doing business, depressing firm productivity by about 40 percent (Escribano, Guasch, and Pena 2008).

For most countries, the negative effect of deficient infrastructure is at least as large as that of crime, red tape, corruption, and financial market constraints. For one set of countries, power emerges as the most limiting factor by far, cited by more than half the firms in more than half the countries as a major business obstacle. For a second set, inefficient functioning of ports and associated customs clearance is equally significant. Deficiencies in transport and in ICTs are less prevalent but substantial in some cases.

Infrastructure not only contributes to economic growth, but it is also an important input to human development (Fay and others 2005). Infrastructure is a key ingredient for achieving all the MDGs. Safe and convenient water supplies save time and arrest the spread of a range of serious diseases—including diarrhea, a leading cause of infant mortality and malnutrition. Electricity powers health and education services and boosts the productivity of small businesses. Road networks provide links to global and local markets. ICTs democratize access to information and reduce transport costs by allowing people to conduct transactions remotely.

Finding 2: Africa's Infrastructure Lags Well behind That of Other Developing Countries

On just about every measure of infrastructure coverage, African countries lag behind their peers in the developing world (Yepes, Pierce, and Foster 2008). This lag is perceptible for low- and middle-income countries in Sub-Saharan Africa relative to other low- and middle-income countries (table O.1). The differences are particularly large for paved roads, telephone main lines, and power generation. For all three, Africa has been expanding stocks much more slowly than other developing regions; so unless something changes, the gap will continue to widen.

To what extent does Africa's current deficit date to a low starting point for infrastructure stocks? Africa started out with stocks that were generally not very different from those in South or East Asia in the 1960s for roads, in the 1970s for telephones, and in the 1980s for power. The comparison with South Asia, which has similar per capita incomes, is particularly striking. In 1970, Sub-Saharan Africa had almost three times the generating capacity per million people as South Asia. In 2000, South Asia had left Sub-Saharan Africa far behind—with almost twice the generation capacity per million people. Also in 1970, Sub-Saharan Africa had twice the main-line telephone density of South Asia, but by 2000, the two regions were even.

Since 1990, coverage of household services has barely improved (figure O.1, panel a). Africa is unlikely to meet the MDGs for water and sanitation. Moreover, on current trends,

universal access to these and other household services is more than 50 years away in most African countries (Banerjee, Wodon, and others 2008). Even where infrastructure networks are in place, a significant percentage of households remains unconnected, suggesting that demand-side barriers exist and that universal access entails more than physical rollouts of networks. As might be expected, access to infrastructure in rural areas is only a fraction of that in urban areas, even where urban coverage is already low by international standards (Banerjee, Wodon, and others 2008) (figure O.1, panel b).

Table O.1 Africa's Infrastructure Deficit

Normalized units	Sub-Saharan Africa low-income countries	Other low-income countries
Paved-road density	31	134
Total road density	137	211
Main-line density	10	78
Mobile density	55	76
Internet density	2	3
Generation capacity	37	326
Electricity coverage	16	41
Improved water	60	72
Improved sanitation	34	51

Source: Yepes, Pierce, and Foster 2008.
Note: Road density is measured in kilometers per 100 square kilometers of arable land; telephone density in lines per thousand population; generation capacity in megawatts per million population; electricity, water, and sanitation coverage in percentage of population.

Finding 3: Africa's Difficult Economic Geography Presents a Challenge for Infrastructure Development

Relative to other continents, Africa is characterized by low overall population density (36 people per square kilometer), low rates of urbanization (35 percent), but relatively rapid rates of urban growth (3.6 percent a year), a relatively large number of landlocked countries (15), and numerous small economies. A further complication is that the continent experiences particularly high hydrological variability, with huge swings in precipitation across areas, seasons, and time, which climate change is likely to exacerbate.

Figure O.1 Access to Household Services

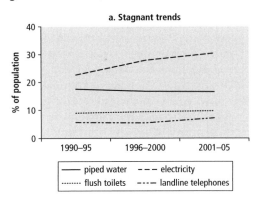

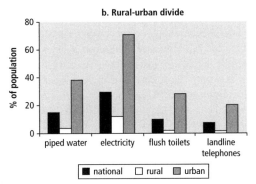

Source: Banerjee, Wodon, and others 2008.

Africa's atomized nation-states are reflected in the region's fragmentary infrastructure networks. Sub-Saharan Africa comprises 48 nation-states, many of which are very small. The bulk of those countries have populations of fewer than 20 million and economies smaller than $10 billion. International frontiers bear little relation either to natural features (such as river basins) or to artificial features (such as cities and their accessibility to trading channels, such as ports). Intraregional connectivity is therefore very low, whether measured in transcontinental highway links, power interconnectors, or fiber-optic backbones. Most continuous transport corridors are concerned with providing access to seaports, whereas the intraregional road network is characterized by major discontinuities. Few cross-border interconnectors exist to support regional power exchange, even though many countries are too small to produce power economically on their own. Until recently, the whole of East Africa lacked access to a global submarine cable to provide low-cost international communications and Internet access. The intraregional fiber-optic network is also incomplete, but growing rapidly. Because of their geographic isolation, landlocked countries in particular suffer from the lack of regional connectivity.

Both the spatial distribution and rapid migration of Africa's population create major challenges for reaching universal access. In rural areas, over 20 percent of the population lives in dispersed settlements where typical population densities are less than 15 people per square kilometer; hence, the costs of providing infrastructure are comparatively high. In urban areas, population growth rates averaging 3.6 percent a year are leaving infrastructure service providers severely stretched. As a result, urban service coverage has actually declined over the last decade, and lower-cost alternatives are filling the resulting gap (Banerjee, Wodon, and others 2008; Morella, Foster, and Banerjee 2008). In addition, population densities in African cities are relatively low by global standards and do not benefit from large economies of agglomeration in the provision of infrastructure services. As a result, the costs of providing a basic infrastructure package can easily be twice as much as in other developing cities (Dorosh and others 2008).

Africa's water resources are abundant, but because of an absence of water storage and distribution infrastructure, they are grossly underused. Therefore, water security—reliable water supplies and acceptable risks from floods and other unpredictable events, including those from climate change—will require a significant expansion of water storage capacity from the current 200 cubic meters per capita (Grey and Sadoff 2006). In other parts of the world, such capacity is in the thousands of cubic meters. The cost of expanding water storage is extremely high in relation to the size of Africa's economies, suggesting the phasing of investments, with initial focus on achieving water security for key growth poles.

Water also needs to be distributed for agricultural use. In a handful of countries, only 7 million hectares are equipped for irrigation. Although the irrigation-equipped area is less than 5 percent of Africa's cultivated area, it produces 20 percent of the value of agricultural production. An additional 12 million hectares could be economically viable for irrigation as long as costs are contained (You 2008).

Finding 4: Africa's Infrastructure Services Are Twice as Expensive as Elsewhere

Not only are Africa's infrastructure networks deficient in coverage, but the price of the services provided is also exceptionally high by global standards (table O.2). Whether for power, water, road freight, mobile telephones, or Internet services, the tariffs paid in Africa are several multiples of those paid in other parts of the developing world. The explanation for Africa's higher prices sometimes lies in genuinely higher costs, and sometimes in high profits. The policy prescriptions for the two cases are, of course, radically different.

Power provides the clearest example of infrastructure with costs genuinely higher in Africa than elsewhere. Many smaller countries have national power systems below the 500-megawatt threshold and therefore often rely on small diesel generation that can cost up to $0.35 per kilowatt-hour to run, about

Table O.2 Africa's High-Cost Infrastructure

Infrastructure sector	Sub-Saharan Africa	Other developing regions
Power tariffs (\$ per kilowatt-hour)	0.02–0.46	0.05–0.10
Water tariffs (\$ per cubic meter)	0.86–6.56	0.03–0.60
Road freight tariffs (\$ per ton-kilometer)	0.04–0.14	0.01–0.04
Mobile telephony (\$ per basket per month)	2.60–21.00	9.90
International telephony (\$ per 3-minute call to the United States)	0.44–12.50	2.00
Internet dial-up service (\$ per month)	6.70–148.00	11.00

Sources: Authors' estimates based on Africon 2008; Bannerjee, Skilling, and others 2008; Eberhard and others 2008; Minges and others 2008; Teravaninthorn and Raballand 2008; Wodon 2008a and 2008b.
Note: Ranges reflect prices in different countries and various consumption levels. Prices for telephony and Internet service represent all developing regions, including Africa.

twice the costs faced by larger countries typically with coal- or hydropower-based systems (Eberhard and others 2008).

High road freight tariffs in Africa have much more to do with high profit margins than high costs (Teravaninthorn and Raballand 2008). The costs for Africa's trucking operators are not much higher than costs in other parts of the world, even when informal payments are counted. Profit margins, by contrast, are exceptionally high, particularly in Central and West Africa, where they reach 60 to 160 percent. The underlying cause is limited competition combined with a highly regulated market based on *tour de role* principles, which allocate freight to transporters through a centralized queuing method rather than allowing truckers to enter into bilateral contracts with customers directly.

The high costs of international telephony and Internet services reflect a mixture of cost and profit factors. Countries without access to a submarine cable must rely on expensive satellite technology for international connectivity and have charges typically twice those in countries that do enjoy such access. Even when access to a submarine cable is secured, countries with a monopoly on this international gateway still have tariffs substantially

higher than those without (Minges and others 2008).

Finding 5: Power Is Africa's Largest Infrastructure Challenge by Far

Whether measured in generation capacity, electricity consumption, or security of supply, Africa's power infrastructure delivers only a fraction of the service found elsewhere in the developing world (Eberhard and others 2008). The 48 Sub-Saharan Africa countries (with 800 million people) generate roughly the same power as Spain (with 45 million people). Power consumption, at 124 kilowatt-hours per capita annually *and falling*, is only 10 percent of that found elsewhere in the developing world, barely enough to power one 100-watt lightbulb per person for 3 hours a day.

More than 30 African countries experience power shortages and regular interruptions to service (figure O.2). The underlying causes vary: failures to bring on new capacity to keep pace with the demands of economic growth, droughts that reduced hydropower in East Africa, oil price hikes that inhibited affordability of diesel imports for many West African countries, and conflicts that destroyed power infrastructure in fragile states. Africa's firms report losing 5 percent of their sales because of frequent power outages—a figure that rises to 20 percent for informal firms unable to afford backup generation. Overall, the economic costs of power outages can easily rise to 1–2 percent of GDP.

A common response to the crisis is to tender short-term leases for emergency power. At least 750 megawatts of emergency generation are operating in Sub-Saharan Africa, which for some countries constitute a large proportion of their national installed capacity. However, emergency generation is expensive at costs of \$0.20–\$0.30 per kilowatt-hour, and for some countries, the price tag can be as high as 4 percent of GDP. Paying for emergency leases absorbs significant budgetary resources, reducing the funds for longer-term solutions.

Figure O.2 Underlying Causes of Africa's Power Supply Crisis

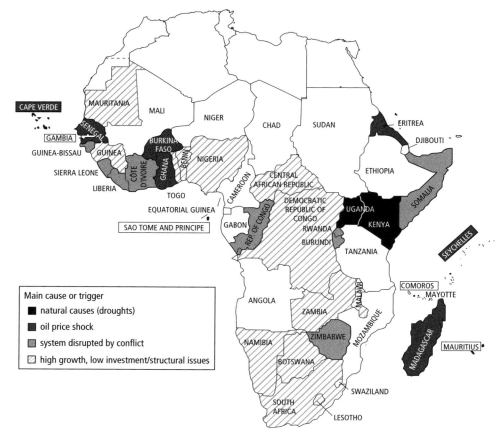

Legend — Main cause or trigger:
- natural causes (droughts)
- oil price shock
- system disrupted by conflict
- high growth, low investment/structural issues

Source: Eberhard and others 2008.

Finding 6: Africa's Infrastructure Spending Needs at $93 Billion a Year Are More than Double Previous Estimates by the Commission for Africa

Meeting Africa's infrastructure needs calls for a very substantial program of infrastructure investment and maintenance:

- Develop an additional 7,000 megawatts a year of new power generation capacity (about half through multipurpose water storage schemes).
- Enable regional power trade by laying 22,000 megawatts of cross-border transmission lines.
- Complete the intraregional fiber-optic backbone network and continental submarine cable loop.

- Interconnect capitals, ports, border crossings, and secondary cities with a good-quality road network.
- Provide all-season road access to Africa's high-value agricultural land.
- More than double Africa's irrigated area.
- Meet the MDGs for water and sanitation.
- Raise household electrification rates by 10 percentage points.
- Provide global systems mobile voice signal and public access broadband to 100 percent of the population.

Implementing such an ambitious program to address Africa's infrastructure needs would cost around $93 billion a year (about 15 percent of the region's GDP). Some two-thirds of this total relates to capital expenditure, and the remaining one-third to operation and maintenance requirements (table O.3; Briceño-Garmendia, Smits, and Foster 2008).

That cost is well over twice the $39 billion of infrastructure spending estimated by the Commission for Africa report in 2005. That figure was based on a cross-country econometric study, rather than the more detailed country-level microeconomic modeling (Estache 2005). A more recent update of the cross-country model used for the Commission for Africa report came up with revised estimates in the range of $80 billion to $90 billion, much closer to those reported here (Yepes 2007).

About 40 percent of the total spending needs are associated with power, reflecting Africa's particularly large deficits. About one-third of the power investment needs (some $9 billion a year) are associated with multipurpose water storage for hydropower and water resource management. After power, water supply and sanitation and then transport are the most significant items.

Given recent escalations in unit costs, these estimates are a lower bound. Although the investment estimates here are based on the most accurate unit-cost data available, development agencies are reporting significant cost escalations on projects under implementation. For road projects, these escalations have averaged 35 percent but in some cases have been as high as 50–100 percent. Closer inspection reveals that no single factor explains this escalation. Domestic inflation, tight construction industry conditions, oil price hikes, and inadequate competition for tenders have all played their role, with the last factor by far the strongest.

The global financial crisis of 2008 can be expected to reduce demand for some types of infrastructure, but it would not hugely alter the estimated spending needs. Planning and social targets rather than economic growth drive a large share of the spending needs, for example, the transport spending needs (which are largely based on connectivity objectives) and the water and sanitation spending needs (which are based on the MDGs). The spending needs with the strongest direct link to economic growth are those for the power sector. However, because of the large investment backlog in the sector, the estimated spending needs contain a strong component of refurbishment and catch-up. Thus, even halving economic growth estimates for the region would reduce estimated power spending needs by only 20 percent. The global recession could also be expected to affect demand for ICT services, as well as trade-related infrastructure, such as railways and ports. However, the weight of these infrastructures in the total spending needs is not much more than 10 percent.

Finding 7: The Infrastructure Challenge Varies Greatly by Country Type

The infrastructure challenge differs markedly across African country groups (Briceño-Garmendia, Smits, and Foster 2008). Because of the widely varying circumstances, distinguishing among middle-income countries (like Cape Verde and South Africa), resource-rich countries with economies heavily reliant on petroleum or mineral revenues (like Nigeria and Zambia), fragile states emerging from conflict (like Côte d'Ivoire and the Democratic Republic of Congo), and the remaining low-income countries that are neither fragile nor resource rich (like Senegal and Uganda) is helpful.

By far the most daunting infrastructure challenges are those facing the fragile states (figure O.3). The recent conflicts affecting these countries usually resulted in the destruction

Table O.3 Overall Infrastructure Spending Needs for Sub-Saharan Africa
$ billions annually

Infrastructure sector	Capital expenditure	Operation and maintenance	Total spending
ICT	7.0	2.0	9.0
Irrigation	2.9	0.6	3.4
Power	26.7	14.1	40.8
Transport	8.8	9.4	18.2
WSS	14.9	7.0	21.9
Total	60.4	33.0	93.3

Source: Authors' estimates based on Banerjee, Wodon, and others 2008; Carruthers, Krishnamani, and Murray 2008; Mayer and others 2008; Rosnes and Vennemo 2008.
Note: Column totals may not add exactly because of rounding errors. ICT = information and communication technology; WSS = water supply and sanitation.

Figure O.3 Burden of Infrastructure Spending Needs

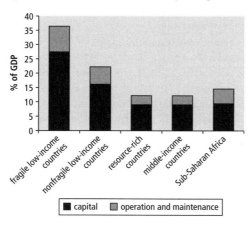

Source: Briceño-Garmendia, Smits, and Foster 2008.
Note: Figures refer to investment (except public sector) and include recurrent spending. Public sector covers general government and nonfinancial enterprises.

or dilapidation of their (already modest) national infrastructure platforms. In the Democratic Republic of Congo, about 50 percent of infrastructure assets need rehabilitation. The fragile states' infrastructure spending needs are especially large, particularly when measured against the size of their economies. Such countries would, on average, need to devote 37 percent of their GDPs to infrastructure spending to build a solid infrastructure platform. With their difficult environments, they attract relatively little external financing, capturing only 10 percent of overseas development assistance and 6 percent of private capital flows allocated to infrastructure. In addition to their huge financing burden, the fragile states do not use their current resource envelope well; they underspend on maintenance and have inefficient service providers.

Nonfragile low-income countries need to allocate, on average, about 23 percent of their GDPs to build and sustain a basic infrastructure platform, a level difficult to envisage in practice. Therefore, these countries will have to make difficult choices about the prioritization of their infrastructure investments, and most of them have a long way to go in improving the efficiency of operating existing infrastructure.

The resource-rich countries are, in principle, much better placed to meet their infrastructure spending needs, though in practice they have not tended to do so. Resource-rich countries could meet their infrastructure spending needs for a more manageable price tag of about 12 percent of GDP. Moreover, the large royalty payments they received during the recent commodity boom provide a ready source of finance. Yet resource rich-countries actually lag nonfragile low-income countries in their infrastructure stocks and spend less on infrastructure. They have been devoting their added wealth not to infrastructure development but to paying off debts. The governance challenges in a resource-rich environment may thus prevent the transformation of wealth into infrastructure.

Meeting the infrastructure needs of the middle-income countries looks to be much more manageable. These countries should be able to meet their infrastructure spending needs with 10 percent of GDP. They are also much stronger in asset maintenance and institutional efficiency. Their more urban populations also facilitate network rollout.

Finding 8: A Large Share of Africa's Infrastructure Is Domestically Financed

Existing spending on infrastructure in Africa is higher than previously thought, amounting to $45 billion a year when budget and off-budget spending (including state-owned enterprises and extrabudgetary funds) and external financiers are taken into account. The latter include the private sector, official development assistance, and financiers that do not belong to the Organisation for Economic Co-operation and Development (OECD). As much as two-thirds of this overall spending is domestically sourced: $30 billion of annual spending is financed by the African taxpayer and infrastructure user, and a further $15 billion is from external sources (table O.4).

The public sector remains the dominant source of finance for water, energy, and transport in all but the fragile states. Public investment is largely tax financed and executed through central government budgets, whereas the operating and maintenance expenditure is largely financed from user charges and executed through state-owned enterprises. Current levels of public

Table O.4 Infrastructure Spending on Addressing Sub-Saharan Africa's Infrastructure Needs
$ billions annually

Infrastructure sector	Operation and maintenance Public sector	Capital expenditure Public sector	ODA	Non-OECD financiers	Private sector	Total	Total spending
ICT	2.0	1.3	0.0	0.0	5.7	7.0	9.0
Power	7.0	2.4	0.7	1.1	0.5	4.6	11.6
Transport	7.8	4.5	1.8	1.1	1.1	8.4	16.2
WSS	3.1	1.1	1.2	0.2	2.1	4.6	7.6
Irrigation	0.6	0.3	—	—	—	0.3	0.9
Total	20.4	9.4	3.6	2.5	9.4	24.9	45.3

Source: Briceño-Garmendia, Smits, and Foster 2008.
Note: Based on annualized averages for 2001–06. Averages weighted by country GDP. Figures are extrapolations based on the 24-country sample covered in AICD Phase 1. Totals may not add exactly because of rounding errors. ICT = information and communication technology; ODA = official development assistance; OECD = Organisation for Economic Co-operation and Development; WSS = water supply and sanitation. — Not available.

finance are substantially higher relative to GDP in the low-income states, typically absorbing 5–6 percent of total GDP (figure O.4). In absolute terms, however, spending remains very low, no more than $20–$30 per capita a year (Briceño-Garmendia, Smits, and Foster 2008).

Looking only at investment, one finds that official development assistance, private participation in infrastructure, and non-OECD financiers together exceed domestically financed public investment (Briceño-Garmendia, Smits, and Foster 2008). The private sector is by far the largest source, on a par with domestic public investment. Much smaller, but still significant, capital flows are provided by official development assistance and, to a lesser extent, non-OECD financiers, such as China, India, and the Arab states. The focus differs markedly in each case. Official development assistance makes an important contribution to water and transport, particularly in fragile states. Non-OECD finance is significant in energy and rail, especially in resource-rich countries. Private participation in infrastructure is heavily concentrated in ICT.

Finding 9: After Potential Efficiency Gains, Africa's Infrastructure Funding Gap Is $31 Billion a Year, Mostly in the Power Sector

Addressing a wide range of inefficiencies could make the existing resource envelope go much

Figure O.4 Infrastructure Public Spending as a Percentage of GDP

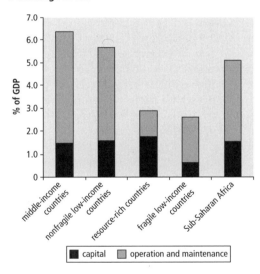

Source: Briceño-Garmendia, Smits, and Foster 2008.

further—to the tune of $17 billion a year. This is Africa's major infrastructure efficiency gap (Briceño-Garmendia, Smits, and Foster 2008).

First, some countries are allocating more resources to some areas of infrastructure than would appear to be warranted (Briceño-Garmendia, Smits, and Foster 2008). This "excess expenditure" amounts to $3.3 billion a year overall. The largest share of this excess expenditure relates to public spending on ICT infrastructure that the private sector could provide, particularly in middle-income countries.

Although some of this "overspending" may be justified by phasing or sequencing, at least part of these resources could possibly be reallocated to underfunded sectors. A need exists to monitor infrastructure expenditure more closely against identified needs and priorities and considering expected economic returns.

Second, African countries are typically executing only about two-thirds of the budget allocated to public investment in infrastructure (Briceño-Garmendia, Smits, and Foster 2008). Put differently, public investment could in theory increase by 30 percent without any increase in spending, simply by addressing the institutional bottlenecks that inhibit capital budget execution. Changes include better planning of investment projects, earlier completion of feasibility studies, more efficient procurement processes, and a move to medium-term multiyear budgeting. Increasing capital budget execution to 100 percent could capture an additional $1.9 billion a year in public investment.

Third, on average, about 30 percent of the infrastructure assets of a typical African country need rehabilitation (figure O.5). This share is even higher for rural infrastructure and for countries affected by violent conflict. The rehabilitation backlog reflects a legacy of underfunding maintenance, a major waste given that the cost of rehabilitating infrastructure is several times higher than the cumulative

cost of sound preventive maintenance. For example, spending $1 on road maintenance provides a savings of $4 to the economy. So some reallocation of resources from investment to maintenance may be warranted, particularly in low-income countries with very low maintenance spending. For roads, an estimated $1.9 billion of capital spending on rehabilitation could have been avoided with sound preventive maintenance.

Fourth, Africa's power and water utilities present very high inefficiency in distribution losses, undercollection of revenues, and overstaffing (figure O.6). Utilities typically collect only 70–90 percent of billed revenues, and distribution losses can easily be twice the technical best practice. According to household surveys, about 40 percent of those connected to utility services do not appear to be paying for them, a share that rises to 65 percent for a significant minority of countries. Undercollection is also a problem for some of Africa's road funds (Gwilliam and others 2008). State-owned telecommunication incumbents employ roughly six times the number of employees per connection than do privately operated enterprises in developing countries. For ICT, countries retaining state-owned incumbents are often incurring significant losses from overstaffing that average 0.2 percent of GDP. Similarly, though to a lesser extent, overemployment in power and water utilities ranges from 20 percent to 80 percent over benchmarks in other developing areas. Overall, the revenues lost through these inefficiencies can easily exceed the current turnover of the utilities by several multiples. For power, these losses are also material at the national level, absorbing 0.5 percent of GDP on the Sub-Saharan African average, or $3.4 billion annually (Briceño-Garmendia, Smits, and Foster 2008). For water, the absolute value of the inefficiencies is smaller, with the average amount accounting for 0.2 percent of GDP, or $1 billion a year.

Fifth, underpricing of infrastructure services is substantial. Although African infrastructure charges are high by international standards, so are the infrastructure costs. Even relatively high tariffs can fail to cover more than the operating costs. The revenues uncollected because of underpricing of power and water amount to

Figure O.5 Rehabilitation Backlog

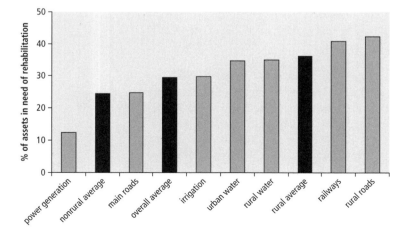

Source: Briceño-Garmendia, Smits, and Foster 2008.

Figure O.6 Hidden Costs of Utility Inefficiencies

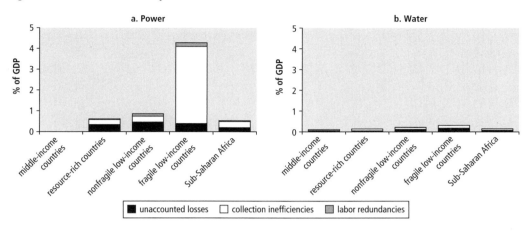

Source: Briceño-Garmendia, Smits, and Foster 2008.

as much as $4 billion a year on aggregate, an implicit subsidy for infrastructure consumers, and that is without taking into account sizable subsidies to large industrial customers that cannot be so readily quantified (Briceño-Garmendia, Smits, and Foster 2008). Because of the very regressive access to infrastructure services in Africa, about 90 percent of those who have access to piped water or electricity services belong to the richest 60 percent of the population (see figure O.9, panel a; Banerjee, Wodon, and others 2008). Thus, better-off households largely capture any subsidy to residential services. In fact, targeting is so deficient that a completely random process for allocating subsidies across the population would perform three times better at reaching the poor.

The overall funding shortfall for meeting Africa's infrastructure needs is given by the difference between estimated infrastructure spending needs and a potential resources envelope that includes existing spending and the potential efficiency gains. Even if all these efficiency gains could be fully realized, a funding gap of about $31 billion a year would remain (table O.5). This gap can be addressed only by raising additional finance or alternatively by adopting lower-cost technologies or less ambitious targets for infrastructure development.

Looking across sectors, about 60 percent of the funding gap relates to power (figure O.7, panel a). The remainder relates to water and

irrigation. There is no significant funding gap for ICT or transport.

Looking across countries, the dollar amount of the funding gap split evenly across income groups. Although the largest financing gaps relate to capital investment, shortfalls in funding for operation and maintenance are substantial, particularly in fragile states. If the infrastructure financing gap is expressed as a percentage of GDP, the level of difficulty involved in closing the gap becomes immediately apparent. The burden associated with the infrastructure financing gap is insurmountable for fragile states. They would need to spend an additional 25 percent of GDP on infrastructure to eliminate their infrastructure deficits. Relative to the size of economies, by far the largest financing gaps are in the energy, transport, and water sectors of fragile states (figure O.7, panel b).

As shown, the size of the funding gap for low-income countries in particular is probably more than they could conceivably raise through available funding channels. For this particularly challenging group of countries, additional measures may need to be taken.

One option is to extend the time horizon for the proposed investment program. Simulations suggest that low-income countries could achieve the proposed investment targets within a period of 20 years without increasing existing spending envelopes, *as long as* they

Table 0.5 Finding Resources: The Efficiency Gap and the Funding Gap
$ billions annually

Item	Electricity	ICT	Irrigation	Transport	WSS	Cross-sector gain	Total
Infrastructure spending needs	(40.8)	(9.0)	(3.4)	(18.2)	(21.9)	n.a.	(93.3)
Existing spending	11.6	9.0	0.9	16.2	7.6	n.a.	45.3
Efficiency gap	6.0	1.3	0.1	3.8	2.9	3.3	17.4
Gain from raising capital execution	0.2	0.0	0.1	1.3	0.2	n.a.	1.9
Gain from eliminating operational inefficiencies	3.4	1.2	—	1.9	1.0	n.a.	7.5
Gain from tariff cost recovery	2.3	—	—	0.6	1.8	n.a.	4.7
Potential for reallocation	n.a.	n.a.	n.a.	n.a.	n.a.	3.3	3.3
Funding gap	(23.2)	1.3	(2.4)	1.9	(11.4)	3.3	(30.6)

Source: Briceño-Garmendia, Smits, and Foster 2008.
Note: ICT = information and communication technology; n.a. = not applicable; — = not available; WSS = water supply and sanitation. Parentheses indicate negative values.

Figure 0.7 Infrastructure Funding Gap by Sector and Country Type

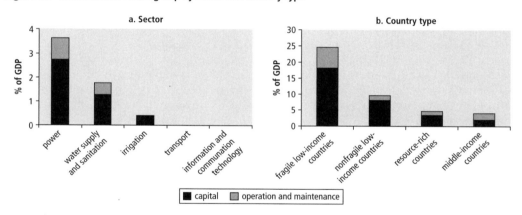

Source: Briceño-Garmendia, Smits, and Foster 2008.

fully exploit efficiency gains. One cannot say the same of fragile states, however. They would still require a substantial increase in spending to meet the investment targets in any reasonable time frame, *even* when inefficiencies are fully captured.

Another possibility is to adopt lower-cost technologies to trim investment needs. Savings of approximately one-third of spending requirements in transport and in water and sanitation are achievable in this way, by adopting lower-cost road designs or lower-end solutions for water and sanitation (such as standposts and improved latrines). Countries face a stark trade-off between the level of service provided and the speed with which they can serve their entire population.

Finding 10: Africa's Institutional, Regulatory, and Administrative Reform Process Is Only Halfway Along

During the last decade, African states have made concerted efforts toward institutional reform in infrastructure. One could probably fairly say that the institutional reform process is halfway along (Vagliasindi and Nellis 2009). They have made progress, but few countries have a modern institutional framework for these sectors. Overall, the greatest progress has been in telecommunications, whereas transport lags furthest behind (figure O.8). The focus also varies. In telecommunications, the

Figure O.8 **Institutional Progress across Sectors**
percentage score on institutional scorecard

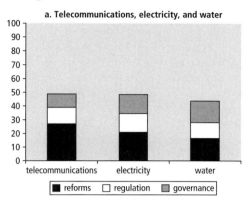

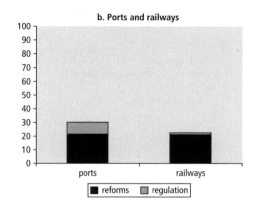

Source: Vagliasindi and Nellis 2009.
Note: See Vagliasindi 2008c for the definition of the *institutional indicators.*

emphasis has been on implementing sector reform, and in water on improving the governance of state-owned enterprises.

Private participation has varied enormously (Vagliasindi and Nellis 2009). Since the mid-1990s, many African countries have experimented with various forms of private participation in infrastructure, with very heterogeneous results (table O.6).

The private sector has proved willing to invest only in mobile telephones, power plants, and container terminals. The number of mobile subscribers and the share of the population receiving mobile signals increased by a factor of 10 in five years, the result of competition among private operators. Private investors have also provided significant finance for thermal power generation (3,000 megawatts) and for container terminals at ports, even if the volumes fall substantially short of requirements. Toll-road concessions are confined to South Africa; traffic volumes elsewhere are not enough to make such endeavors financially self-sustaining.

In power, water, and railways, the private sector has delivered improvements in operational performance but no new finance. The numerous concessions (and related contractual forms) covering railways, power, and water distribution have not delivered significant investment. Because of a combination of low tariffs and low volumes, none of these

businesses delivers cash flows high enough to finance investment. However, these arrangements have often (though not always) been good for operational performance, even if characterized by renegotiation and premature cancellation. A growing area of experimentation is the multiyear performance-based road maintenance contract with the private sector, which shows promise in safeguarding maintenance activities and keeping costs down.

Some progress has occurred with governance reform of state-owned enterprises, where incentive-based performance contracts and external auditing seem to be paying off. Corporate governance reforms, including the establishment of a somewhat independent board of directors, are becoming more prevalent across sectors, even if few enterprises have full corporatization that includes limited liability, rate of return, and dividend policies. Performance contracts with incentives and independent external audits have become dominant features of the reform process for governance of state-owned enterprises, for both electricity and water. When combined with managerial performance incentives, these measures seem to be having a material effect on performance. The introduction of independent audits has also increased efficiency, for both electric and water utilities.

Evidence on the links between introducing an independent regulator and improving

Table O.6 Overview of Private Participation in Infrastructure

Infrastructure sector	Extent of private participation	Nature of experience	Prospects
ICT			
Mobile telephony	Over 90 percent of countries have licensed multiple mobile operators	Extremely beneficial with exponential increase in coverage and penetration.	Several countries still have potential to grant additional licenses
Fixed telephony	About 60 percent of countries have divested state-owned telecommunication incumbent	Controversial in some cases, but has helped improve overall sector efficiency	Several countries still have potential to undertake divestitures
Power			
Power generation	34 independent power projects provide 3,000 MW of new capacity, investing $2.5 billion	Few cancellations but frequent renegotiations; power purchase agreements have proved costly for utilities	Likely to continue, given huge unsatisfied demands and limited public sector capacity
Power distribution	16 concessions and 17 management or lease contracts in 24 countries	Problematic and controversial; one-quarter of contracts cancelled before completion	Movement toward hybrid models involving local private sector in similar frameworks
Transport			
Airports	Four airport concessions, investing less than $0.1 billion, plus some divestitures	No cancellations but some lessons learned	Limited number of additional airports viable for concessions
Ports	26 container terminal concessions, investing $1.3 billion	Processes can be controversial, but cancellations have been few and results positive	Good potential to continue
Railroads	14 railroad concessions, investing $0.4 billion	Frequent renegotiations, low traffic, and costly public service obligations keep investment below expectations	Likely to continue but model needs to be adapted
Roads	10 toll-road projects, almost all in South Africa, investing $1.6 billion	No cancellations reported	Limited because only 8 percent of road network meets minimum traffic threshold, almost all in South Africa
Water			
Water	26 transactions, mainly management or lease contracts	Problematic and controversial; 40 percent of contracts cancelled before completion	Movement toward hybrid models involving local private sector in similar frameworks

Sources: Authors' elaboration based on Bofinger 2009; Bullock 2009; Eberhard and others 2008; Gwilliam and others 2008; Minges and others 2008; Mundy and Penfold 2008; and Svendsen, Ewing, and Msangi 2008.
Note: ICT = information and communication technology; MW = megawatts.

performance is currently mixed (Vagliasindi and Nellis 2009). Some critics argue that regulatory agencies have simply created additional risks because of unpredictable decisions, resulting from excessive discretion and overly broad objectives (Eberhard 2007). Regulatory autonomy remains elusive: in some countries, turnover among commissioners has been high, and the gap between law (or rule) and practice has been wide. For water, where the vast majority of service providers are state-owned enterprises, no evidence exists of any benefit from regulation. For power and telecommunications, some effect is discernible, but it is far from unambiguous. Weak regulatory autonomy and capacity constraints undermine the credibility of independent regulators. Most African regulatory agencies are embryonic, lacking funding and in many cases qualified personnel.

Key Recommendations

Based on these findings, one can make the following 10 key recommendations:

- Addressing Africa's infrastructure efficiency gap is a pressing policy priority with potential dividends of $17 billion a year.
- One of the most flagrant inefficiencies is the failure to maintain infrastructure assets—maintenance needs to be understood as an investment in asset preservation.
- Institutional reform remains essential for tackling utilities' operational inefficiencies, both through private participation and through governance reforms for state-owned enterprises.
- Institutional reform should also go beyond utilities to strengthen the planning functions of the line ministries and address serious deficiencies in the budgetary process.
- Reforms are needed to get full value from existing infrastructure, where widespread administrative and regulatory bottlenecks prevent facilities from being fully used.
- Regional integration can contribute significantly to reducing infrastructure costs, by allowing countries to capture scale economies and manage regional public goods effectively.
- Development of infrastructure networks needs to be strategically informed by the spatial distribution of economic activities and by economies of agglomeration.

- Infrastructure's social policy needs to be rethought, placing more emphasis on recovering costs from those who can afford it and on recasting subsidies to accelerate access.

- Achieving universal access will call for greater attention to removing barriers that prevent the uptake of services and offering practical and attractive second-best solutions.

- Closing Africa's infrastructure financing gap is critical to the region's prosperity, and the global financial crisis has only made infrastructure more relevant.

Recommendation 1: Address Africa's Infrastructure Efficiency Gap as a Pressing Policy Priority

The findings presented underscore the magnitude of inefficiency with which Africa spends its current infrastructure resources. Of Africa's overall infrastructure spending needs of about $93 billion a year, as much as $17 billion could be met simply by using existing resources more effectively.

Reaping this efficiency dividend has to be a major policy priority for the region, and efforts to scale up infrastructure finance need to be made in the context of genuine commitments to address efficiency. Pouring additional funding into sectors characterized by high levels of inefficiency makes little sense. However, postponing increases in finance until efficiency improves is not a valid option: the cost to economic growth and human development is simply too high. Rather, development partner efforts to secure additional resources for infrastructure finance must be matched by government efforts to improve their efficiency in using such resources. Parallel progress is needed on both fronts.

Moreover, investment finance is needed in some cases to allow inefficiencies to be captured (for example, where roads must be rehabilitated before they return to a "maintainable" condition or when meters must be installed to improve revenue collection). These kinds of efficiency-related investments deserve to be prioritized because of the high returns they typically bring.

The current global financial crisis only strengthens the motivation for addressing infrastructure inefficiencies. As African countries begin to feel the pinch of the global financial crisis, and as other sources of funding begin to dry up, measures to improve the efficiency of using existing resources become particularly attractive. Such measures provide an additional internal source of finance at a relatively low monetary cost. Of course, in some cases, significant investments may be needed before efficiency gains can be captured (for example, reducing distribution losses in power or water). In other cases, the economic context of the crisis may simply increase the political cost of taking such measures, such as raising cost recovery or laying off excess employees.

Potential efficiency gains take a wide variety of forms, which are developed in the recommendations that follow. Briefly, they include the following areas:

- Safeguarding maintenance expenditure to avoid wasting resources on the repeated rehabilitation of existing assets, which could save $2.6 billion a year in avoidable capital expenditure for the roads sector alone

- Reforming institutions to improve the operational performance of utilities and other service providers that are currently wasting $6 billion a year on inefficiencies such as overstaffing, undercollection of revenues, and distribution losses

- Addressing deficiencies in the public expenditure framework, where $3.3 billion a year of infrastructure resources appear to be poorly allocated across sectors and low budget execution prevents $1.8 billion a year of public investment funds from being spent

- Modernizing administrative and regulatory frameworks to reduce bottlenecks that prevent services from being provided effectively across existing infrastructure networks and impose substantial costs on infrastructure users

- Reaping the economies of scale and coordination benefits associated with regional integration, which in the case of power alone can be as high as $2 billion a year

- Securing the highest returns from new infrastructure investments by using them to secure economies of agglomeration and to facilitate the development of productive activities along key economic corridors

- Rethinking infrastructure social policy to place more emphasis on cost recovery from those who can afford to pay, and redirecting the current $4 billion a year of subsidies to accelerate access among lower-income groups

- Reducing the costs of meeting key infrastructure targets by adopting lower-cost technologies that provide reasonable levels of service at a price that is affordable to both consumers and the government.

Recommendation 2: Make Greater Efforts to Safeguard Maintenance Spending

The traditional neglect of maintenance expenditure needs to be reversed by rethinking maintenance as asset preservation. One-third of Africa's infrastructure assets need rehabilitation, indicating that historic neglect of maintenance is endemic. For fragile states and for rural infrastructure, the share of assets needing rehabilitation is much higher. The shortfall in road maintenance spending is costing Africa $1.9 billion a year in avoidable capital expenditures. In fact, spending $1 on maintenance can provide a savings of approximately $4 to the economy.

Thus, Africa's infrastructure financing gap is not only about raising investment capital; a substantial part of it relates to maintenance. Yet maintenance offers one of the highest returns to infrastructure spending, so it may be more helpful to think of maintenance as a kind of investment in asset preservation.

The road sector shows that maintenance can be improved through suitable institutional reforms. Since the mid-1990s, the majority of African countries have established road funds as a means of channeling road user charges to network maintenance. Countries with road funds do significantly better at raising adequate maintenance funds as long as the fuel levies paid into these funds are set high enough to provide material financing. Moreover, countries with both road funds and road agencies do significantly better in safeguarding the quality of their road networks. The use

of multiyear performance-based contracts for roads has further contributed to the efficacy and efficiency of road maintenance. These findings illustrate that a combination of funding mechanisms, institutional capacity, and contractual incentives is needed to overcome the maintenance challenge.

Donors have traditionally eschewed funding maintenance, arguing it is more sustainable for funding directly from country budgets. The argument is a good one. However, the willingness of donors to fund asset rehabilitation can create perverse incentives for countries to neglect maintenance, because governments face a choice between raising taxes today to finance maintenance or simply waiting a few years to obtain subsidized donor capital for reconstruction. In low-income, low-capacity environments where maintenance is unlikely to be forthcoming, donors may be well advised to take this choice explicitly into account in project design, rather than simply assume that maintenance will happen. One way of doing so is to choose more capital-intensive, low-maintenance technologies. Even if they represent a higher investment cost in the short run, overall life-cycle costs may be lower if reconstruction can be avoided or postponed. As donors move toward sectorwide budget support, they will have a greater opportunity to ensure that maintenance spending is adequately supported in the budget envelope. In any case, as a general principle, the establishment of a sound framework for financing maintenance should be a prerequisite for the funding of major capital programs.

Recommendation 3: Tackle Inefficiency through Institutional Reform

Since the mid-1990s, the institutional agenda has broadened and deepened (Vagliasindi and Nellis 2009). In the 1990s, the emphasis of institutional reform was on sector restructuring and private participation, transplanting to Africa experiences from other parts of the developing world. This approach yielded dramatic results in telecommunications, but elsewhere the benefits were more limited and the experiences more problematic. Even so, private finance to African infrastructure came from nowhere to provide a flow of funds comparable in scale to overseas development assistance.

A more nuanced, less dogmatic perspective on the private sector has emerged. This perspective values private financing in mobile telephony, power generation, and ports, while recognizing its limits in roads, rail, power, and water (see table O.6). Even for infrastructure where the proven appetite for private finance is very limited, the potential contribution of the private sector to tackling costly management inefficiencies (undercollected utility revenues, low labor productivity, or neglected road maintenance) remains valuable. Indeed, the efficiency gains from such performance improvements are themselves a significant source of sector finance. Moreover, the concept of private participation has undergone significant expansion. More emphasis has fallen on the local (not international) private sector and on hybrid models that experiment with different ways of allocating responsibilities between public and private partners.

Another important way in which the institutional reform agenda has broadened is the greater focus on the quality of governance for enterprises that remain state owned (Vagliasindi and Nellis 2009). The recognition that the private sector will never be a ubiquitous service provider has come with the realization that state-owned enterprises are here to stay. Therefore, it is necessary to recommit to the difficult process of reforming state-owned enterprises.

Renewed efforts on state-owned enterprise reform should favor governance over technical fixes. Fortunately, better governance of state-owned enterprises can improve performance. Past efforts at improving utility management focused too heavily on technical issues at the expense of corporate governance and accountability. Future state-owned enterprise reforms seem justified as long as they focus on deeper institutional issues. Key measures include greater decision-making autonomy for the board of directors, more objective selection criteria for senior managers, rigorous disclosure of conflicts of interest, and more transparent, merit-based recruitment processes.

Parallel efforts can strengthen financial and operational monitoring of state-owned enterprises by their supervisory agencies, whether line ministries or ministries of finance. Transparency and accountability of state-owned enterprises depend on solid systems of financial management, procurement, and management information. Today, basic operational and financial data on firm performance are not produced, reported, or acted on. Without information or, perhaps worse, without action on what information is produced, better outcomes cannot be expected. Key measures include auditing and publishing financial accounts and using comprehensive cost-based accounting systems that allow the functional unbundling of costs and a clearer sense of cost centers. After this foundation is in place, contracting mechanisms can improve performance—within the public sector or with the private sector.

Public sector performance contracts need strong performance incentives. Initial attempts to improve African state-owned enterprises through performance contracts with their line ministry or other supervisory agency were minimally effective. Recent efforts in water (Uganda), however, have had a much more positive effect. The key feature of these contracts is to incorporate incentives for good managerial (and staff) performance and, more rarely, sanctions for failure to reach targets.

Creating effective performance incentives in the public sector can be challenging, making management contracts with the private sector a relevant option. Either expatriate or local management teams can be contracted with, each of which offers advantages. Clarity about what a contract can and cannot achieve, particularly given its short time horizons, is essential. At best, a management contract can improve performance in a handful of relatively manageable aspects of efficiency, such as revenue collection and labor productivity. It cannot solve deficiencies in the broader institutional framework; ideally, these should be addressed beforehand. Nor can a management contract raise investment finance or deliver major effects on service quality that require substantial investments or lengthy gestations.

In principle, regulation can do much; but in practice, regulation has proved difficult. Regulators have been set up across Africa, precisely to insulate utilities from political interference while closely monitoring enterprises. Improving regulatory performance is a long-term process to be pursued where private participation and competitive pressures are significant. The challenge of establishing new public institutions in developing countries is often underestimated. Independent regulation requires a strong political commitment and competent institutions and people. Where some or all are lacking, considering complementary or transitional options that reduce discretion in regulatory decision making through more explicit rules and procedures or by outsourcing regulatory functions to advisory regulators and expert panels may be wise (Eberhard 2007).

Recommendation 4: Include Line Ministries and Budgetary Processes on the Institutional Reform Agenda

Much of the emphasis of recent reforms has been on restructuring the service provider or utility, bringing in private management, applying regulatory oversight, and so on. Little attention has been given to institutional strengthening of the sector line ministries. These line ministries have responsibilities, which, if not adequately discharged, can jeopardize the functioning of the sector. They take the lead in sector planning, participate in the formulation of the public budgets, and execute investments. However, deficiencies exist in all those areas. Unless they are tackled head on, the effect of reforms on service providers will remain limited.

Stronger sector planning is needed in infrastructure line ministries to ensure that the construction of critical new assets begins early enough to come on stream when needed. Too often overlooked or debilitated during the course of sector restructuring efforts, planning is a critical sector function. It is essential to restore this vital planning capability in the line ministries and to develop sound technical methodologies for identifying and selecting infrastructure projects. More rigorous project screening can ensure that infrastructure investments are selected according to their expected returns and are appropriately sequenced and synchronized with one another and with broader development plans to maximize synergies and avoid costly bottlenecks.

A clear example is power generation. Traditionally, planning and procurement of new power infrastructure were the province of the state-owned utility. With power sector reforms and independent power producers, those functions were often moved to the ministry of energy or electricity. The transfer of skills was not always simultaneous, however, so plans were not adequately informed by the complexities on the ground. In many cases, planning has collapsed. New plants are rarely timely, thereby opening power gaps that prompt recourse to temporary power and discourage investors. When procurement is (finally) undertaken, the authorities may not take the trouble to conduct international competitive bidding. This outcome is unfortunate because a rigorous bidding process lends credibility and transparency to procurement and results in more competitively priced power.

Because domestic public spending finances the bulk of Africa's infrastructure investments, development partners need a broader view of the quality of public spending. Across the infrastructure sectors, most investments are by line ministries through the budgetary process. Shortcomings in the way the rest of the sector budget is allocated and spent may offset development finance that focuses too narrowly on specific project interventions. So donor resources are best channeled programmatically as budgetary support or through sectorwide projects, and development partners need to take a broader interest in the overall quality of public spending. Thus, infrastructure interventions must be grounded in a broader understanding of the public expenditure framework in each sector.

Ad hoc political priorities with little or no economic screening too often characterize the budgetary process. The annual budget cycle prevents adequate follow-through on the funding of multiyear infrastructure projects. When it comes to implementation, many countries have significant problems with budgetary execution, with procurement bottlenecks preventing the full budget allocations from materializing in actual spending.

Key aspects of the public expenditure framework need to be addressed. The budgeting process needs to move to a medium-term framework and link sector objectives and resource allocations, underpinned by clear sector plans that go down to specific activities and their associated costs. The careful incorporation of maintenance in medium-term sector-planning tools can prevent the growing need for asset rehabilitation. Project appraisal should underpin the budgetary process for public investment to ensure that all investments under political consideration pass at least a minimum threshold of economic viability. Administrative processes that delay the release of budgeted funds must be overhauled, and procedures for procurement, disbursement, financial management, and accountability must be modernized and streamlined.

Water provides interesting examples of how bottlenecks in the budgetary process can prevent the use of available resources. In West Africa, the binding constraint is not the availability of budgetary resources in many instances but the capacity to disburse them in a timely fashion (Prevost 2009). In Tanzania, steep increases in budget allocations to the sector followed water's identification as a priority in the country's poverty reduction strategy, but disbursements increased at a much slower pace, thus impeding any immediately discernible effect on access (Van den Berg 2009).

Parallel improvements are also needed in the way donor finance is channeled. Given the relevance of external funds, a solid public expenditure management system for African countries requires that donors improve the predictability of their support and streamline and harmonize their procedures. In that sense, a focus on multidonor initiatives that pool funds to provide general budgetary support for a sectorwide program of interventions is preferable.

Recommendation 5: Use Administrative and Regulatory Reforms to Get Full Value from Existing Infrastructure

Africa is failing to get the full development potential even from its existing infrastructure networks. Administrative and regulatory failures create bottlenecks and prevent infrastructure assets from delivering the services they are supposed to. These problems are particularly evident in transport, where high-impact reforms are urgently needed.

Liberalizing the trucking industry can reduce the exorbitant road freight costs in Central and West Africa. The regulation and market structures of the road freight industry, not the quality of road infrastructure, are the binding constraints on international corridors (Teravaninthorn and Raballand 2008). Road freight tariffs, which can reach $0.08–$0.13 per ton-kilometer in Central and West Africa, reflect the high profit margins of trucking services (60–160 percent). The *tour de role* regulatory framework, based on market sharing and centralized allocations of freight, limits vehicle mileage and undermines incentives to improve fleet quality. The alternative is to combine free entry to the market and market pricing with regulatory enforcement of rules for quality and operating behavior. Already practiced in southern Africa, these reforms can reduce road freight tariffs to $0.05 per ton-kilometer. Without such reforms, further investments in upgrading road network quality will simply lead to higher profit margins for the trucking industry without lowering transport costs for consumers.

One-stop border posts are essential to avoid extensive delays in transit traffic along international road corridors. Road conditions along Africa's major international corridors are good, with trucks reaching speeds of 50–60 kilometers an hour, but long delays at borders slow effective velocities to little more than 10 kilometers an hour. A journey of 2,500 kilometers from Lusaka, Zambia, to the port of Durban in South Africa takes on average eight days— four days of travel time and four days spent at border crossings. Compare that total with land border-crossing times of no more than half an hour for industrialized countries. The cost of delays for an eight-axle interlink truck has been estimated at about $300 a day. The investments to develop one-stop border facilities and to modernize customs procedures are relatively modest and would pay back in barely a year. Without such reforms, further investments in the road network will have little effect on overall transit times.

More reliable interconnection services can avoid even longer delays on international rail corridors. Locomotives from one country are generally not allowed to travel on another country's network, mainly because of the inability to provide breakdown assistance to foreign operators. As a result, rail freight crossing borders must wait to be picked up by a different locomotive. These delays can be extensive. A journey of 3,000 kilometers from Kolwezi on the Democratic Republic of Congo border to the port of Durban in South Africa takes 38 days—including 9 days of travel time and 29 days associated primarily with loading and interchange of freight. This delay partly reflects the lack of reliable, well-maintained locomotives, but it also reflects the absence of clear contractual incentives to service traffic from a neighboring country's network. Reducing such delays would require total rethinking of contractual relationships and access rights linking the railways along the corridor. It would also likely require a regional clearing-house to ensure transparency and fairness in reciprocal track access rights.

Slow movement of containers and cargo through Africa's ports imposes very high economic costs. Many firms cite bottlenecks at ports as their most pressing infrastructure constraint in countries as diverse as Burkina Faso, Cameroon, Malawi, Mauritius, and South Africa. Container dwell times in East and West Africa are 12–15 days, twice the international best practice of 7 days. Most delays are caused by long processing and administration times and poor handling in congested port areas, rather than by any real limitations in basic quay capacity. These delays can be very costly. One extra day in port costs more than $35,000 for a 2,200-TEU (20-foot equivalent unit) vessel in 2006 and proportionately more for larger ships. Shipping lines have responded by introducing "congestion charges": for a 20-foot container in 2006, ranging from $35 a day in Dakar, Senegal, to $420 a day in Tema, Ghana.

The solution lies in modernizing customs administration and improving efficiency of cargo handling. The two main bottlenecks within ports are loading and unloading of cargo and customs administration—both need to be addressed simultaneously. Inadequate cranes are part of the problem, but new equipment alone will not deliver better performance unless staff practices are also modernized. Ports with container terminal concessions have

boosted handling rates. Modernizing customs administration requires modern information technology and associated database systems. Such soft infrastructure has traditionally been underfunded, contributing to poor port efficiency. Governance issues may also afflict customs administration.

Port and land distribution infrastructure need to be integrated. The lack of an integrated land distribution system, particularly for transit traffic, further impedes container traffic. Making the most progress are dry and liquid bulk exports, where many port facilities are privately owned and integrated within a comprehensive logistics system. Containerized trade, in contrast, is often only skin-deep. Containers are packed and unpacked near the ports, and the benefits of fully integrated multimodal transport corridors associated with container adoption are not secured. As a result, little containerized traffic moves into the land-locked hinterland, and most of those countries' imports are transported as general cargo.

Overall, the transport regulatory and administrative framework needs to promote seamless multimodal transportation networks more consciously. Transport chains can be no stronger than their weakest links, which are usually the interchanges between different modalities—such as road to rail or rail to sea. The weaknesses are partly physical, where no physical connection exists between the modes and no infrastructure is available for transshipment. However, they are also partly institutional, with responsibility for the interchanges not falling clearly to one modal agency or the other. Finally, they are partly operational, with the government collecting taxes and duties, or staff collecting bribes, slowing movements, and pushing up costs. Even at the sector policy and planning level, Africa's transport modes are too often parceled out across separate line ministries, thereby preventing a cohesive intermodal transport framework from emerging.

Recommendation 6: Pursue Regional Integration to Reduce Infrastructure Costs

Regional integration lowers costs across all aspects of infrastructure. The high cost of infrastructure services in Africa is partly attributable to fragmentary national boundaries preventing achievement of scale economies.

In ICT, power, ports, and airports, regional collaboration essentially provides scale economies that reduce the cost of service. Most African countries are simply too small to develop infrastructure cost-effectively on their own. In ICTs, regional collaboration in continental fiber-optic submarine cables can reduce Internet and international call charges by half, relative to national reliance on satellite communications. In power, 21 countries have national power systems below the minimum efficient scale of a single plant. By sharing large-scale, cost-effective energy resources across countries, regional trade can reduce electricity costs by $2 billion a year. The traffic flows to most of Africa's national ports and airports are too low to provide the scale economies needed to attract services from major international shipping companies and airlines. Regional collaboration in multicountry hubs can help overcome this problem.

In road and rail corridors and transboundary river basins, collaborative management of these regional public goods reduces the cost. Many of Africa's infrastructure assets and natural resources are regional public goods that cut across national frontiers and can be effectively developed and maintained only through international collaboration. Road and rail corridors need to be managed collaboratively to smooth transport and trade services to Africa's 15 landlocked countries, avoiding the extensive border delays that slow international road freight to 10 kilometers an hour. Africa's 63 international river basins call for cooperative water resource management and coordinated investments to increase basin yields of food, power, and other economic opportunities, while strengthening environmental sustainability and mitigating the effects of droughts and floods.

Reaping these benefits poses numerous institutional challenges. Among them are mobilizing political will, developing effective regional institutions, setting priorities soundly, harmonizing regulatory procedures, and facilitating project preparation and finance.

Notwithstanding the economic case for regional integration, the mobilization of political will faces considerable obstacles. Regional infrastructure involves a high level of trust between countries, not least because of the implied dependence on neighbors for key resources, such as energy and water. For example, if regional power trade were pursued fully, 16 African countries would import more than half their power needs. A large share of that power would come from fragile states, such as the Democratic Republic of Congo and Guinea.

Regional institutions are needed to facilitate agreements and implement compensation mechanisms. Some countries have more to gain from regional integration than others do. As long as regional integration provides a substantial economic dividend, one should be able to design compensation mechanisms that make all participating countries better off. Benefit sharing was pioneered through international river basin treaties, such as that for Senegal, and could be applied to other regional infrastructure more broadly. Africa has an extensive architecture of regional political and technical bodies, but they have overlapping memberships, limited technical capacity, and limited enforcement powers. Nor do they currently have the capacity to implement crossborder compensation mechanisms.

Moving on regional projects that deliver quick wins is important. Because of the daunting investment agenda, better sequencing and priority setting for regional projects are needed. Political, economic, and spatial approaches have all been widely discussed. Regional projects range from bilateral cooperation on a transmission line or border post to vast and complex interventions, sometimes with a continental reach. Given the size of the challenges, starting small with projects that deliver tangible high returns and building incrementally on initial successes may be advisable.

Regulatory harmonization needs to go hand in hand with physical integration. Unless regulatory frameworks and administrative procedures are harmonized to allow the free flow of services across national boundaries, physical integration of infrastructure networks will be ineffective. Making progress on regulatory reform has a relatively low monetary cost, but it can have a very high return. A good example is the Yamoussoukro Decision: opening the skies for air transportation across Africa, it has led to greater freedom in the negotiation of bilateral agreements.

Greater efforts are needed to facilitate preparation of complex regional projects, which are particularly costly and time-consuming to prepare. That is especially true when projects are large in relation to the size of the host economy and when they essentially depend on financing from downstream beneficiaries. They also stretch the donor financing systems that are more typically geared toward national investments.

Recommendation 7: Take a Spatial View of Infrastructure Development Priorities

Infrastructure networks are inherently spatial, both reflecting and underpinning the spatial distribution of economic activity. Infrastructure plays a key role in enabling cities to benefit from economies of agglomeration. Transport networks interconnect urban centers with each other and with international trading networks, providing the basis for exchange between the urban and rural economies. Energy, water, and ICT all enhance productivity within urban and rural spaces. Therefore, infrastructure plans and priorities should be strategically informed by a clear understanding of the spatial distribution of economic activity and potential. A clear example of this approach is the Spatial Development Initiative of the New Partnership for Africa's Development (NEPAD).

The spatial lens is a useful basis for prioritization of infrastructure investments and provides insight into cross-sectoral links. Looking at infrastructure through a spatial lens allows identification of the key bottlenecks along various trading corridors, which are typically the highest-return interventions. Cross-sectoral links also become more apparent through a spatial view, shedding light on the need for coordinating interventions across infrastructure sectors and between infrastructure and client economic sectors. An emerging literature suggests that because of synergy effects, the returns from bundling multiple infrastructure interventions in a particular spatial area (Torero and Escobal 2005) or along a given spatial corridor (Briceño-Garmendia and Foster 2009a, 2009b) are higher than those from making the same investments in a

spatially uncoordinated manner. In Africa—too often—the limited infrastructure available is thinly spread out, preventing such synergies from being captured.

The urbanization process calls for a regional development perspective on infrastructure that looks at each city and its rural hinterland as an integrated economic unit. Africa is urbanizing fast, creating change that is predictable and beneficial for both urban and rural areas. Prosperity and density go together, as changes in productivity require agglomeration economies, larger markets, and better connectivity. Concentration and urbanization trigger prosperity in both urban and rural areas, and well-functioning cities facilitate the transition from subsistence agriculture by providing a large market for rural products and supporting nonfarm activities. The debate of rural versus urban development should therefore be replaced by the understanding that rural and urban development are closely linked and mutually dependent—and that economic integration of rural and urban areas is the only way to produce growth and inclusive development.

In urban areas, deficiencies in land policies and planning have become a huge impediment to extending infrastructure services. African cities are growing fast, but with insufficient infrastructure and poor institutions, most new settlements are informal and not covered by basic services. Urban planning should be strengthened to reduce sprawl, enhance densification, prevent development in precarious environmental zones, and provide the appropriate balance between public and private land to safeguard key trunk networks. Property rights must be clearly defined so that land markets can function. Cities frequently lack the financial basis to develop the infrastructure critical to their success. The local tax base, though potentially large, is typically unexploited, leaving municipalities reliant on central government transfers, which are too often inadequate or unpredictable.

Large agricultural sectors and rural economies remain central to economic growth and poverty reduction in Africa. Yet the access of rural populations to infrastructure is extremely low. Rural roads and irrigation systems are together perhaps the most pressing of rural infrastructure needs. The two go hand in hand, and their development should follow the value of agricultural land and the spatial proximity to urban markets. ICT has made huge strides in expanding rural access, with one in two rural Africans now in range of a global systems mobile signal. This platform can contribute to agricultural productivity through simple text-message extension services, through bulletins on agricultural market prices and meteorological conditions, and as a vehicle for financial transactions. The possibilities are only just beginning to be explored.

Recommendation 8: Rethink Infrastructure Social Policy

Although Africa's infrastructure services are relatively expensive, costs remain even higher than prices, and this lack of cost recovery has major detrimental effects. Underpricing infrastructure services is costing Africa $4.7 billion a year in forgone revenues. In addition, because of inequitable access to infrastructure services, these subsidies are highly regressive, largely bypassing the poor (figure O.9). The underrecovery of costs impairs the financial health of utilities and slows the pace of service expansion.

Concerns about affordability are usually the pretext for underpricing services but do not bear much scrutiny (figure O.9). A subsistence-level monthly utility bill priced in cost-recovery terms typically amounts to $6–$10 a month. In the middle-income countries, bills of this magnitude do not appear to present an affordability problem anywhere across the income spectrum. Nor do bills of this magnitude pose affordability issues for the more affluent groups in low-income countries, the main ones to enjoy access to services. Affordability would become a binding constraint in low-income countries only when service coverage starts to exceed 50 percent. Only in the poorest of countries, and those with exceptionally high infrastructure costs, does full cost recovery seem unachievable for today's more affluent consumers. Even in these cases, operating cost recovery should be a feasible objective, with subsidies limited to capital costs. Simulations suggest that raising tariffs to cost recovery would have only minimal effects on poverty rates in most cases.

Figure O.9 Access to and Affordability of Household Services

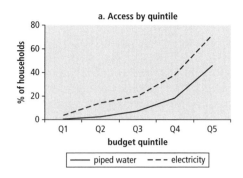

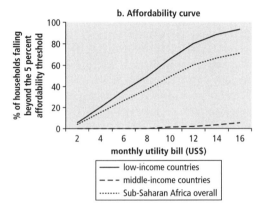

Source: Banerjee, Wodon, and others 2008.
Note: Q1 = first (or poorest) budget quintile; Q2 = second budget quintile; Q3 = third (or middle) budget quintile; Q4 = fourth budget quintile; Q5 = top (or richest) budget quintile.

The affordability of services depends not only on prices, but also on the type of payment arrangements that are made available to consumers. Prepayment (pioneered in the mobile telephone sector) can help households budget their consumption and reduce revenue risks for operators. The same approach is technologically feasible for electricity, and a growing number of power utilities are adopting it.

Subsidies are important, but subsidy design needs major rethinking, with a sharper focus on subsidizing connections, which can be more equitable and effective in expanding coverage. The affordability problems with connection charges are often much more serious than those with use-of-service charges. Moreover, the absence of a connection may itself be a good targeting variable for identifying disadvantaged households, although less so in a low-access environment where coverage may be far from universal, even among affluent households.

An important test of the coherence of a subsidy policy is to see whether it would be affordable for the country under universal access. The existing underpricing of utility services that benefit just a small minority costs many African countries as much as 1 percent of GDP. As countries move toward universal access, that subsidy burden would increase proportionately, rapidly becoming unaffordable for the national budget. Countries should thus consider how the cost of any proposed subsidy policy would escalate as coverage increases. This test of the fiscal affordability of a subsidy is an important reality check that can prevent countries from embarking on policies that are simply not scalable and will keep coverage low.

Recommendation 9: Find Practical Ways to Broaden Access to Infrastructure Services

Universal access to infrastructure services remains distant for most African countries. The vast majority of African households today lack access to modern power, piped water, sewerage, and even all-season roads that service their communities. The very slow progress in expanding this access since the mid-1990s suggests that universal access to infrastructure is more than 50 years away for most countries in Africa.

This situation calls for a different approach to expanding modern infrastructure services and for greater attention to second-best alternatives. Business as usual will not bring about the acceleration of infrastructure access that Africa needs. Moreover, even if access can be accelerated, many people will have to continue to rely on alternatives to modern infrastructure services for many years to come. Therefore, infrastructure social policies in Africa need to give greater thought to improving and expanding second-best alternatives.

In expanding modern infrastructure networks, closer attention should be paid to the demand side of the equation. The mobile telephone revolution has clearly demonstrated that Africa can widely and rapidly adopt modern infrastructure services. Low charges for initial connection make market entry affordable. Prepayment schemes eliminate credit risk and give customers full control over their spending. Services are well tailored to customer demands. Other network services, notably power and water, have tended to view access as a matter of simply rolling out new networks, overlooking the fact that even where networks are available, the hookup rates are relatively low. They need to pay greater attention to demand-side issues that prevent customers from making connections: connection charges that are much higher than household incomes, as well as tenure and urban development issues. The most cost-effective way to increase access for many utilities may be through densification programs that increase hookups to existing networks by using greater community outreach to understand better the demand side of the market.

Second-best alternatives can be fine-tuned to provide feasible and attractive infrastructure services to those otherwise unserved. The vast majority of those without access to modern infrastructure services rely on traditional alternatives, such as candles, wells, or unimproved latrines. Although doing the job, these traditional alternatives tend to be inconvenient, inferior, or unsafe. Second-best solutions, such as street lighting, solar lanterns, standposts, and improved latrines, would provide households with superior services at a cost that is somewhat higher than the traditional alternatives but still falls far short of modern services. Puzzlingly, these second-best solutions are not very prevalent in Africa, and even where they exist, they tend to be available primarily to the more affluent.

A key problem seems to be the public-good nature of many of these solutions (such as standposts and street lighting), which makes it difficult for service providers to recover costs and greatly complicates the administration of the facilities. Effective institutional arrangements must be found to support implementation of these alternatives. Another problem is that some of these alternatives, although cheaper, may simply not be cheap enough to be widely affordable.

Recommendation 10: Close the Infrastructure Funding Gap

Notwithstanding the importance of all these efficiency measures, a substantial infrastructure financing gap of $31 billion a year remains. Such a large shortfall looked daunting even before the onset of the global financial crisis.

As of year-end 2007, many factors had converged to bring about rapid and sustained increases in all major sources of external finance for African infrastructure. Following the Gleneagles Summit, OECD development assistance placed greater emphasis on supporting African infrastructure. Official development assistance flows almost doubled, from $4.1 billion in 2004 to $8.1 billion in 2007. The resurgence of economic growth on the continent led to an upswing in private participation. Since the late 1990s, private investment flows to Sub-Saharan infrastructure almost tripled, going from about $3 billion in 1997 to $9.4 billion in 2006/07 (about 1.5 percent of regional GDP). In addition, non-OECD countries—notably China and India—began to take a growing interest in financing infrastructure within a framework of South-South cooperation. Their commitments rose from almost nothing in the early 2000s to finance about $2.6 billion of African infrastructure annually between 2001 and 2006. Although disbursements tend to lag commitments by several years, if the record commitments of 2007 are fully honored, the disbursements of external finance for African infrastructure may continue to increase over the next few years.

In the absence of any offsetting measures, domestic infrastructure spending would likely fall, compromising economic recovery and deepening poverty. The existing gap of $31 billion a year could widen further as public budgets are squeezed, external capital flows decline, and consumer ability to pay user charges is eroded. The ability to construct new infrastructure, address regional bottlenecks, and maintain existing assets would be severely reduced. In Latin America during the 1990s, some 50 percent of the fiscal compression to balance the public books came from cuts in infrastructure spending. In Indonesia following the Asian crisis, public investment in infrastructure fell from 7 percent of GDP to 2 percent. Growth in Latin America and Asia was compromised in a "lost decade."

Many countries, ranging from China and India to Argentina and Mexico, have used infrastructure-based fiscal stimulus in times of economic crisis. If well targeted to addressing key economic bottlenecks and complemented by policy reforms, infrastructure investments can pave the way for the later resurgence of economic growth. Furthermore, some kinds of public works contracts are labor intensive, creating short-term employment to alleviate poverty. Although Africa could benefit from such a program, the continent does not have the means to finance it without external support. Estimates suggest that a $50 billion stimulus package would be needed to offset the impact of the economic crisis on Africa, and that focusing such a package on infrastructure investments would have the largest short-term effect on GDP growth, boosting projections for 2010 to 4 percent, compared with the postcrisis 1.7 percent. In the long term, Africa would see a permanent increase of 2.5 percent of GDP (ODI 2009).

Any increase in donor finance for African infrastructure should pay particular attention to the power sector and to the fragile states. Donors have neglected power since the 1990s. Although the private sector can contribute to funding power generation, donors will still need to scale up substantially to address the current crisis in the sector. This scale-up was already under way before the onset of the crisis, with donor commitments that first topped $1 billion a year in 2005 reaching a peak of $2.3 billion in 2007. Fragile states stand out as receiving less than their fair share of donor finance for infrastructure. Given the magnitude of the financing gap that these countries face relative to the size of their economies, as well as the importance of infrastructure in regenerating their development, a case exists for channeling incremental donor resources in their direction.

Some of Africa's larger low-income countries have the potential to raise a significant amount of local finance for infrastructure if suitable instruments can be developed. In a handful of African countries, domestic capital markets are beginning to look wide and deep enough to provide significant volumes of infrastructure finance, Nigeria being the most salient example (Irving and Manroth 2009). However, most of this finance takes the form of relatively short-maturity commercial bank lending, often not the best suited for infrastructure projects. A need exists to further develop corporate bond markets and to create regulatory conditions for greater participation by institutional investors in funding infrastructure investments.

Note

The authors of this chapter are Vivien Foster and Cecilia Briceño-Garmendia.

References

Africon. 2008. "Unit Costs of Infrastructure Projects in Sub-Saharan Africa." Background Paper 11, Africa Infrastructure Sector Diagnostic, World Bank, Washington, DC.

Banerjee, Sudeshna, Heather Skilling, Vivien Foster, Cecilia Briceño-Garmendia, Elvira Morella, and Tarik Chfadi. 2008. "Ebbing Water, Surging Deficits: Urban Water Supply in Sub-Saharan Africa." Background Paper 12, Africa Infrastructure Sector Diagnostic, World Bank, Washington, DC.

Banerjee, Sudeshna, Quentin Wodon, Amadou Diallo, Taras Pushak, Hellal Uddin, Clarence Tsimpo, and Vivien Foster. 2008. "Access, Affordability, and Alternatives: Modern Infrastructure Services in Africa." Background Paper 2, Africa Infrastructure Sector Diagnostic, World Bank, Washington, DC.

Bofinger, Heinrich C. 2009. "Air Transport: Challenges to Growth." Background Paper 16, Africa Infrastructure Sector Diagnostic, World Bank, Washington, DC.

Briceño-Garmendia, Cecilia, and Vivien Foster. 2009a. "Democratic Republic of Congo: Prioritizing Infrastructure Investments—a Spatial Approach." World Bank, Washington, DC.

———. 2009b. "Republic of Congo: Prioritizing Infrastructure Investments—a Spatial Approach." World Bank, Washington, DC.

Briceño-Garmendia, Cecilia, Karlis Smits, and Vivien Foster. 2008. "Financing Public Infrastructure in Sub-Saharan Africa: Patterns, Issues, and Options." AICD Background Paper 15, Africa Infrastructure Sector Diagnostic, World Bank, Washington, DC.

Bullock, Richard. 2009. "Taking Stock of Railway Companies in Sub-Saharan Africa." Background Paper 17, Africa Infrastructure Sector Diagnostic, World Bank, Washington, DC.

Calderón, César. 2008. "Infrastructure and Growth in Africa." Working Paper 3, Africa Infrastructure Country Diagnostic, World Bank, Washington, DC.

Carruthers, Robin, Ranga R. Krishnamani, and Siobhan Murray. 2008. "Improving Connectivity: Investing in Transport Infrastructure in Sub-Saharan Africa." Background Paper 7, Africa Infrastructure Country Diagnostic, World Bank, Washington, DC.

Commission for Africa. 2005. *Our Common Interest: Report of the Commission for Africa*. London: Commission for Africa.

Dorosh, Paul, Hyoung-Gun Wang, Liang You, and Emily Schmidt. 2008. "Crop Production and Road Connectivity in Sub-Saharan Africa: A Spatial Analysis." Working Paper 19, Africa Infrastructure Country Diagnostic, World Bank, Washington, DC.

Eberhard, Anton. 2007. "Matching Regulatory Design to Country Circumstances: The Potential of Hybrid and Transitional Models." *Gridlines*, Note 23 (May), Public-Private Infrastructure Advisory Facility, World Bank, Washington, DC.

Eberhard, Anton, Vivien Foster, Cecilia Briceño-Garmendia, Fatimata Ouedraogo, Daniel Camos, and Maria Shkaratan. 2008. "Underpowered: The State of the Power Sector in Sub-Saharan Africa." Background Paper 6, Africa Infrastructure Sector Diagnostic, World Bank, Washington, DC.

Escribano, Alvaro, J. Luis Guasch, and Jorge Pena. 2008. "Impact of Infrastructure Constraints on Firm Productivity in Africa." Working Paper 9, Africa Infrastructure Sector Diagnostic, World Bank, Washington, DC.

Estache, Antonio. 2005. "What Do We Know about Sub-Saharan Africa's Infrastructure and the Impact of Its 1990 Reforms?" World Bank, Washington, DC.

Fay, Marianne, Danny Leipziger, Quentin Wodon, and Tito Yepes. 2005. "Achieving Child-Health-Related Millennium Development Goals: The Role of Infrastructure." *World Development* 33 (8): 1267–84.

Grey, David, and Claudia Sadoff. 2006. "Water for Growth and Development: A Framework for Analysis." Theme Document of the 4th World Water Forum, Mexico City, March.

Gwilliam, Ken, Vivien Foster, Rodrigo Archondo-Callao, Cecilia Briceño-Garmendia, Alberto Nogales, and Kavita Sethi. 2008. "The Burden of Maintenance: Roads in Sub-Saharan Africa." Background Paper 14, Africa Infrastructure Sector Diagnostic, World Bank, Washington, DC.

Irving, Jacqueline, and Astrid Manroth. 2009. "Local Sources of Financing for Infrastructure in Africa: A Cross-Country Analysis." Policy Research Working Paper 4878, World Bank, Washington, DC.

Mayer, Rebecca, Ken Figueredo, Mike Jensen, Tim Kelly, Richard Green, and Alvaro Federico Barra. 2008. "Costing the Needs for Investment in ICT Infrastructure in Africa." Background Paper 3, Africa Infrastructure Sector Diagnostic, World Bank, Washington, DC.

Minges, Michael, Cecilia Briceño-Garmendia, Mark Williams, Mavis Ampah, Daniel Camos, and Maria Shkratan. 2008. "Information and Communications Technology in Sub-Saharan Africa: A Sector Review." Background Paper 10, Africa Infrastructure Sector Diagnostic, World Bank, Washington, DC.

Morella, Elvira, Vivien Foster, and Sudeshna Ghosh Banerjee. 2008. "Climbing the Ladder: The State of Sanitation in Sub-Saharan Africa." Background Paper 13, Africa Infrastructure Country Diagnostic, World Bank, Washington, DC.

Mundy, Michael, and Andrew Penfold. 2008. "Beyond the Bottlenecks: Ports in Sub-Saharan Africa." Background Paper 8, Africa Infrastructure Sector Diagnostic, World Bank, Washington, DC.

ODI (Overseas Development Institute). 2009. *A Development Charter for the G-20.* London: ODI.

Prevost, Christophe. 2009. "Benin Rural Water Public Expenditure Review: Findings, Impacts and Lesson Learned." Paper presented at Water Week, World Bank, Washington, DC, February 17–20.

Rosnes, Orvika, and Haakon Vennemo. 2008. "Powering Up: Costing Power Infrastructure Investment Needs in Southern and Eastern Africa." Background Paper 5, Africa Infrastructure Sector Diagnostic, World Bank, Washington, DC.

Svendsen, Mark, Mandy Ewing, and Siwa Msangi. 2008. "Watermarks: Indicators of Irrigation Sector Performance in Sub-Saharan Africa."

Background Paper 4, Africa Infrastructure Sector Diagnostic, World Bank, Washington, DC.

Teravaninthorn, Supee, and Gael Raballand. 2008. "Transport Prices and Costs in Africa: A Review of the Main International Corridors." Working Paper 14, Africa Infrastructure Sector Diagnostic, World Bank, Washington, DC.

Torero, Maximo, and Javier Escobal. 2005. "Measuring the Impact of Asset Complementarities: The Case of Rural Peru." *Cuadernos de Economia* 42 (May): 137–64.

Vagliasindi, Maria, and John Nellis. 2009. "Evaluating Africa's Experience with Institutional Reform for the Infrastructure Sectors." Working Paper 23, Africa Infrastructure Country Diagnostic, World Bank, Washington, DC.

Van den Berg, Caroline. 2009. "Public Expenditure Review in the Water Sector: The Case of Tanzania." Paper presented at Water Week, World Bank, Washington, DC, February 17–20.

Wodon, Quentin, ed. 2008a. "Electricity Tariffs and the Poor: Case Studies from Sub-Saharan Africa." Working Paper 11, Africa Infrastructure Country Diagnostic, World Bank, Washington, DC.

———. 2008b. "Water Tariffs and the Poor: Case Studies from Sub-Saharan Africa." Working Paper 12, Africa Infrastructure Country Diagnostic, World Bank, Washington, DC.

Yepes, Tito. 2007. "New Estimates of Infrastructure Expenditure Requirements." World Bank, Washington, DC.

Yepes, Tito, Justin Pierce, and Vivien Foster. 2008. "Making Sense of Sub-Saharan Africa's Infrastructure Endowment: A Benchmarking Approach." Working Paper 1, Africa Infrastructure Country Diagnostic, World Bank, Washington, DC.

You, Liang Zhi. 2008. "Irrigation Investment Needs in Sub-Saharan Africa." Background Paper 9, Africa Infrastructure Country Diagnostic, World Bank, Washington, DC.

Part 1

The Overall Story

Introduction

The Africa Infrastructure Country Diagnostic

In 2005, the Commission for Africa drew public attention to the magnitude and urgency of Africa's development challenges and sounded a new appeal to the international community to meet them. In its landmark report, *Our Common Interest*, the commission underscored infrastructure as one of the continent's central challenges:

> Infrastructure is a key component of the investment climate, reducing the costs of doing business and enabling people to access markets; is crucial to advances in agriculture; is a key enabler of trade and integration, important for offsetting the impact of geographical dislocation and sovereign fragmentation, and critical to enabling Africa to break into world markets; and is fundamental to human development, including the delivery of health and education services to poor people. Infrastructure investments also represent an important untapped potential for the creation of productive employment. (Commission for Africa 2005: chap. 7, para. 61, citations omitted)

In the years preceding the commission's report, external capital flows for African infrastructure had reached a historic low. During the 1990s, many donors shifted their priorities to social interventions focused on poverty alleviation, overlooking the central importance of economic growth as an engine of poverty reduction. Moreover, private capital flows in the early 2000s were weak in the aftermath of the Asian crisis. The commission's report stated that

> despite its clear benefits, African governments and their development partners sharply reduced, over the 1990s, the share of resources allocated to infrastructure—reflecting its lower priority in policy discussions. In retrospect, this was a serious policy mistake, driven by the international community, which undermined growth prospects and generated a substantial backlog of investment—a backlog that will take strong action, over an extended period of time, to overcome. (Commission for Africa 2005: chap. 7, para. 63, citations omitted)

The report estimated Sub-Saharan Africa's infrastructure financing needs to be $39 billion per year, divided almost equally between capital expenditure ($22 billion) and spending on operation and maintenance ($17 billion). On this basis, it recommended a doubling of infrastructure spending in the region, to be supported by increased donor allocations of $10 billion up to 2010.

Soon after the publication of the commission's report, the Group of Eight summit at Gleneagles expressed a firm political commitment to scale up donor financing for African infrastructure, which led to the formation of the Infrastructure Consortium for Africa. The consortium became a forum where major bilateral and multilateral donors could work with continental and regional institutions to spearhead economic integration and maintain the momentum behind the political commitment of Gleneagles.

Genesis of the Project

From its inception, the consortium recognized that the paucity of information and analysis on African infrastructure severely constrained scaling up. Even the most elementary data—on quantity and quality of infrastructure stocks, access to services, prices and costs, efficiency parameters, historic spending, and future investment needs—were either nonexistent or limited in coverage. Most standard global databases on infrastructure covered barely a handful of African countries.

A stocktaking paper concluded that the data situation seriously impeded the region's ability to interpret and understand the state of its infrastructure. It asserted that "[w]e don't know precisely how well Sub-Saharan Africa is meeting its infrastructure needs, because the quality and quantity of the data has become so poor. Improving Africa's ability to monitor and benchmark its performance should be a top priority for the international community and is likely to be a major challenge requiring significant coordination across countries and donors" (Estache 2005: executive summary, 1). The consortium concluded that, without such information, evaluating the success of past interventions, prioritizing current allocations, and providing a benchmark to measure future progress would be difficult. Therefore, the consortium decided to unite in a joint knowledge program, the Africa Infrastructure Country Diagnostic (AICD). The goal of the AICD is to improve the knowledge base of the African infrastructure sectors.

A steering committee chaired by the African Union Commission was formed to oversee the AICD project. The committee included representatives from the African Development Bank, the New Partnership for Africa's Development, and the regional economic communities (Common Market for Eastern and Southern Africa, Economic Community of Central African States, Economic Community of West African States East African Community, Economic Community of West African States, and Southern African Development Community). Agence Française de Développement, the U.K.'s Department for International Development, the European Commission, Germany's Kreditanstalt für Wiederaufbau, the Public-Private Infrastructure Advisory Facility, and the World Bank pledged resources to the project. The implementation of AICD was delegated to the Africa Vice Presidency of the World Bank. The steering committee also convened a technical advisory panel of academics from around the world to provide independent review of the studies.

Technical work on the project began in mid-2006 and proceeded in three stages. The first stage, running from mid-2006 to mid-2007, was devoted to primary data collection at the country level, and it produced a suite of new databases on African infrastructure. The second stage, from mid-2007 to mid-2008, focused on data analysis. It led to the production of a number of background papers analyzing key aspects of infrastructure at the continental level (see table I.1). The third stage, from mid-2008 to mid-2009, involved consultation and outreach on preliminary findings and focused on producing this report.

For the purposes of the diagnostic, *infrastructure* is defined to include all the main networks, those associated with information and communication technologies (ICTs), irrigation, power, sanitation, water, and transport (including air, maritime, rail, and road). As far as possible, the diagnostic aims to cover not only physical infrastructure but also the services it provides. The emphasis is on public access infrastructure, so the study does not cover oil and gas pipelines or private port and rail infrastructure dedicated to the exclusive use of particular mineral or industrial activities.

Neither does the diagnostic consider needs for water storage infrastructure required to protect countries from droughts and floods beyond those necessitated by particular downstream uses such as hydropower electricity generation, irrigation, and water supply.

The primary unit of analysis for the diagnostic is the country. The focus is on Sub-Saharan Africa, given the genesis of the project as a response to the major infrastructure deficits in that part of the continent. Owing to budgetary and feasibility constraints, the diagnostic was originally limited to 24 of the 48 countries in the Sub-Saharan region (figure I.1). This Phase I sample covers almost all of the major countries, which together account for about 85 percent of the population and GDP of the region. They were carefully selected to represent the economic, geographic, cultural, and political diversity that characterizes the region (figure I.2). Therefore, the sample of 24 countries is statistically representative, providing an adequate basis for drawing inferences about the overall infrastructure situation of Sub-Saharan Africa.

Later, the project steering committee recommended extending the coverage of the diagnostic to as many of the remaining African countries as possible. Following further fund-raising, Phase II of the project was initiated in mid-2008. It incorporates 16 more countries, raising the total to 40. Although the focus remains on Sub-Saharan Africa, Phase II includes greater coverage of North African countries in a number of areas to complete the African picture and provide a point of comparison with the Sub-Saharan region.

Scope of the Project

The results of Phase II were not available at the time of writing, so the results presented in this volume are based on the analysis of the 24 Phase I countries. However, all financial aggregates in this report have been scaled up to cover the whole of Sub-Saharan Africa. Financial estimates were scaled to reflect the weight of the 24 sample countries in the overall GDP of the region.

The country-level analysis has three pillars, each of which is described below:

Table I.1 AICD Background Papers

Number	Category and title	Authors
	Cross-cutting topics	
BP2	Access, Affordability, and Alternatives: Modern Infrastructure Services in Africa	Sudeshna Banerjee, Quentin Wodon, Amadou Diallo, Taras Pushak, Helal Uddin, Clarence Tsimpo, and Vivien Foster
BP11	Unit Costs of Infrastructure Projects in Sub-Saharan Africa	Willem van Zyl, Lynette Coetzer, and Chris Lombard
BP15	Financing Public Infrastructure in Sub-Saharan Africa: Patterns, Issues, and Options	Cecilia Briceño-Garmendia, Karlis Smits, and Vivien Foster
	Spending needs studies	
BP3	Costing the Needs for Spending in ICT Infrastructure in Africa	Rebecca Mayer, Ken Figueredo, Mike Jensen, Tim Kelly, Richard Green, and Alvaro Federico Barra
BP5	Powering Up: Costing Power Infrastructure Spending Needs	Orvika Rosnes and Haakon Vennemo
BP7	Improving Connectivity: Investing in Transport Infrastructure in Sub-Saharan Africa	Robin Carruthers, Ranga Rajan Krishnamani, and Siobhan Murray
BP9	Irrigation Investment Needs in Sub-Saharan Africa: A Matter of Scale	Liang Zhi You
	State-of-the-sector reviews	
BP1	Stuck in Traffic: Urban Transport in Africa	Ajay Kumar and Fanny Barrett
BP4	Watermarks: Indicators of Irrigation Sector Performance in Sub-Saharan Africa	Mark Svendsen, Mandy Ewing, and Siwa Msangi
BP6	Underpowered: The State of the Power Sector in Sub-Saharan Africa	Anton Eberhard, Vivien Foster, Cecilia Briceño-Garmendia, Fatimata Ouedraogo, Daniel Camos, and Maria Shkaratan
BP8	Beyond the Bottlenecks: Ports in Sub-Saharan Africa	Michael Mundy and Andrew Penfold
BP10	Information and Communications Technology in Sub-Saharan Africa: A Sector Review	Michael Minges, Cecilia Briceño-Garmendia, Mark Williams, Mavis Ampah, Daniel Camos, and Maria Shkratan
BP12	Ebbing Water, Surging Deficits: Urban Water Supply in Sub-Saharan Africa	Sudeshna Banerjee, Heather Skilling, Vivien Foster, Cecilia Briceño-Garmendia, Elvira Morella, and Tarik Chfadi
BP13	Climbing the Ladder: The State of Sanitation in Sub-Saharan Africa	Elvira Morella, Vivien Foster, and Sudeshna Ghosh Banerjee
BP14	The Burden of Maintenance: Roads in Sub-Saharan Africa	Ken Gwilliam, Vivien Foster, Rodrigo Archondo-Callao, Cecilia Briceño-Garmendia, Alberto Nogales, and Kavita Sethi
BP16	Air Transport: Challenges to Growth	Heinrich C. Bofinger
BP17	Taking Stock of Railway Companies in Sub-Saharan Africa	Richard Bullock

- The *spending needs* pillar estimates the cost of future infrastructure requirements.
- The *fiscal costs* pillar documents existing patterns of infrastructure spending.
- The *sector performance* pillar clarifies the scope for improvement in efficiency as well as structural and policy reforms.

Figure I.1 Country Coverage of the Africa Infrastructure Country Diagnostic

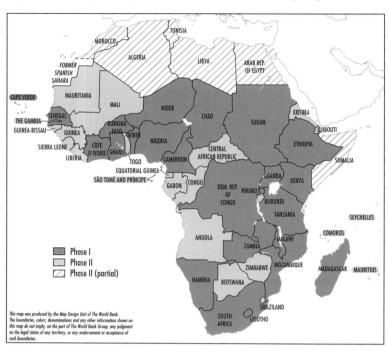

Figure I.2 Representativeness of Phase I Sampled Countries

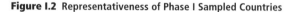
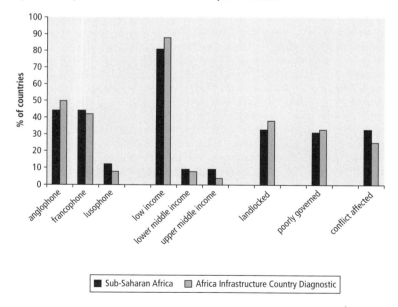

Note: AICD = Africa Infrastructure Country Diagnostic.

Estimating Future Spending Needs

At the outset of the AICD project, only a small number of standardized cross-country studies focused on estimating the magnitude

of Africa's spending needs, and most of them had limited country coverage. The best-known global cross-country studies estimate spending needs using econometric techniques and macroeconomic panel data (Estache 2005; Fay and Yepes 2003; Yepes 2007). These studies identify historical relationships between GDP and physical infrastructure stocks to predict infrastructure requirements given current growth forecasts. Unit costs of infrastructure are then used to convert these predictions into financial estimates. These types of studies provide internationally consistent, first-order approximations of investment needs. They are likely to underestimate requirements, however, because they tend to focus on infrastructure quantity rather than quality; do not take into account repressed demand and social targets; and use single, global (as opposed to country-specific), unit-cost parameters based on efficient implementation.

Country-specific or sector-specific engineering cost studies existed for particular infrastructure packages: the West Africa Power Pool Master Plan, for example, and the African Development Bank's study of the Trans-Africa Highway Network, in addition to various country or regional master plans. These studies tend to be accurate and internalize policy-defined targets, but they have a number of disadvantages. They are costly to produce, are not available for all countries and sectors, and tend to adopt a wide variety of methodologies that limit their comparability across countries.

The AICD project studied spending needs in five sectors: ICT, irrigation, power, transport, and water and sanitation. The objective of the studies was to develop a simple but robust country-based microeconomic methodology that would be significantly more accurate than the "top-down" macro studies, yet substantially more straightforward and standardized than the "bottom-up" engineering studies. The methodology aims to capture both market-driven investments to keep pace with the demands generated by a growing economy and politically determined investment targets to meet social needs that may not be commercially lucrative without government subsidy. As important as estimating the magnitude of investment needs, the models calculate spending requirements for rehabilitation of existing infrastructure assets as well as maintenance needs to sustain operational (existing and new) assets.

The goal was not so much to produce an estimate as to create a model that would allow exploration of spending needs under a variety of different assumptions about economic growth, social objectives, unit costs, and other relevant parameters. Projections were based on World Bank GDP growth projections for the next decade and United Nations demographic forecasts.

In most cases, no clear methodological precedents existed for producing country-level estimates of spending needs based on this kind of microeconomic modeling. A technique adopted across many of these studies was spatial modeling using geographic information systems (GIS) tools. Creation of an African GIS database collated from diverse sources and permitting the overlay of geophysical, agroecological, demographic, and economic features with infrastructure networks made this approach possible (see box I.1). The input parameters needed to run the spending needs models could be derived largely from an extensive desk review of available information.

Although efforts were made to develop methodologies that were consistent across sectors, the specifics of each sector raised particular challenges that called for some adaptation. In all cases, spending needs include new investment, rehabilitation of existing assets, and operation and maintenance associated with new and existing assets.

BOX I.1

The AICD Geographic Information Systems Platform for Africa

Early in the AICD process, it became apparent that geographic information systems (GIS) would be a key input to many aspects of infrastructure analysis. A decision was therefore made to assemble all available geographic databases of relevance to the African infrastructure sectors into a single GIS platform.

The platform includes data sets from different scales, levels of detail, reference years, and coding schemes. In all, more than 20 separate thematic layers of geographic information cover each of the following topics.

- *Infrastructure networks:* power stations, transmission lines, dam sites, irrigated areas, roads (including type, condition, and traffic), railways, ports, airports, submarine cables, fiber-optic backbones, and global systems mobile (GSM) signal coverage
- *Physiographic features:* topography, meteorology, watercourses, river basin boundaries, soil type, land coverage, and agricultural usage and potential
- *Socioeconomic features:* cities, population densities, mines, oil fields, poverty indicators, travel time to nearest urban centers, and household access to services.

The GIS platform was assembled from a wide variety of sources. Public domain data, available from the World Bank and other organizations, such as the Food and Agriculture Organization, the International Food Policy Research Institute, the International Union for Conservation of Nature, the U.S. Geological Survey, the Center for International Earth Science Information Network, the U.S. National Geospatial-Intelligence Agency, and Oak Ridge National Laboratory, were a primary resource. In some cases, government transport or other agencies provided data. Databases were also purchased from private sector sources or constructed from primary country data collected as part of the AICD project. Where possible, an effort was made to update existing data sets with information on condition, status, or other characteristics, based on expert assessment and other sources.

The AICD GIS platform is publicly available on the project Web site, http://www .infrastructureafrica.org, where users may consult preassembled infrastructure atlases for each country, regional economic community, and the continent; make use of the GIS tool to create their own customized maps; or download shape files for more technical GIS analysis.

- For ICTs, the spatial analysis was used to estimate the costs, revenues, and hence financial viability of rolling out services to remote rural communities.

- For irrigation, the financial viability of irrigating crops at different locations was pre-screened as suitable for large- or small-scale irrigation development based on proximity to large dams in one case and the road network in the other.

- For transport, the spatial analysis was used to measure the extent of the road network needed to meet a set of regional, national, urban, and rural connectivity standards. Linking these directly to economic objectives did not prove feasible.

- For power, the model is based on a least-cost optimization model that selects the most cost-effective expansion path for national or regional power sector development to meet a given projection of demand.

- For water and sanitation, the model builds upon existing work (Mehta, Fugelsnes, and Virjee 2005; Water and Sanitation Program 2006) and uses demographic growth trends to analyze the number of new connections needed to meet the Millennium Development Goals (WHO and UNICEF 2006) under a variety of different technological choices.

The results of the AICD spending needs studies are presented in chapter 1 and further detailed in the corresponding sectoral chapters in part 2. Detailed background papers also document the methodology and results for each sector in much greater detail (see table I.1).

All of the spending needs models developed for the project are available online at the project Web site. The Web-based versions allow users to apply sensitivity of spending needs to varying assumptions over a wide range of input parameters for specific countries. The results are displayed both numerically and spatially in the form of maps.

Documenting Existing Spending Patterns

At the outset of the AICD project, almost no information was available about the extent to which African governments and their para-

statals were devoting resources to infrastructure development and maintenance. The International Monetary Fund's *Government Financial Statistics* reports central government budgetary spending for a number of broadly defined infrastructure sectors but does not include the expenditures of state-owned enterprises and special nonbudgetary funds dedicated to infrastructure, both of which are highly significant for the sector. Moreover, it does not break down expenditures according to specific infrastructure sectors and functional outlays, such as capital or maintenance and operating expenditures. Most important, even the very limited data recorded through the Fund's *Government Financial Statistics* were available for only a handful of African countries.

Using the limited information available at the time, researchers made some first-order estimates of Africa's public expenditure on infrastructure (see Estache 2005; Estache, Gonzalez, and Trujillo 2007). Notwithstanding numerous caveats regarding the quality and coverage of the public finance data, the overall picture that emerged showed allocation of a declining share of public budgets to infrastructure from 1980 to 2000.

Without a detailed understanding of expenditure patterns of key public institutions—central governments and state-owned enterprises—pinpointing the magnitude and nature of the region's infrastructure financing gap or assessing the efficiency and effectiveness of public spending is difficult. To overcome these limitations, the AICD project built a new database of standardized cross-country data that seeks to give a detailed yet comprehensive picture of public infrastructure spending, both within and beyond the bounds of central government budgets. Data collection was based on a standardized methodology and covers, as far as possible, the period 2001–06. To ensure the cross-country comparability of the data, a detailed methodology including templates guided data collection in the field and back-office processing and documentation (Briceño-Garmendia 2007).

The methodology is designed to be comprehensive insofar as it covers all relevant budgetary and nonbudgetary areas of infrastructure spending. The collection of data on spending was grounded in an overview of the institutional framework for delivering infrastructure services in each of the countries while aiming to identify all of the channels through which public resources go into infrastructure. The work began with a detailed review of the central government budget. Thereafter, financial statements were collected from all the parastatals and special funds that had been identified in the institutional review.

In countries where infrastructure service providers are highly decentralized (as in municipal water utilities), financial statements could be collected from only the three largest providers. Privatized infrastructure service providers were included if a majority of their shares remained government owned or if they continued to depend on the state for capital or operating subsidies. Thus, telecommunication incumbents were typically included, whereas mobile operators were not.

In some countries, local governments have begun to play an increasingly prominent role in infrastructure service provision, but comprehensive expenditure data at the local government level could not always be collected. In some cases, however, the central government produces consolidated local government accounts. Otherwise, an alternative source of information was the fiscal transfers from central to local governments reported in the budget and on which local governments relied, given limited alternative sources of revenue. In some cases, transfers are earmarked for infrastructure spending; in others, the share allocated to infrastructure could only be estimated.

Data were collected to permit both classification and cross-classification by economic and functional categories. That is, a matrix was established so that spending on each functional category could be decomposed according to the economic nature of the expense and vice versa. Functional classification followed as closely as possible the four-digit category or class level of the functional classification (COFOG) proposed in the International Monetary Fund's *Government Financial Statistics Manual 2001* (IMF 2001), making possible identification of all major infrastructure subsectors. The economic classification of expenses also followed the Fund's framework, making it possible to distinguish to some extent between current expenditures, capital expenditures, and various subcategories.

Much of the necessary data could be lifted directly from the budget documents and financial statements of the relevant parastatals, although in many cases, careful recoding of the data was necessary to align them with the project template. Local consultants undertook fieldwork that was coordinated centrally to ensure quality control and data consistency. The focus of data collection was on executed expenditures, but wherever possible, the budgeted and released expenditures were also collected.

The targeted period for data collection was 2001–06, although a complete time series was not always available. All financial data are presented as annual averages over the period, to smooth out annual variations and maximize available data points. All data were denominated in local currency and centrally normalized using exchange rate, GDP, and population data taken from the World Development Indicators database of the World Bank.

Public expenditure data were complemented by financing data from secondary sources to provide a comprehensive view of financial flows to African infrastructure and the relative importance of the different players. These secondary sources included the World Bank's Private Participation in Infrastructure database, which documents trends in private capital flows; the Development Assistance Committee database of the Organisation for Economic Co-operation and Development (OECD), covering external financial support from bilateral and multilateral OECD donors; and a new database on non-OECD finance for African infrastructure (Foster and others 2008). To make these financial flows methodologically consistent with those for public expenditure, researchers converted commitments made by external financiers into disbursements using typical disbursement profiles for infrastructure projects. Every effort was made to avoid double counting between public expenditure and external finance.

The results of the public expenditure analysis provide the foundation for chapter 2 of this report, but they are reported in much greater detail in Background Paper 15 (see table I.1).

At this time, one can say that the level of public expenditure on infrastructure in Africa is substantially higher than previously thought—and certainly several times higher than earlier estimates. The resulting public expenditure database is now available to the public via the project Web site and can be downloaded by users for a variety of purposes. The database contains detailed information about expenditure patterns by institution, sector, and functional category.

The analysis of public spending patterns was complemented by work on unit costs of infrastructure projects and included a review of the costs and cost structures associated with a sample of donor-funded projects covering roads, power, and water supply. The typical outputs of these projects were standardized to permit the creation of standardized unit costs. Data were collected from the bills of quantities for the public works contracts of these projects and entered into the standardized template. The overall sample included 115 road projects, 144 water projects, and 58 power projects. The resulting database of unit costs illustrates the dispersion that can be experienced in donor-funded infrastructure projects depending on a range of factors.

Understanding Sector Performance

At the beginning of the project, relatively little systematic, comprehensive, and empirically grounded literature was available on the performance of the five infrastructure sectors.

To develop a comprehensive and detailed portrait of the infrastructure sectors in Sub-Saharan Africa, the AICD developed a set of standardized performance indicators covering both the consumer and the service provider perspectives. These indicators are collected for the full range of infrastructure subsectors, including air transport, ICT, irrigation, ports, power, railways, roads, and water and sanitation. In each case, a common conceptual structure was adopted.

A first block of qualitative indicators was generated through a substantial questionnaire that documents the details of the legal, institutional, and regulatory framework, which are summarized in a series of specially developed indexes (see chapter 4 in this volume). Qualitative data,

provide a snapshot of the situation prevailing in 2006 at the time of data collection. A second block of quantitative indicators documents the operational, technical, and financial aspects of sector performance, with particular focus on infrastructure service providers such as utilities. Wherever possible, the quantitative data cover the period 2001 to 2006, and the most recent available year is the one reported.

For each sector, manuals were developed to guide the data collection for the indicators. The manuals map the rationale and conceptual structure of the data collection, provide detailed definitions of the indicators, lay out questionnaire formats to assist in eliciting information, and map a database structure for coding of the data. Such detailed manuals were designed to guide consultants responsible for data collection and to ensure comparability of indicators across countries and ultimately over time, should the process be repeated.

For some sectors (power, railways, roads, water and sanitation), the indicators could be collected only through detailed in-country fieldwork. For a number of other sectors (air transport, ICT, irrigation, ports), the data could be collected remotely through the arm's-length administration of questionnaires with telephone follow-up and the compilation of data from existing publications and sources. The data collection involved contacting several hundred infrastructure institutions around Africa, including more than 16 rail operators, 20 road entities, 30 power utilities, 30 ports, 60 airports, 80 water utilities, and 100 ICT operators, as well as the relevant line ministries in all of the countries.

The data collection focused on the compilation of existing information available from the target institutions through their annual reports, internal databases, and knowledge of their managers. Thus, the coverage of the databases reflects the state of self-knowledge of the institutions. The project did not have the resources to undertake primary survey work to obtain data on missing indicators.

The resulting data were centralized, and two forms of quality control were conducted. The first was a review by specialists knowledgeable about the countries in question. The second consisted of logic and consistency checks on the database as a whole by examining data patterns and outliers.

The survey of infrastructure service providers was complemented by work on patterns of household access to and expenditure on infrastructure services aimed to integrate all existing household surveys conducted in Africa from 1990 to 2005. These sources included 67 demographic and health surveys (DHSs) and multi-indicator cluster surveys containing detailed information on household access patterns, and 30 budget surveys containing detailed information on household expenditure patterns. Data from all of these surveys were standardized (based on a careful comparison of questionnaires) and integrated into a single meta-database, making consistent analysis possible of time trends within countries and diverging patterns across countries. A standardized approach was used to group households socioeconomically according to asset quintiles in the case of the DHSs and expenditure quintiles in the case of the budget surveys. The meta-database covers 39 countries in Africa; time trends are available for 23 of the countries.

The main source of telecommunications data for Africa is the International Telecommunication Union, which compiles time-series data on a number of indicators and publishes information on telecommunications regulation. In addition, a number of one-off reports had been written on the African telecommunication sector. These reports quickly become outdated and are often limited to certain groups of countries. The AICD project has improved the timeliness, detail, and scope of these data sets, including compiling more recent data than are available from intergovernmental sources, verifying the accuracy of existing information, widening and completing coverage for all African countries, and enhancing data to incorporate more detailed and specific indicators for tariffs, regulations, market structure, and the user's perspective, among others. The project has also structured the data into analytical categories and compiled several indexes to facilitate comprehension of the vast amount of data. In summary, the information in the AICD data set for ICT provides a structured framework of comprehensive, inclusive,

and up-to-date information on the status of ICT in Africa not available from any other single source.

In transportation, the Sub-Saharan Africa Transport Policy Program (SSATP) has played an important role in developing the knowledge base through an abundant literature of case studies and policy reports. The SSATP has made some efforts to move toward a set of quantitative indicators for the transport sector, although these remain limited in scope. The program has played a leading role in developing road sector modeling tools, most notably RONET, that enable road maintenance costs to be estimated based on a detailed physical specification of the road network. In addition, there have been important contributions to the understanding of institutional reform in the road sector (Benmaamar 2006) and some work on the performance of African rail concessions. At the outset of the AICD, however, no unified database existed on road type, condition, and traffic. These data were collected on a georeferenced, link-by-link basis that allows the information to be presented graphically in a map and that underpins detailed financial analysis of the road network using the RONET model.

At the outset of the project, relatively little continent-wide analysis of the African water utilities existed (Estache and Gassner 2004b). The starting point for water utility data collection was the databases developed by the Water Utilities Partnership and the International Benchmarking Network (IBNET). Both sources were sparse in their country coverage and focused primarily on utility operational performance without covering the institutional framework in any great depth. Both initiatives informed the development of indicators under the AICD, which aimed to be consistent with them in areas of overlap. The data collection process was coordinated with IBNET to increase African country coverage for both projects. Generally speaking, the AICD operational and financial performance indicators are a subset of those collected by IBNET, but the qualitative indicators and tariff schedules collected through AICD go much further than anything done before. Five modules of qualitative data were collected for each country, covering the institutional and regulatory framework for water provision, governance arrangements for specific water utilities, the status of the sanitation sector, the status of the rural water sector in each country, and the prevalence and characteristics of small-scale service providers in the largest city in each country. The quantitative indicators aim to capture the operational and financial performance of utilities from 2001 to 2006, together with their tariff schedules. In countries where service provision is decentralized, comprehensive data could not be captured on all utilities, but efforts were made to cover the three largest utilities in each country.

In the case of irrigation, limited data were available at the country level. Sub-Saharan Africa has little experience with irrigated agriculture. Most performance indicators are limited to specific irrigation systems. The best single source of data on comparable cross-country indicators was the global databases of the Food and Agriculture Organization. They were complemented where needed by data from the World Bank and the International Food Policy Research Institute.

Power was undoubtedly the least documented of Africa's infrastructure sectors at the outset of the project (Estache and Gassner 2004a). Some basic indicators on overall energy balance and national power generation portfolios were available from the International Energy Agency and others, but coverage of African countries remained quite limited, and the available indicators did not provide any real picture of power utility performance. Although the Union of Producers, Transporters and Distributors of Electric Power in Africa (the African power utilities association) has developed its own database of performance indicators, it is not available to the general public. The Africa Energy Commission is also developing a database of energy indicators for the continent, but it was not available in time for this project.

The results of the various sector reviews provide the foundation for the corresponding sector chapters contained in part 2 (chapters 7–17) of this report. In addition, the results of the household survey analysis are reported in chapter 3 on poverty and inequality, while the overall findings of the institutional analysis are summarized in chapter 4 on institutions. The resulting databases of sector performance

indicators are now available to the public on the project Web site, http://www.infrastructureafrica .org, and through the Development Data Platform of the World Bank. Containing detailed information about institutional, operational, technical, and financial indicators relating to each of the sectors covered, the database can be downloaded for a variety of purposes.

The work on these three pillars and cross-cutting issues resulted in the creation of 17 original background papers on which this "Flagship Report" is based (table I.1). The main findings that follow in this report refer to these background papers. Readers seeking further technical details on any of these issues can find these papers through the project Web site (http://www.infrastructureafrica.org). In due course, the background papers will be repackaged as four sectoral volumes on ICT, power, transport, and water and sanitation, which will be technical companions to this Flagship Report.

In addition to these three central pillars of the data collection effort, more than 20 working papers were commissioned, covering a range of ad hoc topics of relevance to African infrastructure (table I.2). The topics include linkages between infrastructure, growth and fiscal sustainability, welfare effects of infrastructure reforms, utility tariffs and subsidies, urban infrastructure services, local private finance of infrastructure, impact of inadequate power supply on firms, and the role of small, independent suppliers of water. The working papers are also available on the project Web site.

Beyond the initial data baseline established here, the AICD project aims to establish a sustainable basis for ongoing data collection on Africa's infrastructure sectors. This Flagship Report presents and analyzes the baseline information on the African infrastructure sectors collected because of this project. The long-term value of the effort depends on the sustainability of data collection efforts to ensure that key infrastructure trends on the continent can be tracked over time and progress against this benchmark can be accurately measured. Plans are under way for the Statistical Department of the African Development Bank to take over the

Table I.2 AICD Working Papers

Number	Title	Author
WP1	Making Sense of Sub-Saharan Africa's Infrastructure Endowment: A Benchmarking Approach	Tito Yepes, Justin Pierce, and Vivien Foster
WP2	Paying the Price for Unreliable Power Supplies: Own Generation of Electricity by Private Firms in Africa	Vivien Foster and Jevgenijs Steinbuks
WP3	Infrastructure and Growth in Africa	César Calderón
WP4	Electricity Reforms in Mali: A Micro-Macro Analysis of the Effects on Poverty and Distribution	Dorothée Boccanfuso, Antonio Estache, and Luc Savard
WP5	Electricity Reforms in Senegal: A Micro-Macro Analysis of the Effects on Poverty and Distribution	Dorothée Boccanfuso, Antonio Estache, and Luc Savard
WP6	Building Sector Concerns into Macro-Economic Financial Programming: Lessons from Senegal and Uganda	Antonio Estache and Rafael Muñoz
WP7	Cost Recovery, Equity, and Efficiency in Water Tariffs: Evidence from African Utilities	Sudeshna Banerjee, Vivien Foster, Yvonne Ying, Heather Skilling, and Quentin Wodon
WP8	Potential for Local Private Finance of Infrastructure in Africa	Jacqueline Irving and Astrid Manroth
WP9	Impact of Infrastructure Constraints on Firm Productivity in Africa	Alvaro Escribano, J. Luis Guasch, and Jorge Pena
WP10	A Tale of Three Cities: Understanding Differences in Provision of Modern Services	Sumila Gulyani, Debabrata Talukdar, and Darby Jack
WP11	Electricity Tariffs and the Poor: Case Studies from Sub-Saharan Africa	Quentin Wodon
WP12	Water Tariffs and the Poor: Case Studies from Sub-Saharan Africa	Quentin Wodon
WP13	Provision of Water to the Poor in Africa: Informal Water Markets and Experience with Water Standposts	Sarah Keener, Manuel Luengo, and Sudeshna Banerjee
WP14	Transport Prices and Costs in Africa: A Review of the Main International Corridors	Supee Teravaninthorn and Gaël Raballand
WP15	The Impact of Infrastructure Spending in Sub-Saharan Africa: A CGE Modeling Approach	Jean-François Perrault and Luc Savard
WP16	Water Reforms in Senegal: A Micro-Macro Analysis of the Effects on Poverty and Distribution	Dorothée Boccanfuso, Antonio Estache, and Luc Savard
WP17	Fiscal Costs of Infrastructure Provision: A Practitioner's Guide	Cecilia Briceño-Garmendia
WP18	Crop Production and Road Connectivity in Sub-Saharan Africa: A Spatial Analysis	Paul Dorosh, Hyoung-Gun Wang, Liang You, and Emily Schmidt
WP19	The Impact of the Yamassoukro Decision	Charles Schlumberger
WP20	Cost Recovery, Equity, and Efficiency in Power Tariffs: Evidence from African Utilities	Cecilia Briceño-Garrmendia and Maria Shkaratan
WP21	What Can We Learn from Household Surveys about Cooking Fuel Use in Sub-Saharan Africa?	Daniel Camos
WP22	Evaluating Africa's Experience with Institutional Reform for the Infrastructure Sectors	Maria Vagliasindi and John Nellis

long-term data collection effort based on the methodological framework developed under the AICD project. The sponsors of the AICD project remain firmly committed to ensuring the sustainability of the data collection effort.

Note

The authors of this chapter are Vivien Foster and Cecilia Briceño-Garmendia.

References

Benmaamar, Mustapha. 2006. "Financing of Road Maintenance in Sub-Saharan Africa: Reforms and Progress towards Second Generation Road Funds." Discussion Paper 6, Road Management and Financing Series, Sub-Saharan Africa Transport Policy Program, World Bank, Washington, DC.

Briceño-Garmendia, Cecilia. 2007. "Fiscal Costs of Infrastructure Provision: A Practitioner's Guide." Working Paper 17, Africa Infrastructure Country Diagnostic, World Bank, Washington, DC.

Commission for Africa. 2005. *Our Common Interest: Report of the Commission for Africa.* London: Commission for Africa.

Estache, Antonio. 2005. "What Do We Know about Sub-Saharan Africa's Infrastructure and the Impact of Its 1990 Reforms?" World Bank, Washington, DC.

Estache, Antonio, and Katharina Gassner. 2004a. "The Electricity Sector of Sub-Saharan Africa: Basic Facts and Emerging Issues." World Bank, Washington, DC.

———. 2004b. "Recent Economic Developments in the Water and Sanitation Sectors of Selected Sub-Saharan African Countries: Overview of Basic Facts and Emerging Issues." World Bank, Washington, DC.

Estache, Antonio, Marianela Gonzalez, and Lourdes Trujillo. 2007. "Government Expenditures on Health, Education and Infrastructure: A Naïve Look at Levels, Outcomes and Efficiency." Policy Research Working Paper 4219, World Bank, Washington, DC.

Fay, Marianne, and Tito Yepes. 2003. "Investing in Infrastructure: What Is Needed from 2000 to 2010?" Policy Research Working Paper 3102, World Bank, Washington, DC. http://ssrn.com/abstract=636464.

Foster, Vivien, William Butterfield, Chuan Chen, and Nataliya Pushak. 2008. *Building Bridges: China's Growing Role as Infrastructure Financier for Sub-Saharan Africa.* Trends and Policy Options no. 5. Washington, DC: Public-Private Infrastructure Advisory Facility, World Bank.

IMF (International Monetary Fund). 2001. *Government Financial Statistics Manual 2001 (GFSM 2001)*. Washington, DC: IMF Statistics Department.

Mehta, Meera, Thomas Fugelsnes, and Kameel Virjee. 2005. "Financing the Millennium Development Goals for Water and Sanitation: What Will It Take?" *International Journal of Water Resources Development* 21 (2): 239–52.

Water and Sanitation Program. 2006. *Getting Africa on Track to Meet the MDGs for Water and Sanitation: A Status Overview of Sixteen African Countries.* Joint Report of African Ministers Council on Water, African Development Bank, European Union Water Initiative, and Water and Sanitation Program. Nairobi: Water and Sanitation Program–Africa, World Bank.

WHO and UNICEF (World Health Organization and United Nations Children's Fund). 2006. *Meeting the MDG Drinking Water and Sanitation Target: The Urban and Rural Challenge of the Decade.* Geneva: WHO and UNICEF.

Yepes, Tito. 2007. "New Estimates of Infrastructure Expenditure Requirements." World Bank, Washington, DC.

Chapter 1

Meeting Africa's Infrastructure Needs

Infrastructure is central to Africa's development.[1] Major improvements in information and communication technology (ICT), for example, added as much as 1 percentage point to Africa's per capita growth rate during the last decade, since the mid-1990s. However, deficiencies in infrastructure are holding back the continent by at least 1 percentage point in per capita growth. In many countries, infrastructure limitations, particularly in power, depress productivity at least as much as red tape, corruption, and lack of finance—the usual suspects in many people's minds when they think of constraints on growth.

In density of paved roads, capacity to generate power, and coverage of telephone main lines, both low-income and middle-income African countries lag behind their peers elsewhere in the developing world.[2] A few decades ago, in the 1960s to 1980s, Africa's infrastructure endowments were similar to those in East and South Asia, but those regions have since expanded their infrastructure stocks more rapidly, surpassing Africa's position. Meeting Africa's infrastructure needs and developing cost-effective modes of infrastructure service delivery will entail a substantial program of infrastructure investment. In addition to building new infrastructure, existing facilities must be rehabilitated and maintained.

The estimated spending needs are $93 billion a year (15 percent of the region's GDP)—more than twice the 2005 estimate by the Commission for Africa.[3] Total spending estimates divide fairly evenly among the middle-income countries, the resource-rich countries, and low-income nonfragile states (in the neighborhood of $28 billion–$30 billion a year), with low-income fragile states accounting for a smaller share of total needs (about $14 billion a year). The burden on their economies varies dramatically per income group, ranging from 10–12 percent of GDP for middle-income and resource-rich countries to 25 percent of GDP for low-income nonfragile states and 36 percent for fragile states. The total cost splits two to one between capital investment and operation and maintenance expenses.

Over 40 percent of the expenditure needed is in the power sector, which must install 7,000 megawatts of new generation capacity each year just to keep pace with demand. Slightly more than 20 percent is associated with achievement of the Millennium Development Goals (MDGs) for water supply and sanitation. A further 20 percent of the spending requirement is associated with the transport sector to achieve a reasonable level of regional, national, rural, and urban connectivity and to maintain existing assets.

Infrastructure: The Key to Africa's Faster Growth

African economies have grown at a solid 4 percent annual average in recent years. The fastest growth has been in resource-rich countries, which have benefited from rising commodity prices. In almost all cases, however, that performance still falls short of the 7 percent growth needed to achieve substantial poverty reduction and attain the MDGs. Although infrastructure has contributed to Africa's recent economic turnaround, it will need to do even more to reach the continent's development targets.

Inadequate infrastructure impedes faster growth in Africa. This view, highlighted by the Commission for Africa (2005), is supported by considerable economic research (table 1.1). Based on a cross-country econometric analysis and a handful of country studies, the research confirms a strong and significant connection between infrastructure stocks and economic growth. Although the relationship undoubtedly runs in both directions—infrastructure supporting growth and growth promoting infrastructure—modern research techniques

allow isolation of the first of these effects with some precision. The estimated effect of raising Africa's infrastructure to some regional or international benchmark shows considerable consistency of 1 or 2 percentage points in per capita growth.

A key question for policy makers is how much infrastructure development contributes to growth relative to other policy parameters. One study finds that expanding and improving infrastructure contributed almost 1 percentage point to per capita economic growth from 1990 to 2005, compared with only 0.8 percentage point for macroeconomic stabilization and structural policies (Calderón 2008). Stabilization policies include measures to control price inflation and rein in fiscal deficits, while structural policies include measures to enhance human capital, increase financial depth, promote trade openness, and improve governance. Central Africa is the region where infrastructure improvements have made the largest contribution to recent growth, totaling 1.1 percentage points. Only in West Africa did the effect of macroeconomic policies on growth exceed that of infrastructure. Over the same period, infrastructure in East Asia contributed

Table 1.1 Links between Infrastructure and Growth in Africa: What the Research Says

Study	Method	Scope	Sector	Conclusions
Easterly and Levine 1997	Multicountry	Africa	Telecommunications, power	Infrastructure is strongly and significantly correlated with growth.
Esfahani and Ramirez 2003	Multicountry	Africa	Telecommunications, power	Africa's growth per capita would be 0.9 point higher with East Asia's infrastructure.
Calderón and Servén 2008	Multicountry	Africa	Telecommunications, power, roads	Africa's growth per capita would be 1.0 point higher with the Republic of Korea's infrastructure.
Estache, Speciale, and Veredas 2005	Multicountry	Africa	Various	Confirms earlier work and underscores equal relevance for coastal and landlocked countries.
Calderón 2008	Multicountry	Africa	Telecommunications, power, roads	Africa's growth per capita would be 2.3 points higher with Mauritius's infrastructure.
Calderón and Servén 2008	Multicountry	Africa	Telecommunications, power, roads	Extends earlier results to show infrastructure also has a negative effect on inequality.
Fedderke and Bogetic 2006	Country study	South Africa	Various	Finds long-term relationship between infrastructure and growth based on robust econometric techniques.
Ayogu 1999	Production function	Nigeria	Various	Finds strong association between infrastructure and output in panel data.
Kamara 2008	Production function	Various Africa	Various	Finds strong association between infrastructure and output in panel data.
Reinikka and Svensson 1999a	Enterprise surveys	Uganda	Power	Unreliable power is a significant deterrent to private sector investment.
Escribano, Guasch, and Pena 2008	Enterprise surveys	Africa	Various	Infrastructure has a substantial effect on total factor productivity.

Source: Authors' elaboration.

1.2 percentage points to per capita growth (figure 1.1).

The substantial contribution of infrastructure to Africa's recent growth is almost entirely attributable to greater penetration of telecommunications (figure 1.2). In contrast, the deficient infrastructure of the power sector has retarded growth, reducing per capita growth for Africa as a whole by 0.11 percentage point and for southern Africa by as much as 0.2 percentage point. The effect of road infrastructure is generally positive, if rather small, perhaps because of the absence of a widely available measure of road quality, which is the critical variable affecting transport costs.

More detailed microeconomic work on the relationship between infrastructure and the performance of firms (see table 1.1) supports these macroeconomic findings. The data consistently show a strong relationship between infrastructure stocks and the output, productivity, and investment behavior of firms. An exhaustive study analyzed the entire set of investment climate surveys in Africa (Escribano, Guasch, and Pena 2008). The central finding was that in most African countries, particularly the low-income countries, infrastructure is a major constraint on doing business and depresses firm productivity by about 40 percent. The study first looked at the relative contribution of infrastructure and noninfrastructure investment variables to firm productivity (figure 1.3). For many countries, such as Ethiopia, Malawi, and Senegal, the negative effect of deficient infrastructure is at least as large as that of crime, red tape, corruption, and lack of financing.

For a subset of countries—among them Botswana, Ethiopia, and Mali—power is the most limiting infrastructure factor, cited as a major business obstacle by more than half the firms in more than half the countries (figure 1.3). Poorly functioning ports and slow customs clearance are significant constraints for Burkina Faso, Cameroon, and Mauritius. Deficiencies in broader transport infrastructure and ICTs are less prevalent but nonetheless substantial in Benin and Madagascar.

Infrastructure is also an important input to human development (Fay and others 2005). As such, it is a key ingredient in the MDGs (table 1.2).

Figure 1.1 Changes in Growth per Capita Caused by Changes in Growth Fundamentals

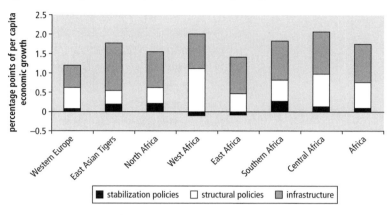

Source: Calderón 2008.

Figure 1.2 Changes in Growth per Capita Caused by Changes in Different Kinds of Infrastructure

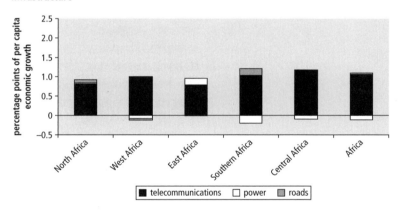

Source: Calderón 2008.

Safe water's effect on health is well documented. Serious illnesses transmitted through unsafe water, such as infectious diarrhea, are a leading cause of infant mortality (Esrey and others 1991). Moreover, better water and sanitation service is associated with less malnutrition and stunting. Waterborne illnesses can be a substantial economic burden, affecting both adult productivity and children's overall health and education. The economic gain of meeting the MDG target for water is estimated at $3.5 billion in year 2000 prices, and the cost-benefit ratio is about 11 to 1, suggesting that the benefits of safe water are far greater than the cost of provision (Hutton 2000; Hutton and Haller 2004). Household members, primarily women and

Figure 1.3 Contribution of Infrastructure to Total Factor Productivity of Firms

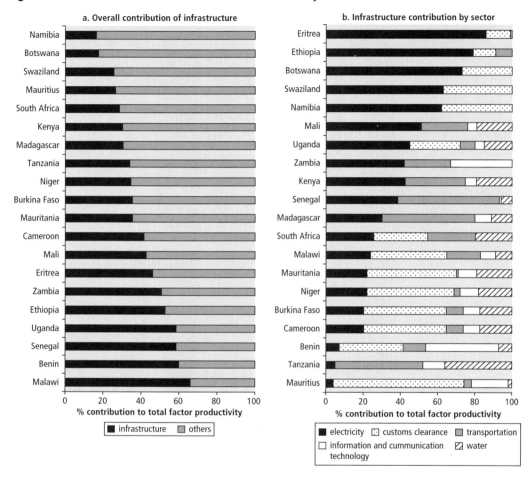

Source: Escribano, Guasch, and Pena 2008.

children, face a substantial opportunity cost in travel time when they have to fetch water. More than 20 percent of the population in Cameroon, Ghana, Mauritania, Niger, and Tanzania must travel more than 2 kilometers to their primary water supply. Rural dwellers tend to travel farther than urban dwellers (Blackden and Wodon 2005; Wodon 2008).

Better provision of electricity has important benefits for health because vaccines and medications can be safely stored in hospitals and food can be preserved at home (Jimenez and Olson 1998). Electricity also improves literacy and primary school completion rates because students can read and study after sundown (Barnes 1988; Brodman 1982; Foley

1990; Venkataraman 1990). Similarly, better access to electricity lowers costs for businesses and increases investment, driving economic growth (Reinikka and Svenson 1999b).

Improved transportation networks enable isolated rural communities to move into commercial agriculture, thereby increasing their income, and to use health and education services some distance away (Barwell 1996; Calvo and others 2001; Davis, Lucas, and Rikard 1996; Ellis and Hine 1998; World Bank 1996). By reducing the time and money it takes to move goods, better transportation improves competitiveness, helping create more jobs and boost incomes (Limão and Venables 1999; World Bank 2000, 2001).

Table 1.2 Evidence on Links between Infrastructure and MDGs in Africa

Study	MDG	Sector	Conclusion
Calvo 1994	Promote gender equality	Water	In four African countries surveyed, women saved over 1 hour per day after they began using a new, improved water source in their villages.
Eberhard and Van Horen 1995	Eradicate poverty	Electricity	In Cape Town, South Africa, households with electricity spent 3–5 percent of their incomes on energy, compared with 14–16 percent for those without access.
Lanjouw, Quizon, and Sparrow 2001	Eradicate poverty	Electricity	In Tanzania, the presence of electricity in a village increased income from nonfarm business activities by 61%. Nonfarm income in villages with electricity was 109 times that in villages without electricity.
Kenny 2002	Eradicate poverty	ICT	In Zambia, a survey of 21,000 farmers found that 50 percent of farmers credited radio-backed farm forums with increasing their crop yields.
Saunders, Warford, and Wellenius 1994	Eradicate poverty	ICT	A survey of transportation costs of an agricultural cooperative in Uganda in 1982 demonstrated that 200 agricultural cooperatives would save an average of $500,000 per year because of telecommunications as a result of avoided transportation costs.
Aker 2008	Eradicate poverty	ICT	In Niger, introduction of cell phones reduced price dispersion of grains, improving farmer and consumer welfare.
World Bank 2000	Eradicate poverty	Transport	In Ghana, after a rural roads rehabilitation project, costs for transporting goods and passengers fell by about one-third on average.
Croppenstedt and Demeke 1996	Eradicate poverty	Transport	In rural Ethiopia, farmers with access to an all-weather road increased their probability of using fertilizer by 10–20 percent because of cheaper transport costs.
Doumani and Listorti 2001	Achieve universal education	Water	In Nigeria, Guinea worm, a parasitic infection caused by poor-quality drinking water, was responsible for 60 percent of all school absenteeism.
Jimenez and Olson 1998	Reduce child mortality	Electricity	Clinics in Uganda and Ghana with photovoltaic cells for power kept refrigerators running for three to four years, whereas in Mali, clinics without these facilities had refrigerator failure about 20 percent of the time.
Telecommunication Development Bureau 1999	Reduce child/maternal mortality	ICT	In Mozambique, telemedicine could save hospitals up to $10,000 a year due to savings in transportation costs for inappropriate referrals.
Davis, Lucas, and Rikard 1996	Reduce child/maternal mortality	Transport	In Tanzania, between one-third and one-half of villagers affected by a rural roads project reported improved access to health care.
McCarthy and Wolf 2001	Reduce child/maternal mortality	Water	Across 20 African countries, access to safe water was found to be the fourth most important determinant of health outcomes, after access to health care, income, and fertility rate.

Sources: Authors' elaboration based largely on Kerf 2003a, 2003b, 2003c, and 2003d.
Note: ICT = information and communication technology; MDG = Millennium Development Goal.

The expansion of ICT networks democratizes access to information. It can be particularly critical for rural populations otherwise cut off from important technological know-how or critical information about market prices (Kenny 2002; Saunders, Warford, and Wellenius 1994). In many cases, telecommunication improvements also reduce transportation spending by allowing people to avoid fruitless journeys or to perform transactions remotely (Telecommunication Development Bureau 1999).

Africa's Infrastructure Deficit

By just about every measure of infrastructure coverage, African countries lag behind their peers in other parts of the developing world (see table 1.3; Yepes, Pierce, and Foster 2008).

The differences are particularly large for paved-road density, telephone main lines, and power generation. The gap exists for both low-income and middle-income groups.

Was Africa's current infrastructure deficit caused by a low historic starting point? Has it always been worse-off than the rest of the world? In the 1960s (roads), 1970s (telephones), and 1980s (power), Africa's stocks were quite similar to those of South or East Asia. (The one exception was paved-road density, in which South Asia already enjoyed a huge advantage over both Africa and East Asia as far back as the 1960s. For household coverage of electricity, both South and East Asia were already far ahead of Africa in the early 1990s, and this gap has widened over time.)

Africa expanded its infrastructure stocks more slowly than other developing regions,

Table 1.3 International Perspective on Africa's Infrastructure Deficit

Normalized units	African low-income countries	Other low-income countries	African middle-income countries	Other middle-income countries
Paved-road density	34	134	284	461
Total road density	150	29	381	106
Main-line density	9	38	142	252
Mobile density	48	55	277	557
Internet density	2	29	8.2	235
Generation capacity	39	326	293	648
Electricity coverage	14	41	37	88
Improved water	61	72	82	91
Improved sanitation	34	53	53	82

Source: Yepes, Pierce, and Foster 2008.
Note: Road density is measured in kilometers per 100 square kilometers of arable land; telephone density in lines per thousand population; generation capacity in megawatts per million population; electricity, water, and sanitation coverage in percentage of population.

opening a gap between Africa and Asia (figure 1.4). The comparison with South Asia—with a similar per capita income—is particularly striking. In 1970, Africa had almost three times more electricity-generating capacity per million people than did South Asia. By 2000, South Asia had left Africa far behind—it now has almost twice the generating capacity per million people. Similarly, in 1970 Africa had twice the main-line telephone density of South Asia, but by 2000, South Asia had drawn even. And in the case of mobile density, low-income African countries are actually ahead of South Asia.

China and India have largely driven the rapid infrastructure expansion in South and East Asia. In particular, China has pursued a conscious strategy of infrastructure-led growth since the 1990s, committing more than 14 percent of GDP to infrastructure investment in 2006 (Lall, Anand, and Rastogi 2008).

At independence, substantial variations in infrastructure existed across different subregions in Africa. Southern Africa started with relatively high infrastructure endowments and achieved some of the highest annual growth rates in infrastructure stocks over the last four decades. In 1980, the subregion had more than three times the generating capacity per million people of other subregions; in 1970, it had five times the telecommunication density of the other subregions. With regard to roads, West Africa was in a much stronger position than the other subregions in the 1960s but was overtaken by southern Africa by the 1980s. In water and

sanitation, the differences between subregions have been relatively small. Today, the Southern African Development Community region has a strong lead over all other subregions on almost every aspect of infrastructure. The weakest infrastructure endowments are in Central Africa (for roads, water, and sanitation) and in East Africa (for ICT and power) (table 1.4).

To better portray the diversity that exists across Africa, this report classifies countries into four types: (a) middle-income countries, (b) resource-rich countries, (c) fragile states, and (d) other low-income countries. (See box 1.1 for full definitions.) These categories were chosen because they capture differences in financing capacity and institutional strength that are relevant in understanding infrastructure outcomes.

Outcomes across these different types of countries are strikingly diverse. The difference in infrastructure stocks between African middle-income countries and other African countries is to be expected, although African *middle*-income countries have only a narrow edge over *low*-income countries elsewhere in the developing world. The lags associated with fragile states are readily understandable, given the disruption of conflict.

Especially striking is the extent to which resource-rich countries lag behind others in their infrastructure endowment, despite their greater wealth. In recent years, resource-rich countries have devoted their additional wealth not to infrastructure development but to paying off their debt. The governance

Figure 1.4 Growth of Africa's Infrastructure Stocks Compared with Asia

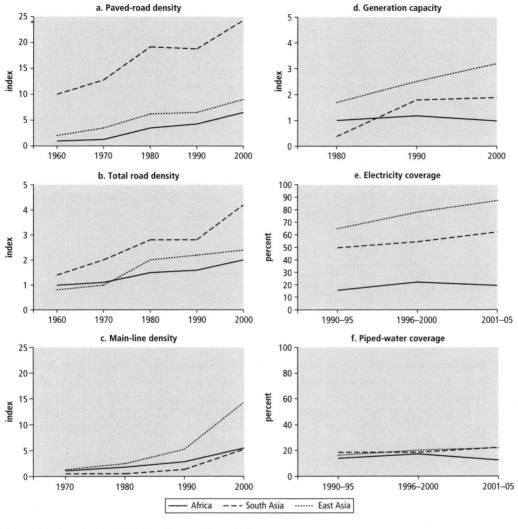

Sources: Banerjee and others 2008; Yepes, Pierce, and Foster 2008.
Note: Road density is measured in kilometers per 100 square kilometers of arable land; telephone density, in lines per 1,000 people; generation capacity, in megawatts per 1 million people.

challenges in a resource-rich environment may also prevent the transformation of that wealth into infrastructure.

Africa's Infrastructure Price Premium

The prices paid by African consumers for infrastructure services are exceptionally high by global standards (table 1.5). The tariffs charged in Africa for power, water, road freight, mobile telephone, or Internet services are several multiples of those paid in other parts of the developing world. Two explanations exist for Africa's high prices. First, the cost of providing infrastructure services in Africa is genuinely higher than elsewhere because of the small scale of production, the reliance on suboptimal technologies, or the inefficient management of resources. Second, the high prices reflect high profit margins caused by the lack of competition in service provision and inadequate price regulation. Of course, the two factors can be simultaneously at play.

Table 1.4 Intraregional Perspective on Africa's Infrastructure Deficit

Normalized units	ECOWAS	EAC	SADC	Central	Middle income[a]	Resource rich[a]	Low income, nonfragile[a]	Low income, fragile[a]
Paved-road density	38	29	92	4	284	14	14	55
Total road density	144	362	193	44	381	66	106	197
Main-line density	28	6	80	13	142	14	7	16
Mobile density	72	46	133	84	277	105	46	53
Internet density	2	2	4	1	8.2	1.6	1.2	3.1
Generation capacity	31	16	176	47	293	67	39	40
Electricity coverage	18	6	24	21	37	26	16	12
Improved water	63	71	68	53	82	57	57	66
Improved sanitation	35	42	46	28	53	32	37	31

Source: Yepes, Pierce, and Foster 2008.
Note: Road density is measured in kilometers per 100 square kilometers of arable land; telephone density in lines per thousand population; generation capacity in megawatts per million population; electricity, water, and sanitation coverage in percentage of population.
EAC = East African Community; ECOWAS = Economic Community of West African States; SADC = Southern African Development Community.
a. Country groupings are discussed in box 1.1.

Table 1.5 Africa's High-Cost Infrastructure

Sector	Africa	Other developing regions
Power tariffs ($ per kilowatt-hour)	0.02–0.46	0.05–0.1
Water tariffs ($ per cubic meter)	0.86–6.56	0.03–0.6
Road freight tariffs ($ per ton-kilometer)	0.04–0.14	0.01–0.04
Mobile telephony ($ per basket per month)	2.6–21.0	9.9
International telephony ($ per 3-minute call to United States)	0.44–12.5	2.0
Internet dial-up service ($ per month)	6.7–148.0	11

Sources: Banerjee and others 2008; Eberhard and others 2008; Minges and others 2008; Teravaninthorn and Raballand 2008.
Note: Ranges reflect prices in different countries and various consumption levels. Prices for telephony and Internet represent all developing regions, including Africa.

Power provides the clearest example of a sector with genuinely higher costs in Africa than elsewhere. Many small countries rely on small-scale diesel generation that can cost up to $0.40 per kilowatt-hour in operating costs alone—about three times higher than countries with larger power systems (over 500 megawatts), which are typically hydropower based (Eberhard and others 2008).

In contrast, high road freight tariffs in Africa are caused more by excessive profit margins than by high costs (Teravaninthorn and Raballand 2008). The costs that Africa's trucking operators face are *not* significantly higher than in other parts of the world, even when informal payments are taken into account. However, profit margins are exceptionally high, particularly in Central and West Africa where they reach levels of 60 to 160 percent. The underlying cause is the limited competition in the sector, combined with a highly regulated market based on *tour de role* principles, whereby freight is allocated to transporters through a centralized queuing method rather than by allowing truckers to enter into bilateral contracts with customers directly.

The high prices for international telephone and Internet service in Africa reflect a mixture of cost and profit. In countries that have no access to a submarine cable and are forced to rely on expensive satellite technology, charges are typically twice as high as in

Introducing a Country Typology

Africa's numerous countries face widely diverse economic situations. Understanding that structural differences in countries' economies and institutions affect their growth and financing challenges as well as their economic decisions (Collier and O'Connell 2006), this report introduces a four-way country typology to organize the rest of the discussion. This typology provides a succinct way of illustrating the diversity of infrastructure financing challenges faced by different African countries.

- *Middle-income countries* have GDP per capita in excess of $745 but less than $9,206. Examples include Cape Verde, Lesotho, and South Africa (World Bank 2007).
- *Resource-rich countries* are countries whose behaviors are strongly affected by their endowment of natural resources (Collier and O'Connell 2006; IMF 2007). Resource-rich countries typically depend on minerals, petroleum, or both. A country is classified as resource rich if primary commodity rents exceed 10 percent of GDP. (South Africa is

not classified as resource intensive, using this criterion.) Examples include Cameroon, Nigeria, and Zambia.
- *Fragile states* are low-income countries that face particularly severe development challenges, such as weak governance, limited administrative capacity, violence, or the legacy of conflict. In defining policies and approaches toward fragile states, different organizations have used differing criteria and terms. Countries that score less than 3.2 on the World Bank's Country Policy and Institutional Performance Assessment belong to this group. Some 14 countries of Africa are in this category. Examples include Côte de Ivoire, the Democratic Republic of Congo, and Sudan (World Bank 2005).
- *Other low-income countries* compose a residual category of countries with GDP per capita below $745 and that are neither resource-rich nor fragile states. Examples include Benin, Ethiopia, Senegal, and Uganda.

Source: Briceño-Garmendia, Smits, and Foster 2008.

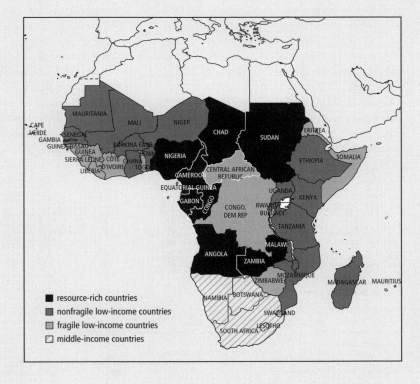

countries that enjoy cable access. Even when access to a submarine cable is obtained, countries with a monopoly on this international gateway have tariffs that are substantially higher than those without a monopoly (Minges and others 2008).

How Much Does Africa Need to Spend on Infrastructure?

Meeting Africa's infrastructure needs and developing cost-effective modes of infrastructure service delivery call for a substantial program of investment, rehabilitation, and disciplined maintenance combined. The physical infrastructure requirements are the grounds for a new set of estimates for spending requirements that are the foundation of this report. In all cases, the estimated spending takes into account both growth-related and social demands for infrastructure, and it incorporates the costs of maintenance and rehabilitation as well as new investment.

The time horizon for estimating spending needs is a decade. The assumption is that over a period of 10 years running up to 2015, the continent should be expected to address its infrastructure backlog, keep pace with the demands of economic growth, and attain a number of key social targets for broader infrastructure access (table 1.6).

Power Spending Needs Are by Far the Largest

Africa's largest infrastructure needs are in the power sector. Whether measured in generating capacity, electricity consumption, or security of supply, Africa's power infrastructure delivers only a fraction of the service found elsewhere in the *developing* world (Eberhard and others 2008). The 48 countries of Africa (with a combined population of 800 million) generate roughly the same amount of power as Spain (with a population of 45 million). Power consumption, which is 124 kilowatt-hours per capita per year and falling, is only 10 percent of that found elsewhere in the developing world, barely enough to power one 100-watt lightbulb per person for 3 hours a day. Africa's firms report that frequent power outages cause them to lose 5 percent of their sales; this figure rises to 20 percent for firms in the informal sector that are unable to afford backup generators. Chapter 8 in this volume contains a more detailed discussion of Africa's power challenges.

Addressing this power shortage will require enormous investments in infrastructure over the next decade. Based on four economic models, covering the Central, East, Southern, and West African Power Pools, potential generation projects in each power pool are identified and ranked according to cost-effectiveness. These models make possible estimating the cost of meeting power demand under a range of

Table 1.6 10-Year Economic and Social Targets for Investment Needs Estimates, 2006–15

Sector	Economic target	Social target
Information and communication technology	Complete submarine cable loop around Africa and 36,000-kilometer fiber-optic backbone network interconnecting national capitals to each other and to submarine cable loop.	Extend GSM voice signal and public access broadband to 100 percent of the rural population.
Irrigation	Develop all financially viable opportunities for large- and small-scale irrigation, potentially some 12 million hectares.	n.a.
Power	Attain demand-supply balance in power production, developing 7,000 megawatts of new generation capacity annually within a regional framework entailing 22,000 megawatts of new cross-border interconnections.	Raise household electrification rate by about 10 percentage points over current levels, entailing an additional 57 million new household connections.
Transport	Attain 250,000 kilometers of good-quality road networks supporting regional and national connectivity goals.	Raise the Rural Access Index from the current level of 34 percent nationally to 100 percent in highest-value agricultural areas.
		Place entire urban population within 500 meters of road supporting motorized access.
Water and sanitation	n.a.	Meet the Millennium Development Goals for water and sanitation.

Sources: Banerjee and others 2008; Carruthers, Krishnamani and Murray 2008; Mayer and others 2008; Rosnes and Vennemo 2008; You 2008.
Note: GSM = global systems mobile. n.a. = not applicable.

alternative scenarios that consider access targets, fuel prices, unit costs of investment, and feasibility of cross-border trade (Vennemo and Rosnes 2008).

Demand for power is almost directly proportional to economic growth. Installed capacity will need to grow by more than 10 percent annually—or more than 7,000 megawatts a year—just to meet Africa's suppressed demand, keep pace with projected economic growth, and provide additional capacity to support the rollout of electrification. Since 1995, expansion of the sector has averaged barely 1 percent annually, or less than 1,000 megawatts a year. Most of that power would go to meet nonresidential demands from the commercial and industrial sectors.

The most cost-effective way to expand Africa's power generation is through regional trade that allows countries to pool the most attractive primary energy resources across national boundaries. Regional trade shaves around $0.01 per kilowatt-hour off the marginal cost of power generation in each of the power pools (and as much as $0.02 to $0.04 per kilowatt-hour for some countries), leading to savings of about $2 billion a year in the costs of developing and operating the power system. Mobilizing the benefits of regional trade depends on developing major untapped hydropower projects in the Democratic Republic of Congo, Ethiopia, and Guinea, which would become major exporters in the Southern, East, and West African Power Pools, respectively (table 1.7). It also hinges on establishing some 22,000 megawatts of interconnectors that will be needed over the next decade (to 2015), to allow power to flow freely from country to country. The financial returns on these interconnectors can be as high as 120 percent in the Southern African Power Pool; it is typically 20–30 percent in the other pools. Regional trade can also put Africa on a path to cleaner development, because it would increase hydropower's share of the continent's generation portfolio from 36 percent to 48 percent, displacing 20,000 megawatts of thermal plant in the process and saving 70 million tons of carbon emissions each year. Finally, raising electrification rates will require extending distribution networks to reach almost 6 million additional households a year over the next decade (to 2015).

The overall costs for the power sector in Africa are a staggering $41 billion a year—$27 billion for investment and $14 billion for operation and maintenance (table 1.8). About half the investment costs are for development of new generating capacity. Approximately 15 percent is earmarked for rehabilitation of existing generation and transmission assets. About 40 percent of the costs are for the Southern Africa Power Pool alone.

Achieving Water Security Remains an Unquantified Challenge

One important infrastructure requirement not explicitly estimated in the investment costs is water storage capacity, which is required to reach water security. Africa experiences huge swings in precipitation across areas, across seasons, and over time (Grey and Sadoff 2006). Climate change will only exacerbate this

Table 1.7 Africa's Power Needs, 2006–15

Pool	New generation capacity (MW)	New cross-border interconnectors (MW)	New household connections (millions)
CAPP	4,395	831	2.5
EAPP	17,108	3,878	20.0
SAPP	33,319	11,786	12.2
WAPP	18,003	5,625	21.5
Island states	368	n.a.	1.2
Total	73,193	22,120	57.4

Source: Adapted from Rosnes and Vennemo 2008.
Note: CAPP = Central African Power Pool; EAPP = Eastern African Power Pool (including Nile basin but excluding the Arab Republic of Egypt); Island states = Cape Verde, Madagascar, and Mauritius; SAPP = Southern African Power Pool; WAPP = Western African Power Pool. n.a. = not applicable.

Table 1.8 Power Spending Needs, 2006–15
$ billions annually

Pool	Investment				Total operation and maintenance	Total spending needs
	Rehabilitation	New generation	New transmission and distribution	Total investment		
CAPP	0.1	0.9	0.3	1.3	0.2	1.4
EAPP	0.3	3.5	3.0	6.8	1.1	7.9
SAPP	2.6	4.5	2.9	10.0	8.4	18.4
WAPP	1.0	3.5	3.7	8.2	4.0	12.3
Island states	0	0.1	0.2	0.3	0.3	0.6
Total	4.0	12.5	10.1	26.6	14.0	40.6

Source: Adapted from Rosnes and Vennemo 2008.
Note: CAPP = Central African Power Pool; EAPP = Eastern African Power Pool (including Nile basin but excluding the Arab Republic of Egypt); Island states = Cape Verde, Madagascar, and Mauritius; SAPP = Southern African Power Pool; WAPP = Western African Power Pool.
Row totals may not add exactly because of rounding errors.

variability. As a result, water security—defined as reliable water supplies and acceptable risks from floods and other unpredictable events, including those from climate change—will require a significant expansion of water storage capacity from the current level of 200 cubic meters per capita. The amount of storage needed to withstand both flood and drought risks has not yet been precisely modeled for most African countries; hence, the needed investment could not be estimated. Even a simplistic approach, however, such as estimating the cost of bringing all African countries from their current storage levels of around 200 cubic meters per capita to South Africa's level of 750 cubic meters per capita, is enough to illustrate the hundreds of billions of dollars that could be required.

Nevertheless, about half the new generation capacity outlined for the power sector relates to water storage infrastructure with multipurpose benefits. These hydropower schemes would therefore also contribute, to an unknown extent, toward achieving the water security objective. The increased storage capacity they represent could—under appropriate multipurpose management principles—help attenuate the shocks associated with floods and droughts. See chapter 14 in this volume for a more detailed discussion of Africa's water resource challenges.

Scope for Expanding Irrigated Areas

Only 7 million hectares, in a handful of countries, are equipped for irrigation. Although it constitutes less than 5 percent of Africa's cultivated area, the irrigation-equipped area represents 20 percent of the value of agricultural production. Chapter 15 in this volume contains a more detailed discussion of Africa's irrigation challenges.

The model suggests that a further 6.8 million hectares are economically viable for irrigation, based on local agroecological characteristics, market access, and infrastructure costs (You 2008). Most of this area, more than 5.4 million hectares, is ideal for small-scale irrigation schemes, assuming that they can be developed for an investment of no more than $2,000 a hectare. A further 1.4 million hectares has the potential for large-scale irrigation schemes that could be retrofitted to dams already serving hydropower purposes or incorporated into the development of new hydropower schemes foreseeable within the next decade, assuming that the distribution infrastructure needed for irrigation can be added for an investment of no more than $3,000 a hectare. Finally, 1.7 million hectares equipped for irrigation have fallen into disuse but could be recovered by rehabilitating the infrastructure. Spreading these investments over a 10-year span would require $2.7 billion annually, plus a further $0.6 billion a year to support maintenance of new and existing systems (table 1.9).

Reaching for the MDGs in Water and Sanitation

The MDG target for access to safe water is 75 percent of the population by 2015; for

Table 1.9 Irrigation Spending Needs, 2006–15

$ billions annually

Total maintenance	Investment				Total
	Rehabilitation	Large-scale schemes	Small-scale schemes	Total investment	
0.6	0.6	0.3	1.8	2.7	3.3

Source: You 2008.

improved sanitation, it is 63 percent. As of 2006, the last year for which official data have been published, the figures for Africa were 58 percent and 31 percent, respectively. To meet the MDG goal, the number of people with access to safe water would need to increase from 411 million to 701 million by 2015—an increase of 29 million a year compared with recent progress of only 11 million per year. To meet the MDG sanitation goal, the number of people with access to improved service would need to increase from 272 million in 2006 to 617 million by 2015—an increase of 35 million a year compared with recent progress of only 7 million a year. Chapters 16 and 17 in this volume offer more detailed discussions of Africa's water supply and sanitation challenges, respectively.

The overall price tag for reaching the water and sanitation MDG access is estimated at $22 billion (roughly 3.3 percent of Africa's GDP), with water accounting for more than two-thirds (table 1.10). Capital investment needs can be conservatively estimated at $15 billion a year (2.2 percent of the region's GDP). These needs include both new infrastructure and rehabilitation of existing assets. Estimates are based on minimum acceptable asset standards. It is assumed that access patterns (or relative prevalence of water and sanitation modalities) remain broadly the same between 2006 and 2015 and that services are upgraded for only a minimum number of customers. The maintenance requirements stand at $7 billion a year (1.1 percent of the region's GDP). Operation and maintenance of network and non-network services, respectively, amount to 3 percent and 1.5 percent of the replacement value of installed infrastructure. Rehabilitation costs have been estimated based on a model that takes into account the maintenance backlog of network infrastructure in each country.

Table 1.10 Water and Sanitation Spending Needs, 2006–15

$ billions annually

Sector	Investment	Maintenance	Total
Water	11.0	5.5	16.5
Sanitation	3.9	1.4	5.4
Total	14.9	7.0	21.9

Source: Banerjee and others 2008.

Transport Needs Are Substantial

Africa's road density seems sparse compared with the vastness of the continent, but it is not unreasonable relative to the continent's population and income. A more detailed discussion of Africa's transport challenges appears in chapters 9–13 in this volume. The adequacy of Africa's current transport network can best be assessed by examining whether it provides an adequate level of connectivity to facilitate the movement of people and goods between regions, within nations, out of rural areas, and across cities. Using a spatial model, one can assess the cost of linking economic and demographic nodes through transport infrastructures so as to achieve regional, national, urban, and rural connectivity.

Regional connectivity within the African continent requires a network that links all capital cities and cities with over 1 million inhabitants to deep-sea ports and international borders. This objective can be achieved with a two-lane network of a little over 100,000 kilometers maintained in good condition. About 70 percent of this network is already in place, but about one-quarter of it needs to be widened from one lane to two lanes, and about three-quarters of it needs to be improved to good quality. The overall cost of meeting this target amounts to $2.7 billion a year, or barely 15 percent of total spending needs for the transport sector. The bulk of this expenditure is for investment.

Regional connectivity also requires a rail network, ports with adequate capacity, and airports. For railways, the main costs are for rehabilitation of the existing track. For ports, more container berths are needed to keep pace with the growth of international trade. For air transport, the model does not suggest any need for new terminals, but some expansion is provided based on passenger traffic projects. For runways, the investments primarily relate to improving the condition of existing runways. No need was found for building new runways, although in a few cases lengthening existing runways to support the use of larger aircraft was relevant.

Connectivity within a country requires extending the regional network to link capital cities to their corresponding provincial centers and to other cities with more than 25,000 inhabitants by at least a one-lane paved road. The overall regional network and such national networks would encompass 250,000 kilometers to meet this objective. About half of this network already exists in the form of paved roads, whereas the other half would need to be upgraded to a paved network. The cost of meeting this target is $2.9 billion a year. A substantial share of that amount is for upgrading existing unpaved roads to paved surfaces.

Rural connectivity is defined as providing accessibility to all-season roads in high-value agricultural areas. Only one-third of rural Africans live close to an all-season road, compared with two-thirds of the population in other developing regions. Because of low population densities in rural Africa, raising this Rural Access Index to 100 percent for Africa would be essentially unaffordable. An alternative approach is to provide 100 percent rural connectivity to those areas with the highest agricultural land value. Limiting access attention to areas with 80 percent of the highest agricultural production value, the cost would be a significant $2.5 billion a year, or close to 13 percent of the overall spending requirement. About half of that sum is for maintenance, whereas the remainder is devoted to improving the condition of existing rural roads, upgrading road surfaces to ensure all-season accessibility, and to a lesser extent, adding new roads to reach isolated populations.

Urban connectivity is defined as ensuring that the entire urban population lives no farther than 500 meters from a paved road capable of supporting motorized access. African cities today have paved-road densities well below the average for well-provided cities in other developing countries, which typically have densities of 300 meters per 1,000 inhabitants. Meeting the objective of 500 meters would require adding 17,000 kilometers to the current urban road network, and upgrading and improving 70,000 kilometers of the existing network, costing $1.6 billion a year, which serves to underscore the significance of urban roads within Africa's overall transport requirements. Most of this sum is needed to widen and pave existing urban roads.

To create a transport network that provides adequate regional, national, rural, and urban road connectivity complemented by adequate rail, port, and airport infrastructure will require significant spending—$18 billion a year, half of which is related to maintenance (table 1.11). Investment requirements are driven primarily by spending needed to upgrade the category of existing assets (for example, from a gravel to a paved road), to improve the condition of existing assets (from poor to good or fair condition), and to expand the capacity of existing assets (for example, from one lane to two lanes). Just over half of this spending would be directed at nonroad transport modes, particularly for their maintenance. The remainder is roughly evenly spread among national connectivity, urban connectivity, and rural connectivity.

ICT Spending Needs Look More Manageable

Africa's progress in ICT is close to that seen elsewhere in the developing world. The percentage of Africa's population living within range of a global systems mobile signal rose from 5 percent in 1999 to 57 percent in 2006 (Minges and others 2008). Over the same period, more than 100 million Africans became mobile telephone subscribers. Indeed, in some countries, household access to mobile telephone services now exceeds that of piped water. Internet penetration lags considerably, with little more than 2 million subscribers and a further 12 million estimated to be making use of public access facilities. The ICT revolution has been accomplished largely through market liberalization and private sector investment, which will continue to be the main driving force behind future investments. The state will need to continue investing in a few critical areas, however. Chapter 7 in this volume contains a more detailed discussion of Africa's ICT challenges.

The private sector will undertake the major expenditures in this sector to service growth in market demand. The urban market for ICT services is well established and profitable. Demand for voice services in this market is expected to grow as penetration rates continue to rise from 20 to 46 lines per 100 inhabitants. In addition, incipient markets for broadband services are expected to expand from 0.04 to 2.54 lines per 100 inhabitants. These demands can be met entirely by private sector investment.

Spatial models are used to simulate the commercial viability of further expanding coverage of voice and broadband signals into rural areas using global systems mobile and WiMAX (Worldwide Interoperability for Microwave Access) technologies (Mayer and others 2008). The models consider the cost of network rollout based on topographical factors and local availability of power. They also estimate local revenue potential based on demographic densities, per capita incomes, and estimated subscriber rates.

With no market barriers, the private sector alone could profitably extend global systems mobile signal coverage to about 95 percent of Africa's population (Mayer and others 2008). The remaining 5 percent, living in isolated rural communities, is not commercially viable and would require a significant state subsidy to connect. The percentage of the population that is not commercially viable varies substantially across countries, from less than 1 percent in Nigeria to more than 20 percent in the Democratic Republic of Congo.

Broadband service, by contrast, is still in its infancy and will expand only if significant investments are made in rolling out high-capacity fiber-optic cable across the continent. Just interconnecting all Africa's capitals would require a network of 36,000 kilometers of fiber-optic cable. If the network were extended to cover all cities with 500,000 or more inhabitants, more than 100,000 kilometers of cable

Table 1.11 Transport Spending Needs, 2006–15
$ billions annually

Sector/area	Investment				Total maintenance	Overall total
	Improve condition	Upgrade category	Add capacity	Total investment		
Regional connectivity	0.5	1.1	0.2	1.8	0.9	2.7
National connectivity	0.5	1.2	0.2	1.9	1.0	2.9
Rural connectivity	0.8	0.4	0.1	1.3	1.2	2.5
Urban connectivity	0.3	0.4	0.4	1.1	0.5	1.6
Railways, ports, and airports	0.2	0.6	1.9	2.7	5.9	8.6
Total	2.2	3.7	2.7	8.6	9.6	18.2

Source: Carruthers, Krishnamani, and Murray 2008.
Note: Railways, ports, and airports include investments by South Africa's Transnet and other demand-driven transport investment needs covered by the private sector.
Column totals may not add exactly because of rounding errors.

would be required. Private finance would likely be forthcoming for the highest-traffic segments. However, the more ambitious the aspirations for extending connectivity, the larger the component of public finance that would be required.

A modest level of broadband service could be provided using WiMAX technology to provide low-volume connectivity to a limited number of institutions and public access telecenters in rural areas. Using this approach, and again in the absence of market barriers, the private sector alone could profitably extend WiMAX coverage to about 89 percent of Africa's population (Mayer and others 2008). The remaining 11 percent, living in isolated rural communities, are not commercially viable and would require a significant state subsidy to support network rollout. As with voice, the percentage of the population that is not commercially viable to cover varies substantially across countries, from less than 1 percent in Nigeria to more than 70 percent in the Democratic Republic of Congo.

Finally, Africa is in the process of completing a network of submarine cables that links it to the global intercontinental network. Several projects are already under way to close the loop around the eastern side of the continent. Some strengthening of the West African submarine system is also needed, plus cable links to service outlying islands, such as the Comoros, Madagascar, and the Seychelles. The private sector is showing considerable appetite to take on this kind of investment.

The investment costs of this additional ICT infrastructure, beyond what would be purely driven by market demand, are relatively modest when compared with other infrastructure sectors. Achieving universal rural access for both voice service and limited broadband service based on WiMAX technology could be accomplished for an investment of $1.7 billion a year, the bulk of which could come from the private sector, with additional public funding amounting to no more than $0.4 billion a year. Completing the submarine and intraregional fiber-optic backbone would entail an annual (private sector) investment of less than $0.2 billion, although this sum would more than double if a more ambitious network connecting all cities with over 500,000 inhabitants were envisaged (table 1.12). Factoring in the market-driven investments needed to keep pace with demand in established urban markets, the estimated ICT sector annual investment need rises to $7 billion a year, plus another $2 billion annually for operation and maintenance.

Overall Price Tag

Africa's overall cost to build new infrastructure, refurbish dilapidated assets, and operate and maintain all existing and new installations is estimated at almost $93 billion a year for 2006 through 2015 (15 percent of African GDP; table 1.13 and figure 1.5).

Comparison with the Commission for Africa

The $93 billion estimate is more than twice the estimate of the Commission for Africa in 2005, which was based on cross-country econometric studies, rather than the more detailed country-level microeconomic modeling of the Africa Infrastructure Country Diagnostic (Estache 2006). A recent update of the cross-country model used for the Commission for Africa report came up with a revised estimate of $80 billion to $90 billion (Yepes 2007).

Some 40 percent of the total is for the power sector, which requires about $41 billion each year (6 percent of African GDP; Rosnes and Vennemo 2008). A significant share of the spending for power is for investment in multipurpose water storage schemes and thus makes an important contribution to water resources management. The second-largest component is the cost of meeting the MDGs for water and sanitation—about $22 billion (3 percent of regional GDP). The third-largest price tag is associated with the transport sector, which comes in at just over $18 billion (3.6 percent of GDP).

Distribution of Spending among Countries

Three groups of countries—the middle-income countries, the resource-rich countries, and the low-income nonfragile states—share roughly equally in the bulk of total spending. Each of these groups needs to spend around

Table 1.12 ICT Spending Needs beyond the Purely Market Driven: Investment Only, 2006–15

$ billions annually

Type of investment	Universal access to voice signal	Universal access to broadband platform	Fiber-optic backbone linking capital cities	Submarine cables
Private	0.58	0.68	—	—
Public	0.20	0.23	—	—
Total investment	0.78	0.91	0.03	0.18

Source: Mayer and others 2008.
Note: In contrast to the preceding tables, the expenditure for operation and maintenance is excluded because of the difficulty of apportioning it across the different subcategories presented.
— Not available.

Table 1.13 Overall Infrastructure Spending Needs for Africa, 2006–15

$ billions annually

Sector	Capital expenditure	Operation and maintenance	Total needs
ICT	7.0	2.0	9.0
Irrigation	2.7	0.6	3.3
Power	26.7	14.1	40.8
Transport	8.8	9.4	18.2
WSS	14.9	7.0	21.9
Total	60.4	33.0	93.3

Sources: Authors' calculations based on Banerjee and others 2008; Carruthers, Krishnamani, and Murray 2008; Mayer and others 2008; Rosnes and Vennemo 2008.
Note: ICT = information and communication technology; WSS = water supply and sanitation.
Row totals may not add exactly because of rounding errors.

Figure 1.5 Africa's Aggregate Infrastructure Spending Needs, by Country, 2006–15

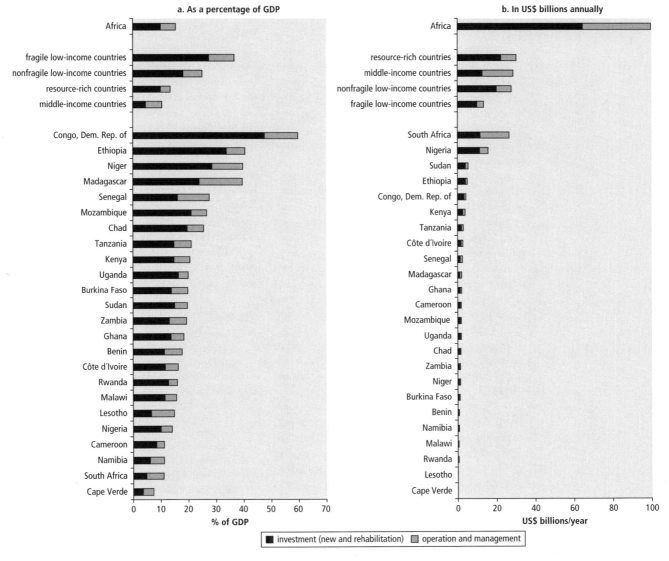

Sources: Authors' calculations based on Banerjee and others 2008; Carruthers, Krishnamani, and Murray 2008; Mayer and others 2008; Rosnes and Vennemo 2008.

$28 billion to $30 billion to meet its infrastructure needs. The price tag for the fragile states is only about half as much at $13 billion. The largest spending needs for an individual country by far are in South Africa, which requires $27 billion a year.

The burden of spending relative to the countries' GDPs is very different across groups. For middle-income and resource-rich countries, the burden appears manageable, amounting to no more than 10 percent to 13 percent of their respective GDPs. For low-income countries, however, as much as 25 percent of GDP would be needed, rising to an implausible 37 percent for the low-income fragile states. Ethiopia, Madagascar, Niger, and above all, the Democratic Republic of Congo face an impossible challenge—their infrastructure needs range from 26 to over 70 percent of GDP (see figure 1.5, panel a).

Distribution of Spending—Investment versus Maintenance

The overall spending requirements break down two to one between investment and operation and maintenance, with the balance between them shifting across country groupings. In the middle-income countries, the spending needs are skewed toward maintenance, which absorbs more than half the total. These countries have already put in place much of the infrastructure they need, and their main challenge is to preserve it in good condition. Across the three other country groupings, almost three-quarters of spending needs are associated with investment and only one-quarter with operation and maintenance. These countries have a vast construction (and reconstruction) agenda to complete before they will have much to maintain.

Will the Price Tag Grow—or Shrink?

These estimates of investment are based on costs prevailing in 2006, the base year for all of the African Infrastructure Country Diagnostic figures. It is well known that the unit costs of infrastructure provision have escalated significantly during the last few years (Africon 2008).

The most reliable evidence available comes from the road sector, where cost overruns reported on multilateral agency projects in 2007 averaged 60 percent. The higher costs are not just from inflation in petroleum and associated input prices, but they also reflect a lack of competition for civil works contracts and the tight position of the global construction industry, as well as lengthy delays in project implementation. Similar escalations in unit costs have been reported anecdotally in other areas of infrastructure, notably power. Possibly, the recent upward pressure on the costs of infrastructure may be reversed as the current global downturn takes its toll, but that is hard to predict. Based on the situation in 2006, the preceding estimates likely represent a conservative lower boundary for the cost of developing infrastructure assets at today's prices.

The global financial crisis of 2008 can be expected to reduce demand for some types of infrastructures, but it would not hugely alter the estimated spending needs. A large share of the spending needs are driven by targets rather than economic growth; this applies, for example, to the transport spending needs (which are largely based on connectivity objectives) and to the water and sanitation spending needs (which are based on the MDGs). The spending needs with the strongest direct link to economic growth are those for the power sector. However, because of the large backlog in that sector, estimated spending needs contain a strong component of refurbishment and catch-up. Thus, even halving economic growth estimates for the region would reduce estimated power spending needs by only 20 percent. The global recession could be expected to affect demand for ICT services and trade-related infrastructure, such as railways and ports. However, the weight of those infrastructures in the total spending needs is not much more than 10 percent.

Notes

The authors of this chapter are Vivien Foster and Cecilia Briceño-Garmendia, who drew on background material and contributions from César Calderón, Alvaro Escribano, J. Luis Guasch, Paul Lombard, Siobhan Murray, Jorge Pena, Justin Pierce, Tito Yepes, and Willem van Zyl.

1. Although the Africa Infrastructure Country Diagnostic project is limited to the study of Sub-Saharan African countries, this book sometimes substitutes Africa for Sub-Saharan Africa. The reader should bear in mind, however, that the information refers only to Sub-Saharan Africa.
2. Road density is measured in kilometers per 100 square kilometers; telephone density in lines per thousand population; electricity generation in megawatts per million population; and electricity, water, and sanitation coverage in percentage of population.
3. Monetary figures are in U.S. dollars unless otherwise noted.

References

Africon. 2008. "Unit Costs of Infrastructure Projects in Sub-Saharan Africa." Background Paper 11, Africa Infrastructure Sector Diagnostic, World Bank, Washington, DC.

Aker, Jenny. 2008. "Does Digital Divide or Provide? The Impact of Cell Phones on Grain Markets in Niger." Center for International and Development Economics Research, University of California, Berkeley.

Ayogu, Melvin. 1999. "Before Prebendalism: A Positive Analysis of Core Infrastructure Investment in a Developing Fiscal Federalism." *African Development Review* 11 (2): 169–98.

Banerjee, Sudeshna, Quentin Wodon, Amadou Diallo, Taras Pushak, Hellal Uddin, Clarence Tsimpo, and Vivien Foster. 2008. "Access, Affordability, and Alternatives: Modern Infrastructure Services in Africa." Background Paper 2, Africa Infrastructure Sector Diagnostic, World Bank, Washington, DC.

Barnes, Douglas F. 1988. *Electric Power for Rural Growth: How Electricity Affects Rural Life in Developing Countries.* Boulder, CO: Westview Press.

Barwell, Ian. 1996. "Transport and the Village: Findings from African Village-Level Travel and Transport Surveys and Related Studies." Discussion Paper 344, World Bank, Washington, DC.

Blackden, Mark, and Quentin Wodon, eds. 2005. "Gender, Time Use and Poverty in Sub-Saharan Africa." Working Series Paper 73, World Bank, Washington, DC.

Briceño-Garmendia, Cecilia, Karlis Smits, and Vivien Foster. 2008. "Financing Public Infrastructure in Sub-Saharan Africa: Patterns, Issues, and Options." AICD Background Paper 15, Africa Infrastructure Sector Diagnostic, World Bank, Washington, DC.

Brodman, Janice. 1982. "Rural Electrification and the Commercial Sector in Indonesia." Discussion Paper D-73L, Resources for the Future, Washington, DC.

Calderón, César. 2008. "Infrastructure and Growth in Africa." Working Paper 3, Africa Infrastructure Country Diagnostic, World Bank, Washington, DC.

Calderón, César, and Luis Servén. 2008. "Infrastructure and Economic Development in Sub-Saharan Africa." Policy Research Working Paper 4712, World Bank, Washington, DC.

Calvo, Christina Malmberg. 1994. "Case Study on the Role of Women in Rural Transport: Access of Women to Domestic Facilities." Sub-Saharan Africa Transport Policy Program Working Paper 11, World Bank, Washington, DC.

Calvo, Christina Malmberg, Colin Gannon, Kenneth M. Gwilliam, and Zhi Liu. 2001. "Transport: Infrastructure and Services—Technical Notes." PRSP Toolkit, World Bank, Washington, DC.

Carruthers, Robin, Ranga R. Krishnamani, and Siobhan Murray. 2008. "Improving Connectivity: Investing in Transport Infrastructure in Sub-Saharan Africa." Background Paper 7, Africa Infrastructure Country Diagnostic, World Bank, Washington, DC.

Collier, Paul, and Stephen O'Connell. 2006. "Opportunities and Choices." Draft chapter for the synthesis volume of the *Explaining African Economic Growth* PRoject of Oxford University and Swarthmore College, Centre for Study of African Economies.

Commission for Africa. 2005. *Our Common Interest: Report of the Commission for Africa.* London: Commission for Africa.

Croppenstedt, Andre, and Mulat Demeke. 1996. "Determinants of Adoption and Levels of Demand for Fertiliser for Cereal Growing Farmers in Ethiopia." Working Paper 96-3, Centre for the Study of African Economies, Oxford, U.K.

Davis, Tony, Kimberly Lucas, and Ken Rikard. 1996. *Agricultural Transport Assistance Program: Impact Study.* Washington, DC: United States Agency for International Development.

Doumani, Fadi M., and James A. Listorti. 2001. "Environmental Health: Bridging the Gaps." World Bank Discussion Paper 422, World Bank, Washington, DC.

Easterly, William, and Ross Levine. 1997. "Africa's Growth Tragedy: Policies and Ethnic Divisions." *Quarterly Journal of Economics* 112 (4): 1203–50. http://ssrn.com/abstract=88828.

Eberhard, Anton, Vivien Foster, Cecilia Briceño-Garmendia, Fatimata Ouedraogo, Daniel Camos, and Maria Shkaratan. 2008. "Underpowered: The State of the Power Sector in Sub-Saharan Africa." Background Paper 6, Africa Infrastructure Sector Diagnostic, World Bank, Washington, DC.

Eberhard, Anton, and Clive Van Horen. 1995. *Poverty and Power: Energy and the South African State.* London: UCT and Pluto.

Ellis, Simon, and John Hine. 1998. "The Provision of Rural Transport Services: Approach Paper." Sub-Saharan Africa Transport Policy Program Working Paper 37, World Bank, Washington, DC.

Escribano, Alvaro, J. Luis Guasch, and Jorge Pena. 2008. "Impact of Infrastructure Constraints on Firm Productivity in Africa." Working Paper 9, Africa Infrastructure Sector Diagnostic, World Bank, Washington, DC.

Esfahani, Hadi Salehi, and Maria Teresa Ramirez. 2003. "Institutions, Infrastructure, and Economic Growth." *Journal of Development Economics* 70: 443–77. http://ssrn.com/abstract=310779.

Esrey, S. A., J. B. Potash, L. Roberts, and C. Shiff. 1991. "Effects of Improved Water Supply and Sanitation on Ascariasis, Diarrhea, Dracunculiasis, Hookworm Infection, Schistosomiasis and

Trachoma." *Bulletin of the World Health Organization* 89 (5): 609–21.

Estache, Antonio. 2006. "Africa's Infrastructure: Challenges and Opportunities." Paper presented at "Realizing the Potential for Profitable Investment in Africa" seminar, IMF Institute and Joint Africa Institute, Tunis, February 28–March 1.

Estache, Antonio, Biagio Speciale, and David Veredas. 2005. "How Much Does Infrastructure Matter for Growth in Sub-Saharan Africa?" World Bank, Washington, DC.

Fay, Marianne, Danny Leipziger, Quentin Wodon, and Tito Yepes. 2005. "Achieving Child-Health-Related Millennium Development Goals: The Role of Infrastructure." *World Development* 33 (8): 1267–84.

Fedderke, Johannes W., and Zeljko Bogetic. 2006. "Infrastructure and Growth in South Africa: Direct and Indirect Productivity Impacts of 19 Infrastructure Measures." Policy Research Working Paper 3989, World Bank, Washington, DC.

Foley, Gerald. 1990. *Electricity for Rural People.* London: Panos Institute.

Grey, David, and Claudia Sadoff. 2006 "Water for Growth and Development: A Framework for Analysis." Theme Document of the 4th World Water Forum, Mexico City, March.

Hutton, Guy. 2000. *Considerations in Evaluating the Cost-Effectiveness of Environmental Health Interventions.* Geneva: World Health Organization.

Hutton, Guy, and Laurence Haller. 2004. *Evaluation of the Costs and Benefits of Water and Sanitation Improvements at the Global Level: Water, Sanitation and Health Protection of the Human Environment.* Geneva: World Health Organization.

IMF (International Monetary Fund). 2007. *Regional Economic Outlook: Sub-Saharan Africa.* Washington, DC: IMF.

Jimenez, Antonio, and Ken Olson. 1998. *Renewable Energy for Rural Health Clinics.* Golden, CO: National Renewable Energy Laboratory. http://www.nrel.gov/docs/legosti/fy98/25233.pdf.

Kamara, Samura. 2008. "Restoring Economic Growth and Stability in Fragile and Post-Conflict Low Income States: Views from the Trench." Paper presented at World Bank Poverty Reduction and Economic Management conference, Washington, DC, April 15–16.

Kenny, Charles. 2002. "The Costs and Benefits of ICTs for Direct Poverty Alleviation." *Development Policy Review* 20: 141–57.

Kerf, Michel. 2003a. "Linkages between Energy and Poverty Alleviation." World Bank, Washington, DC.

———. 2003b. "Linkages between ICT and Poverty Alleviation." World Bank, Washington, DC.

———. 2003c. "Linkages between Transport and Poverty Alleviation." World Bank, Washington, DC.

———. 2003d. "Linkages between Water and Sanitation and Poverty Alleviation." World Bank, Washington, DC.

Lall, Rajiv, Ritu Anand, and Anupam Rastogi. 2008. "Developing Physical Infrastructure: A Comparative Perspective on the Experience of the People's Republic of China and India." Asian Development Bank, Manila.

Lanjouw, Peter, Jamie Quizon, and Robert Sparrow. 2001. "Non-Agricultural Earnings in Peri-Urban Areas of Tanzania: Evidence from Household Survey Data." *Food Policy* 26: 385–403.

Limão, Nuno, and Anthony Venables. 1999. "Infrastructure, Geographical Disadvantage and Transportation Costs." Policy Research Working Paper 2257, World Bank, Washington, DC.

Mayer, Rebecca, Ken Figueredo, Mike Jensen, Tim Kelly, Richard Green, and Alvaro Federico Barra. 2008. "Costing the Needs for Investment in ICT Infrastructure in Africa." Background Paper 3, Africa Infrastructure Sector Diagnostic, World Bank, Washington, DC.

McCarthy, F. Desmond, and Holger Wolf. 2001. "Comparative Life Expectancy in Africa." Policy Research Working Paper 2668, World Bank, Washington, DC.

Minges, Michael, Cecila Briceño-Garmendia, Mark Williams, Mavis Ampah, Daniel Camos, and Maria Shkratan. 2008. "Information and Communications Technology in Sub-Saharan Africa: A Sector Review." Background Paper 10, Africa Infrastructure Sector Diagnostic, World Bank, Washington, DC.

Reinikka, Ritva, and Jakob Svensson. 1999a. "Confronting Competition: Firms' Investment Response and Constraints in Uganda." In *Assessing an African Success: Farms, Firms, and Government in Uganda's Recovery,* ed. Paul Collier and Ritva Reinikka. Washington, DC: World Bank.

———. 1999b. "How Inadequate Provision of Public Infrastructure and Services Affects Private Investment." Policy Research Working Paper 2262, World Bank, Washington, DC.

Rosnes, Orvika, and Haakon Vennemo. 2008. "Powering Up: Costing Power Infrastructure Investment Needs in Southern and Eastern Africa." Background Paper 5, Africa Infrastructure Sector Diagnostic, World Bank, Washington, DC.

Saunders, Robert J., Jeremy Warford, and Bjorn Wellenius. 1994. *Telecommunications and Economic Development.* 2nd ed. Baltimore: Johns Hopkins University Press for the World Bank.

Telecommunication Development Bureau. 1999. *Telemedicine and Developing Countries—Lessons Learned.* Geneva: International Telecommunication Union.

Teravaninthorn, Supee, and Gaël Raballand. 2008. "Transport Prices and Costs in Africa: A Review of the Main International Corridors." Working Paper 14, Africa Infrastructure Sector Diagnostic, World Bank, Washington, DC.

Venkataraman, K. 1990. "Rural Electrification in the Asian and Pacific Region." In *Power Systems in Asia and the Pacific, with Emphasis on Rural Electrification,* ed. Economic and Social Commission for Asia and the Pacific, 310–32. New York: United Nations.

Vennemo, Haakon, and Ornica Rosnes. 2008. "Powering-Up: Costing Power Infrastructure Investment Needs in Africa." Background Paper 5, Africa Infrastructure Country Diagnostic, World Bank, Washington, DC.

Wodon, Quentin, ed. 2008. "Electricity Tariffs and the Poor: Case Studies from Sub-Saharan Africa." Working Paper 11, Africa Infrastructure Country Diagnostic, World Bank, Washington, DC.

World Bank. 1996. "Socio-Economic Impact of Rural Roads: Impact Evaluation Report for the Fourth Highway Project in Morocco." OED Report 15808-MOR, World Bank, Washington, DC.

———. 2000. "Ghana: Building a Stronger Transportation System." Precis 189, Washington, DC.

———. 2001. *Cities on the Move: A World Bank Urban Transport Strategy Review.* Washington, DC: World Bank.

———. 2005. *Global Monitoring Report 2005.* Washington, DC: World Bank.

———. 2007. DEPweb glossary. Development Education Program, World Bank. http://www .worldbank.org/depweb/english/modules/ glossary.html#middle-income.

Yepes, Tito. 2007. "New Estimates of Infrastructure Expenditure Requirements." World Bank, Washington, DC.

Yepes, Tito, Justin Pierce, and Vivien Foster. 2008. "Making Sense of Sub-Saharan Africa's Infrastructure Endowment: A Benchmarking Approach." Working Paper 1, Africa Infrastructure Country Diagnostic, World Bank, Washington, DC.

You, Liang Zhi. 2008. "Irrigation Investment Needs in Sub-Saharan Africa." Background Paper 9, Africa Infrastructure Country Diagnostic, World Bank, Washington, DC.

Chapter 2

Closing Africa's Funding Gap

The cost of addressing Africa's infrastructure needs is estimated at $93 billion, some 15 percent of Africa's GDP—about two-thirds for investment and one-third for maintenance. The burden varies greatly by country type. About half of the capital investment needs are for power, reflecting the particularly large physical deficits in that area.

Existing spending is higher than previously thought. African governments, infrastructure users, the private sector, and external sources together already contribute about $45 billion to directly address the infrastructure needs previously identified. About one-third of this amount is spent by middle-income countries, whereas fragile states barely account for 5 percent of it (about $2 billion in total), mirroring the weakness of their economies and the enormous disparity in terms of financing and institutional capabilities across Sub-Saharan African countries. About two-thirds of the existing spending is domestically sourced, from taxes or user charges, and channeled through public institutions, making the public sector—governments and nonfinancial public enterprises together—the most important financier of capital investment, funding more than half of total investment.

Substantial evidence indicates that a lot more can be done within Africa's existing resource envelope. Inefficiencies of various kinds total about $17 billion a year. If appropriately tackled, fixing these inefficiencies could expand the existing resource envelope by 40 percent.

First, countries and development institutions allocate $3.3 billion in infrastructure spending to areas that appear surplus to the basic infrastructure requirements (as defined in chapter 1 of this volume), which suggests that public and aid flows can be redirected toward areas of greater impact on development.

Second, because only three-fourths of the capital budgets allocated to infrastructure are actually executed, about $2 billion in public investment is being lost.

Third, underspending on infrastructure asset maintenance is another major waste of resources because the cost of rehabilitating infrastructure assets is several times higher than the cumulative cost of sound preventive maintenance. In the road sector alone, addressing undermaintenance can save $1.9 billion a year in rehabilitation, or spending $1 on maintenance can be a savings of about $4 to the economy.

Fourth, Africa's power and water utilities and state-owned telecommunication incumbents waste about $6 billion a year on inefficiencies such as overstaffing, revenue undercollection, and distribution losses.

Fifth, underpricing infrastructure services accounts for $4.7 billion a year in lost revenues.

In all, with existing allocation patterns and even if potential efficiency gains are fully captured, a funding gap of $31 billion a year remains: three-quarters for capital and one-quarter for maintenance. About $23 billion of this gap relates to power and a further $11 billion to water supply and sanitation (WSS). For fragile states, the funding gap is an implausible 25 percent of GDP on average, almost equally divided among energy, water, and transport.

How can Africa close such a sizable funding gap, equivalent to one-third of the estimated infrastructure needs? Additional funds will be required, and in a few countries—mainly the fragile ones—the magnitude of the funding gap calls for considering taking more time to attain targets or using lower-cost technologies. Historical trends do not suggest much prospect of increasing allocations from the public budget: even when fiscal surpluses existed, they did not visibly favor infrastructure. External finance has been buoyant in recent years, and disbursements will likely continue to grow as projects committed move to the implementation stage. In light of today's financial crisis, however, prospects for new commitments do not look good. Private capital flows, in particular, can be expected to decline. Fiscal pressure is growing in donor countries, and to judge by previous crises, foreign aid is likely to slow.

By delaying investment timetables, and assuming that efficiency gains are fully captured, many countries could even attain the infrastructure targets without increasing their spending envelopes. Targeting a high level of service might not always work in the best interest of a country. Lower-cost technologies can permit broadening the portion of the population with access to some level of service.

Closing Africa's funding gap inevitably requires undertaking needed reforms to reduce or eliminate the inefficiencies of the system. Only then can the infrastructure sectors become attractive to a broader array of investors and the countries benefit fully from the additional finance. Otherwise, what is the use of pouring water into a leaking bucket?

Spending Allocated to Address Infrastructure Needs

Africa is spending $45 billion a year to address its infrastructure needs. Existing spending on infrastructure in Africa is higher than previously thought when budget and off-budget spending (including state-owned enterprises and extrabudgetary funds) and external financing (comprising official development assistance [ODA], financiers from outside the Organisation for Economic Co-operation and Development [OECD], and private participation in infrastructure [PPI]) are taken into account. This level of spending is associated with allocations directly targeted to cover the needs identified in chapter 1. In practice, however, some countries spend more on some infrastructure subsectors than the estimated benchmark requirements while incurring funding gaps in other subsectors. This existing spending with potential for reallocation is not counted here but is considered later in this chapter.

The four-way country typology introduced in chapter 1 of this volume—comprising middle-income countries, resource-rich countries, fragile states, and other low-income countries—serves as a basis for summarizing the diversity of infrastructure financing challenges (see box 1.1). Expressed as a percentage of GDP, infrastructure spending is comparable across the different country types, at around 5–6 percent of GDP, with the exception of nonfragile low-income countries, which spend at 10 percent of their GDP. In absolute dollar terms, the middle-income countries spend the most (roughly $16 billion), reflecting their much larger purchasing power. Fragile states, by contrast, account for a tiny amount of overall spending (about $2 billion), reflecting the weakness of their economies (table 2.1).

The public sector, with the lion's share of spending, is by far the most important financier. In the middle-income countries, domestic public sector resources (comprising tax revenues and user charges raised by state-owned

Table 2.1 Spending of Most Important Players Traced to Needs (Annualized Flows)

Country type	Percentage of GDP							$ billions						
	O&M	Capital expenditure						O&M	Capital expenditure					
	Public sector	Public sector	ODA	Non-OECD financiers	Private	Total capital expenditures	Total	Public sector	Public sector	ODA	Non-OECD financiers	Private	Total capital expenditures	Total
Middle income	3.7	1.2	0.1	0.0	0.8	2.1	5.8	10.0	3.1	0.2	0.0	2.3	5.7	15.7
Resource rich	1.1	1.5	0.2	0.7	1.7	4.1	5.2	2.5	3.4	0.5	1.4	3.8	9.1	11.7
Low-income nonfragile	4.0	1.5	2.2	0.5	1.9	6.1	10.1	4.4	1.6	2.5	0.6	2.1	6.7	11.1
Low-income fragile	2.0	0.6	1.0	0.8	1.2	3.6	5.6	0.8	0.2	0.4	0.3	0.5	1.4	2.1
Africa	3.2	1.5	0.6	0.4	1.5	3.9	7.1	20.4	9.4	3.6	2.5	9.4	24.9	45.3

Sources: Africa Infrastructure Country Diagnostic (AICD); Briceño-Garmendia, Smits, and Foster 2008 for public spending; PPIAF 2008 for private flows; Foster and others 2008 for non-OECD financiers.
Note: Aggregate public sector covers general government and nonfinancial enterprises. Figures are extrapolations based on the 24-country sample covered in AICD Phase 1. Totals may not add exactly because of rounding errors. O&M = operation and maintenance; ODA = official development assistance; OECD = Organisation for Economic Co-operation and Development; Private = private participation in infrastructure and household self-finance of sanitation facilities.

enterprises) account for the bulk of spending across all infrastructure subsectors. Across the other country typologies, domestic public sector resources contribute approximately half of total spending. One-third of this aggregate public sector spending (or an equivalent of 1.5 percent of GDP) can be traced exclusively to capital investments.

This level of effort by African governments to develop their infrastructure pales when compared with what East Asian countries have done in recent decades. China, for example, adopted a determined and clear strategy to increase infrastructure investment (publicly and privately financed) as a means of achieving accelerated economic growth. Fixed capital formation in Chinese infrastructure more than doubled between 1998 and 2005. By 2006, only infrastructure investment was higher than 14 percent of GDP, perhaps the highest in the world.

Excluding middle-income countries, external financiers contribute roughly one-half of Africa's total spending on infrastructure. External sources include ODA from the OECD countries, official finance from non-OECD countries (such as China, India, and the Arab funds), and PPI. External finance is primarily for investment—broadly defined to include asset rehabilitation and reconstruction—and in most cases does not provide for O&M. Since the late 1990s, PPI has been the largest source of external finance, followed by ODA and non-OECD finance, which are broadly comparable in magnitude.

Patterns of specialization are clear across the different sources of external finance (figure 2.1). Across sectors, PPI is strongly concentrated on information and communication technology (ICT), which shows the highest commercial returns. ODA has tended to focus on public goods with high social returns, notably roads and water. Much non-OECD finance has gone to energy and, to a lesser extent, to railways, both sectors with strong links to industry and mining. Across countries, PPI has tended to go to middle-income and resource-rich countries, which have the greatest ability to pay for services. Non-OECD finance has shown a preference for resource-rich countries, with a strong pattern linking infrastructure investment and natural resource extraction, and ODA has preferred nonfragile low-income states with limited domestic resources but adequate institutional capacity. The fragile states do not seem to have captured their fair share from any of the external sources.

How Much More Can Be Done within the Existing Resource Envelope?

Africa is losing about $17 billion per year to various inefficiencies in infrastructure operations or spending. In this context, four distinct opportunities can be identified for efficiency gains. First, improving budget execution rates

Figure 2.1 Sources of Financing for Infrastructure Capital Investment, by Sector and Country Type

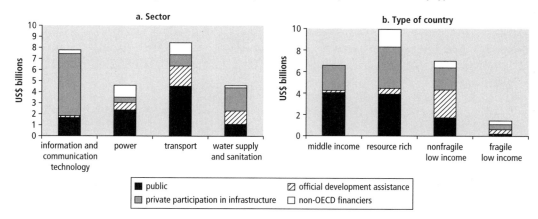

Sources: Africa Infrastructure Country Diagnostic (AICD); Briceño-Garmendia, Smits, and Foster 2008 for public spending; PPIAF 2008 for private flows; Foster and others 2008 for non-OECD financiers.

would increase the potential of fully using resources allocated to public investment. Second, reallocating existing spending toward subsectors in greatest need, therefore with highest economic returns, would allow the existing budget envelope to better cover existing needs. Third, raising user charges closer to cost-recovery levels would provide more efficient price signals and help capture lost revenues. Fourth, reducing operating efficiencies of utilities and other service providers would prevent waste of significant resources, support healthier utilities, and improve service quality.

Raising Capital Budget Execution

African central governments alone allocate, on average, 1.5 percent of GDP, or 6–8 percent of their national budgets, to support the provision of infrastructure (table 2.2). For Africa, this effort translates into about $300 million a year for an average country, which would not take many African countries a long way. To put this figure in perspective, an investment of $100 million can purchase about 100 megawatts of electricity generation, 100,000 new household connections to water and sewerage, or 300 kilometers of a two-lane paved road. It runs well short of covering the investment needs estimated in chapter 1 of this volume (see chapter 1 for details).

As a percentage of GDP, budget spending on infrastructure is comparable across low- and middle-income countries. In absolute terms, however, middle-income countries have a much larger infrastructure budget, with spending per capita at $150–$200, compared with $20–$40 in low-income countries. In other words, per capita budgetary spending on infrastructure by middle-income countries is about five times that of low-income countries.

Overall, spending on transport (notably roads) is the single-largest infrastructure item in general government accounts. It ranges from about half of all general government spending on infrastructure in middle-income countries to 60 percent in low-income countries. Water and sanitation spending is the second-largest category, particularly in the middle-income countries. Energy spending features heavily in resource-rich countries.

From a functional perspective, more than 80 percent of budgetary spending goes to investment. With the exception of middle-income countries and the ICT sector, the central government makes the bulk of public investment, even in sectors in which state-owned enterprises provide most services. Strikingly, relative to central government, nonfinancial public institutions, such as utilities and other service providers, make little infrastructure investment (figure 2.2). The state-owned enterprises are essentially asset administrators. This spending pattern reflects government control of some of the main sources of investment finance, be they royalty payments (in

Table 2.2 Annual Budgetary Flows

Country type	Percentage of GDP						$ billions					
	Electricity	ICT	Irrigation	Transport	WSS	Total	Electricity	ICT	Irrigation	Transport	WSS	Total
Middle income	0.0	0.1	0.1	0.6	0.7	1.5	0.0	0.2	0.2	1.7	1.8	4.0
Resource rich	0.4	0.0	0.1	0.8	0.3	1.6	0.8	0.0	0.3	1.7	0.7	3.6
Low-income nonfragile	0.1	0.1	0.3	0.7	0.3	1.5	0.1	0.1	0.3	0.8	0.4	1.7
Low-income fragile	—	—	—	0.6	0.1	0.7	—	—	—	0.2	0.0	0.3
Africa	0.1	0.1	0.1	0.7	0.5	1.5	0.8	0.4	0.8	4.4	3.1	9.5

Sources: Africa Infrastructure Country Diagnostic; Briceño-Garmendia, Smits, and Foster 2008.
Note: Based on annualized averages for 2001–06. Averages weighted by country GDP. Figures are extrapolations based on the 24-country sample covered in AICD Phase 1. Totals may not add exactly because of rounding errors. ICT = information and communication technology; WSS = water supply and sanitation. — Not available.

resource-rich countries) or external development funds (in low-income countries). It also reflects to some extent the limited capability of state-owned enterprises to fund their capital investment through user fees.

Because central governments are such key players in infrastructure investment, inefficiencies within the public expenditure management systems are particularly detrimental. By way of example, central governments face significant problems in executing their infrastructure budgets. African countries are, on average, unable to spend as much as one-quarter of their capital budgets and one-third of their recurrent budgets in the corresponding fiscal year (table 2.3). The poor timing of project appraisals and late releases of budgeted funds because of procurement problems often prevent the use of resources within the budget cycle. Delays affecting in-year fund releases are also associated with poor project preparation, leading to changes in the terms agreed upon with contractors in the original contract (deadlines, technical specifications, budgets, costs, and so on). In other cases, cash is reallocated to nondiscretionary spending driven by political or social pressures. Historically, the road sector is the worst offender of unused budget allocations, sometimes as much as 60 percent of the budget.

Improving the efficiency of budget execution could make a further $2 billion available for infrastructure spending each year. If the bottlenecks in capital execution could be resolved, countries could on average increase their capital spending by about 30 percent without any increase in current budget allocations. This

Figure 2.2 Split Investment Responsibilities between Governments and Public Enterprises, by Type of Country and Sector

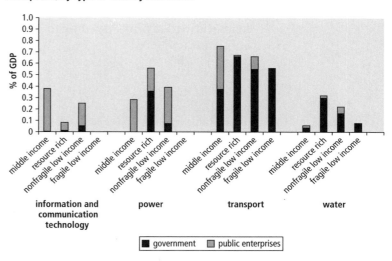

Sources: Africa Infrastructure Country Diagnostic; Briceño-Garmendia, Smits, and Foster 2008.
Note: Based on annualized averages for 2001–06. Averages weighted by country GDP.

finding assumes, arguably a stretch, that budget estimates are realistic and aligned with resources available. Either way, the associated saving suggests that the resolution of these planning, budgeting, and procurement challenges should be central to the region's reform agenda.

Even if budgets are fully spent, concerns exist about whether funds reach their final destinations. A few public expenditure tracking surveys have attempted to trace the share of each budget dollar that results in productive front-line expenditures. Most of the existing case studies concern social sectors, rather than infrastructure, but they illustrate

Table 2.3 Average Budget Variation Ratios for Capital Spending

Country type	Electricity	Communication	Roads	Transport	WSS	Irrigation	Overall infrastructure
Middle income	—	100	75	100	66	60	78
Resource rich	60	37	71	73	43	—	65
Low-income nonfragile	75	64	72	72	72	68	76
Low-income fragile	—	—	—	—	—	—	—
Sub-Saharan Africa	66	72	73	79	66	66	75

Sources: Africa Infrastructure Country Diagnostic; adapted from Briceño-Garmendia, Smits, and Foster 2008.
Note: Budget variation ratio is defined as executed budget divided by allocated budget. Based on annualized averages for 2001–06.
WSS = water supply and sanitation. — Not available.

leakages of public capital spending as high as 92 percent (see Pritchett 1996; Rajkumar and Swaroop 2002; Reinikka and Svensson 2002, 2003; Warlters and Auriol 2005; and references cited therein).

Reallocating Existing Spending to Subsectors in Need

About $3.3 billion a year is spent above the estimated requirements to meet the identified infrastructure needs (see chapter 1 in this volume). This spending—funded by (or through) public budgets—includes domestically raised funds and international aid (OECD and non-OECD sources). Most of this apparent overspending is in telecommunications in countries that have maintained state ownership of the fixed-line incumbent. State ownership not only uses expensive public resources in activities that the already competitive telecommunication market can provide but also forgoes future tax revenues from expanded business activity. To a much lesser extent and only in middle-income countries, the other sector showing potential for reallocation is transport. The overspending in this case is driven by apparent overinvestment in road networks that, as will be seen later, paradoxically coexists with undermaintenance (table 2.4).

How much of that spending in "excess" of infrastructure needs is influenced by political factors? How far are these politics-tainted decisions from economic optimization? How should these resources be reallocated? Estimates of the economic rates of return to key infrastructure interventions can provide some answers.

Across infrastructure interventions in Africa, the rates of return to road maintenance are

the highest, averaging for the continent more than a 100 percent economic rate of return and well above returns for rehabilitation and new construction (table 2.5). By favoring investment over maintenance, African governments have been implicitly equating public investment with productive expenditure, even though not all investment is productive and not all current spending is wasteful.[1] The maintenance of public goods under the jurisdiction of general governments is essential to harness the economic returns to capital and to avoid costly rehabilitation. Highest returns to maintenance are seen in networks already well developed, particularly in middle-income countries and nonfragile low-income countries.

From a sectoral perspective, economic returns to railway investments are the lowest among infrastructure interventions. Railway rehabilitation interventions are justified only for a few higher traffic systems. Investment in water supply and irrigation would bring very solid returns in health benefits and productivity, but returns to power generation need to be compounded by coordinated investment in transmission and distribution networks.

Improving Cost Recovery from User Charges

Two-thirds of African power and water utilities apply tariffs that comfortably cover operating costs, but only one-fifth of those utilities set tariffs high enough to recover full capital costs. Achieving recovery of only operating costs across all African power and water utilities would raise $2.5 billion a year (0.4 percent of the region's GDP). Revising tariffs to make them equal to long-term marginal costs, and thereby enabling all African power and water

Table 2.4 Existing Disbursements above Those Directed to Infrastructure Needs, Annualized Flows

Country type	Percentage of GDP						$ billions					
	Electricity	ICT	Irrigation	Transport	WSS	Total	Electricity	ICT	Irrigation	Transport	WSS	Total
Middle income	—	1.4	—	0.0	0.1	1.5	—	3.7	—	0.0	0.3	4.1
Resource rich	—	—	0.0	0.4	—	0.4	—	—	0.0	0.8	—	0.8
Low-income nonfragile	—	0.1	—	0.2	—	0.3	—	0.1	—	0.3	—	0.4
Low-income fragile	—	—	—	—	—	—	—	—	—	—	—	—
Africa	—	0.5	—	—	—	0.5	—	3.3	—	—	—	3.3

Source: Africa Infrastructure Country Diagnostic.
Note: Based on annualized averages for 2001–06. Averages weighted by country GDP. Figures are extrapolations based on the 24-country sample covered in AICD Phase 1. Totals for Africa differ from the sum of the individual groups because reallocation is allowed only within groups. ICT = information communication and technology; WSS = water supply and sanitation. — Not available.

Table 2.5 Economic Rates of Return for Key Infrastructure

Country type	Railway rehabilitation	Irrigation	Road rehabilitation	Road upgrades	Road maintenance	Generation	Water
Middle income	18.5	19.3	45.4	19.8	143.0	13.6	26.8
Resource rich	10.8	24.2	16.2	17.4	114.5	20.2	37.0
Low-income nonfragile	6.2	17.2	17.6	12.8	125.7	14.3	7.7
Low-income fragile	2.5	—	9.2	12.0	67.6	24.7	36.9
Sub-Saharan Africa	5.1	22.2	24.2	17.0	138.8	18.9	23.3

Source: Africa Infrastructure Country Diagnostic.
Note: — Not available.

utilities to recover capital costs also, would increase the potential for efficiency gains to $4.2 billion a year (0.7 percent of the region's GDP; table 2.6). Although underpricing is equally prevalent in power and water utilities, the value of the lost GDP revenues is slightly higher for power (at 0.4 percent of GDP) than for water (at 0.3 percent).

Raising tariffs to cost-recovery levels is evidently easier said than done and entails a host of social and political challenges. Chapter 3 in this volume examines these issues in greater depth and provides a realistic appraisal of the feasibility of improving cost recovery for utility services in Africa.

In the road sector, a widespread movement exists for using fuel levies and taxes as indirect user charges (see chapter 10 in this volume). For this system to work, fuel levies need to be set high enough to cover the maintenance costs imposed by the use of the road network. Comparing existing fuel levies with the levels needed to secure road maintenance makes it possible to estimate the underpricing in roads.

Underpricing user charges for roads costs the region some $0.6 billion a year (0.1 percent of GDP).

Reducing the Operating Inefficiencies of Utilities

African state-owned enterprises are characterized by low investment and high operating inefficiency. State-owned enterprises account for between 80 percent (energy) and 40 percent (water) of total public expenditures (general government and nonfinancial enterprises). Despite their large resource base, they invest comparatively little—on average, an equivalent of between 15 percent (energy) and 18 percent (water) of the government resource envelope. As a result, governments are typically required to step in to assume most of the investment responsibilities of state-owned enterprises, which are relegated to undertaking daily operation and maintenance. In many cases, investment is unaffordable because of the significant underpricing of services, which barely allows the recovery of operating costs.

Table 2.6 Potential Gains from Increased Cost Recovery

Country type	Percentage of GDP						$ billions annually					
	Electricity	ICT	Irrigation	Transport	WSS	Total	Electricity	ICT	Irrigation	Transport	WSS	Total
Middle income	0.0	—	—	0.0	0.4	0.4	0.0	—	—	0.0	1.0	1.0
Resource rich	0.8	—	—	0.1	0.1	0.9	1.7	—	—	0.2	0.2	2.0
Low-income nonfragile	0.8	—	—	0.2	0.3	1.1	0.8	—	—	0.2	0.3	1.3
Low-income fragile	0.0	—	—	0.1	0.6	0.7	0.0	—	—	0.0	0.2	0.3
Africa	0.4	—	—	0.1	0.3	0.7	2.3	—	—	0.6	1.8	4.7

Source: Africa Infrastructure Country Diagnostic.
Note: Based on annualized averages for 2001–06. Averages weighted by country GDP. Figures are extrapolations based on the 24-country sample covered in AICD Phase 1. Totals may not add exactly because of rounding errors. ICT = information and communication technology; WSS = water supply and sanitation. — Not available.

In addition, most state-owned enterprises operate at arm's length from the central government, failing in practice to meet criteria for sound commercial management. When these enterprises run into financial difficulties, the general government—as the main stakeholder—acts as the lender of last resort, absorbing debts and assuming by default the financial, political, regulatory, and mismanagement risks. Lumpy capitalizations and debt swaps that cover the cumulative cost of operational inefficiencies are frequent events in the African utility sector, which can potentially create a moral hazard that would perpetuate operational inefficiencies if proactive reforms are not undertaken.

This section considers four types of operational inefficiencies and estimates their potential monetary value. First, state-owned enterprises may retain more employees than is strictly necessary to discharge their functions, often because of political pressure to provide jobs for members of certain interest groups. This issue affects state-owned enterprises across the board, including those in ICT, power, and water. Second, utilities incur substantial losses on their power and water distribution networks. Both poor network maintenance, which leads to physical leakage, and poor network management, which leads to clandestine connections and various forms of theft, contribute to these losses. Third, power and water utilities face serious problems in collecting their bills, largely a result of the social and political impediments to disconnecting services, which lead to a nonpayment culture.

Fourth, the undermaintenance of infrastructure assets is widespread but represents a false economy because the rehabilitation of assets is usually much more costly in present-value terms than the preventive maintenance to avoid such asset deterioration.

Overemployment. Overemployment reaches $1.5 billion a year (0.24 percent of GDP; table 2.7). Most overemployment was found in telecommunication utilities in countries that have retained state ownership of their fixed-line incumbent. In Sub-Saharan Africa, such utilities achieve, on average, 94 connections per employee, compared to developing-country benchmarks of 420 connections per employee, an overemployment ratio of 600 percent. Similarly, African power and water utilities have overemployment ratios of 88 percent and 24 percent, respectively, over non-African developing-country benchmarks. These striking results for labor inefficiencies underscore the importance of strengthening external governance mechanisms that can impose discipline on the behavior of state-owned enterprises. Overemployment partially explains why in African countries with a publicly owned operator, the share of spending allocated to capital spending frequently remains below 25 percent of total spending despite pressing investment needs.

Distribution Losses. Distribution losses amount to $1.8 billion a year (0.3 percent of GDP). African power utilities typically lose 23 percent of their energy in distribution losses, more than

Table 2.7 Potential Gains from Greater Operational Efficiency

Operational inefficiencies	Percentage of GDP						$ billions annually					
	Electricity	ICT	Irrigation	Transport (roads)	WSS	Total	Electricity	ICT	Irrigation	Transport (roads)	WSS	Total
Losses	0.2	—	—	—	0.1	0.3	1.3		—	—	0.5	1.8
Undercollection	0.3	—	—	0.1	0.1	0.5	1.9		—	0.5	0.5	2.9
Labor inefficiencies	0.0	0.2	—	—	—	0.2	0.3	1.3	—	—	0.0	1.5
Undermaintenance	—	—	—	0.2	—	0.2			—	1.4	—	1.4
Total	0.5	0.2	—	0.3	0.2	1.2	3.4	1.3	—	1.9	1.0	7.5

Source: Africa Infrastructure Country Diagnostic.
Note: Based on annualized averages for 2001–06. Averages weighted by country GDP. Figures are extrapolations based on the 24-country sample covered in AICD Phase 1. Totals may not add exactly because of rounding errors. ICT = information and communication technology; WSS = water supply and sanitation. — Not available.

twice the best practice of 10 percent. Similarly, African water utilities typically lose 35 percent of their water in distribution losses, nearly twice the 20 percent benchmark. The financial value of those distribution losses is much higher for power at $1.3 billion per year than for water at $0.5 billion per year.

Undercollection of Bills. The undercollection of bills amounts to $2.9 billion a year (0.5 percent of GDP). African power and water utilities manage to collect about 90 percent of the bills owed to them by their customers, short of a best practice of 100 percent. Again, although water utilities perform worse than power utilities at the enterprise level, the financial value of the losses is much greater for power. In many African countries, public institutions are among the worst offenders in failing to pay for utility services. The undercollection of fuel levies for road sector maintenance is also an issue, although the absolute values for this inefficiency are smaller than expected.

Undermaintenance. Deferring maintenance expenditures is perhaps the most perverse inefficiency and the hardest to quantify. Given the precarious financing position of the infrastructure sectors, cutting back on maintenance is often the only way to make ends meet, but spending too little on maintenance is a false economy. Rehabilitating or replacing poorly maintained assets is much more costly than keeping them up with sound preventive maintenance. Moreover, consumers end up suffering as service quality gradually declines. Indeed, not providing maintenance and replacement investment is the most costly way of financing today's operations.

Figure 2.3 Rehabilitation Backlog

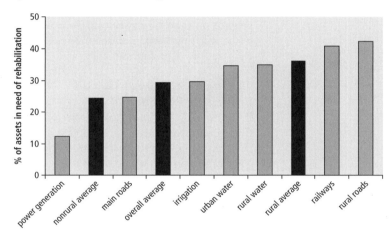

Source: Briceño-Garmendia, Smits, and Foster 2008.

On average, 30 percent of African infrastructure assets need rehabilitation (figure 2.3). Although documenting the exact magnitude of undermaintenance is difficult, the share of today's assets in need of rehabilitation provides a good indicator of past neglect. In general, the state of rural infrastructure is substantially worse than the rest, with 35 percent of assets in need of rehabilitation, compared with 25 percent elsewhere and 40 percent of roads. Wide differences exist across countries. In the best cases (Burkina Faso and South Africa), little more than 10 percent of assets need rehabilitation, and in the worst cases (the Democratic Republic of Congo, Nigeria, Rwanda, and Uganda), more than 40 percent do.

For roads alone, undermaintenance over time leads to additional capital spending of $1.4 billion a year (0.2 percent of GDP).

Although undermaintenance affects all infrastructure sectors, only for roads were sufficient data available to quantify the cost. Every $1 that goes unspent on road maintenance leads to a $4 liability to the economy (Nogales 2009). Therefore, capital spending on roads is much higher than it would otherwise need to be—with continual reconstructing of the same assets rather than creating new ones. The vast majority of Sub-Saharan African countries do not cover road maintenance costs; more than half of the countries have shortfalls of over 40 percent of maintenance needs. However, institutions seem to have an important role to play. Countries with well-designed second-generation road funds seem to do much better in meeting their maintenance needs (see chapter 10 in this volume).

Closing the Efficiency Gap by Promoting Reforms

In sum, $17.4 billion could be captured through improvements in infrastructure management and institutions. The largest potential gains of $7.5 billion a year come from addressing operating inefficiencies. Some of the most pressing and most rewarding would be resolving undermaintenance of roads and increasing the efficiency of the power utilities. The second-largest potential gains of $3.3 billion a year come from improving the allocation of existing resources across sectors, essentially transferring resources from areas that seem to be overfunded to areas that are clearly underfunded. The next-largest potential gain of $4.7 billion a year would come from raising user charges for infrastructure services. Again, better pricing of power produces the greatest dividends. Finally, raising budget execution ratios through improvements in the public expenditure framework could capture an additional $2 billion a year.

Addressing some of the operational deficiencies may require substantial investments in network rehabilitation or system upgrades. Reallocating resources, raising user charges, and reducing overemployment all carry significant political costs, which complicate their implementation. Therefore, expecting that all these efficiency gains could be fully captured is unrealistic. Given the magnitude of the needs, capturing only half of them would much improve the financing and the perspectives for new financing in the African infrastructure sectors.

Even if all these efficiency gains could be fully realized, a sizable funding gap would remain. Chapter 1 of this volume identified spending requirements of $93 billion a year to address Africa's infrastructure needs. Setting these requirements against the $45 billion of existing spending directly traced to these needs and the $17 billion of potential efficiency gains still leaves an annual infrastructure funding gap of $31 billion (table 2.8).

Table 2.8 Finding Resources: The Efficiency Gap and the Funding Gap
$ billions annually

Item	Electricity	ICT	Irrigation	Transport	WSS	Cross-sector gain	Total
Infrastructure spending needs	(40.8)	(9.0)	(3.4)	(18.2)	(21.9)	n.a.	(93.3)
Existing spending	11.6	9.0	0.9	16.2	7.6	n.a.	45.3
Efficiency gap	6.0	1.3	0.1	3.8	2.9	3.3	17.4
Gain from raising capital execution	0.2	0.0	0.1	1.3	0.2	n.a.	1.9
Gain from eliminating operational inefficiencies	3.4	1.2	—	1.9	1.0	n.a.	7.5
Gain from tariff cost recovery	2.3	—	—	0.6	1.8	n.a.	4.7
Potential for reallocation	n.a.	n.a.	n.a.	n.a.	n.a.	3.3	3.3
Funding gap	(23.2)	1.3	(2.4)	1.9	(11.4)	3.3	(30.6)

Source: Briceño-Garmendia, Smits, and Foster 2008.
Note: ICT = information and communication technology; n.a. = not applicable; — = not available; WSS = water supply and sanitation. Parentheses indicate negative values.

Annual Funding Gap

Existing spending and potential efficiency gains can be netted from estimated spending needs to gauge the extent of the shortfall. The result is that Africa still faces an annual funding gap of about $31 billion (5.1 percent of GDP). Over 70 percent of the infrastructure funding gap is for energy, representing a shortfall of $23 billion a year. The rest of the gap is related to WSS, where about an additional $11 billion is needed annually to meet the Millennium Development Goals (MDGs), and to a lesser extent irrigation, which accounts for roughly $2 billion annually of the funding gap. No funding gap was found for ICT and transport, where, on the contrary, close to $1 billion and $2 billion a year, respectively, could be available if efficiencies were captured within each of these sectors (table 2.9).

About 60 percent of the funding gap relates to low-income fragile and nonfragile countries combined. The resource-rich countries generate one-fourth of the funding gap, and a further 18 percent of the gap is attributable to middle-income countries. As a percentage of GDP, the burden of the shortfall for resource-rich and middle-income countries is smallest at 2–4 percent of GDP. Nonfragile low-income countries face a shortfall of 9 percent of GDP, and fragile states face an insurmountable 25 percent. By far, the largest funding gaps relative to GDP are for energy and water in fragile states.

Although the infrastructure funding gap is primarily for capital investment, a shortfall also exists for O&M. About two-thirds of the infrastructure funding gap relates to shortfalls in capital investment. All together, Africa needs to increase infrastructure capital investment by 5 percent of its GDP (approximately $28 billion annually); nonfragile low-income countries need to invest an additional 8 percent, and fragile states an additional 18 percent. The remainder of the infrastructure funding gap relates to O&M: low-income countries cover at most two-thirds of their O&M needs.

Closing the $31 billion infrastructure funding gap is partly about raising additional funds but also about possibly taking more time to attain targets or using lower-cost technologies. The remainder of this chapter evaluates the potential for raising additional finance and very generally explores policy adjustments to reduce the price tag and the burden of the financial gap.

How Much Additional Finance Can Be Raised?

Only a limited number of financing sources are available, and the current global financial crisis is likely to affect them all adversely. First, domestic public finance is the largest source of funding today, but it presents little scope for an increase, except possibly in countries enjoying natural resource windfalls. Second, ODA to African infrastructure has grown substantially

Table 2.9 Funding Gaps, by Sector and Country Group

| Country type | Percentage of GDP | | | | | | | $ billions annually | | | | | | |
	Electricity	ICT	Irrigation	Transport	WSS	Potential for reallocation	Total	Electricity	ICT	Irrigation	Transport	WSS	Potential for reallocation	Total
Middle income	3.9	(0.3)	0.0	(0.1)	0.0	(1.5)	2.0	10.7	(0.9)	0.1	(0.3)	0.0	(4.1)	5.5
Resource rich	2.0	0.2	0.8	(0.6)	1.7	(0.4)	3.7	4.5	0.5	1.8	(1.4)	3.7	(0.8)	8.2
Low-income nonfragile	4.2	(0.2)	0.6	(0.4)	4.7	(0.3)	8.6	4.7	(0.2)	0.7	(0.5)	5.2	(0.4)	9.5
Low-income fragile	7.1	1.9	0.1	5.3	10.2	0.0	24.6	2.7	0.7	0.0	2.0	3.9	0.0	9.4
Africa	3.6	(0.2)	0.4	(0.3)	1.8	(0.5)	4.8	23.2	(1.3)	2.4	(1.9)	11.4	(3.3)	30.6

Source: Africa Infrastructure Country Diagnostic.
Note: Based on annualized averages for 2001–06. Averages weighted by country GDP. Figures are extrapolations based on the 24-country sample covered in AICD Phase 1. Totals do not add because efficiency gains cannot be carried across country groups. ICT = information and communication technology; WSS = water supply and sanitation.

in recent years in line with political pledges, but this assistance could slow down if countercyclical assistance is put in place. Third, non-OECD finance has been rising steeply, but its future is now unclear. Fourth, private participation, also very buoyant during Africa's recent growth upswing, will be particularly vulnerable to the downturn in global markets. Finally, local capital markets have so far contributed little to infrastructure finance outside South Africa, but they could eventually become more important in some of the region's larger economies.

Little Scope for Raising More Domestic Finance

A key question is the extent to which countries may be willing to allocate additional fiscal resources to infrastructure. In the run-up to the current financial crisis, the fiscal situation in Sub-Saharan Africa was favorable. Rapid economic growth averaging 4 percent a year from 2001 to 2005 translated into increased domestic fiscal revenues of just over 3 percent of GDP on average. In resource-rich countries, burgeoning resource royalties added 7.7 percent of GDP to the public budget. In low-income countries, substantial debt relief increased external grants by almost 2 percent of GDP.

To what extent were the additional resources available during the recent growth surge allocated to infrastructure? The answer is surprisingly little (table 2.10). The most extreme case is that of the resource-rich countries, particularly Nigeria. Huge debt repayments more than fully absorbed the fiscal windfalls in these countries. As a result, budgetary spending actually contracted by 3.7 percent of GDP,

with infrastructure investment bearing much of that, falling by almost 1.5 percent of GDP. In middle-income countries, budgetary spending increased by almost 4.1 percent of GDP, but the effect on infrastructure spending was almost negligible, and the additional resources went primarily to current social sector spending. Only in the low-income countries did the overall increases in budgetary expenditure have some effect on infrastructure spending. Even there, however, the effect was fairly modest and confined to capital spending. The nonfragile low-income countries have allocated 30 percent of the budgetary increase to infrastructure investments. The fragile states, despite seeing their overall budgetary expenditures increase by about 3.9 percent of GDP, have allocated only 6 percent of the increase to infrastructure.

Compared with other developing regions, public financing capabilities in Sub-Saharan Africa are characterized by weak tax revenue collection. Domestic revenue generation around 23 percent of GDP trails averages for other developing countries and is lowest for low-income countries (less than 15 percent of GDP a year). Despite the high growth rates in the last decade, domestically raised revenues grew by less than 1.2 percent of GDP. This finding suggests that increasing domestic revenues above what is currently raised would require undertaking challenging institutional reforms to increase the effectiveness of revenue collection and broaden the tax base. Without such reforms, domestic revenue generation will remain weak.

The borrowing capacity from domestic and external sources is also limited. Domestic

Table 2.10 Net Change in Central Government Budgets, by Economic Use, 1995–2004
percentage of GDP

Use	Sub-Saharan Africa	Middle income	Resource rich	Low-income nonfragile	Low-income fragile
Net expenditure budget	1.89	4.08	(3.73)	1.69	3.85
Current infrastructure spending as a share of expenditures	0.00	0.02	0.03	0.00	0.09
Capital infrastructure spending as a share of expenditures	(0.14)	0.04	(1.46)	0.54	0.22

Source: Africa Infrastructure Country Diagnostic, adapted from Briceño-Garmendia, Smits, and Foster 2008.
Note: Based on annualized averages for 2001–06. Averages weighted by country GDP. Totals are extrapolations based on the 24-country sample as covered in AICD Phase 1.

borrowing is often very expensive, with interest rates far exceeding those on concessional external loans. Particularly for the poorest countries, the scarcity of private domestic savings means that public domestic borrowing tends to precipitate sharp increases in interest rates, building up a vicious circle. For many Sub-Saharan countries, the ratios of debt service to GDP are more than 6 percent.

The global financial crisis can be expected to reduce fiscal receipts because of lower revenues from taxes, royalties, and user charges. Africa is not exempt from its impact. Growth projections for the coming years have been revised downward from 5.1 to 3.5 percent, which will reduce tax revenues and likely depress the demand and willingness to pay for infrastructure services. Commodity prices have fallen to levels of the early 2000s. The effect on royalty revenues, however, will depend on the saving regime in each country. A number of oil producers have been saving royalty revenues in excess of $60 a barrel, so the current downturn will affect savings accounts more than budgets. Overall, this adverse situation created by the global financial crisis will put substantial pressure on public sector budgets. In addition, many African countries are devaluing their currency, reducing the purchasing power of domestic resources.

Based on recent global experience, fiscal adjustment episodes tend to fall disproportionately on public investment—and infrastructure in particular.[2] Experience from earlier crises in East Asia and Latin America indicates that infrastructure spending is particularly vulnerable to budget cutbacks during crisis periods. Based on averages for eight Latin American countries, cuts in infrastructure investment amounted to about 40 percent of the observed fiscal adjustment between the early 1980s and late 1990s (Calderón and Servén 2004). This reduction was remarkable because public infrastructure investment already represented less than 25 percent of overall public investment in Latin American countries. These infrastructure investment cuts were later identified as the underlying problem holding back economic growth in the whole region during the 2000s (box 2.1). Similar patterns were observed in East Asia during the financial crisis of the mid-1990s. For example, Indonesia's total public investment in infrastructure dropped from 6–7 percent of GDP in 1995–97 to 2 percent in 2000. Given recent spending patterns, every reason exists to expect that, in Africa, changes in the overall budget envelope will affect infrastructure investment in a similar pro-cyclical manner.

Official Development Assistance—Sustaining the Scale-Up

For most of the 1990s and early 2000s, ODA to infrastructure in Sub-Saharan Africa remained steady at a meager $2 billion a year. The launch of the Commission for Africa Report in 2004 was followed by the Group of Eight Gleneagles

---

BOX 2.1

Does Deficit-Financed Public Investment in Infrastructure Pay for Itself?

Underinvestment in infrastructure, health, and education during much of the 1990s has ignited a lively debate on whether some countries could tolerate a larger public deficit if the additional resources were invested in growth-enhancing sectors. The analysis undertaken by the International Monetary Fund does not explicitly take into account the potential link between public investment and growth—only its short-term costs. Nevertheless, running a short-term deficit now may help produce the growth that will balance the budget later.

By incorporating this long-run growth effect into the standard models used to assess fiscal sustainability, one can see whether taking a longer-term perspective would lead to a more favorable stance for deficit-financed infrastructure. The results turn out to be very country specific, underscoring the difficulty of generalizing in this area.

In Uganda, investment in infrastructure leads to higher output, but also—because of its relatively low productivity—worsens the debt ratio. A better way to finance infrastructure may be to improve the existing capital stock by prioritizing O&M expenditure over new investments. Although increased public expenditure on health and education also leads to higher output, the effect is not as large as for infrastructure.

In Senegal, by contrast, public investment in infrastructure does not seem to be as effective in boosting growth. Both O&M spending on infrastructure and public investment in other sectors such as health and education seem to have a stronger effect on growth. However, no matter how spending is allocated, it seems to worsen the debt-to-GDP ratio, reflecting the low productivity of public expenditure in this case.

Source: Estache and Muñoz 2008.

Summit in July 2005, where the Infrastructure Consortium for Africa was created to focus on scaling up donor finance to meet Africa's infrastructure needs. The main bilateral and multilateral donors committed to double by 2010 the (already higher) 2004 flows to reach $10 billion a year, about 1.6 percent of Africa's GDP at that time. Donors have so far lived up to their promises, and ODA flows to African infrastructure almost doubled from $4.1 billion in 2004 to $8.1 billion in 2007. Close to three-quarters of ODA comes from multilateral donors (African Development Bank, European Community, and International Development Association [IDA]), while Japan and the United States drive the doubling of bilateral commitments.

A significant lag occurs between ODA commitments and their disbursement, suggesting that disbursements should continue to increase in the coming years. The commitments just reported are significantly higher than the estimated ODA disbursements of $3.8 billion (table 2.11). This gap reflects the normal lags associated with project implementation. Because ODA is channeled through the government budget, the execution of funds faces some of the same problems affecting domestically financed public investment, including procurement delays and low country capacity to execute funds. Divergences between donor and country financial systems, as well as unpredictability in the release of funds, may further retard the disbursement of donor resources. Bearing all this in mind, if all commitments up to 2007 are fully honored, ODA disbursements could be expected to rise significantly (IMF 2009; World Economic Outlook 2008).

ODA commitments were also set to increase further before the crisis, but prospects no longer look so good. The three multilateral agencies—the African Development Bank, the European Commission, and the World Bank—secured record replenishments for their concessional funding windows for the three to four years beginning in 2008. In principle, funding allocations to African infrastructure totaling $5.2 billion a year could come from the multilateral agencies alone in the near future. In practice, however, the crisis may divert multilateral resources from infrastructure projects and toward emergency fiscal support. Bilateral support, based on annual budget determinations, may be more sensitive to the fiscal squeeze in OECD countries, and some decline can be anticipated. Historical trends suggest that ODA has tended to be pro-cyclical rather than countercyclical (IMF 2009; ODI 2009; UBS Investment Research 2008; World Economic Outlook 2008; and references cited therein).

Non-OECD Financiers—Will Growth Continue?

Non-OECD countries financed about $2.6 billion of African infrastructure annually between 2001 and 2006 (table 2.12).[3] This sum is not far short of the volumes from ODA; however, the focus of the finance is very different. Non-OECD financiers have been active primarily in oil-exporting countries (Angola, Nigeria, and Sudan). The bulk of their resources have gone to power and to transport. In the power sector, primarily hydroelectric schemes received $1 billion per year, and in the transport sector, railways received nearly $1 billion a year. For electricity, that amounts to 0.17 percent

Table 2.11 Annualized ODA Investment Flows

Country type	Percentage of GDP						$ billions					
	Electricity	ICT	Irrigation	Transport	WSS	Total	Electricity	ICT	Irrigation	Transport	WSS	Total
Middle income	0.01	0.00	0.00	0.03	0.04	0.08	0.03	0.01	0.00	0.09	0.10	0.23
Resource rich	0.03	0.01	0.00	0.11	0.11	0.25	0.08	0.01	0.00	0.23	0.24	0.56
Low-income nonfragile	0.50	0.03	0.00	1.12	0.71	2.36	0.55	0.04	0.00	1.24	0.78	2.61
Low-income fragile	0.10	0.01	0.00	0.64	0.29	1.04	0.04	0.00	0.00	0.23	0.10	0.38
Africa	0.11	0.01	0.00	0.28	0.19	0.59	0.69	0.06	0.00	1.80	1.23	3.77

Source: Africa Infrastructure Country Diagnostic.
Note: Based on annualized averages for 2001–06. Averages weighted by country GDP. Figures are extrapolations based on the 24-country sample covered in AICD Phase 1. Totals may not add exactly because of rounding errors. ICT = information and communication technology; WSS = water supply and sanitation.

Table 2.12 Historic Annualized Investment Flows from China, India, and Arab Countries

Country type	Percentage of GDP						$ billions					
	Electricity	ICT	Irrigation	Transport	WSS	Total	Electricity	ICT	Irrigation	Transport	WSS	Total
Middle income	0.00	0.01	0.00	0.01	0.00	0.02	0.00	0.02	0.00	0.02	0.01	0.05
Resource rich	0.33	0.06	0.00	0.34	0.04	0.76	0.74	0.13	0.00	0.75	0.08	1.69
Low-income nonfragile	0.12	0.15	0.00	0.22	0.05	0.54	0.13	0.17	0.00	0.24	0.05	0.59
Low-income fragile	0.58	0.07	0.00	0.11	0.06	0.82	0.21	0.03	0.00	0.04	0.02	0.30
Africa	0.17	0.05	0.00	0.16	0.03	0.41	1.08	0.34	0.00	1.06	0.16	2.64

Source: Africa Infrastructure Country Diagnostic, adapted from Foster and others 2008.
Note: Based on annualized averages for 2001–06. Averages weighted by country GDP. Figures are extrapolations based on the 24-country sample covered in AICD Phase 1. Totals may not add exactly because of rounding errors. ICT = information and communication technology; WSS = water supply and sanitation.

of African GDP, significantly larger than the 0.11 percent coming from ODA.

China's official economic assistance quadrupled between 2001 and 2005, reaching more than 35 Sub-Saharan countries. Most of the inflows have gone to resource-rich countries, in some cases making use of barter arrangements under the "Angola mode."[4] This type of South-South cooperation builds on economic complementarities between China and Africa. China takes a strategic interest in Africa's natural resource sector, while Africa harnesses China's strengths in construction to develop its economic infrastructure.

India has become a significant financier of energy projects in Africa. India's financial assistance focused initially on export credits to facilitate the purchase of Indian goods. However, India has signaled a bold commitment to support big infrastructure projects, predominantly in energy, with up to $1 billion in Nigeria (including a 9-million-ton per year refinery, a 200-megawatt power plant, and a 1,000-kilometer cross-country railway) and close to $100 million a year in Sudan (for a 700-kilometer oil pipeline from Khartoum to Port Sudan and four 125-kilowatt power plants).

The Gulf States, through their various development agencies, have been funding African infrastructure for some time. Infrastructure projects of a smaller scale than those funded by the Chinese and Indian governments characterize their portfolio, with strong support to such countries as Mali, Mauritania, Senegal, and Sudan. Resources from the Gulf States have been distributed almost equally among water, roads, and small energy projects.

For the three major sources of external finance, significant complementarity exists, despite some overlap. PPI seeks the most commercially lucrative opportunities in telecommunications. Non-OECD financiers focus on productive infrastructure (primarily power generation and railroads). Traditional ODA focuses on financing public goods (such as roads and water supply) and plays a broader role in power system development and electrification.

A similar pattern of specialization emerges geographically, with different countries relying to differing degrees on the various sources of finance. The countries most heavily reliant on PPI are Kenya and Nigeria, supplemented by ODA in Kenya and by Chinese financing in Nigeria. The countries that rely predominantly on non-OECD financiers are often oil producers (Angola, Gabon, Guinea, Mauritania, and Sudan). Most of the remaining countries rely primarily on traditional ODA (Burundi, Mali, Niger, Rwanda, and Tanzania). Other countries (the Democratic Republic of Congo and Guinea) draw on a mixture of OECD and non-OECD sources.

The implementation process for ODA and non-OECD finance is completely different. A key difference between Chinese finance and ODA is that whereas the latter is channeled through the government budget, the former tends to be executed directly by China, often with associated imports of human resources. Although this approach raises significant challenges, it does at least offer the possibility of circumventing some of the capital budget execution problems typically associated with public investment.

Non-OECD finance also raises concerns about sustainability. The non-OECD financiers from China, India, and the Gulf States follow sectors, countries, and circumstances aligned with their national business interests. They offer realistic financing options for power and transport and for postconflict countries with natural resources. However, nongovernmental organizations are voicing concerns about the associated social and environmental standards. Non-OECD financiers also provide investment finance without associated support on the operational, institutional, and policy sides, raising questions about the sustainability of the new assets.

How the current economic downturn will affect non-OECD finance is difficult to predict because of the relatively recent nature of these capital inflows. Coming from fiscal and royalty resources in their countries of origin, they will likely suffer from budgetary cutbacks. The downturn in global commodity prices may also affect the motivation for some of the Chinese infrastructure finance linked to natural resource development.

Private Investors—over the Hill

Since the late 1990s, private investment flows to Sub-Saharan African infrastructure tripled, increasing from about $3 billion in 1997 to $9.4 billion in 2006/07. That is about 1.5 percent of regional GDP for all sectors, more than recent ODA flows (0.6 percent of GDP, or $3.7 billion a year) but still less than half of general government spending (table 2.13).

Close to two-thirds of cumulative private commitments between 1990 and 2006 were in ICT-related projects (Leigland and Butterfield 2006). Power was second. Socially challenging sectors, such as WSS, attracted almost no private activity. The same is true of longer-term and higher-risk projects. Through 2004, greenfield and small projects accounted for 70 percent of all PPI, while concessions and divestitures of incumbent utilities accounted for less than 10 percent. Greenfield transactions, with no long-term risks and little or no investment, are much more prominent than in other regions, and they tend to be small.

Africa's resource-rich countries have been capturing the largest volume of private participation. Relative to their GDP, Africa's middle-income countries are not doing that well, while low-income countries—even fragile states—are capturing flows worth well over 1 percent of GDP.

Since the mid-1990s, a shift has occurred toward projects with longer horizons. Concessions and existing assets increased to 20 percent of the private partnerships in infrastructure. Sectors other than ICT have increased; the most important recorded transactions are in transport, such as the concessions in Sudan for the Juba Port ($30 million) and Uganda's Rift Valley railways ($400 million concession). Moreover, larger greenfield power projects, beyond concessions and management contracts, are starting to emerge.

Private capital flows, in particular, are likely to be affected by the global financial crisis. In the aftermath of the Asian financial crisis, private participation in developing countries fell by about one-half over a period of five years, following its peak in 1997. Existing transactions are also coming under stress as they encounter difficulties refinancing short- and medium-term debt.

Table 2.13 Annual Private Participation Investment Flows

Country type	Percentage of GDP						$ billions					
	Electricity	ICT	Irrigation	Transport	WSS	Total	Electricity	ICT	Irrigation	Transport	WSS	Total
Middle income	0.00	0.60	—	0.16	0.00	0.76	0.01	1.63	—	0.44	0.00	2.08
Resource rich	0.13	1.13	—	0.21	0.00	1.47	0.28	2.52	—	0.47	0.01	3.28
Low-income nonfragile	0.15	1.19	—	0.12	0.00	1.46	0.16	1.32	—	0.13	0.00	1.61
Low-income fragile	0.02	0.72	—	0.04	0.00	0.78	0.01	0.26	—	0.01	0.00	0.28
Africa	0.07	0.89	—	0.16	0.00	1.12	0.46	5.72	—	1.05	0.01	7.24

Source: Adapted from PPIAF 2008.
Note: Based on annualized averages for 2001–06. Averages weighted by country GDP. Figures are extrapolations based on the 24-country sample covered in AICD Phase 1. Totals may not add exactly because of rounding errors. ICT = information and communication technology; WSS = water supply and sanitation. — Not available.

Local Sources of Finance—a Possibility in the Medium Term

Local capital markets are a major source of infrastructure finance in South Africa, but not yet elsewhere. Local infrastructure finance consists primarily of commercial bank lending, some corporate bond and stock exchange issues, and a nascent entry of institutional investors. Because the scale of local financing in South Africa and its advanced state of evolution are so far ahead of those elsewhere, attention here focuses on prospects elsewhere in the region.

Outside South Africa, the stock of outstanding local infrastructure finance amounts to $13.5 billion (table 2.14). This figure comprises transport, the first-ranking sector of all local infrastructure financing, attracting 47 percent of the total, followed by ICT at 32 percent.[5]

The low-income nonfragile countries were the destination for 55 percent of all local infrastructure financing identified in this study. The two low-income fragile countries (Côte d'Ivoire and the Democratic Republic of Congo) attracted just 3.5 percent ($474 million), nearly three-quarters of it in bank financing and the remainder in equity issues by companies in Côte d'Ivoire. For the resource-rich countries, the $4.9 billion in local infrastructure financing was a nearly equal mix of bank and equity financing. For the three middle-income countries, more than half of the $544 million in

local financing was in corporate bonds, all to finance transport.

Only 10 percent of outstanding bank loans are for financing infrastructure investments. At about $5 billion, this sum is a little less than the total for Malaysia alone.

However, a recent trend indicates new issuers (particularly of corporate bonds) are coming to market in several countries, in some cases with a debut issue. More than half (52 percent) of the corporate bonds listed on the markets at year-end 2006 were by infrastructure companies. The share of corporate bonds outstanding at year-end 2006 that had been issued to finance infrastructure exceeded half in 7 of the 11 countries with bond markets reporting these data. West Africa's regional exchange, the BRVM (Bourse Régionale des Valeurs Mobilières), had the highest share of issues financing infrastructure (more than 90 percent). The amount of financing is still small, however.

Local financial markets remain underdeveloped, shallow, and small. Long-term financing with maturities commensurate with infrastructure projects is scarce.[6] The capacity of local banking systems remains too small and constrained by structural impediments to finance infrastructure. Most countries' banks have significant asset-liability maturity mismatches for infrastructure financing. Bank deposits and other liabilities still have largely short-term tenors. More potential may exist

Table 2.14 Outstanding Financing Stock for Infrastructure, as of 2006

$ millions

Outstanding financing for infrastructure	WSS	Electricity	ICT	Transport	Public works	Total	% of total outstanding stock
Middle income (excluding South Africa)	—	82.0	—	440.7	21.3	544.0	4.0
Resource rich	1.7	1,097.6	2,303.9	1,459.1	46.8	4,909.1	36.5
Low-income nonfragile	—	1,496.7	1,984.5	4,065.5	4.4	7,551.0	56.1
Low-income fragile	—	63.0	53.4	346.3	—	462.7	3.4
Total	1.7	2,739.3	4,341.8	6,311.7	72.4	13,466.9	
Share on total outstanding stock (%)	0.01	20.34	32.24	46.87	0.54		100.0

Source: Adapted from Irving and Manroth 2009.
Note: Based on annualized averages for 2001–06. Averages weighted by country GDP. Figures are extrapolations based on the 18-country sample covered in AICD Phase 1. Totals may not add exactly because of rounding errors. Stock includes bank loans, government bonds, corporate bonds, and equity issues. Stock level reported under "Transport" may be an overestimate because many countries report this category together with elements of communications and storage. Based on data from the following 18 countries—middle income: Cape Verde, Lesotho, and Namibia; resource rich: Cameroon, Chad, and Nigeria; low income: Burkina Faso, the Democratic Republic of Congo, Ethiopia, Ghana, Madagascar, Malawi, Mozambique, Niger, Rwanda, Tanzania, Uganda, and Zambia. ICT = information and communication technology; WSS = water supply and sanitation. — Not available.

for syndicated lending with local bank participation—though the increase in new loans over 2000–06 occurred in a favorable external financing environment.

Harnessing the significant potential for local capital markets to finance infrastructure, particularly local bond markets, is contingent on their further development. It is also contingent on further reforms, including those that would deepen the local institutional investor base. Well-functioning and appropriately regulated local institutional investors (pension funds and insurance companies) would be natural sources of long-term financing for infrastructure because their liabilities would better match the longer terms of infrastructure projects. Private pension providers have begun to emerge with a shift from defined-benefit to defined-contribution schemes, viewed as less costly, more transparent, and easier to manage. Moreover, local institutional investors are taking a more diversified portfolio approach to asset allocation.

Regional integration of financial markets could achieve greater scale and liquidity. More cross-border intraregional listings—of both corporate bonds and equity issues—and more cross-border intraregional investment (particularly by local institutional investors) could help overcome national capital markets' impediments of small size, illiquidity, and inadequate market infrastructure. They could also facilitate the ability of companies and governments to raise financing for infrastructure.[7] So far, this intraregional approach to raising infrastructure financing remains largely untapped.[8]

The African banking system did not feel the effects of the global financial crisis at first, but the crisis is slowly but surely affecting financial systems around the region, adding to the already enormous challenge of developing local financial markets.

Costs of Capital from Different Sources

The various sources of infrastructure finance reviewed in the previous sections differ greatly in their associated cost of capital

(figure 2.4). For public funds, raising taxes is not a costless exercise. Each dollar raised and spent by a Sub-Saharan African government has a social value premium (or marginal cost of public funds) of almost 20 percent. That premium captures the incidence of that tax on the society's welfare (caused by changes in consumption patterns and administrative costs, among other things).[9] To allow ready comparisons across financing sources, this study standardized the financial terms as the present value of a dollar raised through each of the different sources. In doing so, it recognized that all loans must ultimately be repaid with tax dollars, each of which attracts the 20 percent cost premium.

Wide variation exists in lending terms. The most concessional IDA loans charge zero interest (0.75 percent service charge) with 10 years of grace. India, China, and the Gulf States, respectively, charge 4 percent, 3.6 percent, and 1.5 percent interest and grant four years of grace.[10]

The cost of non-OECD finance is somewhere between that of public funds and ODA. The subsidy factor for Indian and Chinese funds is about 25 percent and for the Arab funds, 50 percent. ODA typically provides a subsidy factor of 60 percent, rising to 75 percent for IDA resources. In addition to the cost of capital, the different sources of finance differ in the transaction costs associated with their use, which may offset or accentuate some of the differences.

Most Promising Ways to Increase Funds

Given this setting, what are the best ways of increasing the availability of funds for infrastructure development? The place to start is clearly to get the most from existing budget envelopes, which can provide up to $17.4 billion a year of additional resources internally. Beyond that, a substantial funding gap still remains. Before the financial crisis, the prospects for reducing—if not closing—this gap were reasonably good. Resource royalties were at record highs, and all sources of external finance were buoyant and promising further growth. With the onset of the global financial crisis, that situation has changed significantly and in ways that are not yet entirely foreseeable. The possibility exists across the board that all sources of infrastructure finance in Africa may fall rather than increase, further widening the funding gap. Only resource-rich countries have the possibility of using natural resource savings accounts to provide a source of financing for infrastructure, but only if macroeconomic conditions allow. One of the few things that could reverse this overall situation would be the agreement upon a major stimulus package for Africa by the international community, with a focus on infrastructure as part of the effort to rekindle economic growth and safeguard employment.

What Else Can Be Done?

Most of the low-income countries, and in particular the fragile states, face a substantial funding gap even if all the existing sources of funds—including efficiency gains—are tapped. What other options do these countries have? Realistically, they need either to defer the attainment of the infrastructure targets proposed here or to try to achieve them by using lower-cost technologies.

Taking More Time

The investment needs presented in this book are based on the objective of addressing Africa's infrastructure backlog within 10 years. To meet this target, middle-income, resource-rich, and low-income nonfragile states would need to increase their existing infrastructure spending by 50 to 100 percent, while low-income fragile states would need to increase their infrastructure spending by an impossible 350 percent. Extending the time horizon for the achievement of these goals should make the targets more affordable. But how long a delay would be needed to make the infrastructure targets attainable without increasing existing spending envelopes?

By delaying only three years, spreading the investment needs over 13 rather than 10 years, middle-income countries could achieve the proposed targets within existing spending envelopes (figure 2.5, panel a). However, this

Figure 2.4 Costs of Capital by Funding Source

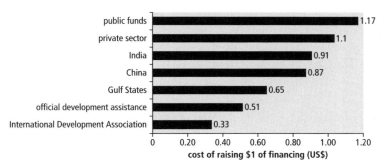

Sources: Average marginal cost of public funds: as estimated by Warlters and Auriol 2005; cost of equity for private sector: as in Estache and Pinglo 2004 and Sirtaine and others 2005; authors' calculations.

conclusion assumes they have first fully captured efficiency gains. Without such efficiency gains, the targets could not be met even over 30 years without increasing spending above current levels (figure 2.5, panel b).

Low-income nonfragile and resource-rich countries would need to delay an additional decade to meet targets with existing spending levels. By spreading the investment needs over 20 rather than 10 years, these countries could achieve the proposed targets within existing spending envelopes (figure 2.5, panel a). Again, this outcome would be possible only if efficiency gains are fully exploited. Otherwise, they would need more than 30 years to reach the target with existing resources (figure 2.5, panel b).

Low-income fragile states would need to delay by more than *two* decades to meet infrastructure targets within existing spending levels. By spreading the investment needs over 30 rather than 10 years, low-income fragile states could achieve the proposed targets within existing spending envelopes (figure 2.5, panel a). However, without efficiency gains, these countries would take much longer than 30 years to meet the associated targets or alternatively would still need to double their existing spending to reach the target in 30 years (figure 2.5, panel b).

Using Lower-Cost Technologies

Many possible alternative technological solutions exist for meeting a given infrastructure target, and each offers a particular combination of financial cost and quality of service.

Figure 2.5 Spreading Spending over Time

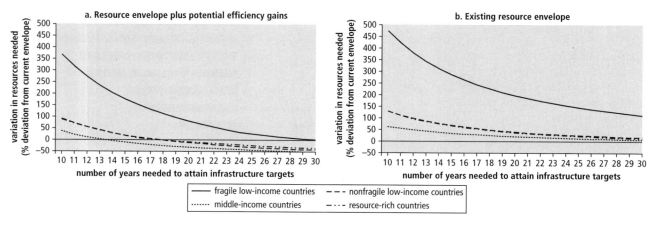

Source: Authors' calculations.

Where budgets are constrained, policy makers face a choice between providing a high level of service to a few people or a lower level of service to a broader cross-section of the population. Critical trade-offs must be considered; thus, one cannot jump to the conclusion that a high level of service is always in a country's best interest. The extent to which cost-saving technologies are available varies considerably across sectors. Two of the clearest cases are water and roads, which are discussed in detail next. Unfortunately, the power sector (which has by far the largest associated investment tag) does not present many technological alternatives for reducing the cost of electricity generation.

Using Alternative Technologies in WSS. In the case of water and sanitation, the cost of achieving the MDGs drops by 30 percent with greater reliance on lower-cost technologies. The MDGs can be achieved using either higher-end solutions, such as piped water and septic tanks, or cheaper solutions, such as standposts and improved latrines. The scenario considered here is one where the MDGs are met by preserving the prevalent mix of high-end and lower-end technologies. That is, the relative share of the population enjoying access to a direct water connection, sewers, or a septic tank—all regarded as high-level services—compared to the share of people with access to lower-end solutions, such as standposts and

unimproved latrines, remains the same as it is today (see chapters 16 and 17 in this volume). Thus, as population grows, the number of people accessing high-level services will be larger in absolute terms. If instead, all additional people served use cheaper solutions, such as standposts and improved latrines in urban areas or boreholes and unimproved latrines in rural areas, the overall cost of meeting the MDGs would fall by 30 percent.

Using Alternative Technologies in Roads. In the case of roads, the cost of reaching regional and national connectivity targets can be reduced by 30 percent by adopting lower standards for trunk roads. Road connectivity targets can be attained by using different engineering standards. The scenario considered here is one in which regional and national connectivity are achieved by a good-condition asphalt road network with at least two lanes for regional and at least one lane for national connectivity. The same connectivity could be achieved at a cost reduction of 30 percent if a single-surface-treatment road in fair condition is substituted for an asphalt road in good condition.

Notes

The authors of this chapter are Cecilia Briceño-Garmendia and Nataliya Pushak, who drew on background material and contributions from William Butterfield, Chuan Chen, Vivien Foster, Jacqueline Irving, Astrid Manroth, Afua Sarkodie, and Karlis Smits.

1. In particular, maintenance is essential to harness the economic returns of capital, but good-quality data on how much of current expenditures go to maintenance is hard to track.

2. Servén (2005) and Hicks (1991) summarize the facts on Latin American and other developing countries. For industrialized countries, see also Roubini and others (1989); De Haan, Sturm, and Sikken (1996) document the experience of industrialized countries.

3. This section draws heavily on Foster and others (2008).

4. Essentially, the Angola mode was devised to enable African nations to pay for infrastructure with natural resources. In a single transaction, China bundles development-type assistance with commercial-type trade finance. A Chinese resource company makes repayments in exchange for the oil or mineral rights. The China Export-Import Bank acts as a broker, receiving money for the sale and paying the contractor for providing the infrastructure. This arrangement safeguards against currency inconvertibility, political instability, and expropriation.

5. Data are as of year-end 2006, or most recent available, for the sampled countries, excluding South Africa.

6. Because South Africa's financial markets are so much more developed than any of those of the other 23 focus countries, this section excludes South Africa.

7. One new initiative is the Pan-African Infrastructure Development Fund, a 15-year regional fund for raising finance for commercially viable infrastructure projects in Africa, which raised $625 million in its first close in 2007, including funds from Ghanaian and South African institutional investors.

8. In addition, the lack of a benchmark yield curve in the vast majority of those African countries that have an organized bond market has limited corporate bond issuance, as has the general absence of credit ratings agencies and a lack of awareness among prospective issuers as well as investors.

9. The marginal cost of public funds measures the change in welfare associated with raising an additional unit of tax revenue (Warlters and Auriol 2005).

10. See Foster and others (2008) for further details.

References

Briceño-Garmendia, Cecilia, Karlis Smits, and Vivien Foster. 2008. "Fiscal Costs of Infrastructure in Sub-Saharan Africa." *Africa Infrastructure Country Diagnostic*. Washington, DC: World Bank.

Calderón, César, and Luis Servén. 2004. "Trends in Infrastructure in Latin America, 1980–2001." Policy Research Working Paper 3401, World Bank, Washington, DC.

De Haan, Jakob, Jan Sturm, and Bernd Sikken. 1996. "Government Capital Formation: Explaining the Decline." *Weltwirtschaftliches Archiv* 132 (1): 55–74.

Estache, Antonio, and Rafael Muñoz. 2008. "Building Sector Concerns into Macro-Economic Financial Programming: Lessons from Senegal and Uganda." Working Paper 6, Africa Infrastructure Country Diagnostic, World Bank, Washington, DC.

Estache, Antonio, and Maria Elena Pinglo. 2004. "Are Returns to Private Infrastructure in Developing Countries Consistent with Risks since the Asian Crisis?" Policy Research Working Paper 3373. World Bank, Washington, DC.

Foster, Vivien, William Butterfield, Chuan Chen, and Nataliya Pushak. 2008. *Building Bridges: China's Growing Role as Infrastructure Financier for Sub-Saharan Africa.* Trends and Policy Options no. 5. Washington, DC: Public-Private Infrastructure Advisory Facility, World Bank.

Hicks, Norman. 1991. "Expenditure Reductions in Developing Countries Revisited." *Journal of International Development* 3 (1): 29–37.

Irving, Jacqueline, and Astrid Manroth. 2009. "Local Sources of Financing for Infrastructure in Africa: A Cross-Country Analysis." Policy Research Working Paper 4878, World Bank, Washington, DC.

IMF (International Monetary Fund). 2009. *The State of Public Finances: Outlook and Medium-Term Policies after the 2008 Crisis.* Washington, DC: IMF.

Leigland, James, and William Butterfield. 2006. "Reform, Private Capital Needed to Develop Infrastructure in Africa: Problems and Prospects for Private Participation." *Gridlines*, Note 8 (May), Public-Private Infrastructure Advisory Facility, World Bank, Washington, DC.

Nogales, Alberto. 2009. "The Cost of Postponing Roads Maintenance." World Bank, Washington, DC.

ODI (Overseas Development Institute). 2009. *A Development Charter for the G-20.* London: ODI.

PPIAF (Public-Private Infrastructure Advisory Facility). 2008. Private Participation in Infrastructure Project Database, http://ppi.worldbank .org/.

Pritchett, Lant. 1996. "Mind Your P's and Q's. The Cost of Public Investment Is Not the Value of Public Capital." Policy Research Working Paper 1660, World Bank, Washington, DC.

Rajkumar, Andrew, and Vinaya Swaroop. 2002. "Public Spending and Outcomes: Does Governance

Matter?" Policy Research Working Paper 2840, World Bank, Washington, DC.

Reinikka, Ritva, and Jakob Svensson. 2002. "Explaining Leakage of Public Funds." Discussion Paper 3227, Centre for Economic Policy Research, London, U.K.

———. 2003. "The Power of Information: Evidence from a Newspaper Campaign to Reduce Capture." Policy Research Working Paper 3239, World Bank, Washington, DC.

Roubini, Nouriel, Jeffrey Sachs, Seppo Honkapohja, and Daniel Cohen. 1989. "Government Spending and Budget Deficits in the Industrial Countries." *Economic Policy* 8 (4): 99–132.

Servén, Luis. 2005. "Fiscal Discipline, Public Investment and Growth." World Bank, Washington, DC.

Sirtaine, Sophie, Maria Elena Pinglo, J. Luis Guasch, and Viven Foster. 2005. *How Profitable Are Infrastructure Concessions in Latin America? Empirical Evidence and Regulatory Implications.* Trends and Policy Options no. 2. Washington, DC: Public-Private Infrastructure Advisory Facility, World Bank.

UBS Investment Research. 2008. "Global Economic Perspectives: The Global Impact of Fiscal Policy."

Warlters, Michael, and Emmanuelle Auriol. 2005. "The Marginal Cost of Public Funds in Africa." Policy Research Working Paper 3679, World Bank, Washington, DC.

World Economic Outlook. 2008. "Estimating the Size of the European Stimulus Packages for 2009."

Chapter 3

Dealing with Poverty and Inequality

Coverage of modern infrastructure services has been stagnant since the mid-1990s and remains strongly skewed toward more affluent households. In urban areas, those who fail to hook up to nearby networks form a significant share of the unserved population, suggesting that demand-side barriers are also at work. In these circumstances, the key questions are whether African households can afford to pay for modern infrastructure services, and if not, whether African governments can afford to subsidize them.

A subsistence power or water bill ranges between $2 and $8 a month. This cost is well within the affordable range for most households in Africa's middle-income countries and for the more affluent segments that currently enjoy access to utilities in low-income countries. However, affordability would definitely become an issue for most people in the poorest low-income countries should access be broadened.

African governments already spend $4.1 billion a year (0.7 percent of GDP) on power and water subsidies that benefit mainly a small group of affluent customers. Expanding these levels of subsidy to the entire population would be fiscally unsustainable for most countries.

In the absence of modern infrastructure services, the next best option would be to reach households with lower-cost, second-best solutions, such as standposts, improved latrines, or street lighting. However, the prevalence of these second-best solutions is surprisingly low in Africa, and those that exist tend to cater more to the higher-income groups than to the middle of the income distribution. The majority of Africans resort instead to traditional alternatives, such as wells, unimproved latrines, or kerosene lamps. Significant challenges exist in increasing the coverage of second-best alternatives, particularly because their public good nature makes some of these technologies more difficult for service providers to operate on a commercial basis.

The business-as-usual approach to expanding service coverage in Africa does not appear to be working. Turning this situation around will require rethinking the approach to service expansion in four ways. First, coverage expansion is not only about network rollout, but also about a need to address demand-side barriers such as high connection charges or legal tenure. Second, cost recovery for household services needs to be improved to ensure that utilities have the financial basis to invest in service expansion. Third, rethinking the design of utility subsidies to better target them and to accelerate service expansion is desirable. Fourth, any approach must consider the actual level of service that households can afford to pay and that governments can afford to subsidize and put greater emphasis on second-best alternatives to modern infrastructure services.

Access to Modern Infrastructure Services—Stagnant and Inequitable

Coverage of modern infrastructure services in Africa is very low by global standards (Estache and Wodon 2007). Coverage of electricity is about 20 percent in Africa; 33 percent in South Asia; and more than 85 percent in East Asia, Latin America, and the Middle East. Coverage of piped water is 12 percent in Africa, 21 percent in South Asia, and more than 35 percent in other developing regions. Coverage of flush toilets is 6 percent in Africa, 34 percent in South Asia, and more than 30 percent in other developing regions. Africa's telecommunications coverage, however, compares favorably with South Asia's and is not so far behind that of other developing regions. Africa's low coverage of infrastructure services in part reflects its relatively low urbanization rates, because urban agglomeration greatly facilitates the extension of infrastructure networks.[1]

Household surveys show only modest gains in access to modern infrastructure services over the period 1990–2005 (figure 3.1). This stagnant overall picture masks two divergent trends. Service coverage in rural areas has seen modest improvements, whereas that in urban areas has actually *declined*. For example, urban coverage of piped water fell from 50 percent in the early 1990s to 39 percent in the early 2000s, and urban coverage of flush toilets from 32 percent to 27 percent. Although many new connections are being made in urban areas, declining urban coverage largely reflects the inability of service providers to keep pace with urban population growth of 3.6 percent a year.

The pace of service expansion differs dramatically across sectors and countries. The

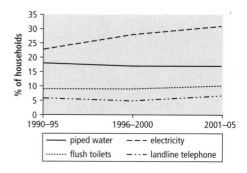

Figure 3.1 Coverage of Network Infrastructure Services, 1990–2005

Source: Banerjee, Wodon, and others 2008.

percentage of the population added annually to the coverage of modern infrastructure services is a good measure of the intensity of effort in service expansion—and it differs dramatically across services (figure 3.2). Less than 0.5 percent of the population is added each year to the network of piped water and flush toilets, whereas about 1.5 percent is added to that of electricity and cellular telephone services. For water and sanitation, the rate of expansion of alternative services such as latrines, standposts, and boreholes is significantly faster than that of piped water and flush toilets. These regional averages mask outstanding performances by individual countries. For piped water, Benin, Côte d'Ivoire, and Senegal reach an additional 1.5–2.0 percent of their population each year, compared with less than 0.1 percent for Africa as a whole.

Universal access to modern infrastructure services lies at least 50 years in the future for most countries. Projecting current rates of service expansion forward and taking into account anticipated demographic growth, one can estimate the year countries will reach universal access to each of the modern infrastructure services. The results are sobering. Under business as usual, less than 20 percent of Sub-Saharan African countries will reach universal access for piped water by 2050, and less than 45 percent will reach universal access to electricity (figure 3.3). In about one-third of countries, universal access to piped water and flush toilets will not be reached in this century.

Coverage varies dramatically across households with different budget levels (figure 3.4).

Among the poorest 60 percent of the population, coverage of almost all modern infrastructure services is well below 10 percent. Conversely, the vast majority of households with coverage belong to the more affluent 40 percent of the population. In most countries, inequality of access has increased over time, suggesting that most new connections have gone to more affluent households (Diallo and Wodon 2005). This situation is not entirely surprising, given that, even among households with greater purchasing power, coverage is far from universal, and well under 50 percent in most cases. Relative to the other modern infrastructure services, electricity coverage is somewhat higher across the spectrum.

Low coverage rates can reflect both supply and demand factors. On the one hand, the household may be physically distant from an infrastructure network (and thus face an absence of supply). On the other hand, the household may choose not to connect to a network even when it is nearby (and thus express a lack of demand). Understanding this difference is important because the policy implications differ radically. By exploiting the spatial distribution of household survey samples in urban areas, one can quantify the relative importance of these supply and demand factors in accounting for low service coverage. Using this approach, one can distinguish between the percentage of population that has *access* to the service (those living physically close to the infrastructure) and the percentage of the population that *hooks up* to the service when it is available.

Lack of coverage for urban electricity supply is equally about demand and supply factors. The power infrastructure for electricity is physically close to 93 percent of the urban population, but only 75 percent of those with access actually hook up to the service. This means that half of the population lacking coverage live close to power infrastructure. One can often observe this phenomenon in African cities, where informal settlements flanking major road corridors lack power service even though distribution lines run overhead.

Overall, the coverage gap for piped water is primarily attributable to supply factors

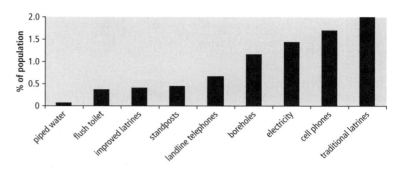

Figure 3.2 Expansion of Access to Infrastructure Services Each Year, Mid-1990s to Mid-2000s

Source: Banerjee, Wodon, and others 2008.

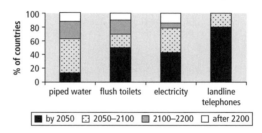

Figure 3.3 Projected Universal Access for Piped Water for Sub-Saharan African Countries, 2050 and Beyond

Source: Banerjee, Wodon, and others 2008.

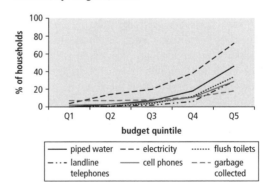

Figure 3.4 Coverage of Modern Infrastructure Services, by Budget Quintile

Source: Banerjee, Wodon, and others 2008.
Note: The data are the latest available as of 2006.

(table 3.1). The physical extent of the piped water network is more limited, reaching only 73 percent of the urban population, and hookup rates for those in proximity are only 48 percent. In general, the role of demand

Table 3.1 Understanding Coverage of Infrastructure Services: The Role of Supply and Demand Factors

percent (population-weighted average)

Infrastructure	Decomposition of coverage			Unserved due to factors	
	Access	Hookup	Coverage	Supply	Demand
Piped water					
Low-income countries	68	42	31	86	14
Middle-income countries	91	74	69	64	36
Overall	73	48	38	81	19
Electricity					
Low-income countries	93	73	69	50	50
Middle-income countries	95	86	81	39	61
Overall	93	75	71	48	52

Source: Banerjee, Wodon, and others 2008.
Note: Access is defined as the percentage of the population that lives physically close to infrastructure. *Hookup* is defined as the percentage of the population that connects to infrastructure when it is available. *Coverage* is defined as the percentage of the population that has the infrastructure service; it is essentially the product of access and hookup. In calculating the *proportion of gap* attributable to demand and supply factors, one considers the hookup rate of the top budget quintile in each geographical area to be an upper bound on potential hookup, absent demand-side constraints.

factors is higher in middle-income countries than in low-income countries, reflecting the fact that infrastructure networks are more highly developed in the former and have a broader geographical reach.

It may appear paradoxical that households do not universally take up connections to modern infrastructure services as networks become physically available. Clear economic reasons exist, however, why this might be so. In some cases, households may have access to cheaper substitutes, such as boreholes. More substitutes are available for piped water than for electricity, which may explain the much lower hookup rates for the former. In other cases, utility connection charges are set prohibitively high for low-income households. For example, 60 percent of the water utilities surveyed for this study apply connection charges in excess of $100. Charges range from about $6 in the Upper Nile in Sudan to more than $240 in Côte d'Ivoire, Mozambique, Niger, and South Africa. The average connection charge across the region is 28 percent of gross national income (GNI) per capita. For Niger, the charge is more than 100 percent of GNI per capita. Similarly, the five water utilities in Mozambique charge more than 75 percent of GNI per capita. These comparisons illustrate how high connection charges present a barrier to affordability.

The tenure status of households may also significantly impede hookup to modern infrastructure services. A study of slum households in Dakar and Nairobi finds that coverage of piped water and electricity is more than twice as high among owner-occupiers as among tenants (Gulyani, Talukdar, and Jack 2008). Even among owner-occupiers, lack of formal legal titles can affect hookup to services.

Affordability of Modern Infrastructure Services— Subsidizing the Better Off

African households exist on very limited household budgets. The average African household of five persons has a monthly budget of less than $180, ranging from about $60 in the poorest quintile to $340 in the richest quintile (table 3.2). Thus, purchasing power—even in Africa's most affluent households—is modest in absolute terms. Across the spectrum, household budgets in middle-income countries are roughly twice those in low-income countries.

Most African households spend more than half their modest budgets on food, with little left over for other items. Spending on infrastructure services (including utilities, energy, and transport) averages about 7 percent of a household's budget, though this can be 15–25 percent in some countries and represents overall a significant share of the nonfood budget. As household budgets increase, infrastructure services absorb a growing share, rising from less than 4 percent among the poorest quintile to more than 8 percent among the richest (figure 3.5). In terms of absolute expenditure, this difference is even more pronounced: whereas households in the poorest quintile spend, on average, no more than $2 per month on all infrastructure services, households in the richest quintile spend almost $40 per month.

Given such low household budgets, a key question is whether households can afford to pay for modern infrastructure services. One measure of affordability is nonpayment for infrastructure services. Nonpayment directly limits the ability of utilities and service providers to expand networks and improve services by undermining their financial strength. Based on

Table 3.2 Monthly Household Budgets
2002 $

Income group	National average	Poorest quintile	Second quintile	Third quintile	Fourth quintile	Richest quintile
Overall	177	59	97	128	169	340
Low-income countries	139	53	80	103	135	258
Middle-income countries	300	79	155	181	282	609

Source: Banerjee, Wodon, and others 2008.

Figure 3.5 Share of Household Budgets Spent on Infrastructure Services, by Budget Quintile

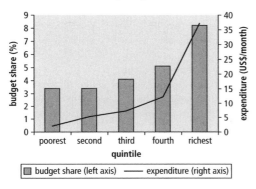

Source: Banerjee, Wodon, and others 2008.

Figure 3.6 Population with Service Connections Who Do Not Pay for Service

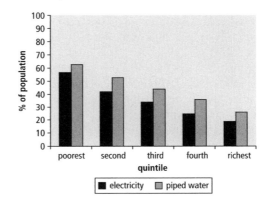

Source: Banerjee, Wodon, and others 2008.

household surveys, one can compare for each quintile the percentage of households that report paying for the service with the percentage of households that report using the service. Those that do not pay include both clandestine users and formal customers who fail to pay their bills. Overall, about 40 percent of people connected to infrastructure services do not pay for them (figure 3.6). Nonpayment rates range from about 20 percent in the more affluent quintile to about 60 percent in the poorest quintile. A significant nonpayment rate, even among the more affluent quintiles, suggests that a culture of payment problems exists in addition to any affordability issues.

The cost of providing subsistence consumption of water *or* electricity ranges from $2 to $8 a month, depending on the extent of consumption and cost recovery (figure 3.7). A more formal method of gauging affordability is to measure the cost of utility bills against household budgets. The cost of a monthly subsistence consumption of piped water can

Figure 3.7 Affordability of Subsistence Consumption Priced at Cost-Recovery Levels

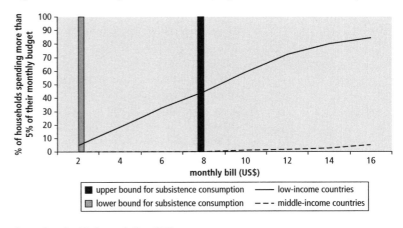

Source: Banerjee, Wodon, and others 2008.

range between $2 (based on an operating cost-recovery tariff of $0.40 per cubic meter and an absolute minimum consumption of 4 cubic meters) and $8 (based on a full cost-recovery tariff of $0.80 per cubic meter and a more typical modest household consumption of 10 cubic meters). The cost of a monthly subsistence consumption of power can range between $2 (based on a low-cost country tariff of $0.08 per kilowatt-hour and an absolute minimum consumption of 25 kilowatt-hours) and $8 (based on a high-cost country tariff of $0.16 per kilowatt-hour and a more typical modest household consumption of 50 kilowatt-hours).

An affordability threshold of 5 percent of household budgets provides a gauge for measuring which utility bills might be affordable to African households. By looking at the distribution of household budgets, one can calculate the percentage of households for which such bills would absorb more than 5 percent of their budgets and thus prove unaffordable. Monthly bills of $2 are affordable to almost the entire African population. Monthly bills of $8 would remain affordable for the entire population of the middle-income African countries, indicating that cost recovery should not be a major problem for these countries.

Cost-recovery tariffs would also be affordable for those currently enjoying access in low-income countries, but not for the remaining population. In low-income countries, monthly bills of $8 would remain perfectly affordable for the most affluent 20–40 percent of the population, the only portion enjoying access. However, such bills would not be affordable to the poorest 60–80 percent that currently lack access even if services were extended to them. The affordability problems associated with a universal access policy would be particularly large for a handful of the poorest low-income countries—Burundi, the Democratic Republic of Congo, Ethiopia, Guinea-Bissau, Malawi, Niger, Tanzania, and Uganda—where as much as 80 percent of the population could not afford a monthly bill of $8.

The immediate poverty-related effect of raising tariffs to cost-recovery levels is generally quite small, although it may have second-order effects. Detailed analysis of the effect of significant tariff increases of the order of 40 percent for power and water services in Senegal and power services in Mali confirms that the immediate poverty-related effect on consumers is small, essentially because very few poor consumers are connected to the service (Boccanfuso, Estache, and Savard 2008a, 2008b, 2008c). As the consequences of higher power or water prices work their way through the economy, however, broader second-order effects on wages and prices of goods in the economy as a whole can lead to more substantial effects on poverty (Boccanfuso, Estache, and Savard 2008a, 2008b, 2008c).

Notwithstanding these findings, most African countries heavily subsidize tariffs for power and water services. On average, power tariffs recover only 75 percent of full costs, and water tariffs only 64 percent. The resulting implicit service subsidies amount to as much as $4.1 billion a year (0.7 percent of Africa's GDP), divided evenly between power and water (see chapter 2 of this volume).

Because electricity and water subsidies are typically justified by the need to make services affordable to low-income households, a key question is whether subsidies reach such households. Results across a wide range of African countries, for both power and water sectors, show that the share of subsidies going to the poor is less than half of the share of the poor in the overall population, indicating a very regressive distribution (figure 3.8). This result is hardly surprising given that connections to power and water services are already highly skewed toward more affluent households. To put these results in perspective, one must compare them with the targeting achieved by other forms of social policy. Estimates for Cameroon, Gabon, and Guinea indicate that expenditures on primary education and basic health care reach the poor better than do power and water subsidies (Wodon 2008a, 2008b).

Can African governments afford to further expand today's subsidy model to achieve universal access? Little justification currently exists for utility subsidies, given that they typically do not reach unconnected low-income households but rather favor more affluent, connected households that do not really need subsidies to afford the service. However, the preceding analysis indicates that affordability would become a major issue to the extent that Africa's low-income countries move aggressively toward universal access. Given the very high macroeconomic cost today of subsidizing even the

Figure 3.8 Extent to Which Electricity and Water Subsidies Reach the Poor, by Country

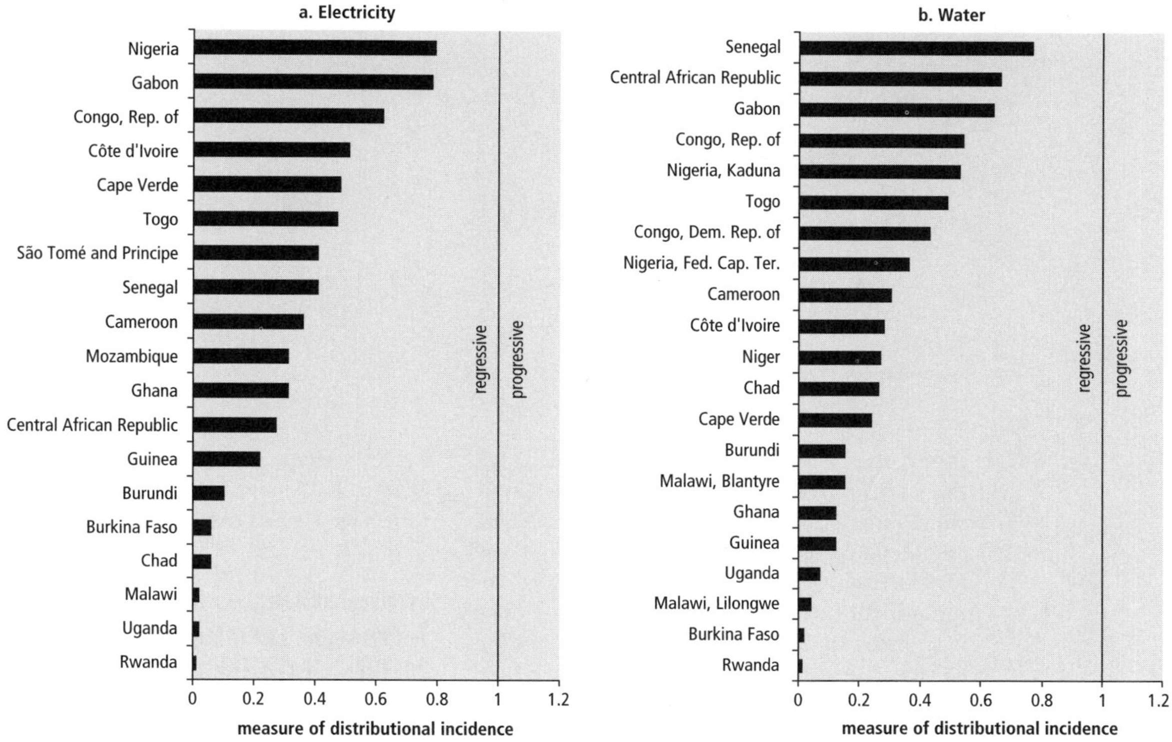

Sources: Banerjee, Wodon, and others 2008; Wodon 2008a, 2008b.
Note: This figure presents a measure of distributional incidence, which captures the percentage of total subsidy value reaching the poor relative to the percentage of the poor in the population. A value greater than 1 implies that the subsidy distribution is progressive (pro-poor), because the share of benefits allocated to the poor is larger than their share in the total population. A value less than 1 implies that the distribution is regressive.

minority of the population with access to power and water, a legitimate question is whether African governments can afford to scale up this subsidy-based model to the remainder of their populations.

Providing universal use-of-service subsidies for power and water would absorb an unaffordable 1.6 percent of GDP above existing spending, about two-thirds for power and one-third for water. These values are high in relation to existing operation and maintenance expenditure, so it is difficult to believe that they would be fiscally affordable for governments (figure 3.9).

One-time capital subsidies could be provided at a lower cost and if spread over 20 years, might just be affordable. The cost of providing a one-time capital subsidy of $200 to cover network connection costs for all unconnected households over 20 years would be substantially low, only 0.35 percent of GDP for power and about 0.25 percent of GDP for piped water. A key difference is that the cost of this one-time subsidy would disappear at the end of the decade, whereas the use-of-service subsidy would continue indefinitely.

The welfare case is quite strong for one-time capital subsidies to support universal connection. Households without access to utility services eventually pay much higher prices and, as a result, limit their consumption to very low levels. Small-scale piped-network operators charge 1.5 times the formal network price, point sources charge 4.5 times the formal network price, and mobile distributors can charge up to 12 times the formal utility tariff (Kariuki and Schwartz 2005). A recent survey of Accra, Dar es Salaam, and Nairobi

Figure 3.9 Amount of Subsidy Needed to Maintain Affordability of Water and Electricity Service, 2005

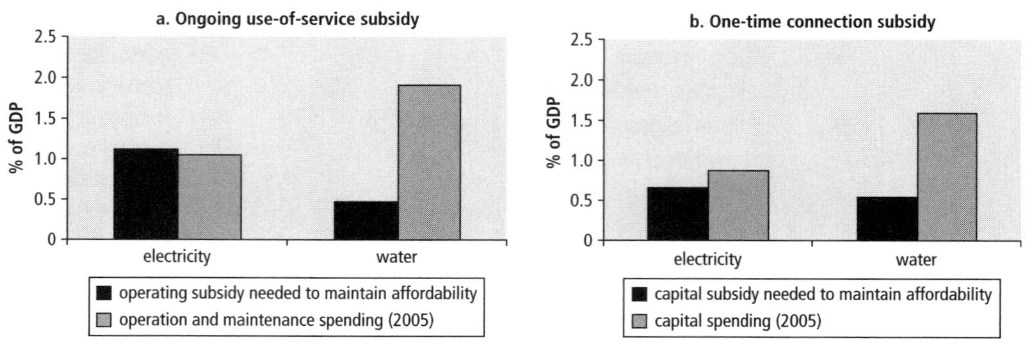

Source: Banerjee, Wodon, and others 2008.

found that the price of utility-piped water ranges from $0.5 to $1.5 a cubic meter, whereas small water enterprises charge between $4 and $6 (McGranahan and others 2006). Similarly, for electricity, the cost of providing basic illumination through candles or kilowatt-hours is an order of magnitude greater than that for electricity per effective unit of lighting (Foster and Tré 2003).

Interestingly, even though nonutility water vendors charge higher unit prices, those purchasing water from vendors do not necessarily spend more than those purchasing water from the public utility—they simply adjust the quantity consumed.

Nonmonetary benefits of connection can also be very significant. Beyond the potential monetary savings, piped water and electricity are associated with a wide range of health, education, and productivity benefits (see chapter 1 of this volume). Better water and sanitation service is associated with less malnutrition and stunting, and it liberates women from the time-consuming chore of collecting water, leaving more time for income-generating activities (box 3.1). Better electricity provision improves literacy and primary school completion rates, because better quality of light allows students to read and study without sunlight.

Finally, affordability concerns also exist for urban transportation services. Transportation represents one of the largest household budget expenditure shares among infrastructure services, absorbing 4–6 percent of the budgets of those households reporting expenditures.

Box 3.2 details some of the access and affordability challenges arising for urban transportation in Africa's burgeoning cities.

Alternatives to Modern Infrastructure Services—the Missing Middle

Even with renewed efforts, most African countries will not realize universal access to modern infrastructure services for some decades. In the meantime, most households will continue to rely on alternative ways of meeting their water and energy requirements (figure 3.10). For the most part, these methods comprise *traditional* alternatives such as wells, unimproved latrines, and kerosene lamps. However, *second-best alternatives* also exist that provide a significantly higher level of service than the traditional solutions but at a substantially lower cost than full-blown piped water or power connections. Examples include standposts for water supply, improved latrines for sanitation, and street lighting for basic neighborhood illumination.

Although traditional alternatives are in widespread use, second-best alternatives have not yet become popular in most countries. The water and sanitation sectors illustrate this point very clearly. In both cases, the traditional alternatives (whether wells or unimproved latrines) provide the largest share of service across the income spectrum. However, the second-best alternatives (whether standposts or improved

BOX 3.1

Access to Basic Infrastructure and Time Use

It is often said that access to basic infrastructure could help increase the earnings of households both by making their work more productive and by freeing time allocated to domestic chores and allocating such time savings to productive work. Some authors have argued that households face a "time overhead" constraint—the minimum number of hours that household members must spend on basic chores vital to the well-being and survival of the family. This burden includes time spent preparing meals, washing clothes, cleaning, transporting water, and gathering fuel for cooking and heating. Access to basic infrastructure can significantly reduce this time overhead, and thereby free time for productive work. Because households that lack access to basic infrastructure tend to be poor and because most of these households have members who want to work longer hours to increase their earnings, access to infrastructure could reduce poverty through a reallocation of household members' time.

Some emerging evidence from household surveys indicates that the time saved from access to basic infrastructure can indeed be substantial. Using data from Sierra Leone, Wodon and Ying (2009) show that women work more than men on domestic tasks and that the domestic workload of children is also high. Access to water and electricity helps reduce domestic work time by up to 10 hours a week. Using data from Guinea, Bardasi and Wodon (2009) find effects on time use of a similar order of infrastructure for access to water. The question remains whether household members could find employment opportunities using the time saved through access to infrastructure. Even if time savings were remunerated at a fraction of the minimum wage, the economic return of these projects is often very large owing to the time savings of households.

latrines) have coverage rates comparable to or even lower than the best alternatives (whether piped water or flush toilets) despite their significant cost advantages. Moreover, coverage of the second-best alternatives is just as regressive as that of the best alternatives. Nevertheless, some countries have made significant progress in expanding coverage of second-best alternatives—such as the Democratic Republic of Congo, Mozambique, Tanzania, and Uganda for standposts; and Burkina Faso, Cameroon, Ghana, Madagascar, and Rwanda for improved latrines. Although data are not available to make a similar comparison for lighting, it is well known that coverage of street lighting lags.

The capital costs of the second-best alternatives are still only a fraction of those associated with the best alternatives, even if they are also significantly more expensive than the traditional alternatives (table 3.3). Thus, the second-best alternatives provide an opportunity to make limited investment budgets go further and accelerate the expansion of service improvements.

Therefore, understanding the factors that lie behind this "missing middle" is important. Once again, both demand and supply issues conspire to limit the extension of the second-best alternatives.

On the demand side, the costs of the second-best alternatives may still be relatively high, given limited household budgets. Water from standposts, though relatively cheap to provide, is often retailed by intermediaries charging substantial markups that outweigh the underlying advantages in construction costs. Improved latrines, though cheaper than flush toilets, are nonetheless substantially more expensive than unimproved latrines, and uneducated households may not be aware of the health benefits.

On the supply side, their public good nature greatly complicates the implementation of second-best alternatives. The provision of standposts and street lighting is unattractive to utilities because of their limited scope for revenue collection as well as the greater potential for revenue loss from increased clandestine connections once networks are provided. For improved latrines, the limited experience of the local construction sector restricts the availability of such designs and may keep their costs higher than they would be in a mass market (see chapter 17 of this volume).

BOX 3.2

Access, Affordability, and Alternatives—Urban Public Transportation

Access to urban transportation services in Sub-Saharan Africa is constrained both by the limited reach of the urban paved-road network and by the limited size of the bus fleet.

Only one-third of the roads in African cities are paved, ranging from barely 10 percent in Kinshasa (Democratic Republic of Congo) and Kigali (Rwanda) to more than 70 percent in Kampala (Uganda). Paved-road density is typically about 300 meters per 1,000 inhabitants, compared with more typical values of 1,000 meters per 1,000 inhabitants for developing cities around the world. Overall, the road network constitutes less than 7 percent of the land area in most African cities, compared with 25–30 percent in developed-country cities. The low coverage of the paved network limits the reach of bus services. In many African cities, numerous outlying neighborhoods can be reached only by two-wheeled vehicles.

The typical availability of bus services in African cities is 30–60 bus seats per 1,000 residents, although the number can be as low as 10 seats per 1,000 in Addis Ababa (Ethiopia), Kinshasa, and Ouagadougou (Burkina Faso). In contrast to middle-income countries that typically have 30–40 large bus seats per 1,000 residents, low-income countries in Africa have only 6 per 1,000.

The proliferation of informal minibus services has been a private response to the financial demise of large, publicly run bus services in most cities. Although minibuses have been very responsive to demand, they pose a variety of social issues, including congestion, pollution, and road safety. Moreover, the lack of effective regulation of minibuses leads to business practices, such as overcrowding, erratic scheduling, and price discrimination, that favor business interests over those of consumers.

Bus fares in African cities tend to be about $0.30 per one-way trip, irrespective of bus size. Evidence from budget surveys indicates that households spend on average $12–$16 a month on urban transportation services. This sum is enough to purchase about 20 round-trip bus tickets per month, which covers the essential travel requirements of one commuter per household, leaving nothing to cover travel needs of other household members. Expenditure levels of the poorest households would be inadequate to cover the transportation costs of even one commuter per household.

A significant minority of urban households do not report any expenditure on urban transportation, suggesting that their transportation needs are met entirely by foot. Data on the modal split of urban journeys show, on average, 37 percent of urban trips taken on buses and another 37 percent on foot. The remainder of trips is spread across a range of private modes. The percentage of trips on foot can be 50 percent or more—Nairobi, Kenya (47); Douala, Cameroon (60); and Conakry, Guinea (78).

The combination of low access and limited affordability for service conspires to seriously constrain the mobility of urban residents, preventing cities from realizing their full potential to bring together people, services, and economic opportunities.

Source: Kumar and Barrett 2008.

Figure 3.10 Access to Alternative Water and Sanitation Services across All Income Levels

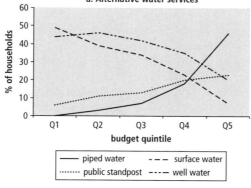

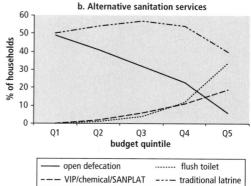

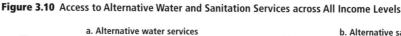

Source: Banerjee, Wodon, and others 2008.

Table 3.3 Capital Cost of Best, Second-Best, and Traditional Alternatives
$ per capita

Alternative	Water		Sanitation		Lighting	
Traditional	Well	21	Unimproved latrine	39	Kerosene lamp	—
Second best	Standpost	80	Improved latrine	57	Street lighting	—
Best	Piped water	283	Flush toilet	125	Electricity	133

Source: Chapter 5 of this volume.
Note: Capital cost estimates are based on a density of 3,272 persons per square kilometer.
— Not available.

Policy Challenges for Accelerating Service Expansion

The business-as-usual approach to expanding service coverage in Africa does not appear to be working. The low and stagnant coverage of household services comes with a major social and economic toll. Most African countries have tackled universal access by providing heavily subsidized best options, such as piped water and electricity. This approach has tended to bankrupt and debilitate sector institutions without bringing about any significant acceleration of coverage. The associated public subsidies have also largely bypassed most needy groups. Few services and countries are expanding coverage at rates high enough to outstrip demographic growth, particularly urbanization.

Turning this situation around will require rethinking the approach to service expansion in four ways. First, coverage expansion is not just about network rollout. Demand-side barriers such as high connection charges or legal tenure must be addressed. Second, cost recovery for household services needs to be improved to ensure a financial basis for utilities to invest in service expansion. Third, rethinking the design of utility subsidies to better target them and to accelerate service expansion is desirable. Fourth, the level of service that households can afford to pay for and governments can afford to subsidize must be considered realistically and greater emphasis placed on second-best modern solutions.

Remembering the Demand Side of the Equation

Overlooking the demand side of network rollout can lead to much lower returns on infrastructure investments. The challenge of reaching universal access is typically characterized as a supply problem of rolling out infrastructure networks to increasingly far-flung populations. However, household survey evidence shows that a significant segment of the unserved population in urban areas lives close to a network. The relatively low rate of hookup to existing infrastructure networks leads to lower financial, economic, and social returns to the associated investment, because the physical asset is operating below its full carrying capacity. This finding has implications for network rollout strategy.

First, hookup—rather than access—needs to be considered the key measure of success. Interventions that aim to expand service coverage too often measure their outcomes by the number of people who can connect to the network provided. As a result, little attention is given to whether these connections actually materialize after the project's completion. Unless the focus of monitoring and evaluation shifts from access to hookup, those involved in service expansion will have little incentive to think about the demand side of service coverage.

Second, the most cost-effective way of increasing coverage may be to pursue densification programs that increase hookup rates in targeted areas. Unserved populations living physically close to infrastructure networks could (in principle) be covered at a much lower capital cost than those living farther away, thereby providing the highest potential return to a limited investment budget. In that sense, they may deserve priority attention in efforts to raise coverage.

Third, expanding coverage requires community engagement. Dealing with the demand-side barriers that prevent hookup requires a more detailed understanding of the potential client base of the utility. What are their alternatives? How much can they afford to pay? What other constraints do they face? This approach in turn suggests a broader skill base than utilities may routinely retain, going beyond standard expertise in network engineering to encompass sociological, economic, and legal analysis of—and engagement with—the target populations.

Fourth, careful thought should be given to how connection costs might be recovered. As noted earlier, high connection charges—widespread across Africa—are one obvious demand-side barrier to hookup, even when use-of-service charges would be affordable. In these circumstances, one may legitimately ask whether substantial one-time up-front connection charges are the most sensible way to recover network connection costs. Alternatives can be considered, including repaying connection costs over several years through an installment plan; socializing connection costs by recovering them through the general tariff and, hence, sharing them across the entire customer base; or directly subsidizing them from the government budget (see box 3.3).

Fifth, expansion of utility networks needs to be closely coordinated with urban development. In many periurban neighborhoods, expansion of utility networks is hampered by the absence of legal tenure and by high turnover rates among tenants, not to mention inadequate spacing of dwellings. Providing services to these communities will require close cooperation with urban authorities because many of these issues can be resolved only if they are addressed in a synchronized and coordinated manner.

Taking a Hard-Headed Look at Affordability

Underrecovery of costs has serious implications for the financial health of utilities and slows the pace of service expansion. Many of Africa's water and power utilities capture only two-thirds of the revenues needed to function sustainably. This revenue shortfall is rarely covered through timely and explicit fiscal transfers. Instead, maintenance and investment activities are curtailed to make ends meet, starving the utility of funds to expand service coverage and eroding the quality of service to existing customers (see chapter 8 on power and chapter 16 on water utilities in this volume).

Affordability, the usual pretext for underpricing services, does not bear much scrutiny. Political economy likely provides the real explanation for low tariffs, with populations currently connected to utility services tending to be those with the greatest voice. The implicit

---

BOX 3.3

Are Connection Subsidies Well Targeted to the Poor?

Within the framework of Niger's poverty reduction strategy, some 11,200 *branchement sociaux* (social connections) to the water network were provided in 2002–04, about half of them in Niamey. To be eligible for a social connection, household members had to be living in a house within 20 meters of the main pipe, and the house had to be built of solid materials (a permanent construction). Some geographic targeting to the poor was achieved by making the social connections in poor and suburban quarters of the city.

To obtain a social connection, a household had to pay a deposit of 17,500 francs (CFAF) (US$39) plus CFAF 2,500 (US$6) of administrative fees. Moreover, the household had to be able to pay the bill each month in a single installment. The 11,200 connections had been originally planned over five years, but they were realized in only a year and a half, and some 600 requests could not be satisfied.

Households that benefited from a social connection belonged to the poorer income quintiles of the population, suggesting that the connections were fairly well targeted.

Source: Tsimpo and Wodon 2009.

subsidies created by underpricing are extremely regressive in their distributional incidence. In all but the poorest African countries, service coverage could be substantially increased before any real affordability problems would be encountered. In the poorest of the low-income countries, affordability is a legitimate concern for the bulk of the population and would constrain universal coverage. Even in the poorest countries, however, recovering operating costs should be feasible, with subsidies limited to capital costs.

How would removal of utility subsidies affect poverty reduction? For most countries, electricity and water spending accounts for only a tiny fraction of total consumption. At the national level, a 50 percent increase in tariffs or even a doubling of tariffs has a marginal effect, with the share of the population living in poverty increasing barely 0.1 of a percentage point. Among households with a connection to the network, the effect is larger but still limited. Indeed, an increase in the share of households in poverty larger than 1 or 2 percentage points rarely occurs. Because the households that benefit from a connection also tend to be better off than other households, the increase in poverty starts from a low base. Thus, the small effect of a tariff increase on poverty could be offset by reallocating utility subsidies to other areas of public expenditure with a stronger pro-poor incidence.

Various tactical measures can improve the acceptability of tariff increases, but ensuring their sustainability is most important. Tariff increases can be phased in either gradually or instantly through a one-time adjustment. Both approaches have advantages and disadvantages. The public acceptability of tariff increases can be enhanced if they are part of wider measures that include service quality improvements. One method to strengthen social accountability is adopting communication strategies that link tariffs with service delivery standards and suggest conservation measures to contain the overall bills. In any event, ensuring that the realignment of tariffs and costs is sustained by providing for automatic indexation and periodic revisions of tariffs is perhaps most important.

Countries have pursued different paths to increase tariffs critical for operational and financial sustainability. In Niger, the standpost and low-volume tariffs have barely increased since 2000, but the industrial and commercial tariffs have grown 6–7 percent in nominal terms (figure 3.11). In Lilongwe, Malawi, the same increases have been applied across all tariff categories. In addition, Botswana, Namibia, South Africa (Eskom), and Tanzania recently increased electricity tariffs as a result of oil price shocks in 2007–08.

A danger always exists that higher tariffs will simply lead to lower revenue collection, but

Figure 3.11 Increased Industrial and Commercial Tariffs, Niger and Malawi

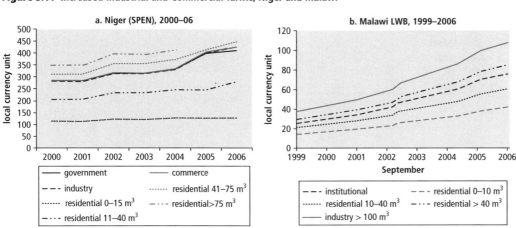

Source: Banerjee, Wodon, and others 2008.
Note: LWB = Lilongwe Water Boards; SPEN = Société de Patrimoine des Eaux de Niger; m³ = cubic meter.

prepayment meters can help. In the absence of a strong payment culture, customers who object to tariff hikes may "retaliate" by refusing to pay their bills. Thus, even before addressing tariff adjustments, utilities must work on raising revenue collection rates toward best practice and establishing a payment culture. At least for power, one technological solution is to use prepayment meters, which place customers on a debit card system similar to that for cellular telephones. For utilities, this approach eliminates credit risk and avoids nonpayment. For customers, it allows them to control their expenditure and avoid consuming beyond their means. South Africa was at the forefront in development of the keypad-based prepayment electricity meter. ESKOM launched the first product, Cashpower, in 1990. Tshwane in South Africa reports universal coverage of its consumers with prepayment meters. In Lesotho, Namibia, and Rwanda, a majority of residential customers use prepayment meters. In Ghana and Malawi, a clear policy exists of rapidly increasing the share of residential customers on prepayment meters (figure 3.12).

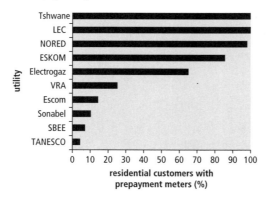

Figure 3.12 Residential Customers Using Prepayment Meters, by Utility

Source: Eberhard and others 2008.
Note: Electrogaz = Rwanda's national electric utility; Escom = Electricity Supply Corporation (Malawi); ESKOM = South Africa's national electric utility; LEC = Lesotho Electricity Company; NORED = Northern Electricity Distribution Service (Namibia); SBEE = Société Béninoise d'Énergie Électrique (Benin); Sonabel = Société Nationale d'Électricité du Burkina (Burkina Faso); TANESCO = Tanzania Electricity Supply Company Limited; Tshwane = Tshwane Local Electric Utility (South Africa); VRA = Volta River Authority (Ghana).

Targeting Subsidies to Promote Service Expansion

Subsidies also have a role to play, but their design requires major rethinking. Subsidies have a valuable and legitimate role in the proper circumstances. They may be appropriate when households genuinely cannot purchase a subsistence allowance of a service that brings major social and economic benefits to themselves and those around them, *as long as* governments can afford to pay those subsidies. However, the design and targeting of utility subsidies must be radically improved to fulfill their intended role. As noted earlier, the utility subsidies provided in Africa today largely bypass the poorest.

African utilities typically subsidize consumption, but subsidizing connection is potentially more equitable and effective in expanding coverage. The affordability problems associated with connection charges are often much more serious than those associated with use-of-service charges. Because connections are also disproportionately concentrated among the more affluent, the absence of connections is disproportionately concentrated among the poorest, which could potentially facilitate the targeting process.

The targeting performance of connection subsidies ultimately hinges on how new connections are allocated. In African countries, where coverage is far from universal even among the higher-income groups, connection subsidies may be just as regressive as consumption subsidies, essentially because the unserved higher-income groups will likely be the first to benefit from coverage expansion. Simulations suggest that—if new subsidized connections mirror the distribution of existing connections—the share of connection subsidies going to the poor would be only about 36 percent of the share of the poor in the population—a highly regressive result no better than that of existing consumption subsidies (table 3.4).

Limiting subsidies to connections in new network rollout rather than densification of the existing network would substantially improve targeting. The share of connection subsidies going to the poor would rise to 74–95 percent of their share in the population, depending on the utility involved, but the outcome would remain regressive. Providing a connection subsidy equally likely to reach all unconnected households would ensure that the percentage going to the poor exceeds their share of the population by 112–118 percent—finally, a progressive result. Improving the distributional incidence beyond this modest level would require connection subsidies to be accompanied by other socioeconomic screens. These findings illustrate that in the low-access environment in most African countries, the absence of a connection remains a relatively weak targeting variable.

Can anything be done to improve targeting of use-of-service subsidies? The poor performance of existing utility subsidies is explained by pro-rich coverage and by the widespread use of poorly designed IBTs. Common design failures in water IBTs include high fixed charges and minimum consumption levels that penalize small consumers, as well as the large size and universal applicability of the first subsidized block (Banerjee, Foster, and others 2008). Common design failures in power IBTs include large subsistence thresholds that allow only consumers with exceptionally high consumption to contribute fully to cost recovery (Briceño-Garmendia and Shkaratan 2008). Achieving major improvements in the targeting of use-of-service subsidies by overhauling the design of increasing block tariffs (IBTs) is difficult. Some improvements in targeting could be achieved by eliminating fixed charges, reducing the size of first blocks to cover only genuinely subsistence consumption, and changing from an IBT to a volume-differentiated tariff in which those consuming beyond a certain level forfeit the subsidized first-block tariff completely. Even with these modifications, however, the targeting of such tariffs would improve only marginally and not become strongly pro-poor in absolute terms.

Global experience suggests that the targeting of utility subsidies can be improved and become reasonably progressive, if some form of geographical or socioeconomic targeting variables can be used beyond the level of consumption (Komives and others 2005). However, such targeting schemes hinge on the existence of household registers or property cadastres that

Table 3.4 Potential Targeting Performance of Connection Subsidies under Various Scenarios

percentage of total poor getting connection subsidies relative to percentage of poor in the population

Utility	New connections mirror pattern of existing connections	Only households beyond reach of existing network receive connection subsidies	All unconnected households receive subsidy
Electricity	37	95	118
Water	35	74	112

Sources: Banerjee, Wodon, and others 2008; Wodon 2008a, 2008b.

support the classification of beneficiaries, as well as a significant amount of administrative capacity. Both factors are often absent in Africa, particularly in the low-income countries.

An important test of the coherence of a subsidy policy is whether the country could afford the policy if it were scaled up to universal access. The underpricing of utility services that benefit just a small minority of the population costs many African countries as much as 1 percent of GDP. As countries move toward universal access, that subsidy burden would increase proportionately, rapidly becoming unaffordable for the national budget. Thus, countries should consider how the cost of any proposed subsidy policy would escalate as coverage improves. This test of a subsidy's fiscal affordability is an important consideration to help countries avoid embarking on policies that are simply not scalable.

Another potentially effective method of targeting is to limit the allocation of subsidies to lower-cost and lower-quality alternatives that encourage self-selection. For services such as water, for which different modes of service provision exist, subsidies could possibly be concentrated on second-best alternatives such as standposts while requiring full cost recovery from private piped-water connections. The theory is that more affluent customers will eschew second-best services and automatically opt to pay the full cost of the best alternative, thus identifying themselves and leaving the subsidized service to less affluent customers. In Africa, however, the use of self-selection may be less effective, because coverage of second-best alternatives such as standposts and improved latrines is just as regressive as coverage of best alternatives such as piped water and flush toilets.

Giving More Consideration to Second-Best Solutions

Second-best solutions appear to provide a happy compromise but face many implementation challenges. As noted earlier, second-best approaches provide modern services that are far preferable in welfare terms to their traditional alternatives and are still much less costly than best modern infrastructure services. So why are these second-best services fairly rare in Africa—and skewed toward more affluent households?

A key problem of many second-best solutions is that their public good nature complicates their adoption. Both public standposts and street lighting are essentially public goods. This characterization makes it difficult for utilities to recover the costs of these services and exposes them to theft by extending the network's reach into lower-income areas. Thus, utilities have no real incentive to provide such loss-prone services. In addition, facilities are vulnerable to maintenance issues, because nobody is responsible for preventing, reporting, or addressing problems. One solution is to introduce an agent responsible for managing the facility, charging for service, and soliciting maintenance activities. However, covering the agent's salary adds significantly to the cost of the second-best alternative, and agents often exploit their controlling position to charge excessive rates.

The African experience with standposts provides pointers for improving the performance of such public facilities (Keener, Luengo, and Banerjee 2008). Where standposts are administered by local agents, the management model should be grounded in the prevailing culture of the beneficiary community. Checks and balances are needed to ensure that the delegated manager behaves responsibly. The utility also must be closely involved in monitoring the status of the standposts, regularly collecting the water revenues, and providing technical assistance to the standpost operators. Therefore, defining a useful set of incentives that bolster the utility's growing interest in participating in the standpost business is essential. In some environments, resale of water by households with private connections can be a practical alternative to standposts, although it is often not legally recognized. In addition, yard taps that serve four or five households—not several hundred—can reduce costs while avoiding some of the most serious public good problems.

Notes

The authors of this chapter are Sudeshna Ghosh Banerjee, Quentin Wodon, and Vivien Foster, who drew on background material and contributions from Tarik Chfadi, Amadou Diallo, Sarah Keener, Taras Pushak, Maria Shkaratan, Clarence Tsimpo, Helal Uddin, and Yvonne Ying.

1. The cross-regional figures for infrastructure coverage are unweighted simple averages.

References

Banerjee, Sudeshna, Vivien Foster, Yvonne Ying, Heather Skilling, and Quentin Wodon. 2008. "Achieving Cost Recovery, Equity and Efficiency in Water Tariffs: Evidence from African Utilities." Working Paper 7, Africa Infrastructure Country Diagnostic, World Bank, Washington, DC.

Banerjee, Sudeshna, Quentin Wodon, Amadou Diallo, Taras Pushak, Hellal Uddin, Clarence Tsimpo, and Vivien Foster. 2008. "Access, Affordability, and Alternatives: Modern Infrastructure Services in Africa." Background Paper 2, Africa Infrastructure Sector Diagnostic, World Bank, Washington, DC.

Bardasi, Elena, and Quentin Wodon. 2009. "Working Long Hours and Having No Choice: Time Poverty in Guinea." Policy Research Working Paper 4961, World Bank, Washington, DC.

Boccanfuso, Dorothée, Antonio Estache, and Luc Savard. 2008a. "Electricity Reforms in Mali: A Micro-Macro Analysis of the Effects on Poverty and Distribution." Working Paper 4, Africa Infrastructure Country Diagnostic, World Bank, Washington, DC.

———. 2008b. "Electricity Reforms in Senegal: A Micro-Macro Analysis of the Effects on Poverty and Distribution." Working Paper 5, Africa Infrastructure Country Diagnostic, World Bank, Washington, DC.

———. 2008c. "Water Reforms in Senegal: A Micro-Macro Analysis of the Effects on Poverty and Distribution." Working Paper 16, Africa Infrastructure Country Diagnostic, World Bank, Washington, DC.

Briceño-Garmendia, Cecilia, and Maria Shkaratan. 2008. "Achieving Cost Recovery, Equity, and Efficiency in Power Tariffs: Evidence from African Utilities." Working Paper 21, Africa Infrastructure Country Diagnostic, World Bank, Washington, DC.

Diallo, Amadou, and Quentin Wodon. 2005. "A Note on Access to Network-Based Infrastructure Services in Africa: Benefit and Marginal Incidence Analysis." World Bank, Washington, DC.

Eberhard, Anton, Vivien Foster, Cecilia Briceño-Garmendia, Fatimata Ouedraogo, Daniel Camos, and Maria Shkaratan. 2008. "Underpowered: The State of the Power Sector in Sub-Saharan Africa." Background Paper 6, Africa Infrastructure Sector Diagnostic, World Bank, Washington, DC.

Estache, Antonio, and Quentin Wodon. 2007. *Infrastructure and Poverty in Sub-Saharan Africa.* Directions in Development Series. Washington, DC: World Bank.

Foster, Vivien, and Jean-Philippe Tré. 2003. "Measuring the Impact of Energy Interventions on the Poor—An Illustration from Guatemala." *In Infrastructure for Poor People: Public Policy for Private Provision*, ed. Penelope Brook and Tim Irwin, 125–78. Washington, DC: World Bank.

Gulyani, Sumila, Debabrata Talukdar, and Darby Jack. 2008. "A Tale of Three Cities: Understanding Differences in Provision of Modern Services." Working Paper 10, Africa Infrastructure Country Diagnostic, World Bank, Washington, DC.

Kariuki, Mukami, and Jordan Schwartz. 2005. "Small-Scale Private Service Providers of Water and Electricity: A Review of Incidence, Structure, Pricing, and Operating Characteristics." Policy Research Working Paper 3727, World Bank, Washington, DC.

Keener, Sarah, Manuel Luengo, and Sudeshna G. Banerjee. 2008. "Provision of Water to the Poor in Africa: Informal Water Markets and Experience with Water Standposts." Working Paper 13, Africa Infrastructure Country Diagnostic, World Bank, Washington, DC.

Komives, Kristin, Vivien Foster, Jonathan Halpern, and Quentin Wodon. 2005. *Water, Electricity, and the Poor: Who Benefits from Utility Subsidies?* Washington, DC: World Bank.

Kumar, Ajay, and Fanny Barrett. 2008. "Stuck in Traffic: Urban Transport in Africa." Background Paper 1, Africa Infrastructure Country Diagnostic, World Bank, Washington, DC.

McGranahan, Gordon, Cyrus Njiru, Mike Albu, Mike Smith, and Diana Mitlin. 2006. *How Small Water Enterprises Can Contribute to MDGs: Evidence from Dar es Salaam, Nairobi, Khartoum, and Accra.* Leicestershire, U.K.: Water, Engineering and Development Centre, Loughborough University.

Tsimpo, Clarence, and Quentin Wodon. 2009. "Who Benefits from Electricity Consumption versus Connection Subsidies? Evidence from Niger." Development Dialogue on Values and Ethics, World Bank, Washington, DC.

Wodon, Quentin, ed. 2008a. "Electricity Tariffs and the Poor: Case Studies from Sub-Saharan Africa." Working Paper 11, Africa Infrastructure Country Diagnostic, World Bank, Washington, DC.

———. 2008b. "Water Tariffs and the Poor: Case Studies from Sub-Saharan Africa." Working Paper 12, Africa Infrastructure Country Diagnostic, World Bank, Washington, DC.

Wodon, Quentin, and Yvonne Ying. 2009. "The Determinants of Domestic Work Time in Sierra Leone." Development Dialogue on Values and Ethics, World Bank, Washington, DC.

Chapter 4

Building Sound Institutions

Institutional competence and capacity are important determinants of the performance of infrastructure providers in every sector. That seems obvious, but systematic analysis has been lacking on the nature and extent of the links between stronger institutions and better outcomes: specifically, broader access, higher service quality, and more financially efficient service. This chapter looks at the different institutional models applied, the approaches to strengthen infrastructure-relevant institutions, and the effect of the various approaches on performance.

The standard infrastructure reform and policy prescription package of the 1990s—market restructuring, private involvement up to and including privatization, establishing independent regulators, and enhancing competition—yielded a fair number of positive results in Africa. This conclusion deserves stress: beneficial outcomes following the application of these reforms have often been unacknowledged or at least underappreciated. Nevertheless, this set of reforms has proved more difficult to apply in Africa than in other regions. One finds in Africa numerous failures to implement, or fully implement, the policy package; renegotiations or cancellations of contracts with private

providers; outcomes below expectations; and a high degree of official and public skepticism about whether the application of the standard package is producing (or even could produce) the desired results. A large part of the explanation for this situation is thought to lie in the relative weakness of African practices, policies, and agencies (that is, institutions) that guide and oversee African infrastructure sectors and firms, public or private.

The statistical analysis for this chapter suggests that institutions make a difference. It reveals strong links between institutional reforms and enhanced governance in the country, sector, and enterprise—and improvements in the quantity and quality of infrastructure services (with sectoral variation). Given the link between institutional development and performance improvements, and the high costs of inaction, strengthening sectoral institutions and country and sectoral governance is a very worthwhile investment.

Most African countries have undertaken preliminary institutional reforms, mainly the broader sectoral policy and legal measures, many of which can be accomplished by the stroke of a pen. What has lagged are regulatory and governance reforms; they have taken much more time to bear fruit. For instance, effective regulation requires building organizations that challenge established vested interests. Governance improvements, particularly in state-owned enterprises (SOEs), require aligning internal and external incentives, which again require broader reforms of the external environment for infrastructure service providers.

Institutional Reforms: A Glass Half Full

Africa's institutional framework for infrastructure is no more than halfway along the path to best practice. The components of the institutional performance indicators developed for this study capture a wide range of characteristics of the institutional environment (box 4.1). A country's aggregate score on this index suggests the extent of institutional reforms. Overall, although

almost all African countries have embarked on institutional reforms, on average they have adopted no more than 50 percent of good institutional practices. The variation in performance across countries is roughly two to one, with the most advanced countries (Kenya) scoring about 70 percent and those furthest behind scoring 30 percent (Benin).

At the country level, progress in one infrastructure sector is no guarantee of progress in another. That is, institutional development in infrastructure sectors is uneven both among and within countries. Countries that perform fairly well in one aspect of infrastructure do not necessarily do so in another. This finding suggests that sector-specific constraints may be as important as country-specific constraints. It also points to the potential for greater cross-fertilization of experiences across sectors within a country.

In addition, the quality of the institutional framework differs across country groupings.

BOX 4.1

Infrastructure's Institutional Scorecard

To analyze the links between institutional factors related to infrastructure and performance outcomes at the sector and enterprise levels, this study devised a standardized survey-based methodology that describes the nature of each institutional reform and measures the intensity of the reform efforts. The methodology builds on, and is compatible with, other recent literature on the subject.

This methodology yields a "scorecard," a succinct snapshot of what has happened, sector by sector, in three key institutional dimensions: (a) broad sectoral policy reforms, (b) amount and quality of regulation, and (c) enterprise governance. First, *reform* is defined as implementing sectoral legislation, restructuring enterprises, and introducing policy oversight and private sector participation. Second, the *quality of regulation* entails progress in establishing autonomous, transparent, and accountable regulatory agencies and regulatory tools (such as quality standards and tariff methodology). Third, *governance* entails the implementation of measures inside the enterprise (such as strengthening shareholder voice and supervision, board and management autonomy, and mechanisms for accounting and disclosure) and measures aimed at improving the external environment in which the enterprise operates (including outsourcing to the private sector and introducing discipline from a

competitive labor and capital market). Note that reform and regulation are country-level indicators, whereas governance is measured at the enterprise level.

The Infrastructure Institutional Scorecard applied in this chapter derives from a detailed survey of African infrastructure sectors and enterprises. The reform and regulatory scorecards cover 24 countries for all sectors (except railways and ports, which included only 21 countries and 15 countries, respectively). The governance scorecards have been collected for the 24 telecommunication providers and 21 railway providers. A sample of 30 utilities in the electricity sector and a sample of 52 utilities in the water sector were examined.

The resulting list of institutional reforms represents a refinement and extension of previous attempts to generate a global scorecard of institutional reforms for infrastructure sectors. The choice of the indicators was made in consultation with infrastructure sector experts. Operationally relevant indicators were selected, each of which had to meet two conditions. First, an action was chosen if a consensus existed that it represented "best practice" and was being applied in different sectors. Second, the data needed to calculate the indicator had to be relatively easy to obtain at the sectoral and enterprise levels.

(continued)

BOX 4.1

(continued)

Reform

Legislation
Existence of de jure reform
Implementation of reform

Restructuring
Unbundling/separation of business lines
State-owned enterprise corporatization
Existence of regulatory body

Policy Oversight
Oversight of regulation monitoring outside the ministry
Dispute arbitration outside the ministry
Tariff approval outside the ministry
Investment plan outside the ministry
Technical standard outside the ministry

Private Sector Involvement
Private de jure/de facto
Private sector management/investment/ownership
Absence of distressed/renegotiation/renationalization

Regulation

Autonomy
Formal autonomy on hiring/firing
Financial autonomy (partial/full)
Managerial autonomy (partial/full)
Multisectoral agency/commissioners

Transparency
Publication of decisions via report/Internet/public hearing

Accountability
Existence of appeal
Independence of appeal (partial/full)

Tools
Existence of tariff methodology/tariff indexation
Existence of regulatory review; length of regulatory review

Internal Governance

Ownership and Shareholder Quality
Concentration of ownership
Corporatization/limited liability
Rate of return and dividend policy

Managerial and Board Autonomy
Autonomy in hiring/firing/wages/production/sales
Size of board
Selection of board members
Presence of independent directors

Accounting, Disclosure, and Performance Monitoring
Publication of annual reports
International financial reporting standards/external audits/independent audit
Audit publication
Remuneration of noncommercial activity
Performance contracts/with incentives
Penalties for poor performance
Monitoring/third-party monitoring

External Governance

Labor Market Discipline
Restriction on dismissing employees
Wages, compared to private sector
Benefits, compared to private sector

Capital Market Discipline
No exemption from taxation
Access to debt, compared to private sector
No state guarantees
Public listing

Outsourcing
Billing and collection
Meter reading
Human resources information technology

Jointly, the three sets of indicators (reform, regulatory, and governance) added together summarize the overall level and type of institutional reforms in any given country.

Separately, each indicator serves as a basis for measuring the (aggregate and disaggregate) effect of progress in reforms and enterprise performance.

Source: Vagliasindi 2008c.

Reflecting countries' broader characteristics, the extent of institutional reforms differs across these groups (figure 4.1). For example, middle-income countries are significantly further ahead with power sector reform, whereas aid-dependent low-income countries are signifi-cantly further ahead with water reform, perhaps reflecting the strong role of donors in this sector. For telecommunications reform, the resource-rich low-income countries have higher scores.

A correlation exists between the quality of *infrastructure* institutions and the *overall*

Figure 4.1 Institutional Progress across Countries, by Income Group, Aid Dependence, and Resource Richness

percentage score on institutional scorecard

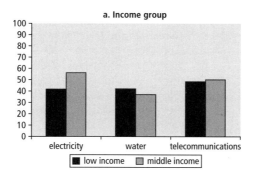

a. Income group

low income middle income

electricity   water   telecommunications

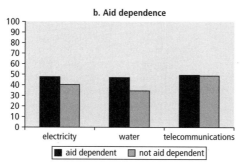

b. Aid dependence

aid dependent not aid dependent

electricity   water   telecommunications

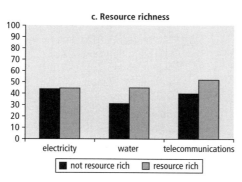

c. Resource richness

not resource rich resource rich

electricity   water   telecommunications

Source: Vagliasindi and Nellis 2009.
Note: See Vagliasindi 2008c for the definition of the *institutional indicators.*

quality of institutions in the country, though this correlation is much stronger for electricity than for water (table 4.1). A key question is the extent to which a country can make progress in reforming infrastructure institutions if its wider governance framework is deficient (Levy 2007). Numerous indicators have been developed in recent years (for example, by Kaufman, Kraay, and Mastruzzi 2008), attempting to capture

the overall level of governance and control of corruption,[1] as well as the quality of public administration. A polity executive constraint indicator also measures the extent of checks and balances within a government (Center for Systemic Peace 2006).

Nevertheless, some countries do well on infrastructure despite broader governance limitations, and vice versa. For Kenya and Niger, lower scores on the country governance indicators have not impeded the achievement of good scores across all utilities' institutional reforms. For Zambia, low scores in budget execution and financial management have not prevented the country from earning reasonably good scores in infrastructure institutional reforms. By contrast, Benin and Lesotho display high country governance and polity executive constraint scores and have decent budgetary and financial management standards, but neither has a high overall institutional score in the utility sectors.

Institutional development in the utilities sector is well ahead of that in the transport sector (figure 4.2). Unsurprisingly, institutional development is furthest ahead in telecommunications, where technological change and competition have driven momentous change, bringing the overall average reform score to just under 50 percent. Electricity and water are not that far behind, with institutional reform scores just over 40 percent. Although institutional actions in power and water lag those in telecommunications for implementing reform agendas, they score somewhat higher in the quality of regulation. Also, the governance framework for the main service providers is significantly better than that for fixed-line telecommunication incumbents. By contrast, institutional scores for ports and railways are only about half those for the utilities. These sectors have made significant progress with reform but lag in developing the regulatory framework.

Across countries and sectors, the greatest progress has been in sector reform. Average scores exceed 60 percent for reform legislation and 50 percent for sector restructuring, policy oversight, and private sector participation (figure 4.3, panel a). Telecommunications, the most advanced, scores about 80 percent of the best-practice index across all areas of sector reform.

Table 4.1 Correlation between Institutional Scores for Infrastructure and Measures of Broader Country Governance

Infrastructure sector	Polity executive constraint	Budget and financial management	Public administration	Overall governance	Control of corruption
Electricity	0.34	0.29	0.53	0.49	0.46
Water	0.08	0.33	0.3	0.18	0.08

Sources: Vagliasindi and Nellis 2009; Center for Systemic Peace 2006 for polity executive constraint scores; IDA 2008 for Country Policy and Institutional Assessment score; Kaufmann, Kraay, and Mastruzzi 2008 for governance and control of corruption.

Figure 4.2 Institutional Progress across Sectors
percentage score on institutional scorecard

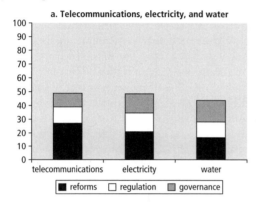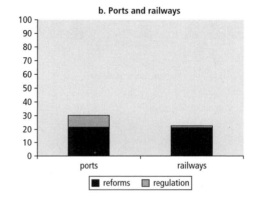

Source: Vagliasindi and Nellis 2009.
Note: See Vagliasindi 2008c for the definition of the *institutional indicators*.

The equivalent score for electricity is about 60 percent, and for water about 50 percent. Transport scores about 50 percent on private sector participation, but this development has not been accompanied by the broader legal and structural reforms seen in the utilities sectors.

Interference from government continues to undermine regulatory independence in many countries. Infrastructure regulation in Africa is still in its early days. Typically, new laws and regulatory bodies have been introduced for telecommunications and electricity, whereas few countries have created water or transport regulators. The quality of regulation can be measured along several dimensions (figure 4.3, panel b). On the technical side, regulation needs to be founded on solid methodological tools, and the resulting decisions need to be communicated to the public in a transparent manner. African regulators score the highest on these dimensions, even if (in absolute terms) they still have some way to go. On the political side, regulation requires a certain degree of autonomy

from government interference while remaining accountable to society. These aspects of regulation have proved more challenging, with scores remaining relatively low.

Governance lags behind other areas of institutional development, and the limited progress shows up mainly in internal managerial practices. Whereas the relevance of sectoral and regulatory reforms has generally been well recognized, the governance regime has received less attention from policy makers and analysts. Almost all Sub-Saharan countries ranked significantly and consistently lower on this dimension of institutional development than on the others (figure 4.3, panel c). Most countries are doing better on internal governance than on external governance. Internal governance relates to structures within the service provision entity, such as the extent to which its structure approximates standard corporate forms; the qualifications and autonomy of its senior management and board of directors; the nature, quality, and timeliness

Figure 4.3 Institutional Progress on Reforms, Regulation, and Governance
percentage score on institutional scorecard

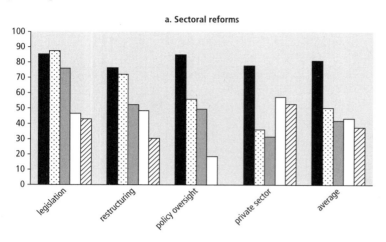

a. Sectoral reforms

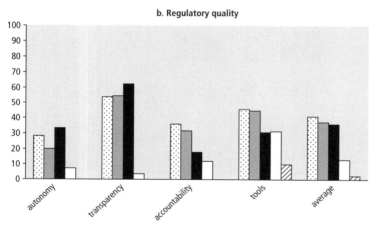

b. Regulatory quality

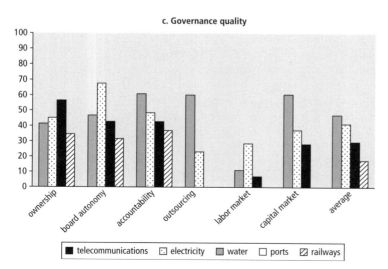

c. Governance quality

■ telecommunications ⋯ electricity ▨ water ☐ ports ⬚ railways

Source: Vagliasindi and Nellis 2009.
Note: See box 4.1 for the definition of the *institutional indicators.*

of the information it submits to its overseers; and the adoption of accounting and disclosure standards. External governance, by contrast, refers to external market disciplines: being subject to private rather than public sector accounting and auditing systems, contracting out noncore activities to private providers, and being obliged to raise debt or equity funds on private capital markets, domestic or international.

Only Kenya and South Africa have raised much from external capital markets. Kenya corporatized its power distribution utility and more recently its generation firm, and then issued a minority of shares in each on the Nairobi Stock Exchange. The 2006 initial public offering of 30 percent of the shares of KenGen raised $35 million, a small but significant start. In South Africa, share issuance was not considered feasible, but the national utility, ESKOM, was corporatized, obtained a credit rating, and then issued corporate bonds—$120 million in 2007 alone.

The data generated in the sectoral chapters and the institutional scorecard analysis shed considerable light on the efficacy of the three central pillars of infrastructure institutional reform, namely, private sector participation (PSP), state-owned enterprise governance, and regulators.

Does Private Sector Participation Work?

The lessons learned from overall experience with PSP demonstrate sectoral nuances. Whereas some sectors display a significant extent of PSP that has brought about valuable outcomes (mobile telephony, power generation, and ports), results are mixed in other sectors (roads, power and water distribution).

The extent of private participation varies significantly across sectors. Despite widespread legislation in the region allowing private operators entry into infrastructure, implementation lags are common, particularly for water and railways (figure 4.4).

In Africa, most private participation in water, electricity, railways, and ports has been by methods other than full divestiture, that is, through management contracts, leases, and concessions. Only in telecommunications has divestiture been widely applied. The amount of private participation, of all sorts, varies by sector, with the most in telecommunications and the least in water (figure 4.5).

As noted previously, private participation in Africa has had some problems. Twenty-five percent of contracts in water have been canceled, as have 15 percent in electricity (table 4.2). Note that these cancellations do not include contracts that have undergone renegotiation because of the complaints of one or both of the parties involved; nor do they account for cases where anticipated renewals of leases or, especially, management contracts have not occurred, leading to a resumption of state management. In all infrastructure sectors, contract negotiation, monitoring, and enforcement have proved more time-consuming and difficult than expected.

Despite these difficulties, the survey undertaken for this chapter reveals significant gains from private participation in some sectors and for certain aspects of performance. A higher degree of private sector involvement is associated with higher labor productivity (connections per employee), though the link is statistically significant only in the case of electricity and ports, and higher but not statistically significant cost-recovery ratios. In telecommunications, the countries with above-average private involvement display higher access in both the fixed and the mobile segments of the market. More extensive private involvement in ports is associated with above-average technical efficiency.

Figure 4.4 Implementation of Private Participation across Sectors

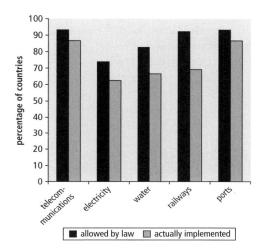

Source: Vagliasindi and Nellis 2009.

Figure 4.5 Private Participation in Management and Investment across Sectors

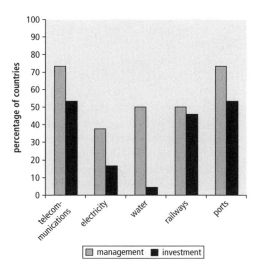

Source: Vagliasindi and Nellis 2009.

Table 4.2 Cancellation of African Private Participation Contracts

Type of contract	Number of contracts	Percentage canceled
Water		
Management contract	15	20
Lease contract	7	45
Concession contract	4	50
BTO/BOO	1	0
Divestiture	1	0
Total	28	25
Electricity		
Management or lease contract	17	24
Concession contract	16	31
Independent power project	34	6
Divestiture	7	—
Total	74	15

Source: Vagliasindi and Nellis 2009.
Note: BOO = build-operate-own; BTO = build-transfer-operate.
— Not applicable.

Earlier empirical studies also find some evidence of positive outcomes, albeit based on case study evidence and by no means in all instances. For example, a recent study of seven infrastructure privatizations in Africa assessed three factors: (a) efficiency gains and losses, (b) nature and competence of the transaction, and (c) who won and who lost (and by how much) in society because of the transaction (BIDE 2006). Three of the seven (Côte d'Ivoire electricity, Senegal Airlines, and Senegal water) were assessed as "unqualified success stories" in efficiency terms, according to a variety of financial and service quality measures. Three others (Mozambique water and Uganda water and telecommunications) were assessed as producing "some positive changes but less than what most expect from privatization." Only Senegal electricity was classified as having "no significant effect" (BIDE 2006: 2). None of the seven was assessed as negatively affecting efficiency.

Such studies found a close correlation between the competence in negotiating the transaction and the efficiency gains by the new private operator. The distributional effect could be assessed fully in two cases (Côte d'Ivoire electricity and Senegal water) and partially in the other five. Even with limited information, the study found a correlation between institutional capacity and wider distribution of benefits. That is, the cases having the better institutional arrangements in conducting the transaction show better outcomes for a broader range of stakeholders than do the cases where the transaction process was rated lower.

Using the analysis of the sectoral chapters in this study, one can further assess the extent and effect of private participation in African infrastructure, from the most extensive and successful involvement to the least.

Telecommunications

Private participation in telecommunications has taken place in the majority of Sub-Saharan countries. In 15 countries, at least partial privatization of the state-owned fixed-line telecommunication incumbent has occurred. Licensing new private mobile operators for greenfield networks has been even more widespread.

Privatization of fixed-line incumbents has affected access and productivity, and quality of services somewhat, though the change is not statistically significant (figure 4.6). The growth in the number of subscribers has been low and in almost all countries negative, except Nigeria, the only country where competition has also been introduced in the fixed-line segment of the market. Productivity is also low, compared with international benchmarks (lines per employee).

Still, several private participation transactions in the fixed-line segment of these markets (the remaining natural monopoly) have run into problems. In the last few years, strategic investors from developed countries have largely withdrawn from African telecommunication privatizations. Only three such sales have occurred since 2001, and in those sales, no traditional strategic partner obtained a controlling stake. Recent telecommunication divestitures have either been public offerings (South Africa and Sudan), sales to developing-country investors (ZTE of China in Niger and Maroc Telecom in Burkina Faso), or sales to domestic investors (Malawi and Nigeria). In several instances, governments have repurchased shares in incumbent operators. That happened in Ghana and is planned in Rwanda. In Tanzania in 2005, the government repurchased shares previously privatized in its fixed-line operator, TTCL. In May 2007, the government placed TTCL under a three-year management contract with a Canadian firm, SaskTel. As of early 2009, the government was considering canceling the contract, claiming that SaskTel had failed in its commitment to raise nonguaranteed debt financing to rehabilitate and expand the network.

Access has spread quickly since 1998 because of the rapid rise of mobile telephony, largely from the combination of private participation and increasingly intense competition. Private investment, the bulk of it greenfield, in cellular phone technology has allowed new providers to enter previously monopolistic markets, resulting in greater access and declining, though still comparatively high, consumer prices. Analysts generally argue that the dramatic increases in African access to and coverage of telecommunication services owe more to the entry of new mobile operators, thereby strengthening competition, than to the improved information and incentives of private managers and owners. Most new mobile operators are controlled by one of five multinational firms operating in the region: France Telecom, MTC (Kuwait), MTN (South Africa), Millicom (Luxembourg), or Vodacom (South Africa).

The salutary effects of competition are apparent. A strong link exists between liberalization in this sector (and others) and better outcomes in access and productivity (figure 4.7). Countries with lower market concentration in the mobile segment of the market, measured by the Herfindahl-Hirschman Index,[2] have much higher penetration rates and productivity in the same segment of the market, as well as in the fixed-line business, though none of these links are statistically significant.

Ports

By 2006, 20 port concessions were operating in Africa, with 6 more in process. Evaluations of these concessions indicate that delays, costs, and thefts were reduced and that port infrastructure started to improve. Cargo-handling rates and the use of better handling systems in African "concessioned" ports are significantly higher than in state-managed ports (figure 4.8).

Private sector involvement has grown greatly in container terminals in the region since 2000 (now in eight countries and in process in several others). Case study evidence for Nigeria and Tanzania confirms the results of the statistical evidence reported here (see box 4.2). Nonetheless, the level of private sector penetration in the African port sector is low, compared with other regions.

Railways

Concessions to the private sector have been applied in 13 of the 24 countries reviewed, and the mechanism is presently under negotiation in 3 countries and under consideration in another 3 countries. Evaluations of several other longer-standing concessions, nonetheless, conclude that railways under concessions perform more efficiently than those remaining in state hands, although the difference is significant only in locomotive availability and coach productivity (figure 4.9).

Figure 4.6 Links between Private Sector Participation and Performance Indicators in Telecommunications

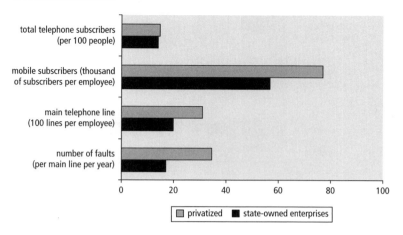

Source: Vagliasindi and Nellis 2009.
Note: None of these performance differentials was found to be statistically significant at 5 percent.

Figure 4.7 Links between Market Concentration and Performance Indicators in Telecommunications

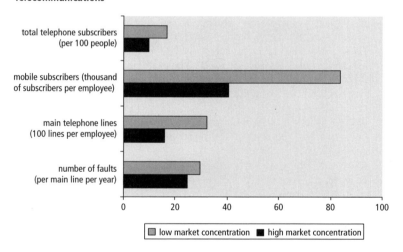

Source: Vagliasindi and Nellis 2009.
Note: None of these performance differentials was found to be statistically significant.

The concession process is not always smooth. For example, the Kenya-Uganda concessionaire, brought in with much fanfare in 2006, has had difficulties in raising the promised investment financing. The contract was renegotiated in late 2008 to reduce the shareholding of the original investor and to allow the owning governments to seek new private partners.

Figure 4.8 Links between Port Concessions and Performance Indicators

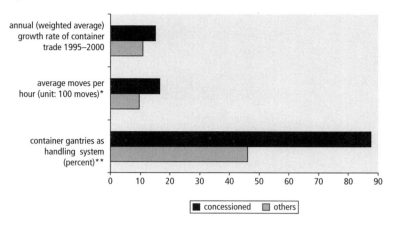

Source: Vagliasindi and Nellis 2009.
Note: *Performance differential is statistically significant at the 10 percent level; **significant at the 5 percent level.

BOX 4.2

Privatization in African Ports

A lease in the container terminal in the port of Dar es Salaam, Tanzania, produced, within five years, a doubling of throughput, a 70 percent reduction in container dwell time, greater customer satisfaction, record profits, and vastly increased government revenues (from taxes, lease fees, and payments of $14 per container cleared). The number of expatriate managers fell from 17 to 4; the number of Tanzanian senior managers doubled. More than half the original workforce was dismissed, but salaries for those remaining increased by an average 300 percent—and postlease expansion in operations created 500 new jobs, far more than the number previously laid off. Dar es Salaam became the fastest container terminal in Africa, with performance exceeding that of many European and Australian ports.

In 2004, Nigeria started a major effort to reform its clogged, inefficient, and very expensive ports. The government enacted "upstream" policy and legal reforms while hiring, through concessions, experienced private operators to manage, operate, and rehabilitate 26 ports. The new autonomous regional port authorities, now the "landlords" of the ports, negotiated the concession contracts. The Federal Ministry of Transport took on the role of sector policy maker. Just a few months after the concessioning of the Apapa-Lagos container terminal, delays for berthing space had dwindled, and leading shipping lines reduced their congestion surcharge from $525 to $75, saving the Nigerian economy an estimated $200 million a year. Observers credit the improvements as much to the upstream reform of the institutional setting as to bringing on board private operators.

Worth noting is that Tanzania and Nigeria are the top two countries in institutional reforms.

Sources: World Bank 2005 for Tanzania; Leigland and Palsson 2007 for Nigeria.

Concessions have not resolved the key issue of mobilizing finance. The drawback of concessions is that they rarely produce the anticipated (and in many cases, contracted) investments for network rehabilitation and expansion. The reason is that service revenues are too low to support investment finance, partly due to low traffic volumes and intense intermodal competition and partly due to the failure by governments to compensate concessionaires for running loss-making obligatory passenger services. Thus, chronic underinvestment and dilapidated infrastructure remain as major railway problems. The limited investment capital forthcoming has been financed by international financial institutions and passed through government to the private railway operators.

Electricity

The most common form of private participation in the electricity sector has been independent power projects (IPPs), with 34 in 11 African countries (Besant-Jones 2006). Assessments of African IPPs have drawn attention to the lack of alternatives, given the severe shortfalls in generation throughout the region and the very important fact that most IPPs do produce the amounts of electricity called for in the contracts. Without IPP production, the number and duration of service disruptions would be far higher than it has been in recent years.

Low transparency in IPP negotiations translated into high costs. Many, if not most, IPPs were negotiated hastily, in periods of crisis, and competitive bidding processes were often amended or skipped entirely. That haste resulted in extremely high costs that now pose a heavy financial burden on the balance sheets of power purchasers: national distribution utilities (and their government owners). This situation, in turn, has led to widespread suspicion that IPP negotiations were incompetently or corruptly managed (Gratwick and Eberhard 2008).

Regulatory benchmarking can be used to enhance transparency. A proposed methodology would facilitate a regulatory review of power purchase agreements by explicitly benchmarking them for price and risk allocation, to identify and ensure that the terms of the agreements are "fair and balanced" to all parties who will be directly and indirectly affected by these transactions (Besant-Jones, Tenenbaum, and Tallapragada 2008). The Nigerian energy regulator has tested the methodology.

Management contracts are the second most common form of electricity PSP, with 17 in 15 countries.[3] Management contracts have produced large and significant labor productivity gains (figure 4.10), though they have not proved sufficient, in and of themselves, to overcome the broader policy and institutional deficiencies of the sector. The effects of these contracts on cost recovery, system losses, and collection rates, however, turn out to be minimal and statistically insignificant (figure 4.10). As with concessions in railways, management contracts in electricity have not been instrumental in generating investment funds.

Several independent evaluations of management contracts conclude that they produced efficiency gains and improved financial performance (Davies 2004). The problem is that they have not been sustained. Only 3 of 17 negotiated contracts remain in operation. A few have been canceled. More commonly, however, although technicians and donors recommend renewal of contracts after their initial phase, African governments, for mainly sociopolitical reasons, choose to reestablish public management. Lessons from this experience include the importance of setting targets not only for commercial performance but also for improvements in quality of supply and service, including expanded access, so that consumers experience tangible benefits. Effective contractual oversight is needed to track performance, to fairly assess and award incentive payments or penalties, and to reduce information asymmetry. Finally, postcontract management succession issues need to be addressed early (Ghanadan and Eberhard 2007).

Water

In water, leases have been applied rather widely, with management contracts as the second most common form of private participation. Concessions have also been used in several African countries (in Chad, Gabon, and Senegal, for

Figure 4.9 Links between Rail Concessions and Performance Indicators

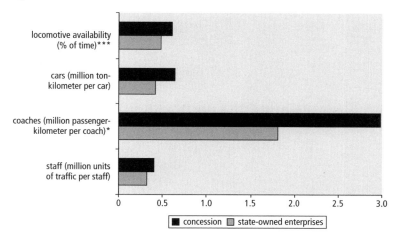

Source: Vagliasindi and Nellis 2009.
Note: *Performance differential is statistically significant at the 10 percent level; ***significant at the 1 percent level.

Figure 4.10 Links between Electricity Management Contracts and Performance Measures

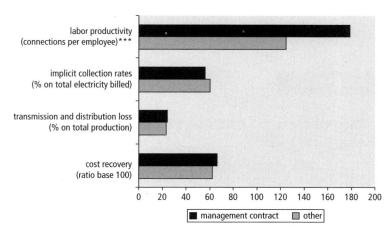

Source: Vagliasindi and Nellis 2009.
Note: ***Performance differential is statistically significant at the 1 percent level.

example, dating from the 1990s). The two in Gabon and Senegal have been judged as successes in producing service improvements, network expansions, and financial stability (BIDE 2006). The long-term leases in Côte d'Ivoire and Niger have been producing positive financial and operational results, despite difficult external conditions (Marin 2008). Only one divestiture has occurred, entailing the sale of 51 percent of equity, which was in the water company in Cape Verde in 1999.

Private participation in water has generated much hostility and opposition. Because water is a commodity essential for life, many feel that its distribution should be free or at a very low price. Despite considerable evidence of persistently poor performance by publicly owned and operated African water companies, many people believe that the service cannot and should not be turned over to private delivery. To support their position, they point to several notable private participation problem cases in water, such as Tanzania (see box 4.3) and Uganda.

A recent detailed empirical review of the main experiences with private sector participation in the African water sector concluded that there had been beneficial effects on enterprise performance in a number of cases but that the extent of these impacts depended on the contractual forms that were used (Marin 2008). In the case of management contracts, which are short term in nature, there had been benefits in terms of revenue collection and service continuity but little effect on other aspects of performance. In the case of lease contracts, which are medium term in nature, broader improvements in operational efficiency had been observed. Access had also improved, although funding continued to come from the public sector.

What Have We Learned?

Any evaluation of the African experience with private sector participation must be nuanced by the wide variation in sector experiences (table 4.3), and both successes and failures considered in tandem. Public and official attention have focused more on the failures and contentious cases, particularly in water, but also in power and transport. However, the lesson from African private participation is not that the approach should be discarded, but that it should be applied selectively and carefully to those areas of infrastructure where it has a proven potential to contribute.

Expectations should also be kept realistic. Experience has shown that there are only a few niches where, either through raising investment finance or improving operational efficiency, the private sector can contribute significantly to investment finance—namely, ICT (particularly mobile networks), power generation, port container terminals, and a handful of high-traffic road segments (table 4.3). While the overall volume of private finance for infrastructure investment is limited, it is nonetheless substantial, having (at least during the mid-2000s) exceeded the volume of ODA for these sectors (recall table 2.1). But even in areas of infrastructure that have not proved attractive for private *finance*—such as most roads, railways, power and water distribution systems—private *management* can still make a significant contribution to improving operational performance, and thereby help to recover the very substantial funds that are currently being lost to various kinds of inefficiency (recall table 2.8).

Of course, one cannot deny the problems in African private participation, or that many of them can be attributed, in all sectors, to institutional deficiencies. Poor sectoral planning, vague or absent sector policies, and long-standing weak financial and operational performance in the utilities helped create the crises of demand and insecurity that led to rushed decisions. In state-owned infrastructure

BOX 4.3

Lessons from the DAWASA Lease Contract (Tanzania)

The failed lease contract of DAWASA, the water authority for Dar es Salaam, Tanzania, is instructive. The contract was signed in August 2002. It was supposed to run for 10 years, but the government canceled it in May 2005, after only 21 months of operation. The government claimed the private provider had failed to meet water production and collection targets, pay the lease and other fees, meet service quality and quantity commitments, and pay the penalties assessed for noncompliance. For its part, the private provider claimed that its bid and business plan were based on inaccurate, out-of-date, or partial information provided by the government. Arbitration in April–May 2005 failed; the government terminated the contract, and the service returned to public management. Critics note that the private provider's lawsuit against the government for breach of contract was rejected (in 2008) by a British court. They argue that this case shows how difficult it is to ensure that private provision of water will fulfill either the anticipated financial objectives or the distributional objectives.

Sources: BIDE 2006; Marin 2008.

Table 4.3 Overview of Experience with Private Participation in Infrastructure

Infrastructure sector	Extent of private participation	Nature of experience	Prospects
ICT			
Mobile telephony	Over 90 percent of countries have licensed multiple mobile operators	Extremely beneficial with exponential increase in coverage and penetration	Several countries still have potential to grant additional licenses
Fixed telephony	Some 60 percent of countries have undergone divestiture of SOE telecommunication incumbent	Controversial in some cases, but has helped improve overall sector efficiency	Several countries still have potential to undertake divestitures
Power			
Power generation	34 IPPs provide 3,000 MW of new capacity, investing $2.5 billion	Few cancellations but frequent renegotiations; PPAs have proved costly for utilities	Likely to continue, given huge unsatisfied demands and limited public sector capacity
Power distribution	16 concessions and 17 management or lease contracts in 24 countries	Problematic and controversial; one-quarter of contracts canceled before completion	Movement toward hybrid models involving local private sector in similar frameworks
Transport			
Airports	Four airport concessions, investing less than $0.1 billion, plus some divestitures	No cancellations but some lessons learned	Limited number of additional airports viable for concessions
Ports	26 container terminal concessions, investing $1.3 billion	Processes can be controversial, but cancellations have been few and results positive	Good potential to continue
Railroads	14 railroad concessions, investing $0.4 billion	Frequent renegotiations, low traffic, and costly public service obligations keep investment below expectations	Likely to continue but model needs to be adapted
Roads	10 toll-road projects, almost all in South Africa, investing $1.6 billion	No cancellations reported	Limited because only 8 percent of road network meets minimum traffic threshold, almost all in South Africa
Water			
Water	26 transactions, mainly management or lease contracts	Problematic and controversial; 40 percent of contracts canceled before completion	Movement toward hybrid models involving local private sector in similar frameworks

Source: Authors' elaboration based on Bofinger 2009; Bullock 2009; Eberhard and others 2008; Gwilliam and others 2008; Minges and others 2008; Mundy and Penfold 2008; and Svendsen, Ewing, and Msangi 2008.
Note: ICT = information and communication technology; IPP = independent power project; PPA = power purchase agreement; SOE = state-owned enterprise.

firms, poor management, inadequate or nonexistent record keeping (at both the firm and higher levels), and lax monitoring created organizational and informational chaos that reduced the interest of potential investors and severely complicated the due diligence processes of those who bid. Nontransparent contract negotiation proceedings, substandard procurement practices, and inadequate contract monitoring and enforcement mechanisms have been among the factors contributing to higher prices, poorer-than-anticipated outcomes, renegotiated or canceled contracts, and governance issues. These institutional deficiencies must be dealt with if private participation is to fulfill its potential.

Despite the inroads of private participation over the past two decades, Africa remains the region with the highest state ownership of its infrastructure utilities. The financial crisis of 2008–09 will further deplete investor appetites for comparatively high-risk ventures in emerging markets, heighten the reluctance of African officials to embark on innovative schemes, and add weight to the notion of the primacy of the public sector. Therefore, the existing level of state ownership is likely to persist, and may indeed increase, in the near to medium term. This likelihood requires renewed attention to a long-standing but recently neglected issue: improving the financial and operational performance of state-owned firms (Nellis 2005; Gómez-Ibáñez 2007).

How Can State-Owned Enterprise Performance Be Improved?

Africa has the highest percentage of state-owned infrastructure utilities of any developing region. Given the mixed record; the absence of investor appetite; and the antipathy of African officials, nongovernmental organizations, and many observers of development toward private participation—and the resulting increasing reluctance of the donor community to push for privatization in infrastructure—state ownership is likely to be the norm for some time.

The track record so far in governance reforms is not encouraging and varies substantially across sectors and countries. One must start with the recognition that a few African state-owned infrastructure firms have sustained good performance in the absence of private participation. Botswana and Uganda show that fully state-owned African utilities can deliver high-quality performance (see box 4.4 and box 4.5, respectively).

The cost of inaction implies high hidden costs. The estimated hidden cost of inefficiency coming from mispricing, unaccounted losses, and collection inefficiency is on average equal to 0.6 percent of GDP in the water sector and 1.9 percent of GDP in the power sector. The inefficiency of SOEs can also be measured by excessive employment. In the telecommunication sector, the hidden cost of excessive employment is on average equal to 0.1 percent of GDP.

Only limited success in achieving full corporatization, including establishing limited liabilities and introducing rate of return and dividend policies, has been recorded in Africa. The telecommunication sector alone can be reported as a success story, with electricity and water lagging, proving that even countries with high scores compare poorly with other regions.

More limited corporate governance reforms have been started more evenly across all sectors and are becoming a dominant feature in electricity and water. These changes include the introduction of boards of directors (even if the size tends to be either too large or too small compared with international standards), selection of board members according to a competitive process rather than direct appointments by line ministries, and the introduction of independent directors (figure 4.11).

Performance contracts with incentives and independent external audits have become dominant features of the governance reform process for both electricity and water (figure 4.12). Independent audits have also been good for efficiency in both cases.

Of governance reforms that appear to be the most important drivers of higher performance, two appear especially promising: performance contracts with incentives and independent external audits (table 4.4). Uganda has had good experience with a performance contract in its water company, providing the utility with incentives for good performance and producing greater accountability (see box 4.5). The introduction of independent audits has also positively affected efficiency for both electricity and water utilities.

What can such cases teach? First, recast and reapply the performance contract approach to SOE reform. Initial attempts to improve African SOEs using this device were minimally effective, but recent efforts have had a stronger and much more positive effect. The more recent performance contracts applied with some success in Uganda (and, reportedly, in Kenya) should be studied and modified for broader application to African utilities across sectors.

Second, renew efforts to strengthen the financial and operational monitoring of SOEs.

BOX 4.4

Lessons from Successful SOE Reforms in Botswana Power Corporation

The state-owned and -operated Botswana Power Corporation has long provided reliable, high-quality service. Over the years, Botswana Power has expanded its network in both urban and rural areas, covered its costs, posed no burden on the government budget, minimized system losses (10 percent), and earned a decent return on assets. Although the availability of cheap imported power from South Africa (now severely threatened) is part of the explanation for good performance, analysts give five institutional factors equal weight in explaining this success: (a) a strong, stable economy, (b) cost-reflective tariffs, (c) lack of government interference in managerial decisions, (d) good internal governance, and (e) competent, well-motivated staff and management.

Source: PPA 2005.

BOX 4.5

Performance Agreement for the National Water and Sewerage Corporation (Uganda)

Between 1998 and 2004, the National Water and Sewerage Corporation (NWSC) system operated under two management contracts with private providers. By the end of the second contract, neither party had an interest in continuing. After 2004, public managers, operating under performance contracts, were responsible for the service. A review of performance during the entire period concluded that the targets set for the private management contracts were fulfilled but that the public management team furnished similarly good performance. The main stages in the enterprise reform process are described below.

From February 1999 onward, the management of the NWSC in Uganda has sequentially implemented a number of reform programs. First, local officials, called area service providers (areas), negotiated with central authorities a set of tightly defined performance targets. Second, area managers were given control over running the process. Third, they were held strictly accountable for specific results.

A number of measures including the 100-day program and the service and revenue enhancement programs resulted in better specification of targets for the areas. The programs

also increased the head office's commitment to provide financial and material resources to enable different areas to implement rehabilitation and investment programs.

In 2002, automatic tariff indexation was introduced. In addition, the Stretch-Out Program increased staff commitment by improving internal communication and setting tougher performance targets and corresponding incentives. A one-minute management system was introduced to further enhance individual staff members' accountability for targets.

The government introduced a three-year performance contract in 2000. The NWSC's debt service obligations were suspended in return for a commitment to operational and financial improvements and an increase in coverage.

In 2003, a second performance contract continued the suspension of debt service and specified that NWSC's debt would be restructured to a sustainable level. A review committee monitored implementation of the agreement. The main incentives of the agreements are bonuses for managers and staff, if performance targets are achieved.

Sources: Baietti, Kingdom, and van Ginneken 2006; Vagliasindi 2008a.

Figure 4.11 Prevalence of Good Governance Practices among State-Owned Enterprises for Infrastructure

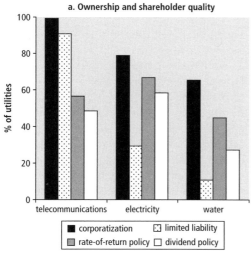

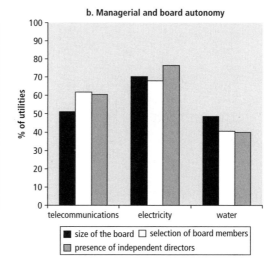

Source: Vagliasindi and Nellis 2009.
Note: See box 4.1 for definitions of institutional indicators.

Some of the structures implied in the Organisation for Economic Co-operation and Development's Principles of Corporate Governance for SOEs (favoring a centralized ownership function through an independent agency versus a decentralized structure) have not yet been sufficiently "tested" in practice and may not suit all developing countries. A centralized

Figure 4.12 Prevalence of Performance Contracts in Electricity and Water

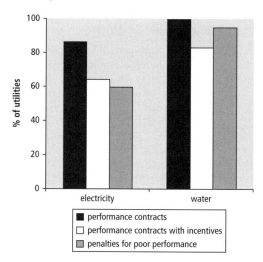

Source: Vagliasindi and Nellis 2009.

Table 4.4 Links between Governance and Performance Indicators for Electricity and Water

Reform/sector	Technical losses		Connections per employee		Access	
	Yes	No	Yes	No	Yes	No
Performance contracts						
Electricity	24.2[a]	23.3[a]	176.8**	103.0	14.6[a]	28.1[a]
Water	36.2	33.6	13.6	6.2	28.1	14.6
Independent audit						
Electricity	22.9	28.3	164.3**	92.7	22.0	9.6
Water	35.2	35.7	7.6	6.0	9.6[a]	22.0[a]

Source: Vagliasindi and Nellis 2009.
Note: **Performance differential is statistically significant at the 5 percent level.
a. The sign of the links between the variables is not as expected.

their economic performance, including the detailed structure of subsidies and intersectoral arrears (Vagliasindi 2008b).

Do Independent Regulators Make Sense?

Countries rank rather low on regulatory independence across all sectors, confirming that the standard model has not fit the challenges in Africa well. Independence in several infrastructure sectors has been challenged across all formal, financial, and managerial dimensions. Evidence on the links between introducing an independent regulator and improving performance is weak, but a significant positive effect is discernible in telecommunications (table 4.5).

In water, where state-owned enterprises still predominate and are likely to for some time, countries with an independent regulator perform no better than those without (table 4.5). This outcome may reflect the fact that donors have tended to be the largest promoters of water regulatory agencies and they tend to assist on the most problematic situations. In addition, many countries (particularly the francophone nations) have opted for regulation by contract rather than create an independent agency.

Nonetheless, hybrid regulatory schemes have not proved to be superior to traditional forms of regulation in the water sector. Africa Infrastructure Country Diagnostic data support no evidence on the superiority of regulation by contract over the traditional form of regulation by agency (see table 4.6 and box 4.6).

For railways and ports, the regulatory function is generally entrusted to ministries of transport. Only Tanzania is establishing two multisector regulatory agencies, one for public services and the other for transport. Mali and Senegal had railway regulatory agencies that were later converted into a common railway-monitoring agency for both countries. In railways, an independent regulator is still considered necessary, not so much to prevent exploitation of the monopoly power of the private sector as to protect the concessionaire from the erratic behavior of governments,

structure, where the owner is the ministry of finance rather than an independent agency, is more suited to the limited physical and human resource bases of most African countries. Moreover, it has been implemented relatively successfully in several developing countries. Under a decentralized or dual model—where the owner is the sectoral ministry or both a central authority (the ministry of finance or treasury) and the sectoral ministry—the central authority can collect and monitor information about the state-owned enterprises and

Table 4.5 Links between Regulation and Performance Indicators for Telecommunications, Electricity, and Water

Sector	Technical losses		Connections per employee		Access	
	Regulation	No regulation	Regulation	No regulation	Regulation	No regulation
Telecommunications	0.2	0.3	0.38***	0.03	0.2***	0.1
Electricity	23.3	25.3	155.3	117.3	22.3	11.9
Water	35.2	34.8	6.8[a]	8.3[a]	36.1	35.9

Source: Vagliasindi and Nellis 2009.
Note: ***Performance differential is statistically significant at the 1 percent level.
a. The sign of the links between the variables is not as expected.

Table 4.6 Links between Type of Regulator and Performance Indicators for Water

Sector	Technical losses (% production)		Connections per employee		Access (% households)	
	Regulation by contract	Regulation by agency	Regulation by contract	Regulation by agency	Regulation by contract	Regulation by agency
Water	39.4	31.5	0.19	0.05	16.9	32.1

Source: Vagliasindi and Nellis 2009.
Note: None of these performance differentials was found to be statistically significant.

BOX 4.6

Regulation by Contract in Senegal

In the highly successful case of Senegalese water, the officials negotiating the contract did a world-class job of structuring a solid transaction and capturing almost immediate gains for consumers by using a creative compensation structure with many of the efficiency properties of two-part utility pricing. By contrast, in the less-successful case of electricity, Senegalese negotiators of the electricity divestiture did not anticipate a predictable problem: "Price was set by a perfectly reasonable price-cap [Retail Price Index – x] formula, but it failed to include a specific escalation factor for key input prices, and only included a general input price adjustment factor. When oil prices roughly doubled shortly after transfer, the operator wanted relief." The government was reluctant to allow the price increases demanded by the private (minority) owner and operator, and the deal collapsed. The firm returned to public hands where, following a failed second attempt at divestiture, it has done rather well.

Source: BIDE 2006.

---

including the nonpayment of passenger service obligations to the concessionaires.

Weak regulatory autonomy and capacity constraints undermine the credibility of the independent regulator (Eberhard 2007). Most Sub-Saharan regulatory agencies are embryonic, lacking funding and in many cases qualified personnel. Budgets vary considerably, ranging from less than $300,000 to about $3 million for electricity. Staffing also varies widely, from one or two to a couple of dozen employees. Although regulatory requirements differ with country size and income, that difference does not fully explain the observed variation in capacity. Contrast Sub-Saharan regulatory budgets to those of the most developed countries: in 2005, the U.S. electricity regulator, the Federal Energy Regulatory Commission, had a budget of about $240 million for 1,200 employees, and the United Kingdom's Office of the Gas and Electricity Markets had a budget of $74 million for about 300 employees.

Notes

The authors of this chapter are Maria Vagliasindi and John Nellis, who drew on background material and contributions from Sudeshna Ghosh Banerjee, Cecelia Briceño-Garmendia, Vivien Foster, Yan Li, Elvira Morella, and Maria Shkaratan.

1. The World Bank's Country Policy and Institutional Assessment indicator reported in IDA 2008.

2. The index is calculated by squaring the market share of each firm competing in the market and summing the results. For example, for a market consisting of four firms with shares of 30, 30, 20, and 20 percent, the index is 2,600 ($30^2 + 30^2 + 20^2 + 20^2 = 2,600$).

3. Management contracts should not be confused with performance contracts. In a management contract, an owning government hires private personnel to operate an SOE. The contractor is paid a fee for service; normally, bonuses are awarded to the contractor if stipulated performance targets are met. A performance contract is a set of negotiations between a government and SOE managers from the public sector, spelling out the obligations and responsibilities of the two parties over a set period. Performance contracts can include incentives to SOE management (and staff); typically, the main issues specified deal with the managers' obligations to meet some targets and the government's obligation to allow price increases, provide investment capital, settle past debts, pay bills on time, and so on.

References

Baietti, Aldo, William Kingdom, and Meike van Ginneken. 2006. "Characteristics of Well-Performing Public Water Utilities." Water Supply and Sanitation Working Note 9, World Bank, Washington, DC.

Besant-Jones, John E. 2006. "Reforming Power Markets in Developing Countries: What Have We Learned?" Energy and Mining Sector Board Discussion Paper 19, World Bank, Washington, DC.

Besant-Jones, John E., Bernard Tenenbaum, and Prasad Tallapragada. 2008. "Regulatory Review of Power Purchase Agreements: A Proposed Benchmarking Methodology." Energy Sector Management Assistance Program Formal Report 337/08, World Bank, Washington, DC.

BIDE (Boston Institute of Development Economics). 2006. Impact of Privatization in Africa: Synthesis of Eight Cases. Washington, DC: World Bank.

Bofinger, Heinrich C. 2009. "Air Transport: Challenges to Growth." Background Paper 16, Africa Infrastructure Sector Diagnostic, World Bank, Washington, DC.

Bullock, Richard. 2009. "Taking Stock of Railway Companies in Sub-Saharan Africa." Background Paper 17, Africa Infrastructure Sector Diagnostic, World Bank, Washington, DC.

Center for Systemic Peace. 2006. Political Regime Characteristics and Transitions. Fairfax, VA: George Mason University.

Davies, Ian C. 2004. Management Contracts in the Electricity Sector: Case Studies in Malawi, Lesotho, Tanzania and Rwanda. Washington, DC: World Bank.

Eberhard, Anton. 2007. "Matching Regulatory Design to Country Circumstances: The Potential for Hybrid and Transitional Models." Gridlines, Note 23. Public-Private Infrastructure Advisory Facility, World Bank, Washington, DC.

Eberhard, Anton, Vivien Foster, Cecilia Briceño-Garmendia, Fatimata Ouedraogo, Daniel Camos, and Maria Shkaratan. 2008. "Underpowered: The State of the Power Sector in Sub-Saharan Africa." Background Paper 6, Africa Infrastructure Sector Diagnostic, World Bank, Washington, DC.

Ghanadan, Rebecca, and Anton Eberhard. 2007. "Electricity Utility Management Contracts in Africa: Lessons and Experience from the TANESCO-NET Group Solutions Management Contract in Tanzania." Management Programme in Infrastructure Reform and Regulation Working Paper, Graduate School of Business, University of Cape Town, South Africa.

Gómez-Ibáñez, José A. 2007. "Alternatives to Infrastructure Privatization Revisited: Public Enterprise Reform from the 1960s to the 1980s." Policy Research Working Paper 4391, World Bank, Washington, DC.

Gratwick, Katharine Nawaal, and Anton Eberhard. 2008. "An Analysis of Independent Power Projects in Africa: Understanding Development and Investment Outcomes." Development Policy Review 26(3): 309–38.

Gwilliam, Ken, Vivien Foster, Rodrigo Archondo-Callao, Cecilia Briceño-Garmendia, Alberto Nogales, and Kavita Sethi. 2008. "The Burden of Maintenance: Roads in Sub-Saharan Africa." Background Paper 14, Africa Infrastructure Sector Diagnostic, World Bank, Washington, DC.

IDA (International Development Association). 2008. IDA: The Platform for Achieving Results at the Country Level, Fifteenth Replenishment. Washington, DC: IDA.

Kaufmann, Daniel, Aart Kraay, and Massimo Mastruzzi. 2008. "Governance Matters VII: Aggregate and Individual Governance Indicators 1996–2007." Policy Research Working Paper 4654, World Bank, Washington, DC.

Leigland, James, and Gylfi Palsson. 2007. "Port Reform in Nigeria." *Gridlines*, Note 17. Public-Private Infrastructure Advisory Facility, World Bank, Washington, DC.

Levy, Brian. 2007. *Governance Reforms, Poverty Reduction and Economic Management.* Washington, DC: World Bank.

Marin, Philippe. 2008. *Public-Private Partnerships for Urban Water Utilities: A Review of Experiences in Developing Countries.* Washington, DC: World Bank.

Minges, Michael, Cecilia Briceño-Garmendia, Mark Williams, Mavis Ampah, Daniel Camos, and Maria Shkratan. 2008. "Information and Communications Technology in Sub-Saharan Africa: A Sector Review." Background Paper 10, Africa Infrastructure Sector Diagnostic, World Bank, Washington, DC.

Mundy, Michael, and Andrew Penfold. 2008. "Beyond the Bottlenecks: Ports in Sub-Saharan Africa." Background Paper 8, Africa Infrastructure Sector Diagnostic, World Bank, Washington, DC.

Nellis, John. 2005. "The Evolution of Enterprise Reform in Africa: From State-Owned Enterprises to Private Participation Infrastructure—and Back?" Research Paper 117, Fondazione Eni Enrico Mattei, Milan.

PPA (Power Planning Associates Ltd.). 2005. "Towards Growth and Poverty Reduction: Lessons from Private Participation in Infrastructure in Sub-Saharan Africa—Case Study of Botswana Power Corporation." Report submitted to World Bank, Washington, DC.

Svendsen, Mark, Mandy Ewing, and Siwa Msangi. 2008. "Watermarks: Indicators of Irrigation Sector Performance in Sub-Saharan Africa." Background Paper 4, Africa Infrastructure Sector Diagnostic, World Bank, Washington, DC.

Vagliasindi, Maria. 2008a. "The Effectiveness of Boards of Directors of State Owned Enterprises in Developing Countries." Policy Research Working Paper 4579, World Bank, Washington, DC.

———. 2008b. "Governance Arrangement for State-Owned Enterprises." Policy Research Working Paper 4542, World Bank, Washington, DC.

———. 2008c. "Institutional Infrastructure Indicators: An Application to Reforms, Regulation and Governance in Sub-Saharan Africa." World Bank, Washington, DC.

Vagliasindi, Maria, and John Nellis. 2009. "Evaluating Africa's Experience with Institutional Reform for the Infrastructure Sectors." Working Paper 23, Africa Infrastructure Sector Diagnostic, World Bank, Washington, DC.

World Bank. 2005. "Second Port Modernization and Railway Restructuring Projects, Project Performance Assessment Report." World Bank, Washington, DC.

Chapter 5

Facilitating Urbanization

Africa is urbanizing fast, a change that is predictable and beneficial. Economic geography indicates that prosperity and density go together because higher productivity requires agglomeration economies, larger markets, and better connectivity. Concentration and urbanization trigger prosperity in urban areas as much as in rural areas, and well-functioning cities facilitate trade and the transformation of rural production and nonfarm activities. The debate over rural or urban development should thus be replaced by the understanding that rural and urban development are mutually dependent and that economic integration of rural and urban areas is the only way to produce growth and inclusive development.

Populated places in Africa need infrastructure to enhance the competitiveness of their businesses and the productivity of their workers. Energy, roads, water, and information and communication technologies (ICTs) give African economies the capacity to develop. Long-run growth requires an efficient system of urban centers that includes small, medium, and larger cities that produce industrial goods and high-value services, along with well-functioning transportation networks (roads, rails, and ports) to link national economies with regional and global markets.

African cities are growing fast, but because of insufficient infrastructure and poor institutions, most new settlements are informal and not covered by basic services. This situation has severe consequences for health, incomes, and market integration. A combination of institutional reform, land policy and planning, housing policies, and basic services is required for urban expansion that is more equitable and inclusive in nature.

Many necessary investments are beyond the limited fiscal and financial base of African cities. Decentralization has increased the responsibilities of cities, but not their powers and incentives to raise (and retain) revenues. Cities need access to predictable streams of revenue and the flexibility to raise additional resources, to safeguard service provision to their constituencies. They also need to improve their technical and managerial capacity to deal with priorities in investment and operation and maintenance, to guide the inevitable expansion, to attract private partners, and to understand their surrounding neighborhoods to develop synergies.

Africa's large agricultural sector and rural economy remain central for overall economic growth and poverty reduction. Better infrastructure is crucial for raising agricultural productivity and facilitating access to markets for agricultural products. The Asian experience suggests that successful economic growth demands higher agricultural productivity, which raises incomes and the demand for nonagricultural products, lowers food prices, and frees up labor for (mainly urban) industrial and service employment (World Bank 2008).[1]

The policy challenge is to harness market forces that encourage concentration and promote convergence in living standards between villages, towns, and cities. Policy makers will be more effective if they look at development strategies for broad economic areas that integrate towns and cities with their surrounding rural hinterland. This chapter discusses and estimates the infrastructure needs of rural and urban areas in the context of rapid urbanization and its challenges for infrastructure, institutions, and targeted interventions.

Viewing Cities as Engines of Growth

The debate on growth strategies has often looked at urban and rural areas as competing for primacy in the national agenda and in investment allocations, but now is the time to frame the debate differently. Cities exist because of the economic and social advantages of closeness. Urban centers contribute to national economic growth by increasing individual, business, and industry productivity through agglomeration economies; by increasing household welfare through social mobility and human development; and by promoting positive institutional change. Cities also drive rural development, serving as primary markets for rural production and generating income that flows back to rural areas. Links between urban and rural areas constitute a virtuous circle, where access to urban markets and services for nonfarm production stimulates agricultural productivity and rural incomes, which in turn generate demand and labor for more goods and

services. Addressing bottlenecks in city performance is an effective entry point into this "virtuous" circle (Kessides 2006).

Proximity to cities (neighborhood effect) is critical for enabling the shift from subsistence to commercial agriculture, for increasing rural incomes, and for making living standards converge. Areas within two hours' travel time of cities of at least 100,000 people seem to have diversified into nonagricultural activities (Dorosh and others 2008). Rural areas located between two and eight hours' travel time from such cities account for more than 62 percent of the agricultural supply and generate a surplus sold to urban areas. In areas farther than eight hours from these cities, agriculture is largely for subsistence, and less than 15 percent of the land's agricultural potential is realized (table 5.1).[2] Similarly, farmers closer to cities tend to use more and higher-quality fertilizers and pesticides and better equipment, resulting in clear improvements in productivity. So the growth of urban markets is a key factor in raising the income of the rural population in the hinterland.

Strengthening Urban-Rural Links

An integrated approach to development recognizes and facilitates the links between urban and rural areas. Urban centers consume rural products and offer inputs for rural production; rural areas serve as markets for goods and services produced in urban areas. Migration produces social and economic links between urban and rural areas. Migrants often remain connected to their families, which they support through remittances. In addition, rural people often receive health services and education from nearby towns and cities. Institutional and fiscal links are often present as well. In most cases, fiscal redistribution takes place—typically from cities to rural areas, given the cities' larger tax base.

Rural-urban links are constrained by inadequate transport networks, poor electricity and water provision, and limited coverage of ICT. Weak institutions add to the constraints. For example, in Ethiopia, the city of Dessie enjoys a strategic location and is a main distribution center for manufacturing products to the surrounding regions (World Bank 2007). However, the lack of a developed agroprocessing industry limits the market opportunities for higher-value agricultural production and the benefits for the surrounding agricultural areas.

Urbanization in Africa

Africa's population remains predominantly rural. About 66 percent of the inhabitants live in rural areas, with significant variation across countries (table 5.2).[3] In African middle-income countries, half of the inhabitants live in rural areas, whereas in the landlocked low-income countries, they account for about 70 percent. The vast majority of Africa's rural population (or half of the overall population) lives in the rural hinterland within six hours' travel time of cities having at least 50,000 inhabitants, whereas about 16 percent of Africa's population lives in isolated areas more than six hours' travel time from the same cities.

The continent is urbanizing rapidly, however, and will become predominantly urban by 2020. The share of urban population rose from 15 percent in 1960 to 35 percent in 2006 and will reach nearly 60 percent by 2020. Urban growth is presently estimated at 3.9 percent a year. Rural migration accounts for one-quarter of that growth, with the remainder attributable to urban demographic growth and administrative reclassification (Farvacque-Vitkovic, Glasser, and others 2008).

In several fragile states, civil war has contributed to urban expansion as people from the affected regions seek refuge in cities. One-third of Africa's urban population is concentrated in the region's 36 megacities with more than 1 million inhabitants. Much of the remainder is spread across 232 intermediate cities of between 100,000 and 1 million inhabitants and in periurban areas. The largest cities are growing fastest, suggesting that Africa's urban population will become more concentrated.

As is typical in the early phases of urbanization, urban household incomes in Africa are much higher than rural incomes, almost twice as high. The 2009 *World Development Report* notes that an economy's transformation is seldom geographically balanced (World Bank 2009). Productivity tends to increase where people and economic activities concentrate to take advantage of agglomeration economies. The initial growth spurt is typically associated with a divergence in living standards between leading regions

Table 5.1 Link between Agricultural Productivity and Distance to Urban Centers

Travel time	Percentage of total area	Percentage of total population	Percentage of total crop production	Per capita production ($ per capita)
Less than 1.7 hours	10.0	41.4	23.6	57.00
1.7–7.6 hours	50.0	46.0	62.5	135.80
More than 7.6 hours	40.0	12.5	13.9	110.70
Total	100.0	100.0	100.0	n.a.

Source: Dorosh and others 2008.
Note: Totals may not add exactly because of rounding errors.
n.a. = Not applicable.

Table 5.2 Distribution of Population by Type of Settlement and Country Type

Country type	GNI per capita ($ per capita)	Percentage of total population					
		Megacities	Intermediate cities	Secondary cities	Periurban areas	Rural hinterlands	Remote rural areas
Sub-Saharan Africa	875	13.4	10.2	0.2	10.3	49.8	16.4
Low-income countries, landlocked	245	8.3	8.3	0.2	7.5	56.5	19.2
Low-income countries, coastal	472	11.1	6.7	0.2	12.0	46.3	23.6
Middle-income countries	5,081	24.6	15.8	0.4	12.5	50.1	1.6

Source: Authors' compilation based on geographic information systems analysis of Global Rural-Urban Mapping Project population density data.
Note: GNI = gross national income. GNI per capita is in current dollars using the Atlas method. Estimates are based on a panel of 20 countries. Megacities have more than 1 million people; intermediate cities have between 100,000 and 1 million people; secondary urban areas have between 100,000 and 50,000 people; periurban areas are less than one hour from the nearest city with more than 50,000 people; rural hinterlands are between one and six hours from the nearest city with more than 50,000 people; and remote areas are more than six hours from the nearest city with more than 50,000 people.

(mostly urban) and lagging regions (mostly rural), but as incomes increase, the divergence is followed by convergence.[4] Essential household consumption converges soonest, access to basic public services next, and wages and income later. Convergence occurs because of the mobility of people and resources across regions and declining economic distances among regions.

African countries stand at the beginning of this process. The difference between urban and rural incomes explains the lower urban poverty rates (35 percent) vis-à-vis rural poverty rates (52 percent) (table 5.3). In absolute terms, the African rural poor are almost three times as numerous as the urban poor. This picture holds for every country regardless of its geography. Similar differences are observed in access to services.

The incomes in urban areas reflect the higher productivity possible thanks to agglomeration economies—the gain in efficiency from having many businesses and workers in proximity. In countries where traditional non-mechanized agriculture still dominates the rural sector, the difference between urban and rural productivity can be large. Assuming that agricultural output originates in rural areas and industry and services originate in urban areas, the African rural sector contributes less than 20 percent of the continent's GDP, despite accounting for more than 60 percent of the population (table 5.4; Kessides 2006). Recent work in Tanzania confirms these values: the country's urban areas are home to 23 percent of the population yet account for 51 percent of the GDP (Maal 2008). One could infer that the average productivity in urban areas is at least three times that of rural areas (Farvacque-Vitkovic, Glasser, and others 2008).

Infrastructure in Urban and Rural Areas

For population centers to realize their full economic potential, the provision of infrastructure and public services must be efficient. Basic services for households in both urban and rural areas can guarantee sustainable urbanization and social equity, enhance living conditions, and prevent disproportionate flows of underserved rural people to the city. Investment in infrastructure can improve productivity in the modern sector and connectivity with and across locations. Deficiencies in infrastructure and services, which limit the potential for agglomeration economies, hinder African economies and may explain the underperformance of businesses in Africa relative to other continents. One-third of African businesses report a worrisome lack of electricity, and 15 percent identify

Table 5.3 Economic Differentials between Rural and Urban Populations, by Country Type

Country type	Monthly household budget			Poverty rate		
	National ($/month)	Rural ($/month)	Urban ($/month)	National (percent)	Rural (percent)	Urban (percent)
Sub-Saharan Africa	144	106	195	48	35	52
Low-income countries, landlocked	86	75	139	49	32	53
Low-income countries, coastal	145	115	209	47	38	51
Middle-income countries	535	256	691	n.a.	n.a.	n.a.

Source: Authors' compilation based on household surveys reported in Banerjee and others 2008.
Note: n.a. = not applicable.

Table 5.4 Sectoral Contributions to GDP and GDP Growth
percentage

Item	1990–95			1996–2000			2001–05		
	Agriculture	Industry	Services	Agriculture	Industries	Services	Agriculture	Industries	Services
Contribution to GDP	17	31	52	17	30	53	19	31	50
Contribution to GDP growth	59	−28	69	14	30	56	26	37	37

Source: Authors' compilation based on National Accounts data.

transportation as a major constraint. Poor-quality roads and other transportation infrastructure endanger connectivity between rural and urban areas, between products and markets, and between workers and labor markets.

The difference in the coverage of basic infrastructure services is huge across urban and rural areas. For the spectrum of household services, urban coverage rates are between 5 and 10 times those in rural areas (figure 5.1). The absolute differences are largest for power and smallest for ICT services. Electricity and improved water supply (such as piped connection or standpost) extend to a majority of the urban population, but to less than one-fifth of the rural. An even smaller share in rural areas uses septic tanks or improved latrines; and access to ICT services remains negligible. In almost half of the countries, energy coverage barely reaches 50 percent of the urban population and 5 percent of the rural. In addition, fewer than 40 percent of African urban households enjoy a private water connection, a septic tank, or an improved latrine, a share that falls to 5 percent in rural areas.

Growth in urban and rural coverage of network infrastructure tends to be positively correlated. Countries with faster expansion of urban coverage of water and electricity also tend to have faster expansion of rural coverage, suggesting that an urban network eases expansion toward rural areas. It may also suggest that urban customers cross-subsidize rural water networks and electrification.

Every year since 1990, an additional 0.9 percent of the urban population has gained access to improved water and 1.7 percent to improved sanitation, whereas the corresponding rural figures stand, respectively, at only 0.3 and 0.4. Electricity service has been expanded to an additional 3 percent of urban residents but to only an additional 0.8 percent of rural residents. Even so, rampant demographic pressure in urban areas has caused coverage rates to decline for all urban services (particularly improved water), whereas coverage of all rural services has increased (particularly power and ICT). As a result, the gap between urban and rural coverage rates has narrowed slightly but at the cost of leaving urban dwellers and businesses without infrastructure for domestic and industrial purposes (figure 5.2). This finding shows that urban service providers have struggled to keep pace with accelerating urbanization.

Africa's sparse road density often leaves rural areas isolated from urban markets. Only one-third of Africans living in rural areas are within 2 kilometers of an all-season road. The paved-road density is 134 kilometers per 1,000 square kilometers of arable land, and the unpaved, 490 kilometers. Moreover, the quality of the rural network is perceptibly lower than that of the main network, with almost half in poor condition (figure 5.3). The lack of adequate urban transport is an obstacle for businesses and for labor mobility.

The spatial footprint of infrastructure networks is larger than the coverage rates would suggest. In the rural hinterlands, where the bulk of Africa's rural population lives, 40–50 percent of people live within range of an infrastructure network. Even in isolated rural areas, the share is as high as 15 percent. This information suggests that hookup rates to infrastructure networks are lower in rural areas. In some cases, that likely reflects much lower rural purchasing power. In others, technical limitations might prevent rural inhabitants from connecting to infrastructure networks, even when close to one.

Infrastructure investment (particularly in rural areas) continues to focus on sector-specific interventions rather than spatially synchronizing and concentrating the provision of different infrastructure services in larger "bundles." Available evidence suggests that bundling of services

Figure 5.1 Access to Infrastructure by Location

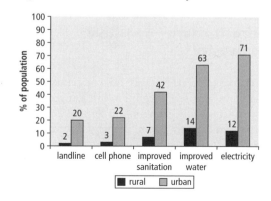

Source: Banerjee and others 2008.

Figure 5.2 Change in Urban and Rural Service Coverage, 1990–2005

Source: Banerjee and others 2008.

Figure 5.3 Quality Differentials between Main and Rural Road Networks

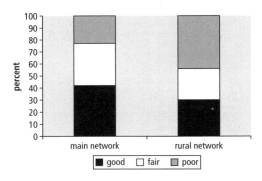

Source: Gwilliam and others 2008.

leads to higher returns among beneficiary households than when the services are provided individually. For example, in Peru joint access to two or more services generates a larger increase in rural household welfare than when services are accessed separately (Torero and Escobal 2005). This finding is valid for urban dwellers as well, at least for water, sanitation, electricity, and telephone services, regardless of how they are combined (Chong, Hentschel, and Saavedra 2007). Access to multiple services also generates a larger reduction of opportunity

costs because the interaction across services compounds positive effects, such as time savings or increased connectivity. With barriers to productivity reduced faster than when services are taken individually, poor households have more chances to access economic opportunities.

In the African context, not only are levels of household service coverage low, but they are also uncoordinated. As a result, the share of households with access to a bundle of multiple infrastructure services is very low, even among the better-off (table 5.5).

The Costs of Providing Infrastructure—Sensitive to Density

The cost of infrastructure network expansion is highly sensitive to population density. For the exact same infrastructure bundle, in both urban and rural spaces, the capital cost (per capita) declines with density. At the highest density, the cost of a bundle of high-quality services is $325 per capita; for medium-density cities, it is $665; for the rural hinterland $2,837; and for isolated areas $4,879 (table 5.6). These

Table 5.5 Households with Access to One or More Modern Infrastructure Services
percentage

Number of services	National	Rural	Urban	Quintile				
				Poorest	Second	Third	Fourth	Fifth
Any one modern infrastructure service	33	15	76	4	17	23	44	78
Any two modern infrastructure services	17	4	47	0	2	7	19	56
Any three modern infrastructure services	9	1	28	0	0	3	11	32
Any four modern infrastructure services	4	0	12	0	0	1	4	16

Source: Banerjee and others 2008.
Note: Household coverage rates are population weighted for the latest available year. Modern infrastructure services include piped water, flush toilet, power, and landline telephone.

Table 5.6 Capital Cost per Capita of Infrastructure Provision, by Density
$ per capita except as otherwise noted

Infrastructure type	Large cities						Secondary cities	Rural hinterland	Deep rural
Density (people/km^2)	30,000	20,000	10,000	5,008	3,026	1,455	1,247	38	13
Water									
Private tap	104.2	124.0	168.7	231.8	293.6	416.4	448.5	1,825.2	3,156.2
Standpost	31.0	36.3	48.5	65.6	82.4	115.7	124.5	267.6	267.6
Borehole	21.1	21.1	21.1	21.1	21.1	21.1	21.1	53.0	159.7
Hand pump	8.3	8.3	8.3	8.3	8.3	8.3	8.3	16.7	50.4
Sanitation									
Septic tank	125.0	125.0	125.0	125.0	125.0	125.0	125.0	125.0	125.0
Improved latrine	57.0	57.0	57.0	57.0	57.0	57.0	57.0	57.0	57.0
Unimproved latrine	39.0	39.0	39.0	39.0	39.0	39.0	39.0	39.0	39.0
Power									
Grid	63.5	71.2	88.5	112.9	136.8	184.3	196.7	487.7	943.1
Minigrid	87.6	95.2	112.5	136.9	160.8	208.3	220.7	485.8	704.2
Solar photovoltaic	92.3	92.3	92.3	92.3	92.3	92.3	92.3	92.3	92.3
Roads									
High quality	31.6	47.4	94.7	189.2	313.1	651.3	759.8	269.1	232.4
Low quality	23.6	35.4	70.7	141.2	233.8	486.3	567.3	224.3	193.6
ICT									
Constant capacity	1.1	1.7	3.3	6.6	10.9	22.8	26.6	39.8	129.7
Actual capacity	1.1	1.7	3.3	6.6	10.9	22.8	26.6	129.7	422.1
Total									
Variable quality[a]	325	369	480	665	879	1,031	1,061	940	836
Constant (high) quality[b]	325	369	480	665	879	1,400	1,557	2,837	4,879

Source: Authors' compilation based on numerous Africa Infrastructure Country Diagnostic sources.
Note: ICT = information and communication technology.
a. For variable quality, technology differs by density and location as follows: (a) water—private tap in large cities, standposts in small cities, boreholes in secondary urban cities, hand pump in rural areas; (b) sanitation—septic tanks in large cities, improved latrines in small and secondary urban cities, traditional latrines in rural areas; (c) power—grid in urban areas, minigrid in rural hinterland, solar in deep rural areas; (d) roads—high-quality scenario; (e) ICT—constant capacity in urban and rural areas.
b. For constant (high) quality, the same technology—the most expensive one—applies at any density except for power (grid at any level of density).

values illustrate the cost disadvantage of African cities (generally less dense), compared with their higher-density Asian counterparts. Africa's urban expansion is occurring with declining densities (urban sprawl), which in itself will make per capita infrastructure costs even higher.

For Africa's largest cities, with a population over 3 million and a median density of 5,000 people per square kilometer, water and sanitation represent the heaviest weight in the infrastructure bundle (54 percent), followed by roads (28 percent), power (17 percent), and ICTs (1 percent).

Economies of density are so important that the rollout of network infrastructure becomes prohibitive at low levels of density. In these cases, it would make sense to shift toward a package of lower-cost technological alternatives, such as solar panels, hand pumps, and on-site sanitation as population density falls. The cost of variable-quality technology rises more gradually—from $325 per capita in high-density cities to $665 in medium-density cities to $940 in the rural hinterland; it then drops back to $836 in isolated areas (table 5.6). The implication is that the highest per capita cost is found in secondary urban areas. Densities there are high enough to demand higher-quality solutions but still not high enough to benefit from significant economies of scale in the delivery of services.

Population density affects not only the cost of network expansion but also the availability of resources to pay for it. Aggregate household spending capacity per square kilometer ranges from some $3,500 a year in deep rural areas to $2.5 million a year in cities with populations over 3 million and a density of 5,000 people per square kilometer. Therefore, in rural areas the cost of a high-quality infrastructure bundle is 10 to 20 times the annual household budgets, making it manifestly unaffordable (figure 5.4). This ratio falls steeply in urban areas, where the cost of the bundle is one to three times the annual household budget. For high-density cities (beyond the range observed in Africa), this ratio falls to less than two-thirds of the annual household budget.

Investment Needs

As noted in chapter 2 of this volume, Africa needs to spend some $93 billion per year to meet its infrastructure needs over the next decade to 2015. About two-thirds of this total relates to capital investment and the remaining third to operation and maintenance (Briceño-Garmendia, Smits, and Foster 2008). These investment needs can usefully be divided into three categories. The first category relates to the investment needed to expand productive infrastructure that underpins the national economy as a whole: for example, generation capacity to serve industrial production;[5] transmission lines; fiber-optic backbones; and the main components of the national transport system including trunk roads, railways, airports, and seaports. The second category relates to infrastructure specifically needed to service the urban space, including urban roads and urban ICT, power, and water distribution networks. The third category relates to infrastructure specifically needed to service the rural space, including rural roads, rural household services, and irrigation.

Historically, Africa has been investing around $26 billion a year in infrastructure,[6] as reported in chapter 2. Of this total, about 30 percent goes to productive infrastructure that underpins the national economy, 50 percent goes to servicing the urban space, and the remaining 20 percent to servicing the rural space (figure 5.5).[7] The lion's share of investment in the power sector has financed the development of energy capacity for industrial production and transmission. Infrastructure linked to the national economy also accounts for an important share of investments in transport. Across all sectors, infrastructure dedicated to servicing the urban space absorbs a greater share of investments than that dedicated to servicing the rural space. The only exception is water and sanitation, where a more even split is observed, although even that represents something of an urban bias, given that the population is predominantly rural.

Looking ahead, Africa will need to invest $60 billion per year, according to the estimates presented in chapter 1 of this volume. The spatial pattern of these future investments will look somewhat different from those of the past: 34 percent of the total will need to go to productive infrastructure that underpins the national economy; another 32 percent will go to servicing the urban space, and the remaining 34 percent to service the rural space (figure 5.6). Thus, the share going to the national economy increases slightly, whereas the share dedicated to servicing urban spaces declines and the share dedicated to rural space increases; this pattern is observable across the individual sectors also.

Infrastructure Financing

The jurisdiction responsible for infrastructure financing and provision differs hugely across sectors and countries. Although ICT and power are usually national responsibilities, responsibility for the water supply in urban areas is widely decentralized (figure 5.7). Nevertheless, in many countries, markedly the francophone countries, operation is entrusted to utilities that remain national. Where municipal utilities do exist, municipal governments own only a few in whole or in part. Responsibility for transport infrastructure is divided between national and local jurisdictions, with boundaries varying from one country to another. The central government is typically responsible for the trunk road network, as well as railways, ports, and airports. Local governments are typically responsible for local roads.

Most local jurisdictions, whether urban or rural, lack the resource base to provide adequate infrastructure services to households and businesses. Municipal budgets are very small in relation to the cost of meeting infrastructure requirements implied by fast urban growth. Data collected from a sample of cities suggest that the average expenditure per person per year rarely exceeds $10 (figure 5.8). South Africa is an exception, with Cape Town at $1,163 and Durban at $1,152.

Transfers from central governments or direct financing have become the most important source of funding for local infrastructure (table 5.7). Cities in most African countries depend on central transfers for more than

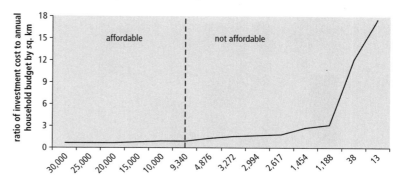

Figure 5.4 Affordability of a Basic Package of Household Infrastructure

population density (no. people/sq. km)

Source: Authors' compilation.
Note: Affordable represents those population densities in which the capital cost per hectare of a basic package of infrastructure services represents no more than one year of income for the inhabitants of that hectare. *Not affordable* represents those population densities in which the capital cost per hectare of a basic package of infrastructure services exceeds, by several multiples, the annual income for the inhabitants of that hectare.

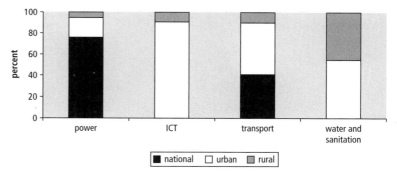

Figure 5.5 Spatial Split of Historic Infrastructure Investments

Source: Authors' compilation.
Note: ICT = information and communication technology. *National economy* refers to productive infrastructure that underpins the national economy and cannot be specifically attributed to servicing inhabitants of urban or rural space (for example, the interurban trunk network, the national power interconnected system, major ports, and airports).
Urban space or *rural space* refers to infrastructure that is primarily oriented toward servicing needs of urban or rural inhabitants, respectively (for example, urban or rural household services, urban or rural roads).

80 percent of their operating revenues. This dependence diminishes the incentives for local governments to raise their own revenues. Transfers are often unpredictable, hindering long-term projects and planning. They often favor small localities over larger cities with serious infrastructure bottlenecks. On the revenue side, local governments have limited

Figure 5.6 Spatial Split of Future Infrastructure Investment Needs

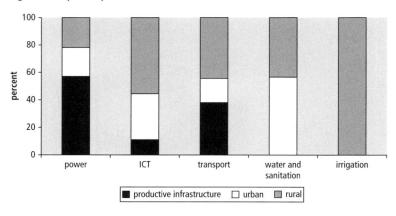

Source: Authors' compilation.
Note: ICT = information and communication technology. *Productive infrastructure* underpins the national economy and cannot be specifically attributed to servicing inhabitants of urban or rural space (for example, the interurban trunk network, the national power interconnected system, major ports, and airports).
Urban or *rural* refers to infrastructure that is primarily oriented toward servicing needs of urban or rural inhabitants, respectively (for example, urban or rural household services and urban or rural roads).

Figure 5.7 Institutional Patterns of Water and Electricity Supply in Urban Areas

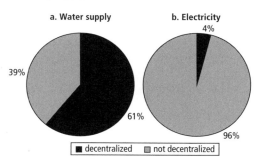

Sources: Banerjee and others 2008; Eberhard and others 2008.

Figure 5.8 Municipal Budgets of Selected African Cities

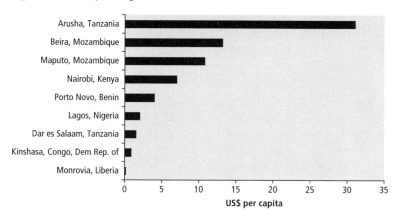

Sources: UN-Habitat 1998; corresponding city budget documents.

taxing authority, even though the potential revenue base is large. For large cities, most of the revenues collected are transferred to the national treasury.

The use of local government budgets varies widely across countries. In Ghana, revenues are mainly dedicated to capital expenses (78 percent), whereas in Côte d'Ivoire and Senegal, current expenditures occupy the largest account (80 percent and 90 percent, respectively). In Ghana, local taxes and local resources are almost nonexistent, whereas in Côte d'Ivoire and Senegal, they make up a significant share of the revenue envelope. Own revenues collected by local governments are less than 1 percent of GDP in all three countries.

Spatial Planning, Land Regulations, and Housing

Urban boundaries have expanded, and zones that were rural in the mid-1980s are now part of the metropolitan areas surrounding major African cities. This trend is particularly evident in the countries with faster urban growth, such as Burkina Faso, Cameroon, and Ghana (Farvacque-Vitkovic, Glasser, and others 2008). The pattern reveals strong physical growth, typified by moderate and patchy densification within the inner-city core, as residential areas give way to commercial users and peripheral growth occurs unguided and at low density.

In many cases, spatial expansion of cities has been faster than population growth, reducing density. Density in African cities ranges between 1,000 and 4,000 people per square kilometer (table 5.8). Density in rural areas is fewer than 100 people per square kilometer. Africa's megacities are denser but still far from their Asian peers. Only a handful of African cities (such as Ifon Osun in Nigeria, Mbuji-Mayi in the Democratic Republic of Congo, or Mombasa in Kenya) attain population densities of 10,000 to 20,000 people per square kilometer, compared with densities of 20,000 to 40,000 in Bangalore, Hyderabad, and Mumbai in India; Guangzhou and Shanghai in China; and Seoul in the Republic of Korea (Bertaud 2003). The more typical densities for African megacities of no more than 5,000 people per square kilometer are comparable to those of cities of

Organisation for Economic Co-operation and Development member states, such as London and New York. Built-in areas are growing faster than urban populations in 7 of 10 African cities, suggesting falling densities (Angel, Sheppard, and Civco 2005).[8] As a result, the already high costs for infrastructure in urban Africa will increase with further sprawl, hindering the affordability of basic services and adding to the environmental and carbon footprints.

In many African countries, land institutions are still incipient, reflecting the political economy and colonial legacy. In Africa, land-ownership is made difficult by the extreme centralization of procedures, the costs of titling, and the rapid depletion of central governments' land reserves. In this context, spontaneous settlements have developed. Limited land supply and high prices affect location decisions and exclude low-income households from the official land market. Many governments have subsidized plots, but supply is much below demand. Governments have tried to help residents excluded from land markets and have expanded infrastructure to new settlements, but the results have been disappointing. Recent work in Burkina Faso, Ghana, and Mali reveals the coexistence of traditional and public systems of property rights, complicating registries and duplicating land rights, which are difficult to enforce (Farvacque-Vitkovic and others 2007, Farvacque-Vitkovic, Raghunath, and others 2008). The limited size of the

land market and the monopoly by traditional landowners lead to shortages of urban land supply and rising prices. Lack of land titles hurts business development and the establishment of new firms. With no access to land and located in underserved and peripheral areas, the poor suffer from poor connectivity and low access to labor markets. The resistance of landowners and the lack of registries also hinder cities from raising revenues on urban land (box 5.1).

African cities face shortages of housing and shelter. In most countries, the real estate market and government agencies supply at most one-fourth of the annual demand for housing; the remaining three-fourths turn to the

Table 5.7 Overview of Local Infrastructure Financing Mechanisms

Mechanism	Urban	Rural
Direct central provision	ICT, power, sometimes water	ICT, irrigation, occasionally power and water
Central government transfers	Not earmarked and usually modest	Not earmarked and usually modest; growing use of rural funds
Local taxes	Significant potential but requires clear property rights and greater formalization of urban economy	Much more limited potential
Municipal debt	Limited number of creditworthy cases	No creditworthiness
Property sales	Significant potential but requires clear prior definition of land titles	Much more limited potential
User fees	Significant potential	Minor potential because of lower purchasing power of households

Source: Authors' compilation.
Note: ICT = information and communication technology.

Table 5.8 Population Density across Country Types

Country type	GNI per capita ($ per capita)	Density in megacities	Density in intermediate cities	Density in secondary urban areas	Density in periurban areas	Density in rural hinterlands	Density in remote areas
Sub-Saharan Africa	875	3,621	1,482	1,281	89	35	13
Low-income countries, landlocked	245	2,529	1,702	1,306	132	71	14
Low-income countries, coastal	472	4,083	1,661	1,492	100	35	13
Middle-income countries	5,081	1,229	574	824	58	45	19

Source: Authors' compilation based on geographic information systems analysis of Global Rural-Urban Mapping Project population density data and Henderson 2002 for megacities.
Note: GNI = gross national income. GNI per capita is in current dollars using the Atlas method. Estimates are based on a panel of 20 countries. Density = number of people per square kilometer. Megacities have more than 1 million people; intermediate cities have between 100,000 and 1 million people; secondary urban areas have between 100,000 and 50,000 people; periurban areas are less than one hour from the nearest city with more than 50,000 people; rural hinterlands are between one and six hours from the nearest city with more than 50,000 people; and remote areas are more than six hours from the nearest city with more than 50,000 people.

BOX 5.1

Land Issues in Tanzania

Tanzania is at the early stage of its urbanization, and the population is growing in most urban areas. Since the 1960s, demand for urban land with services has significantly and systematically exceeded what the government has supplied. Official demand for plots averages 75,000, but the supply is below 6,000 a year. Most applicants lose hope and turn to informal markets to obtain land for their development needs.

Serious difficulties also exist in accessing land for investment purposes. The Tanzania Investment Centre has so far registered 4,210 investment projects, 80 percent of which require access to land parcels. However, the Tanzania Investment Centre estimates that only one-quarter of those registered can acquire land through the existing formal system. Between 2004 and 2007, 440 applications for land allocation were received, but only 13 applicants received their titles, evidence that the formal land delivery system in urban areas is not working. In 1998, informal settlements in Dar es Salaam covered 48 percent of the built-up area, and recent estimates place the share as high as 70–80 percent.

The scarcity of formal plots stems from the underperformance of the public system, the lack of institutional or financial resources, and the competition of the formal system with informal land development, the latter being much cheaper and easier. Institutional constraints also exist. The 1999 Land Act concentrated most powers of land management in the central government, depriving local government authorities of the institutional structures to deal with their land-related responsibilities. Goals for the land are not explicit, and laws are not applied consistently. The division of responsibilities among actors is unclear, and there is no coordination.

Sources: Muzzini and Lindeboom 2008; Raich and Sarzin forthcoming.

informal market and their own construction. In Burkina Faso and Mali, more than 45 percent of the population in the capital city lives in informal settlements (Farvacque-Vitkovic and others 2007). In Ghana, the market produces only 20 percent of the annual demand for shelter (Farvacque-Vitkovic, Raghunath, and others 2008). In Accra, people's increased purchasing power because of remittances has led to higher real estate prices, and zoning and legal restrictions artificially limit the land available for housing.

Many governments have tried to help the poor by subsidizing construction, providing tax incentives to developers, or producing public

housing, but the effect of these incentives has been minimal (Farvacque-Vitkovic, Glasser, and others 2008). Construction costs are very high, especially for landlocked countries.[9] Cement, iron, and other materials are imported, making housing prices unaffordable. Most new houses are captured by medium-income households. According to estimates, of five applications, only one housing unit is allocated to a needy household.[10]

Urban Growth and Informal Settlements

A major problem for Africa's growing cities is the rapid spread of informal settlements. Lack of affordable serviced plots and zoning policies have often excluded the poor from being integrated with urban development, leaving them in underserviced shelters (slums) both in and on the outskirts of major cities. The UN-Habitat standard definition of people living in slums is overcrowding, low access to water and sanitation, lack of secure tenure, and poor housing quality. Based on this definition, as much as 70 percent of Africa's urban population resides in slums (UN-Habitat 2003), and from 1990 to 2001, the slum population grew at 4.4 percent a year, faster than the urban population. If this trend persists, an additional 218 million Africans will be living in slums by 2020, and almost one-third of the world's slum population will be in Africa.

Great heterogeneity exists across cities in the living and income conditions of slum residents. Not all people living in these settlements are income poor, although significant overlap occurs, and living standards differ across countries. In many cases, informal settlements are scattered across cities, side by side with wealthier residences. In Tanzania, urban dwellers in the periurban areas do well, enjoying the freedom of informality, even without land titles or finished walls. Indeed, informal periurban areas are sometimes the most dynamic, precisely because overzealous regulation does not affect them. A strong "city effect" also exists. Thanks to leadership, land security, ownership, and civic participation, the inhabitants of Dakar's slums (Senegal) have living standards far superior to Nairobi's (Kenya) even though the latter have higher incomes and education levels (Gulyani, Talukdar, and Jack 2008).

The main problem of slums and informality is exclusion from basic amenities. Nairobi's slum residents pay up to 11 times more for water sold by private vendors than those who have access to piped water (Farvacque-Vitkovic, Glasser, and others 2008). In Africa as a whole, the price of piped water is $0.50 per cubic meter, whereas water purchased from private vendors in mobile carts is $4.75 per cubic meter. Inadequate access to basic services also has implications for health and human development. Moreover, spatial mismatches and distance constrain accessibility to education and livelihood opportunities.

Policy Issues and Implications

Infrastructure Financing

Cities should be spending more and spending more wisely. Although trunk infrastructure and services with substantial spillover effects are clearly the responsibility of the central government, cities are responsible for solid waste, sewerage, drainage, and lighting. In many cases, they are called on to help with shelter as well. The purported benefits of decentralization are not realized because decentralization policies have given cities more responsibilities (notably in social sectors) but not more resources. Without independent or predictable sources of revenues, African cities can rarely plan or decide on the best way to allocate their resources.

In principle, cities have greater potential to raise local revenues. First, the larger urban economy provides a significant local tax base, although its predominantly informal nature prevents the authorities from capturing taxes. Second, high-value urban properties constitute a major potential tax base, although the lack of clear property titles prevents it from being realized. Third, the higher purchasing power and tighter agglomeration of urban households make recovery of a significant proportion of infrastructure financing requirements with user fees easier.

Long-term debt is always an alternative (at least in theory), but few African cities have the creditworthiness to raise their own debt finance, and the few examples (South Africa and Zimbabwe) have illustrated the weakness of the system and the need for impartial credit ratings.

For larger cities, the economic base is larger, and they have greater autonomy to raise their own taxes. However, tax receipts are often sent to the central governments, and political factors hinder the use of property taxes. Although African cities generate 80 percent of the country's tax revenues, they end up with less than 20 percent of the resources.[11] On the other hand, larger urban areas are likely to have fewer spending responsibilities because they are often covered by national service providers (such as power and water utilities), thus relieving these municipalities of some budgetary expenses they would otherwise incur.

In cities such as Dar es Salaam, Tanzania, and Nairobi, Kenya, improvement in land management institutions could open the door to increased property revenues for municipalities, more land use and sales revenues for the government, and complementary private finance. For example, Cairo has held several auctions of land for conversion, adding 10 percent to the city budget. It has also swapped land permits for private infrastructure in public land. For large Chinese cities, land leases are the usual method to mobilize resources, as well as in Mumbai and Bangalore in India. In 11 African countries, street addressing (or *addressage*) has been established in the major municipalities, increasing municipal tax billings by about 50 percent, with 90 percent collection rates. In Burkina Faso, Mauritania, and Togo, street addressing has helped in inventorying the local tax base and implementing residential taxation (Farvacque-Vitkovic and others 2007; Farvacque-Vitkovic, Glasser, and others 2008; Kessides 2006). In Benin, decentralized management fostered increases in city revenue of 82 percent in Cotonou, 131 percent in Parakou, and 148 percent in Porto Novo, with better collection rates as well (Kessides 2006).

In rural areas, transfers complemented by centralized funds dominate. Many countries have tried to fund rural investment by introducing centralized funding mechanisms to channel earmarked central government funds and donor resources to rural infrastructure. These mechanisms include rural water funds (90 percent of countries), rural electrification funds (76 percent), and rural telecommunication funds (29 percent). For power, rural funds bring faster expansions in the electrified rural population: an annual increase of 0.72 percent is seen in countries with such funds, compared to an annual contraction of −0.05 percent elsewhere. For rural water and rural ICT funds, no significant differential was seen in the rate of service expansion.

Central funds can also support the maintenance of rural infrastructure. To deal with poor maintenance, many countries are allocating part of their national road fund revenues to the maintenance of the rural network (60 percent of countries). This decision may be a good strategy: countries that allocate at least $0.015 per liter of their fuel levies to the rural road networks have a significantly higher share of their rural roads in good condition than those that allocate less, 36 percent versus 21 percent.

Land Policies and Urban and Territorial Planning

Adequate land policies and markets are the backbone of an efficient urban transition. Land management institutions include a comprehensive land registry, credible mechanisms for contract enforcement and conflict resolution, flexible zoning laws, and versatile regulation of subdivisions that help rather than hinder the conversion of land for different uses. Property rights embodied in land titles are essential for converting assets into usable wealth. The transformation of the agricultural sector from communal land rights to individual property rights is important for the rural-urban transformation, but it may take a long time.

Land use and building regulations become more important as urbanization advances. Governments regulate land markets to ensure separation of land between different uses and to ensure the integration of public and private uses of land, such as providing space for transport infrastructure in densely populated areas. Land regulations can be overzealous, however, distorting the incentives for

businesses and households to locate in the city and pushing prices up, thereby leading to a relocation of activities and residents to non-regulated places. Land acquisition delays are very long in Ethiopia and Zambia. In Mozambique, businesses pay on average $18,000 in processing fees for land, and in Nigeria, they must register land to use it as collateral, a process that can take up to two years and cost 15 percent of the land value (Kessides 2006).

Land institutions can improve information, strengthen property rights, record market transactions, and steadily move toward more open land markets. With an endowment of 63 square miles of land, the Tema Development Corporation in Ghana is planning and laying out the Tema area, constructing roads and sewerage systems, preparing and executing housing projects, and managing rental units. Permits for housing construction are submitted to the authority, which charges a permit fee based on the value of the property to be developed (Farvacque-Vitkovic and McAuslan 1993).

Urban planning should guide urban expansion and the associated infrastructure needs. Because of their top-down approach and weak implementation, urban planning and master plans have lost their meaning in many African cities. Urban dynamics are seldom correctly foreseen, and in most cases, the political economy has the last word in determining the location of infrastructure or major developments. To be efficient and useful, planning should be flexible, participatory, and indicative (10–15 years). Urban reference maps should lay out major roads and city services, the areas for urban expansion, and the reserves for amenities.

Planning should check sprawl, enhance densification, prevent development in precarious environmental zones, and enhance the delivery of affordable serviced land and infrastructure. Ideally, planning should be rooted in participatory strategies and linked to local and central budgets. Without realistic projections for resource availability, urban plans often fall into discredit. Dakar (Senegal), Lagos (Nigeria), and Maputo (Mozambique) recently prepared city development strategies as frameworks to encourage participation from the community in discussing challenges and opportunities.

Territorial planning is critical in rural areas to promote a more integrated vision of development and to enhance growth opportunities. Rural development requires the coordinated provision of infrastructure services to support agricultural production and off-farm activities, such as irrigation infrastructure, rural roads, and associated transport services, as well as storage and distribution infrastructure for agricultural products. In rural areas, the limited administrative capacity hinders an integrated vision. Coordination may be further complicated because some services, such as irrigation, may be a central government competency, whereas others (such as roads) are local. Chongqing, China's experience with implementing a territorial development plan on a regional scale provides an example that may be of interest to Africa.

Bundling infrastructure services can substantially increase the return of infrastructure investments. Bundling infrastructure not only secures larger welfare gains to households, urban and rural alike, it also maximizes the economic and social effect of infrastructure service provision in rural areas by granting better access to economic opportunities and reducing the gap between poor and nonpoor. Therefore, investment policies, especially when rural infrastructure is concerned, should more attentively seek complementarities across sectors. This requires that institutional coordination and planning and financial capacity are deployed as needed. Although bundling is an opportunity to realize larger returns on investments, alone it is not enough to drive economic and social development in rural areas. A more far-reaching vision of rural development that maximizes coordination and complementarities across sectors beyond the infrastructure field—for which, however, bundling constitutes an important tool—is needed. This is the scope of territorial development.

Informal Settlements

Preventing the formation of slums and upgrading existing ones are major concerns to policy makers; one of two possible approaches normally prevails. The first approach focuses on improving the living standards of slum dwellers in their existing locations. They are given land tenure; slums areas are equipped with basic infrastructure services, and shelters are upgraded into better and more durable constructions. Investment in transportation and social programs is also used to strengthen links between slum areas and the rest of the city and to facilitate social integration. The Accra District Rehabilitation Project in Ghana is an example of successful upgrading, as are several national upgrading programs in Ethiopia, Kenya, and Uganda.

The second, more controversial, approach focuses on resettling slum dwellers, by moving them either to existing neighborhoods or to new, less crowded, and safer locations. In either case, slum dwellers are compensated for resettlement and disruptions to their livelihoods.

Much can be done, starting with the provision of basic services and infrastructure combined with effective land policy. Legislation that boosts land prices and excludes the poor will need to be revised. Basic packages of services (street lighting, paving, drainage, roads) should be extended to the broadest number of people at the lowest possible cost. In Kenya, Mozambique, and Nigeria, major improvements are possible for a low of $150 per capita, compared with $1,800 or more for finished solutions. Urban transportation can bring the urban poor into the large labor markets. A consistent and extensive policy of land titling would provide clarity and predictability to the land market, develop people's ownership, and promote private investment. In many countries, however, land titling will continue to be difficult (more difficult than extending basic services) because of the political economy and weak administrative capacity.

Six Principles for Efficient Urbanization

Based on the foregoing discussion, there are six key principles for achieving efficient urbanization. First, adopt a solid analytical framework to help define priorities and sequencing. In places that are mostly rural, governments should be neutral and establish the foundations for efficient urbanization (World Bank 2009). Good land policies and universal provision of basic services are central. Where urbanization has accelerated, the priority should be investments in connectivity to ensure that the benefits of rising economic density are widely shared. In highly urban places, targeted interventions may be needed to deal with slums and exclusion.

Second, recognize that the political economy influences the urban transition. African cities are not very powerful. Unlike cities in East Asia or Latin America, African cities have little autonomy and depend on the central government for resources, infrastructure projects, and even land development. Chinese mayors are appointed by the party, but their political careers depend on how well they develop their cities. Especially if they are elected, U.S. and European mayors may see their cities as steps to higher political positions, including the presidency. Mayors in Africa have limited freedom of action. Many of the difficulties African cities have in collecting property taxes are related to the political influence of the major landowners, who oppose such taxes.

Third, be pragmatic. While the long-term goal is to have well-defined property rights and land titling, in the short run, cities may need to "finesse" land titling and use occupancy as a basis for land registration and taxation. Resource-constrained governments should invest in minimum packages of water-sanitation-energy in informal underserviced quarters at the citywide level and resist the idea of transforming slums into perfect neighborhoods. For about $1,200 per capita, many African slum dwellers can be provided with basic services, compared with $18,000 spent in more comprehensive and sophisticated projects in Latin America (Farvacque-Vitkovic, Glasser, and others 2008).

Fourth, focus on cities and areas important for the economy. The priorities should be to improve the institutional framework (especially on land markets), to provide technical and financial resources for planning and developing infrastructure and basic services, to harness agglomeration economies, and to deal with congestion.

Fifth, improve land policies so that markets are more flexible and can respond to the increase in demand. That requires compiling inventories of government land and of formal and informal developers, gathering prices and costs for land plots and construction, and

broadly planning for the extension of urban settlements, taking into account transportation, connectivity, and environmental factors.

Sixth, improve the fiscal soundness of cities: (a) improve transparency and predictability of transfers; (b) strengthen and simplify local taxation, changing the focus of property tax from ownership to occupancy; (c) take advantage of cost recovery from revenue-producing services, such as markets and bus stations—they can make up 70 percent of medium-size city revenues; and (d) use municipal contracts (between central and local governments) and *adressage* to help local governments manage their resources.

Notes

The authors of this chapter are Elvira Morella, Maria Emilia Freire, and Paul Dorosh, who drew on background material and contributions from Alvaro Federico Barra, Catherine Farvacque-Vitkovic, Matthew Glasser, Sumila Gulyani, Darby Jack, Austin Kilroy, Barjor Mheta, Stephen Mink, Siobhan Murray, Madhu Raghunath, Uri Raich, Raj Salooja, Zmarak Shalizi, and Debabrata Talukdar.

1. Note that the early stages of this transition need not involve movements of activities or people; rural households increasingly earn incomes from rural nonagricultural activities (in agricultural processing, construction, commerce, and private services).

2. This correlation between agricultural production and proximity (as measured by travel time) to urban markets holds even after taking agroecology into account.

3. No internationally accepted standard exists for identifying urban areas, and each country tends to use its own definition. This situation hinders any effort to make sensible comparisons across countries. In this chapter, urban areas, from secondary cities to megacities, are identified using a subset of the GRUMP (Global Rural-Urban Mapping Project) urban extents layer (CIESIN 2004). The GRUMP urban extents were joined to a data set of city populations compiled by Henderson (2002) and of urban extents classified by population size. To complete the urban-rural gradient, nonurban areas were classified by distance or travel time to the nearest city. The combination of urban extents and city populations allowed creation of a density-based typology of cities. However, given the limitations associated

with these input data, the calculation of density is approximate at best. Even so, the density-based characterization of "urban" areas allows comparisons across regions and reflects the relation between density and agglomeration economies.

4. *World Development Report 2009* expressed geographic transformation as the development of the leading and lagging regions. Although both regions may consist of both urban and rural areas and hence agriculture and nonagriculture, in South Asia, lagging regions are predominantly rural and agriculture remains the main source of livelihood.

5. As mentioned, the most important hindrance to economic production is the supply of energy. In many countries, it can account for half of the value of the final output.

6. These funds include annual public investments, annualized official development assistance, annualized emerging financiers that do not belong to the Organisation for Economic Co-operation and Development, and annualized private participation in infrastructure.

7. These figures include energy and roads; no data are available on the share of investment on ICT and water that serves industrial production.

8. Population figures are derived from national censuses.

9. The price of construction is estimated at $222 per square meter, so a 75-square-meter home would cost about $17,000 (excluding land) (AGETIPE 2005). Average incomes are $850 a year, producing a ratio of housing price to income of over 2,000 to 1, one of the world's highest.

10. Efforts to develop mortgage systems for low-income households in Africa have encountered several problems: lack of credit history, lack of regular income, shallowness of the financial market, lack of long-term funding, lack of land and house registries, high lending rates, and high credit risks.

11. Too often, the central government appropriates the city-generated taxes and distributes them to sectors that are not necessarily the most productive and certainly not the ones that will feed into the urban economy.

References

AGETIPE (Agence d'exécution des travaux d'intérêt public pour l'emploi). 2005. Contract documents. www.agetipe.org.

Angel, Schlomo, Stephen C. Sheppard, and Daniel L. Civco. 2005. *The Dynamics of Global Urban Expansion*. Washington, DC: Transport and Urban Development Department, World Bank.

Banerjee, Sudeshna, Quentin Wodon, Amadou Diallo, Taras Pushak, Hellal Uddin, Clarence Tsimpo, and Vivien Foster. 2008. "Access, Affordability, and Alternatives: Modern Infrastructure Services in Africa." Background Paper 2, Africa Infrastructure Country Diagnostic, World Bank, Washington, DC.

Bertaud, Alain. 2003. "Order without Design." http://www.alain-bertaud.com.

Briceño-Garmendia, Cecilia, Karlis Smits, and Vivien Foster. 2008. "Financing Public Infrastructure in Sub-Saharan Africa: Patterns, Issues, and Options." Background Paper 15, Africa Infrastructure Country Diagnostic, World Bank, Washington, DC.

CIESIN (Center for International Earth Science Information Network). 2004. *Global Rural-Urban Mapping Project (GRUMP): Urban Extents.* Palisades, NY: CIESIN, Columbia University.

Chong, Alberto, Jesko Hentschel, and Jaime Saavedra. 2007. "Bundling of Basic Public Services and Household Welfare in Developing Countries: An Empirical Exploration for the Case of Peru." *Oxford Development Studies* 35 (3): 329–46.

Dorosh, Paul, Hyoung-Gun Wang, Liang You, and Emily Schmidt. 2008. "Crop Production and Road Connectivity in Sub-Saharan Africa: A Spatial Analysis." Working Paper 19, Africa Infrastructure Country Diagnostic, World Bank, Washington, DC.

Eberhard, Anton, Vivien Foster, Cecelia Briceño-Garmendia, Fatimata Ouedraogo, Daniel Camos, and Maria Shkaratan. 2008. "Underpowered: The State of the Power Sector in Sub-Saharan Africa." Background Paper 6, Africa Infrastructure Country Diagnostic, World Bank, Washington, DC.

Farvacque-Vitkovic, Catherine, Alicia Casalis, Mahine Diop, and Christian Eghoff. 2007. "Development of the Cities of Mali: Challenges and Priorities." Africa Region Working Paper 104a, World Bank, Washington, DC.

Farvacque-Vitkovic, Catherine, Matthew Glasser, Barjor Mehta, Madhu Raghunath, Austin Kilroy, Alvaro Federico Barra, and Raj Salooja. 2008. "Africa's Urbanization for Development: Understanding Africa's Urban Challenges and Opportunities." World Bank, Washington, DC.

Farvacque-Vitkovic, Catherine, and Patrick McAuslan. 1993. "Politiques Foncière des Villes en Développement." World Bank, Washington, DC.

Farvacque-Vitkovic, Catherine, Madhu Raghunath, Christian Eghoff, and Charles Boakye. 2008. "Development of the Cities of Ghana: Challenges, Priorities and Pools." Africa Region Working Paper 110, World Bank, Washington, DC.

Gulyani, Sumila, Debabrata Talukdar, and Darby Jack. 2008. "A Tale of Three Cities: Understanding Differences in Provision of Modern Services." Working Paper 10, Africa Infrastructure Country Diagnostic, World Bank, Washington, DC.

Gwilliam, Ken, Vivien Foster, Rodrigo Archondo-Callao, Cecilia Briceño-Garmendia, Alberto Nogales, and Kavita Sethi. 2008. "The Burden of Maintenance: Roads in Sub-Saharan Africa." Background Paper 14, Africa Infrastructure Country Diagnostic, World Bank, Washington, DC.

Henderson, J. Vernon. 2002. "World Cities Data." http://www.econ.brown.edu/faculty/henderson/worldcities.html.

Kessides, Christine. 2006. *The Urban Transition in Sub-Saharan Africa: Implications for Economic Growth and Poverty Reduction*. Washington, DC: The Cities Alliance.

Maal, Simen Jansen. 2008. "Measuring the Contribution of Urban Centers to the National Economy of Tanzania." Report to World Bank, Dar es Salaam, Tanzania.

Muzzini, Elisa, and Wietze Lindeboom. 2008. *The Urban Transition in Tanzania: Building the Empirical Base for Policy Dialogue*. Washington, DC: World Bank.

Raich, Uri, and Zara Sarzin. Forthcoming. *Financing the Urban Expansion in Tanzania*. Washington, DC: World Bank.

Torero, Maximo, and Javier Escobal. 2005. "Measuring the Impact of Asset Complementarities: The Case of Rural Peru." *Cuadernos de Economia* 42 (May): 137–64.

UN-Habitat (United Nations Human Settlement Programme). 1998. "Global Urban Observatory." http://ww2.unhabitat.org/programmes/guo.

———. 2003. "Global Urban Observatory." http://ww2.unhabitat.org/programmes/guo.

World Bank. 2007. "The Challenge of Urbanization in Ethiopia: Implications for Growth and Poverty Alleviation." Africa Region, Water and Urban Development Unit 2, Washington, DC.

———. 2008. *World Development Report 2008: Agriculture for Development*. Washington, DC: World Bank.

———. 2009. *World Development Report 2009: Reshaping Economic Geography*. Washington, DC: World Bank.

Chapter 6

Deepening Regional Integration

With many small, isolated economies, Africa's economic geography is particularly challenging. Regional integration is likely the only way to overcome these handicaps and participate in the global economy. Integrating physical infrastructure is both a precursor to and an enabler for deeper economic integration, thereby allowing countries to gain scale economies and harness regional public goods. For successful regional integration, countries must start small; build on successes; think globally, linking Africa to more external markets; and compensate the least fortunate, recognizing that benefits are not always evenly distributed.

The benefits of regional integration are visible across all aspects of infrastructure networks. For information and communication technology (ICT) and power, regional infrastructure provides scale economies that substantially reduce the costs of production. Thus, continental fiber-optic submarine cables could reduce Internet and international call charges by one-half. Similarly, regional power pools that allow countries to share the most cost-effective energy resources can reduce electricity costs by $2 billion a year. For transport and water, regional collaboration allows optimal management and development of cross-border public goods. Road and rail corridors linking landlocked countries to the sea are an example of such a regional public good, as are regional airport and seaport hubs. The same can be said of Africa's 63 international river basins.

Reaping these benefits, however, poses institutional challenges:

- *Building a political consensus.* The political obstacles can trump the economic case. Regional infrastructure involves a high level of trust between countries, not least because of the implied dependence on neighbors for key resources such as water and energy.

- *Establishing effective regional institutions.* Regional institutions have to facilitate agreements and compensation. Africa has an extensive architecture of regional political and technical bodies, but these face problems because of overlapping memberships, limited technical capacity, and limited enforcement powers.

- *Setting priorities for regional investments.* Given the daunting investment agenda, better sequencing and priority setting of regional projects has been elusive. Political, economic, and spatial approaches to priority setting have all been widely discussed.

- *Developing regional regulatory frameworks.* Physical integration of infrastructure networks will be effective only with harmonized regulatory frameworks and administrative procedures to allow the free flow of services across national borders.

- *Facilitating project preparation and cross-border finance.* The complexity of regional infrastructure projects makes them costly and time-consuming to prepare. This is particularly true when projects are large in relation to the size of the host economy and essentially depend on financing from downstream beneficiaries.

Why Regional Integration Matters

Regional approaches can address the infrastructure backlog in Africa and propel economic growth, overcoming the region's difficult geography (Limão and Venables 1999). Sub-Saharan Africa has 48 countries, most with small populations—more than 20 countries have a population of less than 5 million. Economies are also very small—20 countries have a GDP of less than $5 billion. The small scale means governments have difficulty funding the large fixed costs associated with infrastructure development. In addition, 15 African countries are landlocked, depending on their neighbors for access to global markets.

Most infrastructure investments share characteristics of public goods, and all benefit to varying degrees from scale economies. Infrastructure sharing addresses the problems of small scale and adverse location. Joint provision increases the scale of infrastructure construction, operation, and maintenance. It reduces costs, pools scarce technical and managerial capacity, and creates a larger market. Economies of scale are particularly important in the ICT and power sectors. Big hydropower projects that would not be economically viable for a single country make sense when neighbors share their benefits. Although new ICT systems—especially mobile telephones—allow provision at the local retail level, connecting Africa to the world requires large up-front investments in undersea cables or satellite communication. For private engagement in ICT or energy, the opportunity to serve a larger regional market makes the extensive up-front investments more attractive. Airports and seaports must be organized as regional hubs to reach the scale necessary to attract airline and shipping services from beyond the continent.

Coordinated management and investment allow countries to reap the best from multicountry infrastructure systems. Some regional infrastructure investments, such as many types of transport investments, provide public goods, or they facilitate access to a common pool resource, as with water resource management for irrigation and other uses. Both public goods and common pool resources require strong coordination. Because the quality of a transport network depends on its weakest link, broad participation is crucial, even where benefits are unequally distributed. Water can be exhausted, and upstream users are in a stronger position than downstream users. Collective agreements, effective monitoring, and conflict resolution mechanisms can ensure a fair distribution of costs and benefits.

The goal of all regional infrastructure efforts is to facilitate the spatial organization of economic activity as a catalyst for faster growth. Lessons from the new economic geography, for which Paul Krugman received the Nobel Prize in Economics in 2008, explain this concept. Natural resource exports will remain important, but they provide few job opportunities and their benefits are seldom widely shared. Dutch disease, greater macroeconomic volatility, and weak governance have slowed growth in some resource-rich African countries (Collier 2007). Fast employment growth and sustained welfare improvements in developing countries require a move toward modern, mostly export-oriented manufacturing activity. The shift in trade that allowed East Asia's rapid growth can also benefit Africa. In the world's fastest-growing regions, the largest increase in trade has been within industries, for parts and components produced in one location and assembled in another. Manufacturing is more about specialized "tasks" than finished products (Collier and Venables 2007).

Splitting up manufacturing processes allows much more specialization, which gives rise to scale economies and, thus, to cost advantages. The result is the concentration of specialized production in new manufacturing centers around the world, linked across national boundaries in regional production networks. Launching such processes in Africa will not be easy, but some general points can be made. The *World Development Report 2009: Reshaping Economic Geography* identifies three principles for regional infrastructure: start small, think global, and compensate the least fortunate (World Bank 2009).

Start Small

Regional infrastructure is an ideal entry point for integration processes, because the costs and benefits and the rights and responsibilities can be more easily defined. In the past, many regional agreements have failed because they were overly ambitious, trying to achieve too much too fast. Regional infrastructure sharing builds institutions that promote closer economic integration, and mutual dependence encourages political stability. Countries will be more willing to cede some sovereignty in exchange for tangible benefits, such as water sharing or lower prices for power or ICT services.

Think Globally

Regional integration should not simply adapt failed import substitution policies to a regional level. Instead, it is the means to greater global integration. African markets, even with regional pooling, are too small to sustain high growth. Regional integration scales up supply by creating larger production networks and beneficial agglomeration. However, the key objective is to connect to world markets for intermediate inputs and intermediate or final outputs. This approach has implications for regional infrastructure development.

For a connection to global markets, primary production centers—more likely in coastal areas—must become regional infrastructure hubs with efficient ports and airports. These large and lumpy investments must be concentrated where they promise the highest economic return. Little point exists in developing several deep-water ports in neighboring countries when the lack of scale deters international shipping firms from serving many African ports. Complementary connective infrastructure (roads, transport services, and smooth border facilitation) encourages regional factor mobility and trade in intermediate inputs. With its many small countries, Africa has a large coordination problem in managing network infrastructure. For instance, to link the major agglomerations in Ghana and Nigeria, regional transport links also pass through Togo and Benin.

Compensate the Least Fortunate

The benefits of concentration mean that growth will most likely be in a small number of existing cities that have location advantages and an existing economic base, such as coastal cities with a good investment climate. Favoring these areas in planning regional infrastructure investments, at least initially, makes economic sense. With the proper complementary policies, other areas in the region will also benefit. Labor mobility will lead to remittances from migrants who find jobs in dynamic growth centers. Specialization means that even small players can find a niche. For instance, car assembly may be possible only in some large African countries such as Nigeria and South Africa. However, smaller countries such as Cameroon or Zambia can specialize in components. For this approach, regional transport and communication costs must come down. For some areas, however, no amount of infrastructure investment will trigger growth. They will need coordinated incentives, preferential allocations of aid in education and health, to create portable assets in the form of human capital that can then migrate to where the employment opportunities exist.

Africa faces severe challenges in diversifying from raw material exports and breaking into world markets for manufactured goods. China and India have unified markets with populations that are 70 percent and 50 percent larger, respectively, than all of Sub-Saharan Africa. Whereas Shanghai or Shenzen, China, draws on a catchment area for labor and products of several hundred million people, the home market for most African growth centers is limited to a few million. Enabling Africa to develop regional manufacturing clusters that can compete globally requires lowering barriers to both productive interaction and (at least temporarily) preferential access to world markets with liberalized rules of origin. Regional integration is essential, and regional infrastructure sharing must be a key priority. National infrastructure programs such as those in India or China (for example, the Golden Quadrilateral highway program) will involve agreement by numerous countries in Africa. However, the payoffs to greater coordination and integration of infrastructure will be large.

Opportunities for Regional Cooperation across Infrastructure Sectors

Africa's regional infrastructure networks have major gaps that increase the costs of doing business and prevent the realization of scale economies. Supply of infrastructure as a public good and management of common pool resources have been deficient. More efficient regional integration of infrastructure is needed in all sectors: ICT, transport, power, and water (figure 6.1).

ICT—Slashing Costs of International Voice and Internet Connectivity

As in other parts of the world, mobile telephones have greatly improved telecommunications in Africa. However, the benefits have been limited to local and domestic communications. The region's national telecommunication networks are poorly integrated with each other and the rest of the world. Optical-fiber technology provides the least expensive and highest-capacity transmission of telephone, Internet, and other data traffic. Submarine and land-based communication cables combine high speed and large capacity. Although initial investments are high, marginal transmission costs are very low.

Access to the global network of submarine cables is low in Africa, especially for landlocked countries that depend on neighbors for access. Both coordination and massive investments are required. The region's main international underwater cable is the South Atlantic 3/West

Africa Submarine Cable (SAT-3), which passes along the Gulf of Guinea and down to South Africa. The entire east coast of Africa lacks access to an underwater cable. Intraregional connectivity by fiber-optic cables is also limited. Most countries rely on satellites for international telecommunications, including Internet access, leading to prices for dial-up and broadband Internet at least twice as high as in other regions. Transmission capacities are low, and costs are high. Countries without access to an underwater cable have only 3 bits of bandwidth per capita, whereas those with access have 24 bits. The average cost of an international fixed-line telephone call within Sub-Saharan Africa is $1.23 a minute, almost twice the cost of a call to the United States ($0.73 a minute). Intraregional call traffic is barely 113 million minutes, compared with intercontinental call traffic of 250 million minutes.[1]

Several projects are already under way to complete the loop of underwater cables around Africa, with an estimated value of $1.8 billion (table 6.1). Most are commercially sponsored and privately financed, such as the Eastern African Submarine Cable System project to link South Africa and the Horn of Africa (box 6.1). The cost of completing the nascent fiber-optic network interconnecting the capital cities of Sub-Saharan Africa and the main submarine cables is modest at $316 million, based on a cost of about $27,000 per kilometer.

The most immediate direct benefits of enhanced connectivity are reduced prices and better service for international voice and Internet connectivity. Prices for most services in countries with underwater cable access are half those in countries without access (table 6.2). Such large price reductions could boost demand for these services and, ultimately, economic productivity. However, too often, access to underwater cables remains with the incumbent operator, which (without adequate regulatory controls) charges monopoly prices that prevent consumers from reaping the full cost advantage of this technology. Countries with multiple international gateways see some competitive pressure, which keeps service prices significantly lower than in countries where an underwater cable is the only international gateway (table 6.2).

Figure 6.1 Africa's Regional Infrastructure Challenge

a. ICT—closing the circle

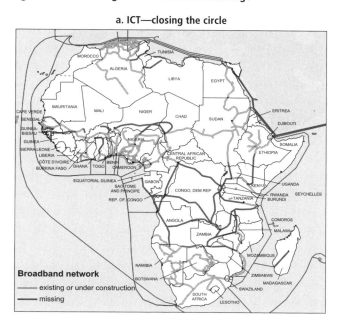

Broadband network
— existing or under construction
— missing

b. River basins—managing common resources

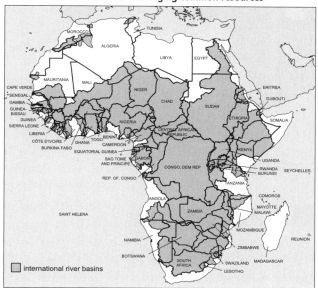

□ international river basins

c. Roads—connecting the dots

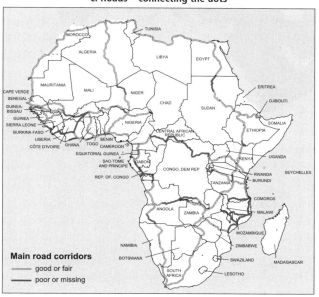

Main road corridors
— good or fair
— poor or missing

d. Power—trading electricity regionally

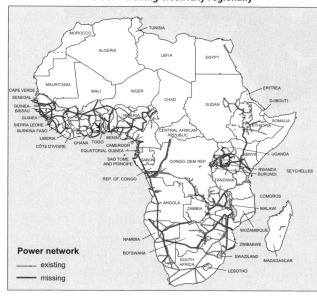

Power network
— existing
— missing

Source: Maps provided by the African Development Bank, 2008.

Beyond direct benefits, enhanced connectivity supports closer regional economic networks and integration with international markets (Leamer and Storper 2001). Good communication is a precondition for the emergence of buyer-supplier networks for specialized production that exploits economies of scale—to move from low-technology, standardized manufacturing to internationally competitive production and to ensure access to global markets for manufactured outputs and business services.

Table 6.1 Costs of Reaching Full Intercontinental and Intraregional Connectivity
$ millions

Region	Intercontinental connectivity		Intraregional connectivity	
	Project	Required investment	Project	Required investment
East Africa	EASSy, TEAMS	260	Connect main hubs within and between subregions and to underwater cables	132
Southern Africa	InfraCo, SRII	510		7
West and Central Africa	Infinity, GLO-1, WAFS	1,010		177
Sub-Saharan Africa total		1,780		316

Source: Mayer and others 2008.
Note: Intraregional data are for 24 countries. EASSy = Eastern African Submarine Cable System; GLO-1 = Globacom-1; SRII = Southern African Development Community Regional Information Infrastructure Initiative; TEAMS = The East Africa Marine System; WAFS = West African Festoon System.

BOX 6.1

Not So EASSy

The Eastern African Submarine Cable System (EASSy) is an underground fiber-optic cable that runs from South Africa to Sudan, allowing all countries along the route to connect to the global submarine cable system.

Developed and owned by a consortium of about 25 telecommunication operators, mostly from eastern and southern Africa, the cable is expected to cost $230 million. About one-third of the funding will come from nonconcessional debt finance provided by five development finance institutions (the International Finance Corporation, the European Investment Bank, the African Development Bank, the French Development Agency, and the German Development Bank), with the remainder from commercial equity.

The project took about three years to develop. The first stage involved discussions and negotiations with stakeholders to determine the project's structure. The second stage focused on the technical and financial details of implementation. The third stage, laying the cable, began in 2008.

Policy makers and development finance institutions have focused on not repeating the experience of the SAT-3 cable, which runs along the west coast. That project was also financed, built, and managed by a consortium of operators, but each member of the consortium has exclusive control over access to the cable in its own country. Lack of competition has meant that prices remain high and the benefits for customers limited.

Designed to ensure effective competition and regulation, EASSy is owned by a consortium, which also includes a special-purpose vehicle owned by a group of smaller operators from the region. Development finance support for EASSy is provided as loans to this special-purpose vehicle, which can sell capacity in any market in the region to licensed operators on an open-access, nondiscriminatory basis, thus competing with other consortium members. As traffic volumes increase, the special-purpose vehicle is required to pass on cost reductions to customers.

Reaching consensus about these access arrangements has been difficult, leading to project delays. Meanwhile, Kenya moved forward with its own underwater cable, The East Africa Marine System (TEAMS), with links to the United Arab Emirates. Technically much simpler, that project enjoys significant private backing. Unless the system can be integrated in a regional network, however, costs will be higher and benefits less broadly shared than with a regional effort. A third, privately funded effort, South Africa–East Africa–South Asia–Fiber Optic Cable (SEACOM), is planned to connect South Africa and several East African countries to global networks by mid-2009.

Source: Based on interviews with staff from the World Bank's ICT Policy Department, 2008.

Power—Capturing Scale Economies to Reduce Energy Costs

Although well endowed with hydropower and thermal energy resources, African countries have developed only a small fraction of that potential. Some of the region's most cost-effective energy resources are far from major centers of demand in countries too poor to

Table 6.2 Benefits of Access to an Underwater Cable

Access level	Share of countries (%)	Price for a call within Sub-Saharan Africa ($ per minute)	Price for a call to the United States ($ per minute)	Price for 20 hours of dial-up Internet access ($ per month)	Price for ADSL broad-band Internet access ($ per month)
No access to submarine cable	67	1.34	0.86	67.95	282.97
Access to submarine cable	32	0.57	0.48	47.28	110.71
Monopoly on international gateway	16	0.70	0.72	37.36	119.88
Competitive international gateways	16	0.48	0.23	36.62	98.49

Source: Minges and others 2008.
Note: ADSL = asymmetric digital subscriber line.

raise the billions of dollars needed to develop them. For example, 60 percent of the region's hydropower potential is in the Democratic Republic of Congo and Ethiopia. Because 21 of 48 Sub-Saharan African countries have total generation capacity of less than 200 megawatts—efficient scale of production below minimum—they pay a heavy penalty: costs reach $0.25 per kilowatt-hour, compared with $0.13 per kilowatt-hour in the region's larger power systems.

The desire to pool energy resources and leverage scale economies in power sector development led to formation of regional power pools in southern and western Africa during the mid-1990s, and more recently in eastern and central Africa. However, trade has yet to take off. Cross-border power trade accounts for only 16 percent of the region's power consumption, more than 90 percent of it within the Southern African Power Pool, and much of that between South Africa and its immediate neighbors. Without physical or regulatory impediments, about 40 percent of eastern and southern Africa's power consumption would be traded across national borders (Rosnes and Vennemo 2008).

If pursued to its full economic potential, regional trade would shave about $0.01 per kilowatt-hour off the marginal cost of power generation in each of the power pools. The resulting overall potential savings of regional power trade would amount to about $2 billion a year in the costs of power system development and operation (equivalent to about 5 percent of total power system costs). The savings come largely from substituting hydropower for thermal power, even if higher immediate investments are required.

Regional trade also puts Africa on a cleaner development path in terms of carbon emissions. Regional power trade would increase the share of hydropower in the continent's generation portfolio from 36 percent to 48 percent, displacing 20,000 megawatts of thermal power in the process and saving 70 million tons a year of carbon emissions (8 percent of Sub-Saharan Africa's anticipated emissions through 2015). Applying the Clean Development Mechanism at $15 per ton of carbon would reduce the region's carbon emissions another 4 percent. Closely integrating power grids will also help balance loads when other renewable energy resources, such as concentrated solar and geothermal energy, are deployed on a large scale.

The 10 largest potential power-importing countries could reduce their long-run marginal cost of power by $0.02–$0.07 per kilowatt-hour (figure 6.2). Those that stand to gain most tend to be smaller countries or those heavily reliant on thermal power, such as Angola, Burundi, Chad, Guinea-Bissau, Liberia, Niger, and Senegal. However, reaping the full benefits of power trade would require a political willingness to depend heavily on power imports. As many as 16 African countries would be better-off (from a purely economic standpoint) importing more than 50 percent of their power needs.

The future of power trade depends on the health of the power sector in a handful of key exporting countries endowed with exceptionally large and low-cost hydropower resources. In descending order of export potential, these include the Democratic Republic of Congo, Ethiopia, Guinea, Sudan, Cameroon, and Mozambique (table 6.3). The first three account for 74 percent of potential

Figure 6.2 Savings from Power Trade for Major Potential Power-Importing Countries

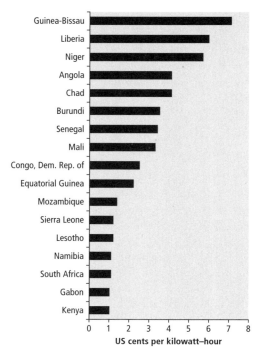

US cents per kilowatt–hour

Source: Derived from Rosnes and Vennemo 2008.

Table 6.3 Profile of Top-Six Potential Power-Exporting Countries

Country	Potential exports (terrawatt hours per year)	Net revenues		Required investment	
		$ millions per year	Percentage of GDP	$ millions per year	Percentage of GDP
Congo, Dem. Rep. of	51.9	519	6.1	749	8.8
Ethiopia	26.3	263	2.0	1,003	7.5
Guinea	17.4	174	5.2	786	23.7
Sudan	13.1	131	0.3	1,032	2.7
Cameroon	6.8	68	0.4	267	1.5
Mozambique	5.9	59	0.8	216	2.8

Source: Derived from Rosnes and Vennemo 2008.
Notes: Net revenue is calculated as the estimated volume of exports multiplied by an illustrative profit margin of $0.01 per kilowatt-hour exported. Required investment represents the investment needed for the country to be able to exploit its full economic power-exporting potential.

power exports, which could become big business for them. Based on a purely illustrative profit margin of $0.01 per kilowatt-hour on power sales, the net export revenues for these top three exporters could be 2–6 percent of their respective GDP. However, the size of the

investments needed to realize these export volumes is daunting. Each of the top three would need to invest more than $700 million a year for the next decade to develop the generation capacity for export, or more than 8 percent of their GDP. Thus, supporting such investments would be difficult without extensive cross-border financing arrangements that allow importing beneficiaries to make upfront capital contributions.

To make trade possible, countries would need to develop some 22,000 megawatts of interconnectors to allow the free flow of power across national borders, at a cost of more than $500 million a year over the next decade. The returns to the interconnectors can be as high as 120 percent for the Southern African Power Pool, and more typically 20–30 percent for the other power pools. For countries with the most to gain from power imports, investments in cross-border transmission have exceptionally high rates of return, typically paying for themselves in less than a year.

Transport Infrastructure—Facilitating Internal and External Trade

Transport infrastructure is critical for linking Africa to the global economy and promoting economic integration *within* the continent. However, the infrastructure demands are quite different in each case.

External Trade. For external trade, the continent's economic geography makes transport connections with the world something of a public good. Major corridors to the sea connect the continent's 15 landlocked countries to the major seaports, through a combination of road and rail infrastructure. The main ports include Douala (Cameroon) for central Africa; Durban (South Africa) and Maputo (Mozambique) for southern Africa; Dar es Salaam (Tanzania) and Mombasa (Kenya) for eastern Africa; and Abidjan (Côte d'Ivoire), Cotonou (Benin), and Dakar (Senegal) for western Africa (table 6.4). About $200 billion a year in imports and exports moves along these corridors, barely 10,000 kilometers long. About 70 percent is in good or fair condition, with donors channeling more resources to improve infrastructure along the routes.

However, regulatory and administrative hurdles continue to inflate costs and prolong delays for freight movements along these strategic arteries (table 6.4). Despite the reasonably good physical condition of the roads, the implicit velocity of freight movement is no more than 10 kilometers per hour (roughly the speed of a horse and buggy). The cause is the extensive delays of 10–30 hours at border crossings and ports. Transit times between major cities are very high by international standards (table 6.4). Member countries have organized corridor associations to address nonphysical barriers to transit, establishing one-stop integrated border posts and improving ports and custom administration.

Tariffs for road freight can be several times higher than in other parts of the developing world (table 6.5), which is attributed not to higher road transport costs in Africa, but to exceptionally high profit margins in the trucking industry (Teravaninthorn and Raballand 2008). These margins in turn reflect cartelization and restrictive regulatory frameworks, such as market entry barriers; technical regulations; and the *tour de role* system that allocates freight business based on queuing, particularly in central and western Africa. This system favors large fleets with mostly older trucks in poor condition. Moreover, it fosters corruption, because a transport operator can increase its volume of cargo only by bribing the freight bureaus, the government entities that allocate freight among transport operators.

Upgrading the remainder of the corridors to the sea to good condition is estimated to cost about $1.5 billion, while the annual cost of maintenance is close to $1.0 billion. Simulations suggest that corridor rehabilitation would yield an internal rate of return of 20–60 percent in eastern Africa's northern corridor. However, low traffic, poor truck use, and an aging fleet in central and western Africa would undermine the economic viability of corridor upgrades. Investments in these regions would likely become attractive only when more fundamental regulatory and institutional reforms improve trucking productivity.

For air transport, the size of the market is simply too small to support a proliferation of national carriers with each centered on

Table 6.4 Average Delivery Time for Containers from Vessel to Consignee

Gateway	Destination	Distance (kilometers)	Transit time (days)
Mombasa, Kenya	Kampala, Uganda	1,100	20
Mombasa, Kenya	Kigali, Rwanda	1,700	27
Dar es Salaam, Tanzania	Bujumbura, Burundi	1,800	21
Abidjan, Côte d'Ivoire	Ouagadougou, Burkino Faso	1,200	7
Abidjan, Côte d'Ivoire	Bamako, Mali	1,200	7
Dakar, Senegal	Bamako, Mali	1,200	10
Cotonou, Benin	Niamey, Niger	1,000	11
Douala, Cameroon	Ndjamena, Chad	1,900	38
Lagos, Nigeria	Kano, Nigeria	1,100	21

Source: Arvis 2005, quoting an international logistics company.

Table 6.5 Key Transport Corridors for International Trade, Sub-Saharan Africa

Corridor	Length (kilometers)	Road in good condition (percent)	Trade density ($ millions per road kilometer)	Implicit velocity[a] (kilometers per hour)	Freight tariff ($ per ton-kilometer)
Western	2,050	72	8.2	6.0	0.08
Central	3,280	49	4.2	6.1	0.13
Eastern	2,845	82	5.7	8.1	0.07
Southern	5,000	100	27.9	11.6	0.05

Source: Teravaninthorn and Raballand 2008.
a. Includes time spent stationary at ports, border crossings, and other stops.

its own airport facility and jet fleet. Instead, regional hubs serving multiple countries are needed, with fleets of smaller commuter jets to move passengers along spokes and into hubs. Liberalization begun under the Yamoussoukro Decision in 1999 should allow carriers serving key routes to consolidate and a better package of intraregional services to emerge. However, implementation has been lagging, especially in harmonizing competition rules and removing nonphysical barriers such as landing rights and tariffs. In eastern and southern Africa, this consolidation of carriers and hubs has already occurred, with Ethiopian Airlines (Addis Ababa), Kenya Airways (Nairobi), and South African Airways (Johannesburg) emerging as the main ones. Yet, in central and western Africa, hubs are conspicuous by their absence (figure 6.3). The collapse of key regional carriers, notably Air Afrique, partly caused this gap. Particularly striking is the failure of Lagos to emerge as a hub for western Africa.

Figure 6.3 Uneven Distribution of Airport Hubs across Africa: Traffic Flows between Top-60 Intraregional City Pairs

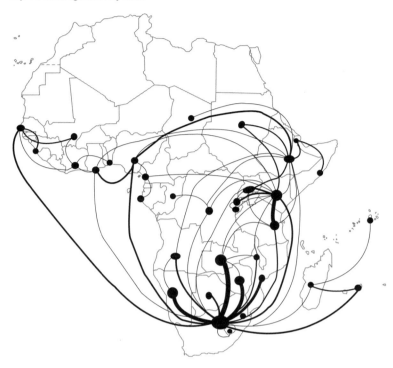

Source: Bofinger 2008.
Note: Thickness of lines reflects traffic volumes.

For seaports, large vessels (more than 200,000 20-foot equivalent units per year that provide scale economies to seaborne trade on east-west ports) are today able to call at only a handful of Sub-Saharan Africa's larger ports (Luanda, Angola; Abidjan, Côte d'Ivoire; Tema, Ghana; Mombasa, Kenya; Maputo, Mozambique; Apapa [Lagos], Nigeria; Dakar, Senegal; Durban and Cape Town, South Africa; Dar es Salaam, Tanzania; and Lomé, Togo). Several of these ports act as regional hubs, but with relatively small transshipment volumes. In theory, coordinating the choice of hub ports on Africa's different seaboards to reach greater economies of scale is desirable, but in practice, it is difficult because of rivalry between national ports.

For the east coast ports, the major regional hubs are already being developed in the Middle East (Djibouti, Djibouti; Jebel Ali, United Arab

Emirates; Jeddah, Saudi Arabia; and Salalah, Oman). For southern Africa, the government of South Africa has decided to develop a sizable hub port in Richards Bay, which will likely capture a significant portion of the seaborne trade between Asia and subequatorial Africa. On the west coast, despite the growth of Tangiers, Morocco, room may still exist for one or two regional hubs. Dakar, with its recent container-terminal concession and port expansion plans, is a strong candidate. Apapa (Lagos), though more centrally positioned, is already struggling with its local market and facing heavy congestion.

Intraregional Trade. Intraregional trade depends on the internal network linking African countries to each other. Except in southern Africa, the rail network does not typically provide such intraregional connectivity, because of the incompatibility of gauges and the isolated parallel corridors to the sea. Even along the more frequented sea corridors, most African railways struggle to reach economic viability because of very low traffic volumes. With traffic volume on intraregional rail routes much lower than even that on corridors to the sea, feasible further intraregional integration of rail networks in the near future is difficult to imagine.

It follows that the road network has the greatest potential to support intraregional trade. In the 1970s, the Trans-African Highway system was conceived as a network of all-weather roads to provide direct routes between the region's capitals; to contribute to the region's political, economic, and social integration and cohesion; and to ensure road transport between important areas of production and consumption (AfDB and UNECA 2000). However, national governments have had difficulty supporting needed investments. The official Trans-African Highway system comprises nine main corridors and reaches just over 50,000 kilometers. In mid-2008, almost half of the network was in poor condition, with about 70 percent of roads paved but 25 percent with either an earth surface or no formed road. Most of these missing links—those with the greatest potential to knit together the continent's economies—are in central Africa (Buys, Deichmann, and Wheeler 2006).

Extending the network to connect all Sub-Saharan African cities with more than 500,000 people would add an estimated 50,000 kilometers of road. The costs of completing an intra-African road network of this kind are of a larger order of magnitude than those associated with the corridors to the sea. Some estimate a one-time cost of $20 billion and an ongoing maintenance cost of $1 billion a year (Buys, Deichmann, and Wheeler 2006). The associated benefits are more speculative. Well-established relationships between trade volumes and transport costs mean that a fully operational Trans-African Highway network could nearly triple intra-African trade, from $10 billion a year to almost $30 billion (Buys, Deichmann, and Wheeler 2006). Even if one assumes rehabilitation costs as high as $20 billion, the benefit-cost ratio over 15 years would be as high as 5 to 1. However, even these higher projected volumes of regional trade look small alongside Africa's existing volumes of international trade, which stand close to $200 billion per year.

Water Resources—Minimizing Conflicts, Maximizing Benefits

Africa has more than 60 transboundary river basins, almost half shared by three or more countries with riparian rights. The region's surface water resources benefit economic development in several ways. Well-managed water resources can create low-cost hydropower, abundant irrigation, and cost-effective surface transport. However, hydrologic variability and limited storage leave economies vulnerable to floods and droughts.

The transboundary nature of most watersheds in Africa implies that regional coordination in water management is important (UNESCO 2003). What happens in an upstream country can benefit or harm its downstream neighbor. Hydropower and water storage infrastructure can provide cheaper electricity and balanced water flows, but excessive extraction or pollution upstream can hurt agriculture and drinking water supplies downstream. Regional coordination based on established international public law governing water sharing can ensure equitable distribution of the benefits of common-pool water resources. For upstream neighbors, apart from greater regional stability, the benefits include sharing of the large investments in hydropower or irrigation infrastructure.

Transboundary water resource management requires strong institutional commitment. Between the 1960s and 1980s, many countries created river basin arrangements such as the Senegal River Development Organization in 1972; the Gambia River Development Organization in 1978; and the Niger River Commission in 1964, later transformed into the Niger Basin Authority. External support, through mediation and financial backing, encouraged initial enthusiasm. However, nearly three decades later, with few exceptions, these transboundary organizations are still in the emergent stages. Some of their challenges included waning political commitment, poor cooperation, management and technical difficulties, armed conflict and political instability, and poorly defined goals or insufficient capacity for proposed plans. As donor support dwindled, basin organizations also lacked the financial backing to carry out their programs.

Coordination costs are high, given the sensitive nature of water resources, especially for countries in arid environments. Technical assistance and capacity building can strengthen basin organizations. One coordination tool is a management system that measures the progress of water resource management in river basins (see UNESCO 2006). Such a system sets benchmarks and defines the monitoring framework to track water discharge, quality, and development effects.

The Senegal River Development Organization is generally considered successful in transboundary cooperation for water management. It built the Manantali and Diama dams, which brought irrigation to some 375,000 hectares of land, enabled 800 gigawatt-hours a year of hydropower generation, and added about 800 kilometers of navigation on the Senegal River from Senegal to Kayes, Mali. Close coordination between riparian neighbors also allows them to address early any negative effects of water management development on agriculture and fisheries.

Meeting the Challenges of Regional Integration of Infrastructure in Africa

The benefits of regional infrastructure development are clear, but reaping those benefits poses political, institutional, economic, and financial challenges that are far from trivial. The starting point is building political consensus among neighboring states that may have diverging national agendas or even recent histories of conflict. Thereafter, effective regional institutions are needed to take forward a collaborative cross-border infrastructure development program and to ensure an equitable distribution of benefits. Given the vast needs and limited resources, some form of priority setting is necessary to guide efforts on the regional integration agenda. Even when priorities are clear, however, funding and implementing extensive project preparation studies and arranging cross-border finance for complex multibillion-dollar projects is far from straightforward. Furthermore, once the regional infrastructure is in place, its efficacy will ultimately depend on harmonizing the associated regulatory and administrative procedures.

Building a Political Consensus

Regional infrastructure is only one aspect of broader regional integration. In contrast to economic or political integration, however, cooperation in infrastructure provision is easier to achieve, because benefits are more clearly defined, and countries need to cede less sovereignty. Regional infrastructure cooperation is therefore an effective initial step on the path to broader integration.

Some countries have more to gain from regional integration than others. Landlocked countries depend particularly on effective road and rail corridors to the sea, as well as on intracontinental fiber-optic backbones that link them to submarine cables. Coastal countries depend particularly on sound management of water resources upstream. Small countries benefit especially from regional power trade that reduces the costs of energy supply. As long as regional integration provides a substantial economic dividend to some of the participating countries, designing compensation mechanisms that benefit all of them should be possible. The concept of benefit sharing was pioneered through international river basin treaties, such as that for the Senegal River, and could be applied to regional infrastructure more broadly.

A key prerequisite for any regional initiative is building political consensus both nationally and across borders. Although methods will vary from country to country, some broad principles apply.

Get High-Level Buy-In. Africa needs more high-level advocacy and leadership to promote regional integration for infrastructure development and beyond. Regional integration issues remain only a small part of parliamentary debate in most countries. Between infrequent regional meetings of heads of state, a sense of inertia and lack of follow-up frequently exist. Governments and international institutions must provide leadership. The African Union has the mandate to coordinate the regional integration program of Africa as spelled out in the Abuja Treaty (1991), which created the African Economic Community, with regional economic communities as building blocks. The African Union identified infrastructure and regional integration as major components of economic growth and poverty reduction in Africa. The main vehicle is the New Partnership for Africa's Development (NEPAD), which has not always received the requisite support from political leaders to build a consensus around financially and economically viable projects. The NEPAD Heads of State Implementation Committee, set up to help remove political blocks to projects, has not been effective and now meets less regularly than originally intended. A strong commitment from regional leaders is essential to move projects forward. When the West African Gas Pipeline ran into political differences, for example, it was the shuttle diplomacy of Nigeria's President Olusegun Obasanjo that kept the project on track.

Build Trust. Trust is important for regional integration—especially when some countries stand to benefit more than others. Countries that do not trust each other may fail to reach a cooperative solution. For example, implementation of the road-railway bridge project between Kinshasa and Brazzaville and extension of the Kinshasa-Ilebo railway are intended to accelerate trade between the Democratic Republic of Congo and the Republic of Congo. Trust between the two countries will be a key factor in the decision to proceed with this project. Starting small, with relatively well-defined projects, is one way to build that trust. Frequent interaction among policy makers at all levels of government builds relationships that help overcome inevitable disagreements. Supranational organizations can be honest brokers for sharing gains and resolving disputes.

Invest in Credible Information. Trust is easier to build when the facts are available to all. Good evidence must be gathered and made accessible to decision makers to gauge the full costs and benefits of regional infrastructure investments, many of which involve large allocations of funds and ceding of some sovereignty. The regional economic communities must communicate the potential benefits to all stakeholders to help build consensus. Countries are unlikely to bear the full cost of public goods if the benefits are not clear. Because regional integration can create winners and losers, assessing the likely benefits and costs will help.

Focus on Sharing Benefits, Not on Sharing Resources. Regional projects often fail because of the perception of unequal access to a natural or infrastructure resource. However, what matters is how the economic benefits from resources or infrastructure are shared. This philosophy is best illustrated in the management of transboundary water resources, where benefits include flood protection, hydropower, irrigation, fisheries, leisure, tourism, and peace and security. One country may benefit most from hydropower, while another requires steady access to water for irrigation. Successful benefit sharing includes the Lesotho Highlands Water Project and the Incomati Basin water-sharing

agreement, contributing to broader political and economic cooperation and stability.

Think Regionally, Even When Developing National Policies. Regional interdependence is a fact of life in all parts of Africa. It is critical for not only landlocked countries but also larger and coastal countries, which deal with regional trade, labor migration, and expanding markets. National policy makers should therefore consider the regional consequences of national policy making. Donors can encourage this approach. For instance, developing an assistance strategy for Burkina Faso without considering its place in the region in relation to Côte d'Ivoire, Ghana, and Mali makes little sense.

Establishing Effective Regional Institutions

No shortage exists of regional institutions in Africa, but few are effective. The institutional architecture that supports African integration comprises more than 30 executive continental bodies, regional economic communities with many overlapping memberships, sectoral technical bodies, and national planning bodies. The result is a high degree of complexity, unclear functional responsibilities for strategy and project development, and uncertain financing strategies. This lack of clarity has slowed progress on coherent regional strategies, realistic programs for integration priorities (such as regional infrastructure and trade integration), and technical plans for specific projects.

Becoming more effective is easier for agencies with a narrow set of tasks and responsibilities than for those with a broader design. The African Union Commission has struggled with its mandate because of a lack of human and financial resources and unclear responsibilities. The regional economic communities have limited capabilities and resources and, above all, weak authority to enforce decisions. A disconnect often exists between what is written in treaties and what happens on the ground. Institutions will be more effective if a greater willingness exists to cede some sovereignty in return for greater economic benefits. Greater use of qualified majority rules in some areas of policy making would lead to more streamlined decision making. This approach has been debated for some time in many regional economic communities, without resolution. Adequate financing is also a problem because member states often fail to pay assessed contributions in full, if at all. Regional economic communities have multiple functions, with infrastructure not necessarily prominent (ICA 2008). As a result, they often fail to attract and retain professional staff with the experience to identify and promote complex regional infrastructure projects.

In 2006, the regional poverty reduction strategy for West Africa by the Economic Community of West African States and the West African Economic and Monetary Union was a significant milestone. Other regions also have completed strategic planning exercises: for example, the Regional Indicative Strategic Plan (developed by the Southern African Development Community) and the East African Community Master Plan. However, links between these regional strategic plans and country programs remain limited. Improved links are critical for coordinated implementation of regional programs, which is essential to leverage outcomes at the country level. For example, the Common Market for Eastern and Southern Africa, the East African Community, and the Southern African Development Community have been successfully coordinating programs through a tripartite task force.

Regional special-purpose entities or sectoral technical bodies have been more effective. A power pool, for example, has a clear mandate, sufficient autonomy to execute its responsibilities, a dedicated funding mechanism, and career opportunities that attract and retain high-caliber staff. It also receives substantial capacity building. The members of a power pool are national electricity utilities, which similarly have clear functions and roles within their national contexts and are less subject to immediate political pressures than less technical public agencies.

The need to increase capacity and streamline decision making extends to national agencies. For complex regional infrastructure projects, several line ministries are often involved in each country. This practice complicates consensus building and assigning of clear responsibilities. A further problem is the frequent lack of follow-up on regional commitments to national

implementation by high-level government officials.

Five actions to improve the effectiveness of institutions can aid regional cooperation in infrastructure provision. First, the roles and responsibilities of regional bodies concerned with regional integration must be clarified. Second, increased legal authority is required for regional entities to improve and accelerate decision-making processes. Third, the key regional bodies must boost their professional capacity. Fourth, national planning agencies must improve their ability to strengthen links between regional strategies and national development plans. Fifth, delivery mechanisms for priority programs (for example, regional infrastructure) should be strengthened to underpin confidence in integration by delivering tangible results.

Africa's efforts to strengthen regional integration have focused on the fifth action. However, national priorities have limited the support for regional programs overall. Poor reflection of regional priorities in national plans has slowed priority programs, sapping government willingness to cede sovereignty to other regional initiatives and creating a vicious circle. Progress requires rebalancing efforts among the five institutional challenges.

Setting Priorities for Regional Infrastructure

With a very large backlog of infrastructure investments as well as limited fiscal space and borrowing ability, countries must set effective priorities for infrastructure investment in Africa. Projects should be well justified to compete with investments in other sectors such as health or education. The long life of infrastructure means that bad decisions are locked in for decades. An unwise investment can saddle governments with an ineffective project that will also require costly maintenance. How should priorities be set? Suitable criteria include predicted economic returns, spatial targeting, and scope for private participation.

Economic Returns. Projects with the highest returns may not always be new infrastructure. Strategic investments that improve the performance of infrastructure systems, such as addressing bottlenecks at ports or border crossings or installing power interconnectors between countries with large cost differentials, are often the most effective. Investments in maintenance and rehabilitation of existing infrastructure, such as roads and rail links in a network, can often yield economic benefits faster than new transport infrastructure.

Spatial Targeting. Too often, political expediency encourages spreading out investments to all parts of a country or region, when a concentration of productive investments in high-potential areas would yield greater economic benefits (World Bank 2009). The spatial development initiative supported by NEPAD aims to link trunk infrastructure with countries' natural resource endowments. The initiative was inspired by the Maputo Development Corridor, which bundled infrastructure investments and used private finance as the catalyst to exploit natural resources along a corridor between Mozambique and South Africa.

South Africa's leadership was key in moving the initiative forward. However, whether similar leadership will emerge in other parts of the region is unclear. Indeed, most of the spatial development initiatives are brownfield initiatives, in which some regional infrastructure already exists. This fact raises the question of why private anchor investments have not yet been seen. A concern is that corridor development will simply facilitate exports of raw materials, whereas the goal should be economic development and employment growth through manufactured exports.

Another example of a spatial approach is the development of better links between the large coastal agglomerations in the Gulf of Guinea (Abidjan, Accra, Cotonou, Lagos, and Lomé) and providing a competitive business environment sustained by policy harmonization along the corridor. Such an initiative would allow all countries to benefit from access to major ports in Abidjan and Lagos and, ultimately, reduce international transport costs for the entire subregion.

Through shared infrastructure and better trade facilitation, Africa can emulate East Asia's economies, which took advantage of economic complementarities in bordering regions to increase investment and facilitate business reforms. The Zambia-Malawi-Mozambique growth triangle—initiated in 2000 and covering northern Zambia, northern and central Malawi, and some central-eastern parts of Mozambique—seems to have facilitated trade and generated new economic activities.[2]

The Economic Community of West African States recently adopted cross-border initiatives between bordering areas with economic complementarities, such as the Sikasso-Korhogo-Bamako initiative (based on the cotton basin shared by Burkina Faso, Côte d'Ivoire, and Mali) and the Kano-Katsina-Maharadi initiative (based on agriculture and cattle in the Nigeria-Niger border region). By identifying what is needed to facilitate cross-border production networks, bordering countries can make regional infrastructure investments based on profitable joint projects.

Scope for Private Participation. ICT, power plants, and ports and airports have significant potential for private provision and operation. The prospect of a larger regional market can attract more interest for private financing or public-private partnerships. Larger private involvement can help overcome the large infrastructure financing gap, but governments must then ratify and implement protocols to facilitate investment. Public control in many countries continues to stifle private investment. For example, regarding ports, only two African countries (Ghana and Nigeria) have adopted the internationally favored landlord model, which aims to strike a balance between public (port authority) and private (port industry) interests.

Priority-setting exercises are under way or planned. A new continental task force will report on a broad set of criteria for helping development institutions set investment priorities in each of the main infrastructure sectors. The report will feed into a joint African Union–NEPAD–African Development Bank study, the Program for Infrastructure Development in Africa, which will elaborate a vision of regional integration on the continent through infrastructure. The program will need to consider other ongoing processes, such as the

Africa-EU Energy Partnership, which aims to agree on an Electricity Master Plan for Africa, and the 2009 African Union Summit, which agreed on a short-list of flagship projects for priority support and investment. In addition, many regional economic communities and other technical regional institutions have 10-year investment plans that present a large investment menu for external financiers.

A requirement for any priority setting is transparency in decision making and agreement on selection criteria. Decision making must be well documented and motivated, using sufficiently detailed data and a clear explanation of assumptions, all publicly accessible. The investments in better information at the country and regional levels will be small relative to the public and private funds at stake, but the benefits of better decision making will be large.

Facilitating Project Preparation and Cross-Border Finance

Project design is complex. The appraisal phase establishes social, economic, financial, technical, administrative, and environmental feasibility (Leigland and Roberts 2007). For regional projects, coordination among national agencies with different procedures, capacity, and administrative constraints adds to the complexity. Thus, the project preparation costs for regional projects tend to be higher, and the process can take longer than that for national projects.

Preparation costs are typically about 5 percent of total financing, or approximately double the cost of preparing national projects. These outlays occur up front when the success of the project and the likelihood of a sufficient return from the investment are still uncertain. Regional institutions and donors have tried to address these issues, setting up more than 20 project preparation facilities, many of which explicitly support regional activities (ICA 2006). However, the resources do not match the regional needs. African countries need to commit more funds and more people with the proper technical, legal, and financial skills for infrastructure planning and project implementation. Timely execution of project preparation activities and a sufficient pipeline of new projects also encourage participation of the private sector. For

operators relying on private financing, a firm planning horizon is even more critical than for the public sector (ICA 2009).

Support for regional projects by the Infrastructure Consortium for Africa grew sharply from about $430 million in 2005 to $2.8 billion in 2007 (ICA 2007).[3] Although the bilateral share has increased over time, multilateral members accounted for 60 percent of total commitments in 2007 (World Bank 2008). Multilateral institutions have been developing specific mechanisms for dealing with regional projects.

The World Bank has four criteria for regional projects to qualify for concessional funding from the International Development Association (IDA): (a) at least three countries must participate, though they can enter the project at different stages; (b) countries and the relevant regional entity must demonstrate a strong commitment; (c) economic and social benefits must spill over country boundaries; and (d) projects must provide a platform for policy harmonization among countries and be priorities within a well-developed and broadly supported regional strategy. A recent evaluation of World Bank regional integration projects concluded that regional programs have been effective, if still on a relatively small scale (World Bank 2007).

The African Development Bank adopted similar principles in 2008, though it requires that only two countries participate. To help with country ownership, both institutions use a one-third, two-thirds principle, whereby participants are expected to use one IDA or African Development Fund (ADF) credit from their country allocation, supplemented by two credits from regionally dedicated resources. Currently, 17.5 percent of ADF and 15 percent of IDA resources in Africa are dedicated to regional programs.

For the EU-Africa Infrastructure Trust Fund, eligible projects must have African ownership and long-term project sustainability. They must also be cross-border projects or national projects with a regional effect on two or more countries. Regional projects funded by the Development Bank of Southern Africa must either involve a minimum of two countries or be located in a single country with benefits to the region.

Some challenges remain. Although recipients of funds from the ADF and the IDA can leverage their country allocations by participating in regional projects, those receiving a small allocation may be reluctant to use a large percentage on one regional project for which the benefits are unclear. How such concessional resources are allocated and whether enough of the overall envelope is dedicated to regional projects remain issues of debate. In addition, limited financing instruments exist for middle-income countries, which is an issue in North Africa (for connectivity with countries south of the Sahara) and in southern Africa (for projects that might involve Botswana or South Africa).

Regional organizations may not always qualify for grants or concessional finance from donor institutions because of their supranational character, limiting the availability of resources for capacity building. Furthermore, some projects with significant regional spillovers may not involve three or more countries and thus not qualify for regional financing, such as the Ethiopia-Sudan interconnector or any national power-generation project that may have export potential.

Developing Regional Regulatory Frameworks

Building physical infrastructure by itself will not yield high economic returns in regional growth and employment. Improving the legal, regulatory, and administrative environment is necessary to ensure infrastructure's efficient use (box 6.2).

Air transport is profitable enough to allow the private sector or public-private partnerships to invest in and improve infrastructure, but the regulatory environment and government safety and security regimes are key to success. The Yamoussoukro Declaration on free access to the African skies has improved intraregional and international connectivity.

A study of 73 African ports concluded that capacity additions and institutional reform must be placed on a fast track to realize the potential. Although some countries are undertaking new master plans for national ports, not all address the need to improve weak labor skills and stifling bureaucracy and to provide independent regulation.

In the energy sector, African borders limit market size through political and regulatory barriers to electricity trade and through physical barriers. Regional power infrastructure requires harmonized power pricing and third-party access regulations, effective cross-border trading contracts, and reliable and creditworthy national utilities. In much of Sub-Saharan Africa, bilateral arrangements between vertically integrated utilities guide cross-border electricity exchanges, although, increasingly, regional power pools are liberalizing the electricity markets.

Worldwide experience in developing power pools has led to a consensus on three key building blocks for success: a common legal and regulatory framework, a durable framework for systems planning and operation, and an equitable commercial framework for energy exchanges (USAID 2008).

The four power pools in Sub-Saharan Africa are at different stages of development, but as countries move from bilateral to multilateral power exchanges, a commercially acceptable framework is essential. In 2006, the West African

BOX 6.2

One-Stop Border Posts to Facilitate Trade

Trade logistics has three components: international shipping, operations at the gateway (final clearance or transit clearance at customs and handling), and inland movement (often under a transit procedure). At the Chirundu crossing between Zambia and Zimbabwe, the average transit times for northbound trucks range from 26 to 46 hours. The border has more than 15 agencies from both governments, each enforcing different pieces of legislation. A joint task force formed by the Common Market for Eastern and Southern Africa, the Southern African Development Community, and the East African Community for harmonization of regional trade arrangements started operating in 2006. The one-stop border posts under this initiative illustrate what political will can achieve. The trade facilitation measures being addressed by the task force include using a single document for customs clearance, harmonizing information technology and electronic customs management systems, harmonizing axle loading and road transit charges, and instituting regional driving license and insurance schemes.

Source: Based on interviews with staff from the World Bank's Africa Transport Department, 2008.

Power Pool was granted special status to reinforce its autonomy, and the 2007 ratification of an overarching legal framework (ECOWAS [Economic Community of West African States] Energy Protocol) will help promote security for investors and enshrine the principle of "open access" to national transmission grids across the region. In 2008, the ECOWAS Regional Electricity Regulatory Authority was established to regulate cross-border electricity exchanges between member states.

Notes

The authors of this chapter are Souleymane Coulibaly, Andrew Roberts, Vivien Foster, and Uwe Deichmann, who drew on background material and contributions from Alvaro Federico Barra, Pinki Chauduri, Siobhan Murray, and Alex Rugamba.

1. Both figures exclude South Africa.
2. See http://www.afrol.com/News/maw008 _growth_triangle.htm.
3. Infrastructure Consortium of Africa members are the Group of Eight countries, World Bank Group, African Development Bank, European Community, European Investment Bank, and Development Bank of Southern Africa.

References

AfDB (African Development Bank) and UNECA (United Nations Economic Commission for Africa). 2000. *Review of the Implementation Status of the Trans-African Highways and the Missing Links.* Volume 2. Tunis and Addis Ababa: African Development Bank and United Nations Economic Commission for Africa.

Arvis, Jean François. 2005. "Transit and the Special Case of Land-Locked Countries." In *Customs Modernization Handbook,* ed. Luc De Wulf and José B. Sokol, 243–64. Washington, DC: World Bank.

Bofinger, Heinrich C. 2009. "Air Transport Sector Review." Background Paper 16, Africa Infrastructure Country Diagnostic, World Bank, Washington, DC.

Buys, Piet, Uwe Deichmann, and David Wheeler. 2006. "Road Network Upgrading and Overland Trade Expansion in Sub-Saharan Africa." Policy Research Working Paper 4097, World Bank, Washington, DC.

Collier, Paul. 2007. "Poverty Reduction in Africa." *Proceedings of the National Academy of Sciences* 104 (43): 16763–68.

Collier, Paul, and Anthony Venables. 2007. "Rethinking Trade Preferences: How Africa Can Diversify Its Exports." *World Economy* 30 (8): 1326–45.

ICA (Infrastructure Consortium for Africa). 2006. *Infrastructure Project Preparation Facilities in Africa: User Guide for Africa.* Tunis: ICA. http://www.icafrica.org/en/documentation.

———. 2007. *Annual Report 2007.* Tunis: ICA.

———. 2008. "Mapping of Donor and Government Capacity-Building Support to African RECs and Other Regional Bodies." Report of Economic Consulting Associates to the Infrastructure Consortium for Africa, Tunis.

———. 2009. *Attracting Investors to African Public-Private Partnerships: A Project Preparation Guide.* Washington, DC: World Bank. http://www.icafrica.org/fileadmin/documents/guides/Attracting-investors-to-African-PPP.pdf.

Leamer, Edward E., and Michael Storper. 2001. "The Economic Geography of the Internet Age." *Journal of International Business Studies* 32 (4): 641–65.

Leigland, James, and Andrew Roberts. 2007. "The African Project Preparation Gap: Africans Address a Critical Limiting Factor in Infrastructure Investment." *Gridlines,* Note 18 (March), Public-Private Infrastructure Advisory Facility, World Bank, Washington, DC.

Limão, Nuno, and Anthony Venables. 1999. "Infrastructure, Geographical Disadvantage, and Transportation Costs." Policy Research Working Paper 2257, World Bank, Washington, DC.

Mayer, Rebecca, Ken Figueredo, Mike Jensen, Tim Kelly, Richard Green, and Alvaro Federico Barra. 2008. "Connecting the Continent: Costing the Needs for Investment in ICT Infrastructure in Africa." Background Paper 3, Africa Infrastructure Country Diagnostic, World Bank, Washington, DC.

Minges, Michael, Cecila Briceño-Garmendia, Mark Williams, Mavis Ampah, Daniel Camos, and Maria Shkaratan. 2008. "Information and Communications Technology in Sub-Saharan Africa: A Sector Review." Background Paper 10, Africa Infrastructure Sector Diagnostic, World Bank, Washington, DC.

Rosnes, Orvika, and Haakon Vennemo. 2008. "Powering Up: Costing Power Infrastructure Investment Needs in Sub-Saharan Africa." Background Paper 5, Africa Infrastructure Country Diagnostic, World Bank, Washington, DC.

Teravaninthorn, Supee, and Gaël Raballand. 2008. *Transport Prices and Costs in Africa: A Review of the Main International Corridors.* Directions in

Development Series. Washington, DC: World Bank.

UNESCO (United Nations Educational, Scientific and Cultural Organization). 2003. *Conflict Prevention and Cooperation in International Water Resources.* Paris: UNESCO.

————. 2006. *The 2nd United Nations World Water Report: Water, a Shared Responsibility.* Paris: UNESCO.

USAID (U.S. Agency for International Development). 2008. "Sub-Saharan Africa's Power Pools: Development Framework." White Paper, USAID, Washington, DC.

World Bank. 2007. *The Development Potential of Regional Programs: An Evaluation of World Bank Support of Multicountry Operations.* Washington, DC: World Bank, Independent Evaluation Group.

————. 2008. "Africa Regional Integration Assistance Strategy." World Bank, Washington, DC.

————. 2009. *World Development Report 2009: Reshaping Economic Geography.* Washington, DC: World Bank.

Part 2

Sectoral Snapshots

Chapter 7

Information and Communication Technologies: A Boost for Growth

Information and communication technologies (ICTs) have been a remarkable success in Africa. Sector reform, particularly in the mobile segment of the market, has transformed the availability, quality, and cost of connectivity across the continent. In less than 10 years, mobile networks have covered 91 percent of the urban population, and coverage in rural areas is growing. However, these high overall levels of coverage hide significant variation between countries, and particularly in the proportion of their populations that have access to services. Some countries have been much more successful in providing basic voice services than others, and some segments of the market, such as fixed-line telephone service and broadband Internet, have been less successful than the mobile segment. Fixed-line penetration rates remain low and are falling in most countries, while broadband Internet is expensive and available to only a small proportion of the population.

Although large parts of the ICT sector have been transformed, much remains to be done. Policy makers need to take the following steps to address the specific challenges facing the ICT sector in Africa:

- Complete the reform agenda by establishing full competition throughout the sector.
- Revise the licensing framework to accommodate rapid technological change and emerging competition.
- Reform the state-owned enterprises (SOEs) that hinder sector growth and development.
- Ensure low-cost international access infrastructure by preventing monopoly control over bottleneck facilities.
- Promote the development of high-bandwidth backbone infrastructure (the networks that carry communications traffic between fixed points in a network).
- Stimulate innovation in the use of wireless technologies by reforming the way the radio spectrum is allocated and managed.
- Promote universal access to ensure that ICT availability is as extensive as possible.

The African ICT Revolution

In Africa, the greatest expansion in ICT has been in voice services. Internet services, in contrast, have grown only slowly. Overall, the ICT sector has had a strong, positive effect on Africa's GDP.

Access to Basic Voice Services

Sub-Saharan Africa has witnessed dramatic growth in the penetration of ICT services since the mid-1990s—mainly in mobile telecommunications, where the number of mobile users grew from 10 million in 2000 to more than 180 million in 2007 (ITU 2008). During the mid-2000s, more than 25 million new mobile subscribers were added each year, and annual growth rates exceeded 30 percent (figure 7.1). The fixed-line market has grown much more slowly, from 10 million fixed telephone lines in 2002 to 11.8 million in 2006.

Competition among mobile operators has created a race to increase the percentage of the population covered by their networks. By 2006, one or more of the mobile networks covered 62 percent of the Sub-Saharan population, which was hence able to access a mobile signal, whether they actually subscribed to the service or not. This coverage continues to increase each year (figure 7.2).

All countries in the region have seen growth in the use of mobile telephones, but with the exception of Nigeria (which added 750,000

Figure 7.2 Global System for Mobile Communications Coverage in Africa, 1998 to Third Quarter of 2006

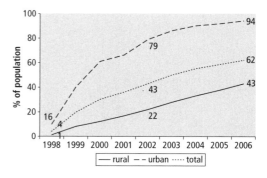

Source: Minges and others 2008.

landlines after introducing competition), growth rates for fixed lines have stagnated or turned negative. For example, the number of fixed lines in South Africa declined by 300,000 between 2000 and 2007.

Access to new ICT services has been remarkably broad. Across Africa, the rural mobile penetration rate is 3 percent, while in middle-income countries it is as high as 13 percent. In urban areas, the penetration rates range from 22 percent in low-income countries to 38 percent in middle-income countries. Even people among the lowest income groups have access to ICT through mobile networks; in the bottom three income quintiles, access ranges from 1.6 percent to 5.5 percent. In middle-income countries, the penetration rate in the lowest-income quintile is 10 percent.

The widespread use of prepaid telephone service has revolutionized access to mobile networks for low-income households. An estimated 97 percent of consumers in Sub-Saharan Africa are prepaid users. With prepaid charging systems, customers can purchase services in small increments and control their expenditures. Operators have introduced other innovative price schemes, some targeted at poor customers: low-cost on-net calling, caller ID (to facilitate callbacks within social and business networks), low and sometimes free off-peak tariffs, and systems to transfer mobile phone credit electronically between subscribers. For operators, these schemes, particularly prepayment, dramatically reduce credit risk and the cost of revenue collection.

Figure 7.1 Growth of Mobile Subscribers in Africa, 1998–2006

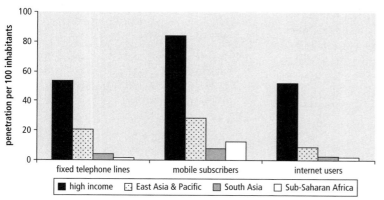

Source: Minges and others 2008.

This rapid growth in access to ICT in Africa has happened despite the relatively high price of services. In 2007, a representative basket of prepaid mobile services cost $12.58 a month, six times the $2 that it cost in Bangladesh, India, and Pakistan. Prices in Africa are declining but not as fast as in other world regions. In 2000, each mobile subscriber paid about $39 a month in African countries and in Bangladesh, India, and Pakistan. By 2005, that figure had fallen to $7 in Bangladesh, India, and Pakistan but only to $20 in Africa. If prices were to fall to the levels seen in South Asia, access to ICT in Africa could be significantly higher.

The average price of international calls in Sub-Saharan Africa has fallen significantly since 2000, but prices for calls to countries outside the region remain much lower than for calls within the region. The average peak price of a one-minute call from Africa to the United States is $0.45, compared with $1.23 for an international call within Africa. These averages mask significant variation among countries (figure 7.3). Price variation is much lower for calls within Africa.

Access to the Internet

Unlike the expanded access to basic voice services, rates of access to the Internet are low and growing only slowly in Africa. High prices and limited availability are key reasons, compounded by poor fixed-line access networks, limited access to the broadband radio spectrum, poor domestic backbone networks, and limited use of computers (figure 7.4).

ICT Sector Developments

Growth in the ICT sector in Africa has taken place primarily in mobile phones through global systems mobile (GSM) networks. The economies of scale generated by the global standardization of GSM equipment have dramatically reduced prices of handsets and network equipment, and international standards allow customers to use networks in more than one country at a low cost. As a result, several pan-African operators have emerged, and they are highly innovative in their tariffs and services. For example, international roaming is a

Figure 7.3 Price of One-Minute, Peak-Rate Call to the United States, 2006

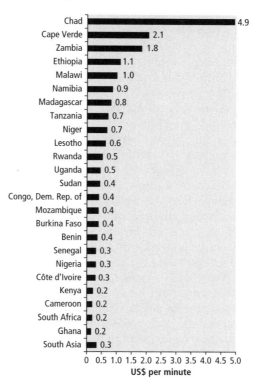

Source: Minges and others 2008.
Note: Peak rate includes taxes.

Figure 7.4 Price Basket for Internet Access, 2005

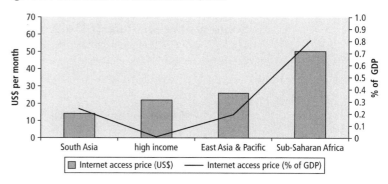

Source: Minges and others 2008.

contentious issue in many parts of the world, but multinational African operators such as Celtel, MTN, Safaricom, and Vodacom have international on-net tariffs offering savings to their customers of about 15 percent per minute in call charges. The major alternative global standard for wireless voice services, Code-Division Multiple Access, is also making slow but steady progress in Africa. Operators in the region have also pioneered innovative services using the mobile telephone networks, such as mobile banking and remittance payments.

The fixed-line market in Sub-Saharan Africa continues to be dominated by incumbents—operators that were either formerly or are currently owned by the state—and their performance remains relatively poor (figure 7.5). The productivity of these operators is low, and most of them have higher levels of personnel than international benchmarks, as measured by the number of lines per employee. In July 2008, the Sub-Saharan operators ranged from 20 to 346 lines per employee, whereas the figure was 427 in Latin America and the Caribbean region, and 700 in Organisation for Economic Co-operation and Development member countries.

The low productivity of African incumbent telecommunication companies creates hidden costs for the economy, through suboptimal allocations of resources to the sector and low consumption of telecommunication services. The cost of this excess labor can be on the order of 0.4 percent of GDP, and even higher in some cases (figure 7.6). For Cameroon, Ghana, and Namibia, among other countries, the level of this inefficiency exceeds the cost of meeting universal access targets.

Economic Impact of the ICT Industry

The ICT sector has positively affected economic growth in Africa. Research shows that increasing investment in ICT services results in higher long-run rates of economic growth (Roeller and Waverman 2001); according to estimates, the ICT revolution in Africa is responsible for about 1 percentage point of the improvement in Africa's per capita economic growth rate between the mid-1990s and the mid-2000s (Calderón 2008). This positive effect will continue as investment in the sector continues and as the use of ICT raises productivity in all types of businesses.

Large-scale private investment, reaching a cumulative value of about $20 billion, has driven the expansion of access to ICT. Between 1992 and 2005, the vast majority of the 82 private sector transactions in the ICT sector were for new operations in mobile communications (World Bank 2009). SOE privatizations and license fees generated a further $3.3 billion of revenues for the state. This investment continues today, as new deals in the region are announced regularly. The current financial crisis has adversely affected investment rates, however, limiting operators' access to finance.

Overall ICT employment has grown as the mobile sector directly and indirectly added jobs in African countries. Multiplier effects and new lines of business (mobile airtime agents and m-transactions) also add to employment growth and income generation. In East Africa, the mobile industry directly and indirectly provides employment for close to 500,000 people (GSMA 2007).

The new ICT infrastructure and related reforms have increased government revenues through one-time fees for licenses and ongoing payments through licenses and taxes. The revenue generated by the ICT industry in African countries ranges from 1.7 percent to 8.2 percent of GDP, with an average of 4.0 percent. The tax and license revenues generated by the industry have also had a significant positive fiscal effect (figure 7.7).

Institutional Reforms in the ICT Sector

Market liberalization has been the most important cause of the ICT sector's growth in Africa. Regulatory reforms and the

Figure 7.5 Net Change in Fixed-Line Market, 2001–05

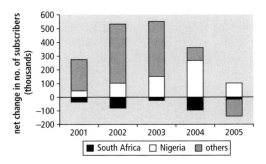

Source: Minges and others 2008.

privatization of SOEs have complemented these market reforms.

Market Reforms

The widespread liberalization of markets in Africa and the emergence of competition, particularly among mobile operators, have been the main drivers of the ICT sector's performance (figure 7.8).

Countries with more competitive markets cover, on average, 64 percent of their population with mobile networks, compared with 57 percent for the less competitive markets. Among the low-income African countries, those with more competitive markets have 31 percent higher mobile penetration rates, 6 percent lower mobile prices, and 39 percent lower international call prices (as measured by the price of a call to the United States).

The benefits of market liberalization increase as competition intensifies. In general, the annual increase in penetration rises as more firms enter the market. Relatively little growth occurs in market penetration in the initial change from monopoly to duopoly, but when a country issues its fourth mobile license, penetration rates increase, on average, by almost 3 percentage points every year. A country's average income also affects the performance of the telecommunication sector. In poorer countries, increased competition is felt most strongly when a market reaches four operators, whereas for middle-income countries, the effect is strongest when a third operator is introduced.

Some countries that have established a legal framework for a liberalized market have nonetheless failed to establish effective competition. Few countries have legislation with outright prohibitions on competition in telecommunications, but many have restrictions on competition arising from exclusivity clauses granted in licenses to existing operators. In 12 countries where data were available, a gap of at least two years elapsed between ending the legal restrictions on competition and granting new licenses. Twelve Sub-Saharan countries have competition in the fixed-line and international markets, but only a few of them have more than two operators in these segments. Even in the mobile segment, barely half of the

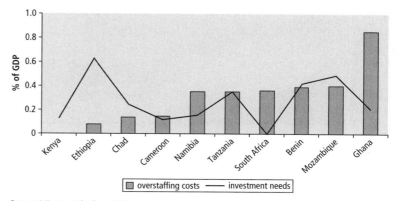

Figure 7.6 Costs of Overstaffing for Fixed-Line Incumbents in Selected Countries

Source: Minges and others 2008.

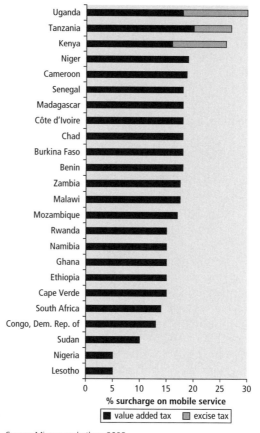

Figure 7.7 Value Added and Excise Taxes on Mobile Telephone Services, 2006

Source: Minges and others 2008.
Note: In Kenya, Tanzania, and Uganda, the excise taxes shown are applicable to mobile calls. Rwanda is planning to implement an excise tax on mobile airtime.

Figure 7.8 Status of Mobile Competition, 1993–2006

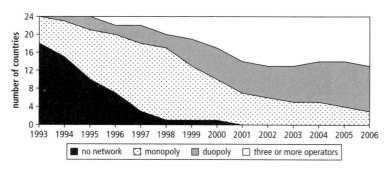

Source: Minges and others 2008.

Figure 7.9 Tariff Rebalancing in African Countries with a Liberalized Telecommunication Sector, 1993–2006

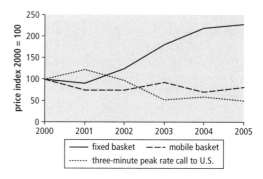

Source: Minges and others 2008.
Note: Price index represents prices as a percentage of their level in the base year 2000 so that only relative changes over time are highlighted.

countries have more than three active operators despite evidence that most markets in the region can support more. Across the region, market reform is far from being complete.

Regulatory Reform

Changes in the legal framework that governs the sector have matched the reforms in market structure. All African countries have laws and regulations covering telecommunications. Typically, a new law (supplemented by decrees and regulations) establishes a national regulatory agency with general provisions for competition, licensing, interconnection, allocation of scarce resources (for example, numbering and spectrum), and pricing. Of the 24 countries sampled, 23 have such a broad institutional framework and independent regulatory authorities, up from 5 in 1996.

Regulators still exert considerable control over incumbent fixed-line operators' tariffs. They have allowed these operators to respond to competition by rebalancing their tariffs, allowing monthly fixed charges to increase and national and international call prices to fall. Regulators have less control over mobile operators' tariffs, which are forced down through competition (figure 7.9).

Some regulators have been successful in setting wholesale tariffs (the charges that operators pay each other for handling calls when they pass from one network to another), which feed directly into the retail price that customers pay for their calls. As competition develops, particularly among mobile operators, regulating these interconnection charges becomes more

important. It can be challenging for regulators with limited technical capacity and legal powers to impose decisions on operators, but some regulators have recently been successful. In Tanzania, the national regulatory authority introduced a phased reduction in mobile termination rates, based on a calculation of operators' costs. Nigeria's regulatory authority has established a target for mobile termination rates, and in Kenya, the regulatory authority recently established a ceiling on mobile termination rates, as well as a cap on the retail price of calls between networks.

Reform of State-Owned Enterprises

As governments have liberalized their markets and reformed the institutions for regulating them, many have also reformed the operators they formerly owned. By the end of 2006, 15 African countries had sold shares in their state-owned telecommunication operator to the private sector. These transactions largely involved equity and management partnerships with strategic investors; only Nigeria and Sudan privatized by issuing shares on local or regional stock exchanges.[1] From 1993 to 2006, the total value of such privatizations was $3.5 billion, half of which was accounted for by South Africa's Telkom.

The nature of strategic partnerships and their success have varied over time. Direct investment by developed-country investors in the fixed-line business has been complemented by sales to developing-country investors, particularly from the Middle East and South Asia. The performance of these privatizations and partnerships has been mixed. In some cases, such as Uganda, the privatization of the state-owned fixed-line incumbent was part of a successful overall reform of the sector. In others, private investors have withdrawn, resulting in the renationalization of ICT assets. Ghana and Rwanda resold the businesses after the first privatization failed, indicating a sustained commitment to reform.

Despite the notable successes, the governments of many African countries retain ownership of at least one telecommunication operator, which distorts the market and creates inefficiencies. Thus, the region has some distance to go before it has a fully privately owned and competitive telecommunication market.

Access to International Connectivity

One of the main drivers of the high cost of Internet and of international voice calls is the price of international connectivity, determined by physical access to submarine fiber-optic cables and the level of competition in the international market. Countries with access to submarine cables have lower international call prices than those without access. Nevertheless, countries that have competitive access have significantly lower prices than those retaining a gateway monopoly (table 7.1).

Access to high-capacity submarine fiber-optic infrastructure is therefore a necessary but insufficient condition for low-price international voice services. Countries also need to ensure that the international facilities segment of the market is competitive if customers are

to benefit from lower prices and better quality of service.

Domestic Backbone Infrastructure

Backbone network infrastructure to carry communications traffic between fixed points in the networks is limited, thus constraining the development of broadband Internet. Mobile operators do not require high-capacity backbone networks to carry voice traffic and have typically developed their own using wireless technologies. Broadband Internet backbone networks need much greater capacity, however, typically using fiber-optic cables. The limited extent of these networks is a constraint on the development of the broadband market in Africa.

Considerable variation exists across the region in how markets for domestic backbone infrastructure operate. In many countries, both implicit and explicit constraints limit development of this type of infrastructure. For example, mobile operators may be required to use the incumbent's backbone network, or they might be allowed to build their own but not to sell backbone network services to other operators on a wholesale basis. These types of regulations limit the development of backbone networks and hinder the development of broadband.

Countries that have fully liberalized the market for backbone networks have seen rapid growth in infrastructure competition. In Nigeria, at least four of the major operators are developing high-capacity fiber-optic cable networks capable of supporting high-bandwidth services, and a similar pattern is emerging in Kenya. These networks are concentrating on major urban areas and on interurban links

Table 7.1 Prices for Access to International Voice and Internet Connectivity

Access level	Share of countries (%)	Price for a call within Sub-Saharan Africa ($ per minute)	Price for a call to the United States ($ per minute)	Price for 20 hours of dial-up Internet access ($ per month)	Price for ADSL broadband Internet access ($ per month)
No access to submarine cable	67	1.34	0.86	67.95	282.97
Access to submarine cable	32	0.57	0.48	47.28	110.71
Monopoly on international gateway	16	0.70	0.72	37.36	119.88
Competitive international gateways	16	0.48	0.23	36.62	98.49

Source: Minges and others 2008.
Note: ADSL = asymmetric digital subscriber line.

where the majority of customers are. If high-capacity backbone networks are to extend beyond these areas, some form of public support will likely be needed, preferably in partnership with the private sector.

Completing the Remaining Investment Agenda

Voice Services

The cost of completing mobile network coverage for voice in Africa is relatively modest. By adopting a spatial approach to modeling the cost of providing access to mobile phone networks, reliable estimates have been developed of the capital and operating expenditures required for completing the rollout of GSM voice signal throughout Africa. Potential revenues are estimated based on population density and income distribution. Potential costs are estimated based on terrain characteristics and cell size and the resulting number of additional base stations needed to complete national GSM coverage. These raw base station numbers drive estimates of capital and operating expenditures.

Reaching all the unserved population would require investments of $0.8 billion a year over 10 years. Currently, 43.7 percent of the population lives in areas not covered by wireless voice networks. If the right competitive environment is established, the private sector could fill most of this gap, reaching 39 percent of the population—the vast majority of the unserved—with a voice signal. Only $0.3 billion per year of public investment would be needed to reach the remaining 4.7 percent of the population in the coverage gap (table 7.2).

Nevertheless, the size of the coverage gap varies immensely across countries (figure 7.10), and in a handful of cases (the Democratic Republic of Congo, Madagascar, and Zambia) can exceed 15 percent of the population.

These analytical results are robust; the size of the coverage gap increases only from 4.4 percent to 5.9 percent of the population if the amount spent on telecommunication services drops from 4 percent of GDP per capita (the baseline assumption) to 3 percent. Similarly, even if costs were three times greater than in the base case, the coverage gap would increase from 4.4 percent of the population to 12.6 percent.

Internet Services

Despite the anticipated positive economic effect that widespread use of broadband would have on African economies, mass-market broadband Internet at speeds seen in other parts of the world is unlikely to be commercially viable in Africa for the near future. The broadband Internet available in most African countries is typically limited to major urban areas and to Internet cafés, businesses, and high-income residential customers. Network coverage is limited, prices are high, and speeds are lower than in other regions of the world. This limited current level of service could be expanded to national coverage using wireless network infrastructure with the same technical and economic advantages as GSM voice networks (lower operating and security costs than wired networks and the potential to use prepaid billing systems). The investment to cover the entire population using limited-performance wireless broadband technology has been estimated at approximately $0.9 billion.

Table 7.2 Investments Needed to Close Gaps in Voice and Broadband Coverage in Sub-Saharan Africa

Indicator	Voice coverage			Broadband coverage		
	Total investment	Efficient market gap	Coverage gap	Total investment	Efficient market gap	Coverage gap
Average annual investment ($ billions)	0.8	0.5	0.3	0.9	0.7	0.2
Percentage of population affected	43.7	39.0	4.7	100.0	89.0	11.0

Source: Mayer and others 2008.
Note: Efficient market gap is the portion of total investment need that the private sector could meet under commercial terms if all regulatory barriers to entry were dismantled to allow the market to function efficiently. *Coverage gap* is the portion of the total investment need that the private sector could *not* meet even under efficient market conditions. This gap would require public subsidy because the service lacks commercial viability.

Figure 7.10 Voice Coverage Gaps in 24 Sub-Saharan Countries

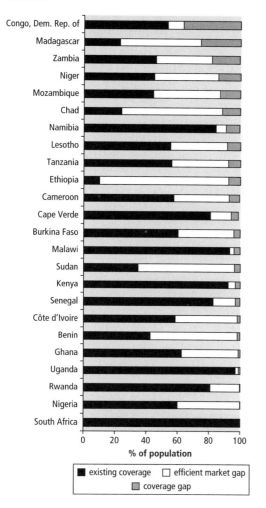

Figure 7.11 Broadband Coverage Gaps in 24 African Countries

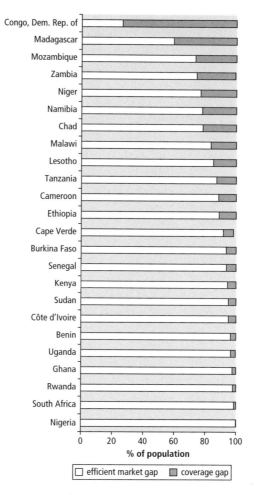

Source: Mayer and others 2008.
Note: Efficient market gap is the portion of the unserved market that the private sector could serve under commercial terms if all regulatory barriers to entry were dismantled to allow the market to function efficiently. *Coverage gap* is the portion of the unserved market that the private sector could *not* serve even under efficient market conditions. This gap would require public subsidy because the service lacks commercial viability.

Source: Mayer and others 2008.
Note: Efficient market gap is the portion of the unserved market that the private sector could serve under commercial terms if all regulatory barriers to entry were dismantled to allow the market to function efficiently. *Coverage gap* is the portion of the unserved market that the private sector could *not* serve even under efficient market conditions. This gap would require public subsidy because the service lacks commercial viability.

As long as the right competitive environment is established, the private sector would cover most of that amount, which could reach 89 percent of the population with this limited-reach broadband access. Only $0.2 billion of public investment would be needed to reach the remaining 11 percent of the population in the coverage gap (table 7.2). However, the coverage gap varies hugely across countries, and in a handful of cases (Chad, the Democratic Republic of Congo, Madagascar, Mozambique, Namibia, Niger, and Zambia) can exceed 20 percent of the population (figure 7.11).

Backbone Networks

Although the existing limited level of broadband service could be expanded at relatively low cost, the shift toward higher-speed mass-market broadband Internet access in Africa at prices that would be affordable for a significant proportion of the population would involve major investments in backbone infrastructure. The revenue generated from customers would be insufficient to make this investment commercially attractive. If governments wished to achieve this level of broadband Internet access, significant levels of public subsidy would likely be required.

High-bandwidth backbone networks are a key part of the investment needed for broadband in Africa. These networks connect towns and cities within countries and across borders. They also link to the international submarine fiber-optic cable networks that carry communications traffic between continents.

Cross-border and interregional connectivity in Africa is currently underdeveloped. One-time investment needs range from $229 million for a minimum set of links to $515 million for an extensive interregional network connecting all African capitals to one another with fiber-optic cables. The private sector will provide much of that investment as regional operators connect their networks across borders. Private investment is also driving international submarine cable infrastructure in Africa. Of the five major submarine fiber-optic cables either already operating or under construction in the region, only one has direct government involvement; four are owned and financed by private operators on commercial terms. These two types of backbone infrastructure are linked. As submarine fiber-optic cables are developed, cross-border links to channel traffic to landing points become more commercially viable.

Aside from routes connecting major urban centers, high-bandwidth backbone networks are unlikely to be commercially viable. Backbone network development in these areas may require some form of public support, either through financial support or through the provision of easier access to existing infrastructure (for example, transport and energy networks).

Policy Challenges

The liberalization of telecommunication markets since the mid-1990s has provided affordable ICT services to the public. It has also radically reshaped the roles of the public and private sectors. The traditional role of the public sector as provider of communication infrastructure has been superseded in most countries by a new role as establisher and regulator of market structure. Few countries in the region, if any, have completed the reform agenda, however. Regulatory frameworks still contain restrictions on investment and competition, and the poor quality of regulation in many countries creates costly inefficiencies. Many incumbent operators remain under state ownership, creating a burden on the public sector, inefficiencies in the market, and conflicts of interest for regulators. Major challenges therefore remain if widespread ICT services at affordable prices are to be available.

Completing the Reform Agenda

Establishing full and effective competition in the ICT sector can deliver rapid and sustained improvements in the availability of communication services. The majority of countries have implemented some reforms, but they still have a long way to go. Completing the reform agenda is therefore the primary challenge facing the ICT sector in Africa.

The most important remaining reform is to increase competition through further market liberalization. In practice, that means issuing more licenses and reforming the licensing structure to allow operators more freedom to innovate and compete across a range of services.

As mobile networks expand into marginal areas, reducing the cost of network rollout and operation will become a more important aspect of the reform agenda. Some form of collaboration among competitors (for example, in the civil engineering aspects of networks, such as masts and towers) could reduce costs enough to allow companies to operate profitably in areas where they would not otherwise be able to do so. Regrettably, this type of collaboration can also enable collusion among operators, so it must be carefully regulated.

The reform agenda will evolve as the market changes. Competition regulation is increasingly becoming part of modern sector legislation in Africa, particularly regarding the behavior of dominant operators and controlling access to essential facilities. Even where a country may not have competition legislation, ICT regulators are applying the tools of competition analysis in telecommunication regulation. They are also adapting their regulatory approach to reflect the evolving marketplace: for example, by relaxing controls on tariffs as competition becomes more effective at controlling them.

African countries will continue to see benefits as competition intensifies and access to ICT increases. As prices fall, even as far as the $0.01–$0.03 per minute range currently seen in South Asia, mobile phone services will become affordable to much of the African population, bringing with it positive economic and social benefits. Governments will also benefit from the expansion of telephone services. First, lower prices will fuel uptake and access to services, directly reducing the costs involved in delivering universal service. Second, greater competition will expose the hidden costs of the incumbent state-owned operators, which represent a burden on government finances and a more general effect on the economy. The expansion of the ICT sector resulting from market liberalization will increase the tax and license-fee revenues earned by governments, and ICT services themselves will become a more effective platform for delivering public services.

Revising the Licensing Framework

The traditional model of licensing is becoming obsolete. In the first wave of market liberalization, licenses were linked to market segments and technologies. GSM licenses granted the right to provide mobile communications in specific spectrum bands using a specific technology, and data licenses were granted to operate in specific value added markets. Two factors are making this traditional approach to licensing obsolete. First, the growth of competitive ICT markets in Africa has demonstrated that multiple players can compete successfully, even in small markets. Managing liberalization through technology and service-specific licenses has therefore proved to be ineffective as a policy tool. Second, technological convergence allows networks to deliver multiple ICT services, thereby reducing costs and promoting service innovation. The traditional approach to licensing often prevents operators from taking advantage of this convergence.

The negative effect of current licensing frameworks is especially evident in Voice over Internet Protocol (VoIP), limited mobility, and Internet protocol television. Many licensing regimes restrict either the VoIP technology or its derived services. Direct consumer access to VoIP allows voice calls over Internet connections instead of the public switched telephone networks. Such services offer much lower prices for long-distance and international calls; however, restrictions are common because the widespread use of VoIP could undermine the main sources of voice revenues for incumbent operators.

Licensing constraints on the mobility of specific wireless telecommunication operators are common in Africa. Operators with limited-mobility licenses can provide wireless telecommunication services while allowing customers to move around within a limited area. No technological reason exists why these networks cannot offer full mobility; the restrictions are often imposed to protect existing mobile licensees. As competition in the full-mobility market increases, these restrictions will seem increasingly anachronistic.

Finally, the use of Internet networks to provide television services is increasing in Africa as the number of broadband subscribers increases. This raises many challenges for regulatory systems that have traditionally dealt with communication and broadcasting media through separate institutions and through separate legal and regulatory frameworks. These separations are creating obstacles to investment and competition as convergence blurs the boundaries between the technologies.

The initial response of policy makers to these trends has been to move toward unified licenses that remove technological distinctions and allow operators to provide a full range of services to customers. The design and implementation of a unified licensing system can be complex, however, magnified by the need to adjust a wide range of existing rights and obligations, annual fees, and acquisition costs. This adjustment can be done in a transparent way through public consultation, but the migration process has to be managed carefully to avoid undue destabilization of the market.

In the medium term, licenses will have to become simpler and less restrictive to facilitate the development of new services at lower prices. Ultimately, the challenge for African countries will be to migrate from the current licensing regime to one in which controls on market entry and the services delivered by market parties would be largely abandoned. The countries of the European Union have taken this approach, moving from a system of individual licenses to a general authorization regime.

Reforming State-Owned Enterprises

Reform of state-owned, fixed-line incumbents remains a major policy challenge for governments in the region. The last decade has seen the fixed-line incumbent operators eclipsed. Compared with the mobile operators, they now play a minor role in telecommunication service in most African countries. Incumbent operators can be a disruptive force in the economy through misallocation of public resources, use of incumbents as social buffers, and the regulatory uncertainty created by their presence in the market. In some cases, preferential treatment of these operators— exclusivity agreements (for example, in control of international gateways and backbone capacity), banning of innovative services such as VoIP, and distortion of prices—inhibits innovation and investment and amplifies the economic burden of SOEs on national economies. This issue has emerged again as some Sub-Saharan governments finance the development of fiber-optic backbone networks through their SOEs.

At a minimum, SOEs should be brought fully within the regulatory and licensing framework so that they are treated in the same way as private operators. This move will stimulate competition and efficiency in resource allocation. Encouraging greater private participation in SOEs to transform and grow the businesses may also be appropriate. Given the state of many incumbent operators' networks, that may require some form of financial and management incentives to attract partners and investors. The challenge for governments will be to ensure that this transition is achieved without distorting the market. It can be done by allocating mobile and other wireless spectrum to these operators, offering management control, and minimizing network coverage commitments.

Providing SOEs with monopoly control over specific segments of the market to make them more attractive to potential buyers will ultimately be unsuccessful, for it will distort the market and constrain its development.

Ensuring Low-Cost Access to International Infrastructure

Creating the conditions for widespread broadband access is a complex policy issue facing the ICT sector in Africa. The markets in the region are so different from those in other parts of the world that governments have no obvious models to draw on. Some lessons are beginning to emerge, however. One, in particular, is the importance of access to high-capacity, low-cost bandwidth via submarine fiber-optic cable infrastructure.

The private sector has demonstrated its capacity to develop, finance, and operate such cables in Africa. The challenge for governments is to minimize the obstacles to this type of investment by readily issuing cable operators permits and licenses. The development of infrastructure, on its own, will not guarantee better services for customers. The experience of the South Atlantic 3/West Africa Submarine Cable (SAT-3) cable on the west coast of Africa shows that physical access to a cable is necessary but not sufficient for low-cost connectivity. A consortium of private operators with little direct regulation controls access to the SAT-3 cable. Because these operators are protected from competition on the cable, customers have not received the full potential benefit of the facility. The challenge for governments seeking to improve access to international infrastructure is to avoid creating infrastructure bottlenecks and to encourage competition between submarine cables and landing stations. Where they cannot do this, regulators should ensure access to the facilities on equitable terms.

Landlocked countries face a special challenge in ensuring that their operators have access to submarine fiber-optic infrastructure. If the private sector does not provide competitive infrastructure in the intervening countries, the government may have a role to play through public-private partnerships.

Promoting the Development of High-Bandwidth Backbone Networks

Domestic backbone networks will become more important as governments focus their attention on delivering affordable broadband Internet. Without these networks, countries will have difficulty making broadband services widely available at prices that significant numbers of people are willing to pay.

Private operators are investing considerable resources in this infrastructure, and the pace is increasing as operators look at broadband as a source of future market growth. Such network development is typically limited to urban areas and interurban routes where the private sector is willing to invest in network development.

No single policy approach exists to backbone network development. Some governments promote a competition-only policy, whereas others invest public resources in publicly owned networks. Regulatory frameworks often constrain investment through restrictions on fixed-network investment and on the services that can be sold. Wholesale markets in backbone services are thus underdeveloped, contributing to the high price and limited availability of broadband Internet in the region.

Successful policy for domestic backbone network development must encourage private investment in commercially viable areas and provide public support for investment in areas that are not commercially viable. Such a policy should encourage infrastructure competition by removing regulatory restrictions and should reduce the cost of investment in fiber-optic infrastructure by providing access to alternative transport and energy infrastructure. Public resources should focus on areas of the country that are not commercially viable. To the extent that public investment is needed, it should be made in partnership with the private sector to ensure that the design of the infrastructure meets the needs of market participants.

Reforming Management of the Radio Spectrum

The rapid evolution of ICT markets in Africa has increased the number of potential users of the radio spectrum and is challenging governments' traditional systems of spectrum allocation and management. When one or two operators and the government dominated the mobile market, management of the radio spectrum did not present major challenges to governments. Market liberalization and technological innovation have increased the number of players wishing to use the radio spectrum, particularly for new broadband wireless Internet services. The way in which access to the radio spectrum is organized is therefore an increasingly important issue for the development of the ICT sector.

The traditional approach to organizing the spectrum's use is to constrain development of the ICT sector. Governments have traditionally accomplished this by deciding how each frequency band is used and who is entitled to use it. This approach is unsuitable for markets with multiple players and spectrum uses that are continually changing. Governments are ill suited to decide the best uses for the radio spectrum and are typically unable to move fast enough in the allocation process. The effect is to constrain market development, particularly in new segments of the market, such as broadband Internet.

The introduction of market forces will improve management of the radio spectrum. Where demand for the right to use certain areas of the radio spectrum exceeds supply, usage rights can be auctioned. Such spectrum auctions are widely used in developed countries, and similar systems are used in Africa to allocate mobile network licenses (which usually include the right to use specified sections of the radio spectrum). Market forces can also be introduced in spectrum management after initial allocations have been made by establishing formal property rights over the spectrum and allowing owners to trade them. Establishing such primary and secondary markets in spectrum usage would free up the spectrum and would help ensure its most efficient use.

Further evolution in how the radio spectrum is managed is possible by establishing a shared-use system for certain bands of spectrum, known as a commons approach.

Recent developments in wireless technology have allowed multiple users of the same radio spectrum bands to operate without undue interference. Allowing anyone to share the radio spectrum, with little or no registration and usually without a fee, reduces the cost of entry into the market and therefore encourages innovation in technology and service delivery.

Changing how the radio spectrum is managed requires political will. The establishment of a property rights scheme can arbitrarily create windfall gains and losses for current and future users. Some users of the radio spectrum may be difficult to incorporate into a pure market-based system. For example, requiring users in the military or emergency services to participate in spectrum markets may be particularly challenging (although not impossible) and would certainly have budgetary implications for those agencies.

Reforming the allocation and management of the radio spectrum would change the role of government. Its primary role in spectrum management would no longer be to make technical and licensing decisions. Rather, the government's role would be to design, operate, and regulate the market in the radio spectrum. Such a change would require changes in the legal framework governing the radio spectrum and the capacity of the regulatory institutions involved.

Promoting Universal Access

As more people in Africa gain access to ICT services, those who remain outside the range of networks are at a disadvantage. Several governments in Africa have attempted to extend access to ICT beyond the perceived limits of the market. The quickest and most effective way of getting infrastructure to poor rural users is through competition. Malawi and Uganda have set up effectively competitive mobile markets that already cover over 80 percent of the population and are continuing to expand.

For the majority of countries in Africa, only competition will result in mobile networks that cover the whole population. With a few exceptions, such as the Democratic Republic of Congo, the additional cost to make voice network coverage universal is modest. In these countries, a service target of 100 percent coverage may be economically feasible. In countries where the gap left by the market is larger, a more modest target will likely be necessary.

When a universal service target is set, the major challenge is to establish a mechanism to achieve it. The majority of countries across the region currently apply a universal service levy on private operators, using the funds for specific ICT projects. This approach has had very limited success, particularly when contrasted with the commercially driven network expansion into rural areas. Universal service funds often suffer from bureaucratic obstacles and political interference in expenditure, and frequently they are not spent on the sector at all. Universal service policy in Africa therefore requires new thinking. The challenge is to meet the government's policy objectives of universal service at minimum cost to taxpayers while harnessing the beneficial effects of competition. An alternative to the traditional fund-based approach is to provide direct incentives for operators to deliver services in rural areas. For example, governments could offer operators a reduction in license-fee payments in exchange for providing services in specified areas, or they could establish pay-or-play schemes in which operators can choose between building networks in specified areas and contributing to a universal service fund, which is then used to subsidize operators that do provide services in unprofitable areas. The major advantage of these approaches is the reduction in transfers between operators and the government, thereby lessening bureaucratic delays or the diversion of funds.

Once a coverage target is defined, governments may also wish to address the issue of access for low-income groups. Call-by-call resale of services has significantly reduced the costs of accessing the network, and these systems are widespread in Africa (for example, the VillagePhone program of cell phone company MTN). Universal service targets could potentially include subsidies for prepayment directed at specific target groups of the population. However, they would have to be carefully designed to avoid mistargeting and leakage.

Notes

The authors of this chapter are Michael Minges, Mark Williams, Rebecca Mayer, Cecilia Briceño-Garmendia, and Howard Williams, who drew on background material and contributions from Mavis Ampah, Alvaro Federico Barra, Daniel Camos-i-Daurella, Ken Figueredo, Richard Green, Mike Jensen, Tim Nelly, Maria Shkaratan, Maria Vagliasindi, and Bjorn Wellenius.

1. Initial public offerings of government stakes in state-owned enterprises in the telecommunication sector have more recently been carried out in Kenya (2008) and Burkina Faso (2009).

References

Calderón, César. 2008. "Infrastructure and Growth in Africa." Working Paper 3, Africa Infrastructure Country Diagnostic, World Bank, Washington, DC.

GSMA (GSM Association). 2007. "Taxation and the Growth of Mobile Services in East Africa 2007." GSMA, London.

ITU (International Telecommunication Union). 2008. *African Telecommunication/ICT Indicators 2008: At a Crossroads.* 8th ed. Geneva: ITU.

Mayer, Rebecca, Ken Figueredo, Mike Jensen, Tim Kelly, Richard Green, and Alvaro Federico Barra. 2008. "Costing the Needs for Investment in ICT Infrastructure in Africa." Background Paper 3, Africa Infrastructure Country Diagnostic, World Bank, Washington, DC.

Minges, Michael, Cecilia Briceño-Garmendia, Mark Williams, Mavis Ampah, Daniel Camos, and Maria Shkaratan. 2008. "Information and Communications Technology in Sub-Saharan Africa: A Sector Review." Background Paper 10, Africa Infrastructure Country Diagnostic, World Bank, Washington, DC.

Roeller, Lars-Hendrik, and Leonard Waverman. 2001. "Telecommunications Infrastructure and Economic Development: A Simultaneous Approach." *American Economic Review* 91 (4): 909–23.

World Bank. 2009. Private Participation in Infrastructure Database. http://ppi.worldbank.org/.

Chapter 8

Power: Catching Up

Africa's chronic power problems have escalated in recent years into a crisis affecting 30 countries, taking a heavy toll on economic growth and productivity. The region has inadequate generation capacity, limited electrification, low power consumption, unreliable services, and high costs. It also faces a power sector financing gap of approximately $23 billion a year. It spends only about one-quarter of what it needs to spend on power, much of which is on operating expenditures to run the continent's high-cost power systems, thus leaving little for the huge investments needed to provide a long-term solution.

Further development of the regional power trade would allow Africa to harness larger-scale, more cost-effective energy sources, thereby reducing energy system costs by $2 billion a year and saving 70 million tons of carbon emissions annually. Economic returns to investments in cross-border transmission are particularly high, but reaping the promise of regional trade depends on a handful of major exporting countries' raising the large volumes of finance needed to develop generation capacity for export. It would also require political will in a large number of

importing countries that could potentially meet more than half their power demand through trade.

The operational inefficiencies of power utilities cost $3.3 billion a year, deterring investments in electrification and new capacity, while underpricing of power translates into losses of at least $2.2 billion a year. Full cost-recovery tariffs would already be affordable in countries with efficient large-scale hydropower- or coal-based systems, but not in those relying on small-scale oil-based plants. If regional power trade comes into play, generation costs will fall, and full cost-recovery tariffs could be affordable in much of Africa.

The key policy challenges are to strengthen sector planning capabilities, too often overlooked in today's hybrid markets. A serious recommitment to reforming state-owned enterprises (SOEs) should emphasize improvements in corporate governance more than purely technical fixes. Improving cost recovery is essential for sustaining investments in electrification and regional power generation projects. Closing the huge financing gap will require improving the creditworthiness of utilities and sustaining the recent upswing in external finance to the sector.

Africa's Chronic Power Problems

Africa's generation capacity, stagnant since the 1980s, is woefully inadequate today. The entire installed generation capacity of the 48 Sub-Saharan countries is 68 gigawatts, no more than Spain's, and without South Africa, the total falls to 28 gigawatts (EIA 2006). As much as one-quarter of that capacity is unavailable because of aging plants and poor maintenance.

The growth in generation capacity has been barely half that in other developing regions. In 1980, Sub-Saharan Africa was at approximately the same level as South Asia in generation capacity per million people, but it has since fallen far behind. Sub-Saharan African countries lag even compared with others in the same income bracket (Yepes, Pierce, and Foster 2008).

Only about one-fifth of the Sub-Saharan population has access to electricity, compared with about one-half in South Asia and more than four-fifths in Latin America. Since 1990, East Asia, Latin America, and the Middle East have all added at least 20 percentage points to their electrification rates, but access rates in Sub-Saharan Africa are relatively stagnant, as population growth and household formation outstrip new connections.

At current trends, less than 40 percent of African countries will reach universal access to electricity by 2050 (Banerjee and others 2008). Overall, household access to electricity in urban areas is 71 percent, compared with only 12 percent in rural areas. Moreover, access rates in the upper half of the income distribution exceed 50 percent, whereas they are less than 20 percent in the bottom half. Given that rural areas account for about two-thirds of the population, extending access presents a major challenge. Only 15 percent of the rural population lives within 10 kilometers of a substation (or within 5 kilometers of the medium-voltage line) and could thus be added to the electricity grid at relatively low cost. As much as 41 percent of the rural population lives in areas considered isolated or remote from the grid[1] and is reachable in the medium term only by off-grid technologies such as solar photovoltaic panels, which typically cost $0.50–$0.75 per kilowatt-hour (ESMAP 2007).

The cost of producing power in Africa is exceptionally high and rising. The small scale of most national power systems and the widespread reliance on expensive oil-based generation make the average total historic cost of producing power in Africa exceptionally high: $0.18 per kilowatt-hour with an average effective tariff of $0.14 per kilowatt-hour.[2] Compare that with tariffs of $0.04 per kilowatt-hour in South Asia and $0.07 in East Asia. Rising oil prices, lower availability of hydropower, and greater reliance on emergency leases have put further upward pressure on costs and prices.

Power consumption is tiny and falling. Given limited power generation and low access, per capita electricity consumption in Sub-Saharan Africa (excluding South Africa) averages only 124 kilowatt-hours a year, barely 1 percent of the consumption typical in high-income countries. Even if that power were entirely allocated to household lighting, it would hardly be enough to power one lightbulb per person for six hours a day. Sub-Saharan Africa is the only region in the world where per capita consumption is falling (World Bank 2005).

Power shortages have made service even less reliable. More than 30 African countries now experience power shortages and regular interruptions in service (figure 8.1). From 2001 to 2005, half of the countries in Sub-Saharan Africa achieved solid GDP growth rates in excess of 4.5 percent. Their demand for power grew at a similar pace, yet generation capacity expanded only 1.2 percent annually. South Africa shows what happens when generation capacity fails to keep up with demand (box 8.1). In some countries, supply shocks exacerbated the situation. Causes of the supply shocks include droughts in East Africa; oil price inflation, which made it difficult for many West African countries to afford diesel imports; and conflicts that destroyed the power infrastructure in some fragile states.

Inadequate power supplies take a heavy toll on the private sector. Many African enterprises experience frequent outages: in Senegal 25 days a year, in Tanzania 63 days, and in Burundi 144 days. Frequent power outages mean big losses in forgone sales and damaged equipment—6 percent of turnover on average for formal enterprises, and as much as 16 percent

Figure 8.1 Underlying Causes of Africa's Power Supply Crisis

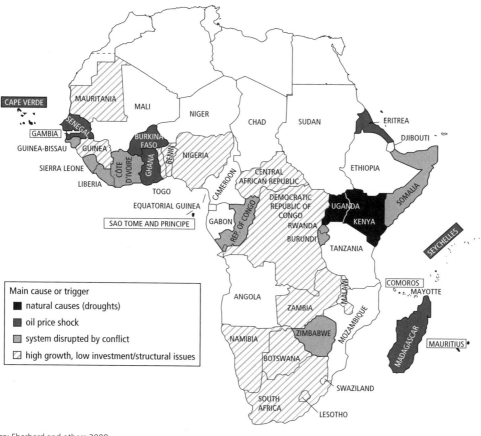

Source: Eberhard and others 2008.

South Africa's Power Supply Crisis

South Africa has long had a reliable and cheap supply of electricity. However, delays in investment by the state-owned electricity provider Eskom (which provides 70 percent of the electricity in Sub-Saharan Africa), breakdowns of power plants, and negligence in coal contracting have eroded spare capacity in the system, leaving the country prone to periodic rounds of rolling power cuts. Many of South Africa's neighbors, dependent on imports, are also feeling the economic costs of power scarcities.

The government had earlier imposed a moratorium on Eskom's building new plants. It considered unbundling the utility and introducing private participation and competition in the market, similar to Nord Pool in Scandinavia or PJM in the United States. But the new market arrangements were never implemented, and with average prices far below the marginal cost of new generation, private investors had no way of entering the sector without special contracting arrangements. After a four-year hiatus, the government abandoned the idea of a competitive market and again charged Eskom with expanding capacity (while retaining the option of contracting with a few independent power producers in the future). These planning and investment failures are typical of hybrid electricity markets.

To help finance investment and reduce demand, electricity prices in South Africa will increase substantially over the next several years. But the supply-demand balance will likely remain tight for at least the next seven years, up to 2015, until new base-load generation capacity comes on line.

Source: Based on interviews with World Bank staff from the Africa Energy Department, 2008.

of turnover for informal enterprises unable to provide their own backstop generation (Foster and Steinbuks 2008). Therefore, many enterprises invest in backup generators. In many countries, backup generators represent a significant proportion of total installed power capacity: 50 percent in the Democratic Republic of Congo, Equatorial Guinea, and Mauritania, and 17 percent in West Africa as a whole. The cost of backup generation can easily run to $0.40 per kilowatt-hour or several times higher than the utility's costs of generating power (Foster and Steinbuks 2008).

The economic costs of power outages are substantial. The immediate economic cost of power shortages can be gauged by looking at the cost of running backup generators and forgoing production during power shortages. These costs typically range between 1 and 4 percent of GDP (figure 8.2). Over time, the lack of a reliable power supply is also a drag on economic growth. From the early 1990s to the early 2000s in Cameroon, Côte d'Ivoire, the Democratic Republic of Congo, Ghana, and Senegal, inadequate power infrastructure shaved at least one-quarter of a percentage point off annual per capita GDP growth rates (Calderón 2008).

A common response to the immediate crisis is to tender short-term leases for emergency power. Unlike traditional power generation projects, this capacity can be put in place in a few weeks, providing a rapid response to pressing shortages. Equipment is leased for up to two years, sometimes longer, and then reverts to the private provider. At least an estimated 750 megawatts of emergency generation is currently operating in Sub-Saharan Africa, representing for some countries a large proportion of their national installed capacity. Because of the preponderance of small diesel units, the costs have typically been $0.20–$0.30 per kilowatt-hour, and for some countries, the price tag can be 4 percent of GDP (table 8.1).

Figure 8.2 Economic Cost of Outages in Selected Countries

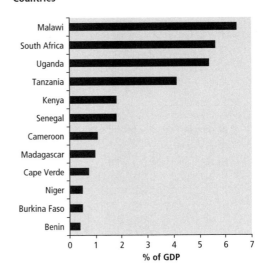

Source: Eberhard and others 2008, using World Bank 2007 data.
Note: Economic cost is estimated as the value of lost load multiplied by the volume of load shedding. Value of lost load is derived from country-specific estimates based on enterprise survey data for sales lost due to power outages.

Table 8.1 Economic Cost of Emergency Power Generation

Country	Emergency generation capacity (megawatts)	Total generation capacity (megawatts)	Emergency generation capacity (% of total)	Cost of emergency generation (% of GDP)
Angola	150	830	18.1	1.04
Gabon	14	414	3.4	0.45
Ghana	80	1,490	5.4	1.90
Kenya	100	1,211	8.3	1.45
Madagascar	50	140	35.7	2.79
Rwanda	15	31	48.4	1.84
Senegal	40	243	16.5	1.37
Sierra Leone	20	15	133.3	4.25
Tanzania	40	881	4.5	0.96
Uganda	100	240	41.7	3.29

Source: Eberhard and others 2008.

A Huge Investment Backlog

Addressing Africa's chronic power problems will require major investments in the refurbishment and expansion of power infrastructure. Of the 70.5 gigawatts of installed generation capacity, some 44.3 gigawatts need to be refurbished. An additional 7,000 megawatts of new generation capacity need to be built each year to meet suppressed demand, keep pace with projected economic growth, and provide additional capacity to support the rollout of electrification. Compare that with expansion of less than 1,000 megawatts a year over the period 1990–2005. The bulk of this new power generation capacity will be needed to meet nonresidential demands. In addition, raising electrification rates will require extending distribution networks to reach an additional 6 million households a year from 1996 to 2005.

The total spending needs of the power sector amount to $40.6 billion a year (Rosnes and Vennemo 2008), or 6.4 percent of the region's GDP, skewed toward capital expenditure (table 8.2). The greatest absolute spending requirements correspond to the middle-income countries, which need to spend $14.2 billion a year, but the largest economic burden is borne by the fragile states, which would have to devote an implausible 13.5 percent of GDP to meet this goal.

Economic growth is an important driver of demand for power generation capacity. The estimates of power investment needs presented earlier are based on growth projections before the onset of the 2008 global financial crisis. The International Monetary Fund reduced its GDP growth projections for Africa from 5.1 percent a year to 3.5 percent a year because of the global economic crisis. Sensitivity analysis suggests that even lowering the original projected growth rates of 5.1 percent to half their levels would reduce estimated power sector spending needs by only about 20 percent in absolute terms, lowering required new generation capacity from just over 7,000 megawatts to just under 6,000 megawatts. The decrease in required spending would be somewhat larger in the Southern and West African Power Pools and somewhat smaller in the Central and East African Power Pools. Even so, when power spending needs are expressed as a percentage of GDP, the effect of a slower-growth scenario is much smaller. Because slower growth reduces GDP as well as power spending needs, the overall economic burden of power sector spending needs is only very slightly lower under a low-growth scenario.

Existing spending on the power sector is $11.6 billion, or just over one-quarter of what is required. The adoption of high-cost generation solutions skews existing spending toward operating expenditure, leaving only $4.6 billion a year to fund the long-term investments to address the continent's power supply crisis, more than half of which comes from domestic public finance. Existing spending represents 1.8 percent of regional GDP, although

Table 8.2 Power Sector Spending Needs

Country type	$ billions annually			Percentage of GDP		
	Capital expenditure	Operation and maintenance	Total spending	Capital expenditure	Operation and maintenance	Total spending
Sub-Saharan Africa	26.60	14.00	40.60	4.20	2.20	6.40
Middle-income countries	6.29	7.90	14.19	2.30	2.92	5.22
Low-income fragile countries	4.50	0.70	5.20	11.70	1.80	13.50
Low-income nonfragile countries	7.60	2.20	9.70	6.90	2.00	8.80
Resource-rich countries	8.40	3.35	11.77	3.79	1.50	5.29

Source: Briceño-Garmendia, Smits, and Foster 2008.
Note: For a more detailed exposition of power sector spending needs, see chapter 2 in this volume. Totals may not add exactly because of rounding errors.

in the nonfragile low-income countries, this share increases to 2.9 percent of GDP. Of the external capital flows, finance from countries not belonging to the Organisation for Economic Co-operation and Development (OECD) is the most significant, accounting for $1.1 billion a year, primarily from the Export-Import Bank of China. Official development assistance follows at $0.7 billion a year and then private capital flows of $0.5 billion a year (table 8.3).

Most of the private sector finance recorded relates to independent power producers (IPPs). In recent years, 34 IPP contracts in Africa have involved investments of $2.4 billion for the construction of 3,000 megawatts of new power generation capacity. Those projects have provided much-needed generation capacity. An independent assessment concluded that they have also been relatively costly because of technology choices, procurement problems, and currency devaluations (calling for adjustments in dollar- or euro-denominated off-take agreements) (Gratwick and Eberhard 2008).

The existing resource envelope would go significantly further if the sector operated more efficiently. Addressing the operating inefficiencies of the power utilities could reduce the funding gap by $3.3 billion a year, improving cost recovery would bring an additional $2.2 billion a year, and $0.3 billion a year could be recouped by improving execution of the capital budget.

Even if all these inefficiencies could be eliminated, a sizable power sector financing gap of $23 billion a year would remain (table 8.4). Three-quarters of this financing gap is a shortfall in capital expenditure, while the remaining quarter is a shortfall in operation and maintenance spending. The largest portion of the gap—nearly $11 billion per year—corresponds to the middle-income countries. However, the largest financing burden relates to the low-income fragile states, where the financing gap amounts to roughly 7 percent of their GDP.

Table 8.3 Financing Flows to the Power Sector
$ billions annually

Country type	Operation and maintenance Public sector	Capital spending Public sector	ODA	Non-OECD financiers	PPI	Total	Total spending
Sub-Saharan Africa	7.00	2.40	0.70	1.10	0.50	4.60	11.60
Middle-income countries	2.66	0.80	0.03	0	0.01	0.80	3.50
Low-income fragile countries	0.60	0	0.04	0.20	0.01	0.30	0.80
Low-income nonfragile countries	2.00	0.40	0.60	0.10	0.20	1.30	3.20
Resource-rich countries	1.60	1.20	0.10	0.70	0.30	2.30	3.90

Source: Briceño-Garmendia, Smits, and Foster 2008.
Note: Operation and maintenance includes other current expenditures. ODA = official development assistance; OECD = Organisation for Economic Co-operation and Development; PPI = private participation in infrastructure. Totals may not add exactly because of rounding errors.

Table 8.4 Composition of Power Sector Funding Gap

Country type	$ billions annually Capital expenditure gap	Operation and maintenance gap	Total gap	Percentage of GDP Capital expenditure gap	Operation and maintenance gap	Total gap
Sub-Saharan Africa	17.6	5.6	23.2	2.7	0.9	3.6
Low-income fragile countries	2.6	0.1	2.8	6.9	0.2	7.1
Low-income nonfragile countries	4.5	0.1	4.7	4.1	0.1	4.2
Middle-income countries	5.5	5.2	10.7	2.0	1.9	3.9
Resource-rich countries	3.5	1.0	4.5	1.6	0.5	2.0

Sources: Briceño-Garmendia, Smits, and Foster 2008; Yepes, Pierce, and Foster 2008.
Note: Totals do not add because efficiency gains cannot be carried across country groups.

The Promise of Regional Power Trade

Although Sub-Saharan Africa is well endowed with both hydropower and thermal resources, only a small fraction of its power generation potential has been developed. Of the 48 Sub-Saharan countries, 21 have a generation capacity of less than 200 megawatts, well below the minimum efficiency scale, which means they pay a heavy penalty: costs reach $0.25 per kilowatt-hour, twice the $0.13 per kilowatt-hour in the region's larger power systems. One reason is that some of the region's most cost-effective energy resources are too distant from major centers of demand in countries too poor to raise the billions of dollars needed to develop them. For example, 61 percent of the region's hydropower potential is in just two countries: the Democratic Republic of Congo and Ethiopia.

Pooling energy resources through regional power trade promises to reduce power costs. The Southern, West, East, and Central African Power Pools, created mainly to support power trade efforts, are at varying stages of maturity. If pursued to their full economic potential, regional trade could reduce the annual costs of power system operation and development by $2 billion per year (about 5 percent of total power system costs). These savings are already incorporated in the power sector spending needs previously presented. They come largely from substituting hydropower for thermal power, substantially reducing operating costs, even though it entails higher up-front investment in capital-intensive hydropower and associated cross-border transmission. The returns to cross-border transmission can be as high as 120 percent for the Southern African Power Pool and more typically 20–30 percent for the other power pools. By increasing the share of hydropower, regional trade would also save 70 million tons of carbon emissions a year.

Under regional power trade, a handful of large exporting countries would serve a substantial number of power importers. The Democratic Republic of Congo, Ethiopia, and Guinea would emerge as the major hydropower exporters. As many as 16 countries would be better-off (from a purely economic standpoint), importing more than 50 percent of their power needs through regional trade. Savings range from $0.01 to $0.07 per kilowatt-hour. The largest beneficiaries tend to be smaller nations without domestic hydropower resources. For those countries, the cost of building cross-border transmission would be paid back in less than one year, once neighboring countries have developed adequate generation capacity to support trade. (For a more detailed analysis of regional power trade potential, see chapter 6 in this volume on regional integration.)

Improving Utility Performance through Institutional Reform

The operational inefficiencies of power utilities cost the region $2.7 billion a year (0.8 percent of GDP on average; figure 8.3). They divide roughly evenly between distribution losses and revenue undercollections. Average distribution losses in Africa are 23.3 percent, more than twice the norm of 10 percent, affecting all countries to some degree. Average collection ratios are 88.4 percent, compared with the best practice of 100 percent. Burkina Faso, Ghana, Niger, and Uganda face much greater undercollections than the rest, up to 1 percent of GDP.

Operational inefficiencies have been holding back the pace of electrification and preventing utilities from balancing supply and demand. They drain the public purse and undermine the performance of the utilities. One casualty of insufficient revenue is maintenance. Utility managers must often choose among paying salaries, buying fuel, or purchasing spares. They must frequently cannibalize parts from other working equipment. The investment program is another major casualty. Utilities with below-average efficiency electrify only 0.8 percent of the population in their service area each year, much lower than the 1.4 percent electrified each year by utilities with above-average efficiency. Utilities with low efficiency also have greater difficulty in keeping pace with demand. The suppressed or unmet power demand in those countries exceeds 13 percent of total demand, twice the

Figure 8.3 Economic Burden Associated with Power Utility Inefficiencies in Selected Countries

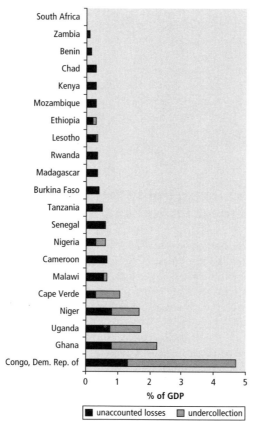

Source: Briceño-Garmendia, Smits, and Foster 2008.
Note: Power utility inefficiencies include undercollection of revenues and unaccounted-for distribution losses.

6 percent in countries with higher efficiency (figure 8.4).

Institutional reform measures hold the key to improving utility performance. Countries that have advanced the institutional reform agenda for the power sector show substantially lower hidden costs than those that have not, as do countries with more developed power regulatory frameworks and better governance of their state-owned utilities (figure 8.5). Measures that seem to have a substantial effect on reducing hidden costs are private participation in the power distribution sector and (among state-owned utilities) performance contracts that incorporate clear incentives. The case of Kenya Power and Lighting Company is particularly striking (box 8.2).

Labor redundancy is another source of utility inefficiencies. Power utilities in Africa have overemployment of 88 percent relative to a developing country benchmark of 413 connections per employee. Overemployment by utilities results in labor overspending in the range of 0.07 percent to 0.6 percent of GDP.

The application of management contracts has been more complex than originally supposed. More than 20 African countries have experimented with private sector participation in power distribution, split evenly between concessions and management contracts. Management contracts have attracted interest

Figure 8.4 Inefficiency in Utility Performance

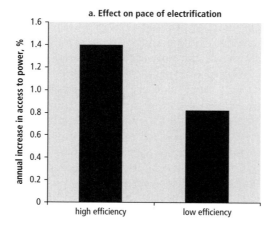

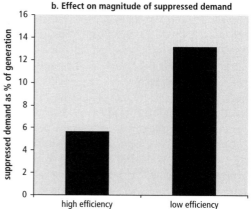

Source: Derived from Eberhard and others 2008.
Note: High efficiency refers to utilities with below-average levels of inefficiency caused by revenue undercollection and distribution losses.
Low efficiency refers to utilities with above-average levels of inefficiency caused by revenue undercollection and distribution losses.

because they are a simpler way of addressing inefficiencies, but their application has proved complex and contentious, and they have not always proved sustainable. Of 17 African management contracts, 4 were canceled before the originally designated expiry date, and at least 5 more were not renewed after their initial term, reverting to state operation. Only 3 management contracts remain in place.

Problems with management contracts have included unrealistic expectations and limited ability to address broader sector challenges. First, many management contracts were undertaken with donor involvement. Donors saw the contracts as an initial step on the road to more extensive sector reform that would be extended

Figure 8.5 Effect of Reform Measures on Hidden Costs

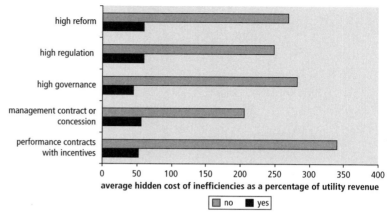

Source: Eberhard and others 2008.

Kenya's Success with Private Participation in Power

Kenya's Electric Power Act of 1997 introduced independent economic regulation, essential for private sector participation. It has since become government policy to put all bids for generation facilities out for competition, open to both public and private firms, and to give no preferential treatment to the national generator.

The sector was unbundled in 1998 when Kenya Electricity Generating Company (KenGen; generation) and Kenya Power and Lighting Company (KPLC; transmission and distribution) were established. KenGen is now 30 percent privately owned, and KPLC is 51 percent privately owned.

Established in 1998, the Electricity Regulatory Board (the Energy Regulatory Commission since 2007) maintains a significant degree of autonomy. It has issued a grid code and rules on complaints and disputes, supply rules, licenses, a safety code, and a tariff policy.

Four independent power producers supply about 12 percent of all power. Four more recently received licenses, and another three are expected to apply for licenses.

In the early 2000s, KPLC had substantial hidden costs in underpricing, collection losses, and distribution losses that absorbed 1.4 percent of GDP. In the run-up to a management contract, revenue collection improved from 81 percent in 2004 to 100 percent in 2006. Distribution losses also began to fall, though more gradually, reflecting the greater difficulty in resolving them. Power pricing reforms also allowed tariffs to rise in line with escalating costs, from

$0.07 in 2000 to $0.15 in 2006 and to $0.20 in 2008. As a result of those measures, the hidden costs of the power sector fell to 0.4 percent of GDP in 2006 and were eliminated by 2008 (see figure). This outcome put the sector on a firmer financial footing and has saved the economy more than 1 percent of GDP.

KPLC'S Success in Driving Down Hidden Costs, 2001–08

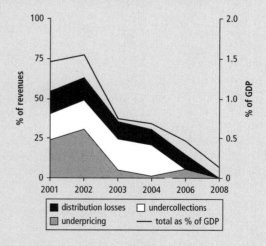

Source: Interviews with World Bank staff from the Africa Energy Department, 2008.

long enough to allow parallel policy and institutional changes to be enacted and to take root. In contrast, many African governments saw them as costly reform measures needed to secure donor finance and had no intention of taking the process any further. Second, although management contracts can produce financial and efficiency gains, they cannot overcome broader policy and institutional weaknesses. Moreover, the efficiency gains do not always provide tangible improvements for customers, even though they impose substantial adjustment costs on management, making political support for these measures hard to build.

Most African power utilities remain state owned and operated. On average, Africa's state-owned power utilities embody only 40 percent of good governance practices for such enterprises (Vagliasindi and Nellis 2009).

Most utilities score better on internal governance criteria, such as board structure and accountability, than on external governance criteria, such as outsourcing and labor and capital market disciplines.

The acute need to improve the management of utilities and the frameworks they operate under has long been acknowledged. Over the years, substantial sums have been spent on institutional reforms: training management, improving internal accounting and external auditing, strengthening boards of directors, providing financial and operational information, building reporting systems, creating and reinforcing supervisory and regulatory agencies, and much more. Some enduring successes have been registered (box 8.3; further discussion of institutional issues can be found in chapter 4 of this volume).

BOX 8.3

Botswana's Success with a State-Owned Power Utility

The Botswana Power Corporation (BPC) is a government-owned monopoly that produces, transmits, and distributes electrical power in Botswana. It was formed by government decree in 1970 with the objective of expanding and developing electrical power potential in the country. From its small beginnings with one power station in Gaborone and a network that extended some 45 kilometers outside the city, the power utility's responsibilities, along with the national network, have expanded enormously. The government has a regulatory role through the Energy Affairs Division of the Ministry of Minerals, Energy, and Water Affairs.

BPC increased access to power to 22 percent in 2006 and is set to reach 70 percent in 2009 and 100 percent by 2016. Through government funding, BPC is extending the electricity grid into rural areas and developing the reach of the national transmission grid. Overall, the power system operates efficiently, with system losses of no more than 10 percent and a decent return on assets.

BPC constantly weighs its options of importing against expanding its own generation facilities, taking into account both economic and strategic factors. The national system provides 132 megawatts, with the remaining 266 megawatts supplied by neighboring countries through the Southern African Power Pool. Since the pool's inception in 1995, Botswana has been a major beneficiary, and its active trading position promoted multilateral agreements among pool members, generally enhancing regional power cooperation.

Part of BPC's strong performance is thanks to cheap imported power from South Africa (now severely threatened by the power crisis). But analysts give institutional factors equal weight: a strong, stable economy; cost-reflective tariffs; lack of government interference in managerial decisions; good internal governance; and competent, well-motivated staff and management. (For a more detailed discussion of institutional reforms, see chapter 4 in this volume.)

Sources: Molefhi and Grobler 2006; PPA 2005.

The Challenge of Cost Recovery

Underpricing power costs the sector at least $2.2 billion a year in forgone revenues (0.9 percent of GDP on average). Underpricing power is widespread across Africa. In the worst cases (Malawi, Tanzania, and Zambia), underpricing can result in utilities' capturing less than half of the revenues they need and creating an economic burden in excess of 2 percent of GDP (figure 8.6).

These figures probably understate the underpricing because of the difficulty of capturing subsidies to large industrial and mining customers, which are usually contained in bilateral contracts and not reflected in the general tariff structure. Key examples include the aluminum-smelting sector in Cameroon and Ghana and the mining sector in Zambia,

where large strategic customers have purchased power at heavily discounted rates of just a few cents per kilowatt-hour. These arrangements were initially justified as locking in base-load demand to support very large power projects that exceeded the country's immediate demands, but they are now questionable because competing demands have grown to absorb this capacity.

Power prices have risen substantially in recent years, but they have nonetheless failed to keep pace with escalating costs. Because of rising oil prices, lower availability of hydropower, and greater reliance on emergency leases, the costs of power production in Africa rose substantially in the early to mid-2000s (figure 8.7, panel a). In response, several countries have increased power tariffs, so that the average revenue of power utilities almost doubled over the same period (figure 8.7, panel b). Even so, because of historic pricing shortfalls, overall average revenues by the end of this period had barely caught up with average operating costs at the beginning of the period.

Most countries are achieving no more than operating-cost recovery. The correlation between average revenues and average operating costs across Sub-Saharan countries is as high as 90 percent, indicating that operating-cost recovery is the driving principle behind power pricing in most cases. Cameroon, Cape Verde, Chad, Malawi, Niger, Rwanda, Senegal, and Tanzania (countries under the 45-degree line in figure 8.8, panel a) fail to meet even operating-cost recovery, and several of them face particularly high operating costs (figure 8.8).

The longer-term cost-recovery situation is somewhat more hopeful. Comparing existing average revenues and average operating costs misrepresents long-term cost recovery for two reasons. First, because of major inefficiencies in revenue collection, the average *revenue* collected per unit of electricity sold is substantially lower than the average effective *tariff* charged today. Second, because of the major inefficiencies in generation technology and the potential for regional trade, for more than two-thirds of the countries the average *incremental* cost of power looking forward is lower than the average *historical* cost of power production looking

Figure 8.6 Underpricing of Power in Selected Countries

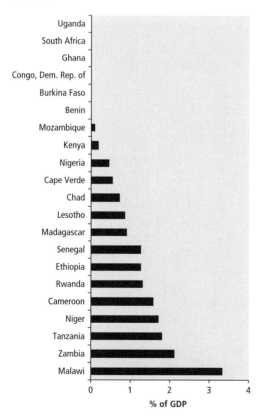

% of GDP

Source: Briceño-Garmendia, Smits, and Foster 2008.

Figure 8.7 Electricity Costs and Revenues by Type of Power System, 2001–05
US$ per kilowatt-hour

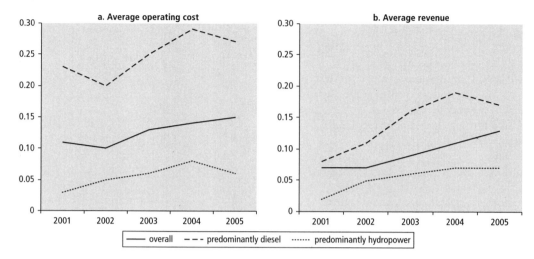

Source: Eberhard and others 2008.

Figure 8.8 Past and Future Cost-Recovery Situation
US$ per kilowatt-hour

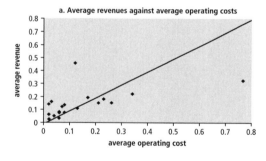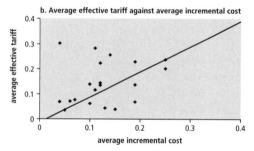

Source: Eberhard and others 2008.

backward and including both historic operating and capital costs.

A truer picture of long-term cost recovery comes from comparing today's average effective *tariff* with the average incremental *cost* looking forward (figure 8.8). At least in some countries, even the current tariff would be adequate for cost recovery, if only all revenues could be collected and the power system could move toward a more efficient production structure. In other countries, however, significant tariff adjustments would still be needed in the long term.

In most cases, the state or donors have almost entirely subsidized the historic capital costs of power development. Although the residential sector accounts for 95 percent of power utility customers in Africa, it contributes only around 50 percent of sales revenue. Thus, the pricing of power to commercial and industrial consumers is just as important for cost recovery. Neither commercial nor residential customers are close to paying full cost-recovery prices.

Subsidies to residential consumers are highly regressive. Across the bottom half of the income distribution, barely 10 percent of households have access to electricity (Wodon 2008). Indeed, three-quarters of the households with electricity come from the top two quintiles of the income distribution. Because poorer households are almost entirely excluded, they cannot benefit from subsidies embedded in electricity prices. In many cases, targeting performance is further exacerbated by poor tariff design, with the widespread use of increasing block tariffs that provide large lifeline blocks of highly subsidized power to all consumers.

With subsistence consumption of 50 kilowatt-hours a month, the cost of a monthly utility bill priced to recover full historic costs of production would be as much as $24.30 in central Africa, which is manifestly unaffordable for the vast majority of the population (table 8.5). Elsewhere in Africa, a subsistence monthly bill priced at full historic cost would range between $7.00 and $10.70 and would be affordable to the relatively affluent sections of the population that already enjoy access to power, but not to the poorer segments of the population that remain unconnected. Indeed, affordability of cost-recovery power bills for existing customers is today really only a problem in low-income countries reliant on small-scale, oil-based generation.

Looking into the future, pricing at the lower long-run marginal cost of power would reduce the subsistence monthly bill to the $3.00–$4.00 range in central and southern Africa where abundant low-cost hydropower would become

available (table 8.5). Such modest bills would be affordable to all but the poorest 25 percent of the population. In eastern and western Africa, the subsistence monthly bill would fall in the $7.00–$9.00 range. Although this amount would likely be affordable for existing customers, it would represent a problem as power access is expanded to lower-income populations. When a more efficient power system develops, full cost-recovery tariffs would be affordable for the vast majority, except perhaps in West Africa.

If regional trade is pursued, the average costs of power production could be expected to fall toward $0.07 in central and southern Africa, $0.12 in eastern Africa, and $0.18 in western Africa. Assuming, again, subsistence consumption of 50 kilowatt-hours a month, a monthly utility bill under full cost-recovery pricing would be about $4 a month in central and southern Africa, $6 a month in eastern Africa, and $9 a month in western Africa. Based on an affordability threshold of 3 percent of household income, full cost-recovery tariffs would prove affordable for the vast majority of the population of low-income countries in central, eastern, and southern Africa (see figure 8.9). In West Africa, about half the population of the low-income countries would face affordability problems. A number of West African countries—notably Côte d'Ivoire,

Table 8.5 Cost and Affordability of Monthly Power Bills at Cost-Recovery Prices: Past and Future
$ per month

Location	Historic cost	Long-run marginal cost
Central African Power Pool	24.30	3.50
East African Power Pool	9.50	7.00
Southern Africa Power Pool	7.00	3.00
West Africa Power Pool	10.70	9.00

Source: Derived from Rosnes and Vennemo 2008.
Note: Dark gray shading: power bill is unaffordable to the vast majority of the population; light gray shading: power bill is affordable to existing customers only, who are typically the richest 25 percent of the income distribution; no shading: power bill is affordable to all but the poorest 25 percent of the income distribution.

Figure 8.9 Affordability of Subsistence Consumption of Power at Cost-Recovery Pricing

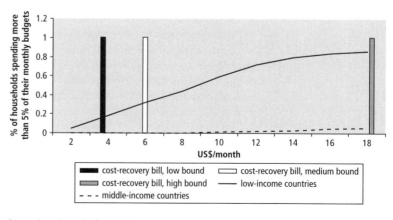

Source: Banerjee and others 2008.
Note: A power bill for subsistence consumption of 50 kilowatt-hours per month is considered affordable if it absorbs no more than 5 percent of household income.

Ghana, Nigeria, and Senegal—already have power coverage of around 50 percent and would face affordability issues as coverage broadens. At any of these levels, power tariffs do not represent a significant affordability issue in the middle-income countries. (For a fuller discussion of the social issues associated with utility pricing in Africa, see chapter 3 in this volume.)

Policy Challenges

The depth and extent of Africa's power crisis and its associated costs demand renewed efforts to tackle the policy and institutional challenges needed to improve performance and financing. The key challenges can be characterized as follows:

- Strengthening sector planning
- Recommitting to the reform of SOEs
- Increasing cost recovery
- Accelerating electrification
- Expanding regional trade in power
- Closing the financing gap.

These interdependent challenges must be dealt with simultaneously. Efforts to boost generation through regional power trade will stumble if the utilities, which will continue to be central actors, remain inefficient and insolvent. Expanding electricity distribution systems without addressing the shortages in generation and improving transmission capacity would clearly be futile. In addition, focusing exclusively on utility reform would be fruitless without a start on substantial, long-gestation investments in both generation and access to improve the quality of service and make the utilities viable. In short, these strategic priorities must progress together.

Strengthening Sector Planning
Most African power markets present an institutional "hybrid," with public and private actors operating in parallel. The 1990s reform prescription of unbundling and privatization, leading to wholesale and retail competition, did not prove very relevant to Africa, not least because most of the region's power systems are simply too small to support any meaningful competition. The new reality is thus one of "hybrid markets," with the state-owned utility remaining intact and occupying a dominant market position. At the same time, because many governments and utilities lack sufficient investment resources, the private sector participates, typically as IPPs. Africa's hybrid electricity markets pose new challenges in policy, regulation, planning, and procurement. The widespread power shortages across the continent and the increasing reliance on emergency power indicate the seriousness of those challenges.

Too often, the planning function has fallen between the cracks. Traditionally, planning and procurement of new power infrastructure were the province of the state-owned utility. With the advent of power sector reforms and the IPPs, those functions were often moved to the ministry of energy or electricity. A simultaneous transfer of skills did not always occur, however, resulting in plans that were not adequately informed by the complexities on the ground: a new hybrid market of private and public actors. In many cases, planning has collapsed. Where still present, planning tends to take the form of outdated, rigid master plans. The lack of strategic policy and planning for the electricity sector at the central government level is a critical weakness. Interventions have been piecemeal rather than integrated; many countries have focused on generation without investing in efficient transmission and delivery of power.

This situation has led to very costly delays in commissioning new plants. In the absence of strong political leadership, good information, and the requisite planning capability, incumbent state-owned utilities often undermine the entry of IPPs by arguing that they can supply power more cheaply or quickly than private alternatives, even if they lack the resources to do so. Poor understanding of the hybrid market deprives policy makers of clear and transparent criteria for allocating new plants between the incumbent, state-owned utility and the IPPs. New plants are rarely ordered on a timely basis, thereby opening power gaps that prompt recourse to temporary power and discourage investors. When procurement is (finally) undertaken, the authorities may not take the trouble to conduct international competitive bidding. This outcome is unfortunate, because a rigorous bidding process lends credibility and transparency to procurement and results in more competitively priced power.

Restoring and strengthening planning capabilities are imperative. Hybrid power markets will not disappear from the African landscape any time soon. To make the best of them, African governments and their development partners must strive to develop a robust institutional foundation for the single-buyer model, with clear criteria for power purchase (off-take) agreements and dispatches of power under those agreements. Governments must restore a strong sector planning capability at the line ministry level, establish clear policies and criteria for allocating new plant opportunities between the state-owned utilities and IPPs, and commit to competitive and timely bidding processes. A well-articulated plan for the sector will allow governments to move beyond the "firefighting" that has reduced their ability to anticipate exogenous shocks, such as drought or high oil prices.

Development partners need to tread carefully in the hybrid marketplace. They can help by providing advice on transparent contracting frameworks and processes and by lending expertise to governments and utilities as the latter seek to reach financial closure with project sponsors and private investors. Lending to public utilities needs to be handled carefully; if done without adequate attention to the peculiarities of the hybrid market, it may have the unintended effect of deepening the contradictions inherent in those markets and even crowding out private investment. What is needed above all is to strengthen public institutions to enable them to engage effectively with the private sector.

Recommitting to the Reform of State-Owned Enterprises

Renewed efforts on SOE reform should favor governance over technical fixes. State-owned utilities are still prevalent across Africa, and their performance is generally poorer than in other regions. Fortunately, improving the governance of SOEs can improve performance. Past efforts at improving utility management focused too heavily on technical issues to the exclusion of governance and accountability. Future SOE reforms seem justified as long as they focus on these deeper institutional issues.

The starting point for SOE reform should be to reform corporate governance. Key measures include greater decision-making autonomy for the board of directors, more objective selection criteria for senior managers, and rigorous disclosure of conflicts of interest, as well as more transparent and merit-based recruitment processes.

Parallel efforts are needed to strengthen financial and operational monitoring of SOEs by their supervisory agencies, whether they are line ministries or ministries of finance. Transparency and accountability of SOEs depend on solid financial management, procurement, and management information systems. Today, basic operational and financial data on firm performance are not produced, reported, or acted on. Without information or, perhaps worse, without action based on whatever information is produced, better outcomes cannot be expected. Key measures include auditing and publishing financial accounts and using comprehensive cost-based accounting systems that allow functional unbundling of costs and a clearer sense of cost centers.

In principle, regulation can be an important part of this process, but in practice, it proves challenging to develop. Electricity regulators have been set up across Africa, precisely to insulate utilities from political interference while closely monitoring enterprise performance. Some critics argue that regulatory agencies have simply created additional risks because of their unpredictable decisions, resulting from excessive discretion and overly broad objectives. Moreover, regulatory autonomy remains elusive; in some countries, turnover among commissioners has been high, while the gap between law (or rule) and practice is often wide. The challenge of establishing new public institutions in developing countries is often underestimated. Independent regulation requires a strong political commitment and competent institutions and people. Where some or all are lacking, it seems wise to consider complementary or transitional options that reduce discretion in regulatory decision making through more explicit rules and procedures, or outsourcing the regulatory functions to advisory regulators and expert panels (Eberhard 2007).

When this foundation is in place, contracting mechanisms can be used to improve performance. These mechanisms could be performance contracts in the public sector or management contracts with the private sector.

Public sector performance contracts need to incorporate strong performance incentives. Initial attempts to improve African SOEs through performance contracts with the line ministry or other supervisory agency were minimally effective. Recent efforts in the water sector (in Uganda, for example) have had a stronger and much more positive effect. The key feature of these contracts is to incorporate incentives for good managerial (and staff) performance and, more rarely, sanctions for failure to reach targets. This approach to more comprehensive performance contracts deserves further consideration.

Creating effective performance incentives within a public sector context can be quite challenging. Management contracts with the private sector are thus a relevant option. They can be applied with either expatriate or local management teams, each of which offers advantages. Nonetheless, clarity about what they can and cannot achieve, particularly given their short time horizons, is important. At best, a management contract can improve performance on a handful of manageable aspects of efficiency, such as revenue collection and labor productivity. It cannot solve deficiencies in the broader institutional framework, which ideally should be addressed earlier. Nor can a management contract raise investment finance or significantly affect service quality if substantial investments or long gestations are required.

Utilities that have the institutional basics in place would likely benefit from technical assistance (box 8.4). In particular, operational efficiency programs are needed to reduce the high rates of technical, nontechnical (electricity theft), and collection losses. Such programs can include capacity building and technical assistance to improve management, business practices, and planning. The priorities are improved load management (to better match supply with priority customer needs), theft reduction initiatives, and increased revenue collection (through enhanced metering and better-run customer service units). Capital spending can also be reduced by using low-cost

---

BOX 8.4

CREST Spreading Good Practices

The Commercial Reorientation of the Electricity Sector Toolkit (CREST) is an experiment under way in several localities served by West African electricity providers. Based on good practices from recent reforms in Indian, European, and U.S. power corporations, CREST is a "bottom-up" approach for attacking system losses, low collection rates, and poor customer service.

To accomplish its objectives, CREST uses technical means (replacing low-tension with high-tension lines, for example, and installing highly reliable armored and aerial bunched cables on the low-tension consumer point to reduce theft) and managerial changes (introducing "spot billing" and combining data recording, data transfer, bill generation, and bill distribution). Transaction times are reduced, and cash flows improve. Early applications of CREST have reportedly produced positive changes in several neighborhoods in Guinea and Nigeria, two difficult settings.

Source: Based on interviews with World Bank staff from the Africa Energy Department, 2008.

technology standards, as in Guinea and Mali. Innovations have included adjusting technical design standards to meet the reduced requirements of low-load systems, maximizing the use of material provided by local communities (such as locally sourced wooden poles), and recruiting employees and supervisors from the local community.

Finally, institutional change is a long-term matter, but well worth the wait. Victories on this front will be small and slow in coming. Donors may prefer the large and the quick, but they must recognize that positive changes in this field lie at the heart of African power sector reform.

Increasing Cost Recovery

The financial viability of incumbent utilities is a key foundation of a healthy power sector. Financially viable utilities are more effective operationally, because they are able to finance timely maintenance activities. They are also more creditworthy and thus may begin to secure their own access to domestic or international capital markets. Achieving this goal demands power tariffs that are high enough to cover operating costs and to contribute as much as possible to covering capital costs as well.

Cost recovery already looks feasible in countries with relatively low-cost domestic power sources. In the continent's larger countries, and in those that rely on hydropower and coal-based generation, cost-recovery tariffs already appear affordable for the majority of the population, and certainly for the affluent minority that enjoys access to power. A case thus exists for these countries seriously to consider moving closer to full cost recovery.

For countries with high-cost domestic power, cost recovery may become feasible in the medium term as regional trade develops. In the continent's smaller countries, and those reliant primarily on oil-based generation, cost-recovery tariffs are largely unaffordable. As regional trade develops and access to more cost-effective sources of power generation open up, however, the total cost of power production will fall, making cost recovery a much more reasonable goal in the medium term. (The possible exception is

West Africa, where the costs of power will remain relatively high even with regional trade.) A case thus exists for these countries to start moving their tariffs toward longer-term cost-recovery levels, accepting that the sector will continue to register financial deficits in the short term.

Cost recovery is particularly important for emergency power leases, to avoid diverting budgetary resources from long-term investments. Numerous African countries have responded to the power crisis by leasing emergency power generation. This solution is rapid and effective but simultaneously costly and temporary. Charges typically amount to $0.20–$0.30 per kilowatt-hour, without considering transmission and distribution costs or associated losses. Given that the cost of backup generation for the private sector is approximately $0.40 per kilowatt-hour, and that the value of lost load may well be higher than that, the private sector should be willing to pay the full cost of this emergency power. Nevertheless, when emergency power is provided without any adjustment to power tariffs, the resulting fiscal drain can be very large, diverting scarce resources from the investments needed to provide a longer-term solution to the power problem. To avoid this fiscal drain, utilities must price emergency power at cost-recovery levels for nonresidential customers.

Power subsidies will still be needed, but they should be well targeted and focus initially on expanding access. Existing power subsidies are captured largely by higher-income groups and do little to broaden access to electricity. Redesigning power subsidies would free scarce fiscal resources that could be redirected to subsidize the expansion of power networks to serve lower-income rural and periurban communities, or for other poverty-alleviation programs. In some of Africa's poorest countries, even low-cost power will remain unaffordable for a significant minority of the population, so well-targeted subsidies would be needed as part of the strategy for reaching universal access. What is clearly untenable, however, is the situation where power subsidies that benefit only a privileged minority of the population create a significant fiscal drag on the economy.

Accelerating Electrification

From a social and political perspective, expanding access is imperative. Yet financing expansion to lower-income households will further strain the financial viability of the power sector. Tackling this dilemma will require significantly higher concessional financing from development partners for access programs, as well as improved financial and operational performance from utilities.

Given the scale of investments needed, a systematic approach to planning and financing new investments is critical. The current ad hoc project-by-project approach in development partner financing has led to fragmented planning, volatile and uncertain financial flows, and duplicated efforts. Engagement across the sector in multiyear programs of access rollout, supported by multiple development partners as part of a coherent national strategy, will channel resources in a more sustained and cost-effective way to the distribution subsector. Coordinated action by development partners will also reduce the unit costs of increasing access, by achieving economies of scale in implementation.

Completing the urban electrification process requires careful attention to the social issues raised. Chapter 3 of this volume found that approximately half of the nonelectrified urban population lives in proximity to the grid. Densification is thus a key challenge. Demand-side barriers, including high connection charges and insecure tenure, need to be addressed as part of this process. Expansion into periurban slums will need to face power theft, for which technical fixes are available (see box 8.4).

For rural electrification, emerging evidence favors more centralized approaches (Mostert 2008). Countries with dedicated rural electrification funds have higher rates of electrification than those without. Of greatest interest, however, are the differences among the countries with funds. Case studies indicate that the countries that have taken a centralized approach to electrification, with the national utility

responsible for extending the grid, have been more successful than those that followed decentralized approaches, where a rural electrification agency attempted to recruit multiple utilities or private companies into the electrification campaign. Therefore, expecting specialized agencies to solve the rural electrification challenge on their own may be unrealistic. They may be most productive in promoting minigrids and off-grid options as extensions of the national utility's efforts to extend the grid, as in Mali (box 8.5).

Rural electrification may need to follow urban electrification. In an African context, one can legitimately ask how far rural electrification can progress when the urban electrification process is still far from complete. Across countries, a strong correlation exists between urban and rural electrification rates, as well as a systematic lag between the two. Countries with seriously underdeveloped generation capacity and tiny urban customer bases are not well placed to tackle rural electrification, either technically because of power shortages or financially because of the lack of a basis for cross-subsidization.

Finding ways of spreading the benefits of electrification more widely is also important. Because universal household electrification is still decades away in many countries, sectorwide programmatic approaches need to ensure that the benefits of electrification touch the poorest households that may be too far from the grid or just unable to pay for a grid connection. Street lighting may be one way of doing that in urban areas. In rural areas, solar-powered electrification of clinics and schools that provide essential public services to low-income communities is another way of allowing them to participate in the benefits of electrification. Another is appropriate technology, such as low-cost portable solar lanterns that are much more accessible and affordable to the rural public. The Lighting Africa initiative is supporting the development of the market for such products.

Expanding Regional Trade

A strategic priority is to tackle head-on the generation capacity deficit through major

BOX 8.5

Rural Electrification in Mali

Among new African rural electrification agencies, AMA-DER (Agence Malienne pour le Développement de l'Énergie Domestique et l'Électrification Rurale, or Malian Agency for the Development of Domestic Energy and Rural Electrification) has had considerable success. The starting point for AMADER is a country in which only about 3 percent of the rural population has access to electricity. Until they are connected, most rural households meet their lighting and small power needs with kerosene, dry cells, and car batteries, averaging monthly household expenditure of $4–$10.

Created by law in 2003, AMADER uses two major approaches to rural electrification: (a) spontaneous, "bottom-up" electrification of specific communities and (b) planned, "top-down" electrification of large geographic areas. The bottom-up approach, which typically consists of minigrids managed by small local private operators, has been more successful. By late 2008, about 41 bottom-up projects had been financed, comprising 36,277 household connections at an average cost per connection of $776. Typically, AMADER provides grants for about 75 percent of the connection capital costs.

Because Mali has limited renewable resources, most of the minigrid systems are diesel fired. Customers on these isolated minigrids typically receive electricity for six to eight hours a day. In promoting these new projects, AMADER performs three main functions: it acts as a (a) provider of grants, (b) supplier of engineering and commercial technical assistance, and (c) de facto regulator through its grant agreements with operators. The grant agreement can be viewed as a form of "regulation by contract" that establishes minimum technical and commercial quality of service standards and maximum allowed tariffs for both metered and unmetered customers.

To ensure that the projects are financially sustainable, AMADER permits operators to charge residential and commercial tariffs that are higher than the comparable tariffs charged to similar customers connected to the national grid. For example, the energy charge for metered residential customers on isolated minigrids is about 50 percent higher than the comparable energy charge for grid-connected residential customers served by Énergie du Mali (the national electric utility). Many of the minigrid operators also provide service to unmetered customers, who are usually billed a flat monthly charge per lightbulb and outlet, combined with load-limiting devices to ensure that a customer does not connect lightbulbs and appliances beyond what he or she has paid for.

Financing has been a problem for both AMADER and potential operators. AMADER has been hindered by insufficient and uncertain funding for providing capital cost grants. Potential operators have had difficulty raising equity or obtaining loans for the 20–25 percent share of capital costs not funded by AMADER. Promoting leasing arrangements and instituting a loan guarantee program for Malian banks that would be willing to lend to potential operators have been discussed as methods of reducing financial barriers for operators.

Source: Interviews with World Bank staff from the Africa Energy Department, 2008.

---

regional projects. Africa's considerable hydropower, gas, and coal resources remain underexploited. The best way to scale up generation at the lowest unit cost is to develop a new generation of large power generation projects. A substantial number of these transformational projects should be developed in the near term to begin to make a material difference on the supply-demand balance. However, individual countries do not have the necessary investment capital, or even the electricity demand, to move forward with these large projects. A project finance approach predicated on regional power off-take is needed, blending private participation and donor funding.

Power pool development must proceed in parallel so that this new capacity can be transmitted to users. Challenges common to all the pools are rehabilitating and expanding the cross-border transmission infrastructure to increase the potential for trade and harmonizing regulations and system operating agreements. Equally important is formulating market trading mechanisms so that the additional energy generated from large projects can be priced and thus allocated efficiently and fairly (for example, through competitive pool arrangements).

Although the economics of large regional generation projects are convincing, they may give rise to significant political challenges. Africa could potentially save $2 billion a year in energy costs if trade were pursued to its fullest desirable extent, but the gains are much larger for some countries than for others. Small thermal power–dependent countries and a handful of major exporters are likely to benefit the most. About one-third of African countries would end up importing more than half of their power needs, and self-sufficiency sometimes has more political weight than access to low-cost power.

Moreover, reaping the benefits of regional power trade essentially depends on realizing massive investments in three challenging countries. The Democratic Republic of Congo, Ethiopia, and Guinea would be the major power exporters under a regional trading system. To become major exporters, however, all three would need to invest massively in hydropower, which could easily absorb more than 8 percent of their GDP for a decade. Even with support from cross-border finance, the limited financial capacity of these countries and the numerous governance challenges faced by the fragile states (the Democratic Republic of Congo and Guinea) make this quite a tall order.

These considerations call for an incremental approach to developing regional trade. The initial emphasis needs to be on quick wins by building bilateral exchanges between neighbors where a particularly strong economic case exists and where the political context is supportive. This strategy will allow trading experience to build up gradually, paving the way for adding more complexity over time. Even if Africa's first-best generation options cannot always be developed or if the ultimate pattern of power production on the continent turns out to be driven more by financial muscle than by economic expansion, the benefits of interconnection remain clear. Given the small scale and undiversified nature of most countries' power systems, cross-border transmission will always make sense as a means of boosting the efficiency and reliability of power production.

Closing the Funding Gap

Africa's power funding gap is particularly daunting, even more so in the global financial crisis. At $23 billion, the funding gap in Africa's power sector is the largest of any infrastructure sector. The global financial crisis will likely exacerbate the problem. As noted earlier, slower growth could reduce spending needs by as much as 20 percent, but tighter global financial markets could similarly reduce available funding, widening the funding gap even further.

Improving creditworthiness is an important first step that could eventually assist in accessing capital markets. The immediate subsidy savings from addressing operational efficiencies and cost recovery, though substantial, do not come close to closing the gap. In principle, utilities achieving operational efficiency and cost recovery (whether state owned or privately run) could aspire to raising their own capital on domestic or international markets, but that ability is still some way off. External finance to Africa's power sector had been very low for some time but has picked up in recent years (figure 8.10).

Official development assistance to public investment in power has risen substantially. In response to the power crisis, donors have increased their emphasis on the power sector. Commitments averaged $1.5 billion a year for 2005–07, reaching a peak of $2.3 billion in 2007. This is an important turnaround in funding, but more will be needed if any substantial inroads are to be made into Africa's power sector challenges.

Non-OECD countries have emerged as major new power financiers in Africa (Foster and others 2008). Commitments of non-OECD countries, particularly the Chinese and Indian export-import banks, came from nowhere to average about $2 billion a year in 2005–07. Most of the Chinese financing has gone to 10 large hydropower projects with a combined generating capacity of over 6,000 megawatts. Once completed, these projects will increase Sub-Saharan Africa's installed hydropower capacity by 30 percent. China is also financing 2,500 megawatts of thermal power, and the Indian Bank has financed significant thermal generation projects in Nigeria and Sudan.

Private finance was also buoyant until 2007, but significantly lower than official finance. Private commitments to Africa's power sector averaged about $1 billion a year in 2005–07, putting it in third place behind non-OECD finance and traditional official development assistance. The bulk of private resources has gone into 3,000 megawatts of independent power projects. Although it will not be enough to close the financing gap, private finance is very much needed. Successful private investments in energy projects in Africa are still rare, however, and increased private investment will not materialize simply because of large financing gaps. The lessons from past failures must be addressed because private investment will flow only where rewards demonstrably outweigh risks. Some early but encouraging signs indicate that scaling up generation capacity through large private sector–led projects is starting to gather momentum. A prominent example is the privately owned 250-megawatt Bujagali hydropower plant in Uganda, supported by World Bank Group guarantees and funded by a private consortium. Ambitious regional projects undoubtedly present technical, financing, and political risks and will continue to be underpinned by substantial public sector and donor contributions.

Shorter-term measures on energy efficiency can ease the transition. Most of the measures described here are medium term and cannot be implemented overnight. Many Sub-Saharan countries will continue to face a very tight demand-supply balance in the coming years. Therefore, shorter-term measures to soften the economic and social effects of power scarcity must complement longer-term efforts at addressing the underlying structural causes of the power supply crisis. Recent experiences from countries such as Brazil show that well-designed demand-side management measures (for example, a quota system with price signals, combined with a public energy-efficiency campaign) can go a long way toward trimming peak demand, substantially reducing power rationing at fairly low economic and social cost.

Figure 8.10 External Financing Commitments for the African Power Sector, 1994–2007

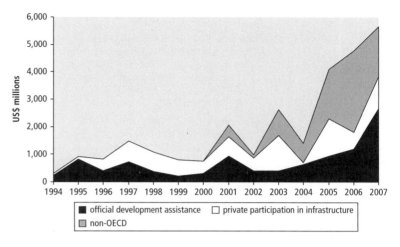

Source: Briceño-Garmendia, Smits, and Foster 2008.
Note: OECD = Organisation for Economic Co-operation and Development.

Notes

The authors of this chapter are Anton Eberhard, Vivien Foster, Cecilia Briceño-Garmendia, and Maria Shkaratan, who drew on background material and contributions from Daniel Camos-i-Daurella, Gabriel Goddard, Jaakko Hellaranta, Rob Mills, Fatimata Ouedraogo, Timo Reiss, Orvika Rosnes, Jevgenijs Steinbuks, Prasad V. S. N. Tallapragada, Maria Vagliasindi, Tjaarda Storm P. Van Leeuwen, and Haakon Vennemo.

1. Isolated areas are more than 50 kilometers from a substation and are either in the power plant buffer (within 10 kilometers for capacity below 10 megawatts, 20 kilometers for capacity below 100 megawatts, and 50 kilometers for capacity below 100 megawatts) or within 10 kilometers of a lit urban area or lit pixel. Remote areas are more than 50 kilometers from a substation and are not in the power plant buffer or within 10 kilometers of a lit urban area or lit pixel.

2. These costs are calculated at the consumption level of 100 kilowatt-hours a month.

References

Banerjee, Sudeshna, Quentin Wodon, Amadou Diallo, Taras Pushak, Hellal Uddin, Clarence Tsimpo, and Vivien Foster. 2008. "Access, Affordability and Alternatives: Modern Infrastructure Services in Africa." Background Paper 2, Africa Infrastructure Country Diagnostic, World Bank, Washington, DC.

Briceño-Garmendia, Cecilia. 2008. "Quasi-Fiscal Costs: A Never Ending Concern." Internal note, Africa Infrastructure Country Diagnostic, World Bank, Washington, DC.

Briceño-Garmendia, Cecilia, Karlis Smits, and Vivien Foster. 2008. "Financing Public Infrastructure in Sub-Saharan Africa: Patterns, Issues, and Options." Background Paper 15, Africa Infrastructure Country Diagnostic, World Bank, Washington, DC.

Calderón, César. 2008. "Infrastructure and Growth in Africa." Working Paper 3, Africa Infrastructure Country Diagnostic, World Bank, Washington, DC.

Eberhard, Anton. 2007. "Matching Regulatory Design to Country Circumstances: The Potential of Hybrid and Transitional Models." *Gridlines*, Note 23 (May). Public-Private Infrastructure Advisory Facility, World Bank, Washington, DC.

Eberhard, Anton, Vivien Foster, Cecilia Briceño-Garmendia, Fatimata Ouedraogo, Daniel Camos, and Maria Shkaratan. 2008. "Underpowered: The State of the Power Sector in Sub-Saharan Africa." Background Paper 6, Africa Infrastructure Country Diagnostic, World Bank, Washington, DC.

EIA (Energy Information Administration). 2006. *International Energy Annual*. Washington, DC: U.S. Department of Energy. http://www.eia.doe.gov/emeu/international/contents.html.

ESMAP (Energy Sector Management Assistance Program). 2007. "Technical and Economic Assessment of Off-Grid, Mini-Grid and Grid Electrification Technologies." ESMAP Technical Paper 121/07, World Bank, Washington, DC.

Foster, Vivien, William Butterfield, Chuan Chen, and Nataliya Pushak. 2008. *Building Bridges: China's Growing Role as Infrastructure Financier for Africa*. Trends and Policy Options no. 5. Washington, DC: Public-Private Infrastructure Advisory Facility, World Bank.

Foster, Vivien, and Jevgenijs Steinbuks. 2008. "Paying the Price for Unreliable Power Supplies: In-House Generation of Electricity by Firms in Africa." Policy Research Working Paper 4913, World Bank, Washington, DC.

Gratwick, Katharine Nawaal, and Anton Eberhard. 2008. "An Analysis of Independent Power Projects in Africa: Understanding Development and Investment Outcomes." *Development Policy Review* 26 (3): 309–38.

Molefhi, Benjamin O. C., and L. J. Grobler. 2006. "Demand-Side Management: A Challenge and Opportunity for Botswana Electric Energy Sector." North-West University, Potchefstroom, South Africa.

Mostert, Wolfgang. 2008. *Review of Experience with Rural Electrification Agencies: Lesson for Africa*. Eschborn, Germany: EU Energy Initiative Partnership Dialogue Facility.

PPA (Power Planning Associates). 2005. "Towards Growth and Poverty Reduction: Lessons from Private Participation in Infrastructure in Sub-Saharan Africa—Case Study of Botswana Power Corporation." Summary report, World Bank, Washington, DC.

Rosnes, Orvika, and Haakon Vennemo. 2008. "Powering Up: Costing Power Infrastructure Investment Needs in Southern and Eastern Africa." Background Paper 5, Africa Infrastructure Sector Diagnostic, World Bank, Washington, DC.

Vagliasindi, Maria, and John Nellis. 2009. "Evaluating Africa's Experience with Institutional Reform for the Infrastructure Sectors." Working Paper 23, Africa Infrastructure Country Diagnostic, World Bank, Washington, DC.

Wodon, Quentin, ed. 2008. "Electricity Tariffs and the Poor: Case Studies from Sub-Saharan Africa." Working Paper 11, Africa Infrastructure Country Diagnostic, World Bank, Washington, DC.

World Bank. 2005. *African Development Indicators*. Washington, DC: World Bank.

———. 2007. Enterprise Surveys database. http://www.enterprisesurveys.org/.

Yepes, Tito, Justin Pierce, and Vivien Foster. 2008. "Making Sense of Sub-Saharan Africa's Infrastructure Endowment: A Benchmarking Approach." Working Paper 1, Africa Infrastructure Country Diagnostic, World Bank, Washington, DC.

Chapter 9

Transport: More Than the Sum of Its Parts

So much variety exists among the transport modes and their infrastructure, in both policy and technical matters, that the following four chapters deal with them separately. Those modes interact and interconnect in complex ways, however, raising common issues.

Many movements of passengers and freight involve more than one mode of transport, with impediments at the point of interchange, often caused by corrupt customs administration, or restrictions on entry to the transport market. In freight, Sub-Saharan Africa suffers particularly from such blockages, which delay shipments, increase costs, and hinder the development of logistics systems so critical in sophisticated global markets. Because Africa has so many landlocked countries, this problem is multinational and must be confronted on a regional or a corridor basis.

One of the main sources of restrictive entry is the perceived need to protect national carriers or the existing carriers. Although this protection has largely withered away in international shipping and inter-African air transport, it still prevails in road freight.

Increasing the scope for competition among carriers is a challenge confronting most transport modes. In most parts of the world, competition has involved extending the role of the private sector. Franchises and concessions permit this extension without loss of government influence over activities regarded as strategic. Bus transport and trucking are already predominantly private. Many African railways are now concessioned, and the role of the private sector is increasing in ports and air transport. However, the regulation of these markets often remains obstructive rather than constructive, with *tour de role* traffic allocation and dispatching[1] reducing efficiency and increasing costs.

A common reason for restricting competition is the belief that the government can ensure provision of socially desirable services only when they are supplied by a public enterprise or strongly protected private enterprises. However, this belief is largely fallacious, particularly if the protected suppliers have no incentive to be efficient or no segment of the market is profitable enough to support unremunerative "social" services. Publicly owned airlines, railways, shipping companies, and bus companies have all fallen short. Thus, much work remains, both nationally and regionally, in developing regulatory regimes that reconcile public and private interests.

Integrating Multimodal Transport

Inland transport costs often seriously inhibit foreign trade, which passes through a seaport or airport and then one or more land modes. For example, inland transport accounts for an estimated 40 percent of the total cost from the point of origin to the port of destination for West African cocoa and coffee exports.

The transport chains are no stronger than their weakest links, usually the interchanges. The weaknesses are partly physical, with no physical connection between the modes and no infrastructure for transshipment; partly institutional, with responsibility for the interchanges not falling clearly to one modal agency or the other; and partly operational, with the government collecting taxes and duties or staff collecting bribes, slowing movements, and pushing up costs.

The port-rail link is the first major weakness. Although rail transport is advantageous for long-distance, time-insensitive commodities, it depends heavily on internationally traded traffic. To hold this traffic, it must be linked efficiently to good port connections, but conflicts between rail and port jurisdictions over rail segments in port areas often inhibit this link. Except in South Africa, inland transport and facilities are poorly aligned with port development. The stripping and stuffing of containers in port areas also increases congestion in many ports. It is no accident that some of the most successful rail lines in Africa operate in national corridors where specialized rail and port facilities are vertically integrated (for example, Spoornet coal and ore lines and Gabonese manganese ore).

Good links between complementary rail systems are also essential. Some railway organizations already contribute to this. The binational railways in Côte d'Ivoire–Burkina Faso and Senegal-Mali provide good examples, as does the operation of contiguous railways by the same concessionaire (Central East African Railways in Mozambique and Malawi). However, they also create local monopolies that can increase their profits through predatory practices, as in Zambia's treatment of copper exports by the Democratic Republic of Congo (see chapter 11 in this volume). In East Africa, joint concessioning of railways is part of a donor–funded corridor, where border-crossing arrangements have been reformed. Some countries are now trying to develop coordinated corridor systems, as in the Ghana Gateway and Maputo corridors.

Other transport modes may also be involved. Inland waterway transport historically carried primary products from landlocked countries but is now in decline. The three major lakes in East and Central Africa—Victoria, Tanganyika, and Malawi—used to be important in transit and intraregional trade. Particularly on Lake Victoria, the lake services were part of the railway systems linking the railheads at the inland ports of Bell (Uganda), Kisumu (Kenya), and Mwanza (Tanzania). The Kenya and Uganda lake operations were concessioned together with the railways in those countries, whereas in Tanzania, the lake services were separated from the railways. Only one service now operates on Lake Victoria, and some of the railway track leading to the ports is in poor repair, especially in Kenya.

The story is similar in West and Central Africa, where the Congo basin has a navigable network of 12,000 kilometers, covering nearly 4 million square kilometers in nine countries. In principle, this waterway could be a very valuable resource in a multimodal transport network serving the region, particularly given low associated transport costs of $0.05 per ton-kilometer versus $0.15 per ton-kilometer for road or rail freight in Central Africa, albeit at significantly lower speeds. In practice, however, the river corridor suffers from an outdated and insufficient infrastructure, inadequate channel markings and maintenance, feeble regulation, and numerous nonphysical barriers to movement. Thus, it is ever more marginal in transport. Recognizing this untapped potential, in October 2005, the Executive Secretary of the Economic and Monetary Community of Central Africa encouraged the governments of Cameroon, the Central African Republic, the Democratic Republic of Congo, and the Republic of Congo to establish the Commission Internationale du Bassin Congo-Oubangui-Sangha to improve the physical and regulatory arrangements for inland navigation. A consultancy study is examining the current arrangements in the four participating countries and identifying steps to begin an effective redevelopment of inland navigation (CICOS 2007).

Developing Logistics Systems

The transport problems of doing business in Africa are not just a matter of poor infrastructure or high transport costs. Modern logistics systems also emphasize the efficiency of customs and other border agencies, the ease and affordability of arranging international shipments, the competence of the local logistics sector, the ability to track and trace shipments, and their timeliness. These various aspects of logistic performance are encapsulated in a logistic performance index (figure 9.1). Except for South Africa, Sub-Saharan African countries perform poorly not only on infrastructure quality, but also on all the main aspects of logistics competence.

Africa is thus viewed as logistics-unfriendly; third-party logistics systems, so important in increasing production and distribution efficiency in the industrial countries, are poorly developed in Africa. Whatever the main mode of transport, the most serious impediments are administrative. For example, in road transport, regulation and market structures of the road freight industry, rather than the quality of the road infrastructure, are the binding constraints on international movements (Teravaininthorn and Raballand 2008). African governments must understand the importance of the qualitative aspects of logistic performance and act to remove administrative obstacles to that performance.

Corruption, through bribery of a range of officials having a combination of discretionary power and a quasi-monopoly position in the logistics chain, is a critical problem. For example, corruption can increase the total shipping costs, including costs of overland transport, port clearance, and ocean shipping, of a standard 20-foot container traveling between South Africa's economic hub and eastern Africa or the Far East by up to 14 percent and the total port costs by up to 130 percent. Contrary to common belief, no robust evidence links corruption with low wage levels or lack of job rotation. Rather, it is highly correlated with the extent to which rules, regulations, and the organizational features of bureaucracies give public officials the

Figure 9.1 Africa Registers Low Scores on the Logistics Performance Index, 2007

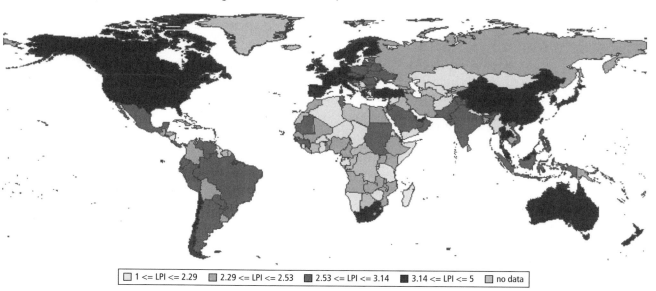

☐ 1 <= LPI <= 2.29   ☐ 2.29 <= LPI <= 2.53   ☐ 2.53 <= LPI <= 3.14   ■ 3.14 <= LPI <= 5   ☐ no data

Source: World Bank 2007.
Note: LPI = Logistics Performance Index; 1 is the lowest score and 5 is the highest score.

bargaining rights to extort bribe payments from shippers. In a comparison between the ports of Maputo (Mozambique) and Durban (South Africa), bribery of *customs* officials accounted for 80 percent of total bribery in Maputo, but only 10 percent in Durban (Sequeira and Macchi 2009). The explanation was that, in Maputo, a low level of automation existed and both monitoring and sanctioning were weak, whereas in Durban, the opposite was the case. In contrast, bribery of *port* officials was lower in the privately concessioned Maputo port, where a higher level of automation, monitoring, and sanctioning exists than in the publicly operated Durban port, where automation is low and monitoring and sanctioning are weak.

Developing Transit Corridors for Landlocked Countries

The weakness of logistics systems impinges most on the landlocked countries. In southern Africa, operating costs are not excessively higher than in Europe ($0.08 per ton kilometer in 2008), but queues at borders and restrictions on access to the market mean that rates on international routes are higher by 10–30 percent. Being landlocked adds four days to exports and nine days to imports for land distribution of equivalent distances within a seaport country. However, this difference is usually less than the sea transit time. Much more problematic is the high variability of transit time, especially for imports. The unreliability of import and export chains stems largely from inadequate transit procedures, overregulation, multiple controls, and poor border service (World Bank 2008). In addition, bribes and unnecessary charges can add 50 percent to the transport costs between a port and a landlocked country. Because of these impediments, landlocked countries have a much smaller involvement in world trade than the coastal countries, and they have remained predominantly dependent on exports of raw materials. Although increasing prices for raw materials over the past five years have helped landlocked countries in Africa, they remain vulnerable to a change in that trend.

Most of the critical trade facilitation impediments stem from the procedure and services in the transit country, which often sees no advantage for its own economy in addressing the needs of transit traffic. This view may, in fact, be mistaken if transit traffic contributes to scale economies in the transit country's own port and maritime or air service sectors, and particularly if the goods transported complement, rather than compete with, its own products. Even in those circumstances, however, the vested interests of the beneficiaries of bribes and providers of unnecessary border service may be difficult to overcome. Furthermore, governments of transit countries with potential benefits may give the wrong signals (see box 9.1).

These problems with transit countries are increasingly recognized. In August 2003, attendees at an intergovernmental conference at Almaty, Kazakhstan, agreed to a Program of Action calling for joint efforts by landlocked and transit countries to revise their regulatory frameworks and improve transit-related infrastructure and procedures with the assistance of other countries and microfinance institutions.

Some critical elements of a reform program can be identified. Reform of trucking regulation is essential and is discussed further in chapter 10 of this volume. This must be supplemented by a reengineering of the transit system. In the longer term, something similar to the European Transports Internationaux Routiers (TIR), which provides a reliable system based on a single manifest (the TIR carnet) and a chain of guarantees, could speed freight through international borders, though the immediate introduction of a system is doubtful. More immediately, one-stop border posts, in which the two border countries share the information provided, could eliminate duplication and speed transit. Customs must be automated, limiting direct contact between officials and agents; monitoring and sanctioning must be strengthened; and port management must be privatized to reduce corruption. Inland clearance centers or dry ports, which deal with traffic under bond, can circumvent the traditional impediments of the seaports. Development of airfreight can also overcome the constraints for some traffic.

BOX 9.1

Impediments to Transit Traffic Growth in the Maputo Corridor

Maputo is the closest port to the industrial center of South Africa in Gauteng province (581 kilometers compared with 750 kilometers between Durban port and Johannesburg) and current congestion at Durban port gives it an apparent advantage for shippers with time-sensitive goods. If Maputo could capture 1 percent of the 700 million tons of traffic from and to Gauteng and Mpumalanga provinces, its total throughput would be doubled. However, despite major road investment in the Maputo-Gauteng corridor and a rather successful port concession process, transit traffic accounted for less than 40 percent of Maputo's total traffic in 2007, and the port operated at less than 30 percent of its capacity. With so much spare capacity at Maputo and so much congestion in Durban, both countries would seem to benefit if transit traffic were increased.

Why has this not yet happened? Road conditions are not a major obstacle, and transport prices are not abnormally high along the international corridor. However, many large South African shippers are reluctant to shift their transport routes from Durban because they perceive the business climate in Mozambique to be too unpredictable to invest in redirecting their logistics routes. Mozambique has a logistics performance index below the Sub-Saharan Africa average and much below that of South Africa. Maputo port users must face increased transport unpredictability because of the absence of direct calls by shipping lines (except Mitsui O.S.K. Lines) due to low volumes. Corruption is also greater in Maputo, averaging 15 percent of a one-way overland shipping rate for a standard 40-foot container, compared with only 7 percent for Durban (Sequeira and Macchi 2009).

Above all, the Mozambique government has not been acting to overcome this lack of confidence, as exemplified by its policies on traffic scanning. In April 2006, the government granted the concession of a scanner to Kudumba, a private sector operator. Initially, all exports had to be scanned, including bulk cargo with a fee per ton and exported cars from South Africa. Although scanning fees have decreased considerably since 2006 for certain terminal operators (for example, from $100 per car to $15 per car), fees continue to be high compared to world practices. The absence of transparency and participation in the decision to introduce scanning technology and the determination of fees and the lack of a transparent bidding process in the award of the concession to Kudumba have further strengthened the perception of uncertainty in the business environment.

Source: Raballand and Macchi 2008.

Some progress has been made in this direction. Trucking regulation is more liberal in southern Africa than in other parts of Sub-Saharan Africa. Transit system reform is being introduced to facilitate transit traffic through Cameroon to Chad and the Central African Republic (see box 9.2).

One-stop border post initiatives apply to the border between Kenya and Uganda at Malaba; between Zambia and Zimbabwe at Chirundu; between Zimbabwe and Mozambique at Forbes/Machipanda; along the Trans-Kalahari Corridor; and in West Africa on selective borders of Burkina Faso, Ghana, Mali, and Togo. Some landlocked countries already have bonded warehouses at the ports in West Africa, and rail concessionaires are developing facilities to speed transits, such as the Sitarail intermodal terminal proposal in Ouagadougou, Burkina Faso; the ZRS company customs bond at the Victoria Falls border crossing between Zambia and Zimbabwe; and the planned Madarail bonded container terminal near Antananarivo, Madagascar.

Much remains to be done to fill gaps in the implementation of the Almaty program. Generally accepted corridor-monitoring indicators are required to check progress. Trucking markets and the associated freight-forwarding sector reforms need to be extended. Agreement between neighboring countries on transit system reforms must be encouraged by donor contributions and facilitated by the development of best practice standards.

Increasing Competition

Competition between suppliers of an individual transport mode improves service quality and reduces costs, as shown in chapter 10 on road transport and chapter 13 on air transport in this volume. Competition between modes may also result in the replacement of one by

BOX 9.2

A New Attempt to Reform the Transit System in the Cameroon–Central African Republic–Chad Corridor

A major reform is being piloted as part of the Central Africa Transport and Transit Facilitation Project financed by the African Development Bank, the Agence Française de Développement, the European Commission, and the International Development Association. The object is to meet the needs of two landlocked countries, the Central African Republic and Chad, that suffer some of the highest international transport costs and worst logistics conditions among developing countries. Freight bureaus enforcing mandatory freight allocations and queuing manage international transport between the two countries and the port of Douala, Cameroon, under bilateral conventions. The main problems with the existing transit regime include very slow release of goods from the port of Douala, requiring seven documents, all of which must be cleared by three separate offices. Multiple checkpoints and controls also exist on the roads to the landlocked countries. Both transport charges and the guarantees required from banks are significantly more costly than for comparable services in other countries.

A TIR (Transport Internationaux Routiers)-based international road transit convention (TIPAC, or Transit Inter-États des Pays de l'Afrique Centrale), signed in 1991, was never followed. In 2008, despite the reluctance of the vested interests to lose the multiple rents in the existing system, and thanks mainly to strong leadership and pressure for reform from the Cameroonian government and customs, agreement was eventually reached on a substantially revised transit system. The main elements are introduction of one common transit document, removal of all checkpoints on the roads, and use of information technology based on ASYCUDA (Automated SYstem for CUstoms Data) by the United Nations Conference on Trade and Development. The last adds a bar code to the transit document and container that is read optically at the start, destination, and border to simplify transit procedures for authorized freight forwarders who have obtained a standing customs guarantee from the banking system. If implemented, the changes are expected to yield substantial benefits of shorter delivery times, greater predictability, and lower prices.

Source: World Bank 2008.

the other. For example, road improvement in Mauritania effectively eliminated domestic air transport, and all African railways have had difficulty retaining passenger traffic where a road alternative exists. However, various modes may be complementing each other or competing with each other at the same time. Reconciling these tensions is very difficult.

Where modes compete, efficient allocation of traffic between them would normally depend on their relative prices reflecting their relative costs; however, that can be difficult to interpret. Where traffic is heavily imbalanced (as in international trade) and cost structures differ between modes, both commercial pressure and economic efficiency may call for widely varying price–marginal cost ratios, and predatory pricing is difficult to define.

Attention to the fairness of competitive conditions is important. Roads are publicly provided at costs to users that do not even cover maintenance, whereas privately provided

rail service is expected to cover its full costs, including track. The viability of privately concessioned railways can be hurt by undercharging for road maintenance and not enforcing axle load limits on road traffic.

National transport strategies that put infrastructure charging for road and rail on a common basis would probably reduce budget burdens and improve road conditions. The net effect on modal split is more difficult to predict because of security, reliability, and other noncost items considered in determining choices. For example, a comparison of road and rail tariffs on five concessioned railways showed road tariffs exceeding rail tariffs by 44–213 percent. More competition between road and rail, abetted by increasing road costs, might reduce trucker profit margins rather than increase the mode share or pricing power of rail. Given the cartels and high profit rates in road haulage, even greater benefits could likely be obtained by promoting competition in road haulage.

Revisiting Attitudes toward Private Supply and Profit

Private participation in supply, central to competition, can increase the efficiency of operation and the mobilization of private capital. However, to activate these benefits, governments must understand the commercial realities that motivate private business. Excess private profit from a monopoly should be constrained. Yet private firms will not participate if governments deny them a reasonable return on investment, a necessity for a private operation and not a sin.

Consistent policies to attract private sector finance and management should include an explicit determination of the objectives of private participation. Policy makers should recognize that private participation can bring efficiency benefits not only in cases of marginal commercial viability, but also in sectors deemed highly profitable (ports) or deemed desirable albeit highly unprofitable (some railway concessions). That awareness calls for a wider range of forms of private participation, including negative concessions and *affermage* arrangements.[2] A specialist national agency dealing with privatization could help in producing such policies and forms of participation.

Government use of public sector monopoly powers to generate excess revenues can be equally damaging, even if ostensibly to support other unprofitable services. Internal cross subsidies have usually had adverse effects. For example, South Africa's Spoornet draws cross subsidies for loss-producing freight and passenger services both from the ostensibly profitable ore and coal services and, through Transnet, from ports and pipelines.

In practice, the effect has been to denude the core services of investment. In Africa, the average age of locomotives is 25 years and of freight wagons, 25–30 years, both nearly twice the international best practice. In the ore services, a capacity gap exists, and Spoornet's safety record appears to be low and deteriorating. The port system is also being denied investment. Despite the high technical competence of the South African system, the recent *National Freight Logistics Study* concluded, "Restoring rail reliability is fundamental and is the single most important challenge facing the freight logistics sector in South Africa" (Department of Transport 2005: 13). The dangers of exploiting public monopoly powers also arise in airports in several countries where the benefits of private managerial efficiency are forgone by keeping such activities in the public sector.

Careful consideration must therefore be given to establishing appropriate oversight and regulatory institutions. Creation and exploitation of monopoly powers by cartelization need to be under continual review, covering both industrial structure and commercial behavior. Many countries could develop a small but skilled unit to advise governments and specialized modal regulators on the principles of regulation.

One further concern about private foreign involvement in supply merits consideration. Concerns about reliance on private foreign control of services critical to national security have been widely used as an argument for maintaining national air transport and shipping fleets and for limiting foreign capital in national infrastructure finance. In practice, uneconomically small airlines and shipping fleets protected by cargo reservation tend to push up costs and drain national resources (to the detriment of national security). In addition, resistance to involving the global container port terminal operators denies countries the efficiency and investment that such participation could bring.

Thus, countries need mechanisms to reconcile private (and foreign) participation in financing transport infrastructure with economic, social, and strategic objectives. This approach calls for more fundamental consideration of the nature and appropriateness of social and strategic objectives and for analysis of the relative effectiveness of different instruments in achieving those objectives. Developing a range of contract designs appropriate to different objectives is part of this challenge.

Meeting Social Obligations

Most African governments, wishing to be seen as keeping down costs of public passenger transport, have maintained low bus and rail passenger fares. Where fares are commercially unviable, however, they are likely to undermine the supply of the public services. Even where the controls are enforced only on publicly provided modes (notably rail or conventional large bus services), they typically shift business to an informal sector with higher fares or lower service quality, failing to assist poorer citizens.

Governments could pay compensation for the imposed social obligations. However, only in rare cases, such as the support of the public bus company in Addis Ababa, are public service obligation payments adequate and timely. More generally, the failure to achieve this timeliness postpones, but does not avoid, the collapse of public bus service. The same appears to be happening with the provisions for subsidizing rail passengers in some rail concessions. Where subsidized rail services have economically viable road alternatives, the subsidy (if paid) drains resources from the economy. More comprehensive and well-thought-out strategies for fare controls and subsidies, probably by procuring subsidized services through competitive tendering, can ensure the most effective use of transport infrastructure.

Notes

The author of this chapter is Kenneth Gwilliam, who drew on background material and contributions from Jean Francois Arvis, Rodrigo Archondo-Callao, Jose L. Guasch, Alberto Nogales, Gael Raballand, Sandra Sequeira, and Kavita Sethi.

1. *Tour de role* dispatching is a system in which service suppliers are allocated traffic strictly in turn. It is widely applied in the public transport and trucking markets. This system limits direct competition and usually results in low vehicle use and high unit costs.

2. A negative concession is one offered for a loss-making service, in which the competition is conducted in terms of the minimum public subsidy required by the operator to take on the loss-making service. An *affermage* contract is similar to a management contract, but the private operator takes responsibility for all operation and maintenance functions, both technical and commercial.

References

CICOS (Commission Internationale du Bassin Congo-Oubangui-Sangha). 2007. *Plan d'action strategique pour la promotion de la navigation dans le bassin Congo-Oubangui-Sangha.* Hamburg: HPC Hamburg Port Consulting GmbH.

Department of Transport. 2005. "National Freight Logistics Strategy." Department of Transport, Republic of South Africa.

Raballand, Gaël, and Patricia Macchi. 2008. *The Critical Importance of Strengthened Regional Integration for Growth and Development in Mozambique.* Washington, DC: World Bank.

Sequeira, Sandra, and Patricia Macchi. 2009. "The Importance of Soft Transport Infrastructure: Customs Officials in Maputo versus the Port Operators in Durban." *Afrique Contemporaine* 230 (2).

Teravaininthorn, Supee, and Gaël Raballand. 2008. *Transport Prices and Costs in Africa: A Review of the Main International Corridors.* Directions in Development Series. Washington, DC: World Bank.

World Bank. 2007. *Connecting to Compete: Trade Logistics in the Global Economy—the Logistics Performance Index and Its Indicators.* Washington, DC: World Bank.

———. 2008. *Improving Trade and Transport for Landlocked Developing Countries.* Washington, DC: World Bank.

Chapter 10

Roads: Broadening the Agenda

African governments have been addressing the low density and poor condition of their road networks. Institutional reform since the mid-1990s has progressed well, with a remarkable consensus on the content. Most countries have second-generation road funds supported by fuel levies, and many others have autonomous road agencies. Specialist maintenance management agencies have been established, and new forms of contract-based maintenance are being introduced. Although important funding gaps remain, results are discernible. On average, 80 percent of the main road network is in good or fair condition, and the current value of the national road networks is at least 70 percent of their potential. The limited time series available also suggests that a number of countries have improved road conditions over time.

Despite this progress, the reform agenda is incomplete. In many cases, fuel levies have been set too low to be effective, and road funds and agencies do not always meet all good-practice design criteria. Modern contracting and contract management methods are far from universal. Furthermore, while policy makers' attention has focused on the institutions and financial flows for the interurban roads, other challenges have surfaced that will require different types of solutions.

First, the reforms to the interurban road network have affected rural roads much less. Even though agriculture is viewed as an engine of growth, only one-third of rural inhabitants live within 2 kilometers of an all-season road. Doubling this percentage would be very costly, absorbing more than 1 percent of GDP a year for a decade. The rural environment presents particular institutional challenges for road maintenance.

Second, surface transportation is about more than good roads. Africa continues to be handicapped by very high road freight tariffs, driven primarily by high profit margins rather than high costs (or defective roads). In Central and West Africa particularly, trucking industry cartels and restrictive *tour de role* traffic allocation and dispatching practices are responsible for low vehicle mileage and poor fleet quality. The most urgent reforms are to liberalize trucking while mitigating associated social effects. Without such measures, further improvements in road quality will only translate into higher profit margins for the trucking industry.

Third, Africa's rapidly growing cities face major mobility problems. Urban road density is low by developing-country standards. Moreover, following the demise of large buses in many cities, myriad informal minibus operators largely dominate urban transport services. Services are costly, and availability is inadequate. Few countries capture sufficient financial resources to develop and maintain the urban road network. Overlapping national, metropolitan, and municipal jurisdictions present serious institutional challenges. Furthermore, the cross-sectoral links between urban transport and land use planning are unexploited.

Road Infrastructure—Lagging Other Regions Somewhat

The region's trunk road network comprises strategic trading corridors linking deep-sea ports to economic hinterlands. These corridors, which carry about $200 billion of trade a year, include no more than 10,000 kilometers of road. The concept of an intraregional trunk network, or Trans-African Highway, remains a distant reality because of missing links and poor maintenance on key segments. Between 60,000 and 100,000 kilometers of road are required to provide such intracontinental connectivity.

Africa's national road density is substantially lower than that in other developing regions: only 204 kilometers of road per 1,000 square kilometers of land area, with only one-quarter paved, compared with a world average of 944 kilometers per 1,000 square kilometers, with more than half paved. That density is less than 30 percent of the next-lowest region, South Asia. However, Sub-Saharan African road density in relation to population is slightly higher than South Asia's and only slightly lower than the Middle East's and North Africa's.

Relative to GDP, however, Sub-Saharan Africa has a large road network. In Madagascar, Malawi, Mozambique, and Niger, the asset value of the road network exceeds 30 percent of GDP, an indication of the consequently large economic burden of maintenance. As a result,

the road conditions lag somewhat behind those of other developing regions, but not so much for the main trunk road network as for other roads (Gwilliam and others 2008).

With accelerating urbanization, Africa needs to develop intraurban roads, but networks in 14 African cities were found to be substandard (Kumar and Barrett 2007). Road density (paved-road density in particular) lags far behind that in other developing cities. Capacity is generally limited. The majority of roads have one lane in each direction, and where roads are wider, pedestrians and parked vehicles often take up one lane. Intersections are close together and are ill designed for turning. Service lanes are absent, pavement is deteriorating, and street lighting is minimal. Because traffic management is limited, accidents are frequent, with pedestrians accounting for two-thirds of fatalities.

For rural roads, beyond the classified tertiary network, which is typically the responsibility of local government, a vast unclassified network of tracks providing service to rural areas is usually the responsibility of local communities. Nevertheless, African rural communities have by far the lowest accessibility to an all-season road in the developing world. Evidence indicates that physical isolation prevents large areas of the continent from reaching their agricultural potential. With low population density, achieving good overall rural accessibility would imply at least doubling the length of the classified network for most countries (Starkey and others 2002).

Traffic volumes remain low and heavily concentrated on the main road network (table 10.1). In most countries, at least 90 percent of reported traffic on the classified network is carried on the main networks.[1] Except in Nigeria and South Africa, the traffic on the main road network in Africa averages only about 500 vehicles a day.

Rural networks typically carry less than 10 percent of the classified network's traffic; however, in Ethiopia, Malawi, and Nigeria, they carry more than 20 percent. Except in Nigeria, the absolute volumes of traffic on the rural network are very low, averaging about 30 vehicles a day.

Table 10.1 Average Daily Traffic on the Main Road Network

Country type	Classified network	Classified network			Paved network	Unpaved network
		Primary	Secondary	Tertiary		
Low income	236	934	182	28	1,054	50
Lower middle income	341	1,186	303	39	1,474	95
Upper middle income	1,066	5,469	117	24	2,883	5

Source: Gwilliam and others 2008.

Road Infrastructure Institutions and Finance—Promising Developments

The initial thrust of institutional reform has been to create an independent source of funding for road maintenance, based on road user charges, segregated from the general government budget, and administered by an autonomous board.

Funding Arrangements

Donors have played a major role in promoting this institutional framework. Most countries already have such second-generation road funds, and most others, except Nigeria and South Africa, are establishing them. Not all funds have good-practice designs, however, and their performance varies substantially (figure 10.1).

Despite widespread application of fuel levies to fund road maintenance, the level of the fuel levy, hence its utility, varies enormously across countries. The range extends from symbolic levels of about $0.03 a liter, nowhere near high enough, to about $0.16 a liter, which covers most road maintenance needs. Many countries have major difficulties in collecting the levies, whether because of evasion (Tanzania) or delayed transfers of revenues (Rwanda), and capture perhaps as little as half the planned resources. Therefore, the road funds in Benin, Côte d'Ivoire, Ethiopia, Gabon, and Zambia still depend on budget allocations for more than three-quarters of their resources rather than being funded largely from fuel levies, as is the intention of road funds.

Toll roads affect barely 0.1 percent of the region's classified road network, almost entirely in South Africa. Toll-road concessions have captured fewer than $1.6 billion in investment commitments, small in relation to the region's needs. Less than 10 percent of the region's road network attracts the 15,000 vehicles a day that are the minimum traffic flow needed to make concessions economically viable. Toll roads have potential only in South Africa and to a lesser extent, in Nigeria.

Implementation Agencies

A second stage of reform has created road agencies, independent from line ministries, with responsibility for contracting out public works. About two-thirds of the 24 countries sampled have a road agency, and others are planning one, but only one-third of the agency boards have private representation. Nigeria, Senegal, and South Africa have a road agency but not a road fund. Autonomy varies from full responsibility for road network management to limited responsibility for road maintenance programs defined by the road department or ministry.

About half of the countries sampled contract out more than 80 percent of maintenance work. Some road agencies are adopting performance-based maintenance contracts, under which a private contractor maintains a public road to achieve and maintain specified condition standards for periods ranging from 3 to 10 years in return for a fixed payment stream. The advantages of such contracts are that they can provide a strong incentive for contractors to undertake effective maintenance, and they can reduce expenditure uncertainties for the road fund. The contracts started in Canada in the late 1980s, and industrialized countries have now adopted them. In developing countries, they were first applied in Argentina in mid-1990, but they rapidly spread

Figure 10.1 Progress with Road Fund Reforms

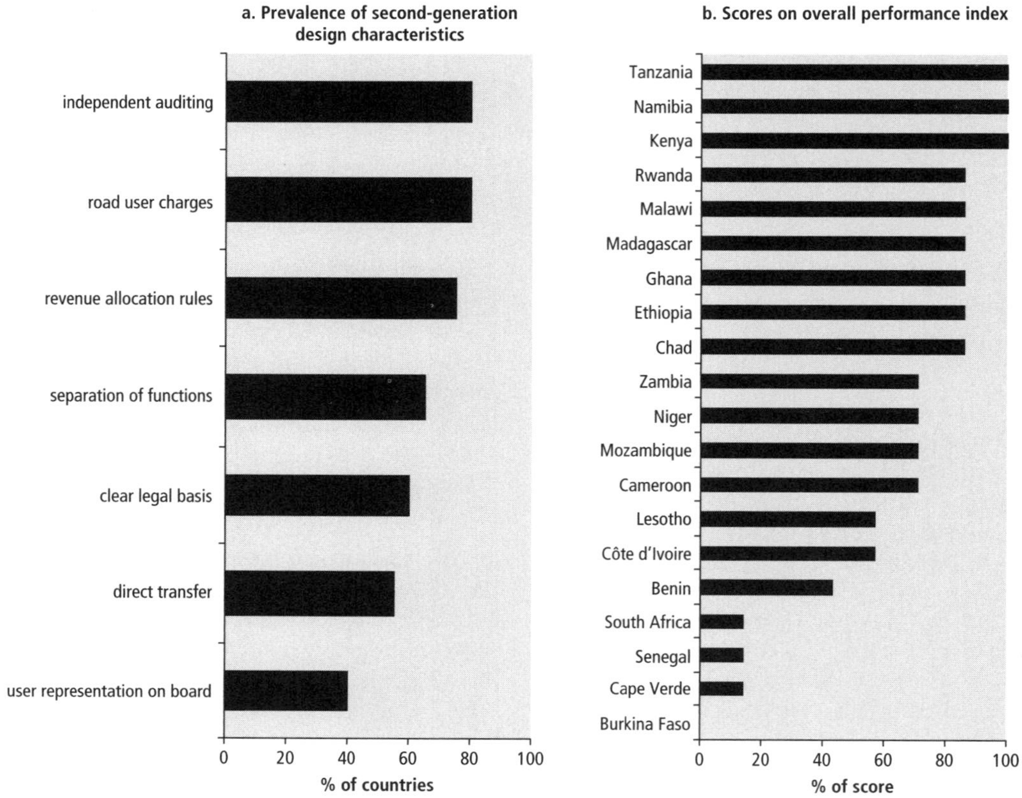

Source: Gwilliam and others 2008, based on data collected by World Bank 2007.

to neighboring countries so that more than 40,000 kilometers of Latin American roads are now being maintained under such contracts. In Africa, Ethiopia, Ghana, and Zambia have begun to use them.

Cost savings from performance-based maintenance contracts on paved roads have ranged between 10 and 40 percent in industrialized countries and between 10 and 20 percent for several developing countries (Stankevich, Qureshi, and Queiroz 2005). Even where such cost savings were not achieved, the benefits have been substantial. In Chad, the only example in francophone Africa, the cost per kilometer of routine maintenance under a performance-based maintenance contract for a set of gravel roads was significantly higher ($5,000) than under a traditional maintenance contract ($1,500) but with the benefit that the contractor was

responsible for maintaining a level of service linked to the condition of the road surface. Under a performance-based maintenance contract, the condition of the road improves steadily, whereas under the traditional approach, the road condition improves for a short period following the work and then starts deteriorating quickly until new maintenance is carried out.

A parallel institutional development, particularly relevant to rural roads, involves delegating project management to specialist agencies. In many countries, these agencies, *agences d'exécution des travaux d'intérêt public* (AGETIPs; public works implementing agency), now manage private consultants and contractors on behalf of the public authority and perform all the necessary functions for contract preparation, implementation, and supervision (box 10.1).

BOX 10.1

The Role of AGETIPs

Delegating the function of managing the planning, procurement, and implementation of public works to a specialist private agency is well established in French public administration. In many African countries, an AGETIP was attractive to international financial institutions as a means of obtaining more effective implementation of donor-funded works, particularly in rural sectors, where administrative skills were weakest.

Following the creation of the first AGETIP in connection with a donor–financed sites and services project in Senegal in 1989, the greatly improved administration of public works and timely payment enable a substantial increase in the participation of small and medium-size enterprises in public works programs, often using labor-intensive techniques. Roads, particularly rural roads, are an important part of

their work. There are now 19 such agencies in 17 countries, mostly in francophone West Africa. The international association AFRICATIP (Association Africaine des Agences d'Exécution des Travaux d'Intérêt Public) develops and shares best practices among its members.

The agencies play three roles: (a) competent technical agencies using private sector recruitment and payment procedures, (b) managers of special funds, and (c) directors of the planning and programming of the investments of local authorities. They also provide technical manuals and contractor training. Although originally established to facilitate donor financing, they now handle mostly national funds and have become instruments for indigenous business development.

Source: Diou, Henry, and Demy 2007.

Road Expenditures—More Maintenance, Less Rehabilitation

On average, countries spend $9,000 a kilometer for main road networks in Sub-Saharan Africa, just below 2 percent of GDP, compared with 1 percent in typical industrial countries and 2–3 percent in fast-growing emerging economies (figure 10.2). Although the effort is high relative to the size of Africa's economies, it remains low in absolute terms, with low-income countries spending no more than $7 per capita a year. For the main road network, maintenance spending ranges from barely $200 per kilometer in Chad to more than $6,000 per kilometer in Zambia. Maintenance spending per kilometer of the main network tends to be about twice that of the rural network.

Paradoxically, low-income countries spend 50 percent more per kilometer overall than do middle-income countries, while countries with road agencies and high fuel levies seem to spend somewhat less than those without. The explanation is a pronounced capital bias

in road spending, with investment accounting for two-thirds of total spending in the resource-rich and low-income countries, particularly those without adequate institutional mechanisms for funding road maintenance. Middle-income countries and those with high fuel levies tend to spend *more* on maintenance *without* incurring higher road expenditure overall. This finding clearly shows that timely attention to maintenance reduces the expenditure needed to sustain the road system in the long term (Harral and Faiz 1988). Aid has partly fueled this capital bias. For example, aid financing covers just over 50 percent of road investment in Senegal and almost 90 percent in Rwanda.

The capital bias would be even more pronounced if capital budgets were fully executed. On average, countries have budgeted 50 percent more on road investment than they spend during a given budget cycle. This underspending produces a capital budget execution ratio averaging about 70 percent. Deficiencies in project planning and delays in procurement processes

Figure 10.2 Average Annual Spending on Road Transport, by Country, 2001–05

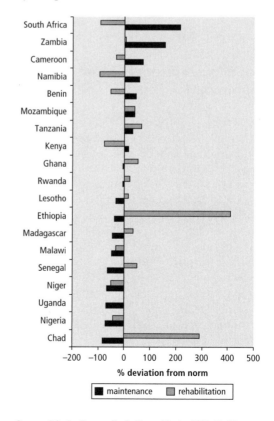

Source: Briceño-Garmendia, Smits, and Foster 2008.

are the main culprits. Middle-income countries and those with road funds and fuel levies fare best in executing their capital budgets.

High capital spending may be justified by large rehabilitation backlogs. Except for Chad and Ethiopia, capital spending for many sampled countries indeed falls well below or is close to what is needed to clear rehabilitation backlogs within (a reasonable) five years. However, such high levels of spending on rehabilitation make sense only when a broader policy is in place to ensure proper maintenance of these roads after they have undergone rehabilitation. In practice, half of the countries sampled are not devoting adequate resources to maintain the main road network, and about half of this subset is not even spending enough for routine maintenance (figure 10.3). In Chad, Niger, Nigeria, Senegal, and Uganda, maintenance spending is less than half the norm.

Unit costs of road construction have recently escalated, with cost overruns on multilateral agency projects rising from 30 percent in 2005 to more than 60 percent in 2007, threatening to dilute further the adequacy of current budget allocations. Inflation has been substantial for the basket of road construction inputs linked to oil prices, but it does not tell the whole story. The lack of effective competition for civil works contracts, with a small number of bidders and

Figure 10.3 Rehabilitation and Maintenance Spending Relative to Norms

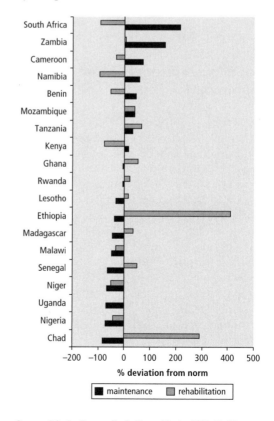

Sources: Briceño-Garmendia, Smits, and Foster 2008; Gwilliam and others 2008.

wide price spreads across bids, looks to be the main culprit (Van Zyl, Coetzer, and Lombard 2008). Substantial delays in project implementation also add to the costs.

These higher costs double the importance of ensuring that engineering standards are the most cost-effective possible. Network analysis reveals that on average, about 30 percent of main road networks are overengineered relative to observed traffic volumes, and only 10 percent are underengineered. Particularly where rapidly expanding the extent of the passable road network is desirable, as in the Democratic Republic of Congo, adopting lower standards may be sensible, upgrading only when traffic growth or local bottlenecks make it necessary. About 15 percent of rural networks are underengineered. Greater efforts are needed to adapt road design standards to local conditions and materials to avoid excessive costs in road construction, particularly for low-volume sealed roads.

Road Conditions—Reflecting Quality of Sector Governance

About half of the main network is in good condition, and an additional one-third is in fair condition—whereas only one-quarter of the rural network is in good condition and a further one-quarter in fair condition (figure 10.4).

The large variation in road quality reflects several interacting factors. First is affordability. GDP per capita is most strongly correlated with the percentage of the main road network in good condition, suggesting that richer countries tend to spend more on maintenance. However, no such clear relationship exists for rural roads. Second are some fundamental topographic and climatic influences. Mountainous and wet countries generally have poorer conditions, in both main and rural networks, associated with climate rather than traffic.

Even controlling for income and climate, however, substantial variation still exists in observed road quality across countries, varying with the quality of their road sector institutions and financing framework. Countries with both road funds and road agencies show

substantially better road conditions than do those that lack either. Moreover, both the road fund design and the level of the fuel levy appear to significantly affect the quality of the main road network, although again the effect on rural road quality is much less pronounced. The main exception, South Africa, has very good primary roads without a conventional second-generation road fund, but it does have a very effective road agency and consistent government commitment to finance road maintenance adequately.

Surprisingly little variation exists in the road network's asset value as a percentage of its potential value if it all were in good condition. All countries realize at least 70 percent of this potential, suggesting that maintenance efforts are fairly well concentrated on preserving the high-value paved-road network. Moreover, the limited time series available suggests that most countries have improved the quality of their roads in recent years.

Good governance is thus critical for safeguarding road quality through good budget finance and a professionally competent public sector implementation agency. Countries with road funds and high fuel levies are substantially more successful at raising finance that translates into higher road maintenance expenditures. Countries with road funds and quasi-independent road agencies show substantially higher quality on main road networks.

Infrastructure Spending Needs—an Average of 1.5 Percent of GDP a Year

A modest set of connectivity objectives might include the following: (a) connecting large cities and international frontiers with a good-quality, two-lane paved road; (b) connecting intermediate cities and the provincial capital with a good-quality, one-lane paved road; (c) increasing to 100 percent the proportion of the rural population living within 2 kilometers of an all-season road in the agricultural areas comprising the 80 percent highest production value within each country; and (d) putting the urban population within 500 meters of a road supporting all-season bus access.

Figure 10.4 Distribution of Road Network Length across Condition Classes, by Country

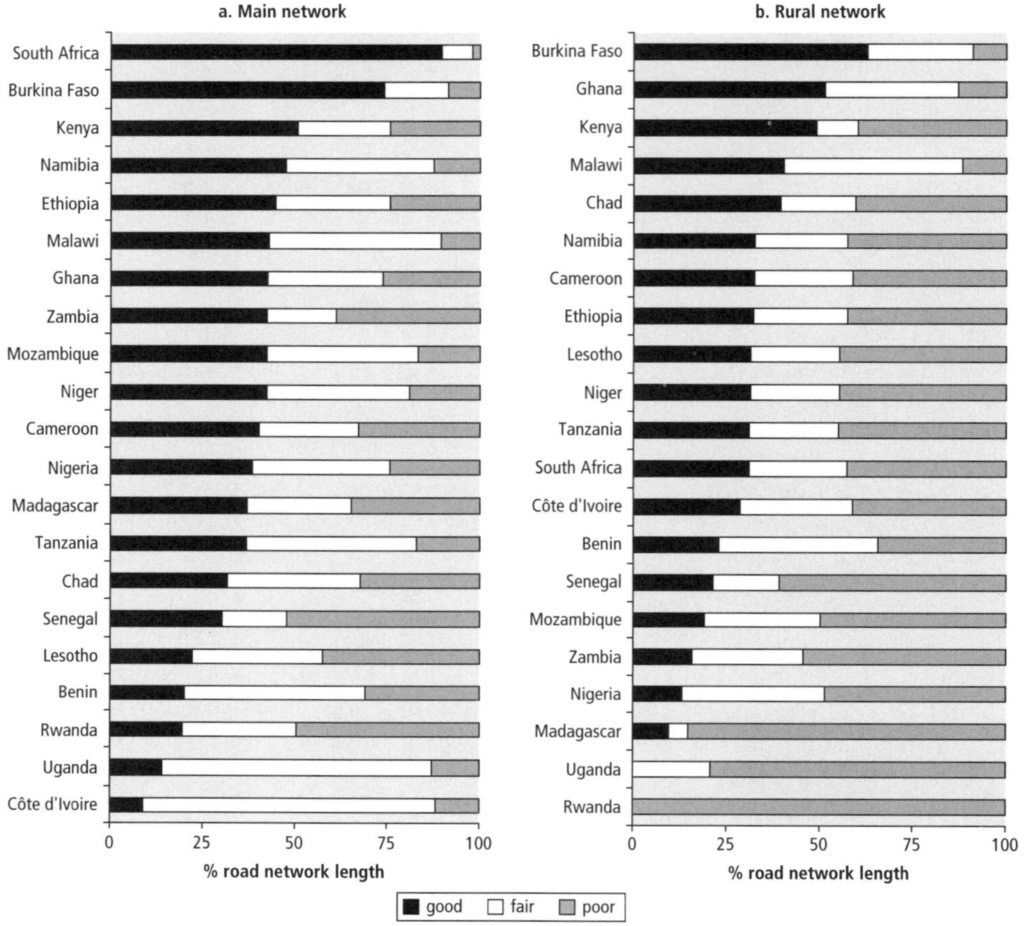

a. Main network

b. Rural network

% road network length

% road network length

■ good   □ fair   ▨ poor

Source: Gwilliam and others 2008.

On the basis of this package, spending needs for the road sector amount to $9.6 billion a year, skewed toward capital expenditure (table 10.2). Because of their mature road network, the middle-income countries account for little more than 10 percent of this total. Except in middle-income countries, about two-thirds of spending requirements relate to capital expenditure, with the remainder attributable to operation and maintenance. Thus, overall, the region needs to spend 1.5 percent of GDP on roads, of which 0.6 percent of GDP is needed for road maintenance. However, the burden for low-income fragile states is very high—in excess of 7 percent of GDP.

Existing spending on the sector amounts to $6.9 billion a year, significantly less than what is needed (table 10.3). Spending in the fragile states is particularly low, barely one-tenth of what is required. The public sector finances two-thirds of road sector spending and more than one-half of road sector investment. In the low-income countries—whether fragile or not—about half of road sector expenditure is donor financed. The contribution of the private sector to road finance in Africa is almost negligible. Financiers from outside the Organisation for Economic Co-operation and Development are not making a major contribution to this sector.

Implementation of efficiency-oriented reforms could raise a total of $3.8 billion a year,

Table 10.2 Road Sector Spending Needs

Country type	$ billions annually			Percentage of GDP		
	Capital expenditure	Operation and maintenance	Total spending	Capital expenditure	Operation and maintenance	Total spending
Sub-Saharan Africa	5.98	3.65	9.63	0.93	0.57	1.50
Middle income	0.40	0.46	0.86	0.15	0.17	0.32
Low income, fragile	1.89	0.83	2.72	4.92	2.15	7.07
Low income, nonfragile	1.84	1.23	3.07	1.67	1.11	2.78
Resource rich	1.86	1.14	3.00	0.84	0.51	1.35

Source: Carruthers, Krishnamani, and Murray 2008.
Note: Totals may not add exactly because of rounding errors.

Table 10.3 Financing Flows to the Road Sector
$ billions annually

Country type	Operation and maintenance Public sector	Capital spending					Total spending
		Public sector	ODA	Non-OECD financiers	PPI	Total	
Sub-Saharan Africa	1.45	3.22	1.80	0.37	0.05	5.44	6.88
Middle income	0.41	1.21	0.09	0.02	0.05	1.37	1.77
Low income, fragile	0.06	0.19	0.23	0.03	0	0.45	0.50
Low income, nonfragile	0.61	0.58	1.24	0.14	0	1.96	2.57
Resource rich	0.31	1.29	0.23	0.17	0	1.69	2.01

Source: Briceño-Garmendia, Smits, and Foster 2008.
Note: Operation and maintenance includes other current expenditures. ODA = official development assistance; OECD = Organisation for Economic Co-operation and Development; PPI = private participation in infrastructure. Totals may not add exactly because of rounding errors.

largely eliminating the funding gap, except in fragile states. The greatest scope for efficiency gains lies in practicing sound preventive maintenance, which in the medium term would substantially reduce the investments needed to clear the rehabilitation backlog, saving an estimated $1.9 billion per year. Low ratios of capital budget execution are also holding back public investment in roads. Addressing this issue would capture a further $1.3 billion annually. Finally, some countries face difficulties in collecting revenues owed to their road funds; solving this problem would capture another $0.6 billion a year of resources.

Transport Services—the Forgotten Problem

Road sector interventions have traditionally focused on constructing and improving the

"hard" infrastructure. However, what ultimately matters from an economic perspective is the extent to which roads support efficient, reliable, and safe transport services for various kinds of freight, as well as for urban and rural populations. Although the private sector typically provides these services, the government has a critical role to play as regulator and facilitator of service provision. These "soft" transport issues deserve more attention.

Road Freight

The regulation and market structures of the road freight industry, rather than the quality of the road infrastructure, are the binding constraints on performance in the international corridors (Teravaninthorn and Raballand 2008). Although the associated road infrastructure is generally in good condition, the administrative bottlenecks at borders and ports keep the effective velocity of transit along these routes very low (typically less than 10 kilometers an hour). Even for national traffic, the exceptionally high road freight tariffs in parts of Africa—reaching $0.13 per tonne-kilometer in Central Africa—are attributable more to high profit margins (60–160 percent) than to any inherent cost disadvantage (table 10.4).

Marked performance differences occur across subregions. Performance is worst in Central and West Africa and best in southern Africa, with East Africa in between. The difference can be explained by industry cartels in Central and West Africa, together with the *tour de role* regulatory framework. That framework is based on market sharing and centralized allocation of freight that limits vehicle mileage and undermines incentives for improving fleet quality. In southern Africa, by contrast, a much larger share of freight traffic is allocated through competitive bilateral contracts between clients and shippers.

Rural Road Transport

Most rural transport takes place near villages. Trips generally involve short distances and small loads carried on paths, typically for marketing, collecting water and firewood, and tending crops and animals. Most trips are walking trips. Nonmotorized transport, such as a bicycle, is often unaffordable, and where mechanical transport is available to the household, it tends to be appropriated by a male household head. Changing this practice may be a demanding cultural task; in some parts of Africa, women's use of bicycles may be considered unseemly. Nevertheless, when enough women begin to use them and the benefits to the whole household become apparent, the practice may rapidly gain social acceptance, as it has in parts of Burkina Faso.

Out-of-village travel by motorized transport, from villages to market towns and from towns to cities, is less common. Supply is typically fragmented and informal, and rural communities are often captive markets for local monopolists.

Urban Road Transport

Buses are the common mode of public transit in most cities (Kumar and Barrett 2007). Except in a handful of cases, however, minibuses are much more prevalent than large buses. About twice as many trips are taken by minibuses and shared taxis than by large buses. The use of motorcycles for commercial transport has also grown very rapidly in recent years, mainly because of the poor state of the roads and the inability of bus companies to meet growing demand. Small-scale suburban rail networks exist in a few cities, but nowhere do they account for more than 2 percent of the market.

Supply is inadequate and tariffs are high. Most African cities have 30–60 public transport vehicle seats per 1,000 residents, but only 6 large bus seats per 1,000 residents (compared with 30–40 in middle-income countries). Low fleet capacity is exacerbated by poor use of the limited vehicle fleet, with vehicles achieving fewer than 200 kilometers a day. The quality of public transport is consequently poor, with long walking and waiting times typically doubling the in-vehicle time. Extreme overcrowding is also common, particularly on large buses. The average cost of a one-way trip, at about $0.30, is high in relation to household budgets. Regulations that keep fares for large buses below those of minibuses and inappropriate cost benchmarks have contributed to the demise of large buses.

Table 10.4 Overview of Key Road Freight Parameters on Main International Corridors

Corridor	Roads in good condition (%)	Trade density ($ millions per kilometer)	Implicit velocity (kilometers per hour)	Freight tariff ($ millions per tonne-kilometer)	Profit margins (%)
Western	72	8.2	6.0	0.08	80
Central	49	4.2	6.1	0.13	70–160
Eastern	82	5.7	8.1	0.07	70–90
Southern	100	27.9	11.6	0.05	20–60

Source: Teravaninthorn and Raballand 2008.

Minibus ownership is generally highly fragmented, with most individual entrepreneurs owning no more than one or two vehicles, generally rented out to drivers. Powerful unions, associations, or syndicates that organize the sector and provide a degree of self-regulation, typically based on equitable sharing of the market in the *tour de role* system, offset the highly fragmented ownership. This approach contributes significantly to poor vehicle use and to long walking times and waiting times at terminals.

Although not confined to the urban transport situation, road safety is also a very serious issue in most African countries. In the early 2000s, nearly 3,000 people were killed on Kenyan roads annually, about 68 deaths per 1,000 registered vehicles, 30 to 40 times the rate in highly motorized countries. Traffic accidents are the third-leading cause of death after malaria and HIV/AIDS, presenting major public health problems in disability and health care costs.

Moving Forward—Broadening the Reform Agenda

The institutional reform agenda needs to be completed and broadened to encompass the demands of urban and rural connectivity. This connectivity is not just about physical infrastructure; it is also about the regulatory framework governing transport services. The recent (and likely continuing) escalation of unit road costs will strain already stretched transport budgets. Road safety also remains a concern. To deliver on these challenges will require continuing emphasis on creating efficient agency structures to manage road programs and strengthen government capabilities for oversight. The agenda comprises the following:

- Completing institutional reforms
- Increasing rural accessibility
- Developing urban transport services
- Liberalizing road freight transport
- Dealing with escalating unit costs
- Improving road safety.

Completing the Institutional Reforms

Countries with road funds are more successful in safeguarding road maintenance expenditures and spending on segments that maximize network value, while those that also have road agencies see greater funding going to better road quality. Although sector reforms are widespread, closer inspection reveals that the quality and depth of those reforms are quite variable across countries.

Road funds need to be designed in line with accepted good-practice criteria. Key areas of deficiency include (a) a lack of user representation on road fund boards, (b) the absence of direct transfer mechanisms to ensure that fuel levy revenues go directly to the fund (circumventing national budgets), (c) a strong legal foundation for road funds to safeguard their autonomy, (d) clear allocation rules for road fund revenues, and (e) a lack of systematic economic analysis guiding resource allocation. Some evidence indicates that the benefits of road funds are larger where countries adopt the full set of good-practice design criteria.

Fuel levies need to be set at an adequate level and supported by an effective revenue collection mechanism. Although many countries have fuel levies, only a subset is high enough (over $0.10 a liter) to generate revenues commensurate with road maintenance requirements. Even where levies are right, difficulties in revenue collection can prevent their full capture. Effective administration is thus equally important.

Efficient road implementation agencies are a necessary complement to road funds, ensuring that resources are well spent; however, quasi-autonomous road agencies are not yet as widespread as road funds. Moreover, many of them fall short of good practice, particularly in autonomy and user representation on boards. A key element for their success appears to be the adoption of performance-based maintenance contracts, which are still less developed in Africa than in other regions.

Although agencies can overcome constraints of public sector salaries and processes, government structures must still carry out key functions: (a) determining road standards, (b) carrying out road classifications, and (c) setting long-range planning goals. Governments will continue to formulate transport policy and to regulate and oversee the new road institutions. If they do not perform these functions effectively, the new institutions are bound to suffer. For example, road funds will not get the revenue increases they need, and road agencies will be unable to deliver realistic network improvement programs.

Increasing Rural Accessibility

Providing full road accessibility to 100 percent of Africa's rural inhabitants would entail a vast expansion in the all-season road network, virtually tripling its length. For many countries, this goal is unlikely to be affordable in the medium term, highlighting the need to carefully select and prioritize rural road investments. One way of doing so is to strategically align rural road investments with agricultural development programs at the national level, to prioritize those rural roads likely to have the largest effect on agricultural productivity and market access. Recent analysis of Central Africa suggests that the most attractive rural road investments may lie in areas that are at some distance from major urban markets but still within reasonable reach, because in these cases, rural road investments may be the critical intervention needed to open up market accessibility (Briceño-Garmendia and others 2009a, 2009b). By contrast, road investments in very isolated rural areas may be less attractive because they would not make enough of a difference in overall travel times to provide adequate market access.

Given the vast scale of Africa's potential rural road network, the issue of keeping down unit costs becomes particularly critical. Policy makers face a stark trade-off between the standard to which rural roads are built and the length of the rural network that can be developed for any given budget envelope. This choice raises questions about what kind of rural roads farmers really need. In many rural communities, volumes of production may be well below the threshold needed to justify the use of a truck to collect produce, and simpler roads targeted more at ensuring accessibility for two-wheeled vehicles or animal-drawn carts may be more suitable (Raballand and others 2009). In other settings, ensuring all-season accessibility may

be achievable simply through spot improvements at vulnerable points (such as creeks and riverbeds) without the need to upgrade the surface of the road along its entire length.

Whatever the chosen objective for rural road development, financing will likely remain a challenge. Local governments mobilize only modest revenues of their own, with market and business taxes as the main sources. Intergovernmental transfers are thus the main source of domestic funding for local government spending in many countries. This situation poses three main problems. First, throughout most of Sub-Saharan Africa, less than 5 percent of aggregate public revenue is generally made available to local governments managing rural networks. Second, general budgets rarely allocate adequate funds for maintaining main roads, much less rural roads. Third, capital and recurrent allocations to local governments are usually not fungible, and the allocation for recurrent expenditures may barely cover the salaries of the rural road unit. Moreover, the budget cycle dictates such transfers, so that central-to-local transfers are unlikely to be adequate and timely for maintaining local government roads.

Adequate, steady funding for local government maintenance is more likely to be forthcoming from a dedicated road fund, as long as some formal commitment exists in the road fund law to ensure that it accepts responsibility and provides for local roads. Although 60 percent of road fund revenues is typically allocated to the main interurban road network, countries have, to varying degrees, channeled portions to the maintenance of rural road networks. This approach appears to be effective. Countries that allocate at least $0.015 of their fuel duties to rural roads have 36 percent of their rural networks in good condition, compared with 21 percent for those that do not.

Building full capacity for all management functions in each local government and community is unrealistic and inefficient. Individual local government networks are small, and the management contract for an individual local government may be too modest to attract competent consulting firms. In Madagascar, the average network for a local government is 140 kilometers; in Cameroon and Nigeria, it is 180 kilometers; and in Tanzania and Zambia, it is 280 kilometers. All fall far short of the 500–2,000 kilometers needed to justify employing an engineer in a local unit. Joint service committees of local authorities can achieve economies of scale in procurement for the authorities they represent, but they usually require substantial technical assistance from central ministries or from the regional offices of a main road authority. In countries with an autonomous road authority responsible for main roads, local governments can contract with the road authority to manage the roads on their behalf or to assist with planning and procurement.

Some countries centralize the technical responsibility for rural roads. Relying on a road ministry or another central ministry to manage rural roads has the advantage of a formal channel for technical support. However, the disadvantage is that the ministry often operates completely independently of the local government structure and thus is poorly connected to local needs and developments. In principle, a central coordinating unit for local government roads should perform as well as a central government rural roads department. In practice, however, coordinating units for local government roads are not always as strong as they need to be, as is illustrated by the experience of Tanzania and Zambia in the late 1990s.

Delegation of planning, procurement, and management has already been improved in many countries through the establishment of AGETIPs, and the national institutions have benefited from their association in AFRICA-TIP and from donor assistance. Considerable room for improvement exists in the work of the AGETIPs, however, particularly with respect to their technical capacity, the quality of preparatory studies and contract supervision, and delays in project implementation (Diou, Henry, and Demy 2007).

The options are not mutually exclusive. For example, a joint services committee can use private consultants, hired through a contract management agency. The best option for managing local roads depends on many local factors, including the size of the authorities, the nature of the network, and the competence of the private sector or higher public authority units.

Community infrastructure, including mainly unclassified roads and paths for which no level of the formal government accepts responsibility, faces particular problems. Community contributions in cash and kind are suitable primarily for community roads and paths, but in-kind contributions may be inefficient, and other sources of money are necessary. Cost sharing between local communities and other government or external agencies can help raise the volume of resources mobilized and thereby increase the proportion of the network that receives regular maintenance. Well-structured donor financing through rural road projects or through social and community or rural infrastructure funds can support investment in community infrastructure. Cost sharing may also be effective in maintaining community roads. Many local authorities in Africa have more roads to maintain than they can afford, so cost sharing with communities has merit.

Lack of technical know-how often impedes community management. Communities in Sub-Saharan Africa need technical advice (on road design and standards, appropriate materials, work planning) and managerial advice (on financial accounting, contract management, procurement) to perform the responsibilities that come with ownership.

For rural transport services, the main issues are increasing service quantity and keeping services affordable. The priority in transport services in rural areas must be to maintain basic year-round vehicle access for the types of vehicles likely to be operating. The quantity of access is even more important than the quality. Better rural telecommunications can provide the means of more effectively matching vehicles to loads. Given the monopoly power of service providers, communities can organize to increase their bargaining power through a collective lobby. Operating subsidies are usually infeasible, but providing credit for vehicle purchases, possibly through piggybacking on agricultural credit programs, is an option.

Developing Urban Transport Services

Urban public transport requires simultaneous and integrated attention to planning urban structures, building and maintaining infrastructure, and organizing transport services. In practice, these three primary functions are seldom housed in the same institution, and even where they remain with the central government, several ministries are usually involved. Only a handful of African cities have agencies with metropolitan responsibilities and overarching functions, and even those agencies lack the executive powers to implement their vision and must work through other units of government.

The institutional arrangements for urban roads are frequently complex. Legislation pertaining to roads is usually separate from that governing transport services, and several national and local bodies often share jurisdiction. In Conakry, Guinea, several institutions are responsible for segments of the road network. In Accra, Ghana, responsibility for urban transport has been devolved from central to local government—at least in principle. However, local governments have neither the resources nor the technical know-how to carry out their assigned functions, so the ministry of transportation (through the department of urban roads) is effectively responsible for road maintenance and development.

In the passenger transportation market, the self-regulation of operators associations and cartels has ossified fragmentation of informal operations and wasteful institutionalized procedures. Supply is inadequate and expensive. Two main options exist to remedy this situation: small and medium-size vehicles and, in the largest cities, light rail.

In principle, traditional, disciplined large-vehicle services could be reintroduced, but such attempts—in Dakar (Senegal), Accra, and other cities—have failed. The association of large vehicles with traditional large public monopoly companies made them vulnerable to political intervention and to the failures in cost control that destroyed them in the first place. Moreover, although subsidies may be required to sustain service levels and fare aspirations, open-ended subsidies of a public operator will almost certainly pass the benefit of subsidies to managers and employees rather than to passengers.

For some time, the small and medium-size vehicles must be part of the structure, not least because few governments have the fiscal

resources to reestablish a large-bus sector while the private sector remains wary of investing in large vehicles. The short-term options are thus to rely on self-regulation of the sector, which has usually failed, or to devise competitive structures, either "for" or "in" the market to build private confidence in a managed private market. Attempts can also be made to stimulate increased vehicle size, as in South Africa. This sort of strategy has achieved limited success in some central Asian countries.

In the very largest cities, exclusive road-based track systems, such as bus rapid transit or (more costly) light rail, may have a role. Such developments are being considered in Dar es Salaam in Tanzania and Lagos in Nigeria, but they are still experimental.

Liberalizing Road Freight Transport

Freight tariffs in much of Africa are unnecessarily high because of restrictive regulation and weak competition among truckers. The most damaging aspect of trucking organization is the combination of self-regulation with national protection. Both militate for the interests of the incumbent national operators at the expense of their customers. They create scope for corruption while leaving socially costly problems (vehicle overloading) relatively untouched. Both areas offer alternatives.

Self-regulation is a means of maintaining on-the-road discipline in an excessively fragmented market. It fills a vacuum created by the absence of effective public regulation. By its nature, it concentrates on ensuring an equitable distribution of traffic between members of the association, typically through the wasteful operating procedure of *tour de role* dispatching. The alternative is a combination of freedom of entry and market pricing, with independent enforcement of rules on quality and operating behavior, as in efficient road-haulage markets in Europe and the United States.

National protection appears to secure a "fair" share of traffic for the haulers of each of the national partners in a transit market. It operates through quotas that reduce the use of vehicles and thus increase the costs. It is often supported by enforcing regulated rates, which deny the shipper the opportunity to shop around for a better deal. The alternative is to combine free entry to the market with rigorous enforcement of national safety and operational behavior rules in all countries. Regulatory systems would combine strict quality control with liberal approaches to pricing and market entry. Moving in this direction would include developing internationally agreed strategies to improve the range of elements on the main transit corridors and to strengthen enforcement on overloading.

Breaking the regulatory status quo in Central and West Africa is difficult because of a coalition of interest groups opposing change. Truckers have strong leverage on high-level authorities because they have enough monopoly power to block trade. Governance issues also intrude because some high-level authorities own or indirectly control trucks or trucking companies and thus benefit from the status quo and current market-sharing schemes.

Deregulating the trucking industry in Central and West Africa is thus more of a political and social challenge than a technical one. The main concern is the potential reduction in the number of trucks to match demand in road transport. That reduction could lead to a drop in trucking employment and profits, because some companies (or owner-operators) would disappear and others would shrink, and these social effects would need to be mitigated. Some chance exists that the coalition of interest groups opposing change in the transport market in most countries in Central and West Africa might not resist reforms if compensation schemes pay, at least partly, for the social costs.

The southern African international transport market is a good model for the rest of the continent because it combines liberalizing entry with enforcing quality and load-control rules applicable to all operators. Operations to and from South Africa are governed by bilateral agreements that provide for sharing information on traffic development and define the types of permits that can be issued. This system restricts the carriage of bilateral trade to operators from the two countries concerned and prohibits cabotage.[2] It does not establish quotas, however, and it allows rates to be determined by the market to enable direct contracting between shippers and transporters and giving incentives to efficient operators.

Dealing with Escalating Unit Costs

The recent escalating costs of roadwork can be attributed to rising input costs against a backdrop of growing demand for contracting, which appears to have been exploited in an environment of generally low competition for contracts. No one solution exists. Inflation in input costs lies beyond the control of policy makers, but they can take other measures.

A key issue is to ensure effective competition for contracts. Road agencies should actively market contracts to obtain a set of good bidders. If at any stage in the bidding a competitive choice set of bidders does not surface (say, at prequalification), something is seriously wrong, and the agency should consider postponing the process until it has identified and corrected the underlying issues. Continuing the bid without a proper choice set in the hope of achieving an acceptable bid price is an unnecessary gamble.

A better understanding of the underlying cost trends and their links to contract pricing is also critical. Although cost inflation lies beyond the control of sector authorities, they can increase the accuracy of the design cost estimates, improve the allowance for cost fluctuations, and monitor cost increases through the procurement period. To this end, agencies need to understand the cost structure underlying road contracts more clearly and to track international price trends for key inputs over time.

The capacity of project-executing agencies also needs to be strengthened to support the timely implementation of contracts. Delays often result from deficiencies in the planning and procurement of sector agencies, making this a third area for attention.

Whatever the improvements to road agency procurement processes, the unit costs of road infrastructure are likely to remain on an upward path, straining already limited sector budgets. Beyond measures to improve procurement, considering how to design roads to keep costs down is important. Overengineering of roads—beyond the surface type needed for the anticipated traffic volume—is an issue in parts of Africa and represents a waste of resources that should be avoided. Careful economic analysis of road investments can avoid the overengineering of networks observed in some countries. In addition, experimentation with innovative technologies that keep costs down, for example, by making greater use of locally available materials, deserves consideration.

Improving Road Safety

Governments recognize the seriousness of the road safety problem. The February 2007 Pan-African Road Safety Conference, held in Accra, Ghana, resolved to set road safety as a national health and transport priority. Areas for funding include (a) strengthening prehospital emergency services; (b) mainstreaming safety design issues in road investment programs; (c) collecting reliable road accident statistics; and (d) enacting national legislation to deal with speeding, driving unroadworthy vehicles, failing to use safety helmets, using mobile phones when driving, and driving under the influence of alcohol.

For institutional arrangements, the choice lies between establishing a special agency and broadly injecting safety skills and procedures (such as safety audits on projects and policies) in all relevant agencies. Involving transport, education, and health agencies is a minimum, which probably requires at least a national coordination agency, such as the National Transport Safety Committee in Ghana. To have authority, the agency needs to be directly responsible to the chief minister or the cabinet. The urban equivalent would be a special unit in the mayor's office.

For program composition, the choice lies between a sequence of consistent measures and a comprehensive "big bang" approach. Evidence from various parts of the world suggests that the greatest success is through concentrated, multidimensional programs of action. For example, Japan turned a situation from disastrous to exemplary over a fairly short period by combining more stringent rules on vehicle condition, speeding, and drunk driving with very high-profile publicity campaigns and strict enforcement by traffic police. One of the most successful initiatives in Africa has been the comprehensive program introduced in the Richards Bay area of KwaZulu-Natal, based on a model already introduced in Victoria, Australia.

Above all, enforcement will have to be drastically improved. Eliminating corruption in licensing, enforcing on-road behavior, and inspecting and controlling vehicle conditions are essential. Using technology to eliminate arbitrariness in implementation, together with carefully designed market incentives, has worked well in privatizing vehicle inspections in Mexico.

Notes

The authors of this chapter are Kenneth Gwilliam, Kavita Sethi, Alberto Nogales, and Vivien Foster, who drew on background material and contributions from Rodrigo Archondo-Callao, Fanny Barrett, Cecilia Briceño-Garmendia, Robin Carruthers, Arnaud Desmarchelier, Ranga Krishnamani, Ajay Kumar, Gael Raballand, Karlis Smits, and Supee Teravaninthorn.

1. These networks typically comprise a centrally administered primary network plus secondary networks, but in Malawi, Nigeria, South Africa, and Uganda, only the primary network is centrally administered and included here.

2. *Cabotage* is the provision of transport within a country by a foreign operator.

References

Briceño-Garmendia, Cecilia, Vivien Foster, Hyoung Wang, Alvaro Federico Barra, and Ranga Rajan Krishnamani. 2009a. "Prioritizing Infrastructure Investments in the Democratic Republic of Congo: A Spatial Approach." Report, Sustainable Development Department, Africa Region, World Bank, Washington, DC.

————. 2009b. "Prioritizing Infrastructure Investments in the Republic of Congo: A Spatial Approach." Report, Sustainable Development Department, Africa Region, World Bank, Washington, DC.

Briceño-Garmendia, Cecilia, Karlis Smits, and Vivien Foster. 2008. "Financing Public Infrastructure in Sub-Saharan Africa: Patterns, Issues, and Options." Background Paper 15, Africa Infrastructure Country Diagnostic, World Bank, Washington, DC.

Carruthers, Robin, Ranga R. Krishnamani, and Siobhan Murray. 2008. "Improving Connectivity: Investing in Transport Infrastructure in Sub-Saharan Africa." Background Paper 7, Africa Infrastructure Country Diagnostic, World Bank, Washington, DC.

Diou, Christian, Michel Henry, and Babaly Deme. 2007. *La Délégation de Maîtrise d'Ouvrage en Afrique en 2007.* Republic of Senegal,

Public-Private Infrastructure Advisory Facility, and AFRICATIP. http://www.africatip.net/fr/publications/downloads/2008-11-11%2006:28:29/Rapport_AGETIP_MOD_vfinale.pdf.

Gwilliam, Ken, Vivien Foster, Rodrigo Archondo-Callao, Cecilia Briceño-Garmendia, Alberto Nogales, and Kavita Sethi. 2008. "The Burden of Maintenance: Roads in Sub-Saharan Africa." Background Paper 14, Africa Infrastructure Country Diagnostic, World Bank, Washington, DC.

Harral, Clell, and Asif Faiz. 1988. *Road Deterioration in Developing Countries.* Washington, DC: World Bank.

Kumar, Ajay, and Fanny Barrett. 2007. "Stuck in Traffic: Urban Transport in Africa." Background Paper 1, Africa Infrastructure Country Diagnostic, World Bank, Washington, DC.

Raballand, Gaël, Somik Lall, Arnaud Desmarchelier, and Patricia Macchi. 2009. "Economic Geography and Aid Effectiveness in Transport in Sub-Saharan Africa." Report, Transport Department, Africa Region, World Bank, Washington, DC.

Stankevich, Natalya, Navaid Qureshi, and Cesar Queiroz. 2005. "Performance-Based Contracting for Preservation and Improvement of Road Assets." Transport Note TN-27, World Bank, Washington, DC.

Starkey, Paul, John Hine, Simon Ellis, and Anna Terrell. 2002. "Improving Rural Mobility: Options for Developing Motorized and Non-Motorized Transport in Rural Areas." Technical Paper 525, World Bank, Washington, DC.

Teravaninthorn, Supee, and Gael Raballand. 2008. "Transport Prices and Costs in Africa: A Review of the Main International Corridors." Working Paper 14, Africa Infrastructure Country Diagnostic, World Bank, Washington, DC.

Van Zyl, Willem, Lynette Coetzer, and Chris Lombard. 2008. "Unit Costs of Infrastructure Projects in Sub-Saharan Africa." Background Paper 11, Africa Infrastructure Country Diagnostic, World Bank, Washington, DC.

World Bank. 2007. "Road Maintenance Initiative Matrix." Sub-Saharan Africa Transport Program, World Bank, Washington, DC.

Chapter 11

Railways: Looking for Traffic

African railroads have changed greatly in the past 30 years. Back in the 1980s, many railway systems carried a large share of their country's traffic because road transport was poor or faced restrictive regulations, and rail customers were established businesses locked into rail either through physical connections or (if they were parastatals) through policies requiring them to use a fellow parastatal. Since then, most national economies and national railways have been liberalized. Coupled with the general improvement in road infrastructure, liberalization has led to strong intermodal competition. Today, few railways outside South Africa, other than dedicated mineral lines, are essential to the functioning of the economy.

Rail networks in Africa are disconnected, and many are in poor condition. Although an extensive system based in southern Africa reaches as far as the Democratic Republic of Congo and East Africa, most other railways are disconnected lines reaching inland from the ports, serving small markets by modern railway standards. Most were built relatively lightly, and few, other than Spoornet in South Africa, have invested in rehabilitating and renewing infrastructure and rolling

stock. Moreover, various conflicts and wars have rendered several rail sections unusable. As a result, some networks have closed and many others are in relatively poor condition, with investment backlogs stretching back over many years.

Few railways are able to generate significant funds for investment. Other than for purely mineral lines, investment has usually come from bilateral and multilateral donors. Almost all remaining passenger services fail to cover their costs, and freight service tariffs are constrained by road competition. Moreover, as long as the railways are government operated, bureaucratic constraints and lack of commercial incentives will prevent them from competing successfully. Since 1993, several governments in Africa have responded by concessioning their systems, often accompanied by a rehabilitation program funded by international financial institutions.

For the most part, concessions have improved operational performance. Although results have been mixed, many concessionaires have increased traffic volumes and have generally performed more efficiently, and there has been little evidence of monopolistic behavior. Relations with governments have often been uneasy, however, especially concerning adequate compensation for loss-making passenger service obligations, and many governments clearly had unrealistic expectations about the private sector's ability to improve operations and generate investment.

Concessionaires appear willing to spend their own funds only on day-to-day maintenance, not on infrastructure. Financing asset renewal and upgrading remains an open question for most of the African rail network. Without infrastructure investments, the competition from road networks will thwart railway survival except to carry large-scale mineral traffic. Although concessioning has generally improved service and reduced the financial burden on governments, it does not appear to be a full solution to financing the investment needs of African railways.

Africa's Rail Networks

At the end of 2008, 47 railways were operating in 32 countries in Africa. Railway development has followed a similar pattern in almost all African countries. Typically, isolated lines headed inland from a port to reach a trading center or a mine, and over time, a few branch lines were built. Many of the lines were state owned, but some were constructed as concessions or, in the case of some mineral developments, as part of a mining company's operation. Although continental rail master plans have existed for over a century, most of the African network remains disconnected, operating within a single country or linking a port and its immediate regional hinterland. The only significant international network is centered in South Africa and stretches north to Zimbabwe, Zambia, and the Democratic Republic of Congo (figure 11.1). Trade between African countries (other than to and from South Africa) has always been minimal, largely because of the similarity in the products exported, which suggests that interregional links would be lightly used even if they existed.

Low Rail and Traffic Density

African railway networks' spatial density, a metric that compares track mileage with the size of a country, is low (UIC 2008).[1] The highest measurement of spatial density is 16 in South Africa, but most other countries fall in the range of 1 to 6, and 13 countries have no operating railway at all. Too much should not be read into this indicator, however; network density is strongly affected by the pattern of population. Australia, Canada, China, and the Russian Federation, all with vast undeveloped and sparsely populated areas, have densities of between 5 and 7, whereas most European countries range from 20 to 100.

A complementary indicator is the network density per million inhabitants, which is highest in Gabon (520) and Botswana (480), followed by South Africa (460). Most other African countries range from 30 to 50. European countries range from 200 to 1,000, and Australia and Canada exceed 1,500. China is much lower, at 50.

These metrics alone cannot justify network expansion in Africa. To be an economical investment, a new line needs a minimum level of traffic, and the geographical distribution of potential customers within a country and the

Figure 11.1 Map of African Rail Networks

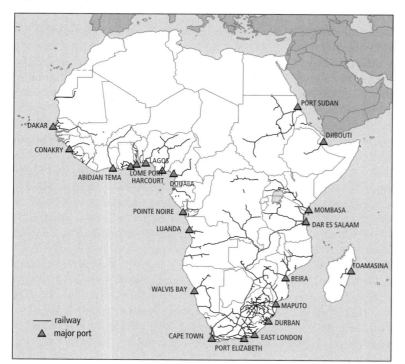

Figure 11.2 Rail Network Size and Traffic by Region

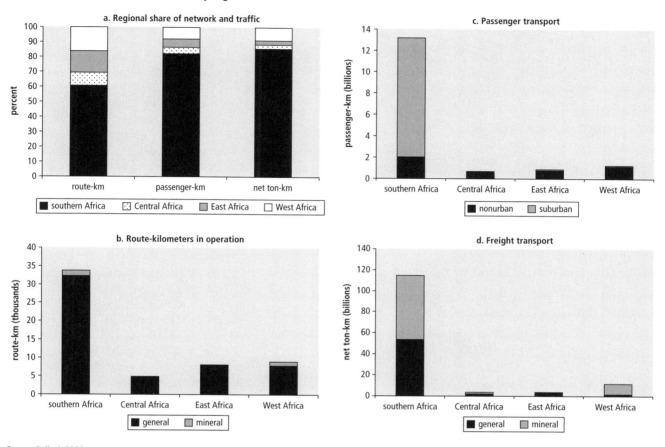

Source: Bullock 2009.
Note: Southern Africa = Angola, Botswana, Madagascar, Malawi, Mozambique, Namibia, South Africa, Swaziland, Zambia, and Zimbabwe; Central Africa = Cameroon, the Democratic Republic of Congo, Gabon, and the Republic of Congo; East Africa = Djibouti, Eritrea, Ethiopia, Kenya, Sudan, Tanzania, and Uganda; West Africa = Benin, Ghana, Guinea, Mali, Mauritania, Nigeria, Senegal, and Togo.

level of usage that can be expected are more important than these national averages.

South Africa has the most important network (figure 11.2). Specialized mineral lines in western and southern Africa carry over half of the region's freight, most of it on the Spoornet coal and ore export lines. Southern Africa dominates general rail freight, handling over 80 percent of the freight traffic on the nonmineral lines. Southern Africa also dominates the passenger business, with over 70 percent of passenger traffic, largely because of its heavy commuter passenger business in cities. Some other African cities also operate commuter services, but with the exception of Dakar, Senegal, they mostly provide one or two trains at peak hours along a short line.

Traffic density on African railways is generally low.[2] The highest average network traffic density outside Spoornet is in Gabon (2.7 million traffic units), with Cameroon and Swaziland having the only other railways over 1 million; many railways average fewer than 300,000 units (figure 11.3). By comparison, the average traffic density of the Maghreb systems (Algeria, Morocco, and Tunisia) is nearly 2 million units, and the Arab Republic of Egypt, with its heavy passenger traffic, exceeds 8 million. Most European systems average 2 million to 5 million, with densities under 1 million found only in Albania and Montenegro. With such light usage, many networks struggle to generate enough funds just to maintain, much less renew, their infrastructure.

Figure 11.3 Average Railway Network Traffic Density, 2001–05

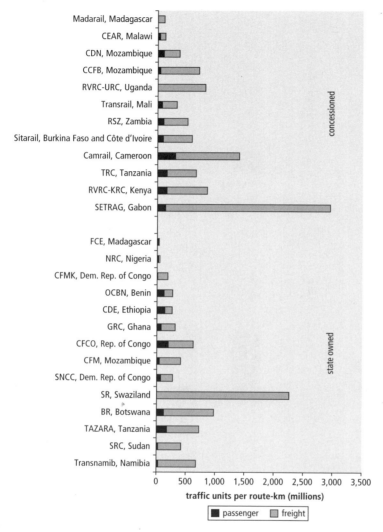

Source: Bullock 2009.
Note: The overall traffic units carried by a railway are the sum of the passenger-kilometers and the net tonne-kilometers of freight carried. This simple standard measure is widely used as a means of aggregating freight and passenger traffic. The relative weighting of passenger and freight is conventionally taken as 1:1. BR = Botswana Railways; Camrail = Cameroon Railway Corporation; CCFB = Companhia dos Caminhos de Ferro da Beira (Mozambique); CDE = Chemin de Fer Djibouto-Ethiopien; CDN = Corredor de Desenvolvimento do Norte (Mozambique); CEAR = Central East African Railways Corporation (Malawi); CFCO = Chemin de Fer Congo-Océan (Republic of Congo); CFMK = Chemin de Fer Matadi-Kinshasa (Democratic Republic of Congo); CFM = Caminhos de Ferro do Mocambique; FCE = Fianarantsoa Côte Est (Madagascar); GRC = Ghana Railways Corporation; NRC = Nigeria Railways Corporation; OCBN = Organisation Commune Bénin-Niger; RSZ = Railway Systems of Zambia Ltd; RVRC-KRC = Rift Valley Rail Corporation-Kenya Railways Corporation; RVRC-URC = Rift Valley Rail Corporation-Uganda Railways Corporation; SETRAG = Société Transgabonnaise (Gabon); SNCC = Société Nationale des Chemins de Fer du Congo (Democratic Republic of Congo); SR = Swaziland Railways; SRC = Sudan Railways Corporation; TAZARA = Tanzania-Zambia Railway; TRC = Tanzania Railways Corporation.

Dilapidated Infrastructure

Most networks outside South Africa still operate with their original facilities. Limited upgrading has occurred, but the lines can still be characterized as relatively low axle-load, low-speed, small-scale, undercapitalized networks ill suited to modern requirements. Many structures and some of the track work are now over 100 years old. Many sections of track have deteriorated almost beyond repair. Although this situation can be tolerated on low-volume feeder lines, and indeed may be the only way some can be viably operated, it is a major handicap when competing against the modern roads being constructed in major corridors.

Most rail systems have considerable sections of track in need of repair or replacement. Some have major sections that are not in operation and will require rehabilitation before operations can resume. Even where service exists, poor track condition forces speed restrictions, resulting in lower railway competitiveness and rolling-stock productivity.

In some countries, parts of the network are not operated because of war damage, natural disaster, or general neglect. Much of the Mozambican central and northern networks and railways in Angola, Côte d'Ivoire, Eritrea, Ethiopia, and the Republic of Congo either have been damaged or have had to suspend operations for as long as 20 years. The total African rail network is about 69,000 kilometers, of which some 55,000 kilometers is currently being operated (see figures 11.1 and 11.2). Almost all the network is single track, except for sections of the Spoornet network. Much of the South African network is electrified, but the only other electrified sections in Sub-Saharan Africa are in the mining region of the Democratic Republic of Congo and a short section in Zimbabwe (the latter is not in use).

Signaling on many networks still relies on manual systems. On lines with low train density, mechanical signals are adequate from a capacity viewpoint, but significant safety problems can result from human error. Where power signaling has been installed, it often does not operate because of short circuits, lack of electrical power, and dilapidated cable networks. Telephone exchanges in many companies are similarly obsolete, with limited capacity and the need for spare parts that are virtually impossible to find.

Most African railways use either the Cape gauge (1.067 meters or 3 feet, 6 inches) or the meter gauge. The main network in southern and central Africa uses the Cape gauge, which is also used in some anglophone countries farther north. The meter gauge is used in most of francophone Africa and much of East Africa. A number of isolated standard-gauge lines are used primarily for mineral traffic, although Nigeria is developing a new standard-gauge network to serve its capital, Abuja. Narrow-gauge lines have operated at various times, but most are now derelict. Apart from the network in East Africa and the one extending north from South Africa, few railways cross international borders. Instead, they reach railheads from which traffic can be carried farther by road.

Despite the multiplicity of gauges, interoperability is not a major problem in Africa. Two gauges exist in the same location in only three places—two in Tanzania and one in Guinea. However, mixed gauges will become a problem if some of the proposed connecting lines are constructed.

In summary, most African railways are confronting major infrastructure problems primarily associated with aging track: insufficient ballast, rail wear, deteriorating earthworks and formation, decrepit structures, and rail signaling and telecommunications with obsolete equipment and lack of spare parts. The cost of rehabilitating the networks is large compared with the existing traffic volumes and revenues. The means by which rehabilitation can be done on a sustainable basis is the central question faced by most African railways.

The African Rail Market

Typically railways in Africa are small, carrying no more traffic than a moderately busy branch line in other parts of the world. African railways carry far more freight than passengers, with freight averaging about 80 percent of traffic between 1995 and 2005. Almost all railways carry passenger traffic; only Swaziland and Uganda have freight-only railways. The passenger business is steadily shrinking, however, and several of the railways still retaining a reasonable passenger business do so only because competing road networks are in poor condition or do not exist.

Traffic—Low and Growing Slowly

Outside South Africa, the traffic volumes serviced by African railways are very small; about half of the 26 railway operators surveyed carried traffic of less than 500,000 traffic units annually, while only 5 of them exceeded 1 million traffic units annually—a volume comparable to a moderately busy branch line on other railways (figure 11.4). By comparison, Spoornet in South Africa carries 1 million traffic units every three days (Thompson 2007). In some cases, the light traffic is caused by a lack of demand; in others, it is caused by shortages of rolling stock, particularly locomotives.

Although the average haul on African networks is relatively long with regard to their size, it is not especially so vis-à-vis road transport. Some railways carry mostly end-to-end traffic; Tanzania Railways Corporation, Tazara (Tanzania-Zambia Railway Authority), and Transrail (Dakar-Bamako Railway) all haul freight an average distance of 1,000 kilometers, and some smaller railways, such as Uganda Railway or CEAR (Central East African Railways), act as feeders to other systems, which carry the traffic a few hundred kilometers farther. These systems have a good chance of competing for general freight traffic, even as a road network improves, as long as satisfactory service levels can be achieved, but the shorter systems that require transshipment to road at railheads will generally find they can compete effectively only for bulk traffic.

Most systems operate only limited passenger commuter services, if any, and the average distance of passenger trips is the distance between the capital of a country and major provincial centers. The only significant cross-border flows are on the Sitarail (Côte d'Ivoire), Tazara, and Transrail networks.

Since the mid-1990s, most African countries experienced steady economic growth. Average annual GDP grew 4 percent, with corresponding increases in trade. Per capita GDP grew by about 1.5 percent a year. Countries such as Mali, Mozambique, and Tanzania that avoided political upheaval grew as much as 50 percent faster. Despite the generally favorable economic background, only four African railways increased both their passenger and

Figure 11.4 Average Railway Traffic Volumes, 2001–05

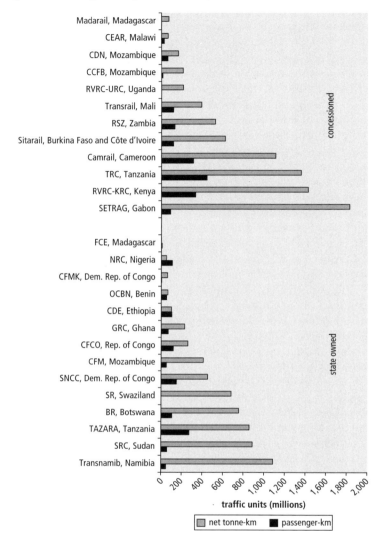

Source: Bullock 2009.
Note: Traffic units are passenger-kilometers in the case of passenger traffic and net tonne-kilometers in the case of freight traffic. BR = Botswana Railways; Camrail = Cameroon Railway Corporation; CCFB = Companhia dos Caminhos de Ferro da Beira (Mozambique); CDE = Chemin de Fer Djibouto-Ethiopien; CDN = Corredor de Desenvolvimento do Norte (Mozambique); CEAR = Central East African Railways Corporation (Malawi); CFCO = Chemin de Fer Congo-Océan (Republic of Congo); CFMK = Chemin de Fer Matadi-Kinshasa (Democratic Republic of Congo); CFM = Caminhos de Ferro do Mocambique; FCE = Fianarantsoa Côte Est (Madagascar); GRC = Ghana Railways Corporation; NRC = Nigeria Railways Corporation; OCBN = Organisation Commune Bénin-Niger; RSZ = Railway Systems of Zambia Ltd; RVRC-KRC = Rift Valley Rail Corporation-Kenya Railways Corporation; RVRC-URC = Rift Valley Rail Corporation-Uganda Railways Corporation; SETRAG = Société Transgabonnaise (Gabon); SNCC = Société Nationale des Chemins de Fer du Congo (Democratic Republic of Congo); SR = Swaziland Railways; SRC = Sudan Railways Corporation; TAZARA = Tanzania-Zambia Railway; TRC = Tanzania Railways Corporation.

have been concessioned, freight traffic has generally increased, whereas passenger traffic has generally stagnated or declined.

The growth or decline of traffic on many systems over the last decade often had little to do with changes in the underlying demand. War or natural disaster has had a major effect in some cases; on other railways, the volume carried reflects the availability of rolling stock, particularly locomotives. Many railways are short of locomotives. When this situation improves with new or secondhand locomotives or through a locomotive rehabilitation project, traffic will increase accordingly.

Passenger Services—in Decline

Several African cities have announced plans to introduce modern heavy-rail suburban commuter networks. Such services are currently limited to South Africa and Dakar, Senegal. Experiences elsewhere in the world suggest that any new services will need substantial external financial support for both capital and recurrent operating costs and should be operated by new independent transport authorities. Almost all other passenger services face strong competition from buses and shared taxis in both price and service frequency, and few corridors remain in which rail passenger services are the only means of transport. Bus fares are typically about 30–50 percent higher than the economy rail fare, but on most routes buses are faster (sometimes twice as fast) and more frequent. Buses have the lion's share of the market, although they suffer from the same problems as rail: unreliable departures, delays and breakdowns, and overcrowding.

The long-term prospects for nonurban rail services are generally poor (Amos and Bullock 2007). Rail services start competing with roads at speeds higher than 70 kilometers per hour. However, the cost of maintaining track and signaling systems that would enable these commercial speeds is significantly more than the cost of maintaining the 30- to 40-kilometer-per-hour commercial speed needed for a freight railway. In addition, a very large capital investment would be required to construct new medium-speed (for example, 200 kilometers per hour) interurban railways. Such investment is justified

freight traffic over the period, two of which had been concessioned. One other railway saw an increase in average passenger traffic, and all others saw a reduction. Fifteen railways increased their freight traffic. Where railways only on the basis of substantial demand (several million passengers a year) and relatively high-income passengers who can afford to cover at least operational costs. Few, if any, corridors in Africa could justify such investments, at least for the medium term.

Formal compensation schemes, such as public service obligations, have been introduced in a few cases to support passenger rail services, but they rarely provide timely compensation for service operations. Payment may be delayed several years or may otherwise take the form of a subsidy calculated to break even, limiting the ability of railways to increase their maintenance and negating any attempts to improve the financial performance of the freight services. As a result, most long-distance passenger services in Africa are trapped in a cycle of minimal investment, deteriorating services, declining patronage, and financial losses.

The few instances in which local trains serve villages with no road connection pose a different problem. These trains are used by traders bringing goods to and from regional centers, and although heavily loaded with passengers, they nonetheless incur major losses. Although such services can be funded through government subsidy, the long-term solution is to create feeder roads for motorized access, enabling more cost-effective means of transporting goods and greatly improving accessibility to such locations.

Freight—Needs Improving

Freight traffic on railways is mostly bulk and semibulk commodities, principally to and from ports. The actual commodities transported by rail reflect the economic structure of countries served by the railway, with mining products important in several countries and timber and export crops important in West Africa. Imports are mostly manufactures, such as cement and petroleum products, and general freight. On some systems, much of the general freight is containerized (cash crops with high value are increasingly traveling this way), particularly when the trip involves crossing an intermediate border before reaching the port. Unlike passenger services, significant imbalances between traffic in the two directions are common. Even where tonnage is approximately balanced, the

differences in the commodity mix, with many requiring specialized cars, mean freight trains are rarely fully loaded in both directions. In some cases, this natural imbalance in traffic is accentuated for rail because road vehicles delivering imports tend to backload freight at marginal cost, leaving rail to transport the remaining freight without a compensating return load.

Average freight tariffs range from $0.03 to $0.05 per net tonne-kilometer, similar to tariffs on other general freight railways in comparable countries. Tariffs are generally constrained by competition, either from road or alternate routes (particularly in the Great Lakes region, Malawi, West Africa, and Zambia) and are also influenced by the traditional value-based tariff structures, the relative cost of carrying different commodities (as reflected in net tons per railcar round-trip), direction of travel, and volume. Although most rail rates are well below comparable road rates, especially for containers, rail typically carries only 20–50 percent of the traffic in a corridor, and some of the smaller state-owned railways have an even smaller share.

Line-haul tariffs are only part of the cost equation for freight traffic. Much is often made of the inherent lower cost of rail compared to road. This is true where minerals must be transported from a rail-connected mine to a rail-connected port but is not so clear for medium-distance general freight that also must be transported by road to and from railheads. Haulage between the railway and the ultimate origin and destination can be surprisingly expensive, often as much as the equivalent of 200–300 kilometers of line-haul transport, negating any advantage rail may have in pure line-haul tariffs. New sidings are sometimes constructed, but they need a certain amount of traffic to be economical. Traffic that needs to be collected at a central depot before being dispatched by rail is more vulnerable to road competition, and even bulk traffic is not immune if distances are not too long. In many countries, collection and distribution chains are being streamlined, often eliminating up-country depots and distribution centers, and marketing channels have become more diversified. The railways have often been slow to respond, steadily losing market share.

Level of service is a key factor in the freight business. For rail to play a significant role in the general freight transport system, it must improve its service (specifically, overall transit time, reliability, security, and service frequency) and ensure that it is addressing the needs of customers. Too often, what rail has offered as transport has been quite different from what the competing road hauler can offer, and road carriers can charge a significant premium. In general, freight markets in Africa require reliable services (a commercial speed of 40 kilometers per hour is usually sufficient) rather than high-speed services, with (a) rail infrastructure and rolling stock maintained for service, (b) operating discipline to ensure that schedules are maintained, and (c) commercial arrangements that ensure that customers fulfill their contractual responsibilities.

Most railways can win bulk mineral traffic when it is offered, but general freight requires a reasonable level of service from rail if it is to compete with road without offering a significant price discount. By 2025, any remaining monopolies for general freight will have run their course, and the only traffic on which African railways will have an undisputed grip will be minerals (although mining companies are increasingly running even this traffic directly, either as third-party operators or on their own private networks). Experience in many countries has shown that general freight transport requires operators to be flexible, responsive, and adaptable. Fewer customers are fellow parastatals under order to use a state-owned railway, and few government-owned organizations, no matter how corporatized they may be, have the commercial freedom to operate effectively in a fully competitive environment.

Rail in Africa must become a transport business in the broadest sense and must be able to adapt to new markets. The predicaments of the remaining government-owned railways, however, show that rail cannot compete effectively while it is handicapped by the bureaucratic constraints and lack of commercial incentives and accountability of a government organization. Achieving an acceptable level of service, combined with flexible pricing policies and a strategy of providing a transport service as opposed to merely a line-haul operation, can reduce the price discount between rail and road, increasing the contribution that freight can make to the maintenance and renewal of infrastructure. This improvement is one of the major benefits a concessionaire can offer a state-owned railway.

Moreover, because of the lack of interconnection services and cross-border service contracts, rail freight suffers huge delays in crossing national borders. For example, a rail freight journey of 3,000 kilometers from Kolwezi on the Democratic Republic of Congo border to the port of Durban in South Africa takes 38 days to complete, an effective speed of only 4 kilometers per hour. Only 9 of these days are spent traveling, with the remainder (a staggering 29 days) taken up primarily with loading and interchanging freight, as well as some time for customs clearance. Each day of delay costs $200 per railcar. The main cause of the problems in the rail sector is the absence of reliable interconnection services when trains cross borders. Locomotives from one country are currently not allowed to travel on another country's network, mainly because of the inability to provide breakdown assistance to foreign operators. As a result, rail freight crossing borders must wait to be picked up by a different locomotive. The delays are often extensive, partly because of the lack of reliable, well-maintained locomotives. Delays also reflect the lack of clear contractual incentives to service traffic from a neighboring country's network. Reducing such delays would therefore require totally rethinking the contractual relationships and access rights linking the railways along the corridor. It would also likely require the establishment of a regional clearinghouse to ensure transparency and fairness in reciprocal track access rights.

How Much Investment Can Be Justified?

Providing an estimate of the investment needed by African railways is a daunting task (Carruthers, Krishnamani, and Murray 2009). In addition to building detailed inventories and assessments of infrastructure and determining how much needs to be repaired or replaced, the question of how much investment is economically justified must be asked. Lines that have been superseded by road developments and those with low traffic levels will rarely merit reconstruction and investment, and funds should instead be directed to those parts of the network with long-term value. Although a government's desire to reinstate such links is understandable, doing so is often extremely expensive.

Investment has historically been used for new construction and rolling stock, for replacement of rolling stock, and sometimes for rehabilitation and replacement of track. Long-term maintenance neglect has caused a huge backlog investment of up to $3 billion for Africa's railways. In practice, this one-time expenditure needed to eliminate the rehabilitation backlog could be spread over a 10-year period at an annual rate of $300 million.

After the network is restored to good condition, the annual bill would fall substantially to cover only what was needed for ongoing track rehabilitation and renewal. Excluding South Africa, the Sub-Saharan network consists of about 44,000 kilometers of track, of which about 34,000 kilometers is operational. The infrastructure on this network will have a life of at least 40–50 years, given the generally low traffic volumes; the cost of periodic reconstruction (about $350,000 per kilometer) is thus equivalent to an annual cost of about $8,000 per kilometer. Few lines with an average density of fewer than 1 million net tons a year are likely to warrant this kind of major rehabilitation expenditure, because traffic would need to earn $0.08 per net tonne-kilometer to fund the reconstruction, whereas typical rail freight tariffs are no more than $0.05 per net tonne-kilometer. Lines with a density under 250,000 tons a year probably cannot support anything more than routine maintenance. Even if low-volume lines are reconstructed using cheaper, secondhand materials, this level of expenditure is unlikely to be justified for more than 20,000 kilometers of the network. Overall, the ongoing annual cost of track reconstruction would thus average approximately $100 million a year.

Sustaining an adequate fleet of rolling stock will cost an additional $80 million a year. The cost of replacing rolling stock can be estimated by using assumed average asset lives. Excluding South Africa, the Sub-Saharan network carries about 15 billion net tonne-kilometers a year, excluding the mineral lines, and about 4 billion passenger-kilometers. That level of traffic will require, on average, replacing 500 freight cars, 20 passenger cars, and about 20 locomotives a year. As with infrastructure, much of that stock will be secondhand (from India or South Africa), but the estimated cost will still average about $80 million a year, equivalent to about $0.04 per net tonne-kilometer or passenger-kilometer. The steady-state investment in the African network north of South Africa should thus be about $200 million a year (allowing $20 million for facilities, maintenance, equipment, and other costs).

That amounts to a combined annual program of about $500 million for 10 years, after which investment would drop to the steady-state level of $200 million (Bullock 2009). The $500 million a year requirement refers to the period during which the rehabilitation backlog is being cleared. These calculations are only broad order-of-magnitude estimates. However, the amount needed to overcome these problems is large, equal to the annual revenues of some of the railways and well beyond their capacity to self-finance. The only option in most cases is to seek large concessional loans or grants from third parties.

In addition to reinvestment in the current network, investment in new projects is a possibility. For years, proposals have been floated to create new routes for landlocked countries and to integrate the isolated networks. The most comprehensive proposal was the 1976 master plan of the Union of African Railways for a pan-African rail network that included 26,000 kilometers of new construction. Designed to create a grid to support intra-African trade development and regional economic integration, the plan was approved by the Organization of African Unity in 1979, but few, if any, of the proposed links have gone beyond the drawing board. The Union of African Railways is now concentrating on a revised plan containing a subset of 10 corridors, some of which are already partially constructed, and the proposal has generated a number of regional studies and action plans.

Several proposals for individual segments have been made, and mining companies have proposed a number of dedicated mineral lines.

Few of these projects will be financially or economically viable. The cost of new construction of a single-track, nonelectrified railway on relatively flat terrain is at least $1.5 million per kilometer, increasing to about $5 million in more rugged country. In many cases, the proposed new routes would compete with existing road and rail routes, which would constrain the rates that typically could be charged to at most $0.05 per net tonne-kilometer. In the case of export mineral traffic, the potential rate is generally constrained to about $0.02–$0.03 per net tonne-kilometer by the long-term delivered market price. Because a serviceable two-lane road can generally be constructed for approximately $1 million per kilometer, the additional rail investment would be economically justified only if expected traffic was at least 2 million–4 million tons a year. If the capital costs of the infrastructure do not have to be recovered, the lines can probably be operated successfully at 0.5 million–1.0 million ton.

Institutional Arrangements and Performance

Until the 1980s, almost all African railway companies were publicly owned corporations, with varying degrees of financial and management autonomy. Attempts at commercialization while retaining public ownership were generally unsuccessful, and concessions were introduced in the 1990s. Under concessional arrangements, the state remains the owner of all or some of the existing assets, typically the infrastructure, and transfers the other assets (normally the rolling stock) and the responsibility to operate and maintain the railway to a concessionaire.

Most countries in Central, East, and West Africa have moved all or part of the way to concessioning, often under the pressure of multilateral and bilateral organizations that have until recently been the only source of large loans for asset rehabilitation and renewal. With the exception of southern Africa (Botswana, Namibia, South Africa, and Swaziland) and

countries suffering or recovering from civil disruption (Angola, the Democratic Republic of Congo, and Zimbabwe), most countries are at various stages of reform. Of the 30 African countries with publicly owned railways, 14 have opted for a concession arrangement and 1 operates under a management contract (figure 11.5). Four others have begun the process.

Concessions—Becoming the Norm

The introduction of concessions has required substantial changes in the legal and regulatory framework in many countries. In the francophone countries, concessions can generally be done within the existing legal system, but most anglophone countries have had to amend their railway acts. Arrangements have also been made for the economic and safety regulation of concessions, and new government bodies have been established to own the assets leased to the concessionaires.

Those railways that have not been concessioned remain subject to significant political and governmental influence. Arrangements vary across countries, but the sectoral ministry (normally transport) exercises political and administrative control, while the ministry of finance exercises financial control. Board directors are generally a combination of ministry officials and internal senior management, who are often appointed by the government. Oversight is nominally assigned to the parliament, but in practice such control may be limited to an audit of the company accounts in its annual report (often several years in arrears). Although the governing regulatory frameworks nominally provide financial and management autonomy, in practice this arrangement is considerably limited by the many opportunities for state intervention permitted under the legal and regulatory frameworks at both the institutional and jurisdictional levels. This conflict between the control and decision functions, as well as frequent reviews by political authorities of initiatives taken by the government's authorized representatives in the corporation, discourages management initiative and effectiveness.

The first railways to be concessioned were in West Africa, beginning in 1995 with the Sitarail concession linking Burkina Faso and Côte d'Ivoire and followed in the late 1990s by

Cameroon, Gabon, and Malawi. The reform momentum accelerated in the 2000s, but implementation has often been a slow process, typically taking three to five years, sometimes much longer.

Most African networks leave little room for competition, and few governments have seriously considered the European model of full vertical separation. However, third-party operators run on government lines in Kenya and Senegal, and a through freight service has operated for some years from South Africa to Tanzania. Concessions do not always include the entire network, with lightly used branch lines sometimes excluded.

The initial duration of concessions varies from 15 to 30 years, and the concessionaire is free to operate its activity as a business, with freight tariffs generally determined by supply and demand, and passenger fares subject to some form of indexation. Formal regulatory structures with real teeth are rare in Africa, and many rail concessions are potentially open to market abuse, even though concession agreements generally include some protection, at least on paper. For example, the Zambian rail concessionaire flagrantly price-discriminates by charging freight tariffs of $2.00 per tonne-kilometer on transit traffic from the Democratic Republic of Congo to Dar es Salaam, Tanzania, while charging only $0.05 per tonne-kilometer on other freight. The reason is to divert the Democratic Republic of Congo traffic southward toward the port of Durban in South Africa and over the Beit Bridge, which the same concessionaire operates. As a result, most of the Democratic Republic of Congo's copper exports end up going to Durban by road.

A number of consumer protection devices exist, but they are rarely invoked. The two most common protections are (a) the power to refer rail tariffs to either the government or an independent authority and (b) the power to allow third-party operators onto the railway to compete with the concessionaire. Where a concessionaire fails to comply with the terms of the concession, whether by design or by force of circumstance, procedures exist for terminating the concession. These procedures have rarely been applied. Only one or two concessions

Figure 11.5 Private Participation in African Railways since 1990

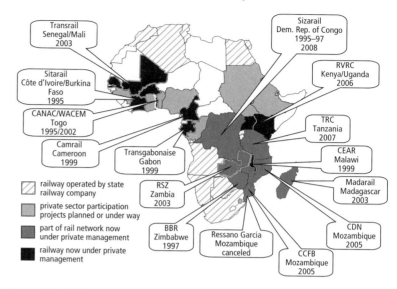

railway operated by state railway company

private sector participation projects planned or under way

part of rail network now under private management

railway now under private management

Transrail
Senegal/Mali
2003

Sitarail
Côte d'Ivoire/Burkina Faso
1995

CANAC/WACEM
Togo
1995/2002

Camrail
Cameroon
1999

Transgabonaise
Gabon
1999

RSZ
Zambia
2003

BBR
Zimbabwe
1997

Ressano Garcia
Mozambique
canceled

CCFB
Mozambique
2005

CDN
Mozambique
2005

Madarail
Madagascar
2003

CEAR
Malawi
1999

TRC
Tanzania
2007

RVRC
Kenya/Uganda
2006

Sizarail
Dem. Rep. of Congo
1995–97
2008

Source: Bullock 2009.
Note: BBR = Beitbridge Bulawayo Railway; CANAC/WACEM = CANAC Railway Services Inc./West African Cement; CCFB = Companhia dos Caminhos de Ferro da Beira; CDN = Corredor de Desenvolvimento do Norte; CEAR = Central East African Railways Corporation; RSZ = Railway Systems of Zambia Ltd; RVRC = Rift Valley Rail Corporation; TRC = Tanzania Railways Corporation.

have been terminated (for example, Ressano Garcia in Mozambique), and two concessions (Transrail and Rift Valley) changed the operator.

Rail concessions in Africa have attracted a limited pool of mostly foreign private operators. These operators fall into two distinct groups: (a) those seeking vertical integration of the distribution chain by acquiring dominant positions in specific production and transport sectors, and (b) those specializing in a single transport activity (such as railways or ports). The business cases for these rail investments often appear weak, however, suggesting that the companies that seek these concessions focus on the financial benefits that can be extracted from managing large investment plans (financed for the most part by governments) rather than concentrating on business cash flows.

Private companies are the majority shareholders in all concessions to date. State participation is highest in Mozambique, which holds 49 percent of both CCFB (Companhia dos Caminhos de Ferro da Beira–Mozambique) and CDN (Corredor de Desenvolvimento do

Norte–Mozambique) and is also a significant shareholder in the adjacent CEAR concession. In Madagascar, the government holds 25 percent of Madarail, while governments own 10–20 percent in Abidjan-Ouagadougou Railway (Sitarail), Dakar-Bamako Railway (Transrail), and Cameroon Railway Corporation (Camrail). Local private participation in concessions has generally been relatively low and is often fraught with problems during the bidding process. Employee shareholding remains under 5 percent where it exists at all.

Operational Performance— Concessioning Helps

Both labor productivity and asset productivity (locomotive and railcar use) are low in most African networks, compared with railways elsewhere, because of the poor condition of the infrastructure and rolling stock, low traffic levels, and government ownership. Under concessions, however, these indicators have improved sharply, partly because of growth in traffic but mostly from major reductions in the workforce.

Since about 1990, almost all railway companies have streamlined their workforces. This measure has often been the prelude to concessioning, but in some cases, it has also been a general policy to improve efficiency. Still, labor productivity on most African systems is relatively low by world standards, with few railways achieving over 500,000 traffic units per staff a year, compared with an average 3.3 million traffic units per staff a year for the South African operator Spoornet (figure 11.6). This low productivity not only reflects the continuing use of labor-intensive methods with relatively little outsourcing, but it is also the consequence of a decline in traffic without adjustments to staff levels. With low wages, the direct financial impact is not always catastrophic, but having a large number of underemployed staff members corrodes morale and is a strong disincentive for those who wish to improve efficiency. An important effect is that railways have difficulty recruiting and retaining technically competent staff or introducing the technology required to improve service levels, for which a better-paid and more skilled workforce is essential. Asset

productivity is similarly low, with the source generally being low availability caused by a lack of spare parts.

Labor and asset productivity have improved steadily in most concessions, typically doubling because of workforce reductions either before or at the time of concessioning, the scrapping of obsolete rolling stock, and increased traffic volumes (figure 11.7).

Safety is also an important aspect of operational performance. Rail travel is still safer than road travel, but rail's record in Africa is much worse than that of comparable railways elsewhere, caused by obsolete track infrastructure, poorly maintained rolling stock, and lack of operational discipline. As with productivity, however, safety has generally improved following concessioning.

Financial Performance—Generally Unsustainable

Most state-owned railways in Africa just about break even cashwise after receiving government support. Often, this balance occurs only because a significant amount of maintenance has been deferred; when the maintenance backlog becomes too great, it is typically addressed by a loan that is treated as investment. The two companies that have been concessioned the longest (Camrail and Sitarail) make modest operating profits. The performance of RSZ (Railway Systems of Zambia) is unknown, and the cases of Kenya and Tanzania are too early to judge.

Passenger services generally do not contribute significantly to the cost of maintaining infrastructure or to covering corporate overhead. In a few cases, they cover their marginal costs (train crew, rolling-stock maintenance, fuel or traction electricity, and passenger-handling costs). Passenger tariffs on many railways are essentially regulated, often within a framework that includes only a subset of total costs. However, many of the poorer performing systems in Africa would be unable to cover above-rail working expenses on a systemwide level even if they could set their own tariffs.

Freight services normally cover their avoidable operating costs. Some also earn enough to cover infrastructure costs and even capital costs for rolling stock. Earnings are a function of the tariff rate and the average carload on the revenue side, and factors such as train size, commercial speed, and rolling-stock use and availability on the cost side. In general, freight can earn enough to make operating services worthwhile, but only in some cases can it fund replacement of rolling stock, and very rarely can it earn enough to finance infrastructure renewal.

Where railways have been concessioned, low-interest sovereign loans to concessionaires have usually made a substantial contribution to the financing of investments. Concessionaires provide a relatively low proportion of the equity. Most plan to finance over 80 percent of their investment with debt, and the share of the privately financed investments is in many cases well below 50 percent. Concessions that planned a substantial contribution from commercial borrowing have faced consistent criticism for their lack of investment in practice. Because the value of the rolling stock transferred to the concessionaire more than compensates for the equity put into the concessions in most cases, the result is a significant transfer of the financial risks associated with infrastructure investment from the private sector to the public sector. The business fundamentals of many concessions are insufficient to support major investment on a commercial basis, and they are all too prone to significant liquidity problems. Major asset maintenance and reinvestment are thus likely to be problems.

Concessions normally pay the government concession fees as well as a series of taxes (for example, value added tax, personnel social taxes, income tax), often of the same order of magnitude. Given the relative size of taxes (largely income tax) and concession fees, governments should consider the combined effect of both revenue streams when negotiating a concession. Regardless of the mix of fees and taxes and of any promises made during the bidding process, a concessioned railway's strategy will always be constrained by the business fundamentals of the proposed railway privatization deal. A concessionaire will be able to bear only a finite level of charges, whether they are concession fees,

Figure 11.6 Labor Productivity on African Rail Systems

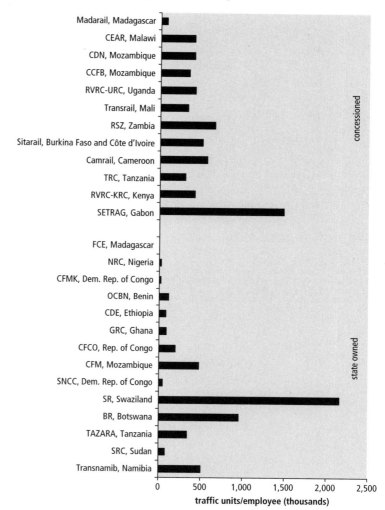

Source: Bullock 2009.
Note: Common averages have been used for Kenya and Uganda, which are included in a single concession, and for Nacala (Mozambique) and Malawi, which share common resources.
The overall traffic units carried by a railway are the sum of the passenger-kilometers and the net tonne-kilometers of freight carried. This simple standard measure is widely used as a means of aggregating freight and passenger traffic. The relative weighting of passenger and freight is conventionally taken as 1:1. BR = Botswana Railways; Camrail = Cameroon Railway Corporation; CCFB = Companhia dos Caminhos de Ferro da Beira (Mozambique); CDE = Chemin de Fer Djibouto-Ethiopien; CDN = Corredor de Desenvolvimento do Norte (Mozambique); CEAR = Central East African Railways Corporation (Malawi); CFCO = Chemin de Fer Congo-Océan (Republic of Congo); CFMK = Chemin de Fer Matadi-Kinshasa (Democratic Republic of Congo); CFM = Caminhos de Ferro do Mocambique; FCE = Fianarantsoa Côte Est (Madagascar); GRC = Ghana Railways Corporation; NRC = Nigeria Railways Corporation; OCBN = Organisation Commune Bénin-Niger; RSZ = Railway Systems of Zambia Ltd; RVRC-KRC = Rift Valley Rail Corporation-Kenya Railways Corporation; RVRC-URC = Rift Valley Rail Corporation-Uganda Railways Corporation; SETRAG = Société Transgabonnaise (Gabon); SNCC = Société Nationale des Chemins de Fer du Congo (Democratic Republic of Congo); SR = Swaziland Railways; SRC = Sudan Railways Corporation; TAZARA = Tanzania-Zambia Railway; TRC = Tanzania Railways Corporation.

borrowing costs, or rolling-stock acquisition costs, and concessions with high levels of both debt and concession fees will be prime candidates for renegotiation.

Figure 11.7 Rail Concession Labor Productivity

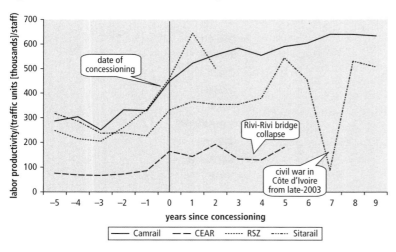

Source: Bullock 2009.
Note: The overall traffic units carried by a railway are the sum of the passenger-kilometers and the net tonne-kilometers of freight carried. This simple standard measure is widely used as a means of aggregating freight and passenger traffic. The relative weighting of passenger and freight is conventionally taken as 1:1. Rivi-Rivi bridge refers to the Rivi-Rivi River bridge in Balaka, Malawi. Camrail = Cameroon Railway Corporation; CEAR = Central East African Railways Corporation (Malawi); RSZ = Railway Systems of Zambia Ltd; Sitarail = railway operator for Burkina Faso and Côte d'Ivoire.

The Verdict on Concessions—Generally Beneficial but Not the Full Answer

Since 1992, there have been 16 rail concessions in Africa. Two of the 16 have been canceled, 1 has been badly affected by war, and 1 has suffered from natural disasters and procedural delays. Six have operated for five years or more but only 2 of those without a significant dislocation of some sort.[3]

Except for the railways immediately adjacent to South Africa, those that have not been concessioned have deteriorated continuously since the mid-1990s. In a number of cases, these declines will prove to be terminal. Many governments in Africa will consider concessions only as a last-ditch solution, but in many cases, the railways have been left to deteriorate for too long, and rectifying the situation will be a struggle.

The concessions have not been without their problems. In many cases, finding more than a few bidders has been difficult, and in several cases, bidders' financial resources have been insufficient to finance the major investments required. As a result, the state has had to guarantee investments; even then, mobilizing the financing has been slow. Concessionaires

have generally been unenthusiastic about running passenger services, which do not generate the same revenues as freight; this situation has not been helped by delays and disputes about the payment of government compensation for unprofitable services. Further problems have arisen over the level of concession fees, the length of the concession, and arrangements for redundant staff. In some cases, these issues have led to renegotiation of the concession contract.

Despite these vicissitudes, the results to date are encouraging. Even if not all expectations have been met, most of the concessioned railways have improved their traffic levels and their productivity and are providing better service to users, albeit after a solid injection of investment by donors and international financial institutions. Arguably, some of this improvement might have occurred anyway. In addition, responsibility for the ongoing rehabilitation and maintenance of track is rapidly emerging as a key issue between concessionaires and governments. A key government objective in many railway concessions is to obtain finance (whether private or through international financial institutions) to rehabilitate track infrastructure. For most private operators, however, track rehabilitation, especially track renewal, is a major expense that drains available funds, but it is also one that can be easily deferred.

The greatest effect of concessionaires has been improved operations. Given the weak investment and regulatory climate in many African countries, investment flows have been limited. Under concessioning, operations have been positive, and efficiency has clearly improved. Labor productivity has increased steadily in all the concessions in operation for over five years, and similar figures will likely come from recent concessions. Asset productivity has also generally increased. Although concessionaires in Africa typically have a more appropriate cost structure than their predecessors, it is rarely the ideal cost structure. Operating costs on railways are a function of capital invested, as well as operating efficiency, and many African railways have been starved of capital, substantially increasing overall operating costs.

Allocative efficiency is difficult to measure directly, but the evidence is generally positive.

Improved productivity, an active search for new traffic by concessionaires, and better internal business practices have all improved railway cost and pricing structures and lifted the level of service, thus helping attract traffic to the mode that can carry it most efficiently and improve intermodal competition.

Most concessionaires have fulfilled the passenger service requirements in their concession agreements, even where it has been operationally difficult or where agreed public service obligation payments have not been forthcoming. Many of these services were inherited, and passenger service would often be more economical with a road-based system.

A recent review of four concessions found little evidence of monopolistic behavior by concessionaires (Pozzo di Borgo and others 2006; World Bank 2006). This review examined freight rates and whether services were being reduced so resources could be redeployed to favored users, beyond changes in services that any commercialized railway undertakes in response to changing traffic patterns. Few concessions are immune from road competition, except in the few cases where roads still must be constructed or where heavy mineral movements occur. No evidence exists that personal travel has been made more expensive for the poor.

The greatest disappointment for governments has been the lack of infrastructure funding from sources other than international financial institutions. Concession agreements clearly put the responsibility of financing track maintenance and renewal on private operators. Likewise, rolling-stock financing has been left to concessionaires under their contracts. However, most concessionaires initially rely on loans from international institutions, with below-market borrowing costs, lengthy loan terms, and grace periods to finance infrastructure. (The exceptions are the Beitbridge Railway [Zimbabwe to South Africa], which relies on take-or-pay clauses that guarantee minimum revenues; the Nacala Railway in Mozambique, which is being funded at semicommercial rates; and Zambia and the Rift Valley Railways [covering Kenya and Uganda], where the investment program is modest and is funded directly by the concessionaire.) Loans have been provided for rolling stock in some cases, but for many of

the low-volume operators, the sensible choice is to find secondhand equipment. Much of the investment to date has been for maintenance and renewal backlogs, without which the railway often would not function, and can be characterized as one-time investment to get the systems running. Even that investment has been slow, more than four years in Cameroon and five years on the Nacala line—a long time to wait when a business is barely breaking even.

Are concessions a long-term answer? Or are they merely quick fixes that are living off investment by third parties and will prove unsustainable in the long term? What more must be done to ensure a sustainable sector? Many of the answers to those questions must come from governments.

Key Issues for Governments

Classic concession schemes[4] in Africa are unlikely to be financially attractive to bidders other than those who can secure financial benefits not directly linked to the railway operations.[5] Consequently, unless the structure of African rail concessions changes or the market environment in which they operate alters favorably, private operators will continue to show limited interest in African railway concessions. Two key areas need to be addressed: the financing of passenger services and major track renewals and rehabilitation, both requiring substantial public funding in most concessions. If this funding is provided, governments will also need to strengthen their regulatory capacity to ensure that the conditions are met and that the effect on the rail sector in general, and concessionaires in particular, is properly considered when policies in other sectors of the economy are developed.

Passenger Services

If governments want the concessionaire to operate passenger services, they should make clear compensation arrangements that can be monitored. Few passenger train services will likely cover even their above-rail costs. Their financial contribution to infrastructure costs is minimal, and few services would justify investment in rolling stock, whether hauled by locomotive or self-propelled. If these services are to operate for more than the initial years of a concession, governments need to develop a simple compensation scheme with timely payments. Any scheme should enable the concessionaire to keep all the revenue, which will encourage maximum operation, and should include a public contribution, possibly per carriage-kilometer, toward the cost of running unprofitable passenger services. The scheme should be easily audited and should be reviewed periodically, perhaps every five years.

If such schemes are not introduced, passenger services will be a constant source of conflict between the government and the operator. Moreover, the issue will divert the focus of the concessionaire from the freight services, where improvement is far more important economically for the country.

Capacity or Willingness of Private Operators to Finance Track Renewal

Few, if any, concessions are generating significant profits for their operators and certainly not enough to fund long-term renewals. Although most concessionaires pay fees into general government revenue, none can afford to do so and accrue funds for future renewals at the same time. Whether a purely privately financed rail concession model is sustainable in much of Africa remains doubtful. Track structures have (or should have) lives of several decades, given the traffic volumes typically carried on an African railway. On a small system, track renewal is needed somewhere on the network only about every 20 years. It is almost always possible to defer renewals for several years, albeit at the cost of deteriorating track conditions and reduced operating speeds. For any concessionaire who is uncertain about the future, the safest decision is to do as little track renewal as possible.

Even if they do want to renew track, private operators will often struggle to generate sufficient cash flow for it. Few concessions are strong financially. If a government makes the level of the concession fee or rolling-stock purchase price the ultimate measure of a successful deal, it will limit the successful bidder's ability to renew infrastructure. Even if an operator has sufficient

cash, on a small network when the expenditure may not occur for 5 or 10 years, a concessionaire is unlikely to reserve funds annually and hold them in reserve that long. Furthermore, raising debt financing for rail repair will generally be possible only through a general corporate loan, which is almost impossible for a small stand-alone railway.

Profits to the concessionaire need to be boosted, or supplementary funding sources need to be developed, or both. Today, African railway concessions offer two models for financing infrastructure. In the first, governments finance initial track rehabilitation and renewal costs, generally by securing loans from international financial institutions. These loans are then made to private operators and tend to cover only the initial five-year investment plan in the hope that they will propel each concessionaire's traffic to a level that will then enable it to self-finance future track investments. This approach is commonly used for railways with a high ratio of initial track investment compared with revenues and that are thus unlikely to be able to mobilize sufficient private financing. In the second model, governments do not finance initial track renewal but commit to compensating concessionaires for their investment by the end of the concession (for example, Kenya, Uganda, and Zambia railways). In such cases, the initial amount to be invested is relatively small in relation to expected revenues, and private operators are assumed to be able to secure private financing on the merits of their business case. Under both models, governments usually agree to purchase at the end of their concessions the nonamortized portion of any infrastructure investment concessionaires have financed. However, the ability of many governments to make such a payment is uncertain, which often affects infrastructure investment in the later stages of a concession, although a partial risk guarantee can strengthen the government's reimbursement commitment.

Three conditions must be met to secure privately financed track investment: (a) governments ensure that the concession (and thus the proposed track investment) is financially sound, (b) the nonamortized value of the assets owed to the concessionaire at the end of the concession period remains reasonable, and (c) the concession agreement allows for a possible extension of the concession period.

Often, however, governments will still need to assist. Notwithstanding the likely improvements in efficiency from concessioning, many agreements will probably fail the first hurdle of financial soundness. If the government still wishes to pursue a concession because of the benefits of rail transport, it will need to contribute grant funds regularly. One option is to partially finance infrastructure renewal independently of the concessionaire through a land transport renewal fund, which could be an extension of a road fund, created as a common pool of funds by both the road and rail sectors. For example, concession payments could be paid into the fund rather than into general revenue. A rationale for this option can be developed from the external costs avoided by the carriage of passengers and freight by road rather than rail.

Effective and Efficient Regulation of Private Rail Operators

In practice, many concessions ignore many or all of their reporting obligations under the concession agreements. In some cases, this situation obtains because of operator intransigence, in others because of a lack of expertise or initiative. Not surprisingly, both politicians and bureaucracies are often ill informed about the problems facing a concessionaire and the remedies being attempted. Most concessions have a long list of requirements for the concessionaire to meet, and allowing reporting to be ignored inevitably creates plenty of scope for later disputes. Regulatory bodies must strengthen their capacity and impose annual independent financial and operational audits as part of concession contracts. One solution for funding the regulatory bodies is to use the concession fees, but funding from a land transport fund, if one can be established, may be preferable.

Consistent Government Behavior toward Railway Concessionaires Aligned with Good Business Practice

Uncoordinated actions from ministries within governments have negatively affected the performance of a number of concessions. Examples range from administratively imposed salary levels to restrictions on access to container facilities and unfunded public service requirements. Most of these actions could be avoided by establishing a properly staffed and funded oversight body (the concession counterparty is generally the obvious choice for this). A government should ensure that such a body has the necessary political and technical powers to coordinate and control government actions toward private rail operators. In practice, that means the agency should meet regularly to discuss pending issues with the concessionaire. The oversight body should include, or have ready access to, a railway technical expert and a railway financial expert, and someone should head it whose sole responsibility is to monitor the railway concession and who reports directly to the transport and finance ministers at least.

Consistent Government Approach to Infrastructure Cost Recovery

Governments should also develop a coherent and realistic policy regarding infrastructure cost recovery. The road sector has an articulate and organized lobby. Advocates for government railways, where they exist, have generally been ineffectual and poorly prepared, although concessionaires are generally able to make aggressive representations. The lower the road costs are and the greater the degree of overloading permitted, the lower the freight rates by both road and rail will be—and less money will be available from a concessionaire to maintain and upgrade the railway infrastructure.

Road competition is strongest in southern Africa, which has the most liberal market structure, the largest trucks, and the best roads. In addition, the level of road user charges and the prevalence of overloading heavily affect rail. Requiring rail to fund all its long-term maintenance and upgrades, while tolerating road cost underrecovery and overloading on arterial routes, may help government budgets in the short run, but it is an almost impossible handicap for most general freight railways to overcome.

The Way Ahead

A wide gap often exists in the minds of government officials between their expectations of what concessioning can achieve and what actually happens after they award the concession. Service volumes on most African railways are low, often about that of a moderately busy branch line in many countries. These low volumes can commercially justify no more than the minimum infrastructure maintenance, which allows operation at a speed of 40–60 kilometers per hour. That speed does not permit an attractive passenger service except where no practical alternative exists—an increasingly rare situation. Governments that are unprepared to invest substantial sums of their own funds in upgrading and maintaining infrastructure should therefore expect only a "fit for purpose" freight railway operating at moderate speeds but doing so reliably and safely. This type of railway can be operated successfully under concession at typical African traffic densities. If traffic volumes are very low (250,000 tons a year or less) or if a high standard of passenger service is expected, continuing financial support from the government will be necessary.

After a concession is awarded, the government must monitor concessionaire behavior and ensure that the government's interests are fulfilled. Most important, a government must ensure that the infrastructure does not deteriorate over the life of the concession, as is often the case. Deterioration generally occurs when concessionaires have short- or medium-term financial objectives that do not align with the longer-term economic objectives of the government. A concession agreement should try to reconcile these two objectives as much as possible, and compliance should then be monitored regularly.

Despite these problems, well-run railways should still offer the most economical solution to transporting general freight that is not time sensitive in major corridors for distances over 500–800 kilometers and bulk commodities over shorter distances. The revival of a railway through concessioning is warranted when the business fundamentals supporting it are sound. At the same time, better solutions must be devised to ensure that while governments continue to reap the substantial potential economic benefits of concessions, private operators' financial returns are high enough to attract broad and competitive investor participation.

Notes

The authors of this chapter are Dick Bullock and Kenneth Gwilliam, who drew on background material and contributions from Pierre Pozzo di Borgo.

1. Spatial density is measured in route-kilometers per 1,000 square kilometers.
2. Traffic density is expressed as traffic units per route-kilometer. The traffic units carried by a railway are the sum of the passenger-kilometers and the net tonne-kilometers of freight carried. It is a simple standard measure that is widely used, although it has some limitations as an indicator (for example, a first-class passenger-kilometer in a commercial high-speed TGV train is treated identically with a passenger-kilometer in a crowded suburban train). The relative weighting of passenger and freight is conventionally taken as 1:1, although alternative weightings have been used on some railways from time to time, usually trying to reflect relative costs.
3. For more detailed discussions, see Bullock 2005.
4. Classic concession schemes require the private operator to take on a significant debt burden in relation to revenues.
5. That is, by controlling the entire distribution chain or through the supply of rail equipment and services.

References

Amos, Paul, and Richard Bullock. 2007. "The Financial Performance of Non-Urban Passenger Services." Transport Paper 14, World Bank, Washington, DC.

Bullock, Richard. 2005. "Results of Railway Privatization in Africa." Transport Paper 8, World Bank, Washington, DC.

———. 2009. "Taking Stock of Railway Companies in Sub-Saharan Africa." Background Paper 17, Africa Infrastructure Country Diagnostic, World Bank, Washington, DC.

Carruthers, Robin, Ranga R. Krishnamani, and Siobhan Murray. 2008. "Improving Connectivity: Investing in Transport Infrastructure in Sub-Saharan Africa." Background Paper 7, Africa Infrastructure Country Diagnostic, World Bank, Washington, DC.

Pozzo di Borgo, Pierre, Alain Labeau, Raphael Eskinazi, Julien Dehornoy, Alan Parte, and Marouane Ameziane. 2006. "Review of Selected Railway Concessions in Sub-Saharan Africa." World Bank, Washington, DC.

Thompson, Louis. 2007. "Spoornet and Transnet Sectoral Reference Paper." World Bank, Washington, DC.

UIC (International Union of Railways)-Statistics Centre. 2008. *Railway Time-Series Data 2007*. Paris: Railway Technical Publications.

World Bank. 2006. "Sub-Saharan Africa: Review of Selected Railway Concessions." Africa Transport Sector Report 36491, World Bank, Washington, DC.

Chapter 12

Ports and Shipping: Landlords Needed

African shipping has been largely deregulated. However, many African countries are trapped in a vicious circle of high tariffs discouraging traffic and further increasing costs. Poor inland links and wasteful and costly port administration accentuate this problematic situation. The lack of an integrated land distribution system, particularly for transit, impedes container traffic.

Since the mid-1990s, both general cargo and containerized cargo passing through African public ports have trebled. Southern Africa has had the fastest growth in general cargo traffic and West Africa in container traffic, albeit from a low base. Dry bulk traffic (coal, grain, and some chemicals) and liquid bulk traffic (mostly oil) have also been growing rapidly. By international standards, however, these traffic categories are unbalanced, increasing the costs for African trade. Export volumes greatly exceed import volumes for dry and liquid bulks, while imports dominate exports for general cargo and container trades.

Many ports handle the traffic, few of them large by world standards. The main transshipment points for regional traffic (Abidjan, Côte d'Ivoire; Dar es Salaam, Tanzania; Djibouti, Djibouti; Durban, South Africa; and Mombasa, Kenya) are not major hubs on the main international itineraries, and they appear unlikely to become so. Several ports suffer from low capacity, particularly in terminal storage, maintenance, and dredging capability. Overall, however, total use of African port capacity is estimated at 80 percent and likely to remain at this level in the near future.

Many ports are poorly equipped and inefficiently operated. Container handling rates fall well below international norms. Port charges for both containers and general cargo are substantially higher than in other regions. Security standards are still extremely variable, and few ports are prepared for the dramatic changes in trade and shipping patterns now occurring.

The main requirements are organizational. Many capacity constraints could be overcome simply by making the existing ports more efficient. Regional port planning is required to counter the costs of fragmentation. Port pricing and regulatory policies need to be more commercial and to better respond to the international shipping market. Comprehensive policies are required for modal integration and administrative simplification, and modern port management structures are essential.

The landlord port system has been more successful than the service port in Africa (as elsewhere) and is best suited to introduce the private sector. Within a landlord port structure, attracting container line operators and major international terminal operators could produce efficiency improvements. Ghana and Nigeria have moved toward the landlord port, and several francophone countries operate a hybrid model. However, development is slow, and the involvement of the efficient private global operators is very low.

The African Shipping Market

Africa's maritime traffic has been growing rapidly across all cargo types, although container traffic is highly imbalanced and faces major challenges because of the lack of efficient transportation links back to the hinterland. Shipping markets are small and thin, contributing to relatively high costs.

Maritime Traffic—On the Rise but Out of Balance

Except in South Africa, container transport in Sub-Saharan Africa is still at an early stage of development; however, it is growing rapidly from a very low base, with an average annual growth rate of 7.2 percent and as high as 13.8 percent in West Africa (table 12.1). Of the 7.6 million 20-foot equivalent units (TEUs) handled by all Sub-Saharan African ports in 2005, Durban handled nearly 2 million TEUs, and the three main South African ports together handled more than 3 million TEUs. West Africa

accounts for less than 1 percent of total world container traffic and for little more than 2 percent of all African traffic. East Africa has a heavy concentration in Mombasa (6 percent of the Sub-Saharan African total, according to the United Nations Conference on Trade and Development) while West Africa has five ports handling more than 350,000 TEUs each.

The lack of an integrated land distribution system, particularly for transit traffic, impedes container traffic. Handling of dry and liquid bulk exports is making the most progress, with many port facilities privately owned and integrated in a comprehensive logistic system.

From 1995 to 2005, general cargo has grown at an average annual rate of 6.6 percent and at a rate as high as 15.7 percent in southern Africa (table 12.2), rates higher than in the rest of the world because of later containerization. General cargo has traditionally been the major type of cargo moved to landlocked countries. Little congestion occurs in the ports, but handling is inefficient, and the transfer of some of this traffic to containers is contingent on inland distribution systems.

Dry bulk traffic is sometimes handled at common-user general cargo facilities, but the major flows (grain from Mombasa, ferrochrome from Maputo, and coal from Richards Bay [South Africa]) pass through privately owned and operated dry and liquid bulk terminals, for which the traffic volumes are generally not well reported. In 2007, the total throughput of Richards Bay was 66 million tons, making it the world's ninth-largest bulk exporting port. Because major global interests control these businesses, the port and shipping arrangements likely conform to the best international standards. Some dry bulk traffic is still handled on general cargo quays, suggesting the possibility for further specialization, though that depends on having a large enough basic flow.

Liquid bulk traffic is predominantly oil, with 11 countries (dominated by Nigeria and Angola) supplying 12 percent of world demand and 19 percent of U.S. demand. In 2006, oil made up 85 percent of exports by value from West and Central Africa. It is a growing sector, with Asian countries (China, in particular) and the United States making significant investments in Africa, including placement of the

Table 12.1 Traffic Trends for Container Trade, Sub-Saharan Ports, by Region, 1995–2005

Region	TEUs		Overall percentage change	Average annual percentage change
	1995	2005		
East Africa–Indian Ocean	505,100	1,394,956	176	5.8
Southern Africa	1,356,000	3,091,846	128	2.5
West Africa	673,400	3,126,901	364	13.8
Total	2,534,500	7,613,703	200	7.2

Source: Mundy and Penfold 2008.
Note: TEU = 20-foot equivalent unit.

proper export platforms. Again, international standards are generally met.

For the most part, African countries are exporters of minerals (including oil) and agricultural products, handled either by specialized or dedicated dry or liquid bulk terminals or by general cargo facilities. For example, agricultural products are often handled over the quay at general cargo facilities by grabs or mobile conveyors. Export volumes (loadings) greatly exceed import volumes (unloadings) for dry and liquid bulks, while imports dominate exports for general cargo.

The dominance of imports is most pronounced in the container trades, increasing the costs. Of Africa's outgoing containers, 23 percent are full, and for West Africa, 12 percent. Only the southern African ports approach trade levels of most other world regions, with containers 30–40 percent full on the backhaul to Asia (figure 12.1).

Traffic Patterns—Low Volumes, High Costs

African shipping has been largely deregulated, and Africa has been integrated into the global liner network through global players' acquisition of regional operators and replacement of direct calls by transshipments from elsewhere. For example, Maersk uses Salalah (Oman) as the hub for its East African trade and Algeciras (Spain) and Tangier (Morocco) as the hubs for its West African trade. As a result, the number of direct calls is falling in some areas, and container vessel capacity serving African ports is relatively small, mostly under 2,000 TEUs.

The proliferation of ports and the limitations on traffic volumes add to the high costs of shipping to Africa. Greater port efficiency and regional integration to provide better links between the port and its hinterland are the only solutions for small ports to increase traffic. Without greater port and distribution efficiency, several maritime countries will continue to be served by feeder services (particularly in East Africa) and by regional liner services (in West Africa).

Delays at the ports are very costly. In 2006, one extra day in port cost more than $35,000 for a 2,200-TEU vessel, and proportionately more for larger ships. Shipping lines have responded

Table 12.2 Traffic Trends for General Cargo, 1995–2005

Region	Thousand tons		Overall percentage change	Average annual percentage change
	1995	2005		
East Africa–Indian Ocean	13.84	38.42	177	5.9
Southern Africa	2.73	14.52	431	15.7
West Africa	19.57	51.68	164	5.1
Total	36.14	104.62	189	6.6

Source: Mundy and Penfold 2008.

Figure 12.1 Balance of Sub-Saharan African Container Trade, 2005

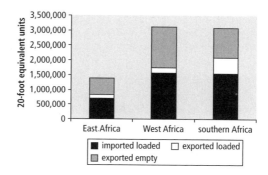

Source: Mundy and Penfold 2008.

by introducing "congestion charges," ranging from $35 per day for a 20-foot container in Dakar to $425 per day in Tema (Ghana) in 2006. Delays are often caused by long processing and administration times and by poor handling in congested port areas, rather than by lack of basic quay capacity. Where customs allow the transport of boxes under bond, some ports have developed off-dock terminals to move container yards to a less congested area.

Most landlocked countries have alternative outlets to the sea. For example, the five landlocked countries in West Africa have 15 transit possibilities, and Zambia alone has five competing corridors. The total cost (including border and port delays) determines the choice of shippers. In southern Africa, much traffic takes the longer route to the congested and fairly inefficient Durban port because of the more liberal and efficient land transport and border arrangements on that route, as well as the more frequent sailings. More competition among corridors could lower the administrative blockages to free flows of goods on the corridors.

African Ports

Africa has many small and medium-size ports, with a low concentration by world standards. West Africa has about 25 significant ports, but none is among the 70 largest world ports. In addition, new port developments are increasing the proliferation (figure 12.2).

Port Configuration—Need for a Better Hub-and-Feeder System

All three regions, eastern, western, and southern, claim to suffer from specific capacity problems. Mombasa and Dar es Salaam have reached their storage limits for containers in their terminals. Durban is struggling to bring in new capacity to meet container handling and storage demand. In West Africa, Luanda and Tema are short of container capacity, and Luanda, Douala (Cameroon), and Tema are under pressure for general cargo. Numerous factors contribute. Location in a major urban area limits the capacity of some ports (Apapa [Lagos], Nigeria). For many ports, equipment availability and maintenance

are constraints. Maintenance dredging is often inadequate (and much more costly than a few years ago) because of the reliance on ad hoc contracting rather than long-term performance contracts. In addition, many ports have poor navigational aids.

Despite these circumstances, one source considers total use of African port capacity to be 80 percent overall and likely to remain there through 2010 (Drewry Shipping Consultants Ltd. 2006, 2008). Making ports more efficient could overcome many of the capacity constraints, because handling rates are below international standards. For example, the Durban Container Terminal manages only about 17 moves per crane hour, short of an international norm of 25 to 30 moves.

On the East African coastline, Mombasa and Dar es Salaam are competing as regional transshipment points, but both face severe capacity constraints in the short term. Feeders serve both, mainly Salalah (Oman) and Dubai (the United Arab Emirates). For example, Europe's main port, Rotterdam (the Netherlands), has no direct container flows to either port. Traffic through Dar es Salaam has increased greatly since Hutchison Port Holdings took over the management contract for the container terminal held by International Container Terminal Services, Inc.; however, Hutchison did not undertake infrastructure investment responsibility. A combination of many factors resulted in terminal congestion, leading to terminal dwell times for containers of up to 30 days and increased waiting times for vessels. The present contract terminates in 2010, and negotiations are in progress to extend the contract for a much longer period with further equipment purchases planned. In Mombasa, a contract is being awarded to deepen the port, and a new container terminal to compete with Dar es Salaam is being discussed. In the near future, however, both ports are likely to remain relatively poor in facilities, performance, and hinterland connections. Meanwhile, Djibouti may soon provide competition for Salalah and Dubai, with DP World scheduled to bring on stream a new container terminal facility at Doraleh, targeted specifically at offering significant transshipment capacity for East Africa and the Indian Ocean. In addition, container terminal facilities in Jeddah (Saudi Arabia) are

Figure 12.2 African Ports, by Size

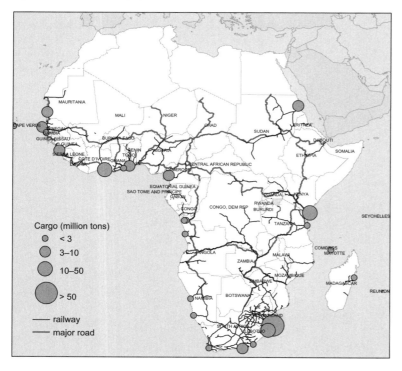

being extended, and in 2008, DP World signed a concession for the operation and further development of the Aden Container Terminal in Yemen. Since 2008, a consultant has been finalizing the National Port Strategy project for Tanzania.

In South Africa, Durban struggles to handle its own national traffic and experiences recurring berth congestion crises during the peak season. Shipping lines are threatening to reintroduce a surcharge for berthing delays, as existed between 2002 and 2005. Durban also has problems of environment, security, hinterland connections, and space. Although plans exist to bring on stream major new capacity, such as the new Pier One scheme, demand is very strong, and over the short to medium term, it may well outstrip the new capacity. The number of carriers seeking alternative locations for transshipment in the Indian Ocean islands (notably Mauritius) reflects Durban's problems. Although superstructure and infrastructure usually are separated in South Africa, the common ownership of both within the publicly owned Transnet has clearly failed to deliver the necessary improvements required of a great world port ideally located to act as a transshipment center for southern Africa. Currently, South Africa is an end-of-the-line country, and unlike other major or global hubs located on one of the very large east-west routes that make economies of scale possible, its problems arguably lie at least partly in the organization and the provision and management of equipment and handling space, as much as in basic quay capacity. The significance of that distinction is that the solution lies in institutional reform and the mobilization of private sector capabilities in port service management, as well as in public sector investment.

On the West African coast, Abidjan has enjoyed some success as a container transshipment center, but it has suffered because of the country's internal strife and the specific problems relating to ownership of operating rights for the container terminal. The need for an alternative to Abidjan is indicated by the Maersk Line's (and its affiliate Safmarine) using the Spanish port of Algeciras and the new container terminal at Tangier (Morocco)

as its main hubs for West African container trade, relaying West African cargo moving to and from Europe and Asia. Nevertheless, the number of public-private partnerships is increasing, and competition between the private port operators in the area is fierce. Consequently, some of the big global operators have become willing to look at medium-size and even small terminal projects, which they previously snubbed (Harding, Pálsson, and Raballand 2007).

Port Ownership and Management—Still Mainly a Public Service Model

Port planning and management are generally outdated, though seven sampled countries are developing new port master plans, several with a focus on institutional reform. Port regulation is normally undertaken by a ministry of transport, rather than by a quasi-independent agency; thus, it tends to be highly politicized. With its independent regulator, South Africa is the exception.

The dominant port management model in Africa is still the public service port: the state enterprise owns the port infrastructure and undertakes all port operations. This model is beginning to change. Some statutory incorporated port agencies are being reestablished as limited liability commercial companies. Ghana and Nigeria have moved toward the landlord port, where the state owns and operates major port infrastructure but allows the private sector to provide basic services. In addition, several francophone countries have a hybrid model, called *amodiation*, in which the port authority rents on-dock storage space to privately owned, licensed stevedoring companies hired by shipping lines for cargo handling.

Since 2000, some major container terminals have been concessioned to the major international terminal operators (table 12.3). However, involvement of the efficient private global operators is still low; in 2007, the top 20 global terminal operators handled only 16 percent of throughput in Africa, compared with about 70 percent in other regions of the world. Concessioning has proved controversial in some cases, with the results contested in both Luanda and Dakar. No generally accepted "clean" model exists, and influence and corruption remain.

Table 12.3 Private Transactions for All Port Sectors, 2000–07

Transaction	Countries	Ports	Number of transactions	Number of canceled transactions	Royalty payments to government ($ millions)	Investment in facilities ($ millions)
Management or lease contract	Cameroon, Kenya, Mozambique	Douala, Mombasa, Maputo	4	1	0	0
Concession contract	Angola, Comoros, Equatorial Guinea, Gabon, Ghana, Madagascar, Mozambique, Nigeria, Sudan, Tanzania	Luanda, Mutsamudu, Luba, Owendo, Tema, Toamasina, Beira, Maputo, Quelimane, Apapa (Lagos), Calibar, Harcourt, Lilypond, Onne, Warri, Tin Can, Juba	32	0	1,366	1,052
Greenfield projects	Côte d'Ivoire, Equatorial Guinea, Ghana, Kenya, Mauritius	Abidjan, Luba, Tema, Mombasa, Freeport	6	0	316	236
Total			42	1	1,683	1,288

Source: Mundy and Penfold 2008.

Port Performance—Room for Improvement

Container handling falls below international standards in most ports. Even when container gantry cranes are available, the number of container moves per crane hour is usually 10 to 20, compared with 25 to 30 moves in the world ports (figure 12.3).[1] When ships' gear is used, the performance is even worse, with only 7 to 10 moves per hour in Dakar, East London (South Africa), Matadi (the Democratic Republic of Congo), and Walvis Bay (Namibia). The low performance is partly explained by the lower number of containers handled per call with smaller vessels. However, management is even more important. Higher handling rates are generally achieved in locations where private operators have been in residence for some time; although the hybrid Mozambique model, in which the government retains a major share, has not been so successful.

Rates for general cargo handling are also lower in Africa at 7 to 25 tons per crane hour, compared with more than 30 tons in other world ports.[2] Almost all handling is through public ports.

Specialized oil and coal terminals usually do not fall under public port management. Traditionally, state-owned organizations, private interests, or a combination have developed the facilities, which fall outside the mainstream of port operations and follow an integrated supply-chain logic. Because of the private involvement in dry and liquid

Figure 12.3 Average Moves per Hour by Category of Port

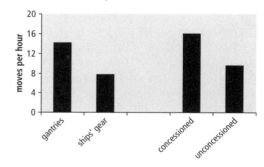

Source: Mundy and Penfold 2008.

bulk port facilities, less documentation exists about their efficiency, but a recent study of South African ports showed the bulk ports performing well on international benchmarks (Bell and Bichou 2007).

The growing interest in Africa as a source of energy products, agricultural products, timber, and minerals might aid in creating the proper maritime export capacity. The funding for this new capacity is invariably provided as part of a turnkey project, not under a traditional port authority budget. Thus, financial impediments are not envisaged.

The quality of container handling inland is indicated by the cycle times of trucks dropping off and picking up containers at the terminal and the average container dwell times in a terminal. The typical target for an efficient truck cycle is 1 hour. Average cycle times are estimated at 5–6 hours in East Africa, 4 hours in southern Africa, and 10 hours or more in West Africa (table 12.4). Average container dwell times are 6 days in southern Africa, 12 days in East Africa, and 15 days or more in West Africa, more than an accepted international standard of 7 days or less. The range of dwell times in southern Africa (4–8 days) is a much tighter band than in East and West Africa, thanks largely to better organization and control of container storage at the terminal.

Like all ports in countries that are signatories to the International Convention for the Safety of Life at Sea, African ports have been required, since 2004, to comply with the International Ship and Port Facility Security Code. Although standards of security are still extremely variable, the estimated costs of compliance for African ports—averaging about $2 per TEU and about $.04–$.05 per ton of general cargo—have not increased overall costs significantly and may have generated compensating benefits, including reduced losses through pilferage and higher customs yields (Kruk and Donner 2008). The long-term concern is a sensible balance between security and costs.

Port charges for both containers and general cargo are substantially higher in African ports than in other regions (table 12.5). For container handling, the charges applied in Sub-Saharan Africa can be more than twice those typically applied for the same service in other parts of the world, with at least 50 percent more as the norm. Normal charges for general cargo handling per ton offloaded from a vessel in Sub-Saharan Africa are also about 40 percent above world rates.

Policy Issues and Implementation Challenges

World trade and shipping patterns are changing. Expanding containerization, in ever-larger vessels, requires port facilities to handle large vessels quickly and efficiently. The financial crisis of 2008–09 adds to the turmoil. By international standards, African public port capacity is low, and its performance is poor, bringing higher costs and further losses in world trade shares. African governments are thus faced

Table 12.4 Average Port Delays

Region	Range of truck cycle times	Range of container dwell times
East Africa	3.5 hours to 1 day	5 to 28 days
Southern Africa	2 to 12 hours	4 to 8 days
West Africa	6 hours to 1 + day	11 to 30 days

Source: Mundy and Penfold 2008.

Table 12.5 Typical Gateway Container and General Cargo Handling Charges in World Markets
dollars

Region	Container handling from ship to gate	General cargo over the quay per ton
West Africa	100–320	8.00–15.00
East Africa	135–275	6.00–15.00
Southern Africa	110–243	11.00–15.00
Southeast Asia	80	8.00
Far East	144	8.00
Middle East/South Asia	96	7.00
United Kingdom	100	8.50
Northern Europe	110	7.50
Southern Europe	95	7.00
Latin America	154	9.00
Australasia	130	9.00

Source: Mundy and Penfold 2008.

with finding appropriate responses to changes in international trade and shipping markets.

Responses to Changes in the International Shipping Market

The problem is not just port capacity. East Asian ports use vessels in the 8,000–11,000 TEU range, but most African ports cannot efficiently handle container vessels above 2,000 TEUs. Moreover, an upper limit exists to optimal vessel capacity because of the low total volume of freight to African ports. Serving multiple African ports directly with vessels of 8,000 TEUs or more is therefore unlikely in the near future. Thus, a tendency will exist to transship through a small number of African regional hubs with container transshipment facilities to distribute traffic along the coasts.

The direction of the trade may also be changing as some lines consider liner services from Asia by way of southern Africa to the east coast of Latin America and the Caribbean.

For this trade, however, average vessel size is unlikely to increase because ships are cascaded down from longer-distance trade.

As the shipping industry has grown more capital intensive, more technically demanding, and more subject to global regulatory change, the number of active African shipping lines has severely decreased. Liberalizing the shipping market has already brought down deep-sea shipping costs; it should also facilitate the development of less-costly feeder services for container shipping. As the major traders attract the global operators, they may also develop a niche market in African feeder services, reestablishing African-owned shipping companies. For example, the establishment of Togo-based Ecomarine in the West African feeder market in 2003 was the first indigenous development since the decline of West African national companies in the 1990s.[3] Where collusion or barriers to market entry remain in the shipping market, governments will need to assess the level and distribution of benefits from the restraints and compare them to the widely distributed benefits of lower shipping costs in a deregulated market.

Strategic Port Planning

The expected changes have implications for port planning. Africa can support only a few regional hubs and possibly one major hub (in South Africa). Competition already exists for the hub in East Africa (between Dar es Salaam and Mombasa) and will intensify as facilities are upgraded in Djibouti, and regional collaboration—though desirable—seems unlikely. Simply investing in port capacity will not turn a port into a hub unless it has a strategic location, adequate water depth, and the facilities and performance to ensure low handling costs.

A strong corridor for transit traffic also helps. This requires facilitating traffic on the main trade corridors from the port to the landlocked hinterland. A common problem is the failure to address international, intermodal transport holistically. Inland movement, particularly across green borders, has been slow and expensive, thereby stifling trade. Although logistics chains are a commercial matter, they require the facilitation of integrated port, customs, and inland transport arrangements—a matter for government.

Governments will need to choose how best to develop state-of-the-art ports, with appropriate technologies and management skills. This determination will almost certainly involve the international private sector, particularly in the container terminal business. Strategic port planning must set the roles of the public and private sectors and identify the processes to attract and select private partners.

Countries with congested city ports or with draft limitations will need to consider whether to rehabilitate existing ports or develop new ones. Developments in the deep-sea shipping markets may also trigger the need to change location. For example, an east-west axis between Asia and Latin America would be economical only for vessels of 6,000 TEUs or larger. Any such service would necessitate a port of call in South Africa, unlikely to be satisfied by Durban. Cape Town is developing a new container terminal, but it is too far from the industrial heart of the country in Gauteng province to be a strong South African hub port. Richards Bay, which has deep water and a spacious environment, might be better. It recently launched plans for the staged development of a megaport, including a container terminal.

Port Pricing and Regulation

Having the economy benefit from lower transport costs typically requires regulating port tariffs to obtain the most efficient supply and the lowest real costs, thereby preventing any monopoly, whether state owned or private, from exploiting its advantage in the market. In many countries, however, a single port is a natural monopoly, tempting governments to maintain direct ownership and operation and, thus, to use the port as a "cash cow" to support other government activities. For example, in South Africa, all major ports are owned and operated by the National Ports Authority (responsible for infrastructure) and South African Port Operations (responsible for port operations), both part of the state-owned Transnet, a wider monopoly covering rail, pipelines, and ports. Transnet has presided over an extensive but opaque structure of cross subsidies, allowing the whole operation to exist without government subsidy. Thus, South African ports suffer from underinvestment. This type of port strategy inevitably reduces the broader benefit to the economy of having lower transport costs.

Port Management

African ports do not necessarily lack basic quay capacity (though some ports appear to be straining their limits). However, they are inefficient in using the basic infrastructure. The lack of modern superstructure, particularly cranes, inhibits fast vessel turnarounds and imposes costs on customers. Continuing reliance on the public service port structure accentuates overmanning and forgoes the advantages of the modern technologies and management practices that have revolutionized world markets for shipping and cargo handling (see table 12.4). The prevalence of state-owned service ports is also associated with the low concentration of global operators in African ports. Having global terminal operators in this business would almost certainly improve matters: they are well acquainted with the advantages of scale in terminal operations and with the benefits of an efficient hub-and-feeder structure in the deep-sea trade.

The need is thus to mobilize private capital and management skills to improve efficiency and develop a logistics system. In Africa, as elsewhere, the landlord port system has generally enjoyed greater success than the public service port and is the best way to attract the private sector. Attracting major international container lines and terminal operators can increase efficiency. However, mobilization of that potential still requires appropriate public sector actions in the administration of customs and the regulation of inland transport, as recent experience in Lagos demonstrates (see box 12.1).

Private participation by the most efficient international port operators must be stimulated by a landlord port philosophy conducive to their participation and by transparent tendering. Such port reforms are likely to involve retrenchment and compensation. Governments should develop advance strategies to

BOX 12.1

Private Participation and Port Efficiency: The Case of Apapa Container Terminal, Lagos, Nigeria

Lagos port has long been notorious for inadequate facilities and congestion. As part of a broader program of port reform in early 2006, the Nigerian Ports Authority awarded a concession to APM Terminals to manage, operate, and develop the Apapa container terminal, increasing capacity from 220,000 TEUs per year to 1.6 million TEUs. Within months of the award of that concession, delays for berthing space dwindled significantly, and shipping lines reduced their congestion surcharge from $740 to $105 per TEU, saving the Nigerian economy $200 million a year. By early 2009, new gantry cranes had been acquired to triple the original capacity.

However, that was not the end of the story. Although the port's equipment is able to handle more than 500 containers per day for customs examinations, the majority of the containers are returned to stacking by the end of each day. By January 2009, the port was clogged by uncollected containers, and at the end of February, the head of the Nigerian Ports Authority announced a temporary suspension of ship entry with immediate effect, lasting until sometime in mid-April, to enable terminals to clear "alarming" backlogs. The controller of the Nigeria Customs Service for Apapa blamed the low clearance volume on the need to physically examine every container because of the high incidence of concealment and false declaration by importers. However, even cleared containers were not being collected. At the end of January, of the reported 9,741 containers in the port for delivery to the importers, only 851 had been cleared by customs, with all charges paid and documentation completed but not picked up by agents. The Nigerian Ports Authority consequently proposed introducing demurrage charges of $4 per TEU in a bid to force owners to move their containers out of the ports. In their turn, however, the containers' agents blamed a lack of trucks, arguing that many had been booked to empty containers. Although the moratorium on entry of new vessels was lifted in early March, some backlogs and delays remained and significant organizational and regulatory problems still remain.

Source: Press reports assembled by C. Bert Kruk, World Bank.

create employment alternatives and to handle the administration and finance of the adjustment in the terms of the concession contracts.

Comprehensive Policies for Modal Integration

Governments must decide how best to foster and finance integrated port and transport facilities and associated land uses. A national port plan covering modal integration and port-specific issues is the key. Allocating enough land for integrated development should be considered in the early stages of port planning, particularly for new ports. Links between rail and port concessions, while having some risk of exploitation in downstream markets, may provide the best incentive to good modal integration.

Governments of both coastal and landlocked countries must decide which transit corridors to support and develop. The key to exploiting the major scope for traffic growth is coordinated system development similar to that for the Ghana Gateway and for the Maputo Corridor between the port of Maputo and South Africa, Swaziland, and Zimbabwe. Landlocked countries will likely want more than one alternative. Where the bottlenecks are at the seaports, planning and developing inland ports (dry ports) deserves consideration, particularly for landlocked transit countries.

Investment for Quality—the Communications Needs

To reduce dwell times and handling costs, countries need to invest in information systems, communications technology, and modern customs practices. Customs procedures, in particular, act as a bottleneck to port efficiency when they are outdated or open to corruption. As an extreme example, one port had to close for an extended period because of customs problems. Modern customs procedures and other soft infrastructure have a major role in delivering efficient port and freight transportation systems.

Striving for efficient ports must be complemented by associated measures to increase transparency and reduce corruption in customs administration. The African ports, like all world ports, must create port community systems not only to improve productivity and efficiency (and thereby reduce costs), but also to respond to the growing importance of and future obligation in supply chain security.

Notes

The authors of this chapter are Mike Mundy and Kenneth Gwilliam, who drew on background material and contributions from Michel Luc Donner, Bradley Julian, Cornelis Kruk, and Andrew Penfold.

1. Some concession contracts specify required performance in TEUs per crane hour. Moves per hour is preferred here as an indicator because moving a 20-foot box requires the same time as moving a 40-foot box.
2. This comparison must be viewed cautiously because the productivity depends on the type of cargo handled, which is not allowed for in this crude statistic.
3. Those national companies include Sitram of Côte d'Ivoire, NNSL (Nigerian National Shipping Line) of Nigeria, Black Star Line of Ghana, Sotonam of Togo, and Camship of Cameroon.

References

Bell, Michael G. H., and Khalid Bichou. 2007. "The Port Sector in South Africa: Towards an Integrated Policy and Institutional Reform." World Bank, Washington, DC.

Drewry Shipping Consultants Ltd. 2006. *Global Capacity Issues: Annual Review of Global Container Terminal Operators*. London: Drewry Shipping Consultants Ltd.

———. 2008. *Annual Review of Global Container Operators*. London: Drewry Shipping Consultants Ltd.

Harding, Alan, Gylfi Pálsson, and Gaël Raballand. 2007. "Port and Maritime Transport Challenges in West and Central Africa." Working Paper 84, Sub-Saharan Africa Transport Policy Program, World Bank, Washington, DC.

Kruk, C. Bert, and Michel Luc Donner. 2008. "Review of Cost of Compliance with the New International Freight Transport Security Requirements: Consolidated Report of the Investigations Carried Out in Ports in the Africa, Europe and Central Asia, and Latin America and Caribbean Regions." Transport Paper 16, Transport Sector Board, World Bank, Washington, DC.

Mundy, Michael, and Andrew Penfold. 2008. "Beyond the Bottlenecks: Ports in Sub-Saharan Africa." Background Paper 8, Africa Infrastructure Country Diagnostic, World Bank, Washington, DC.

Chapter 13

Airports and Air Transport: The Sky's the Limit

Air transport can stimulate regional economic development. In Africa, 120,000 people are employed directly in air transport, and 20 percent of tourism jobs are associated with travelers by air. Air cargo is also important in some export trades (such as flowers from Kenya and fish from Tanzania). Overall, traffic has been growing at about 6 percent a year from 1997 to 2006. In southern and eastern Africa, the market growth is strongest, with three vigorous hubs and three major African carriers dominating international and domestic markets. In central and western Africa, however, the market is stagnating, with the vacuum created by the conflict in Côte d'Ivoire and the demise of several regional airlines still unfilled.

Air transport in Sub-Saharan Africa is still expensive by international standards. Landing charges are high, partly caused by the absence of the support from concessions revenue enjoyed by many airports in the world. Because of relatively low volumes of traffic on many routes in Africa, airfares are also high, despite the efforts of some governments to subsidize domestic fares from protected intercontinental routes. In many cases, the protection of small national carriers, as an instrument for this cross subsidy, adds to the budget burden and hinders efficient service.

Generally, infrastructure capacity is not a serious problem. The number of airports is stable, and enough runways exist to handle traffic with better scheduling and modest investment in parallel taxiways and some terminal facilities. Aircraft fleets are being modernized, but air traffic control facilities need substantial improvement. Revenues from airports and air traffic are probably high enough to finance the necessary investments, but the sector does not capture them. The problem is both political and organizational.

Two other serious challenges remain. First, liberalization of the international regime within Africa must be completed, as committed to in the Yamoussoukro Decision of 1999. Many international agreements within Africa have been liberalized, resulting in routes and aircraft sizes that are better adapted to the market and some large, viable indigenous carriers that are expanding. However, the domestic and intercontinental markets often remain protected, and many small, nonviable state-owned operations continue, particularly in southern Africa, that are protected at the expense of potential users of air transport.

Second, air safety must be addressed. Sub-Saharan African carriers have the world's worst accident record. Contrary to many accounts, this unenviable record is largely attributable to poor pilot capabilities and weak safety administration rather than the age of aircraft. Supervisory oversight of operators is particularly lax.

The African Air Transport Market

Air traffic in Africa has been growing, but at the same time concentrating, so that fewer routes are served. Lack of competition keeps costs relatively high, and the safety record remains very worrisome. However, fleet renewal has been substantial in recent years, downsizing aircraft toward a city-jet size.

Traffic Trends—on the Rise

All segments of the air passenger transport market in Sub-Saharan Africa have been growing steadily since 1997, with a small hesitation following September 11, 2001, and a larger downturn in West and Central Africa associated with the collapse of Air Afrique in 2004 (figure 13.1).

A notable acceleration has occurred in all main traffic categories (measured in number of seats) since 2004, including domestic, international, and intercontinental (table 13.1). Intercontinental traffic, which relies heavily on the three major gateways of Johannesburg, Nairobi, and Addis Ababa, grew at an average of 6.2 percent a year between 2001 and 2007. Although the South African routes to Germany and the United Kingdom are still the most heavily trafficked, the most notable feature of this growth has been the significant rise in service through the Middle East from all of the main gateways.

International traffic within Sub-Saharan Africa grew slightly faster, at an average of 6.5 percent a year between 2004 and 2007, with the same three major hubs handling 36 percent of such traffic (figure 13.2). The national airline dominates the interregional traffic of each hub: South African Airways (33 percent of the international traffic at the hub), Kenya Airways (70 percent), and Ethiopian Airlines (83 percent). Both Kenya Airways and Ethiopian Airlines have been developing new routes as the sole carrier, while most of South African Airways' international routes have more than one carrier in competition. East Africa has the more developed network. In West and Central Africa, only Nigeria has a significant number of intercontinental and international connections.

Domestic traffic grew fastest, at more than 12 percent a year between 2004 and 2007. But that growth—as high as 67 percent in Nigeria—varied greatly and actually declined in about half of the countries in the region between 2001 and 2007. Overall, the number of domestic city-pairs served dropped by 229 in that same period. In addition, excluding Mozambique, Nigeria, and South Africa, domestic traffic showed an average annual decline of 1 percent a year and a loss of 137 routes between 2004 and 2007.

The steady growth of traffic overall disguises some severe problems at the subregional level. The Banjul Accord Group of countries, including Nigeria, has shown the fastest growth, followed by the more developed, yet healthily growing regions of East and southern Africa (figure 13.3). Because of regional airline collapses, a swath of nations surrounding the

Figure 13.1 Growth of Air Traffic, 1997–2006

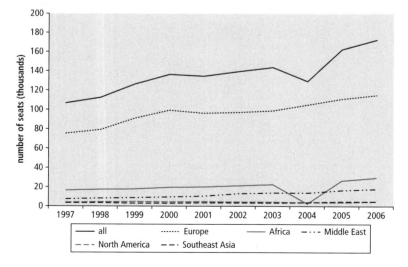

Source: Bofinger 2009.

Table 13.1 Air Traffic Growth in Sub-Saharan Africa, 2001–07

Market	Estimated number of seats			Percentage of growth		
	2001	2004	2007	2001–04	2004–07	2001–07
All Sub-Saharan Africa	50,410,448	54,544,861	72,338,706	2.66	9.87	6.20
Domestic Sub-Saharan Africa	18,184,071	19,356,818	27,477,027	2.11	12.39	7.12
International Sub-Saharan Africa	11,758,107	11,868,280	14,327,728	0.31	6.48	3.35
Intercontinental Sub-Saharan Africa	19,544,122	22,051,174	28,068,536	4.11	8.38	6.22
Between North Africa and Sub-Saharan Africa	924,148	1,268,588	2,465,415	11.14	24.79	17.77
Other	1,036,932	1,076,010	794,621	1.24	−9.61	−4.34

Source: Bofinger 2009.

Banjul Accord Group of countries has experienced negative growth. Of 19 countries that lost international connections since 2004, 16 are in these areas of West and Central Africa. Most worrisome are the Central African Republic (only one flight a week in November 2007), Chad, Eritrea, Mauritania, and the Seychelles. Not only are they minimally connected, but also their connectivity plunged between 2004 and 2007.

Air Transport Supply—the Process of Concentration

In the early 1960s, many of the newly independent African states created their own, mostly government-owned, national air carriers. Most pursued a business strategy designed to protect profits on international routes through restrictive use of the bilateral permission system in order to cross subsidize costly yet extensive domestic route networks. Until 1991, nearly all African carriers were state owned. Some very small carriers failed early or were assimilated into Air Afrique. Since 2001, however, several medium-size airlines have ceased operations, including Air Afrique, Air Gabon, Ghana Airways Corporation, and Nigeria Airways. Countries now fall into one of four distinct groups. Countries in the first group (Ethiopia, Kenya, and South Africa) have succeeded in establishing an efficient state-owned carrier. The 17 countries in the second group continue to operate weak, highly subsidized, state-owned carriers mainly operating in very small, protected markets and often in domestic and shorter-distance international sectors. The 25 countries in the third group have

Figure 13.2 Top-60 International Routes within Sub-Saharan Africa, 2007

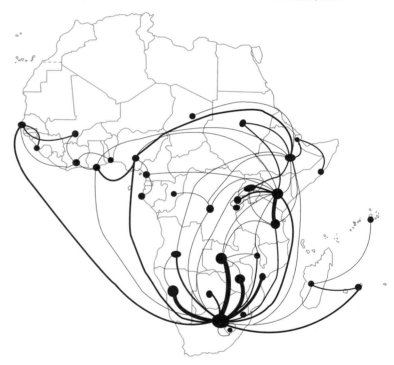

Source: Bofinger 2009.
Note: The thickness of the lines is on a continuous scale, with the thickest line (South Africa–Zambia) representing nearly 1 million seats for 2007 and the thinnest (Ethiopia–Ghana) representing 62,000 seats. The size of the end points results from the thickness of the lines.

withdrawn from state-owned carriers and left their markets to private operators only. The three countries (the Central African Republic, Lesotho, and Niger) in the final group have no known operators and rely on services from other countries.

The combined effect of airline failures and regulatory restrictions on competition has

Figure 13.3 Regional Growth Zones in Seats Offered, All Travel Categories

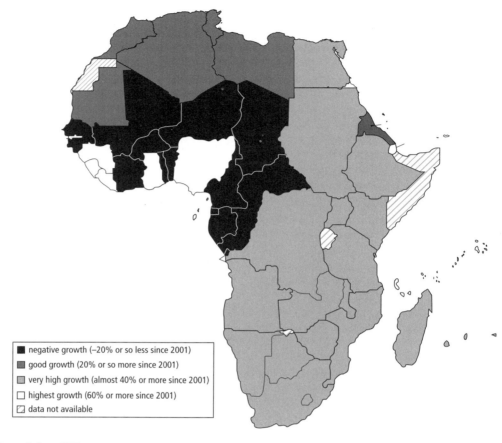

■ negative growth (−20% or so less since 2001)
▨ good growth (20% or so more since 2001)
▨ very high growth (almost 40% or more since 2001)
☐ highest growth (60% or more since 2001)
▨ data not available

Source: Bofinger 2009.

been to increase concentration, both in the total market and on individual routes. By early 2008, 15 airlines accounted for 59 percent of all seat capacity offered in Africa. The top-20 intercontinental routes each average 3.45 competing airlines. International service within Sub-Saharan Africa is less competitive, with just 15 airlines providing more than 82 percent of capacity, and the big 3 (Ethiopian Airlines, Kenya Airways, and South African Airways) providing 57 percent.

Sixteen of the top 60 routes, and 66 of the 206 total routes, have only one carrier. Ethiopian Airlines and, to a lesser extent, Kenya Airways have contributed to this concentration by developing new routes as sole carriers. In most cases, domestic travel is serviced by the national flag carrier and is highly concentrated. Of the 286 routes with service in 2007, only 54 had more than one service provider—generally, the national flag carrier. Standing out among the larger countries for allowing competition are South Africa, where competition occurs only on the heaviest routes, and Tanzania, where more than one service provider exists on all of its 17 domestic routes.

The Equipment Operated

The two most significant trends for Sub-Saharan African air transport have been the downsizing of aircraft toward the city-jet size (Boeing 737 or Airbus 319) and, contrary to many accounts, the renewal of the fleet. The proportion of seat miles flown on older Western aircraft has increased to accommodate growth quickly and inexpensively only in some domestic markets, and even that proportion is only 4 percent of seat miles overall. A slight increase has already occurred in the use of commuter propeller aircraft on the low-volume routes in Tanzania and in West and Central Africa, and such aircraft may have an important role in the recovery of the air transport market in that subregion.

Fares—More Expensive Within Africa than Outside

Air travel within Africa is considerably more expensive per mile flown than intercontinental travel, especially on routes of less than 2,000 nautical miles (figure 13.4). This cost reflects the fact that domestic and international markets are less dense and less competitive than the longer distance intercontinental markets. Moreover, aircraft landing charges are generally high by international standards, partly because of the absence of nonflight revenues from airport concessions. In some cases, the skewed cost is limited by subsidized or fixed pricing on domestic routes operated by a national flag carrier.

Flying in Africa—a Dangerous Business

The most notable problem of the African air transport industry is safety. In 2004, Africa experienced 22.0 percent of all accidents worldwide, despite accounting for only 4.5 percent of all sectors flown globally. In 2006, African carriers lost 4.31 aircraft per million departures, compared with 0.65 aircraft worldwide.

The major intercontinental carriers, most of them Asian, European, or U.S. registered, have an excellent safety record. In contrast, companies operating Western-built aircraft that are still in use in most developed countries but registered in a Sub-Saharan African country have had 15 fatal accidents since the mid-1990s, involving 1,080 deaths. Even worse, African carriers operating older Western- or Eastern-built aircraft have reported at least 29 accidents over same period (and suspicions exist that many others are not reported). In addition, many accidents involve flights conducted by the air force, which in many African countries transports civilian passengers and cargo.

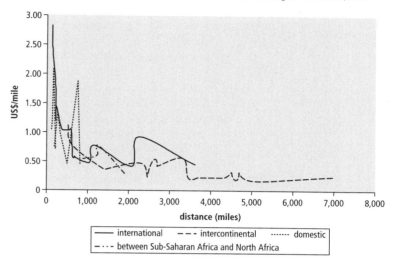

Figure 13.4 Airfares by Distance on African Routes, Including North Africa, 2008

Source: Bofinger 2009.

Some commentators have ascribed this bad record primarily to the use of Eastern-built aircraft. Certainly, the hull loss rate per million departures of Eastern-built aircraft reached 54.35 in 2006 in Africa, 10 times the world average for such aircraft (5.61). However, a study by the Interstate Aviation Committee concluded that the flight safety of most Soviet-made types of aircraft is no worse and, in some cases, is better than that of their Western equivalents. Much more significant is that mainly small, poorly regulated fringe carriers fly these aircraft. The high accident rate in Sub-Saharan Africa is thus primarily a result of poor safety standards and lax supervision, not operation of Eastern-built or older aircraft.

Air Transport Policy in Africa

Much of the world has moved from a strictly regulated air transport industry to a more liberalized one. In the United States, deregulation resulted in the failure of weaker carriers, emergence of new low-cost carriers, rearrangement of routes, and evolution of the hub-and-spoke system. Fares fell on average, and load factors generally increased through differentiated pricing. In Europe, too, the rise of low-cost carriers was a highly visible effect of deregulation.

On October 17, 1988, the ministers in charge of civil aviation in African states met in Yamoussoukro, Côte d'Ivoire, and expounded a new African Air Transport Policy, later called the Yamoussoukro Declaration. Although the ministers foresaw the gradual elimination of traffic restrictions, the declaration was aimed primarily at cooperation among African air carriers to better compete with non-African carriers. Nevertheless, it did stimulate the United Nations Economic Commission for Africa to initiate a further conference in Yamoussoukro, which resulted in the historic agreement on pan-African liberalization of air services, the 1999 Yamoussoukro Decision (Schlumberger 2008).

The decision's main objective was the gradual liberalization of scheduled and nonscheduled intra-African air services, abolishing limits on the capacity and frequency of international air services within Africa, universally granting traffic rights up to the fifth freedom,[1] and liberalizing fares. Signatory states were obliged to ensure the fair opportunity to compete on a nondiscriminatory basis. A monitoring body would supervise and implement the decision, and an African air transport executing agency would ensure fair competition. The decision paid special attention to improving air transport safety. However, even though the decision is a pan-African agreement to which most African states are bound, the parties decided that separate regional economic organizations should implement it.

The monitoring body has met only a few times. Competition rules and arbitration procedures remain pending. Although an executing agency was finally created in 2007 by assigning the responsibilities and duties to the African Civil Aviation Commission, a specialized institution of the African Union, the commission has yet to prove its effectiveness. In contrast, operational implementation has been much more productive (table 13.2), with

Table 13.2 Air Service Liberalization in African Regional Groupings

Community	Members	General status of Yamoussoukro Decision implementation	Status of air services liberalization	Percentage of flights under fifth and seventh freedoms
Banjul Accord Group	Cape Verde; Gambia, The; Ghana; Guinea; Liberia; Nigeria; and Sierra Leone	Principles of YD have been agreed upon in a multilateral air service agreement.	First through fifth freedoms have been granted, tariffs are free, and capacity and frequency are open.	43
Economic and Monetary Community of Central Africa	Cameroon; Central African Republic; Gabon; Equatorial Guinea; Congo, Rep. of; Chad	Principles of YD have been agreed upon in an air transport program. Some minor restrictions remain.	First through fifth freedoms have been granted, tariffs are free, and capacity and frequency are open. A maximum of two carriers per state may participate.	28
Common Market for Eastern and Southern Africa	Most East and southern African states except Botswana, Lesotho, South Africa, and Tanzania	Full liberalization has been agreed upon, but implementation is pending until a joint competition authority is established.	Liberalization is pending. When it is applied, operators will be able to serve any destination (all freedoms), and tariffs and capacity and/or frequency will be unregulated.	14
East African Community	Kenya, Tanzania, Uganda	EAC Council issued a directive to amend bilaterals among EAC states to conform to YD.	Air services are not liberalized because the amendments of bilaterals remain pending.	16
Southern African Development Community	Most countries south of Tanzania	No steps were taken toward implementation, even though civil aviation policy includes gradual liberalization of air services within SADC.	No liberalization within SADC has been initiated.	6
West African Economic and Monetary Union	Benin, Burkina Faso, Côte d'Ivoire, Guinea-Bissau, Mali, Niger, Senegal, Togo	Within WAEMU, YD is fully implemented.	All freedoms, including cabotage, have been granted. Tariffs are liberalized.	44

Source: Bofinger 2009.
Note: EAC = East African Community; SADC = Southern Africa Development Community; WAEMU = West African Economic and Monetary Union; YD = Yamoussoukro Decision.

greater freedom to negotiate bilateral agreements in all of the subregions.

In West Africa, the Economic Community of West African States was unable to take any significant steps toward liberalizing air services, but the smaller West African Economic and Monetary Union went even beyond the Yamoussoukro principles with a regime that includes cabotage rights. The Banjul Accord Group, also in West Africa, agreed to a multilateral air service agreement, fully compatible with the Yamoussoukro Decision. In Central Africa, the Economic and Monetary Community of Central Africa has implemented all the necessary legislative and regulatory elements to comply with the provisions of the Yamoussoukro Decision. In East and southern Africa, the Common Market for Eastern and Southern Africa achieved the most progress, but full application of the decision principles remains suspended. The East African Community has chosen the effective strategy of directing the bilaterals to conform to the decision, but signing of the agreement remains pending. The Southern African Development Community has progressed the least. Apparently, the dominant position of South Africa remains the main obstacle toward implementing the decision. Overall, about two-thirds of air transport service within Africa is now liberalized.

African Air Transport Infrastructure

The existing air transport infrastructure can fairly well accommodate Africa's current air traffic and foreseeable growth; only a handful of cases warrant investments in taxiways or terminal upgrades. Instead, the main investment need lies in air traffic control and surveillance equipment, which with few exceptions is largely inadequate.

Airports—a Declining Number in Service, but Adequate Runway Capacity

At least 2,900 airports exist in Africa, of which an estimated 261 in Sub-Saharan Africa received scheduled services in 2007. These airports fall into three groups. First, three major international airports (Addis Ababa, Johannesburg, and Nairobi) act as gateways to the continent for intercontinental traffic and as hubs for its distribution. They currently handle 36 percent of all international traffic in Africa. Lagos could perform a similar function for West and Central Africa but is lagging. Second, about 40 medium-size airports are connected to the hubs and primarily serve international and domestic traffic. Third, more than 200 small and often nonviable airports act as the distribution points for frequently declining domestic air traffic. Except for those in the Banjul Accord countries (Cape Verde, the Gambia, Ghana, Guinea, Liberia, Nigeria, and Sierra Leone), the number of airports with scheduled service dropped by 20–40 percent between 2001 and 2007.

Nearly all airports that had scheduled advertised service in November 2007 have at least one paved major runway. Only a dozen or so airstrips are unpaved, most of them in countries either in or just out of military conflict. An exception is Tanzania, which has five airports with scheduled service and with alternatively surfaced runways, though projects for resurfacing are in progress.

Airports in Africa do not often have "pure" runway capacity constraints. With a five-minute separation between flights, a single-runway airport could accommodate 144 flights in 12 hours, or more than 1,000 flights a week. With an average load of 120 passengers, more than 17,000 passengers a day could be handled. Even with a 20-minute separation, passenger numbers would not exceed 4,300 a day. Very few airports in Africa handle more passengers than this. Capacity constraints may appear, however, on taxiways, aprons, and jetways.

In many African airports, aircraft must taxi to the turning bay, turn around, and taxi back toward the access to the apron, usually in the center of the runway. This procedure is acceptable in most airports where enough time elapses between departing and arriving aircraft to do so. Only a relatively few high-volume airports require parallel taxiways with multiple turn-off ramps from the runway. Despite this generally adequate flight capacity, policy makers in several countries are urging the construction of entirely new international airports for which no economic justification exists.

The airside infrastructure in such major hubs as Johannesburg and Nairobi meets high international standards in runway length, instrument landing systems, and so on. For airports with lower traffic volumes, however, significant differences in the quality of the infrastructure are apparent. Fewer than 50 percent of airport runways are in excellent or very good condition, compared with 96 percent in North Africa. Although traffic to airports without paved runways is low, the number of airports with poor runways is relatively high in some countries (table 13.3). Fortunately, 87 percent of the seats landed are on excellent or very good runways, and only about 4 percent of the traffic is to airports with marginal or poor ratings.

Instrument landing systems can be found at nearly all airports with an estimated capacity of 1 million seats or more, but their presence drops off rapidly below this traffic volume. In many smaller, older airports, nondirectional beacon systems—now very outdated—still prevail. However, this circumstance does not necessarily imply that new investment is needed in ground-based navigation infrastructure; today's satellite technology can easily replace many of the ground-based systems at a much lower cost. Nevertheless, in practice, few plans have been made to replace obsolete technologies.

Airport Terminals—Few Capacity Constraints

Some evidence exists of inadequate capacity of passenger terminals, though data are not readily available. Many Sub-Saharan African terminals report traffic volumes at or above their declared capacity, and in some cases,

capacity issues are already being addressed. For example, Nairobi's passenger terminal is going through an extensive upgrade to allow more than 9 million passengers a year. In other cases, the declared capacity needs to be examined. For example, Malawi's airport in Lilongwe, though clearly in need of some upgrades, does not appear on the ground to be as deficient as the figures suggest. Rescheduling to prevent the simultaneous arrival of too many flights can be of great help.

Airport Management—Limited Privatization

Airports usually have some quasi-independent operating agency, whether government owned or not. Even the company that owns South Africa's nine most important airports, including Johannesburg, is only partially privatized, with majority ownership still held by the state. Cameroon, Côte d'Ivoire, and Madagascar have concessioned their major airport groups, although in Madagascar, the government has a majority shareholding in the concessionaire. Kenya has concessioned the development of the cargo terminal at Nairobi's international airport. South Africa has divested some smaller airports completely. Even without full airport concessions, the range of airport service providers is wide. In Tanzania's Dar es Salaam International Airport, passenger services are performed by Swissport, and at Nairobi's Jomo Kenyatta International Airport, a broad range of competition exists for landside services. Navigation and air traffic control still typically fall directly under governmental agencies, with some services subcontracted.

Table 13.3 Runway Quality in Sub-Saharan Africa, 2007

Rating	Airports (number)	Percentage of total airports	Seats (millions)	Percentage of total seats
Excellent	31	18	67.75	68
Very good	50	29	18.49	19
Fair	46	27	8.51	9
Marginal	10	6	2.29	2
Poor	36	21	2.42	2
Total	173	100	99.50	100

Source: Bofinger 2009.

Air Traffic Control—the Critical Infrastructure Deficiency

Air traffic control infrastructure in Africa is wanting, with the exception of airports in South Africa and Kenya.[2] Addis Ababa uses no civilian radar, forcing extra distance and time separations between aircraft. In Malawi, as equipment has aged and become too expensive to maintain, surveillance has fallen into disrepair. Even when the equipment exists, radar procedures (and radar separations) are not always implemented. In Kenya, only the airport in Nairobi has full-time radar vectoring, while that in Mombasa switches to radar only if weather so demands. In Tanzania, Dar es Salaam's airport has a good radar installation, with a secondary radar range in excess of 200 miles, but has no radar vectoring because of a lack of radar-certified controllers.

Closely related to traffic surveillance is the capability for aircraft communication to and from the ground. In certain areas of Africa, an airliner could fly for more than an hour and be unable to make contact with the ground. The lack of adequate surveillance also raises concerns about search and rescue operations.[3] Weather installations are also sparse, often relying on physical observation using manual techniques now commonly automated in the West. Moreover, broadband infrastructure is not available in most airports.

Policy Challenges

Countries in Africa face five main challenges in developing their airports and air transport:

- Deciding what to do with national flag carriers
- Improving air safety
- Liberalizing air transport markets
- Financing infrastructure
- Developing and maintaining skills.

A Strategy for National Flag Carriers

Most national flag carriers in Sub-Saharan Africa have been small by international standards, with a very weak base of demand. They usually experienced political pressures to maintain unremunerative services without direct subsidies, often performing politically determined services for no return at all. Even with protection of the home market, they lacked the potential to be commercially viable. Consequently, many of them have failed, as did the multinational Air Afrique.

Despite the failures, Africa still has many small, nationally owned flag carriers that were established decades ago. They survived initially through protection of both the domestic market and the national share of international markets. Even when losses mounted, governments often argued that the national flag carrier should be retained in a restructured form, because subsidized domestic routes would be dropped without a national carrier, causing regional isolation, and revenues from foreigners traveling within the country would be lost. However, restructuring has often simply meant strengthening protection and investing in new aircraft, without improving the basic economics of the operation.

Africa has some successful nationally owned flag carriers, usually the dominant carrier in an intercontinental hub. However, they are rare. In most cases, instead of protecting a flag carrier, countries should pursue a better alternative of opening the market to allow a successful operator to provide service. This approach could include a successful flag carrier from another country. In principle, the merger of several regional airlines should create some strength, but the experience of Air Afrique shows the dangers of political intervention and noncommercial operation. A possible compromise is to paint one of the successful operator's aircraft in the flag carrier's colors and hire a crew for passenger services in the country.

Improvement of Air Safety

According to the African Airlines Association, the age of the fleet is the greatest concern: nearly one-third of the total fleet of 750 aircraft is more than 20 years old, with a prevalence of ex-Soviet types in certain countries. That view is not widely accepted. Although most accidents in 2006 involved old, Soviet-built turboprop aircraft, more recent, devastating crashes have involved mainly Western-built aircraft. Worldwide averages suggest that, vintage for vintage, Russian-built aircraft are as safe as Western-built aircraft if properly maintained and operated. The problem is that many small carriers acquire one or more old aircraft on the nontransparent aircraft supply market and operate them without supervision by the civil aviation authorities. Their pilots work long hours and regularly operate aircraft in a dangerous environment, resulting in crashes. Even for U.S.-built aircraft, U.S. National Transportation Board inquiries highlighted several cases of pilot error, in which poor pilot training and assessment contributed to an accident.

In general, the International Air Transport Association identifies poor regulatory oversight as the top threat to safety in Africa, followed by inadequate safety management systems. Similarly, the International Civil Aviation Organization's Universal Safety Oversight Program shows that safety implementation in Africa is very deficient. For example, West and Central Africa, and East and southern Africa perform below the world average in all the critical elements of safety implementation—in most cases, by a factor of two (figure 13.5). These deficiencies are highly correlated with accident rates, suggesting that institutional failings explain much of Africa's poor accident record. The U.S. Federal Aviation Administration and the European Union also rate air safety in many African countries as poor.

Because of the interaction between national systems, air safety is a regional problem that needs to be addressed regionally. ASECNA (Agence pour la Sécurité de la Navigation Aérienne en Afrique et à Madagascar), founded in 1959, has 15 member states aiming to pool air navigation services and other infrastructure. In addition to navigation infrastructure, the organization manages eight airports. Further steps are under way. In East Africa, a centralized East African civil aviation authority has just been formed with support from the U.S. Department of Transportation's Safe Skies for Africa program. Though not yet fully implemented, the organization, now headquartered at the East African Community in Arusha, Tanzania, would supplement the existing civil aviation authorities in the member countries by providing resources in a central pool available to community countries. Also, two projects for the Cooperative Development of Operational Safety and Continuing Airworthiness Program are being planned for the Southern African Development Community and the Economic and Monetary Community of Central Africa. Thus, regional pooling of resources is addressing Africa's shortcomings in oversight.

Liberalization of Air Transport Markets

Formal implementation of the Yamoussoukro Decision remains very slow, particularly in southern Africa. Many national airline officials have advised their governments that the airlines are not ready for a free market and still need protection. Many are concerned that an open skies policy for intercontinental transport, particularly to Europe, would drive African carriers from the intercontinental market, with adverse secondary effects for international and domestic services in Africa.

This attitude almost certainly hinders regional development. Ample evidence already exists of the benefits for southern Africa from wider liberalization. For example, liberalizing the domestic market in South Africa in 1990 fueled passenger growth of 80 percent between 1994 and 2004, and eventually led to the establishment of domestic low-cost carriers.

Figure 13.5 International Civil Aviation Organization Analysis of Safety Implementation in Africa, 2004

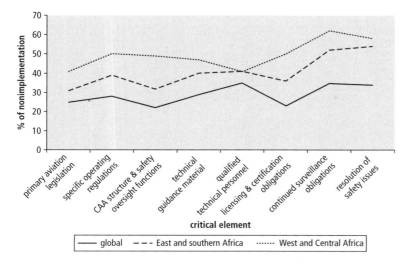

critical element

—— global   – – – East and southern Africa   ······· West and Central Africa

Similarly, liberalizing the Nairobi-Johannesburg route in 2000 increased flights from 4 a day to 14 and increased passenger volumes by 69 percent. Competition is important here. On the Johannesburg-Lusaka route (for which South African Airways had been the only carrier for over 10 years), designating the South African low-cost carrier, Kulula, as the Zambian carrier reduced fares by 33–38 percent and increased passengers by 38 percent.

Recent modeling suggests that full liberalization in the Southern African Development Community would reduce airfares by 18–40 percent with a low-cost carrier entering the market and would increase traffic volume by 20 percent (Genesis Analytics and others 2006). Another half a million foreign tourists would arrive by air each year, spending more than $500 million. The multiplier effect would increase the Southern African Development Community's GDP by about $1.5 billion, or 0.5 percent growth. Another study on liberalizing routes on 20 city-pairs to and from Addis Ababa came to a similar conclusion (Abate 2007).

Financing of Infrastructure

Two agencies are typically concerned with air transport infrastructure. Air traffic control is usually the function of a national civil aviation authority, whereas airport infrastructure (both airside and landside) is usually the responsibility of a separate airports agency. Both have financing problems.

Civil aviation authorities survive on fees. Where the land mass is large and the geographic location important, significant air navigation charges (exceeding many of the other service charges relied on by authorities) can be gained from overflights. However, reallocating those charges can be politically contentious. A truly independent regulatory body could improve services, but in many cases, the revenues end up in the national treasury.

The same situation applies to airports. In a study by the International Civil Aviation Organization using 2005 data (ICAO 2008), the main access airports in Africa were considered inherently profitable. However, the nonpayment of tariffs by weak flag carriers in small countries undermines airport finance, as does the allocation of many airport revenues (such as those for overflight) to the state treasury, with only a small part left to the sector. The sensible investment strategy would seem to be investment in existing infrastructure, not new airports, and use of newer, cheaper technologies for air traffic surveillance and navigation systems.

Development and Maintenance of Skills

The International Air Transport Association has identified the lack of effective flight crew training and proficiency as a major source of safety problems. Even where training is adequate, highly trained flight crews in the poorer countries can usually command higher salaries when working for a larger foreign airline. A similar drain of skills affects regulatory staff. Safety inspectors trained with donor funding abandon oversight almost immediately to earn much more working for an airline.

Many issues are interconnected. Poor countries trying to maintain a domestic flag carrier do not pay enough to train and maintain good flight crews. Because funds are usually insufficient to provide competitive salaries for safety inspectors, oversight standards also fall. Maintaining staff is thus linked to the policies for flag carriers, market liberalization, and sector finance. Only a coherent and fiscally affordable set of policies in these challenging areas can produce a more sustainable air transport sector in Sub-Saharan Africa.

Notes

The authors of this chapter are Heinrich Bofinger and Kenneth Gwilliam, who drew on background material and contributions from Michel Iches, Pierre Pozzo di Borgo, and Charles Schlumberger.

1. The eight "freedoms of the air" are the focus of international regulation of air transport. The first and second freedoms are technical freedoms to overfly a foreign country or to land for refueling. The third and fourth freedoms are commercial freedoms to carry passengers from a carrier's home country to another or vice versa. The fifth to seventh freedoms concern the rights to carry passengers between two foreign countries, either as an extension of a flight from the home country (fifth), through

a stop in the home country (sixth), or without ongoing service to the home base (seventh). The eighth freedom, pure cabotage, is the right to carry traffic between two points in a foreign country.

2. The lack of radar installations should be discussed as the lack of surveillance infrastructure, because radar is now an obsolete technology. Newer, much more accurate, and much less costly technologies are now being installed, as in the United States. Similarly, navigation aids are being supplanted by technologies based on global positioning systems in modern aircraft.

3. In a recent accident in Cameroon involving a new Boeing 737, the aircraft could not immediately be located because the last known position was the departure end of the runway.

References

Abate, Megersa A. 2007. "The Economic Effects of Progressive Air Transport Liberalization in Africa." School of Graduate Studies, Addis Ababa University, Ethiopia.

Bofinger, Heinrich C. 2009. "Air Transport: Challenges to Growth." Background Paper 16, Africa Infrastructure Country Diagnostic, World Bank, Washington, DC.

Genesis Analytics, Andrew Myburgh, Fathima Sheik, Fatima Fiandeiro, and James Hodge. 2006. *Clear Skies over Southern Africa*. Woodmead, South Africa: ComMark Trust.

ICAO (International Civil Aviation Organization). 2004. "An Update of the ICAO Universal Safety Oversight Audit Programme." Presentation to the ICAO TCB Seminar, Singapore, January 12–14, pp. 9 and 11. http://www.icao.int/icao/en/tcb/TCB-Singapore-2004/Attachements/Presentations/Acrobat/ICAO%20USOAP%20&%20Follow-up%20Programme.pdf.

———. 2008. "Financial Situation of Airports and Air Navigation Service Providers 2005." ICAO, Montreal, Canada.

Schlumberger, Charles E. 2008. "Air Transport Policy Research: The Implementation of the Yamoussoukro Decision." Working Paper 20, Africa Infrastructure Country Diagnostic, World Bank, Washington, DC.

Chapter 14

Water Resources: A Common Interest

Water management is critical for meeting Africa's development challenges. Though water is vital for agriculture, only 5 percent of Africa's cultivated land is irrigated. Hydropower is also largely undeveloped in Africa; less than 10 percent of its potential has been tapped. Water for people and animals is vital for health and livelihoods, yet only 58 percent of Africans have access to safe drinking water.

African economies depend on a reliable and adequate supply of water, but high rainfall and hydrological variability result in frequent droughts and floods that stifle economic growth. Moreover, water resources shared by countries pose complex political and management challenges.

Achieving water security to support growth and to build climate resilience is at the heart of water resource management in Africa. Water security reflects a country's ability to function productively in the face of water vulnerability. It is a precondition for sustaining and increasing investment returns and achieving dynamic economic growth. A minimum capacity of infrastructure and institutions, backed by robust water information systems, is needed to ensure basic national water security.

Building water infrastructure will fuel growth, reduce weather-induced risk, and alleviate water-related conflicts. Both large and small infrastructure projects need to be part of a balanced water investment program that provides reliable water supplies for human health and economic activities and that protects natural water and environmental assets. Development of large multipurpose storage facilities (often combined with hydropower generation) is necessary for mitigating the economic effects of hydroclimatic variability, for ensuring reliable water supply, and for using available water. Small-scale approaches to water management improve the ability of the rural poor to cope with water shocks by increasing agricultural productivity and providing cost-effective water supply and drought mitigation. Sound water management institutions are necessary to ensure sustained returns on infrastructure investments and to optimize the use of the water by multiple users and across administrative and political borders.

The estimated annual capital cost of water resource infrastructure is approximately $10 billion, of which almost 80 percent is for development of large multipurpose hydropower storage, and about 10 percent each is for development of large storage capacity for urban water supply and investment in developing small-scale infrastructure projects. As a complement to these physical investments, Africa will need an additional $1.0 billion a year to develop hydrological networks, meet gaps in water information, and develop water management institutions.

Water Resources and Economic Development: Challenges for Africa

Africa faces difficult water legacies in the form of high hydrological variability and a multiplicity of transboundary river basins. Both challenges can be impediments to the continent's economic growth.

Africa's Water Legacies

Africa faces a complex challenge in water resource management because of two legacies. The first is its natural legacy of high hydroclimatic variability. The amount of water in Africa is comparable to that in other regions of the world; the continent has 9 percent of the world's water resources and 11 percent of its population. However, Africa's water endowment conceals the fact that rainfall across much of the continent is variable and unpredictable, both between and within years. Interannual rainfall variability in Africa, especially in eastern and southern Africa, is high. These regions experience year-to-year variations exceeding 30 percent around the mean, a rate much greater than the temperate climates in Europe and North America (figure 14.1). High seasonal variability compounds these effects, causing droughts and floods. Runoff in Africa is extraordinarily low, only half that in Asia, Australia, Europe, and North America, despite having the same average precipitation. Low runoff coupled with high rainfall variability explains the unpredictable, and relatively low, seasonal and annual flows in many African rivers.

Climate change is expected to increase this variability. The Intergovernmental Panel on Climate Change forecasts that Africa will experience a significant rise in temperature

of about 3–4 degrees Celsius by the end of the 21st century, compared with the period from 1980 to 1990 (IPCC 2007). The semiarid margins of the Sahara and the central part of southern Africa will be most affected, whereas equatorial latitudes and coastal areas will be least affected. The Intergovernmental Panel on Climate Change projects that the mean annual precipitation and runoff will decrease for northern and southern Africa and increase for eastern Africa by midcentury. Precipitation intensity will also likely increase for the entire continent; the benefit of increased rainfall in the wetter areas may be negated by the rainfall being concentrated in more extreme weather events and thus less usable. In the drier areas, the spread between high and low runoff will likely increase, substantially complicating the challenge of water resource management.

The second challenge is Africa's political and geographic legacy in which several countries share the same river basins. Africa has more than 60 transboundary rivers, with many countries sharing the same basin. International river basins cover more than 60 percent of the continent, and virtually all the region's rivers cross several borders: the Nile crosses 10, the Niger 9, the Senegal 4, and the Zambezi 8 (figure 14.2).

Shared water resources present a management challenge and require investment in transboundary water management capacity and institutions, even if they also offer opportunities for joint action and cooperation. Cross-border rivers have further implications for regional security and development, particularly as Africa tries to develop and manage its water resources for economic development.

These legacies, compounded by underdevelopment of water infrastructure, present significant social, economic, and political risks. The region's weak capacity to buffer the effects of hydrological variability creates uncertainty and risk for economic activity. The expectation of variability and unpredictability in rainfall and runoff can encourage risk-averse behavior at all levels of the economy. It discourages investment in land, advanced technologies, or agriculture. An unreliable water supply is also a significant disincentive for investments in industry and services. Growing demands for water generate competition over water use,

Figure 14.1 Interannual Hydroclimatic Variability in Africa, by Selected Regions and Countries

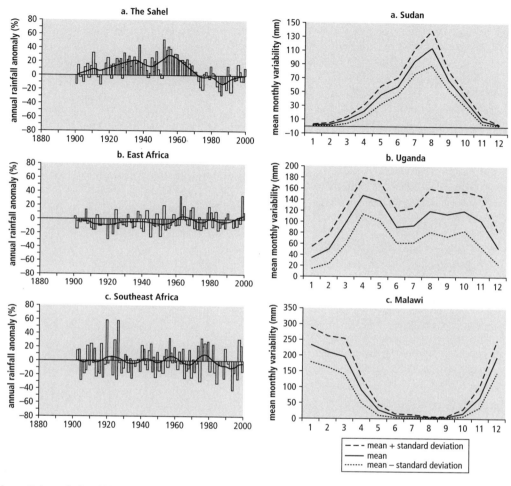

Source: Hulme and others 2001.

posing social risks to poorer communities. Weak international relations and institutions for managing the international river basins may cause regional tensions and possible conflicts among riparian countries.

Effects on Economic Development

Hydrological variability causes significant economic loss and constrains growth (Grey and Sadoff 2006b). Africa lacks the capacity to buffer the shocks of frequent droughts and floods. The abundance or shortage of rainfall affects national agricultural outputs. In Kenya, losses from flooding caused by El Niño in 1997–98 and drought caused by La Niña in 1998–2000 ranged from 10 to 16 percent of GDP during those years (World Bank 2004). Mozambique's GDP growth is reduced by over 1 percentage point annually because of water shocks (World Bank 2007). In Zambia, a study of how hydrologic variability affects the economy found that rainfall variability will cost the country $4.3 billion in lost GDP over 10 years, and it lowers the country's agricultural growth by 1 percentage point each year (World Bank 2008).

Underdevelopment of water resources leads to underuse of economic potential. Water resources in Sub-Saharan Africa compare well in absolute terms with other countries in the world. The region has 9 percent of the world's water resources and about 6,000 cubic meters of annual renewable water resources per capita

Figure 14.2 Africa's International River Basins

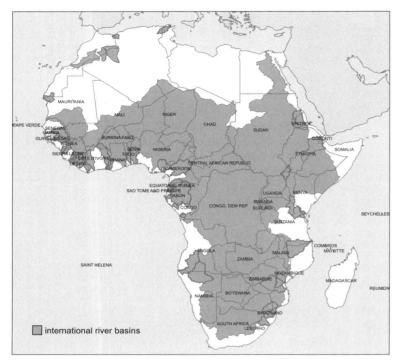

international river basins

Source: Oregon State University 2005. Reprinted with permission.

compared with Asia's 4,000 cubic meters and the Middle East and North Africa's 1,500 cubic meters. However, Africa has the lowest water withdrawal per capita in the world (about 170 cubic meters) because of hydrologic variability, underdeveloped water infrastructure, and current water resource management. Asia and Europe use about three times the water per person; the water-scarce Middle East withdraws more than four times as much and North America more than eight times as much (table 14.1).

The low level of water mobilization leads to underdevelopment of Africa's economic potential: less than 5 percent of cultivated land is irrigated, and less than 10 percent of hydropower potential is developed (figure 14.3). Irrigated land contributes only about 10 percent of the agricultural production in Africa, with only about 8.5 percent of cultivated land irrigated (figure 14.4). Less than 58 percent of Africa's population has access to drinking water, and 31 percent to sanitation services (WHO/UNICEF 2006).

Weak institutional capacity in river basin planning and management creates potential conflicts and lost benefits. Conflicts are emerging over water allocation and use in different parts of the region. Competing claims over water have been asserted over many of the lakes (for example, Lake Victoria and Lake Tana) and river basins for economic and environmental uses. The growing demand for water from the major sectors of African economies, especially agriculture, imposes a serious constraint on the medium- and long-term growth in water availability in some river basins. The expected growth in hydropower production will likely require an increase in peak capacity that will add to the competition. However, the water management institutions needed to address these conflicts in many African countries are weak and fragmented. Agencies with authority over a particular economic sector often make uncoordinated decisions about water allocation and use, which lead to inefficiency and degradation of the resource. The absence of water rights regimes and incentives for efficient water allocation and conservation contributes to the problem.

Cooperative management of water resources in international river basins is necessary to increase the basins' yield of food, power, and economic opportunities while strengthening environmental sustainability and mitigating the effects of droughts and floods. The cost of noncooperation is high, including the economic cost of negative environmental impacts, suboptimal water resource development, political tensions over shared resources, and the forgone benefits of joint water resource development (Sadoff, Whittington, and Grey 2003).

Lack of water infrastructure and inadequate water management mostly affect the poor. Africa's poverty is closely linked to its dependence on rain-fed subsistence farming. About 28 percent of Africa's working population is engaged in agricultural production, ranging from 4 percent in South Africa to 47 percent in Rwanda (You 2008). Because subsistence agriculture is the dominant livelihood, rainfall, droughts, and floods, combined with the weak marketing network and difficult physical access to many areas, affect food security across

Table 14.1 Water Availability and Withdrawal
cubic meters per person

Region	Per capita actual renewal water resources	Per capita annual total water withdrawals
Asia (excluding the Middle East)	4,079.0	631
Central America and the Caribbean	6,924.4	603
Europe	10,655.1	581
Middle East and North Africa	1,505.0	807
North America	19,992.5	1,663
South America	47,044.0	474
Oceania	54,636.8	900
Sub-Saharan Africa	6,322.5	173

Source: FAO 2003.

the region. These factors, along with limited irrigation and underdevelopment of water infrastructure, increase the rural economy's vulnerability to water shocks. Annually, some 220 million Africans are exposed to drought, and more than 1.5 million were affected by floods in 2007.

Degradation of water catchments undermines investments already made in water resources. Loss of vegetation, erosion, and sedimentation are major threats to surface-water resources, because they cause lower base flows and higher flood peaks. Poor management of Africa's water catchments has led to excessive soil erosion, increased costs of water treatment, rapid siltation of reservoirs, decline in economic life, and disruption of water supplies. In Malawi, any new dam is expected to fill with sediment within a few years of commissioning. The most important dams in the country are the hydropower facilities on the Shire River, which are badly affected by sedimentation. In Kenya, the rate of sediment outflow from the Athi-Galana-Sabaki River into the Indian Ocean increased from about 50,000 tons a year in the 1950s to 8.4 million tons a year by 1992 (World Bank 2004). In countries with degraded water catchments, development of water storage infrastructure needs to be accompanied by improved protection of watersheds to sustain the investment.

Reliable hydrological and water quality data are needed for effective water resource management and informed decision making. Hydrographic networks are outdated or in need of rehabilitation in many countries.

Figure 14.3 Africa's Hydropower Potential

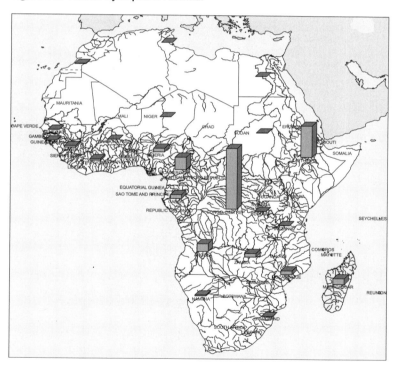

Source: International Energy Agency 2006 (El-Gazzar and others 2007, p.7).

Regular monitoring of the hydrological system (such as meteorological stations, rain gauges, and river flows) is steadily declining, and most African countries have not updated their assessments. Africa also lags behind the rest of the world in the number of meteorological stations where data can be systematically collected for dissemination to users. According to the World Meteorological

Figure 14.4 Sub-Saharan Africa's Irrigation Potential

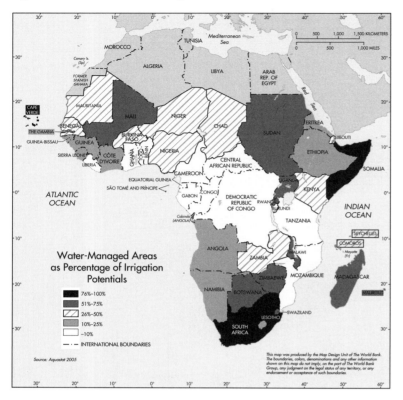

Source: ECA 2006.

Organization, Africa has only 1,150 observation stations—one-eighth the recommended number (UNFCCC 2006).

Addressing the Challenges

Achieving water security is a prerequisite for attracting investment and promoting economic growth in Africa.

Water Security, Investments, and Growth

Minimum water infrastructure and institutional capacity are required to ensure basic national water security (Grey and Sadoff 2006b). *Water security* is the ability of a country to function productively despite its inherent water vulnerability. A country's water security depends on both its inherent water supply-and-demand patterns and its capacity to confront

water vulnerability. It is a precondition for sustaining and increasing investment returns and achieving dynamic economic growth.

The more vulnerable an economy is to water variability, the greater is the required investment to achieve water security. If a country cannot provide water security, it will not be resilient to water shocks, and it will not have reliable water supplies (figure 14.5, scenario 1; Subramanian, Yu, and Dankova 2008). When an acceptable level of water security is achieved along with basic climate resilience and risk mitigation, vulnerability is no longer a severe constraint on growth. Beyond this point, further investment in water infrastructure contributes to economic growth (figure 14.5, scenario 2). Climate change will likely impose additional costs for achieving and sustaining water security through its effect on the spatial and temporal pattern of water demand and availability, as well as by increasing hydrological variability in certain areas.

Water security is a dynamic state. Its definition varies in different parts of the world, reflecting geographic, social, and political factors and the stage of economic development. In Africa, hydrologic variability and extremes are at the heart of water vulnerability because they weaken growth and retard development. African countries must achieve water security to keep the risks of droughts, floods, and unreliable water supplies at a socially and economically acceptable level. Several studies have pointed to the strong correlation between rainfall variability and national GDP in countries as diverse as Ethiopia, Kenya, Lesotho, Mozambique, and Zambia (World Bank 2004, 2006, 2007, 2008, 2009). Emerging evidence

Figure 14.5 Water Security and Growth

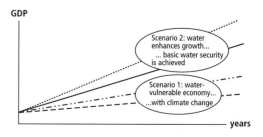

Source: Authors' elaboration.

also indicates a correlation between availability of water storage and road infrastructure and inflows of foreign direct investment (Brown and others 2008).

Achieving Water Security: Priority Areas for Action

Balanced investments in water resource infrastructure and institutions are needed to increase productive uses of water, to mitigate the effect of recurrent floods and droughts, and to achieve basic water security as a platform for Africa's economic growth. Priority should be given to investments that (a) focus on growth, (b) reduce rural poverty, (c) build climate resilience and adaptation, and (d) foster cooperation in international river basins.

Focusing on Growth

Governments should link their water interventions with their development objectives and poverty-reduction targets. To achieve higher economic returns and promote national growth, focusing infrastructure investments around main growth centers and along primary development corridors where production, industrial development, and trade are concentrated makes sense. The availability of reliable water supplies in growth centers protects investments against the risks of hydrologic variability and improves the performance of the manufacturing and service sectors. It attracts new investments and enables industries to adopt water-saving technologies when the economic incentives are in place. For municipal utilities, a mix of hydrological risk mitigation measures and rising industrial and domestic water demands in the growth areas allows them to take advantage of economies of scale in production and distribution, to extend coverage, and to improve the systems' operation and maintenance. An example of a growth-oriented policy is the Metolong Dam and Water Supply Program in Lesotho (box 14.1)

Reducing Rural Poverty

Water is an important asset for the rural poor in Africa. However, high rainfall variability and insecure access to water for consumption and

---

BOX 14.1

The Metolong Dam and Water Supply Program in Lesotho

Development of Lesotho's water sector is part of the government's effort to diversify the economy and improve the provision of essential services.

The greater Maseru area is the center of the country's garment industry. It includes more than 50 firms employing approximately 50,000 people. This industry has resulted in an almost fourfold increase in exports since 2000, and it contributed $567 million in foreign exchange earnings in 2006 (38 percent of GDP). Water and wastewater services are essential to the continued economic contribution of these companies. They currently account for half of all water consumed in Maseru, and the lack of water and wastewater infrastructure presents a major constraint to continued economic growth. The industrial growth has also stimulated an increase in urban migration. Maseru, the capital of Lesotho, experienced population growth of 5.5 percent a year between 1996 and 2006, expanding to more than 350,000 people. Currently, the only source of raw water for treatment and supply to Maseru comes from a single intake on the Mohokare (Caledon) River, which is unreliable, inadequate, and of inferior quality.

To address the need for long-term, secure water supplies to the lowlands, the government commissioned a feasibility study of the Lesotho Lowlands Water Supply Scheme in 2004 with support from the European Development Fund. That study, as well as a separate study financed by the Arab Bank for Development in Africa in 2003, identified the construction and implementation of the Metolong Dam and Water Supply Program as the least-cost long-term solution for bulk water supply to Maseru and the surrounding lowlands. With the ability to provide 75,000 cubic meters of treated water a day, the dam, in conjunction with existing supplies, will ensure a secure supply of 115,000 cubic meters of water per day, enabling Maseru to meet domestic and industrial requirements for at least the next 40 years. The construction of the Metolong Dam is scheduled to begin in 2012.

Source: World Bank 2009.

---

agriculture are major constraints to poverty reduction in rural Africa.

A recent Food and Agriculture Organization report (Faurès and Santini 2008) describes potential reductions in rural poverty through water resource interventions in Africa, specifically in southern and eastern Africa and along the east-west central belt (figure 14.6). These areas have high levels of rural poverty, broad opportunities for agricultural growth, and sufficient water in absolute physical terms.

Figure 14.6 Water Interventions and Poverty

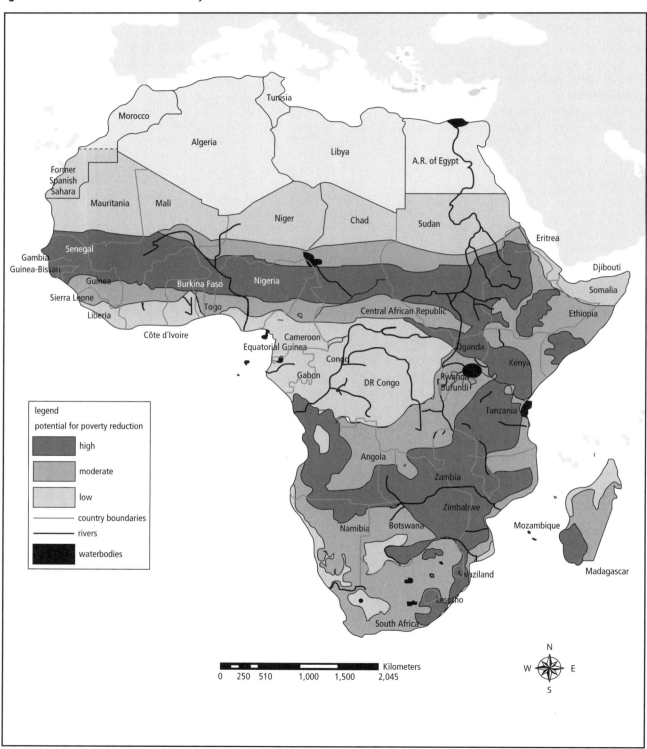

Source: Faurès and Santini 2008.

However, at the same time, water is a limiting factor for these rural livelihoods because of significant seasonal and interannual variability and lack of water control. Such zones offer the greatest opportunities for expanding food production through irrigation, rain-fed agriculture, rainfall harvesting, and conservation of soil moisture.

Community-based management and development of local watersheds and groundwater resources in the poorest areas are crucial for sustaining local livelihoods against the effects of climate variability. These measures include constructing small hydraulic structures, introducing local-scale hydropower units, harvesting water, developing smallholder irrigation, and installing flood protection measures.

Building Climate Resilience
Managing rainfall variability is a critical task for African countries. Expanding water storage capacity (as well as improving management of the existing hydraulic structures) would mitigate the effects of water shocks and build climate resilience. Along with large storage and hydraulic structures, small multiobjective water development is an important opportunity for new investment. These investments should take into account the potential effects of climate change. Appropriately designed irrigation investments would increase agricultural productivity and significantly mitigate the danger of rainfall variability. Investments to reduce climate vulnerability should also include hydrometeorological services and monitoring, catchment protection and management, and risk assessment and mitigation.

Fostering Transboundary Cooperation
Optimizing economic productivity and environmental sustainability means managing rivers as hydrological units at the basin level. The great hydrologic challenges that countries face at the national level of water resource management (such as rainfall and runoff variability, degrading water quality, and flood protection) create opportunities to gain significant benefits from cooperation over shared river basins. Cooperative management of water resources increases a basin's yields of food, power, and other economic goods while strengthening

environmental sustainability and mitigating the effects of droughts and floods. Countries around the Senegal and Niger Rivers have started to reap the benefits of a cooperative and joint approach to managing their shared waters (Andersen and others 2005; Yu 2008). Countries surrounding Lake Victoria are gaining environmental benefits from their joint efforts to eliminate encroaching water hyacinth and other weeds. The systemwide yield of water in the Nile could likely be increased by several percentage points a year if cooperation led to water storage upstream and coordinated reservoir operation in the arid plains downstream (Sadoff, Whittington, and Grey 2003). The countries will also likely benefit from joint investments in water infrastructure, thereby reducing infrastructure costs and maximizing returns. Unilateral and uncoordinated decisions on water resources by riparian countries, in contrast, may lead to increased political tensions and conflicts, reducing development opportunities in the basins.

Investing in Africa's Water Security

Because most African countries have low stocks of hydraulic infrastructure, emphasizing investments in infrastructure is appropriate for them. However, institution building and reform, improvements in water management and operations, and strengthening of water information systems must complement growth in infrastructure. Development of institutions is a lengthy and costly process, and adequately sequenced and balanced, it should be advanced in parallel with infrastructure investments, paying particular attention to the development of river basin organizations.

Investing in Storage Infrastructure: Both Large and Small
Development of water infrastructure is a prerequisite for water security in Africa and for meeting the targets of the eight Millennium Development Goals. Artificial water storage of adequate capacity is needed to ensure reliable water supply during droughts and to retain excessive water during periods of flooding.

Despite Africa's vulnerability to frequent droughts and floods, storage capacity remains underdeveloped. Average per capita storage capacity in Africa is about 200 cubic meters a year, much less than that of countries in other regions (figure 14.7).

Irrigation and hydropower have been the main drivers for dam construction in Africa, but a storage facility designed for a single purpose has limited capacity to serve other economic and social needs, and its investments often have higher opportunity costs. For example, the Cahora Bassa Dam on the Zambezi River was constructed for the sole purpose of generating hydropower. The devastating 2000 floods in Mozambique showed that the dam could play an important flood mitigation role, but its operational rules do not permit use of its storage capacity to mitigate water shocks. To convert this dam into a multipurpose reservoir would be too costly. Despite the need for power, other considerations, such as flood control, salinity repulsion, irrigation development, and environmental requirements, call for multipurpose storage development. Multipurpose water projects generally result in optimal water development, maximize economic returns on investments, and need to be implemented in the basinwide context. Two important principles for developing large water infrastructure are equitable sharing of the benefits with the people affected and mitigation of possible negative environmental effects. Thus, stakeholder participation is necessary at all stages of decision making, project design, and implementation.

The direct and indirect long-term economic benefits of investing in large storage capacity are many, but they require considerable initial capital investments. The aggregate spending needs for African infrastructure were reported in chapter 1 of this volume, but because water resource investments are typically buried within investment programs for other sectors, such as irrigation, power, and water supply, the specific water resource components are explicitly highlighted here.

Table 14.2 details the component of power sector investment needs explicitly attributable to water storage in large dams. If regional power trade could be effectively harnessed, some 50,000 megawatts of new hydropower capacity would need to be built from 2006 to 2015, but without expanding regional trade, only 33,000 megawatts of hydropower capacity could be developed. The trade scenario would translate into an annual average investment requirement of $7.8 billion in large-scale water storage to support generation of electricity over the 2006–15 period (Rosnes and Vennemo 2008, 2009).

Not only would expanded regional trade lead to the development of more water storage, but it would also improve the cost-effectiveness of water storage. The unit capital cost of hydropower investments would fall from $5.9 million to $5.4 million per megawatt (table 14.2) because cross-border collaboration allows larger and more efficient storage sites to be developed.

The key challenge is how to finance the multibillion-dollar large-scale water storage projects needed to make this savings a reality. Often the countries with the best storage sites are those with the least financial capacity to develop them. Regional collaboration offers the possibility of cost-sharing arrangements among countries for large water infrastructure, allowing downstream beneficiary countries with greater solvency to provide up-front capital contributions. For example, a cooperative effort by Burundi, Rwanda, and Tanzania to design and build the Rusumo Falls hydroelectric project on the Kagera River could bring 60 megawatts of renewable power to an area where only 2 percent of households have access to electricity.

Figure 14.7 Water Reservoir Storage per Capita in Selected Countries, 2003

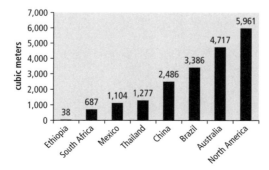

Source: Grey and Sadoff 2006a.

Table 14.2 Capital Investment Needs in Large Multipurpose Hydropower Storage by 2015

Region	Large storage-based hydropower production (megawatts)		Capital costs per unit ($ millions per megawatts)		Total capital costs ($ billions per year)	
	Regional power trade expansion	No power trade expansion	Regional power trade expansion	No power trade expansion	Regional power trade expansion	No power trade expansion
Southern Africa	16,764	10,797	0.96	1.21	1.95	1.59
Eastern Africa	10,675	4,170	1.81	1.96	2.35	0.99
Western Africa	17,260	14,845	1.32	1.37	2.77	2.48
Central Africa	4,847	3,567	1.28	1.37	0.75	0.59
Total	49,546	33,379	5.37	5.91	7.82	5.65

Source: Authors' calculations based on Rosnes and Vennemo 2008.
Note: These investment cost estimates are based on actual planned large storage-based (multipurpose) hydropower projects presented for each region in Rosnes and Vennemo 2008 and 2009. Totals do not add exactly because of averaging.

Governments have traditionally shouldered the responsibility for financing large hydraulic structures, including most multipurpose dams. Private sector participation in such investments is possible, however, for multipurpose projects with revenue-creating components (such as hydropower production, commercial irrigation, and urban water supply functions) combined with nonrevenue and public-good functions (such as flood control, fish breeding, recreation, small-scale irrigation, and so forth). Promoting public-private partnerships to finance multipurpose water resource projects is a key challenge of decision makers.

A continuum of options from large to small infrastructure projects needs to be part of a balanced investment approach. Small water storage facilities can increase climate resilience and improve food security. Small-scale approaches to water management help the rural poor by providing cost-effective solutions to water supply and drought mitigation. They improve the ability of the rural poor to address food insecurity by increasing agricultural productivity. Small storage options include (a) off-stream reservoirs, (b) on-farm ponds and networks of multipurpose small reservoirs, (c) groundwater storage, and (d) water storage through a root zone with a variety of water-harvesting techniques and conservation of soil moisture. Structures to harvest rain require little space and are not labor intensive, but they must be designed in accordance with intended usage and local circumstances to ensure cost-effectiveness.

Studies in Botswana and Zimbabwe show that 80–85 percent of all measurable rain can be collected from outside catchment areas and stored (Dixit and Patil 1996).

The estimated cost for small reservoir facilities is based on an assessment of small-scale irrigation development potential from 2006 to 2015 (You 2008). This analysis used a spatial allocation model on a 10-kilometer global grid, considering economic profitability, crop pattern, prices, crop water productivity, water balance and availability, and distance to market for each pixel. A macroscale hydrology model used climatic data to calculate runoff for each pixel. The total small-scale irrigation area was estimated at about 10 million hectares, and the total water storage requirement was estimated at about 35 billion cubic meters for the countries sampled. The total cost for small irrigation storage facilities was based on the irrigation development area, required storage volume, and their average costs.

A certain amount of storage is also needed to keep pace with growing demands for the urban water supply. The associated investment can be estimated based on demographic growth, Millennium Development Goal targets, trends in water consumption, as well as unaccounted for water and the availability of supply from various sources. The storage need is put at 5.4 billion cubic meters.

Total capital investment needs for the development of water resource infrastructure for 2006–15 are estimated at approximately $10 billion a year, included within estimates for power ($7.8 billion), water supply ($1.3 billion), and irrigation ($0.8 billion) presented in chapter 1 of this volume.

Investing in Institutions and Information: Managing Water Resources across Sectors and Jurisdictions

Sound water management institutions in Africa will ensure sustained returns on infrastructure investments and optimize the allocation and use of water by multiple economic sectors and across administrative and political borders.

Despite low water use for productive purposes in Africa, conflicts are emerging over water in areas of concentrated economic activity. These conflicts often intensify during periods of water shortages. The drop in Lake Victoria's level because of increased withdrawals and the drought of 2003–06 affected other users of water around the lake. In Ethiopia's Lake Tana, reduced inflows and increased water abstractions in 2003–04 highlighted the need for coordinated water planning and management. The need for improved water allocation regimes for multisectoral use can be seen in the conflicting water demands in the Inner Niger Delta in Mali and in the emerging competing claims of irrigation expansion plans, hydropower production, and environmental water demands in the Kafue basin in Zambia. Establishing priorities for water investments and clear policy rules to govern optimal water allocation across economic sectors will be key to enabling or constraining their relative growth. All of this should result from sound medium-term river basin planning.

Full realization of Africa's water potential and the optimal allocation of water among various sectors require the right institutional arrangements at the national level, including (a) capable water management organizations, (b) provisions for public participation in water management decisions, (c) water rights regimes, and (d) tailored incentive systems. Many African countries are beginning to develop national institutions for water management. Tanzania, for example, has identified nine river basins for which it will develop sustainable development plans. This institutional arrangement envisages stakeholder forums to address multiple uses and optimize benefits across sectors and administrative jurisdictions. South Africa has enacted far-reaching water legislation, and Botswana is restructuring its water-related institutions. African countries have relatively rich experience in managing water supply and sanitation through utilities. This is not the case with water resource management, where for the majority of African countries, robust and sustainable institutions have yet to be developed.

Africa has a longer history of developing regional institutions to manage transboundary waters. The first regional river basin organizations were established in the mid-20th century (the Niger River Commission in 1964, later transformed into the Niger Basin Authority in 1980; the Senegal River Basin Organization in 1972; and the Gambia River Development Organization in 1978). Burundi, Rwanda, and Tanzania established the Kagera Basin Organization in 1977. The Lake Chad Basin Development Fund was set up in 1973 to support the Lake Chad Basin Commission's activities. More recently, the riparian countries of the Nile formed the Nile Basin Initiative in 1999 as a prelude to a more permanent institution. In 2005, the countries around Lake Victoria established the Lake Victoria Basin Commission under the auspices of the East African Community.

Despite these early starts, with only a few exceptions, these transboundary river basin organizations are still in their emerging stages and remain relatively weak (UN-Water/Africa 2006). They suffer from waning political commitment, poor cooperation, management and technical difficulties, armed conflict and political instability in member states, lack of defined goals or weak incentives for regional cooperation, and insufficient capacity to carry out their plans. As donor support dwindled, basin organizations had insufficient financial backing to carry out their programs. Today, the organizations are at various stages of development (figure 14.8).

In a few cases, however, river basin organizations have been backed by strong government ownership and commitment and have enjoyed support from multiple donors, enabling them to successfully complete several years of institutional development, confidence-building measures, and cooperative investment programming. The Niger Basin Authority, for example, undertook an institutional assessment to prepare for reorienting its efforts in early 2000. Subsequently, it introduced an organizational structure approved by the Niger Basin Council of Ministers, competitively recruited a team of professionals, and strengthened its fiduciary systems. The authority has also agreed on a water charter that spells out the rules of engagement for the riparian countries, including procedures for sharing information and formulating investment programs. The nine countries on the Niger have agreed to a 20-year sustainable development action plan and a related investment program.

The experience of these organizations indicates that the process of river basin development requires political leadership, government commitment, confidence building among countries, and realization of concrete benefits. Substantial investments are needed for assessments, project preparation, and feasibility studies. Investments in facilitating greater regional cooperation within the river basin organizations will also be critical. These investments can support a regional forum for dialogue, conflict resolution, and cooperation around a shared resource (Sadoff and Grey 2005).

Relevant, adequate, and reliable information enhances institutional capacity for decision making. An effective water information system requires action on both the demand and supply sides. Planners and decision makers must be aware of the importance of information in decision making. Information managers must be able to develop the appropriate mix of formal and informal knowledge and communication systems to support decision makers. Thus, a water information system should include the following components:

- *Hydrological information:* Collection system (including instrumentation, quality control, coding) for data capture for surface water, groundwater, and water quality parameters, and environmental information,

Figure 14.8 Degree of Regional Water Cooperation

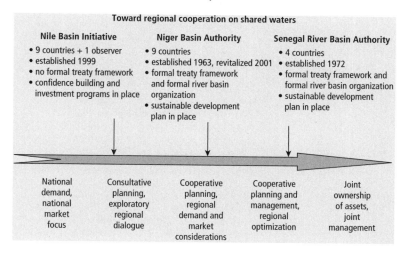

Source: Adapted from Grey and Sadoff 2006a.

such as sediments and fisheries. The process should include computers to analyze and store information. It will also include support services for periodic calibration of instruments.

- *Spatial data:* Satellite imageries, aerial surveys, ground surveys, bathymetry, and other data sets from geographic information systems.

- *Information management:* Hydrological design aids (such as maps of probable maximum precipitation and regional flood frequency studies) for use by project designers.

- *Knowledge management:* A model and decision support system to interface with the water information system.

- *Dissemination:* Protocols to supply end users.

Recent experience with water resource projects indicates that investments in information and institutions will require close to 10 percent of the investment in water infrastructure. Given the estimated annual $10 billion investment for water infrastructure, close to $1 billion a year of additional resources will be needed to advance the institutional and information agendas.

Note

The authors of this chapter are Rimma Dankova, Satoru Ueda, Ashok Subramanian, Winston Yu, and Jyothsna Mody, who drew on background material and contributions from Vahid Alavian.

References

Andersen, Inger, Ousmane Dione, Martha Jarosewich-Holder, and Jean-Claude Olivry. 2005. *The Niger River Basin: A Vision for Sustainable Management*. Katherin George Golitzen, ed. Washington, DC: World Bank.

Brown, Casey, Daniela Domeisen, Robyn Meeks, Kenneth Hunu, and Winston Yu. 2008. "Exploring the Effect of Hydro-Climatic Variability on Economic Growth in Sub-Saharan Africa: A Water Security Index." Technical Report 08-04, Water and Growth Report 2, International Research Institute for Climate and Society, New York.

Dixit, Medha J., and Subhash M. Patil. 1996. "Rain Water Harvesting." Discussion paper presented at the 22nd Water, Engineering and Development Centre International Conference, New Delhi, India, September 9–13.

ECA (Economic Commission for Africa). 2006. "Water in Africa: Management Options to Enhance Survival and Growth." Addis Ababa, Ethiopia: ECA.

EI-Gazzar, Mohamed, Yassin Ibrahim, Mohamed Bedrous, and Aziz Maher. 2007. "Hydro and Nuclear Power for African Less-Carbon Development." Paper presented at the World Energy Congress, Rome.

FAO (Food and Agriculture Organization). 2003. FAO statistical database. http://www.fao.org/corp/statistics/en/.

Faurès, Jean-Marc, and Guido Santini, eds. 2008. *Water and the Rural Poor: Interventions for Improving Livelihoods in Sub-Saharan Africa*. Rome: Food and Agriculture Organization of the United Nations and International Fund for Agricultural Development.

Grey, David, and Claudia Sadoff. 2006a. "The Global Water Challenge: Poverty Growth and International Relations." Paper presented at Global Issues Seminar Series, World Bank, Washington, DC, January 25.

———. 2006b. "Water for Growth and Development: A Framework for Analysis." Theme document of the 4th World Water Forum, Mexico City, March.

Hulme, Mike, Ruth Doherty, Todd Ngara, Mark New, and David Lister. 2001. "African Climate Change: 1900–2100." *Climate Research* 17: 145–68.

IPCC (Intergovernmental Panel on Climate Change). 2007. *Climate Change 2007: Synthesis Report*. Geneva: IPCC.

Oregon State University. 2005. Transboundary Freshwater Dispute database. http://www.transboundarywaters.orst.edu/database/.

Rosnes, Orvika, and Haakon Vennemo. 2008. "Powering Up: Costing Power Infrastructure Investment Needs in Sub-Saharan Africa." Background Paper 5, Africa Infrastructure Sector Diagnostic, World Bank, Washington, DC.

Sadoff, Claudia W., and David Grey. 2005. "Cooperation in International Rivers: A Continuum of Securing and Sharing Benefits." *Water International* 30 (4): 1–8.

Sadoff, Claudia W., Dale Whittington, and David Grey. 2003. *Africa's International Rivers: An Economic Perspective*. Washington, DC: World Bank.

Subramanian, Ashok, Winston Yu, and Rimma Dankova. 2008. "Sharing Water, Sharing Benefits, Sharing Costs." Paper presented at the Expo Zaragoza 2008 Water Tribune, Zaragoza, Spain, June 16–September 10.

UNFCCC (United Nations Framework Convention on Climate Change). 2006. "Background Paper on Impacts, Vulnerability and Adaptation to Climate Change in Africa for the African Workshop on Adaptation Implementation of Decision 1/CP.10 of the United Nations Climate Change Convention, Accra, Ghana, September 21–23, 2006." http://unfccc.int/files/adaptation/adverse_effects_and_response_measures_art_48/application/pdf/200609_background_african_wkshp.pdf.

UN-Water/Africa. 2006. *African Water Development Report, 2006*. Addis Ababa, Ethiopia: UN-Water/Africa.

WHO/UNICEF (World Health Organization/United Nations Children's Fund). 2006. *MDG Assessment Report*. Geneva and New York: WHO/UNICEF Joint Monitoring Programme for Water Supply and Sanitation.

World Bank. 2004. "Towards a Water-Secure Kenya: Kenya Water Resources Sector Memorandum." World Bank, Washington, DC.

———. 2006. "Ethiopia Country Water Resources Assistance Strategy." Agriculture and Rural Development Department, World Bank, Washington, DC.

———. 2007. "Mozambique Country Water Resources Assistance Strategy." Africa Region Water Resources Unit, World Bank, Washington, DC.

———. 2008. "Zambia Country Water Resources Assistance Strategy." Draft, Africa Region

Water Resources Unit, World Bank, Washington, DC.

———. 2009. "Lesotho Water Sector Improvement Program (Second Phase): Metolong Dam and Water Supply Project." Report 46272-LS, World Bank, Washington, DC.

You, Liang Zhi. 2008. "Irrigation Investment Needs in Sub-Saharan Africa." Background Paper 9, Africa Infrastructure Country Diagnostic, World Bank, Washington, DC.

Yu, Winston. 2008. "Benefit Sharing in International Rivers: Findings from the Senegal River Basin, the Columbia River Basin, and the Lesotho Highlands Water Project." Working Paper 1, Africa Region Water Resources Unit, World Bank, Washington, DC.

Chapter 15

Irrigation: Tapping Potential

A large segment of Sub-Saharan Africa's population lives in rural areas and depends heavily on agriculture. Agricultural growth is clearly key to poverty reduction and to achieving the Millennium Development Goal of halving poverty by 2015. Agricultural performance has significantly improved since 2000; nevertheless, agricultural productivity remains the lowest in the world. Climate change and the global food price crisis provide additional challenges. A comprehensive effort is required to increase investment in agricultural intensification. Water for agriculture is a critical ingredient of such programs.

Africa's agricultural water remains comparatively underdeveloped, despite economically viable potential to expand irrigated areas. Today, only 3.5 percent of Africa's agricultural land is equipped for irrigation, some 7 million hectares concentrated in a handful of countries. However, further expansion of the irrigated area would be profitable. At least 1.4 million hectares could be developed using existing or planned dams associated with hydropower development, at a total additional one-time investment of $2.6 billion in distribution of agricultural water. In addition, at least 5.4 million hectares would be viable for small-scale

irrigation, involving an additional one-time investment of $17.8 billion. In general, economic returns on small-scale schemes (on average 26 percent) are substantially higher than those on large-scale schemes (on average 17 percent).

These results, however, are critically dependent on keeping investment costs down to best-practice levels of $3,000 per hectare for the water distribution component of large-scale irrigation and $2,000 per hectare for small-scale irrigation, rather than the significantly higher levels often observed at the project level in the recent past. Another key finding is that irrigation is in most cases viable only for cash crops or high-value food crops (such as horticulture) that raise revenues in excess of $2,000 per hectare; relatively few hectares are viable for irrigation of staple food crops.

What would be the effect on development of an aggressive expansion of Africa's irrigated agricultural area? If Africa does not increase its slow growth in irrigated area, the food supply on the continent will gradually diminish because of climate change, leading to a huge surge in cereal imports and a significant increase in child malnutrition. In contrast, if Africa's irrigated area could be tripled by 2050, the food supply would increase markedly, with a huge decline in cereal imports. There would be 2 million fewer malnourished children than under the lower irrigation scenario, or about the same level that would be expected in the absence of climate change. Thus, aggressive agricultural water development could reverse the adverse effects of moderate global warming on food security.

Aggressive scaling up of investments in agricultural water raises issues associated with the performance and sustainability of irrigated agriculture. Considerations of economic viability, farm-level profitability, and sustainability should guide future investment decisions. In particular, investments in agricultural water should be considered as part of a comprehensive package, including (a) empowered farmer organizations; (b) sustainable, efficient, and accountable agricultural support services; and (c) accessible, profitable markets. Furthermore, efforts to expand irrigation should be made in the context of national agricultural water development strategies that emphasize the importance of a more conducive institutional environment and that form the foundation for sectoral programs that combine investment in infrastructure with investment in institutional reforms.

Agriculture and Poverty Reduction

Agricultural growth is a key to reducing poverty. More than half of Sub-Saharan Africa's population lives in rural areas, and agriculture accounts for a significant percentage of GDP. Of Africa's poor, 85 percent live in rural areas and depend largely on agriculture for their livelihoods. GDP growth originating in agriculture is about four times more effective in raising incomes of extremely poor people than GDP growth originating outside the sector—and the potential multipliers from agricultural water investment are even higher (World Bank 2008).

Agricultural performance in the region has improved significantly since 2000. Growth in agricultural GDP in Sub-Saharan Africa has accelerated from 2.3 percent a year in the 1980s to 3.8 percent a year from 2000 to 2005. Average incomes in Sub-Saharan Africa have been rising in tandem with those in other regions since the mid-1990s.

Despite these encouraging developments, agricultural productivity is the lowest in the world, with per capita output only 56 percent of the world average. Output has not kept pace with population increases, and growth has occurred largely through expansion of harvested area (rather than through more intensive use of existing cropland): more than 80 percent of output growth since 1980 has come from expansion of cropped area, compared with less than 20 percent for all other regions.

Climate change and the global food price crisis, developments likely to hit Africa disproportionately, further challenge agricultural performance. Water sources will become more variable. Droughts and floods will stress agricultural systems. The seas will inundate some coastal food-producing areas, and food production will fall in some places in the interior. Nevertheless, substantial uncertainty remains about where the effects will be greatest.

A comprehensive effort is required to advance agricultural productivity. Investments in more reliable access to agricultural water[1] are critical in support of that objective (World Bank 2008). More reliable access to agricultural water increases the opportunity to use productivity-enhancing inputs and thus supports intensification and diversification, as well as the scope for agricultural wage employment. In addition, it reduces local food prices, improving real net incomes. It can also reduce poverty indirectly through increased rural nonfarm and urban employment. Moreover, investments in irrigation improve access to markets. A more reliable, year-round supply of products, a higher and more uniform quality of products, and the option to manipulate harvest dates to capture higher seasonal prices put a high premium on irrigation.

African leaders have identified agricultural water development as a key area for investment. The Comprehensive Africa Agricultural Development Program prepared under the New Partnership for Africa's Development in 2002 adopted land and water management as the first of its four pillars for priority investment. It proposed extending the area under sustainable land management and reliable water control systems to 20 million hectares (more than twice the area currently under water management in

Sub-Saharan Africa) by 2015 (NEPAD 2003). In response to this call for action, the Partnership for Agricultural Water in Africa was recently launched to scale up investments in agricultural water and to harmonize donor programs.

Current State of Irrigation

Irrigation carries significant potential to increase agricultural productivity. Across Sub-Saharan Africa, irrigated agriculture accounts for about 25 percent of the value of agricultural output (table 15.1). This share is produced on just 3.5 percent of the cultivated land, confirming the potential of irrigation to improve livelihoods in Sub-Saharan Africa and suggesting that more investment in irrigation would yield substantial benefits.

However, Sub-Saharan Africa's agricultural water remains underdeveloped. Of a cultivated area of 197 million hectares, only 7 million hectares is equipped for irrigation, with a further 2 million hectares under some other form of water management. Overall, this area amounts to only 23 percent of the 39 million hectares that is believed to be physically suitable (though not necessarily economically viable) for irrigation. The share of cultivated area equipped for

irrigation in Sub-Saharan Africa varies considerably by country but is generally very low, with only a few countries reaching the 20 percent mark (figure 15.1). In absolute terms, more than 60 percent of the total area is concentrated in just three countries—Madagascar, South Africa, and Sudan—each with over a million hectares of irrigated area.

Donor investments in agricultural water have declined sharply. From 1994 to 1996, the total value of projects funded by all donors for irrigation and drainage was less than 10 percent of the levels 20 years earlier—just $127 million from all sources (World Bank 2007). Significant scope exists for scaling up investments. Average agricultural water withdrawals are 1.3 percent of renewable water resources; groundwater use is less than 20 percent of renewable supplies, indicating significant scope for further surface water and groundwater development. Expansion of irrigated area has been slow in Sub-Saharan Africa. Over the last 40 years, only 4 million hectares of new irrigation has been developed, by far the smallest expansion of any region. Over the same period, China added 25 million hectares, and India 32 million. Annual growth in irrigation development in the region was 2.3 percent from 1973 to 2000 and slowed further from 2000 to 2003, but it has

Table 15.1 Selected Irrigation Investment Indicators for Sub-Saharan Africa
percentage

Region	Cultivated area equipped for irrigation	Irrigation potential realized	Agricultural water withdrawals as percentage of total renewable water resources	Dam capacity as percentage of total available surface water	Groundwater pumped as percentage of total renewable groundwater	Average annual expansion of irrigated area, 1973–2000	Value of irrigated output as percentage of total value of agricultural output
Sudano-Sahelian	6.9	50	21.8	9.7	38.1	2.7	58.3
Eastern	2.6	11	4.9	5.5	3.1	2.4	5.0
Gulf of Guinea	1.5	7	1.2	47.1	0	2.2	6.3
Central	0.7	1	0.1	1.7	0	0.5	7.3
Southern	4.2	36	6.2	99.0	17.8	3.2	6.6
Indian Ocean Islands	30.4	71	4.2	0.1	8.7	3.5	0
Sub-Saharan Africa average	3.5	18	1.3	11.2	17.5	2.3	24.5
Asia average	33.6	67	15.8	12.0	—	2.6	—

Source: Svendsen, Ewing, and Msangi 2009.
Note: The regions shown are those adopted in Frenken (2005). The grouping of countries within these regions is based on geographical and climatic homogeneity, which directly influences irrigation. Sudano-Sahelian: Burkina Faso, Cape Verde, Chad, Niger, Senegal, Sudan; Eastern: Ethiopia, Kenya, Rwanda, Tanzania, Uganda; Gulf of Guinea: Benin, Côte d'Ivoire, Ghana, Nigeria; Central: Cameroon, the Democratic Republic of Congo; Southern: Lesotho, Malawi, Mozambique, Namibia, South Africa, Zambia; Indian Ocean Islands: Madagascar. — Not available.

Figure 15.1 Percentage of Cultivated Area Equipped for Irrigation, by Country

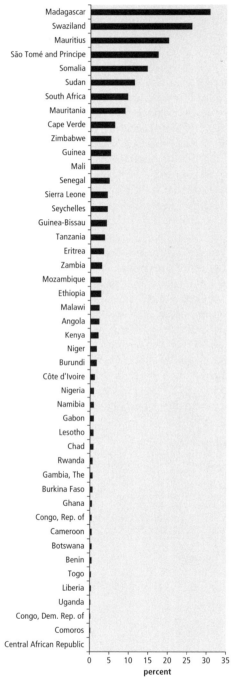

Source: Svendsen, Ewing, and Msangi 2009.
Note: Djibouti, with 100 percent of its cultivated area equipped for irrigation, is not shown here for easier visibility of other countries. The percentage of area equipped for irrigation that is actually irrigated spans a wide range in Sub-Saharan Africa. Overall, the average use rate is 71 percent in the region, compared with a similar but slightly lower 67 percent in Asia.

picked up in the last several years, particularly for the Central African Republic, Kenya, Mauritius, Nigeria, Senegal, and Zambia. An appropriate institutional framework is required to manage water for growth. Sub-Saharan Africa's framework of irrigation-related institutions is undeveloped. These institutions are important for managing and sharing water over agroecologically and hydrologically diverse areas and over transboundary basins. The establishment and sound functioning of water management bodies will provide the institutional framework and will specify the location of investment planning and implementation responsibilities for irrigation infrastructure projects.

Economic Investment Potential and Needs

Some 39 million hectares of agricultural land in Africa is deemed physically suitable for irrigation; however, physical suitability does not necessarily entail economic viability (box 15.1). Economic potential for irrigation is highly sensitive to initial investment costs and requires market access, complementary inputs, extension of credit, and a supportive enabling environment. Both large-scale irrigation schemes (distributing water collected in major dams) and small-scale irrigation schemes (collecting water locally at the farm level) are relevant for Africa.

Profitable dam-based, large-scale irrigation appears feasible on 1.35 million hectares (table 15.2), if the attention is confined only to those projects that pass a threshold of 12 percent for internal rate of return. The associated one-time, on-farm investment is $2.6 billion, which would nonetheless need to be spread out over at least a decade. The countries with the greatest potential for dam-associated large-scale investments are Ethiopia, Nigeria, Sudan, and Zimbabwe, all with more than 100,000 hectares of potential. These estimates are based on the assumption that dam construction would be deemed profitable purely from a hydropower perspective and that the only costs that would need to be covered by related irrigation schemes would relate to water distribution infrastructure.

The small-scale irrigation potential is much greater because large, existing rain-fed areas

BOX 15.1

Assumptions for Irrigation Investment Potential Study

For this study, a spatial analysis was conducted that combined hydrogeographic and economic parameters to estimate investment potential. Two categories of irrigation development were assessed: (a) dam-based, large-scale irrigation associated with hydropower reservoirs (both existing and planned) identified by a companion study for hydropower; and (b) small-scale irrigation based on small reservoirs, farm ponds, treadle pumps, and water-harvesting structures collecting local runoff. The main data sets were (a) spatially explicit current crop distribution, (b) spatially explicit crop-specific biophysical potential, and (c) potential runoff and effective rainfall from a hydrological model for small-scale irrigation. Crop prices, based on commodity-specific world prices for 2004–06, were adjusted for country differences in price policy and market transaction costs.

Small-scale irrigation assumed a five-year cycle of investment, a medium investment cost of $2,000 per hectare for on-farm investment, and $80 per hectare for operation and maintenance. Three hours' travel time to the nearest market was set as the cutoff value for market access, excluding all pixels that fell beyond this range. Runoff use efficiency for small systems was set at 30 percent; that is, only 30 percent of the captured runoff can be used for small-scale irrigation.

Large-scale irrigation assumed a medium investment cost of $3,000 per hectare for on-farm development, $0.25 per cubic meter for water delivery and conveyance, a proxy for canal operations and maintenance, and $10 per hectare for on-farm operations and maintenance. A 50-year investment horizon was used. Dam costs were not included because they are assumed to be fully justified and fully covered by the hydropower schemes associated with the relevant dams. Overall irrigation efficiency for large systems was assumed to be 40 percent.

Source: You 2009.

Table 15.2 Potential Investment Needs for Large-Scale, Dam-Based, and Complementary Small-Scale Irrigation in Sub-Saharan Africa

Region	Large-scale irrigation			Small-scale irrigation		
	Increase in irrigated area (million hectares)	Investment cost ($ millions)	Average IRR (%)	Increase in irrigated area (million hectares)	Investment cost ($ millions)	Average IRR (%)
Sudano-Sahelian	0.26	508	14	1.26	4,391	33
Eastern	0.25	482	18	1.08	3,873	28
Gulf of Guinea	0.61	1,188	18	2.61	8,233	22
Central	0.00	4	12	0.30	881	29
Southern	0.23	458	16	0.19	413	13
Indian Ocean Islands	0.00	0	—	0.00	0	—
Total	1.35	2,640	17	5.44	17,790	26

Source: You 2009.
Note: See table 15.1 for definitions of regional groupings. The average value for IRR was weighted by the increase in irrigated area. Benin, Chad, and Madagascar have no profitable large-scale irrigation. IRR = internal rate of return. — Not available.
a. Unlike cost estimates presented elsewhere in this report, these are *one-time* investment costs rather than *annualized* figures.

could be profitably converted to small-scale irrigation. Costs would be only slightly lower because for small-scale irrigation, on-farm water storage would need to be built in addition to water distribution infrastructure. Only land within three hours' travel time to a significant town is deemed suitable for the development of small-scale irrigation, restricting it to about 30 percent of the cultivated land. Again, restricting attention to those projects that pass a threshold of 12 percent for internal rate of return, profitable small-scale irrigation could take place on 5.44 million hectares at a one-time cost of $17.8 billion that would nonetheless need to be spread out over at least a decade (see table 15.2 and figure 15.2). In all regions except southern Africa, small-scale irrigation has a higher internal rate of return than does large-scale irrigation. By far the greatest potential is found in Nigeria, which accounts for more than 2.5 million (or almost half) of the suitable hectares. Countries such as Cameroon, Chad, Ethiopia, Mali, Niger, South Africa, Sudan, Tanzania, Togo, and Uganda each have at least 100,000 hectares of potential.

Full development of economic irrigation potential doubles the share of cultivated land under irrigation, raising the share of cultivated land under irrigation from 3.5 percent to 7.0 percent. Annualized investment costs over 10 years would constitute 1.8 percent of 2000 GDP and account for 88 percent of agricultural spending. For many countries, that would imply a substantial increase in agricultural spending. However,

under the Comprehensive Africa Agricultural Development Program of the New Partnership for Africa's Development, African countries have already committed themselves to raising allocations of national budgetary resources to agricultural and rural development up to 10 percent of the total by 2015. This planned increase in spending could go some way toward meeting the costs of an expanded irrigation program.

Most of the hectares found to be viable for irrigation would be dedicated to higher-value crops (table 15.3). In most cases, irrigation is found to be viable only when high-revenue-yielding crops are cultivated, be they traditional cash crops (such as coffee) or higher-value food crops (such as horticulture). More than half of the viable hectares identified are associated with crops that can yield in excess of $2,000 per hectare annually. Relatively few hectares are found where irrigation investments can be justified simply to grow staple food crops.

The investment cost estimates used here reflect best-practice experience, but actual costs may often be higher. Studies suggest that well-designed and well-implemented irrigation projects in Africa can lead to costs of no more than $2,000 per hectare for small-scale irrigation schemes and $3,000 per hectare (the distribution component) for large-scale irrigation schemes. Therefore, they are the central parameters used in this modeling exercise. Nevertheless, in practice, irrigation projects in Africa may incur investment costs well in excess of $4,000 per hectare (Inocencio and others 2005). Therefore, considering the sensitivity of these results to possible changes in unit investment costs is important.

Estimates for both large- and (particularly) small-scale irrigation potential are highly sensitive to assumptions about investment costs (table 15.4). Results are sensitive to the assumptions about investment costs per hectare and other parameters (see box 15.1). For large-scale irrigation, the number of viable hectares would decline to 54 percent of the base case if investment costs rose from $3,000 to $6,000 per hectare. This situation might be the case, for example, if irrigation were required to contribute to water storage costs and not simply to water distribution infrastructure. For small-scale irrigation, the story is much more dramatic.

Figure 15.2 Investment Potential for Dam-Based and Small-Scale Irrigation

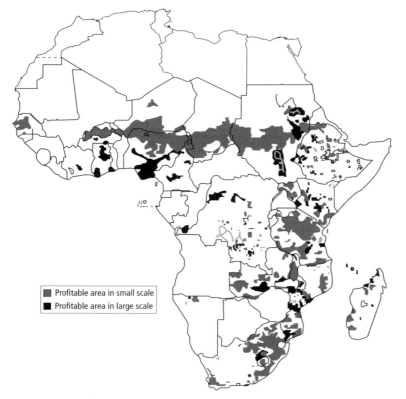

Profitable area in small scale
Profitable area in large scale

Source: You 2009.
Note: Dark gray areas indicate positive internal rate of return for dam-based irrigation. Light gray areas indicate profitable areas for small-scale irrigation. Countries left blank were not covered in the sample.

Table 15.3 Share of Crops under Irrigation, Irrigation Investment Needs Assessment

Crops	Average revenue ($/hectare/year)	Percentage total viable hectares
Sugarcane, barley, soybeans, other pulses	< 100	16
Bananas, beans, potatoes, sorghum, sugar beets, ground nuts, cassava, maize, cotton lint	100–500	14
Coffee, rice, sweet potatoes, millet	500–1,000	16
Horticulture and other high-value crops	> 2,000	54

Source: Derived from You 2009.

Table 15.4 Sensitivity of Irrigation Potential to Assumed Investment Cost

Large-scale irrigation		Small-scale irrigation	
Initial investment cost/ hectare (US$)	Hectares (percentage baseline)	Initial investment cost/ hectare (US$)	Hectares (percentage baseline)
1,000	112	600	226
3,000	**100**	**2,000**	**100**
6,000	54	5,000	5

Source: You 2009.
Note: The base case is in boldface and considers all projects that have a positive net present value including those whose internal rate of return may be below the 12 percent threshold.

Raising the investment cost from the baseline case of $2,000 per hectare to $5,000 per hectare would all but eliminate the economic case for small-scale irrigation. This finding underscores the fact that the economic viability of much of Africa's potentially irrigable land depends critically on containing investment costs to best-practice levels.

Effect of Expanding Agricultural Water Development

What would be the development effect of an aggressive expansion of Africa's irrigated agricultural area? It has already been established that an economic case exists for developing an additional 6.8 million hectares of irrigation with respectable returns of at least 12 percent. This conclusion comes with two important caveats. First, investment costs would need to be contained to the $2,000–$3,000 per hectare range. Second, to ensure viability, most irrigation development would need to focus on higher-value crops. Assuming such conditions were met, what would be the broader development effect? An illustrative modeling exercise is used to see how the higher agricultural yields resulting from irrigation scale-up would affect the food economy looking ahead to 2020 and beyond.

A high but feasible 3.6 percent annual increase in investments in irrigation would triple the irrigated harvested area to 22 million hectares in 2050. The irrigated yield would grow by 10 percent in parallel with a gradual 10 percent increase in rain-fed crop productivity (by increasing effective rainfall by 5 percent by 2020 and 10 percent by 2050). The effects of these investments are discernible in three areas: food prices, food imports, and nutritional outcomes.

Greater availability of food would help contain major projected increases in food prices (table 15.5). Food prices in Africa are projected to increase from the 2000 baseline level of $117 per ton of cereals to $205 by 2050. The greater food production brought about by irrigation scale-up would help limit this inflationary pressure, keeping the price of a ton of cereals down to $177 by 2050.

Irrigation scale-up would also reduce Africa's reliance on food imports (table 15.5). As of 2000, Africa was importing more than 23,000 tons of cereals annually. Africa's food trade deficit is projected to grow dramatically to more than 98,000 tons in 2050, reflecting a substantial rise in food demand from growing and increasingly urban populations combined

Table 15.5 Food Price Changes for Various Indicators, 2020 and 2050

Year	Average world price for cereals ($/metric ton)	Net cereal imports (thousand tons)	Number of malnourished children (thousands)	Caloric availability (kilocalories/ person/day)	Rain-fed area, cereals (thousand hectares)	Irrigated area, cereals (thousand hectares)	Rain-fed production, cereals (thousand metric tons)	Irrigated production, cereals (thousand metric tons)
Projection of current investment levels with climate change								
2000	117	23,638	32,669	2,277	74,303	3,783	75,283	6,829
2020	187	4,370	44,041	2,241	87,109	4,847	132,184	12,851
2050	205	75,417	33,756	2,761	92,908	6,294	203,680	26,011
Projection of current investment levels without climate change								
2000	117	23,638	32,669	2,277	74,303	3,783	75,283	6,829
2020	179	6,398	43,646	2,263	86,908	4,858	132,125	12,891
2050	159	98,963	31,894	2,886	92,441	6,441	204,427	26,454
Increased investments with climate change								
2000	117	23,638	32,669	2,277	74,303	3,783	75,283	6,829
2020	182	−7,331	42,507	2,235	85,793	7,666	138,904	18,625
2050	177	11,134	31,640	2,852	89,560	21,722	220,820	86,003

Source: Estimates provided by International Food Policy Research Institute, Washington, D.C., 2009.

with relatively slow expansion of output. By expanding homegrown food production, irrigation investments could reduce food imports to only 11,000 tons by 2050.

Some discernible (though far from dramatic) effects on malnutrition would occur (table 15.5). Because of the adverse market trends noted, child malnutrition is projected to increase slightly in the coming decades, from 32.7 million cases in 2000 to 33.8 million in 2050. The greater availability of food associated with irrigation investments would help relieve this problem, keeping the number of cases down to 31.6 million in 2050, albeit a rather modest reduction.

Overall, irrigation investments help offset some of the adverse effects anticipated from climate change (table 15.5). Climate change is an important factor driving the projected deterioration of the food supply situation in Africa. Irrigation investments can be viewed as an adaptation measure insofar as they help offset the negative supply-side effects of climate change. Thus, irrigation offsets the effect of climate change on child malnutrition, and it more than offsets the effect on the food trade balance. Food prices would remain somewhat higher than they would have been without climate change, but still considerably lower than without irrigation.

Implementation Challenges

Considerably increasing investments in irrigation raises issues about the performance and sustainability of these investments. A recent multidonor irrigation performance diagnostic identified challenges that need to be addressed to improve the performance of irrigation investments. This section summarizes the findings and recommendations of that report (World Bank 2007).

Adopt a Strategic Vision
National agricultural water development strategies need to be promoted. They should recognize (a) the potential contribution of agricultural water to poverty reduction and growth; (b) the imperatives of farm-level profitability and economic viability; and (c) the need for policies, legal frameworks, and organizations that foster profitable, sustainable water-managed farming by smallholders. The strategies would analyze trade-offs and capture synergies of the various investment options. Key areas to be covered by such strategies include (a) increasing the productivity and profitability of existing irrigation schemes; (b) expanding or developing new irrigation (including systems based on water harvesting); (c) testing and disseminating rainwater harvesting technologies; (d) developing

sustainable supply chains for agricultural water equipment; and (e) investing in research on agricultural water management.

Agricultural water strategies need to be incorporated into wider sectoral strategies for agriculture, rural development, and water. Water strategies should be based on integrated water resource management principles that promote an economically efficient allocation of water to the agricultural sector, ensure that water allocation and management take into account the needs of the poor, and provide for effective participation by smallholders in basin planning. Agricultural water needs to be more clearly reflected in Poverty Reduction Strategy Papers or similar national development strategies.

Invest in Institutional Reforms

The new agricultural water strategies should form the basis for sectoral programs that combine investment in infrastructure with investment in institutional reforms. A starting point for reforms is to improve coordination among the government organizations responsible for infrastructure development (a ministry of water) and those responsible for irrigated farming (a ministry of agriculture) and to build capacity and incentives for public agencies to adopt a new agricultural water development paradigm (box 15.2). It is also desirable to develop the instruments needed for private sector involvement through public-private partnerships.

Responsibility for development should be decentralized as much as possible, based on the principle of subsidiarity. In almost all cases, reforms will focus on empowering potential users of agricultural water to cope with their new roles and responsibilities and to deal effectively with service providers, including irrigation agencies (which should become accountable to their clients), credit organizations, and input supply and output markets. This measure should be accompanied by investment in capacity building for farmer organizations. More generally, the role of farmers in cost sharing and in operation and maintenance should be transparent.

Monitoring and evaluation should be an essential management tool for farmers, implementing agencies, and financing partners. As

An Enabling Environment for Reform: Office du Niger

Initiated by the French in 1932, the Office du Niger is one of the oldest and largest irrigation schemes in Sub-Saharan Africa. Located in Mali, the scheme was originally developed to supply the French textile industry with cotton and to increase food security for the Sahel region. Despite a disappointing performance in the first several decades, including limited area development, poor infrastructure maintenance, and low yields, the project was rehabilitated in the early 1980s with assistance from the European Union; the World Bank; and the governments of France, Germany, the Netherlands, and the United States. Comprehensive reforms and rehabilitation tripled average paddy yields to 5 tons per hectare, increased the area under cultivation to about 80,000 hectares, boosted settler population by over 220 percent, and increased paddy production per capita from 0.9 ton to 1.6 tons, reducing poverty and increasing food security.

The project's success is attributed to technical, institutional, and economic factors. Technical factors include water management through physical rehabilitation of irrigation and drainage networks, a comprehensive package of improved technologies, and appropriate agricultural mechanization. Institutional and economic factors include liberalized paddy marketing and processing, land-tenure security, infrastructure improvements, institutional reforms, and stronger partnerships with farmers. Also important were donor coordination, government commitment, and the right macroeconomic and policy environment.

Source: Based on interviews with World Bank staff from the Africa Water Resources Department, 2008.

a minimum requirement, monitoring and evaluation systems should measure inputs; costs; and changes in production, incomes, employment, health, and the environment.

Undertake Viable and Sustainable Projects

Future designs and investment decisions should be based solely on economic viability, farm-level profitability, and sustainability. Nonviable investments for "social" or "strategic" purposes should be avoided. Subsidies (if any) should be limited to (a) items having a medium- to long-term economic life (headworks and main canals on larger schemes), the cost of which is beyond the financial capacity of most farmers, rather than for lower-cost investments with a short economic life (treadle pumps or on-farm development for improved infield rainwater management); and (b) technology development and promotion. Subsidies for support services and operation and maintenance should preferably be avoided or otherwise carefully targeted and provided only in the short term to kick-start commercial production.

Reducing per hectare development costs is critical for success. The cost of public irrigation development in Sub-Saharan Africa has been excessively high. Many irrigation schemes failed to capture significantly higher yield levels and cropping intensities and failed to transition to production of higher-value crops. Under these circumstances, high development costs rapidly erode returns on investment. Costs have come down in recent years because of competition among contractors; the emergence of new contractors, particularly from low-income countries; and the introduction of affordable irrigation technologies. Keeping down development costs is important, because projects with low returns have per hectare development costs four times those of projects with good returns. Designing for maximum profitability is thus critical and involves both cost-effective design and an effective strategy to increase output. A new generation of well-designed and well-implemented irrigation projects has proved only marginally more costly than those of other regions.

Provide Agricultural Water as Part of a Comprehensive Package

Investments in agricultural water are part of a comprehensive package to increase outputs, including empowered farmer organizations; sustainable, efficient, and accountable agricultural support services; and accessible, profitable markets. Therefore, investments in agricultural water not only should focus on infrastructure delivery but also should address agricultural intensification in a holistic way (box 15.3). Indeed, without complementary efforts to improve agricultural productivity through other channels, irrigation is unlikely to deliver the sizable increases in yield necessary to justify the original investment.

Investments need to be pro-poor. Project preparation studies should provide an understanding of how investments in agricultural water can assist beneficiaries to improve their

---

BOX 15.3

Nigeria's Fadama Water User Association: Expanding Irrigation

Community-driven development can expand irrigation in Sub-Saharan Africa, particularly among homogeneous groups with high social equality. The Fadama II agricultural development project in Nigeria supported water user associations. It increased access to productive assets and infrastructure, including agricultural inputs, irrigation infrastructure, and postharvesting equipment. Community groups were organized into user groups based on their agricultural sector (livestock, crops, forestry, and the like) and were paid 10 percent of the asset costs. As a result, the value of productive assets for water and irrigation, which included water pumps, boreholes, and tube wells, increased nearly 3,000 percent. In addition, the irrigation investment raised crop productivity in dry regions, increasing incomes in the dry savannahs nearly 80 percent.

Source: Based on interviews with World Bank staff from the Africa Water Resources Department, 2008.

---

livelihoods. This understanding will make the investment more pro-poor by selecting technology options that are low risk and affordable to the poor, and by seeking to maximize farm-level profitability and agricultural wage employment, as well as other indirect employment opportunities. In addition, institutional design should ensure that the role of women in production systems and their management is taken into account and built on.

Notes

The authors of this chapter are Mark Rosegrant, Claudia Ringler, and IJsbrand de Jong, who drew on background material and contributions from Salah Darghouth, Mandy Ewing, Stephen Mink, Siwa Msangi, Siobhan Murray, Mark Svendsen, and Liang Zhi You.

1. Agricultural water and irrigation are used interchangeably, and both refer to the supply of additional water to augment rainwater (if any) for crops and livestock. In this report, agricultural water and irrigation include drainage, where appropriate.

References

Frenken, Karen, ed. 2005. *Irrigation in Africa in Figures: AQUASTAT Survey—2005.* FAO Water Report 29. Rome: Food and Agriculture Organization of the United Nations.

Inocencio, Arlene, Masao Kikuchi, Manabu Tonosaki, Atsushi Maruyama, and Hilmy Sally. 2005. "Costs of Irrigation Projects: A Comparison of Sub-Saharan Africa and Other Developing Regions and Finding Options to Reduce Costs." Report of component study for Collaborative Programme, International Water Management Institute, Pretoria, South Africa.

NEPAD (New Partnership for Africa's Development). 2003. Comprehensive Africa Agricultural Development Programme. http://www.nepad-caadp.net/.

Svendsen, Mark, Mandy Ewing, and Siwa Msangi. 2008. "Watermarks: Indicators of Irrigation Sector Performance in Sub-Saharan Africa." Background Paper 4, Africa Infrastructure Country Diagnostic, World Bank, Washington, DC.

World Bank. 2007. *Investment in Agricultural Water for Poverty Reduction and Economic Growth in Sub-Saharan Africa: Synthesis Report.* Washington, DC: World Bank.

———. 2008. *World Development Report 2008: Agriculture for Development.* Washington, DC: World Bank.

You, Liang Zhi. 2008. "Irrigation Investment Needs in Sub-Saharan Africa." Background Paper 9, Africa Infrastructure Country Diagnostic, World Bank, Washington, DC.

Chapter 16

Water Supply: Hitting the Target?

Sub-Saharan Africa as a whole is unlikely to meet the Millennium Development Goal (MDG) for water supply. Coverage in urban areas has been declining as utilities have struggled to keep pace with population growth. In rural areas, more than 40 percent of the population continues to rely on surface water. Overall, wells and boreholes are the fastest-growing sources of supply.

The price tag for reaching the MDG for access to an improved water source is estimated at $16.5 billion a year (roughly 2.6 percent of Africa's GDP). For many countries, these costs look prohibitive. By emphasizing lower-cost technologies, such as standposts and boreholes, those countries could reduce the cost of meeting the MDG. However, standpost use is affected by institutional challenges that remain to be addressed.

Spending on the water sector today is $3.6 billion, one-fourth of what is required. However, some $2.7 billion available to the sector is currently being wasted due to inefficiency.

An important example of inefficiency is underpricing of services. Average water tariffs are about $0.67 per cubic meter, below the cost-recovery threshold of just over $1.00 per cubic meter. By underpricing water, the sector forgoes at least $1.8 billion a year in revenues. Typically, capital costs have been subsidized, but the subsidies are highly regressive. Full capital cost recovery should be affordable for half of the population, including the bulk of those that enjoy piped water access today, but would not be affordable to the remainder.

Furthermore, the operational inefficiencies of water utilities cost the region $0.9 billion a year and impede service expansion. Institutional reforms of legal and regulatory frameworks hold the key to improving performance. Private participation, particularly lease contracts, has significantly affected utility performance, but state-owned utilities will remain the central actors, and greater efforts are needed to improve their governance frameworks.

Even if all these inefficiencies could be eliminated, the overall financing gap for the water sector would still be $7.8 billion a year (1.2 percent of GDP).

Looking ahead, the institutional reform agenda remains as relevant as before, even if the focus has shifted toward a more pluralistic view of public and private sector roles. The reform agenda also needs to move beyond utilities to encompass line ministries and the whole public expenditure framework that underpins, and too often hinders, sector investment programs. Room also exists for more cost recovery, so that scarce subsidy resources are redirected to promote access among the poorest. For the majority that does not enjoy access to a piped-water connection, greater thought needs to be given to how standposts can become a more effective part of urban water supplies. The burgeoning use of wells and boreholes for supply in urban areas demands urgent attention from policy makers both to improve their understanding and to develop suitable regulatory tools. In rural areas, the big challenge, in addition to continuing to expand access, is the high breakdown rate from lack of maintenance, which threatens the sustainability of what has already been achieved.

The Millennium Development Goal for Water—Elusive for Many

Whereas the rest of the world is on track to achieve the MDG for water supply,[1] Sub-Saharan Africa reports that only 58 percent of its population enjoys access to safe drinking water vis-à-vis a target rate of 75 percent to be reached by 2015 (WHO/UNICEF 2006).[2] Progress has been modest, with access increasing by only 9 percentage points between 1990 and 2006, or less than 1 percentage point a year. To meet the target, growth should stand at over 2 percentage points a year. As a result, Sub-Saharan Africa lags all other regions, including South Asia, whose performance was broadly comparable to that of Sub-Saharan Africa in the past but which has moved at a much faster pace in recent years.

Some countries are closer to meeting the MDG targets than others. According to the most recent WHO/UNICEF Joint Monitoring Programme data for 2006, five African countries have already met the MDG target: Burkina Faso, Ghana, Malawi, Namibia, and South Africa. Moreover, an additional 12 countries had reasonable prospects of meeting the target by 2015 if they continued to make steady progress: Cameroon, the Central African Republic, the Comoros, Côte d'Ivoire, Eritrea,

Guinea, Mali, Mauritania, Senegal, Sudan, Uganda, and Zimbabwe. At the other end of the spectrum, some of Africa's most populous countries, such as the Democratic Republic of Congo and Nigeria, are a long way from meeting the target. The proximity of 2015 and the daunting challenges highlight the importance of understanding the performance of the water sector in the region, its achievements and shortcomings, and the factors most critical in expanding coverage.

Service options for water supply can be organized on a hierarchical ladder according to the delivery method and quality of the associated service. At the top of the ladder is piped water, which is both potable and convenient. Standposts offer the same potability, but through a less convenient channel and with some risk of the water becoming contaminated during collection. Next come wells and boreholes, which, depending on their location, can be more or less convenient than standposts. The water delivered can be of good quality, though that depends on the local aquifer and protection from contamination. Surface water is at the bottom of the ladder, because its quality is in most cases questionable, and it is seldom convenient. Although the objective may be to provide universal piped-water access to the population, it may not be feasible or affordable in the short run. An important first step is to move people away from surface water to one of the lower rungs of the water supply ladder.

Differing Patterns of Urban and Rural Access

In rural areas, reliance on surface water remains prevalent. The share of the population relying on surface water fell quite steeply in the 1990s, from 50 percent to just over 40 percent, where it has remained through 2005 (table 16.1). Boreholes are the main source of improved water, accounting for a further 40 percent of the population. Access to piped water and standposts is very low, barely increasing over the last 15 years. Indeed, in many countries, less than 1 percent of the rural population receives piped water. Strikingly, in countries

Table 16.1 Evolution of Water Supply Coverage in Africa, by Source
percentage of population

Period	Piped supply		Standposts		Well and boreholes[a]		Surface water	
	Urban	Rural	Urban	Rural	Urban	Rural	Urban	Rural
1990–95	50	4	29	9	20	41	6	50
1995–2000	43	4	25	9	21	41	5	41
2001–05	39	4	24	11	24	43	7	42

Source: Banerjee, Wodon, and others 2008.
Note: The figures are based on household surveys.
a. The WHO/UNICEF Joint Monitoring Programme (2006) considers protected wells and boreholes to be improved water sources. However, disaggregating the data into protected and unprotected wells and boreholes from the household surveys used in the Africa Infrastructure Country Diagnostic study is not possible.

with higher levels of urbanization, access to piped water and standposts in *rural* areas is substantially higher.

In urban areas, rapid population growth has caused piped-water coverage to fall markedly over the last 15 years. However, at close to 40 percent, it is still the single-largest source of water supply. Standpost coverage has similarly declined, whereas that of boreholes has risen, so that each of these types of service reaches about 24 percent of the urban population. The lower coverage of standposts compared with piped water is particularly striking, given their relatively low cost and the pressure to expand services rapidly. Reliance on surface water, at 7 percent of the urban population, has hardly changed.

Utilities are the central actors responsible for water supply in urban areas. Overall, about two-thirds of the urban populace depends on utility water. In the middle-income countries, utilities are essentially the only players, reaching about 99 percent of the urban population, the vast majority through private piped-water connections. In low-income countries, only 49 percent of urban residents benefit from utility water, fewer than half through private piped connections (table 16.2). For the rest, informal sharing of connections through resale between neighbors (15 percent of the urban population) is almost as prevalent as formal sharing through standposts (19 percent of the urban population). In Maputo, Mozambique, one-third of unconnected households purchase water from their neighbors, and in Maseru, Lesotho, household resellers provide water to 31 percent of the population, including almost half

Table 16.2 Services Provided by Utilities in Their Service Areas
percentage

Country type	Population already enjoying access to utility water				Population gaining access to utility water each year		
	Piped water	Standposts	Resale of neighbor's water	Total	Piped water	Standposts	Total
Low income	30	19	15	68	1.9	1.0	2.9
Middle income	89	10	0	99	4.5	−0.2	4.5
Average[a]	44	14	6	86	2.5	0.9	3.2

Source: Banerjee, Skilling, and others 2008.
Note: The figures are based on utility data for utility service areas. The coverage is higher than that obtained from household surveys because utility service areas do not cover the entirety of urban areas and because for some countries, data were available only for utilities in larger cities.
[a]Average is population weighted.

of the unconnected households. Household resale, while prevalent, is often illegal, although Côte d'Ivoire illustrates the potential benefits of legalization (box 16.1).

Utilities report providing around 20 hours of service daily, and just over 80 percent of their samples pass chlorine tests (table 16.3). They typically produce just over 200 liters per capita served, though the amount for middle-income countries is about twice that for low-income countries. If the utilities' total water production could be evenly distributed to the entire population residing in the utility service area, it would amount to 74 liters per capita a day, just about adequate to meet basic human needs.

Urban households that do not benefit from utility water rely on several alternatives. The rapid expansion of boreholes in urban areas has already been noted. Water vendors, another alternative, may retail water from utilities, boreholes, or surface sources, either

BOX 16.1

Legalizing Household Water Resellers in Côte d'Ivoire

Côte d'Ivoire legalized household resellers in informal settlements to help the poor receive safe water. This legislation enables the Société de Distribution d'Eau de la Côte d'Ivoire (SODECI) to indirectly influence the price and quality of the water in these areas. The utility has issued about 1,000 licenses to water resellers, who can invest in last-mile network extensions to cater to demand in poor neighborhoods. SODECI reduces the risk of nonpayment by requiring a sizable deposit (about $300) and invoicing resellers monthly.

Nevertheless, the scheme faces implementation challenges. Household resellers pay SODECI twice: their reseller payments and a price markup for network extensions in these areas. Furthermore, no special tariff applies to household resellers; they pay the high consumer tariff. Therefore, the motivation to become a household reseller is limited, and most households pay the regular domestic consumer price.

Source: Collignon and Vézina 2000.

Table 16.3 Quality of Services Provided by Utilities in Their Service Areas

	Availability of utility water		Quality of water supply	
Country type	Liters per capita available for residents in service area	Liters per capita available for utility customers	Hours/day of continuous service	Percentage of samples passing chlorine test
Low income	74	149	19	83
Middle income	272	277	24	99
Average[a]	167	224	21	83

Source: Banerjee, Skilling, and others 2008.
[a] Average is population weighted.

from trucks and carts, or sometimes through their own private distribution networks. Water vendors account for only 3 percent of the African urban market, rising to 7 percent for West Africa. In some countries, however, their contribution to the urban water supply is much larger: Nigeria (10 percent), Chad (16 percent), Niger (21 percent), and Mauritania (32 percent). In 15 large cities in Africa, the cost of vendor water, particularly when transported directly to the household, can be 2 to 11 times more expensive than having a household connection (table 16.4). This strong willingness to pay for vendor water is a potential revenue source that the utilities are typically unable to capture.

The dynamics of service expansion reveal a similar overall pattern in both urban and rural areas: the absolute number of people depending on surface water continues to grow, a grim statistic in its own right (figure 16.1). Across the board, wells and boreholes are expanding

coverage much more rapidly than all the utility-based alternatives together. Within the purview of the utility, access to standposts seems to be growing faster than access to piped water. But the combined growth rates of the various improved forms of water supply in urban areas (less than 1 percent a year) still fall short of population growth (more than 4 percent a year).

Access to improved water sources is highly inequitable across the income distribution (figure 16.2). Piped water and standposts are heavily concentrated among the more affluent segments of the population, typically in urban areas. The poorest 40 percent of the population, by contrast, depends on surface water and on wells and boreholes in almost equal measure. Piped supply covers only 10 percent of African households in the bottom 60 percent of the population. For the middle-income countries, access to piped water and standposts among the poorest quintiles is substantially higher than in the low-income countries.

Financing the MDG

The overall price tag for reaching the MDG target for access to water is estimated at $16.5 billion (roughly 2.6 percent of Africa's GDP), which is somewhat higher than previously thought (Mehta, Fugelsnes, and Virjee 2005). Capital investment needs based on minimum acceptable asset standards and accounting for

Table 16.4 Average Price for Water Service in 15 Largest Cities, by Type of Provider

	House connection	Small piped network	Stand post	Household reseller	Water tanker	Water vendor
Average price ($/cubic meter)	0.49	1.04	1.93	1.63	4.67	4.00
Markup over house connection (%)	100	214	336	402	1,103	811

Source: Keener, Luengo, and Banerjee 2008.

Figure 16.1 Increases in Access to Water by Source, 1990s to Early 2000s

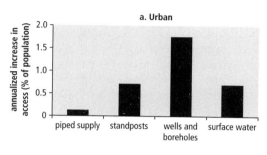
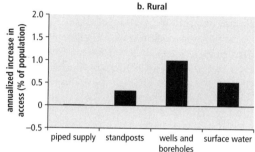

Source: Banerjee, Skilling, and others 2008.

Figure 16.2 Coverage of Water Services, by Budget Quintile

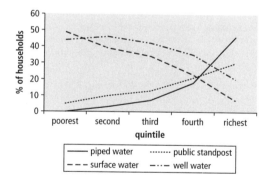

Source: Banerjee, Skilling, and others 2008.
Note: In terms of household spending, poorest quintile = poorest 20 percent of the population; second quintile = second-poorest 20 percent of the population; third quintile = middle 20 percent of the population; fourth quintile = second-richest 20 percent of the population; richest quintile = richest 20 percent of the population.

Table 16.5 Estimated Annual Financing Needed to Meet the Water MDG

Country type	$ billions annually			% of GDP		
	O&M	Capital	Total	O&M	Capital	Total
Sub-Saharan Africa	5.53	11.01	16.54	0.86	1.72	2.58
Low-income fragile	0.98	2.41	3.39	2.55	6.27	8.81
Low-income nonfragile	1.91	4.36	6.27	1.73	3.95	5.68
Middle income	1.19	1.19	2.38	0.44	0.44	0.88
Resource rich	1.47	3.12	4.59	0.66	1.40	2.06

Source: Briceño-Garmendia, Smits, and Foster 2008.
Note: O&M = operation and maintenance. Row totals may not add exactly because of rounding errors.

both new infrastructure and rehabilitation of existing assets can be conservatively estimated at $11.0 billion a year (1.7 percent of the region's GDP). The maintenance requirements are $5.5 billion a year (0.9 percent of the region's GDP) (table 16.5).

The cost of achieving the water MDG is very high for nonfragile low-income countries (5.7 percent of GDP), and particularly high for fragile states (8.8 percent of GDP).

Although donors have been financing the associated capital costs, low-income countries face a maintenance bill of approximately 2 percent of GDP, perhaps even more of a challenge given weaknesses in sector institutions and budgeting processes. The challenge to resource-rich countries, though not insignificant, appears much more manageable. Middle-income countries should comfortably meet their financing needs.

Existing spending on water and sanitation is $7.6 billion, or less than half of what is required. (Because of the difficulty of accurately separating water and sanitation, spending for both services is presented together here. The more detailed discussion of sanitation can be found in chapter 17 of this volume.) African countries are already devoting significant resources to meeting the water and sanitation MDG targets. Domestically funded spending accounted for over half of total spending. For capital investment, donors have had a predominant role, particularly in low-income countries, where they finance most of the investment (table 16.6). Financiers outside the Organisation for Economic Co-operation and Development have also played a role in the low-income countries, whereas private finance has been negligible. However, household self-finance of on-site sanitation facilities—such as latrines—is estimated to be substantial.

Public investment in water and sanitation is almost exclusively the domain of the central government. Within the public sector, general governments[3] carry out most capital spending, whereas public enterprises tend to execute most spending for operation and maintenance. Therefore, the institutional effectiveness of the line ministries is just as important as the institutional effectiveness of the utilities in ensuring that resources are well used. Thus, better public expenditure management, good selection of projects, and clear strategic guidance for investment should all be considered integral aspects of the sector reform agenda.

The existing resource envelope for Africa's water supply sector would go considerably further if various serious inefficiencies—amounting to $2.7 billion a year—could be

addressed. Improving cost recovery of water utilities could reduce the gap by $1.8 billion a year, addressing operating inefficiencies would bring an additional $0.9 billion a year, and raising capital budget execution could recoup some $0.2 billion a year. A larger part of these gains is for the low-income countries, whose utilities should focus equally on improving cost recovery and on reducing operating inefficiencies. For middle-income countries, much of the gain would come from reducing operating inefficiencies.

Even if all of these efficiencies could be addressed, the water sector would still face a sizable financing gap of $9.3 billion a year (1.5 percent of GDP; table 16.7). The gap for capital requirements is more than twice that for operation and maintenance, suggesting that the MDG challenge is mainly about expanding access to improved water sources and rehabilitating existing assets in poor condition.

Although the costs of investment appear high, the health dividends of meeting the MDG target are substantial. Every dollar invested in water supply generates economic benefits of at least $1.50 (Hutton and Haller 2004). Access to improved water brings a variety of benefits, particularly improved health and reduced time spent collecting water. Serious illnesses transmitted through unsafe water, such as infectious diarrhea, are a leading cause of infant mortality. Waterborne illnesses can be a substantial economic burden, causing adult deaths and workdays lost and affecting children's health and education.

Table 16.6 Existing Financial Flows to Water Supply and Sanitation
$ billions annually

	O&M	Capital expenditure						Total
Country type	Public sector	Public sector	ODA	Non-OECD financiers	PPI	Household self-finance	Total	
Sub-Saharan Africa	3.06	1.06	1.23	0.16	0.01	2.13	4.58	7.64
Low-income fragile	0.13	0.03	0.11	0.02	0.00	0.16	0.32	0.45
Low-income nonfragile	0.30	0.25	0.78	0.05	0.00	0.45	1.54	1.83
Middle income	2.17	0.15	0.10	0.01	0.00	0.21	0.47	2.64
Resource rich	0.15	0.72	0.24	0.08	0.01	0.52	1.57	1.72

Source: Briceño-Garmendia, Smits, and Foster 2008.
Note: ODA = official development assistance; OECD = Organisation for Economic Co-operation and Development; O&M = operation and maintenance; PPI = private participation in infrastructure.

Table 16.7 Composition of Water Sector Funding Gap

Country type	$ billions annually			Percentage of GDP		
	O&M	Capital	Total	O&M	Capital	Total
Sub-Saharan Africa	2.74	6.60	9.34	0.43	1.03	1.45
Low-income fragile	0.75	2.00	2.76	1.96	5.22	7.17
Low-income nonfragile	1.43	2.92	4.35	1.30	2.64	3.94
Middle income	0.00	0.00	0.00	0.00	0.00	0.00
Resource rich	1.06	1.74	2.80	0.48	0.78	1.26

Source: Briceño-Garmendia, Smits, and Foster 2008.
Note: O&M = operation and maintenance.

Household members, primarily women and children, face a substantial opportunity cost in time to fetch water. More than 20 percent of the population in Cameroon, Ghana, Mauritania, Niger, and Tanzania must travel more than 2 kilometers to the primary water supply. Rural dwellers tend to travel farther than urban dwellers. Therefore, the time savings from accessing water from a nearby source are enormous even when valued at a discounted wage rate.

Using Appropriate Technologies

For many countries, the costs of meeting the water MDG look prohibitive. Although the cost of meeting the MDG amounts to 2.3 percent of GDP on average, for a handful of countries (including Benin, the Democratic Republic of Congo, Kenya, and Madagascar), the cost would be in excess of 7 percent of GDP, well beyond what could be feasibly attained. So these countries must choose between achieving the MDG at a lower rung of the water supply ladder with lower-cost technologies and substantially postponing their achievement of the goal. Concentrating all coverage expansion in lower-cost technologies, such as standposts and boreholes, would lower the cost of meeting the MDG to 1.6 percent of GDP on average. For Benin, Kenya, and Madagascar, the cost could be reduced to less than 4 percent of GDP, which would be more affordable. The Democratic Republic of Congo would be the only country still experiencing an overall cost above 7 percent of GDP.

This strategy, however, runs contrary to current practice, which sees piped water serving the majority of those gaining access to improved water in utility service areas each year. A survey of 51 water utilities shows that about 2 percent of the population in utility service areas gains access to a formal utility water service each year—1.5 percent to piped water and 0.5 percent to standposts. Given the higher unit cost of piped water, utilities are not maximizing the effect on coverage from their limited investment budgets. Indeed, utilities could double the value for money of their investment programs (dollars per capita gaining access to improved water) if they weighted their investment programs toward standposts rather than private connections.

Standposts provide safe water in urban areas at about one-third the per capita cost of a private tap. Therefore, it is striking that the coverage of public standposts in urban Africa lags so far behind that of private taps and that their distributional incidence is skewed toward the better-off households.

Several institutional challenges prevent standposts from being more widely adopted (Keener, Luengo, and Banerjee 2008). Standposts describe a range of public water supply arrangements, from an unattended public access tap to a kiosk with a human operator. Despite their low investment cost, standposts are in practice often beset by poor maintenance and high retail prices. The service provided by the standpost may be very low because the utility's claims about the number served by a single standpost are highly variable and often unrealistic, ranging from just a few customers to 5,000, with an average of about 700. Official utility data indicate that about three-quarters of standposts are in good working order, but more detailed surveys suggest that fewer than half may be functioning normally at any one time.

The utility manages about half the standposts, but a growing number are being delegated to private or community management. Although this arrangement helps ensure sustainability, price markups to the final consumer can be large, and local elites can capture the service. Many utilities originally offered standpost services free of charge and later moved toward charging preferential rates for standpost water, typically half the price charged for a private connection. When delegated management is introduced, however, markups are added to cover the salaries of the standpost operators, often with significant profit markups. As a result, standpost prices rise to 3 times the utility rate, and as much as 20 times in some extreme cases (for example, in Kinshasa in the Democratic Republic of Congo). Community engagement can increase the accountability of kiosk operators, but it can also lead to corruption and mismanagement in countries that lack social cohesion or oversight by supporting institutions.

Even so, a handful of countries are making headway with the expansion of standposts. Each year in Rwanda, an additional 3 percent of the population resident in the service area of the national utility Electrogaz gains access to standposts (box 16.2). Similarly, Lusaka Water and Sewerage Company in Zambia adds 3 percent of its resident population to this category every year. Another intermediate approach sometimes adopted is to install yard taps, shared by four or five households. They are lower in cost than private taps, and they avoid

---

BOX 16.2

Standposts in Kigali, Rwanda

The water production capacity of Electrogaz, the main utility in Kigali, is inadequate to meet network demand. The lack of bulk supply causes rolling shortages throughout the city, often forcing residents with private connections to seek water from public sources, such as standposts.

The financial sustainability of standposts in Kigali can be estimated from the tariff paid by standpost operators ($0.42 per cubic meter), the total cost of Electrogaz's production ($0.36 per cubic meter), the rate of unaccounted-for water in distribution and selling (35 percent and 5 percent, respectively), and the volume and price of water sold at the standposts. Three hypothetical operators selling 100 jerricans each per day at $0.02, $0.03, and $0.05 per jerrican would earn estimated monthly net incomes of about $314, $949, and $1,584, respectively (the 2007 GDP per capita was $341), making this an attractive business proposition for them. However, from the utility's perspective, the combination of a low tariff and the 35 percent rate of unaccounted-for water in distribution creates a loss-producing scenario: each cubic meter supplied to a standpost costs $0.55 per cubic meter to supply when distribution losses are fully accounted for but brings in only $0.42 in revenue.

Kigali has roughly 240 standposts, of which an estimated 193 (80 percent) were operating in December 2008. Utility officials estimate that about 60,000 people use standposts, though this figure includes consumers who use them only when their primary source is unavailable. According to the total water volume recorded by public standpost meters, the standposts could supply only 48,500 people with 20 liters per capita a day. This figure would be more indicative of the upper bound of the population that primarily depends on standposts (about 6 percent of the city's population).

The utility's limited production capacity has affected both the level of peak demand at standposts and the cost of production. Observations and interviews with consumers indicate that prices have often been higher in areas when and where water service has been cut and have been lower after periods of precipitation that increase the availability of other supply options, such as rainwater and natural springs.

Source: Keener and others forthcoming.

some of the issues associated with standposts, which serve hundreds of customers.

The Challenge of Cost Recovery

By underpricing water, the sector forgoes at least $1.8 billion a year in revenues (0.3 percent of GDP). Underpricing of water—a common problem throughout the world—is also widespread across Africa. In the worst cases, such as Côte d'Ivoire, Madagascar, and Senegal, underpricing can result in utilities' capturing less than 40 percent of the revenues they need and can lead to an economic burden of around 0.7–0.9 percent of GDP (figure 16.3). The associated utility deficit is often concealed within

a set of complex financial arrangements with the central government that prevents optimal resource allocation, financial sustainability, and economically efficient use of water resources (Briceño-Garmendia, Smits, and Foster 2008). As a result, the utility management postpones basic investment and rehabilitation decisions to "make it through the day" financially. Thus, although these policies appear to be socially benign, by debilitating the financial position of the utility, they ultimately lead to delayed investment and hence hold back service expansion to reach the unserved population.

Average water tariffs in Sub-Saharan Africa are about $0.67 per cubic meter, two-thirds of a cost-recovery threshold of just over $1.00 per cubic meter. Tariffs are already relatively high by international (even developing-country) standards (box 16.3). In 2004, average water tariffs were about $1.00 per cubic meter in members of the Organisation for Economic Co-operation and Development, around $0.35 in middle-income countries, and as low as $0.10 in South Asia (GWI 2005). Tariffs of about $0.40 per cubic meter are considered more than adequate to cover operating costs in most developing-country contexts. In low-income African countries, however, operating costs are as high as $0.60 per cubic meter on average, reflecting inadequate selection of technologies, low population density, country risk premiums, and the high cost of inputs. Current tariffs cover operating costs on average but do not contribute much toward capital costs.

In most cases, the state or donors have subsidized capital costs almost entirely. Subsidies to residential consumers are highly regressive (Banerjee, Wodon, and others 2008). Across the bottom half of the income distribution, barely 10 percent of households have access to piped water. Indeed, more than 80 percent of households with piped water come from the top two quintiles of the income distribution. Because poorer households are almost entirely excluded, they cannot benefit from subsidies embedded in prices for piped water. In many cases, targeting performance is further exacerbated by poor tariff design, with widespread use of minimum charges and rising block tariffs that provide large lifeline blocks of highly subsidized water to all consumers.

Figure 16.3 Economic Burden of Water Underpricing, by Country

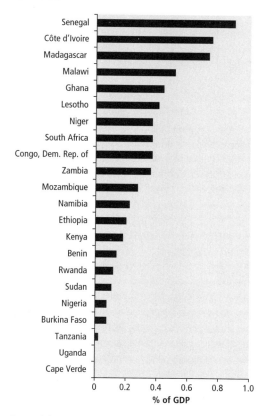

Source: Briceño-Garmendia, Smits, and Foster 2008.
Note: The economic burden of underpricing is defined as the difference between the average effective tariff and the full cost-recovery tariff multiplied by the total volume billed. It is the total revenue shortfall attributable to underpricing.

BOX 16.3

Cost Recovery, Equity, and Efficiency in Water Tariffs in Africa

During a 2006–07 survey of 23 African countries, tariff structures for 45 water utilities were collected and analyzed. These tariff structures were assessed using criteria of cost recovery, efficiency, and equity. Many countries in Africa have adopted a two-part tariff structure that incorporates both a fixed charge and a water-use charge. The block structure can add to the complexity of tariffs; the number of blocks ranges between two and seven with an average of three. Only four utilities practice a one-block or linear tariff.

Cost Recovery

The experience of recovering operating costs in Africa is positive, with many utilities setting tariffs at levels high enough to recoup operation and maintenance costs. The performance of African utilities in this respect is superior to that found elsewhere in the world. In Africa, the tariff structures are designed in a way that is more conducive to meeting operation and maintenance costs at the high or low ends of consumption. Capital cost recovery is largely elusive for residential consumers; only four utilities in Cape Verde, Namibia, and South Africa charge more than $1.

Efficiency

The relatively high levels of metering and tariffs in Africa suggest that consumers receive a price signal to economize on water use. A significant number of utilities apply fixed charges with minimum consumption attached, however, and in these cases, low-volume consumers may not receive any kind of price signal over their consumption range. However, the necessity of water demand management is less

important in Africa than elsewhere: most consumers already survive on little more than subsistence quantities of water.

Equity

More generally, African water tariff structures do not perform all that well in equity terms. A number of factors contribute to this inequity. First, the subsidy to the low block under the current increasing block tariff structure does not all go to small consumers (usually the poor); instead, a substantial amount of the subsidy leaks to large consumers. Second, because of the fixed and minimum consumption charges and the large size of the low blocks, small consumers often end up paying higher effective prices per unit than large consumers. In almost three-fourths of the cases, consumers with water intake at the survival level pay as much as or more than average consumers pay. Despite the prevalence of rising block tariffs, the smallest consumers do not always pay the lowest price in Africa. Third, the connection cost is high for many utilities compared with gross national income per capita, indicating significant affordability problems for expanding networks into unserved areas. Fourth, the retail standpost price is significantly higher than the utility-imposed price because of rent-seeking behavior on the part of operators.

African utilities operate in an environment of high-cost service provision and high-cost recovery. What emerges is a tariff structure that is relatively efficient and that recovers at least the operation and maintenance cost. However, several utilities have enforced high connection costs and inequitable tariff structures that limit the ability of poor households to secure access to service or to be able to afford the service even when they have access.

Source: Banerjee, Foster, and others 2008.

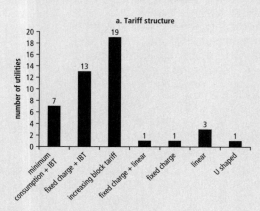

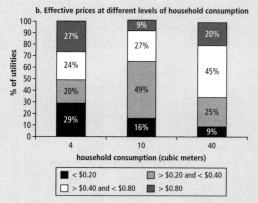

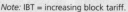

Note: IBT = increasing block tariff.

Full capital cost recovery is generally affordable in the middle-income countries but in the low-income countries would be affordable to only 40 percent of the population. Assuming household subsistence consumption of 10 cubic meters per month (or about 65 liters per capita a day), a monthly utility bill under full cost-recovery pricing of $1 would be around $10. Based on an affordability threshold of 5 percent of household income, full cost-recovery tariffs would prove affordable for 40 percent of the population in low-income countries (figure 16.4). With about 10 percent of the national population already enjoying a direct water connection, an additional 30 percent of the population could be added to service and be able to afford it. The majority of the remaining 60 percent of the population would be able to afford bills of around $6 a month that would result either from operating cost recovery or from full cost recovery at a more modest consumption of about 6 cubic meters per month (or 40 liters per capita a day).

Improving Utility Performance through Institutional Reform

The operational inefficiencies of water utilities, including revenue undercollection, distribution losses, and labor inefficiencies, cost the region $0.9 billion a year (or as much as 0.15 percent of GDP). Operating inefficiencies are rampant among Africa's water utilities, divided roughly evenly between revenue undercollection and distribution losses. Average collection ratios are relatively high in Africa at 90 percent but still short of the best practice of 100 percent. Average distribution losses in Africa are 35 percent, far above the common norm of 20 percent, with all countries affected to some degree. The overall magnitude of these inefficiencies can be quantified by comparing the revenues available to the utility with the revenues available to an ideal utility that is able to charge cost-recovery tariffs, collect all its revenues, and keep distribution losses to the technical minimum (Ebinger 2006; Saavalainen and ten Berge 2006). In the worst cases, such as the Democratic Republic of

Figure 16.4 Affordability of Cost-Recovery Tariffs in Low-Income Countries

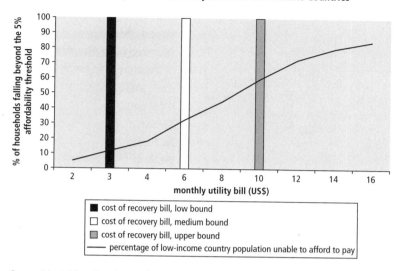

Source: Adapted from Banerjee, Wodon, and others 2008.
Note: Tariffs are described as affordable if a monthly bill based on subsistence consumption absorbs no more than 5 percent of the household's budget.

Congo, Ghana, and Zambia, operating inefficiencies can create an economic burden of 0.7–1.0 percent of GDP (figure 16.5).

Another source of inefficiency is overemployment. State-owned enterprises can be social buffers to (very inefficiently) transfer rents or resources to the population. African utilities have an average of five employees per 1,000 connections, more than twice the two employees per 1,000 connections frequently used as the international benchmark for developing countries (Tynan and Kingdom 2002).

Operating inefficiencies have been impeding expansion. Inefficiencies not only drain the public purse but they also seriously undermine the performance of utilities.

One casualty of insufficient revenue is maintenance. The rate of bursts per kilometer of water main provides some indication of the condition of the underlying infrastructure, and hence the extent to which it is adequately operated and maintained. Among African utilities, a huge variation occurs between low- and middle-income countries, with bursts ranging from five per kilometer in the latter to just over one per kilometer in the former. Utility managers must often choose among paying salaries, buying fuel, or purchasing spares. Frequently, they must cannibalize parts from

Figure 16.5 Economic Burden of Water Utility
Operational Inefficiencies, by Country

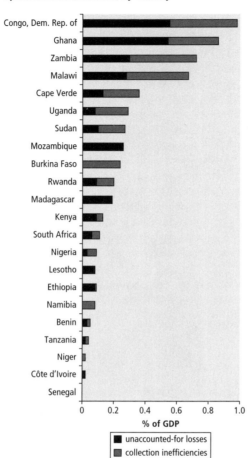

Source: Briceño-Garmendia, Smits, and Foster 2008.
Note: Utility inefficiency is defined as the revenue lost from undercollection of water billed, as well as the value of technical and
nontechnical losses of water on the distribution network valued at
the full cost-recovery tariff.

other working equipment. The investment
program is another major casualty.

Service expansion (measured as a percentage
of the population resident in the utility service
area that every year gains access to either piped
water or standposts) is significantly higher for
more efficient utilities. In particular, utilities
with low hidden costs achieve an average annual
increase in coverage of more than 3 percent of
the resident population, essentially twice as
much as that registered by utilities with high
hidden costs (figure 16.6).

For similar reasons, more efficient utilities deliver better-quality water (figure 16.6).

Utilities with fewer employees per connection
manage to have, on average, 85 percent of the
water supplied with adequate chlorine, in contrast to 75 percent of the remaining utilities.
Conversely, utilities with higher hidden costs
tend to deliver slightly higher-quality water.

Institutional reforms hold the key to improving utility performance. Good institutional
frameworks pay off in lowering the inefficiency
of utilities. Utilities that have decentralized
or adopted private sector management have
hidden costs that are substantially lower than
those that have not (figure 16.7). In addition,
unbundling has a considerable effect on utility
efficiency; however, unbundling is rare in Africa
and is concentrated exclusively in middle-
income countries, whose superior performance
can be explained by many other reasons. Conversely, higher levels of regulation and governance, as well as corporatization, are associated
with higher efficiency.

Nevertheless, introducing reforms is easier
said than done. In recent years, many African
countries have initiated water sector reforms
to improve performance (figure 16.8). This
reform agenda has had two major thrusts:
encouraging private participation and improving governance from within.

The first thrust has focused on experiment-
ing with private participation. Overall, 26
private sector transactions have occurred in
African water, affecting the majority of countries in one way or another. Most have been
lease contracts (or *affermage*). Experience
with private sector participation is disproportionately concentrated in the francophone
countries of West Africa (Côte d'Ivoire, Guinea,
Niger, and Senegal), with some exceptions
(Mozambique and Uganda). Another distinc-
tive feature of the African experience has been
the use of concessions for joint power and
water utilities, as in Gabon and Mali.

The rate of cancellation of private sector contracts for water supply in Africa has been much
higher than elsewhere. Some 29 percent of private contracts for water supply in Africa have
been terminated prematurely, a much higher
rate than in any other developing region. As a
result, the number of active private operators
has shrunk to just a handful, with four in South
Africa and one each in Cameroon, Cape Verde,

Figure 16.6 Effect of Utility Inefficiency on Access Expansion and Water Quality

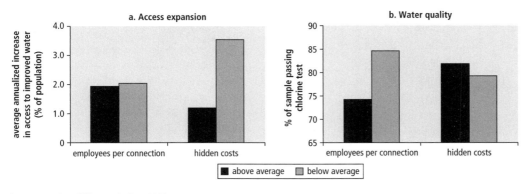

Source: Banerjee, Skilling, and others 2008.
Note: Hidden cost is a measure of utility inefficiency that sums the revenues lost from underpricing, distribution losses, and undercollection of billed revenues. Employees per connection is a second measure of utility inefficiency that focuses on the extent of overstaffing.

Figure 16.7 Hidden Costs and Institutional Frameworks

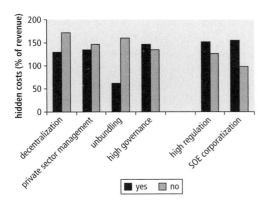

Source: Banerjee, Skilling, and others 2008.
Note: Hidden cost is a measure of utility inefficiency that sums the revenues lost from underpricing, distribution losses, and undercollection of billed revenues. High governance means the utility scores above average on the Africa Infrastructure Country Diagnostic indicator of the quality of state-owned enterprise governance (see box 4.1 in chapter 4 of this volume). High regulation means the country scores above average on the Africa Infrastructure Country Diagnostic indicator of the quality of regulation (see box 4.1 in chapter 4 of this volume). SOE = state-owned enterprise.

Figure 16.8 Overview of Reforms Affecting Urban Utilities

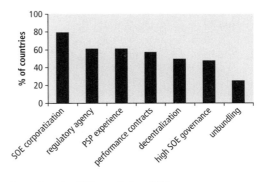

Source: Banerjee, Skilling, and others 2008.
Note: PSP = private sector participation; SOE = state-owned enterprise.

Côte d'Ivoire, Gabon, Ghana, Mozambique, Niger, and Senegal.

At their best, private sector contracts have accelerated access while boosting efficiency. Private sector participation has had favorable results in improving utility performance (table 16.8), with Senegal being particularly noteworthy (box 16.4). Management contracts, being relatively short-term instruments, have had a material effect on improving revenue collection

and service continuity, but they have had little effect on more intractable issues, such as unaccounted-for water and access. Lease contracts have had a substantial effect on improving access and have generally improved operational efficiency. With the exception of Côte d'Ivoire, however, the associated investments have been publicly financed. The lease contracts in Guinea and Maputo, Mozambique, have been affected by problems of coordination between the private contractor and the government that have held back their progress in some key areas, such as unaccounted-for water. Overall, private sector contracts accounted for (though did not necessarily finance) almost 20 percent of the increase of household connections in the region, twice the amount that would be expected given

Table 16.8 Overview of Private Sector Participation's Effect on Utility Performance

Country or city	Private sector participation	Unit change in performance before and after private participation					
		Household connections	Improved water	Service continuity	Unaccounted-for water	Collection ratio	Labor productivity
Gabon	Concession contract	+20	—	—	−8	—	—
Mali		+15	+29	—	−14	—	—
Côte d'Ivoire	Lease contract or affermage	+19	+22	—	—	—	+2.6
Guinea		—	+27	—	0	—	—
Maputo (Mozambique)		—	+2	+10	−1	+24	—
Niger		+9	+3	—	−5	—	+3.2
Senegal		+18	+17	—	−15	—	+2.8
Johannesburg (South Africa)	Management contract	—	—	—	0	+10	—
Kampala (Uganda)		—	—	+6	−2	+12	—
Zambia		—	—	+5	−28	+19	—

Source: Adapted from Marin 2009.
Note: Household connections and improved water are measured as additional percentage points of households with access; service continuity is measured as additional hours per day of service; unaccounted-for water is measured as reduced percentage points of losses; collection ratio is measured as additional percentage points of collection; labor productivity is measured as additional thousands of connections served per employee. — Not available.

BOX 16.4

Senegal's Successful Experience with Private Sector Participation

Senegal's experience with private sector participation in water supply is characterized by two remarkable results: (a) an impressive expansion of access and (b) a large increase in operational efficiency that mainly originated from a reduction of nonrevenue water.

The first result was mainly attributable to a massive subsidized connection program sponsored by donors and in part to the cash-flow surplus generated by the private operators. In particular, the social connection program implemented with donor support provided some 129,000 connections (75 percent of all new connections installed), benefiting poor households living in targeted neighborhoods. A portion of the new connections ended up losing service because of nonpayment, however, despite tariffs that had been declining in real terms up to 2006 and a social tariff targeted at poor households that covered the first monthly block of 6 cubic meters of subsistence consumption.

The second result owed much to contractual innovations geared toward increasing the private operator's incentives to perform efficiently. In particular, the contract included targets for nonrevenue water reduction and bill collection, backed by financial penalties for noncompliance. These targets were then applied to a notional sales volume based on the amount of water actually produced, which was used to determine the operator's remuneration in lieu of the actual water sold. Whenever the operator fell short of the non-revenue water and bill collection targets, the notional sales volume would be lower than the actual sales, penalizing the operator.

Another innovation in Senegal's public-private partnership was the responsibility of the private operator to finance part of the network's rehabilitation using cash flow. This approach provided the operator with more flexibility to identify and reduce water losses, lessening its dependence on the public asset-holding company.

The effect of these innovations on efficiency has been remarkable, making Senegal's *affermage* a prominent example of private participation in Africa. Today, Senegal can report a level of nonrevenue water comparable to the best water utilities in western Europe, but these results also confirm that operational efficiency is perhaps the area in which private operators can make the most positive and consistent effect, since the parallel progress in service expansion required substantial public sector support.

Source: Adapted from Marin 2009.

their market share of only 9 percent. Half of those gains were made in Côte d'Ivoire alone (Marin 2009).

Anglophone and francophone countries have taken two distinct approaches to sector regulation. About half of the countries (mainly anglophone) have established distinct regulatory agencies for the water sector, although a significant number of them have not adopted private sector participation. Conversely, a number of francophone countries with private participation have adopted regulatory frameworks contractually, without establishing an independent regulatory agency. No evidence appears to support the superiority of either of these two approaches to regulation. Neither does any evidence indicate that the creation of a regulatory entity has led to discernible improvements in utility performance. Even where explicit regulatory frameworks have been established, they typically meet only about half of the corresponding good-practice criteria.

The second thrust of the reform agenda has focused on improving the governance of the sector from within. This approach was based on the recognition that the standard infrastructure reform prescriptions were not always as relevant or as easily applied to the water sector as to other areas of infrastructure, and that service provision would remain dominated by public enterprises in the near future. The focus of these reforms has been on moving toward corporatization of state-owned enterprises and on decentralizing responsibilities to lower levels of government. In addition, some measures have been taken to improve the governance of state-owned enterprises, aimed at adopting commercial principles and modern management methods. About 80 percent of Africa's larger water utilities have now been corporatized, thereby laying the foundation for a more commercial form of management. Close to half of the countries sampled have decentralized their water utilities since the mid-1990s to bring responsibility closer to local communities; however, all the francophone countries studied retain centralized organization of the sector.

Africa's state-owned water utilities typically fulfill only about half of the good-practice criteria for enterprise governance. Since the mid-1990s, some serious efforts have been made to improve internal processes and corporate governance mechanisms, more so than in other infrastructure sectors. In particular, a growing number of utilities are using performance contracts, for instance, in Lesotho, Uganda, and Zambia, although not all of them incorporate the penalties, performance-based remuneration, and third-party monitoring that make these mechanisms truly effective. Uganda's use of performance contracts to underpin substantial improvements in sector performance is particularly noteworthy (box 16.5).

Reforms in the Rural Space

Africa remains a predominantly rural continent. About 400 million rural inhabitants have no form of utility-provided water. Rural coverage of piped-water supply and standposts has barely risen in the past 15 years, and most of the gains have come from rural inhabitants moving up the water supply ladder from surface water to wells and boreholes. Until improved water sources serve more of the rural population, MDG goals will continue to be elusive.

In rural areas, the central challenge is to reduce reliance on surface water through a sustainable network of water access points, which are most typically boreholes. About half of the sampled countries are reducing the share of the rural population reliant on surface water and in the best cases (Lesotho, Mozambique, and Uganda) are managing to shift 2–3 percent of the rural population away from this option each year. In the other half of the countries sampled, however, the share of the rural population reliant on surface water is actually *increasing*. In Chad, Kenya, and Rwanda, an additional 1 percent of the rural population is forced to rely on surface water, whereas in Burkina Faso that number rises to 3 percent, and it is nearly 10 percent in the Democratic Republic of Congo.

Even in countries that are successful in expanding rural access to improved water sources, sustainability is still a concern. A recurring problem in rural water systems is the lack of technical or financial capacity to maintain assets. Decentralization and the breakdown of community management arrangements have

BOX 16.5

Uganda's Successful Case of State-Owned Enterprise Reform

The National Water and Sewerage Corporation (NWSC) is an autonomous public corporation wholly owned by the government of Uganda. The NWSC is responsible for providing water and sanitation services in 23 towns to 2.2 million people, 75 percent of the population in Uganda's large urban centers.

Before 1998, large inefficiencies posed the urgent need to revamp operations. They included poor service quality, very low staff productivity, and high operating expenses, with a collection rate of only 60 percent and a monthly cash deficit of $300,000.

Turnaround strategies culminated in establishing area performance contracts between the NWSC head office and a number of area managers. The head office performs contract oversight, capital investment, and regulation of tariffs, rates, and charges; the area managers, acting as operators, are therefore responsible for management, operation and maintenance services, revenue collection, and rehabilitation and extension of networks. The objective was to enhance each area's performance by empowering managers and making them accountable for results. A comprehensive system of more focused and customer-oriented targets was designed. Typical performance indicators included working ratio, cash operating margin, nonrevenue water, collection efficiency, and connection ratio. Performance evaluation looked at both processes and outputs and was conducted through regular as well as unannounced inspections. Incentives were both monetary, including penalties for below-target performances, and nonmonetary, including trophies to the best-performing areas and departments and publication of monthly, quarterly, and yearly best, as well as worst, performance.

In fiscal year 2003/04, the area performance contracts were changed to internally delegated area management contracts, aimed at giving more autonomy to operating teams and based on clearer roles, better incentive plans, and a larger risk apportioned to operating teams. The contract framework was later consolidated by using competitive bidding as a basis for awarding contracts to the operating units.

A review of 10 years of NWSC operations shows that gains in operational and financial efficiency and service expansion have been substantial and impressive relative to the performance of NWSC's peers in Africa.

NWSC Efficiency Gains

Performance indicator	1998	2008
Service coverage (percent)	48.0	72.0
Total connections	50,826	202,559
New connections per year	3,317	25,000
Metered connections	37,217	201,839
Staff per 1,000 connections	36	7
Collection efficiency (percent)	60.0	92.0
Nonrevenue water (percent)	60.0	32.5
Proportion of metered accounts (percent)	65.0	99.6
Annual turnover (U Sh billions)	21	84
Profit (after depreciation) (U Sh billions)	−2.0	+3.8

Note: U Sh = Uganda shillings.

Key success factors are identified in the empowerment of staff; the devolution of power from central to regional operations; the increased customer focus; and the adoption of private sector–like management practices, including performance-based pay, "customer pays for a good service" principle, and so forth. Also, the emphasis on planning, systematic oversight and monitoring, information sharing through benchmarking, and the continuous challenging of management teams with new and clear performance targets has created a strong system of checks and balances and powerfully triggered involvement, engagement, and sense of pride on the side of staff, beyond what simple financial incentives might obtain.

Sources: Adapted from Muhairwe 2009; NWSC 2006.

put greater strain on local governments to manage services. This situation leads to rapid deterioration of rural water points to where they no longer provide the intended service, and populations are forced to return to relying on surface water. On average, one in three rural water points needs rehabilitation, and for a significant number of countries, the share rises to at least one in two (the Democratic Republic of Congo, Madagascar, Malawi, Nigeria, and Tanzania). Nevertheless, in the best-case scenarios, the share needing rehabilitation can be as low as 10–20 percent (Benin and Uganda).

Inadequate maintenance of rural water systems reflects both institutional weaknesses and inappropriate technology choice. Besides weak institutional capacity, undermaintenance is worsened by inadequate attention to technology choice, low pump density, restrictive maintenance systems, and lack of a supply chain to adequately maintain complex machinery (Harvey and Reed 2006; Oyo 2006). In a number of countries, problems have been caused by divorcing the supply of hand pumps from the supply of associated spare parts. Suggested solutions include governments' taking a leading role in initial supply chain management and coordinating with donors until the private sector is capable of taking over (Oyo 2006). The unavailability of private supply chains is a result of limited population density and income levels of African economies. Several initiatives, including market demand assessments (Mozambique in 2003), coordination among links in the chain, and development of supply chain products, are under way in Africa.

Several countries have made progress with institutional reforms of rural water. Understanding what factors drive these differences in performance across countries is important, particularly whether the institutional reforms implemented have made a difference. The reform agenda for rural water comprises five key components: (a) adopting an explicit rural water policy to guide interventions in the sector; (b) developing a map of rural water points so that their functionality can be monitored; (c) adopting cost-recovery policies to improve the financial sustainability of systems; (d) establishing a dedicated central budget funding source for rural water; and (e) creating a water agency to spearhead the implementation of rural water projects.

However, progress on key rural reform measures has been uneven. The extent of progress on each of these reform steps is used to create a Rural Reform Index for water. Burkina Faso, Côte d'Ivoire, and Uganda score 100 percent on this index, whereas Niger scores only 20 percent. The most widely adopted reform measures are rural water policies and rural water funds, which can be found in almost all the sampled countries. The least widely adopted are rural water agencies and mapping of rural water points, which are found in fewer than half of the countries sampled (figure 16.9).

A strong link exists between institutional reforms and progress toward the MDG in rural areas. The most successful countries in reducing the rural population's reliance on surface water are all—without exception—among the most aggressive reformers in Africa (table 16.9). Benin, Côte d'Ivoire, Mozambique, Namibia, Nigeria, Senegal, and Uganda are outstanding performers in reducing the share of the population consuming surface water and rank highest in rural reform. Conversely, the Democratic Republic of Congo, Kenya, Malawi, Niger, and Zambia increasingly rely on surface water and score very low on the Rural Reform Index. Burkina Faso and Tanzania are two countries that perform poorly on access expansion, which is

Figure 16.9 Overview of Rural Water Reforms

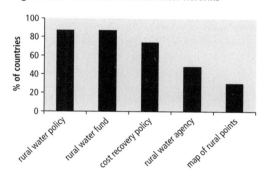

Source: Banerjee, Skilling, and others 2008.

Table 16.9 Relationship between Rural Reform Index and Success in Expanding Rural Service Coverage

Reform score	Success in getting people off surface water	
	Decreasing reliance on surface water	**Increasing reliance on surface water**
Aggressive reformers scoring more than 80% on Rural Reform Index	Benin Côte d'Ivoire Mozambique Namibia Nigeria Senegal Uganda	Burkina Faso Tanzania
Moderate reformers scoring 40–80% on Rural Reform Index	Ethiopia Lesotho	Chad Rwanda
Slow reformers scoring less than 40% on Rural Reform Index		Congo, Dem. Rep. of Kenya Malawi Niger Zambia

Source: Banerjee, Skilling, and others 2008.

surprising given their strong track record on institutional reforms. For moderate reformers, the results can go either way (box 16.6).

The degree of reform also affects whether rural water points are maintained adequately. The percentage of rural water points needing rehabilitation tends to be lower for countries with more advanced rural reform processes.[4] Thus, Benin and Uganda score high on sector reform as well as on maintaining rural water points. The converse is true for the Democratic Republic of Congo and Malawi.

Policy Recommendations

On the basis of this diagnostic, the water sector evidences a number of key areas for policy attention. The institutional reform agenda remains as relevant as before, even if the focus of the agenda has shifted toward a more pluralistic view of public and private sector roles. The reform agenda also needs to move beyond utilities to encompass line ministries and the entire public expenditure framework that underpins, and too often hinders, sector investment programs. Room for improvement exists in cost recovery so that scarce subsidy resources are redirected to promote access among the poorest. For the majority that do not enjoy access to piped water, greater thought needs to be given to how standposts can become more effective for urban water supply and how to get the best out of small-scale independent providers. The burgeoning use of wells and boreholes for supply in urban areas demands urgent attention from policy makers, both to improve their understanding of this phenomenon and to develop suitable regulatory tools.

BOX 16.6

Issues Constraining Rural Water Supply in Cross River State, Nigeria

Cross River State, one of Nigeria's 36 states, is located in the rain forest belt of Nigeria. About 75 percent of its population, 3.25 million people, lives in rural areas and is engaged in subsistence farming. More than 70 percent lives on less than $1 a day.

Water supply in Cross River State is in crisis. Coverage stands at only 25 percent in urban areas and 31 percent in semi-urban and rural areas. Rural water is supplied mainly through boreholes with hand pumps and wells, 65 percent of which are not functioning. Moreover, no water treatment is provided. To meet the MDG for water, an additional 10,098 boreholes with hand pumps and 2,525 motorized boreholes will need to be built across the state by 2015, a daunting task given its current financial, institutional, and technical capacity.

Cross River State has recently been the subject of an assessment of rural water supply based on public expenditure reviews covering the period from 2002 to 2007. The review shows that lack of adequate budgetary funding and low disbursement efficiency are major constraints. Rural water captures only 0.5 percent of the state's capital budget, and execution ratios average less than 20 percent. Weak institutions and fragmented responsibilities translate into feeble leadership and rural water falling behind in the political agenda. The sector is the responsibility of the State Rural Water Supply and Sanitation Agency, which remains a section of the Rural Development Agency. Unlike in other states, no dedicated ministry champions reforms and allocations. More important, although a rural water policy exists nationally, state policies do not necessarily reflect national policy, and effective cooperation is not pursued between national and state governments. Responsibilities are decentralized locally, but the State Rural Water Supply and Sanitation Agency continues to be characterized by a weak and poorly funded mandate and loose connections to the national water sector.

Maintenance and rehabilitation of rural water schemes are jeopardized by the lack of skilled labor and the substantial underdevelopment of a local private sector. Technical capacity for routine maintenance remains low; spare parts for boreholes are difficult to find and are very expensive where available.

Finally, no effective strategy to promote community participation has been put in place, resulting in local community involvement in rural water provision that remains shallow at best. Absent any sense of ownership, rural communities do not take responsibility for preserving and repairing facilities. Neither would they have the capacity to do so without adequate training.

Source: Iliyas, Eneh, and Oside 2009.

Continue to Pursue Institutional Reforms

Institutional reforms are the key to improving water sector performance. Countries pursuing institutional reforms create more efficient and effective sector institutions and promote more rapid expansion of higher-quality services. The potential dividend is large because addressing utility inefficiencies alone could make a substantial contribution to closing the sector funding gap in many countries.

Although the majority of African countries have embarked on the sector reform agenda, few have completed it. The glass is still half full, but the experience of those countries that are furthest ahead provides some guidance for the region.

In rural areas, a few critical interventions can make a difference. Establishing a clear sector policy, creating a strong central capability for sector financing and project implementation, moving to greater cost recovery, and developing a system to monitor the condition of rural water points are all measures that, when implemented as a package, can boost performance.

In urban areas, the story is more complex. The traditional reform agenda of the 1990s has not fully proved its relevance to the sector. Perhaps surprisingly, no clear evidence indicates that regulation has made a positive contribution to sector performance across the board. Private sector participation, although controversial in implementation, has in many cases proved a useful tool for improving operational performance and efficiency (Marin 2009). Expectations that the private sector would finance new infrastructure for water utilities have not been met, with negligible private capital flows that are dwarfed by public and donor finance. However, the private sector has contributed to expanding access, though typically with public funding (Marin 2009).

The new reform agenda for water retains a role for private participation. Lease contracts may be the form of private participation best suited to African water utilities. By transferring more responsibility to the private sector than in a management contract, they have provided greater scope for operational improvements. In contrast to concessions, recognition is explicit that investment will need to be publicly funded,

even if the private sector can sometimes help execute it. A key lesson from Africa's experience with lease contracts is the difficulty of achieving seamless coordination on investment plans between the contractor and the public holding company. In addition, incorporating clear contractual incentives for efficiency improvements (for example, by basing the contractor's revenues on ideal rather than actual performance parameters) is important (Marin 2009).

The new agenda places greater emphasis on broader reforms within governing state-owned enterprises. Given the limited scope of private participation, state-owned utilities remain center stage. Without addressing the typical deficiencies that afflict such enterprises—including numerous and conflicting objectives, political interference, and lack of transparency—the sector will have difficulty exiting low-level equilibrium. Three key areas for attention are (a) internal process improvements, (b) increased managerial autonomy, and (c) more stringent performance monitoring. Incorporating measures to streamline corporate processes, such as procurement, financial management, and performance management, is essential for strengthening the application of commercial principles and accountability mechanisms. Measures to broaden the board of directors, to increase the use of external audit and independent audit of accounts, and to incorporate independent members from beyond the public sector would help depoliticize decision making and consolidate the arm's-length relationship. Adopting performance-based monitoring arrangements that mimic private sector contracts is also of interest, but only to the extent that they create credible incentives by incorporating meaningful rewards and penalties at the personal and corporate levels and are subject to third-party monitoring.

Improve Efficacy of Public Expenditure

The bulk of investment in the water sector is by line ministries through the budgetary process, often with external support. The existing patterns of spending clearly show that although utilities are instrumental in delivering services, the general government (using either domestic or external capital) continues to make most of the investment decisions. Therefore, a solid public investment appraisal system and strong public spending management are prerequisites for improving both urban and rural water supply.

Major bottlenecks hold back the disbursement of public investment funds. Capital budget execution ratios for public investment in water are relatively low, 75 percent on average. In many instances, the capacity to disburse budgetary resources in a timely fashion is the binding constraint, rather than their availability (Prevost 2009). In Tanzania, steep increases in budget allocations to the sector followed its identification as a priority in the country's poverty reduction strategy; however, disbursements increased at a much slower pace, so there was no immediately discernible effect on access (Van den Berg 2009).

Key aspects of the public expenditure framework must be addressed. The budgeting process needs to move toward a medium-term framework and make stronger links between sector objectives (such as MDG targets) and resource allocations. Clear sector plans that detail specific activities and their associated costs should underpin the budget process. The careful incorporation of maintenance needs into medium-term sector planning tools is critical to prevent asset rehabilitation. Administrative processes that delay the release of budgeted funds also need to be overhauled. At the same time, procedures for procurement, disbursement, financial management, and accountability should be modernized and streamlined.

Donor resources are best channeled programmatically as budgetary support or through sectorwide projects. Given the sector's strong dependence on external funds, a solid public expenditure management system for African countries also requires that donors improve the predictability of their support and make progress on streamlining and harmonizing administrative procedures. In that sense, a focus on multidonor initiatives that pool funds to provide general budgetary support for a sectorwide program of interventions is preferable.

Technical assistance to the sector has traditionally been understood as improving the management practices of utilities. However, technical assistance to support line ministries in improving the framework for identifying, appraising, prioritizing, planning, and procuring investment projects has an equally important role. Donors can support countries in developing good project identification and appraisal tools that systematically consider the technological alternatives for expanding access and that examine the importance of spending on maintenance and rehabilitation against new investment.

Experiment with Different Institutional Models for the Unconnected

The modest role played by standposts in urban water supply is striking. In most countries, government and utility attention continues to focus on expansion of piped-water connections. This battle is being lost, however, because of a combination of rapid urbanization and financially debilitated utilities. Standposts are very limited in the African urban water scene, are expanding relatively slowly, and remain concentrated among the more affluent segments of the population. Simple simulations suggest that if utilities were to shift their existing investment budgets from piped connections to standposts, the rate of service expansion could potentially double. However, as long as urban households are inconvenienced by higher payments and longer water collection times, standposts are not necessarily going to be a superior solution even if they are a cheaper alternative to private piped connections. In low-income countries, resale of water by neighbors through informal standpost arrangements is almost as prevalent as formal standposts.

The key to this paradox could lie in the problematic institutional arrangements associated with standposts in African cities. Utilities charge little or nothing for standpost water, and standpost revenues constitute a negligible portion of the revenue base. Therefore, utilities have little financial incentive to expand the service. Standpost operators, where they exist, often charge large markups that make the service prohibitively expensive and that may generate significant revenues never captured by the utility. The quality of service provided by standposts can be very low because of the high rates of malfunction and the very large (sometimes implausibly large) numbers of people expected to rely on each one.

Solving this conundrum demands serious attention. The way forward is not yet clear, but it calls for intensive experimentation with alternative network designs and institutional setups. Standposts cover a wide range of communal arrangements or delegated management models, some of which may be more promising than others. One option would be to increase the density of standposts to increase competition, with an immediate effect on convenience and price of water supply. Yard taps, which provide communal access to a smaller group of four or five contiguous households, lower costs but only partially address the problem of maintenance and management. Whatever the approach, an important component of the solution will be to ensure a fairer distribution of revenues between utilities and standpost operators or other secondary water retailers. The experiences of the handful of low-income countries that have achieved more than 20 percent urban coverage of standposts—notably Côte d'Ivoire, Rwanda, and Senegal—deserve some study.

The popularity of the household resale option could also be exploited by making it an explicit part of the utility's rollout strategy. Household resale of water through yard taps appears to be a widely used option in many African cities. Survey evidence highlights a variety of reasons why residents may find this approach preferable to official standposts. Neighbors can offer more convenient operating hours and better water pressure; because they are nearby, less time is required to collect water. In addition, they offer more flexible payment mechanisms than either public standposts or a private connection (Keener, Luengo, and Banerjee 2008). Therefore, increasing recognition should be given to this water supply modality, removing any legal barriers and potentially considering the creation of such household-based water retail enterprises as an integral component of utilities' expansion plans.

Ultimately, investing in utility production and distribution of water is the best policy for keeping down the costs of alternatives. Within cities, water markets are strongly connected in the final price offered to the consumer. The more disrupted the formal piped system, the higher the price will be in the informal sector compared with the formal one. Increasing water production capacity and improving the efficacy of the distribution network can significantly affect the welfare of the unconnected as well as the connected, because it drives down the premium on alternative sources of water supply (Keener, Luengo, and Banerjee 2008).

Increase Cost Recovery with Careful Social Policies

Underpricing water is contributing to the financial weakness of utilities, slowing access expansion, and holding back the quality of service. Given that utility customers are drawn from the upper end of the income distribution, the result is a highly regressive incidence of subsidies to the sector. A large (and generally poor) segment of the urban population is paying multiples of these prices to access utility water indirectly, and in many cases more than the utility cost-recovery price.

Countries need to make progress toward further cost recovery while considering the economic circumstances of their populations. The key principle is to verify the affordability of water tariffs with reference to household budgets, rather than simply to assume that they will be unaffordable. Although the purchasing power of African households is quite limited, the analysis confirms that operating cost recovery is a perfectly feasible objective for just about all African countries. Tariffs that recover full capital costs also look to be affordable for the richest 40 percent of the population in low-income countries, where today's piped water coverage is concentrated. Thus, little economic justification exists for today's subsidies. Countries would be better served by recovering full costs from their existing customer base and using the resulting cash flow to accelerate access expansion in poor neighborhoods. In the longer term, however, as access to piped water increases, low-income countries will need social tariffs that provide water priced at operating cost recovery levels for a minimum level of consumption to the substantial share of their population that cannot afford full capital cost-recovery tariffs.

Government entities need to become better customers. Government entities can easily account for 20–30 percent of total billings. They can be the worst offenders in paying bills as well, with a significant lag in payment time. Often, a large chunk of arrears is paid back to the utility books with little indication of future payment schedules. This uneven payment culture has significant implications not only for the investment planning of utilities, but also for developing a broader payment culture across society as a whole.

The design of tariff structures for water utilities deserves serious rethinking. Most African utilities are applying increasing block tariffs, in the expectation that they will make water tariffs more equitable. However, these expectations are not always being met (Banerjee, Wodon, and others 2008). About half of the utilities using increasing block tariffs incorporate fixed charges or minimum consumption thresholds that actually *inflate* the costs of water for poor households with modest levels of consumption, which becomes counterproductive. A significant share of utilities with increasing block tariffs also has very high subsistence blocks (in excess of 10 cubic meters), and as a result they end up providing subsidized water to the vast majority of consumers, rather than to a targeted group of low-volume users.

Connection charges should be kept as low as possible, and subsidies could be reoriented toward connection. The majority of African water utilities levy piped-water connection charges in excess of $100, an insurmountable barrier for low-income households. Utilities intent on universalizing access should explore ways to radically reduce connection charges to levels that are more in line with household affordability. A number of alternative ways exist to recover connection charges, including payment plans that spread them out over time or sharing of connection costs across the whole customer base through the general tariff. Connection costs may also be more suited to public subsidy than water usage tariffs. They have the advantage of being one-time payments linked to a concrete and monitorable action that addresses a real affordability constraint. Simulations suggest that connection subsidies can potentially be much more pro-poor than general subsidies to the water tariff, particularly if some simple targeting mechanisms are used (Wodon 2007).

Improve Understanding of Groundwater's Role in the Urban Supply

Although wells and boreholes have long been a dominant source of improved water in rural areas, they have also become the fastest-growing source of improved water supply in African cities. Groundwater, from water wells (boreholes and hand-dug wells), now supplies one-fourth of urban dwellers and is the fastest-growing source of improved water supply in African cities by far. This is true in more than just those cities where groundwater has long been a major source of utility supply (such as Lusaka in Zambia and Abidjan in Côte d'Ivoire). With utility coverage rates falling in urban Africa, groundwater has essentially stepped into the breach, and the rapid growth of boreholes shows the appetite for lower-cost solutions. Investments in boreholes provide the opportunity to reach a larger proportion of the population with relatively modest resources. One in four urban Africans relies on wells and boreholes for improved supply; that ratio rises to one in two urban Africans in the low-income countries. In Burkina Faso, Malawi, Mali, Mozambique, Uganda, and Zimbabwe, the share rises as high as three in four. In Malawi, Nigeria, and Rwanda reliance on urban wells and boreholes is increasing particularly rapidly, with more than 3 percent of the population gaining access to this water source each year.

Not enough is known about the physical, institutional, and financial characteristics of groundwater use. Household surveys provide a good picture of overall reliance but leave many questions unanswered. The relative prevalence of simple, shallow hand-dug wells versus professionally drilled boreholes is unknown and so then is the extent to which groundwater supplies are adequately protected from direct wellhead contamination. The institutional arrangements associated with groundwater supplies are also unclear, particularly the extent to which they constitute stopgap services provided by municipalities versus private or communal self-supply initiatives. Depending on the conditions and arrangements, the capital costs of such wells could be anywhere from $5,000 to $25,000 (or $10 to $20 per capita) (Foster 2008).

In addition to growing groundwater reliance, African cities are characterized by heavy use of low-grade in situ sanitation, mainly in the form of unimproved latrines (see chapter 17 of this volume). Deployment of latrine sanitation at excessive population densities or with lack of proper latrine operation can lead to increased groundwater contamination that can affect the entire urban aquifer providing the groundwater supplies (Xu and Usher 2006).

Furthermore, extensive unregulated use of groundwater by private actors may prevent the most rational and efficient exploitation of the resource for public water supply. In particular, it prevents cities from reaching economies of scale in groundwater exploitation and from following the principle of conjunctive surface water and groundwater use that allows groundwater to play its natural role as a backup supply in times of drought (Foster 2008).

Developing an improved understanding of the benefits and risks of groundwater use in fast-growing African cities and towns and of how those benefits and risks vary with the hydrogeological setting is urgent (Foster, Tuinhof, and Garduño 2008). This objective should begin with a city-level appraisal of (a) the quantity and quality of available urban groundwater resources; (b) the drivers, dynamics, and patterns of usage; and (c) an assessment of the vulnerability of urban aquifers to pollution from the land surface. Creating a groundwater-monitoring framework and promulgating appropriate construction and operation protocols for wells and in situ sanitation facilities (mainly latrines) would help safeguard groundwater quality, but guidelines for safe use of groundwater sources should accompany this framework. Appropriate governance arrangements also need to be established, recognizing the broad reach of groundwater resources, and should involve water utilities, public health authorities, and municipal agencies, including a suitable channel for public consultation.

Notes

The authors of this chapter are Sudeshna Ghosh Banerjee, Elvira Morella, Cecilia Briceño-Garmendia, and Vivien Foster, who drew on background material and contributions from Tarik Chfadi, Piers Cross, Alexander Danilenko, Sarah Keener, Manuel Luengo, Dennis Mwanza, Eustache Ouayoro, Heather Skilling, Caroline van den Berg, Quentin Wodon, Guillermo Yepes, and Yvonne Ying, and received extensive support from the Water and Sanitation Program network in Africa.

1. The MDG for water supply commits countries by 2015 to halving the percentage of their populations without access to an improved water source relative to the baseline situation in 1990. For the purposes of the MDG, "improved water" includes access to piped water or standposts, as well as some types of wells and boreholes that are adequately protected.

2. The Joint Monitoring Programme of the World Health Organization and the United Nations Children's Fund systematically tracks access to improved water supply and sanitation, but the data constraints are immense. Systematic information and data about suppliers' characteristics and institutional environments are poor when they exist. Often, even the well-performing service providers are unrecognized outside their immediate environments, and lessons learned are not widely shared. Under the auspices of the Africa Infrastructure Country Diagnostic, a limited effort has been made to use a specially designed questionnaire on institutional environment, governance structure, and technical and financial performance to collect data covering 51 utilities in 23 countries. This novel database covering the period from 1995 to 2005 is paired with household survey data of various years from 1990 to 2005.

3. General government includes central and local governments and special funds when off the budget.

4. Rural water indexes are negatively—if admittedly weakly—correlated.

References

Banerjee, Sudeshna G., Vivien Foster, Yvonne Ying, Heather Skilling, and Quentin Wodon. 2008. "Cost Recovery, Equity, and Efficiency in Water Tariffs: Evidence from African Utilities." Working Paper 7, Africa Infrastructure Country Diagnostic, World Bank, Washington, DC.

Banerjee, Sudeshna G., Heather Skilling, Vivien Foster, Cecilia Briceño-Garmendia, Elvira Morella, and Tarik Chfadi. 2008. "Ebbing Water, Surging Deficits: Urban Water Supply in Sub-Saharan Africa." Background Paper 12, Africa Infrastructure Country Diagnostic, World Bank, Washington, DC.

Banerjee, Sudeshna G., Quentin Wodon, Amadou Diallo, Taras Pushak, Helal Uddin, Clarence

Tsimpo, and Vivien Foster. 2008. "Access, Affordability, and Alternatives: Modern Infrastructure Services in Africa." Background Paper 2, Africa Infrastructure Country Diagnostic, World Bank, Washington, DC.

Briceño-Garmendia, Cecilia, Karlis Smits, and Vivien Foster. 2008. "Financing Public Infrastructure in Sub-Saharan Africa: Patterns, Issues, and Options." Background Paper 15, Africa Infrastructure Country Diagnostic, World Bank, Washington, DC.

Cardone, Rachel, and Catarina Fonseca. 2003. "Financing and Cost Recovery." Thematic Overview Paper 7, IRC International Water and Sanitation Centre, Delft, the Netherlands.

Collignon, Bernard, and Marc Vézina. 2000. *Independent Water and Sanitation Providers in African Cities: Full Report of a Ten-Country Study.* Washington, DC: UNDP–World Bank Water and Sanitation Program.

Ebinger, Jane. 2006. "Measuring Financial Performance in Infrastructure: An Application to Europe and Central Asia." Policy Research Working Paper 3992, World Bank, Washington, DC.

Foster, Stephen S. D. 2008. "Urban Water Supply Security in Sub-Saharan Africa: Making Best Use of Groundwater." Paper presented at the Africa Groundwater and Climate Conference, Kampala, Uganda, June 24–28.

Foster, Stephen S. D., Albert Tuinhof, and Hector Garduño. 2008. "Groundwater in Sub-Saharan Africa: A Strategic Overview of Development Issues." In *Applied Groundwater Studies in Africa: IAH Selected Papers in Hydrogeology,* vol. 13, ed. Segun Adelana and Alan MacDonald, 9–21. London: Taylor & Francis.

GWI (Global Water Intelligence). 2005. "The GWI 2005 Water Tariff Survey." *Global Water Intelligence* 6 (9).

Harvey, Peter A., and Robert A. Reed. 2007. "Community-Managed Water Supplies in Africa: Sustainable or Dispensable?" *Community Development Journal* 42 (3): 365–78.

Hutton, Guy, and Laurence Haller. 2004. *Evaluation of the Costs and Benefits of Water and Sanitation Improvements at the Global Level: Water, Sanitation and Health Protection of the Human Environment.* Geneva: World Health Organization.

Iliyas, Mohammed, Dozie Eneh, and Igiri Oside. 2009. "Public Expenditure Review in the Rural Water and Sanitation Sector for Cross River State—Nigeria." World Bank, Washington, DC.

Keener, Sarah, Sudeshna G. Banerjee, Nils Junge, and Geoff Revell. Forthcoming. "Informal Water Service Providers and Public Stand Posts in Africa." World Bank, Washington, DC.

Keener, Sarah, Manuel Luengo, and Sudeshna Banerjee. 2008. "Provision of Water to the Poor in Africa: Informal Water Markets and Experience with Water Standposts." Working Paper 13, Africa Infrastructure Country Diagnostic, World Bank, Washington, DC.

Marin, Philippe. 2009. *Public-Private Partnerships for Urban Water Utilities: A Review of Experiences in Developing Countries.* Washington, DC: Public-Private Infrastructure Advisory Facility and World Bank.

Mehta, Meera, Thomas Fugelsnes, and Kameel Virjee. 2005. "Financing the Millennium Development Goals for Water Supply and Sanitation: What Will It Take?" *International Journal of Water Resources Development* 21 (2): 239–52.

Muhairwe, William T. 2009. "Fostering Improved Performance through Internal Contractualisation." Paper presented at World Bank Water Week, Washington, DC, February 17–20.

NWSC (National Water and Sewerage Corporation). 2006. "Corporate Plan 2006–2009." NWSC, Kampala, Uganda.

Oyo, Anthony. 2006. "Spare Parts Supplies for Handpumps in Africa: Success Factors for Sustainability." Field Note 15, Water and Sanitation Program, Africa Region, Nairobi.

Prevost, Christophe. 2009. "Benin Rural Water Public Expenditure Review: Findings, Impacts and Lesson Learned." Paper presented at World Bank Water Week, Washington, DC, February 17–20.

Saavalainen, Tapio, and Joy ten Berge. 2006. "Quasi-Fiscal Deficit and Energy Conditionality in Selected CIS Countries." Working Paper 06/43, International Monetary Fund, Washington, DC.

Tynan, Nicola, and Bill Kingdom. 2002. "A Water Scorecard: Setting Performance Targets for Water Utilities." Viewpoint Note 242, World Bank, Washington, DC.

Van den Berg, Caroline. 2009. "Public Expenditure Review in the Water Sector: The Case of Tanzania." Paper presented at Water Week, World Bank, Washington, DC, February 17–20.

WHO/UNICEF (World Health Organization/ United Nations Children's Fund). 2006. *MDG Assessment Report.* Geneva and New York: WHO/UNICEF Joint Monitoring Programme for Water Supply and Sanitation.

Wodon, Quentin. 2007. "Water Tariffs, Alternative Service Providers and the Poor: Case Studies from Africa." World Bank, Washington, DC.

Xu, Yongxin, and Brent Usher, eds. 2006. *Groundwater Pollution in Africa.* London: Taylor & Francis/Balkerma.

Chapter 17

Sanitation: Moving Up the Ladder

Target 7 of the Millennium Development Goals (MDGs) for sanitation access calls for halving by 2015 the percentage of the population in 1990 without improved sanitation. At the present pace, Africa will unlikely meet the target either at the regional or (with few exceptions) at the country level. The Joint Monitoring Programme (JMP) of the World Health Organization and the United Nations Children's Fund is charged with assessing the state of sanitation and progress toward the MDG target. The JMP's latest data show only modest improvement, from 26 percent of the population with access in 1990 to 31 percent in 2006 (United Nations 2008; box 17.1), and many countries face difficulty in making progress (Water and Sanitation Program 2006).

Today, about 30 percent of the population practices open defecation (40 percent in rural areas) and about half of the population, urban and rural, rich and poor alike, relies on unimproved latrines, a heterogeneous collection of facilities with poorly understood health effects. Flush toilets, mostly connected to septic tanks rather than sewers, remain a luxury, as do improved latrines, which have made headway in only a handful of countries. The prevalence of open defecation has finally started to fall,

but coverage of unimproved latrines is growing much faster than coverage of any of the improved alternatives.

Although a bleak picture overall, some countries *have* expanded or upgraded sanitation, each year moving as much as 3 percent of their population up the "ladder" to better forms of sanitation. Ethiopia has done so with unimproved latrines; Burkina Faso, Madagascar, and Rwanda with improved latrines; and Senegal with septic tanks.

To meet the MDG target for sanitation, countries need to spend an estimated 0.9 percent of GDP a year, of which 0.7 percent is for investment and 0.2 percent for operation and maintenance. A few countries already invest in new sanitation facilities up to the recommended level, but many do not. Households pay for most of the investment bill, but whether they are spending enough on operation and maintenance is doubtful. Based on limited evidence, governments contribute only a small fraction of investments. The health benefits attaching to these investments are considerable, including significant reductions in the incidence of diarrhea, intestinal worms, and trachoma.

The challenges and policy options differ substantially across and within countries.

BOX 17.1

What Is Improved Sanitation?

The improved sanitation category in the data from the Joint Monitoring Programme of the World Health Organization and the United Nations Children's Fund includes both flush toilets and improved latrines. It also includes half of the traditional latrines, an adjustment that is made because this modality cannot be disaggregated exactly between improved and unimproved sanitation.

The household analysis presented here, based on Demographic and Health Surveys and Multiple Indicator Cluster Surveys, does not adopt this kind of adjustment. Instead, the analysis disaggregates the different types of improved and unimproved sanitation to allow a richer discussion of sanitation options and issues. Notwithstanding these methodological differences, findings are broadly consistent with those reported by the JMP.

Source: Banerjee and others 2008.

Individual countries or urban and rural regions thereof may face three patterns of access to sanitation; each requires appropriate policy responses.

Where open defecation remains prevalent, people must be encouraged to use latrines, if available. Key factors in changing behavior are a community's commitment to cultural change and peer pressure. Relatively modest government expenditure to promote hygiene education can raise awareness.

Where unimproved latrines are prevalent, they should be upgraded to improved models. However, upgrading faces constraints on both the demand and supply sides. The significant cost of improved facilities suggests a demand problem and the need for capital subsidy. Lack of domestic construction capacity suggests a

supply problem and the need for training and local market development. Both responses are relevant, but by starting from the supply side, policy makers can minimize the need for a subsidy and promote cost-reducing innovations.

Where septic tanks predominate, the challenge is providing access to improved sanitation to a larger, lower-income population. As population densities increase and water consumption rises, Africa's burgeoning cities will eventually need to develop more extensive sewerage networks. Thus, reducing the cost of networks through technological innovation is critical.

The State of Sanitation in Africa

Rungs on a Ladder

One can think of the different types of sanitation as rungs on a ladder, with each rung having a higher investment cost and greater health benefits than the one below (figure 17.1). The bottom of the ladder is open defecation, a practice harmful to public health. The first rung is unimproved latrines, which comprise various kinds of pits that vary greatly in their efficacy but provide at best only basic sanitary protection.[1] The next rung is improved latrines, including a variety of engineered facilities such as SanPlat and Ventilated Improved Pit (VIP) latrines, and basic pits with slabs.[2] When appropriately used, these provide adequate sanitary protection at reasonable cost. The final rung of the ladder is the flush toilet, which may be connected to either a septic tank or (where it exists) the sewerage network. From a health perspective, the most critical movement is from no service (open defecation) or unimproved service (unimproved latrine) to an improved or sanitary service. Once the basic level of sanitary protection is reached, returns in health benefits diminish with each higher rung on the sanitation ladder.

Unimproved latrines are the most prevalent sanitation option in Africa, but understanding the health benefits they can deliver is difficult. Classifying unimproved latrines is complicated by the variety of installations under

Figure 17.1 The Sanitation Ladder

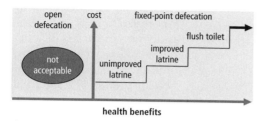

Source: Morella, Foster, and Banerjee 2008.

Figure 17.2 Percentage of the Population Sharing Toilet Facilities

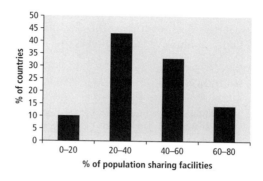

Source: Banerjee and others 2008.

this basic label. Sometimes, an unimproved latrine can, with some modification, provide enough sanitary protection to be regarded as improved. The extent to which latrines deliver the intended health benefits depends on how they are used. Even basic latrines can provide protection if they are covered and emptied in a timely fashion, and if hands are washed after use. Conversely, improved latrines will not provide sanitary protection if people do not use them properly or do not use them at all, for example, if their installation is not accompanied by sufficient efforts in hygiene promotion and social marketing.

Waterborne sewerage systems are rare in Africa. Only half of the large cities operate a sewerage network at all. Only in Namibia, South Africa, and the exceptional case of Senegal do some of the utilities covering the largest cities provide universal sewerage coverage. More typical (as in Côte d'Ivoire, Kenya, Lesotho, Madagascar, Malawi, and Uganda) are sewer networks that reach barely 10 percent of the population within the service area of an urban utility. Little more than half of the households with piped water also have flush toilets, which are often connected to septic tanks rather than to sewers.

Typical urban sanitation includes the sharing of facilities by multiple families (figure 17.2). More than 40 percent of all urban households share their toilet facilities with other households; in Benin, Burkina Faso, Ghana, Guinea, Madagascar, and the Republic of Congo, the figure is more than 50 percent. Sharing sanitation facilities implies that not only must household members wait

to access the facilities but also they may have to pay significant surcharges to facility owners. More important, maintenance of shared facilities is often poor, which poses health risks and may discourage use.

Differing Patterns of Access

More than one-third of the population—mostly in rural areas—must still defecate in the open (table 17.1). Unimproved pit latrines are by far the most prevalent facilities in both urban and rural areas. Improved sanitation reaches less than 20 percent of the national population, less than 10 percent in rural areas. Coverage of improved latrines is no greater than that of septic tanks, despite the significant cost difference between them. Only 10 percent of the national population has the advantage of a septic tank; coverage in rural areas is practically negligible. In urban areas, septic tanks are much more common than improved latrines.

Access to sanitation varies dramatically across income groups (figure 17.3). Unimproved latrines are by far the most egalitarian form of sanitation, accounting for about 50 percent of households across income ranges. Open defecation is widely practiced in the lowest income quintile and not practiced at all in the highest. Conversely, improved latrines and septic tanks, virtually nonexistent among the poorest quintiles, are used by the richest 20–40 percent of the population. Access to improved latrines parallels that of septic tanks, suggesting that despite their lower cost, improved latrines remain something of a luxury, with little success in penetrating the middle of the income distribution. More important, the minimal presence of improved sanitation across poorer groups highlights a crucial issue: the most vulnerable populations are failing to benefit from efforts to improve sanitation.

Not only are unimproved latrines the most prevalent facilities in Africa, but also their use is the fastest growing. In recent years, they have been used by an additional 2.8 percent of the population each year in urban areas and an additional 1.8 percent in rural areas, which is more than twice the rate of expansion of septic tanks and improved latrines combined (figure 17.4). Growth in the use of unimproved latrines is concentrated among the poorer quintiles, whereas growth in the use of improved latrines and septic tanks is concentrated among the richer quintiles. Because the MDG target focuses on the two most improved sanitation options, the expanding use of unimproved latrines does not always fully register in policy discussions. Meanwhile, the prevalence of open defecation in Africa has finally begun to decline, albeit at a very modest pace.

Notwithstanding the overall dismal picture of sanitation in Africa, a number of countries have made major strides in recent years, moving more than 3 percent of their populations up the sanitation ladder annually. Côte d'Ivoire and Ethiopia have achieved these results with unimproved latrines (figure 17.5), Madagascar and Rwanda with improved latrines (figure 17.6), and Senegal with septic tanks (figure 17.7). Ethiopia is making the most rapid progress in reducing open defecation, each year moving more

Table 17.1 Patterns of Access to Sanitation in Africa
percentage of population

Area	Open defecation	Traditional latrine	Improved latrine	Septic tank
Urban	8	51	14	25
Rural	41	51	5	2
National	34	52	9	10

Source: Morella, Foster, and Banerjee 2008.

Figure 17.3 Coverage of Sanitation by Budget Quintile

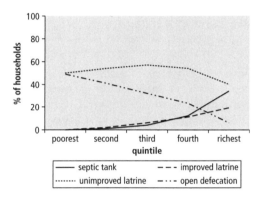

Source: Morella, Foster, and Banerjee 2008.
Note: In terms of household spending, poorest quintile = poorest 20 percent of the population; second quintile = second-poorest 20 percent of the population; third quintile = middle 20 percent of the population; fourth quintile = second-richest 20 percent of the population; richest quintile = richest 20 percent of the population.

Figure 17.4 Annual Growth in Coverage of Sanitation Types, 1990–2005

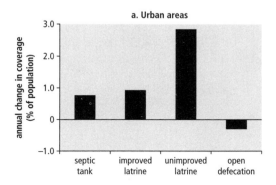
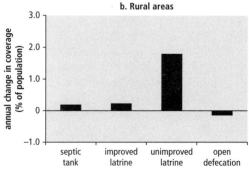

Source: Morella, Foster, and Banerjee 2008.

Figure 17.5 Moving Up to the Bottom Rung of the Sanitation Ladder: Côte d'Ivoire and Ethiopia, 1990–2005

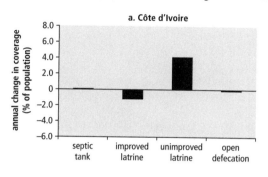
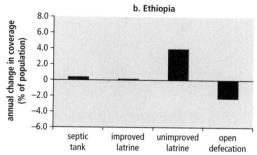

Source: Morella, Foster, and Banerjee 2008.

Figure 17.6 Upgrading Latrines: Madagascar and Rwanda, 1990–2005

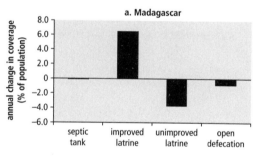
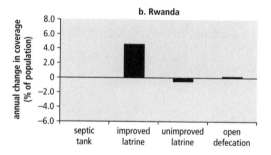

Source: Morella, Foster, and Banerjee 2008.

Figure 17.7 Mainstreaming Septic Tanks: Senegal, 1990–2005

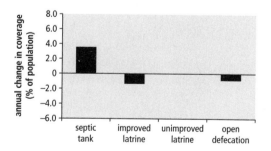

Source: Morella, Foster, and Banerjee 2008.

than 2 percent of its population away from the practice.

These overall trends conceal contrasting patterns across groups of countries and across urban and rural areas within countries that can help structure policy alternatives (figure 17.8). Urban areas tend to follow one of three possible patterns. The most common is where unimproved latrines are the dominant mode of sanitation; the second is where improved latrines prevail, but unimproved latrines still constitute a large share; the third is where half of the population uses septic tanks and half uses unimproved latrines, but where coverage of improved latrines is nearly nonexistent. Rural areas similarly tend to follow one of three possible patterns. As in urban areas, the most common is where unimproved latrines dominate; the second is where open defecation is most prevalent; and the third is where coverage of improved latrines is increasing, though most people rely on unimproved latrines or open defecation.

Figure 17.8 Characterizing Patterns of Access to Sanitation across Urban and Rural Areas

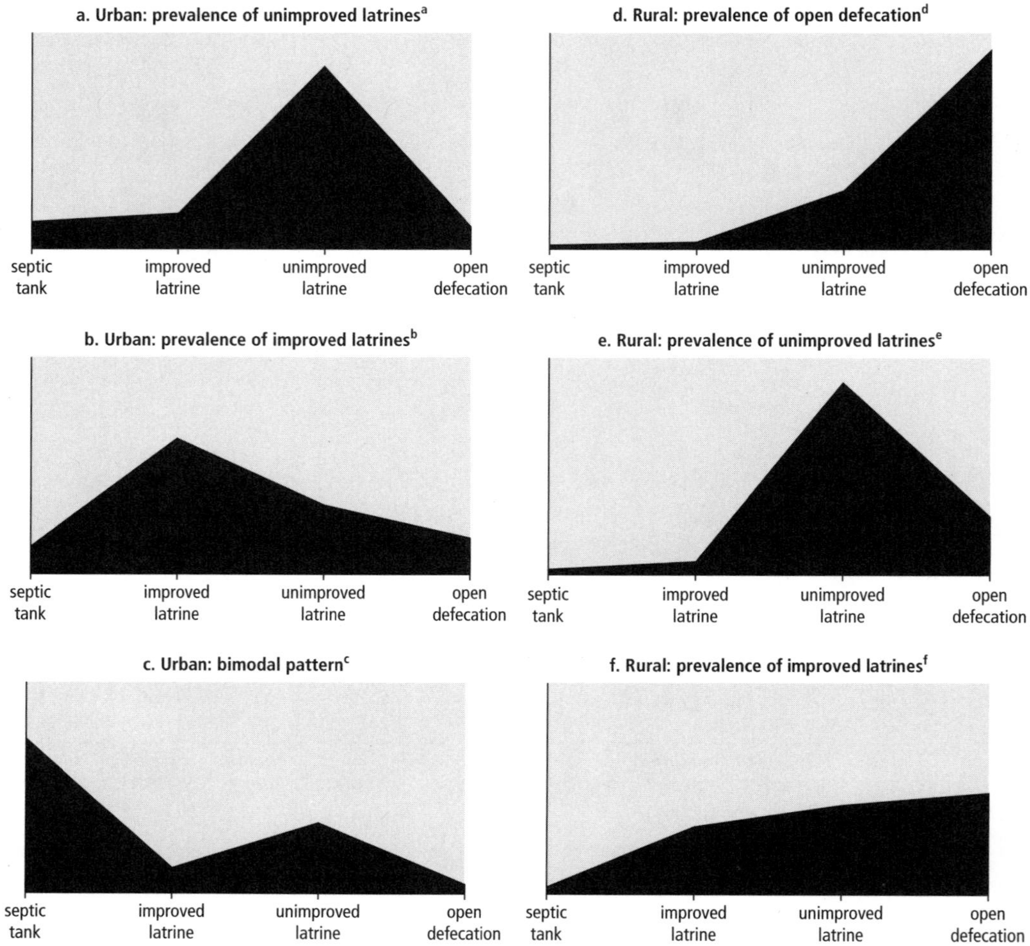

a. Urban: prevalence of unimproved latrines[a]

(x-axis: septic tank, improved latrine, unimproved latrine, open defecation)

d. Rural: prevalence of open defecation[d]

(x-axis: septic tank, improved latrine, unimproved latrine, open defecation)

b. Urban: prevalence of improved latrines[b]

(x-axis: septic tank, improved latrine, unimproved latrine, open defecation)

e. Rural: prevalence of unimproved latrines[e]

(x-axis: septic tank, improved latrine, unimproved latrine, open defecation)

c. Urban: bimodal pattern[c]

(x-axis: septic tank, improved latrine, unimproved latrine, open defecation)

f. Rural: prevalence of improved latrines[f]

(x-axis: septic tank, improved latrine, unimproved latrine, open defecation)

Source: Morella, Foster, and Banerjee 2008.
a. Data include the Central African Republic, Chad, Comoros, the Democratic Republic of Congo, Ethiopia, Guinea, Lesotho, Malawi, Mali, Mauritania, Mozambique, Nigeria, the Republic of Congo, Sudan, Tanzania, and Uganda.
b. Data include Benin, Burkina Faso, Cameroon, Ghana, Madagascar, Niger, and Rwanda.
c. Data include Côte d'Ivoire, Gabon, Kenya, Namibia, Senegal, South Africa, Zambia, and Zimbabwe.
d. Data include Benin, Burkina Faso, Chad, Côte d'Ivoire, Ethiopia, Mauritania, Mozambique, Namibia, Niger, and Sudan.
e. Data include Cameroon, Comoros, the Democratic Republic of Congo, Gabon, Ghana, Guinea, Kenya, Malawi, Mali, Nigeria, the Republic of Congo, South Africa, Tanzania, Uganda, and Zambia.
f. Data include the Central African Republic, Lesotho, Madagascar, Rwanda, Senegal, and Zimbabwe.

Dispersed Institutional Effort

As shown by an institutional survey of sector institutions in 24 countries, complexity, a multiplicity of actors, and lack of accountability for sector leadership are the three salient features of the institutional framework governing the sanitation sector. Unlike water, many parts of the supply chain for sanitation (hygiene promotion, latrine construction, and latrine emptying, for example) are in the hands of different public and private players, which prevents one agency from championing the sector and contributes to sanitation's falling between the cracks. The recent trend toward government decentralization has complicated the capture of adequate public resources for sanitation and allocated responsibilities to entities that lack technical capacity. Fifteen countries have adopted formal national sanitation policies, and most countries have an accepted definition of sanitation and a hygiene promotion program. But only seven countries have policies that include cost recovery, and only eight have a sanitation fund or a dedicated budget line (in some cases, funded exclusively by donors, as in Chad and Ethiopia, or by a combination of the government, sector levies, and donors). Côte d'Ivoire has the only fund financed entirely by sector levies.

Households Foot the Bill

Building on earlier work (Mehta, Fugelsnes, and Virjee 2005), one can estimate the overall price tag for reaching the sanitation MDG at $6 billion a year, or roughly 0.9 percent of Africa's GDP (Morella, Foster, and Banerjee 2008). Capital investment needs based on minimum acceptable asset standards and accounting for both new infrastructure and rehabilitation of existing assets can be conservatively estimated at $4.5 billion a year (0.7 percent of the region's GDP). The maintenance requirements are $1.5 billion a year (0.2 percent of the region's GDP).

No reliable data exist on sanitation expenditures because individual households undertake so much of the expense. However, recent investment can be estimated from household surveys, using the number of households acquiring access in successive years and a standard unit cost. Because this method treats all new or improved facilities as newly built, it may overestimate the cost of increasing access mainly by upgrading unimproved latrines. This approach suggests that, on average, African countries are investing about 0.5 percent of GDP in new sanitation facilities, quite close to the recommended investment level. Half of the countries appear to invest less than 0.7 percent of GDP, which is the level needed to meet the sanitation access MDG. Some countries, particularly Madagascar and Rwanda, appear to have made rapid progress, investing as much as 1.0 percent of GDP. At the other end of the spectrum, Kenya, Lesotho, Namibia, and Zambia spend less than 0.2 percent of GDP.

How much of the estimated total spending on sanitation comes from the public purse is hard to pin down. The few countries with available evidence report negligible public investment on sanitation of 0.02 percent of GDP, on average, although serious measurement problems mean a large portion of public investment in sanitation is likely not separately coded from water supply (Briceño-Garmendia, Smits, and Foster 2008). Nevertheless, households appear to be footing the bulk of the investment bill. In countries with very low current spending, whether households alone will be able to increase investment up to the level needed is uncertain. In addition, nothing is known about their spending on operation and maintenance, which is estimated to require an additional 0.2 percent of GDP in the future. Public spending on operation and maintenance appears to have already reached this level, but evidence is limited, and spending refers mostly to sewer networks. Operation and maintenance of on-site sanitation remain a household responsibility, and facilities are notoriously poorly maintained.

Although the costs of meeting the MDG sanitation target are high, so is the associated health dividend (Hutton and others 2007). Sanitation reduces the risk of intestinal worms, diarrhea, and trachoma, and it is very important—more than access to safe water— in fighting hookworm infection (Esrey and others 1991). Access to adequate sanitation reduces diarrhea incidence by an estimated 36 percent. Trachoma incidence was reduced by 75 percent in Gambian villages solely by controlling flies that breed when excreta are not safely disposed of (Emerson and others 2000). One study estimates that reaching the MDG for both water and sanitation in Africa would prevent 172 million diarrhea cases a year, saving $1.8 billion in treatment costs (Hutton 2000).[3]

Challenges and Policy Options

One of the strongest findings emerging from this review is how much the sanitation challenge differs across countries and between urban and rural areas within the same country. Decisions about where to focus policy efforts along the sanitation ladder should be informed by access patterns. Recommendations will therefore distinguish the different groups identified in figure 17.8. Judicious and low-cost public interventions can leverage household spending for construction of latrines.

The ultimate objective should be to provide universal access by expanding service and reducing open defecation as much as possible. Policy makers are often tempted to focus on rungs of the sanitation ladder well above the realities of their societies: for example, channeling limited public resources into sewer networks that serve only a few thousand people while overlooking the urgent need to lift millions more people away from open defecation. Policy attention needs to focus on moving people up from the lowest rungs of the ladder. More expensive options should be left to households with the resources to take them up.

African countries may face high prevalence of open defecation, especially in rural areas; dominance of unimproved latrines; or significant development of septic tanks that reach a small share of the population, mainly wealthier urban residents. The policy options for each issue are presented as separate cases below, and countries may need to use different combinations of these approaches. The first priority is to stimulate demand for sanitation and behavior change where open defecation prevails. The second is to ensure an adequate supply of improved sanitation options in settings dominated by unimproved latrines, before evaluating the need for policy interventions on the demand side of the market. The third is to expand access to improved sanitation across larger shares of the population, which in high-density settlements requires making sewerage more affordable.

Stimulate Demand for Sanitation and Behavior Change Where Open Defecation Prevails

Unlike other infrastructure services, demand for sanitation cannot be assumed. Populations accustomed to open defecation may require a substantial change in cultural values and behavior to use a fixed-point facility. Without such change, people may not use latrines at all or they may use them in a way that undermines the potential health benefits. A study in southern India showed that large public investment in latrines without accompanying hygiene education led to only 37 percent of men using the facilities despite 100 percent coverage (World Bank 2002). Hygiene education is critical regardless of the type of sanitation challenge a country faces; safe disposal of feces and hand washing with soap protect health in all sanitation settings. Promoting hygiene can start a virtuous cycle that builds demand for better sanitation, raising awareness of the benefits of sanitation and establishing codes of conduct and new life standards.

Incorrect use of latrines can dramatically reduce or even reverse their health benefits. A facility is sanitary and safe not only because of the technology and material used but also because of good practices and behaviors, such as keeping the facility contained and clean. An improved latrine that is not correctly used and emptied still poses high risks of environmental contamination and disease. Thus, rolling out a physical investment program without accompanying promotion of hygiene makes little sense. Moreover, effective hygiene promotion alone may stimulate self-financed household investment in better facilities. Too often, these "soft" aspects of sanitation are overlooked, and priority is given to the "hard" aspects, such as installing and upgrading infrastructure.

Changing behavior requires sustained communication and public education at the community level. Understanding the motivations that interest people in hygiene and sanitation is important. Health is one consideration, but not necessarily the foremost in people's minds: convenience, dignity, and social status may be more important. Adapting hygiene and sanitation promotion programs to cultural and institutional norms and intensely marketing them to stimulate communitywide involvement are critical. Peer pressure—to improve one's status—can also help. When a community recognizes preferred behaviors, pressure to conform arises, and social structures and leaders begin to contribute. A successful example is the Southern Nations Regional Health Bureau's sanitation advocacy campaign launched in 2003 in southern Ethiopia. It increased latrine coverage from 13 percent of the population to 78 percent in just two years (box 17.2). Once

BOX 17.2

Ethiopia's Success with a Community-Led Program

The southern region of Ethiopia—home to diverse cultures and scores of ethnic groups—has a population of 15 million, much larger than many African countries. Population density varies, peaking at 1,100 people per square kilometer in the Wanago district.

In early 2003, access to on-site sanitation was lower than 13 percent, below the national average of 15 percent (see figure). Traditional latrines were most prevalent but scarcely used, poorly maintained, smelly, and dangerous to children and animals. Meanwhile, population expansion, growing household densities, and deforestation were combining to reduce private options for open defecation.

Latrine Construction, 2002/03–2005/06

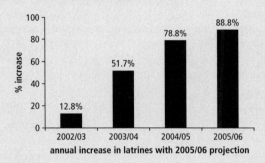

Source: Southern Nations Regional Health Bureau.

The Southern Nations Regional Health Bureau, charged by the national Ministry of Health with promoting sanitation and hygiene, applied a community-led total sanitation approach,

including zero subsidies but allowing the community to devise its own innovative and affordable models.

With a modest but dedicated sum of money, a mass communication campaign was launched using the slogan "Sanitation is everyone's problem and everyone's responsibility." It promoted sustainable and affordable sanitation by creating awareness and encouraging self-financing across all income quintiles. Close collaboration with all stakeholders helped to build consensus and capacity to facilitate community involvement in hygiene promotion and supervision of construction.

At the household level, women were identified as the main drivers of latrine construction. At public consensus-building meetings, they complained about how open defecation directly affects their lives, highlighting the health risks of contact with feces in the banana plantations and in the fields where they collect fodder for cattle. They also complained about the bad smell and the embarrassment of seeing people defecate openly. Featured stories cited shame as an important factor in consensus building and a strong motivator for latrine construction. Volunteer community health promoters went house to house across villages with health extension workers and members of the subdistrict health committee to persuade households to build latrines, and then they supervised construction.

Alongside other gains in public health, pit latrine ownership rose from less than 13 percent in September 2003 to more than 50 percent in August 2004. By August 2005, it had reached 78 percent, and a year later was on track toward reaching 88 percent.

Source: Reproduced from Water and Sanitation Program 2008.

---

a culturally appropriate formula is found, dramatic change can be achieved with modest public spending focused on promoting sanitation rather than on financing hardware.

Ensure Adequate Supply before Addressing Demand in Settings Dominated by Unimproved Latrines

Where unimproved latrines prevail, the central problem is how to upgrade them to more hygienic facilities so that the full health benefits of fixed-point defecation can be achieved. Countries where unimproved latrines are widely used have already overcome the behavioral challenge

of moving people away from open defecation. The problem is rather about improving facilities. The debate centers on whether the main impediment to upgrading latrines comes from the supply side or the demand side.

Using standardized unit costs from Senegal's sanitation sector, one can estimate the percentage of a household's monthly budget that would be absorbed by the up-front investment in different types of sanitation facilities (table 17.2). Although unimproved latrines are affordable across all income levels, improved latrines cost much more than a month's household income in Senegal—even for households

Table 17.2 Cost of Sanitation Facilities in Senegal
percentage of monthly household budget

Facility	National	Rural	Urban	Poorest quintile	Second quintile	Third quintile	Fourth quintile	Richest quintile
Septic tank	289	427	209	641	491	396	292	167
Improved latrine	194	286	140	430	330	266	196	112
Unimproved latrine	22	32	16	48	37	30	22	13
Monthly household budget (2002 $)	227	154	315	102	134	166	225	394

Source: Morella, Foster, and Banerjee 2008.

in the highest income group. These findings are consistent with the patterns of access to sanitation observed across the socioeconomic spectrum in Africa. The fact that half of African households have invested in unimproved latrines in the absence of any subsidy suggests that these modest investment costs are affordable across the income spectrum. The fact that improved latrines are found only among the wealthiest households indicates that affordability may well be an issue in this case. In addition, in urban areas, poor dwellers in slum settings often do not own their land or house and so have fewer incentives to invest in improving their living conditions.

The appropriate policy response to these demand-side constraints likely entails a public subsidy for the additional capital costs associated with a standard package of improved facilities. However, a subsidy may have drawbacks, including distorting demand and markets. Subsidies can reduce the demand of households with the ability to pay. Moreover, suggesting a standard package may make poor households feel entitled to such a facility, regardless of whether it is the most appropriate for their circumstances and geographic location. Widespread adoption of a standard could also discourage innovations that may lower costs. Therefore, in the African context, many other policy measures likely need to be taken before subsidies become relevant.

From the supply side, poor knowledge in the construction sector about required designs, a lack of skilled construction workers, and a shortage of materials can explain the low prevalence of improved latrines. Access patterns already provide some clues that supply-side issues are a real constraint in Africa. First, the prevalence of improved latrines is low, even in middle-income countries, except in a handful of cases. Second, 40–50 percent of the population use unimproved latrines, even among the highest-income groups who may be able to pay for more advanced facilities.

A weak private sector dominated by small entrepreneurs at the local level compounds the supply problem. Latrine construction demands skills not widely available, and small enterprises often do not have the resources to develop new skills or adopt new technologies.

Supply bottlenecks should be tackled first. Otherwise, subsidy resources may be wasted on households that could have financed the facilities on their own. Allowing the local market to develop also provides space for innovation that can lower the cost of improved latrines. Technological innovation is needed to secure greater health benefits with cheaper variants that are tailored to a locality. This innovation should be grounded in a better understanding of the most prevalent designs for unimproved latrines in any given locality and should explore how relatively minor changes in these designs could help achieve health benefits.

Policies need to address supply-side limitations. Government support is best channeled toward (a) conducting research and developing products, (b) marketing latrines, and (c) opening supply channels for key inputs. Training small service providers and providing access to credit can also help. The National Sanitation Program in Lesotho, established 20 years ago, is dedicated to sanitation promotion and private sector training. Households directly employ private latrine builders trained under the program. The program has increased national sanitation coverage from 20 percent of the population to 53 percent.

Make Sewerage More Affordable in High-Density Settlements

In much of Africa, on-site sanitation is the most cost-effective and only practical way to secure the health benefits of hygienic disposal of excreta. Nevertheless, on-site sanitation has its limits. As the urban population grows, water consumption also increases, creating the challenge of safely returning large volumes of wastewater. In addition, given the growing urban population densities, limited land constrains the use of latrines (particularly the simpler types), which require rotation of sites. At high population densities, sewerage systems are both more suitable and more cost-effective.

Whereas the annual population growth in Africa averages 2.5 percent, the urban population is growing at 3.9 percent. By 2020, nearly 60 percent of Africa's population will be in urban areas, and within 20 years, the population of most African cities will have doubled. Eventually, Africa's burgeoning cities will need to develop more extensive sewerage networks. The statistics on affordability in table 17.2 are particularly worrisome. If households are struggling to afford improved latrines, they are much less likely to be able to afford waterborne sewerage, and the public subsidies to support such sewerage networks are equally unaffordable. Reducing the cost of sewer networks through technological innovation is therefore critical.

One lower-cost alternative that was developed in Latin America but that could be explored in Africa is condominial sewerage. These networks are designed to keep costs down by having the public collection network just touch each housing block (or condominium) instead of surrounding it, with the pipes serving each household then laid within the block itself at the residents' initiative. Decentralized microsystems of treatment and disposal can also replace the conventional centralized treatment system. Construction costs are reduced by using small-diameter pipes, buried at relatively shallow depth, with work partially carried out by residents. Experiences in Latin America reveal savings of up to 65 percent (Melo 2005). Pilot condominial systems are being implemented in several African countries, most notably in the periurban areas of Dakar, Senegal. By 2009, the Dakar system is expected to furnish 60,000 households (270,000 people) with on-site sanitation and to support 160 condominial schemes serving 130,000.

Several Common Challenges Remain for All Countries

Irrespective of a country's position on the sanitation ladder, several common challenges cut across all sanitation settings: (a) securing fiscal space for sanitation, (b) coordinating the numerous players in the sector, and (c) developing a more refined approach to measuring progress.

Securing Additional Resources

The unglamorous nature of sanitation puts it at a disadvantage in the competition for fiscal resources. Government decentralization and poor accounting for sector expenditures impede understanding of the exact amount of public funds allocated. Fewer than half of the countries surveyed reported any spending on sanitation, and those that did averaged no more than 0.23 percent of GDP, including both investment and operation and maintenance (Briceño-Garmendia, Smits, and Foster 2008).

At the 2008 African Conference on Sanitation and Hygiene in Durban, South Africa, governments committed themselves to raising public expenditure on sanitation to 0.5 percent of GDP by 2010. This commitment would require spending close to the levels needed to reach the MDG target, but reaching the target will still be difficult because of the need to make up for lagging past performance. Better accounting of public expenditure on sanitation will also be needed to monitor progress toward the target.

Although governments are called on to provide more resources, innovative financing approaches that help providers and operators are also needed. Cost recovery has proved to be a limited incentive because the only tariffs in sanitation are those on sewerage, and they apply only to the minority of the population served by that network. Moreover, most African utilities responsible for providing wastewater services also supply water, and the lack of accounting separation between these services makes it likely that water pays for sanitation. Burkina Faso has taken an innovative approach by levying a sanitation tax on the water bill, which is then used to subsidize access to improved sanitation facilities in Ouagadougou (box 17.3).

Needed—a Champion for the Sanitation Sector

Given that on-site sanitation, rather than waterborne sewerage, will likely continue to dominate sanitation in Africa, households rather than governments will remain center stage. Even so, the government's role in promoting demand and addressing supply bottlenecks remains. Too often, dispersion and duplication

of sanitation functions, even within the public sector, prevent one entity from leading, and sanitation issues fall between the cracks.

A key policy issue is therefore to identify and empower a clear sanitation champion within the public sector. In Senegal, the decision to take sanitation seriously was expressed through the creation of a dedicated sanitation utility. Senegal was also the first country to establish a government body at the national level—the Ministry for Prevention, Public Hygiene and Sanitation (recently reorganized as the Ministry of Urban Affairs, Housing, Urban Water, Public Hygiene and Sanitation)—to coordinate sector activity. Although creating a ministry in the central government may not always be necessary, Senegal provides an important lesson in singling out one entity with a clear mandate to lead.

Measuring Progress

Although the JMP has made strides in monitoring progress toward the MDG target for sanitation, no commensurate effort has been made to create detailed and frequent country-level monitoring and evaluation systems critical to guiding policy interventions. Most countries have no system, and in the countries that are developing a system, providing a clear picture of the sector is not yet possible. Moreover, monitoring and evaluation systems rarely measure the effect of improved sanitation on health.

At the country level, better monitoring and evaluation systems could be built by ensuring more coordination at the ministerial level, for instance, between the ministry in charge of sanitation and the ministry in charge of health. In addition, a larger role should be played at the local level, especially by the decentralized technical departments, in collecting data and monitoring progress. This would require more capacity and resources from the central government.

A limitation of the JMP's framework is the inability to discriminate among the levels of sanitary protection provided by different variations within the large class of unimproved latrines, which will continue to dominate African sanitation. Unimproved latrines include a heterogeneous collection of installations, only some of which can be regarded

---

BOX 17.3

Burkina Faso's Sanitation Tax

The on-site sanitation problems in Ouagadougou are specifically addressed in the Sanitation Strategic Plan being implemented by the national public utility in charge of water supply and sanitation.

A sanitation marketing approach has enhanced construction services offered to households by small providers and stimulated household demand for improved sanitation facilities. Some 700 masons and social workers have been trained since the beginning of the program.

Burkina Faso's national utility offers to provide part of the material free to households—equivalent to about a 30 percent subsidy—with the households financing the rest. The utility finances the subsidy through a small sanitation tax on the water bill.

This example shows that on-site sanitation corresponds to a strong demand from urban dwellers, with more than 60,000 pieces of sanitation equipment subsidized so far—latrines as well as gray water–removal systems. It also demonstrates the importance of a local financing mechanism. Donors have contributed to the mechanism, but only modestly. Most of the funds come from the tax on the water bill.

Source: Reproduced from Water and Sanitation Program 2008.

as improved sanitation. Unfortunately, the JMP's household survey instruments that track progress toward the MDG target cannot discriminate among the qualities of installations within the unimproved latrine category. As a result, the data on progress in sanitation in Africa are blurriest precisely where most of the progress is taking place. The precision of household survey instruments should be improved in this respect.

Tracking the intermediate goal of increasing the share of households making use of some kind of sanitation facility, even if it is an unimproved latrine, may also be relevant, given that this is where Africa has been making the greatest progress.

Notes

The authors of this chapter are Elvira Morella, Sudeshna Ghosh Banerjee, and Vivien Foster, who drew on background material and contributions from Piers Cross, Pete Kolsky, Marianne Leblanc, Eustache Ouayoro, and Ede Perez.

1. Unimproved latrines refer to various kinds of pits for excreta disposal. Well known in Africa, Asia, and Latin America, they normally consist of a simple pit covered with logs, not usually roofed, and sometimes with no walls.

2. Improved latrines—comprising SanPlat, VIP latrines, and basic pits with slabs—ensure more hygienic separation of excreta from the immediate living environment. Improved versions have walls and a roof and may include a ventilation pipe or a cover plate for the squat hole. The collection chamber may vary from an unlined pit to a composting chamber. The superstructure may be a crude shelter or an attractive brick or thatch construction with or without a vent pipe and with or without a seat. SanPlat latrines are slightly elevated for ease of use in the dark. They can be located close to the house and have a fitted lid to prevent odors and keep away flies. VIP latrines consist of the normal pit but are fitted with a screened vent pipe.

3. Hutton (2000) uses health care unit costs from the World Health Organization to estimate the cost of treating diarrhea, to which he adds other expenses (such as transport) incurred by the patient. A number of assumptions are made regarding treatment (such as number of visits or length of hospitalization). As a result, the mean cost per case of diarrhea for the patient is $10–$23, and the additional costs per visit

are estimated at $0.50 or less. As for economic losses from lost time at work and school and from death, Hutton relies on the concept of minimum wage rates for his estimates, adjusted to reflect the varying productivity of the different countries (for each country, the value of the minimum wage rate must be no larger than the local gross national product per capita and no smaller than the manufacture added value). Both health and economic benefits are presented, assuming that all interventions were implemented within 2000. To account for population growth, the projected population figures for 2015 are used.

References

Banerjee, Sudeshna G., Quentin Wodon, Amadou Diallo, Taras Pushak, Helal Uddin, Clarence Tsimpo, and Vivien Foster. 2008. "Access, Affordability and Alternatives: Modern Infrastructure Services in Sub-Saharan Africa." Background Paper 2, Africa Infrastructure Country Diagnostic, World Bank, Washington, DC.

Briceño-Garmendia, Cecilia, Karlis Smits, and Vivien Foster. 2008. "Financing Public Infrastructure in Sub-Saharan Africa: Patterns, Issues, and Options." Background Paper 15, Africa Infrastructure Country Diagnostic, World Bank, Washington, DC.

Emerson, Paul M., Sandy Cairncross, Robin L. Bailey, and David C. Mabey. 2000. "Review of the Evidence Base for the 'F' and 'E' Components of the SAFE Strategy for Trachoma Control." *Tropical Medicine and International Health* 5 (8): 515–27.

Esrey, Steven A., James B. Potash, Leslie Roberts, and Clive Shiff. 1991. "Effects of Improved Water Supply and Sanitation on Ascariasis, Diarrhea, Dracunculiasis, Hookworm Infection, Schistosomiasis and Trachoma." *Bulletin of the World Health Organization* 69 (5): 609–21.

Hutton, Guy. 2000. *Considerations in Evaluating the Cost-Effectiveness of Environmental Health Interventions.* Geneva: World Health Organization.

Hutton, Guy, U-Primo E. Rodriguez, Lydia Napitupulu, Pham Ngoc Thang, and Phyrum Kov. 2007. *Economic Impacts of Sanitation in Southeast Asia: A Four-Country Study Conducted in Cambodia, Indonesia, the Philippines and Vietnam under the Economics of Sanitation Initiative (ESI).* Jakarta, Indonesia: World Bank, Water and Sanitation Program.

Mehta, Meera, Thomas Fugelsnes, and Kameel Virjee. 2005. "Financing the Millennium Development Goals for Water Supply and

Sanitation: What Will It Take?" *Water Resources Development* 21 (2): 239–52.

Melo, Jose Carlos. 2005. *The Experience of Condominial Water and Sewerage Systems in Brazil: Case Studies from Brasilia, Salvador and Parauapebas.* Lima, Peru: Water and Sanitation Program—Latin America, World Bank.

Morella, Elvira, Vivien Foster, and Sudeshna G. Banerjee. 2008. "Climbing the Ladder: The State of Sanitation in Sub-Saharan Africa." Background Paper 13, Africa Infrastructure Country Diagnostic, World Bank, Washington, DC.

United Nations. 2008. *The Millennium Development Goals Report 2008.* New York: United Nations.

Water and Sanitation Program. 2006. *Getting Africa on Track to Meet the MDGs on Water and Sanitation: A Status Overview of Sixteen African Countries.* Joint Report of the African Ministers' Council on Water, African Development Bank, the European Union Water Initiative, the United Nations Development Programme, the Water and Sanitation Program–Africa, and the World Bank. Nairobi, Kenya: Water and Sanitation Program–Africa.

———. 2008. "Can Africa Afford to Miss the Sanitation MDG Target? A Review of the Sanitation and Hygiene Status in 32 Countries." Joint Initiative of the African Ministers' Council on Water, African Development Bank, World Bank, and Water and Sanitation Program, Washington, DC.

World Bank. 2002. "Urban Environmental Strategic Sanitation Planning: Lessons from Bharatpur, Rajasthan, India." Field Note 23771. Water and Sanitation Program–South Asia, New Delhi.

Index

Boxes, figures, notes, and tables are indicated with b, f, n, or t following the page number.

sanitation, 325, 326, 327f, 329
transport infrastructure, 150, 151t
utility connection charges, 90
water supply, 300, 301, 302b, 307, 315, 319, 320
water utilities, 310, 311, 313
Country Policy and Institutional Performance Assessment, 51
country typology of AICD, 48, 51b, 66
CREST (Commercial Reorientation of the Electricity Sector
        Toolkit), 196b

DAWASA lease contract, 116, 116b
debt service expenditures, 76–77
deficit-financed public investment, 77b
Democratic Republic of Congo
    affordability issues, 92
    backup generators, 184
    broadband access, 173
    drinking water access, 300
    external financing, 79
    hydropower projects, 53, 149, 187
    infrastructure as constraint on economic growth, 2
    local capital markets and, 81
    mobile phone coverage, 172, 178
    multimodal transport network, 204–205
    paved road density, 96b
    ports and shipping, 254
    power outages, 184
    power trade, 149, 150f, 187, 200
    railways, 204, 230, 232, 238, 239
    regional integration, 155
    road standards, 217
    spending estimates, 59
    standposts, 95
    undermaintenance, 73
    urban public transportation, 96b
    utility inefficiencies, 309
    water MDG and, 305
    water supply, 313, 314, 315, 316
demographic and health surveys (DHSs), 39, 324b
demographic trends
    basic infrastructure access and, 88
    spending needs estimates and, 36
    urbanization and, 127–128
density
    infrastructure costs and, 130–132
    paved road, 96b
    railway traffic, 230–231
    sewerage affordability and, 333
    telecommunications networks, 60n2
    transportation networks and, 56, 60n2, 129
    urban growth and, 4, 134, 135t, 141n3
    urban infrastructure needs and, 132, 133f
Department for International Development (UK), 32
Development Assistance Committee, 37

disease
    sanitation access and, 329
    water resources and, 45–46, 304–305
distribution losses
    power sector, 187
    utilities, 11, 11f, 66, 72–73, 73t
    water resources, 309
domestic finance sources, 76–77
DP World, 252–253
drinking water. See water resources

East Africa. See also specific countries
    airports and air transport, 268, 268f
    hydroclimatic variability, 272, 273f
    ICT investment, 4, 147, 148b, 148t
    ICT sector impact on, 168
    infrastructure, 48
    maritime traffic growth, 250–251t, 251f
    port system, 252, 255
    railways, 204
    water resource management, 277
The East Africa Marine System (TEAMS, Kenya), 148b, 148t
East African Community
    AICD and, 32
    airports and air transport, 264t
    Lake Victoria Basin Commission, 282
    Master Plan, 156
    regional integration, 156, 159b
East African Power Pool, 52, 53, 53–54t, 185, 187
East Asia
    basic infrastructure access, 88
    capital budgets for infrastructure, 77
    economic growth and infrastructure, 44–45
    electricity access, 182
    infrastructure, 47–48, 49f
    public sector expenditures, 67
Eastern Africa Submarine Cable System (EASSy), 146, 148b, 148t
Economic and Monetary Community of Central Africa
    AICD and, 32
    airports and air transport, 264–265, 264t
    multimodal transport network, 204
Economic Community of West African States (ECOWAS), 32,
        156, 157
    Regional Electricity Regulatory Authority, 160
economic development
    agriculture and, 125–126, 288–289
    ICT sector impact, 43, 45f, 52t, 168
    infrastructure linked to, 2, 44–47, 44t, 45–46f
    irrigation, 52t
    power sector and, 45f, 52–53, 52t, 141n5, 183–186, 184f, 184t
    regional integration and, 156–157
    transportation sector, 52t
    urban areas as engine for, 126
    water resources and, 52t, 272–276, 276f, 277, 277b